Studies in Church History

50

RELIGION AND THE HOUSEHOLD

John Doran

RELIGION AND THE HOUSEHOLD

PAPERS READ AT
THE 2012 SUMMER MEETING AND
THE 2013 WINTER MEETING OF
THE ECCLESIASTICAL HISTORY SOCIETY

EDITED BY

JOHN DORAN (†)

CHARLOTTE METHUEN

and

ALEXANDRA WALSHAM

PUBLISHED FOR
THE ECCLESIASTICAL HISTORY SOCIETY
BY
THE BOYDELL PRESS
2014

First published 2014

A publication of the Ecclesiastical History Society
in association with The Boydell Press
an imprint of Boydell & Brewer Ltd
PO Box 9, Woodbridge, Suffolk IP12 3DF, UK
and of Boydell & Brewer Inc.
668 Mt Hope Avenue, Rochester, NY 14620-2731, USA
website: www.boydellandbrewer.com

ISBN 978-0-95468-102-9

ISSN 0424-2084

A CIP catalogue record for this book is available
from the British Library

The publisher has no responsibility for the continued existence or accuracy
of URLs for external or third-party internet websites referred to in this
book, and does not guarantee that any content on such websites is, or will
remain, accurate or appropriate.

Details of previous volumes are available from Boydell & Brewer Ltd

This publication is printed on acid-free paper

Printed and bound in Great Britain by
TJ International Ltd, Padstow, Cornwall

MIX
Paper from
responsible sources
FSC
www.fsc.org   FSC® C013056

CONTENTS

Preface   ix

List of Illustrations   x

List of Contributors   xv

List of Abbreviations   xviii

Introduction   xxi

John Doran (1966–2012): An Appreciation   1
   BRENDA BOLTON

Relationships, Resistance and Religious Change in the Early   5
Christian Household
   KATE COOPER

Material Christianity in the Early Medieval Household   23
   JULIA M. H. SMITH

Households of St Edmund   47
   SARAH FOOT

'A faithful and wise servant'? Innocent III (1198–1216) looks   59
at his Household
   BRENDA BOLTON

The College of Cardinals under Honorius III: A Nepotistic   74
Household?
   THOMAS W. SMITH

Perfection and Pragmatism: Cathar Attitudes to the Household   86
   BERNARD HAMILTON

Daily Commodities and Religious Identity in the Medieval   97
Jewish Communities of Northern Europe
   ELISHEVA BAUMGARTEN

Holy Families: The Spiritualization of the Early Modern   122
Household Revisited (*Presidential Address*)
   ALEXANDRA WALSHAM

Richard Whitford's *Werke for Housholders*: Humanism,   161
Monasticism and Tudor Household Piety
   LUCY WOODING

The Syon Household at Denham, 1539–50   174
PETER CUNICH

Reforming Household Piety: John Foxe and the Lollard   188
Conventicle Tradition
SUSAN ROYAL

The Decalogue, Patriarchy and Domestic Religious   199
Education in Reformation England
JONATHAN WILLIS

Living with the Bible in Post-Reformation England: The   210
Materiality of Text, Image and Object in Domestic Life
TARA HAMLING

Adoramus te Christe: Music and Post-Reformation English   240
Catholic Domestic Piety
EMILIE K. M. MURPHY

Needlework and Moral Instruction in English Seventeenth-   254
Century Households: The Case of Rebecca
AMANDA PULLAN

Catechesis, Socialization and Play in a Catholic Household,   269
*c.*1660: The 'Children's Exercises' from the Blundell Papers
LUCY UNDERWOOD

'A dose of physick': Medical Practice and Confessional   282
Identity within the Household
SOPHIE MANN

'My house shall be called the house of prayer': Religion   294
and the Material Culture of the Episcopal Household, *c.*1500
to *c.*1800
MICHAEL ASHBY

'Conscientious attention to publick and family worship   307
of God': Religious Practice in Eighteenth-Century English
Households
W. M. JACOB

Sons of the Prophets: Domestic Clerical Seminaries in Late   318
Georgian England
SARA SLINN

'Idle reading'? Policing the Boundaries of the Nineteenth- 331
Century Household
GARETH ATKINS

The Spiritual Home of W. E. Gladstone: Anne Gladstone's 343
Bible
DAVID BEBBINGTON

The Death of Charlotte Bloomfield in 1828: Family Roles 354
in an Evangelical Household
ANTHONY FLETCHER

The Oxford Movement, Marriage and Domestic Life: John 366
Keble, Isaac Williams and Edward King
JOHN BONEHAM

Islam at Home: Religion, Piety and Private Space in Muslim 378
India and Victorian Britain, c.1850–1905
JUSTIN JONES

'Domestic charms, business acumen, and devotion to 405
Christian work': Sarah Terrett, the Bible Christian Church, the
Household and the Public Sphere in Late Victorian Bristol
LINDA WILSON

Who is Living at the Vicarage? An Analysis of the 1881 416
Census Returns for Clerical Households in Lincolnshire
JOHN W. B. TOMLINSON

The Missionary Home as a Site for Mission: Perspectives 428
from Belgian Congo
DAVID MAXWELL

Christian Family, Christian Nation: Raymond Johnston and 456
the Nationwide Festival of Light in Defence of the Family
ANDREW ATHERSTONE

Unfettering Religion: Women and the Family Chain in the 469
Late Twentieth Century
CALLUM G. BROWN

Household Sovereignty and Religious Subjectification: 492
China and the Christian West compared
ADAM YUET CHAU

PREFACE

This, the fiftieth volume of Studies in Church History, explores the theme 'The Church and the Household'. It offers a selection of the plenary papers and communications presented at the Summer Conference of the Ecclesiastical History Society held at the University of Bangor in July 2012 and the Winter Meeting in London in January 2013, both conceived under the able presidency of Professor Alexandra Walsham.

The production of this volume has been marked by the tragedy of John Doran's sudden death in October 2012, soon after the selection of the communications had been made. John had been appointed co-editor of Studies in Church History in January 2012, and his death was a great loss to the society. This volume is dedicated to him and includes an appreciation of his life. In the wake of John's death, Alexandra Walsham has taken on significant additional responsibilities in bringing this volume to completion, and both I and the society's committee are very grateful to her.

Thanks are due also to all who chaired sessions at the Summer Conference and peer-reviewed the communications, to the authors of the papers included in this volume for their contributions, and to Dr Tim Grass for his able and assiduous work as Assistant Editor. The society continues to fund this essential post. We are grateful to the University of Bangor conference team and to Professor Tony Claydon for their efforts, which contributed to the success of the Summer Conference, and to Dr Williams's Library for hosting the Winter Meeting. Professor Michael Walsh organized both: his work and energy are very much appreciated.

Charlotte Methuen
University of Glasgow

ILLUSTRATIONS

Frontispiece: John Doran. Reproduced by courtesy of the University of Chester.

Material Christianity in the Early Medieval Household
Fig. 1: Twelfth-century Spanish reliquary-casket. Silver   24
repoussé over oak core, 15.9 x 25.4 x 14.5 cm. Kate S.
Buckingham Endowment, 1943.65, The Art Institute of
Chicago. Photography © The Art Institute of Chicago.
Figs 2a–2b: Glass bottle with stylite saint. Mould-blown   27
dull green hexagonal bottle, probably of Syrian manufacture,
mid-fifth to seventh century, 22.5 x 6.5 cm. British Museum
1911,0513.1. Images © Trustees of the British Museum.
Fig. 3: Lamp with Chi-Rho monogram, North Africa/Tunisia,   27
mid- to late fifth century, hard-fired clay, 5.0 x 14.0 x 8.0 cm.
Malcove Collection, University of Toronto Art Centre, Gift of
Dr Lillian Malcove 1982, M82.354. Courtesy of the University
of Toronto Art Centre. Photography by Toni Hafkenscheid.
Fig. 4: Reliquary amulet, Early Christian/Byzantine, date   27
unknown, bronze, 2.5 x 7.5 x 3.2 cm. Malcove Collection,
University of Toronto Art Centre, Gift of Dr Lillian Malcove
1982, M82.387. Courtesy of the University of Toronto Art
Centre. Photography by Toni Hafkenscheid.
Fig. 5: Pilgrim token or disc depicting St Menas, Early   28
Byzantine/Coptic, fifth to sixth century, terracotta, diameter
7.0 cm. Malcove Collection, University of Toronto Art Centre,
Gift of Dr Lillian Malcove 1982, M82.260. Courtesy of the
University of Toronto Art Centre. Photography by Toni
Hafkenscheid.
Fig. 6: Pilgrim flask. Terracotta, sixth century, from the shrine   29
of St John the Evangelist, Ephesus, 5.0 x 5.0 x 1.8 cm. Musée
du Louvre, MNB2066. Image: Marie-Lan Nguyen, © Wikimedia
Commons.
Fig. 7: Pilgrim flask of St Sergios. Tin–lead alloy, 5.4 x 3.81   29

x 1.59 cm. Walters Art Museum, 55.105. Image: © Wikimedia Commons.

Fig. 8: The Emly Shrine. Irish house-shaped shrine, late   41
seventh to early eighth century. Champlevé enamel on
bronze over yew wood with gilt bronze mouldings and
inlay of lead-tin alloy, 9.2 x 4.1 x 10.5 cm. Museum of Fine
Arts, Boston, Theodora Wilbour Fund in memory of Charlotte
Beebe Wilbour, 52.1396. Image: © 2014 Museum of Fine Arts,
Boston.

Fig. 9: Purse-shaped reliquary. Carolingian, third quarter of   41
the eighth century (?), from Enger (Germany). Gold- and
silver-alloy with gems, pearls and cloisonné enamel, over oak
core, 16.0 x 14.0 x 5.3 cm. Kunstgewerbemuseum, Berlin,
1888,632. Image source: Wikimedia Commons.

Fig. 10: House-shaped reliquary. Italian, tenth century.   41
Bone and copper-gilt on wood, 19.7 x 18.6 x 8.3 cm. The
Metropolitan Museum of Art, The Cloisters Collection, 1953
(53.19.2). Image: © The Metropolitan Museum of Art.

*Daily Commodities and Religious Identity in the Medieval Jewish
Communities of Northern Europe*

Fig. 1: Leipzig, UL, MS Voller 1102/I, Leipzig Mahzor   98
(Worms, *c.*1310), fol. 130ᵛ.

Fig. 2: Moses hitting the rock: London, BL, North French   106
Miscellany, fol. 309ʳ. © The British Library Board, Add.
MS 11639.

Fig. 3: List of *Tekufot*: BL, North French Miscellany, fol. 643ᵛ.   107
© The British Library Board, Add. MS 11639.

Fig. 4: *Matzah* Baking: Jerusalem, Israel Museum, 180/057, The   108
Bird's Head Haggadah (Southern Germany, *c.*1300), fols 25ᵛ–26ʳ.
Photo © The Israel Museum, Jerusalem.

*Holy Families: The Spiritualization of the Early Modern Household
Revisited*

Fig. 1: Guides to domestic piety: Matthew Griffith, *Bethel, or*   125
a forme for families (London, 1634), title page. Reproduced by
permission of the Syndics of Cambridge University Library,
shelfmark Syn. 7.63.150.

Fig. 2: The godly family: *Tenor of the whole psalms in foure partes*   129

(London, 1563). By permission of the Folger Shakespeare Library, Washington DC, shelfmark 11/9/43.

Fig. 3: The Protestant patriarch: *The good hows-holder* (London,   131
1607). © Trustees of the British Museum. Image number
AN163671001.

Fig. 4: The Family of Love at home: H. N., *A benedicitie or*   142
blessinge to be saide over the table ([Cologne], 1575). By permission
of the Bodleian Library, Oxford, shelfmark Douce. S.Subt. 67 (4).

Fig. 5: The extended Holy Family: Mary, Christ, Joseph, Anna   147
and Joachim: woodcut by Albrecht Durer (1511). © Trustees
of the British Museum. Reference E.3, 108. Image number
AN00551033.

*The Decalogue, Patriarchy and Domestic Religious Education in
Reformation England*
Fig. 1: Detail from T. T., *Some fyne gloves devised for newyeres*   203
gyftes (London, 1559). Reproduced by permission of The
Henry E. Huntington Library and Art Gallery, San Marino,
California, USA. Image published with permission of ProQuest.
Further reproduction is prohibited without permission. Image
produced by ProQuest as part of *Early English Books Online*,
<http://www.proquest.com>.

*Living with the Bible in Post-Reformation England: The Materiality of
Text, Image and Object in Domestic Life*
Fig. 1: Wall paintings at 3 Cornmarket St, Oxford, dating from   220
c.1564–81. Image courtesy of the Oxford Preservation Trust.
Fig. 2: View of the painted wall decoration in the first-floor   221
north-east room at Calico House, Newnham, Kent.
Reproduced by permission of English Heritage.
Fig. 3: Wall painting of Adam and Eve dating from the second   222
half of the seventeenth century, photographed in an attic room
of 'The Springs' farmhouse, Meadle, Buckinghamshire.
Reproduced by permission of English Heritage.
Fig. 4: Carved wood overmantel of *c*.1612–20 in a second-   223
floor chamber at 90 High St, Oxford. Reproduced by
permission of English Heritage.
Fig. 5: View of the painted decoration on the cross-wing of a   226
ground-floor room at Ansells End Farm, Kimpton,
Hertfordshire. Reproduced by permission of English Heritage.

Fig. 6: Wall paintings at 1 Church Lane, Ledbury,   230
Hertfordshire. Image courtesy of Ledbury Town Council.

Adoramus te Christe: *Music and Post-Reformation English Catholic
Domestic Piety*
Fig. 1: *Adoramus te Christe*, attributed to Thomas Jollett,   245
c.1606–1608, Oxford, Bodl., MS. Eng.Th.B.2.137. Reproduced
by permission of the Bodleian Libraries, University of Oxford.
Fig. 2: John Dowland, *First book of Book of Aires*, 1597, fols   248
C1^v–C2^r. Reproduced by permission of The Huntington
Library, San Marino, California, USA.

*Needlework and Moral Instruction in English Seventeenth-Century
Households: The Case of Rebecca*
Fig. 1: Rebecca and Eliezer, from Gerard De Jode, *Thesaurus*   257
Sacrarum Historiarum Veteris Testamenti (Antwerp, 1585).
Reproduced by permission of the Master and Fellows of
St John's College, Cambridge.
Fig. 2: Sacrifice of Isaac, Bourne cabinet. Museum of   262
Lancashire, Preston. Photographs of figs 2–6 by the author,
and reproduced by courtesy of Lancashire County Council's
Museum Service.
Fig. 3: Abraham sending Eliezer, Bourne cabinet.   262
Fig. 4: Rebecca and Eliezer at the well, Bourne cabinet.   263
Fig. 5: Travelling scene with Rebecca and Eliezer portrayed as   264
Mary and Joseph, Bourne cabinet.
Fig. 6: Rebecca meeting Isaac, Bourne cabinet.   266

*'My house shall be called the house of prayer': Religion and the Material
Culture of the Episcopal Household, c.1500 to c.1800*
Fig. 1: G. Hollis, 'The Palace, Ely', engraving in William   297
Stevenson, *Supplement to the Second Edition of Mr Bentham's
History* (London, 1817). Reproduced by permission of the
Syndics of Cambridge University Library.
Fig. 2: Tripartite niche on the eastern tower of the Old   302
Bishop's Palace, Ely. Photograph by the author.
Fig. 3: Detail from an upstairs fireplace of the palace, Ely,   304
c.1771–80. Photograph by the author.

The Death of Charlotte Bloomfield in 1828: Family Roles in an Evangelical Household
Fig. 1: Charlotte Bloomfield (1815–28) by Mrs Mee. In the   355
ownership of the author; image reproduced by kind
permission of Yale University Press.

Islam at Home: Religion, Piety and Private Space in Muslim India and Victorian Britain, c.1850–1905
Fig. 1: A sketch illustrating 'the arrangement of native   383
houses of the better sort in the towns of the North-Western
Provinces' by M. Kempson (Director of Public Instruction,
N.W.P., 1862–78): M. Kempson, ed., *Taubatu-n-Nasuh*, 2nd edn
(London, 1886), 320–1.

The Missionary Home as a Site for Mission: Perspectives from Belgian Congo
Fig. 1: William Burton on trek. Reproduced by courtesy of   435
the Central Africa Mission [hereafter: CAM] (Preston 26).
Fig. 2: Preparing for a trek. Reproduced by courtesy of CAM   436
(Preston 3).
Fig. 3: The Mission house at Mwanza. Reproduced by   439
courtesy of CAM (Preston 53).
Fig. 4: Brick making. Reproduced by courtesy of CAM   440
(Preston 44).
Fig. 5: An evangelist and his family. Reproduced by courtesy   443
of CAM (Preston 75).
Fig. 6: Pastors' wives: (left to right) Ndokasa, Luisa and   443
Jennifer. Reproduced by courtesy of CAM (Preston 73).
Fig. 7: Pastors: (left to right) Yoela Kapumba, David   444
Katontoka, Samsoni Kashamo, Abraham Nyuki, Tshango
Menge. Reproduced by courtesy of CAM (Preston 50).
Fig. 8: Hettie Burton and baby Mangasa. Reproduced by   451
courtesy of CAM (Preston 76).
Fig. 9: Mangasa. Reproduced by courtesy of CAM   451
(Preston 14).
Fig. 10: Banze Inabanza Jacques, Mwanza, Democratic   452
Republic of Congo, 22 May 2007. Photograph by the author.

CONTRIBUTORS

Michael ASHBY
  Postgraduate student, University of Cambridge

Andrew ATHERSTONE
  Tutor in History and Doctrine, and Latimer Research
  Fellow, Wycliffe Hall, Oxford

Gareth ATKINS
  Research Fellow, Magdalene College, Cambridge, and
  Postdoctoral Fellow, Centre for Research in Arts, Social
  Sciences and Humanities, Cambridge

Elisheva BAUMGARTEN
  Associate Professor, Departments of Jewish History and
  History, Hebrew University of Jerusalem

David BEBBINGTON
  Professor of History, University of Stirling

Brenda BOLTON
  Formerly Senior Lecturer in History, Queen Mary and
  Westfield College, University of London

John BONEHAM
  Postgraduate student, Aberystwyth University

Callum G. BROWN
  Professor of Late Modern European History, University of
  Glasgow

Adam Yuet CHAU
  University Senior Lecturer in the Anthropology of Modern
  China, University of Cambridge

Kate COOPER
  Professor of Ancient History, University of Manchester

Peter CUNICH
  Associate Professor, Department of History, University of
  Hong Kong

Anthony FLETCHER
Emeritus Professor of English Social History, University of London

Sarah FOOT
Regius Professor of Ecclesiastical History, University of Oxford

Bernard HAMILTON
Professor Emeritus of Crusading History, University of Nottingham

Tara HAMLING
Senior Lecturer in History, University of Birmingham

W. M. JACOB
Visiting Research Fellow, King's College, London

Justin JONES
Lecturer in the Study of Religion, University of Oxford

Sophie MANN
Postgraduate student, King's College, London

David MAXWELL
Dixie Professor of Ecclesiastical History, University of Cambridge

Emilie K. M. MURPHY
Postgraduate student, University of York

Amanda PULLAN
Postgraduate student, Lancaster University

Susan ROYAL
Postgraduate student, Durham University

Sara SLINN (*Michael J. Kennedy Postgraduate Prize*)
Postgraduate student, University of Nottingham

Julia M. H. SMITH
Edwards Professor of Medieval History, University of Glasgow

Thomas W. SMITH
Postgraduate student, Royal Holloway, University of London

John W. B. TOMLINSON
Lecturer, Lincoln College

Lucy UNDERWOOD
　　Fellow, British School at Rome

Alexandra WALSHAM (*President*)
　　Professor of Modern History, University of Cambridge

Jonathan WILLIS
　　Lecturer in Early Modern History, University of
　　Birmingham

Linda WILSON
　　Senior Lecturer, University of Gloucestershire

Lucy WOODING
　　Senior Lecturer in Early Modern History, King's College,
　　London

ABBREVIATIONS

ActaSS	*Acta sanctorum*, ed. J. Bolland and G. Henschen (Antwerp etc., 1643–)
AFP	*Archivum fratrum praedicatorum* (1931–)
AHR	*American Historical Review* (1895–)
AnBoll	*Analecta Bollandiana* (1882–)
ARG	*Archiv für Reformationsgeschichte* (1903–)
AV	Authorized Version
BAV	Biblioteca Apostolica Vaticana
BHL	*Bibliotheca hagiographica latina antiquae et mediae aetatis*, 3 vols (Brussels, 1898–1901)
BL	British Library
Bodl.	Bodleian Library
BN	Bibliothèque nationale de France
CChr	Corpus Christianorum (Turnhout, 1953–)
CChr.SL	Corpus Christianorum, series Latina (1953–)
CERS	Church of England Record Society
ChH	*Church History* (1932–)
CICan	*Corpus iuris canonici*, ed. E. Richter and E. Friedberg, 2 vols (Leipzig, 1879–81)
CQR	*Church Quarterly Review* (1875–1968)
CRS	Catholic Record Society
CSEL	Corpus Scriptorum Ecclesiasticorum Latinorum (Vienna, 1866–)
EETS	Early English Text Society
EHR	*English Historical Review* (1886–)
ET	English translation
GH	*Gender and History* (1989–)
HistJ	*Historical Journal* (1958–)
HR	*Historical Research* (1986–)
JAH	*Journal of African History* (1960–)
JBS	*Journal of British Studies* (1961–)
JECS	*Journal of Early Christian Studies* (1993–)
JEH	*Journal of Ecclesiastical History* (1950–)
JEMH	*Journal of Early Modern History* (1997–)

JFH	*Journal of Family History* (1976–)
JRS	*Journal of Roman Studies* (1911–)
JThS	*Journal of Theological Studies* (1899–)
LCL	Loeb Classical Library
LPL	Lambeth Palace Library
LW	*Luther's Works*, ed. J. Pelikan and H. Lehmann, 55 vols (St Louis, MO, 1955–75)
MGH	Monumenta Germaniae Historica inde ab a. c. 500 usque ad a. 1500, ed. G. H. Pertz et al. (Hanover, Berlin, etc., 1826–)
MGH Capit.	Monumenta Germaniae Historica, Capitularia regum Francorum (1883–97)
MGH Epp.	Monumenta Germaniae Historica, Epistolae (1887–)
MGH SRG i.u.s.	Monumenta Germaniae Historica, Scriptores rerum Germanicarum in usum scholarum seperatum editi (1871–)
MGH SRM	Monumenta Germaniae Historica, Scriptores rerum Merovingicarum (1884–1951)
MGH SS	Monumenta Germaniae Historica, Scriptores (in folio) (1826–)
n.d.	no date
NH	*Northern History* (1966–)
n.s.	new series
ODNB	*Oxford Dictionary of National Biography*, ed. H. C. G. Matthew and Brian Harrison (Oxford, 2004)
OECT	Oxford Early Christian Texts
OED	*Oxford English Dictionary*
OHCC	Oxford History of the Christian Church
P&P	*Past and Present* (1952–)
PL	Patrologia Latina, ed. J.-P. Migne, 217 vols + 4 index vols (Paris, 1844–65)
PS	Parker Society
RH	*Recusant History* (1951–)
s.a.	*sub anno* ('under the year')
SC	Sources Chrétiennes (Paris, 1941–)
SCH	Studies in Church History
SCH S	Studies in Church History: Subsidia
SCJ	*Sixteenth Century Journal* (1970–2006)
SEHT	Studies in Evangelical History and Thought
SHCM	Studies in the History of Christian Missions

s.n.	*sub nomine* ('under the name')
s.v.	*sub verbo* ('under the word')
TNA	The National Archives
TRHS	*Transactions of the Royal Historical Society* (1871–)
UL	University Library
WUNT	Wissenschaftliche Untersuchungen zum Neuen Testament

INTRODUCTION

In its infancy, Christianity was a religion of the household. Lacking dedicated buildings for worship, the congregations of the faithful met in domestic environments. Like the ancient Hebrews before them, early Christians instinctively described themselves using the language of kinship, equating their biological ties with blood relatives with the spiritual links they shared with fellow believers. In the pages of Scripture they spoke of the latter as their brothers and sisters and God as their loving Father. In the centuries since, the same vocabulary has repeatedly been utilized to conceptualize the Church as an institution and to delineate the relationship between the inhabitants of heaven and human beings on earth. The Holy Family has been the subject of enduring devotion and has offered a model for lay piety in the home. The household has also provided a blueprint for all kinds of religious communities: monastic orders, confraternities, reform movements, dissenting sects and evangelical organizations.

In the Christian West, as in other civilizations, the family and the household have long been regarded as microcosms of the social and political order, basic building blocks of the state and society. Hovering on the boundary between the public and the private, throughout history they have been a focus of both optimism and anxiety. They have simultaneously been seen as sources of sedition, corruption and moral degeneration and as key arenas in which to educate, nurture and indoctrinate the next generation. The connection between religious cultures and the household has been marked by an equally curious mixture of intimacy and tension. Surrounded by ambivalence, the family and the home have both buttressed and subverted the ecclesiastical status quo. They have fostered religious solidarity and cohesion, but they have also served to foment internal conflict and friction. They operate at once as symbols of stability and of danger.

It was with this rich range of possible avenues of enquiry in mind that 'Religion and the Household' was chosen as the theme for the Summer and Winter Conferences in 2012–13. These meetings attracted papers and communications on the household as a physical space and setting for collective prayer and personal meditation; as a network of people bound together by ties of kinship, emotion, service and obligation; and as a metaphor and symbol of structures and systems of authority that operated essentially outside it. Collectively they fostered lively discussion about the complex intersection between religion and the domestic realm from antiquity to the present day. This volume of essays endeavours to deepen our understanding of how that nexus has developed and how it has been shaped by the varying social and cultural conditions to which Christianity has been exposed in a wide range of geographical locations. While many of the papers published here concentrate on England, others investigate Germany, France, Italy, Africa, India and North America, as well as the biblical Middle East. The conferences also sought to foster fruitful reflection on the comparisons between the Christian Church and different religious traditions, especially Islam and Judaism, and this collection includes contributions that centre on these faiths, as well as upon indigenous religious practice in modern China. A further aim was to prompt consideration not merely of the household's role in the growth of Christianity, but also of the part played by the private home and family unit in its gradual eclipse and decline – in other words, in the processes of secularization that have gathered momentum in Western Europe over the last two centuries. This introduction offers a brief overview of the main themes that emerge from the chronologically arranged essays which follow. It highlights the wider, cumulative insights they yield and draws out a series of common threads that weave them together.

SITES OF RESISTANCE OR BULWARKS OF THE SOCIAL ORDER

The first of these is illuminated by the opening contribution to the volume, Kate Cooper's thought-provoking discussion of how the household became an 'ideological battleground' in the first centuries of the Christian faith. Initially presenting a challenge to the domestic hierarchies of Roman society, over time the new religion aligned itself with the values of the empire and became formally adopted by Constantine as its official creed. Where the earliest narratives celebrated the conscientious resistance of converts to their parental and patriarchal elders, later writings discouraged this kind of pious disobedience. Cooper presents the Christian faith as a 'paradoxical formula', with the capacity both to unsettle the household and to resolve the 'tangle of potentially volatile tensions' it contained. She explores the process by which 'the family of faith was reconciled with the reproductive family', but also highlights the seeds for generational discord that were implicit in Christianity from the very beginning.

The contradictory tendencies Cooper detects in the patristic era continued into the late antique and early medieval period. Focusing upon domestic space and the material objects that occupied it, Julia Smith explores the worries that emerged about relics and miracles in the Carolingian Church and its efforts to assert institutional control over sources of supernatural power by transferring them from elite households into ecclesiastical ownership. The rise of the monasteries as the setting for saintly intercession and asceticism was accompanied by the retreat of the private chamber and home from prominence in early medieval Christian discourse.

Bernard Hamilton's study of the Cathar heresy in twelfth- and thirteenth-century southern France sheds light on an intriguingly different pattern of development. Suspicious of sex and procreation as mechanisms by which evil overtook the world, Cathar theology fostered the creation of celibate communities of initiated perfect living in ordinary houses but aloof from secular society, which formed the only true households recognized by its hierarchy. After the onset of the Albigensian Crusade and the introduction of the Inquisition, however, Cathar leaders were compelled to recognize that families of married believers and their dependents were critical to their Church's survival. Lay residences likewise provided a place of asylum for the Bridgettine monks and nuns expelled from Syon Abbey after its suppression by Henry VIII in 1539, as Peter Cunich shows, but once again the secular household could only provide a temporary solution for a community dedicated to cloistered contemplation, offering shelter during a time of intense crisis, yet eroding the distinctiveness of monastic life as it did so.

The blurred boundary that often exists between church and household, family and sect is also evident in the case of Lollardy. Household conventicles in which Lollards prayed together, read the Bible and engaged in other forms of spiritual sociability were a vital but divisive element of the ecclesiological legacy of the

Lollard heresy: 'privy assemblies' were at once an edifying echo of the primitive *ecclesia* and an inspiration for extra-parochial gatherings which the Elizabethan regime regarded as insidious and subversive. Susan Royal's careful scrutiny of how John Foxe represented them in his *Actes and Monuments* casts fresh light on the radicalism of the martyrologist's religious outlook. My own essay explores some of these competing impulses as they were played out on both sides of the confessional divide erected by the Reformation. It examines the significance both Protestantism and Catholicism attached to the household as a haven for churches under the cross alongside the fraught relations that the experience of being a repressed minority sometimes engendered between wives and husbands, parents and children. It probes warm endorsement of the home as a site for cementing orthodox piety in tandem with ongoing concern about its capacity to become a hotbed of separatist dissent. And it assesses how an institution the authorities regarded as critical to enforcing religious uniformity ironically became one of the means by which English society found ways of accommodating diversity.

Some of these suggestions find unexpected parallels in other periods and distant regions of the world. Adam Chau analyses the importance attached to household sovereignty in modern Chinese culture and its uneasy relationship with external forms of religious authority from an anthropological perspective. He suggests that the resilience of a household idiom of religious engagement, centred on the hosting of spirits, is not merely a function of the unwillingness of the state to sanction the erection of places of worship but also of the persistent desire of people to venerate these divinities in domestic environments. The Christian Church, by contrast, proved to be far more successful in usurping the independent agency of the household as a locus for liturgical activity. Justin Jones's sophisticated study of the evolution of a programme of reform of the Muslim home in nineteenth-century north India is alive to similar ambiguities. Fearing that such households were sites of rebellion and fanaticism, the colonial state subjected them to increased scrutiny; this was the other face of the Victorian cult of domesticity, which in turn coloured Islam's own efforts to police morality and renew spirituality within the family. Regarded as a terrain in which religious purity could be recovered, the Muslim home testifies to forms of 'cross-cultural pollination' that defy the hostile polarities which have dominated the historiography of colonial encounter in the Indian subcontinent.

The Spiritualization of the Household: Nurseries of Morality and Piety

A second theme running through this volume is the significance of the household as a forum for religious education and didactic instruction. Andrew Atherstone's essay highlights the resurgence of this idea in pre-Thatcherite Britain in the guise of the vigorous campaign waged by the Nationwide Festival of Light and its Anglican lay director, Raymond Johnston, in the 1970s and 1980s. Johnston's reassertion of the home as a 'microchurch' and a bastion of Christian values was a conservative reaction to its perceived erosion by the combined forces of communism, feminism, liberalism, television and cinema. In seeing the old-fashioned family as the key instrument for restoring a sick society to health, this movement mimicked many earlier attempts to bring about what Christopher Hill famously called the 'spiritualization of the household'.

One particular phase of Christian history in which this impulse can be discerned is the late Middle Ages. Lucy Wooding examines the Bridgettine monk Richard Whitford's bestselling *Werke for Housholders* (1530). Reflecting clerical awareness of the lay demand for guidance in domestic affairs, Whitford's work also served to diffuse monastic ideals about prayer, work, piety and discipline beyond the cloister. Wooding proposes that rather than seeing humanism as the precursor of the godly Protestant household, the latter should perhaps be regarded as the 'leftover wreckage' of aspects of traditional religion that were too valuable to be completely abandoned. Jonathan Willis examines another species of the prolific early modern English literature on domestic devotion: tracts on the Decalogue. If their discussions of the fifth Commandment ('Honour your father and your mother') laid unprecedented stress on obedience to patriarchal authority, they also acknowledged that heads of households had reciprocal obligations to their inferiors. Amanda Pullan investigates a novel and neglected medium of moral instruction: the art of embroidery. Needlework was an activity that not only embodied the duty of eschewing idleness, but also inspired young women to emulate the example of the biblical figures who were often their subjects. As a model of industry and virtue, modesty and motherhood, the story of Rebecca was particularly popular, but sometimes it also enabled those who stitched it to articulate alternative messages regarding female behaviour.

The notion of the family as an effective nursery of piety retained its purchase in eighteenth-century elite society, as Bill Jacob's wide-ranging assessment of the Church of England in this period demonstrates. His concluding speculations about the role of Methodism in offering a rival focus for the religious experience of servants, and in consequently contributing to the decline of ideals of domestic piety, would repay fuller investigation. In evangelical circles, however, these ideals continued to exert formative influence. Bridging the gap between prescription and practice, David Bebbington uses the annotations in Anne Gladstone's Bible to illuminate the religious ethos that shaped the everyday life of the future prime minster and his sister, while Anthony Fletcher's poignant retelling of the story of Charlotte Bloomfield casts light on how her terminal illness at once tested and strengthened the piety of her household. Transforming this family tragedy into a triumph, the manuscript narrative of the death of this child became a memorial but also a manual for the instruction of later generations. Gareth Atkins, by contrast, focuses upon the threats to the integrity of the religious family presented by 'idle reading' of sensational novels. He shows how evangelical authors and godly households responded to the spread of consumer culture and envisaged the home as a safe environment in which the young could be nurtured to resist infection by secular values.

As Lucy Underwood's investigation of the 'children's exercises' surviving in the Blundell papers reveals, Roman Catholics developed their own modes of domestic pedagogy and catechesis, including autodidactic drama performed by boys and girls in recusant households. Offering a glimpse of the child's perspective, these texts illustrate how civility and decorum were taught through contained misbehaviour and how play could be an agent of socialization. They underline the centrality of the home in what Underwood calls 'the domestication of emergency'.

Private Spaces and Public Places

A third theme that repeatedly emerges in this collection is the fluidity of the boundary between the private household and the public world. The existence and rigidity of the division between these two spheres, and their gendered dimensions, have been much discussed, especially in the context of the nineteenth century. The increasing consensus that the distinction was far more nuanced and complex than often assumed is reinforced by Linda Wilson's exploration of the Nonconformist Bible Christian Church and the household of the Bristol couple William and Sarah Terrett. Comradeship rather than difference emerges as the keynote of the Terretts' relationship, and Wilson also highlights how women repeatedly broke out of their allotted 'female' role in the home to participate in philanthropy, business and forms of social activism such as the temperance movement. Jones's discussion of India also underlines the porosity of the public/private divide in this society, in which Victorian dichotomies clashed with prevailing Mughal ideas. It is equally difficult to sustain these distinctions in the medieval and early modern eras. The early thirteenth-century papal household of Innocent III examined by Brenda Bolton was at once 'a consummate private space' and 'secretive enclave' and a public space from which the pontiff dispensed charity and alms to impoverished visitors and in which he projected himself as a shepherd of the faithful. In the post-Reformation period, as Tara Hamling observes, the domestic environment was likewise 'the meeting place of public and personal lives and agendas'. The word 'family' was used expansively to encompass not merely the nuclear unit of parents and children, but also servants and co-resident kin.

Furthermore, the home was an environment into which outsiders regularly penetrated. Despite the image of homogeneity and cohesiveness conveyed by our sources, families and households were also arenas in which there was scope for interaction with people of different denominations and faiths. They are laboratories in which we can learn much about interconfessional relations and about religious coexistence and toleration. Elisheva Baumgarten illustrates how the everyday routines of medieval northern European Jewish households entailed cooperation with the Christians among whom they resided in an era prior to the advent of the ghetto. Jews lived 'an entangled existence in which they were both part of their surroundings and a distinct minority' and in which negotiation rather than aggression was the *Leitmotif* of social relations. Forms of cooperation and exchange that belie claims of stark separation are also highlighted in Sophie Mann's study of religion and medicine in the early modern English household. The plurality of the religious landscape was matched by an equally complex medical marketplace. Catholics and Protestants were eclectic in the remedies to which they resorted and their interactions with a range of practitioners sometimes provided proselytizing opportunities. The same was true of the missionary households in Belgian Congo discussed by David Maxwell: these were sites for contact between Western evangelists and Africans.

EVERYDAY LIFE, IDENTITY FORMATION AND THE MATERIAL CULTURE OF DOMESTIC ENVIRONMENTS

At the same time, the household was a critical forum in which religious identities were forged. As Baumgarten demonstrates, the rituals that developed around bread, water, cloth and candles demarcated Jews culturally from the Christian majority. The picture that Hamling paints of domestic life in Protestant England is one in which everyday practices were similarly transformed into devotional acts. The quotidian rhythms of life in the home (from cooking and eating to sleeping and reading), as well as the rooms in which they took place (bedchambers, closets, kitchens and parlours), acquired spiritual meaning and moral significance. They too operated as confessional markers, distinguishing adherents of the reformed religion from those loyal to the Church of Rome. Emilie Murphy offers insight into the other half of this equation by investigating how music was implicated in Catholic processes of identity formation. She shows how the performance of martyr narratives within the household assisted in sacralizing domestic space and fostering a sense of belonging to a heroic but persecuted faith.

These and other essays reflect an interest in how the material culture of the domestic environments (their architecture, furniture, fabric and accessories) shapes, and is in turn shaped by, religious belief and praxis. Smith's study of the place of relics in Carolingian households finds echoes in Hamling's work on how English Protestants lived in close proximity with the Bible, laying it beside them at the dinner table, like early medieval men and women who kept holy objects in their private *cubicula*. Michael Ashby uses surviving physical evidence and antiquarian notes to reconstruct the changing appearance of the episcopal household at Ely between 1500 and 1800. He demonstrates how its iconographical schemes reflected the self-conception of bishops as examples of self-restraint and as godly patriarchs and the changes in style and taste that accompanied the growth of consumption in the eighteenth century. He rightly warns against regarding the latter as a reliable barometer of the rise of secular values within society and the Church and stresses the continuing role of interior decoration as a source of religious edification.

ECCLESIASTICAL HOUSEHOLDS

While many essays in this collection focus on the households of the laity, a substantial cluster place their ecclesiastical counterparts under the microscope. Bolton casts fresh light on how Innocent III sought to reincarnate the apostolic virtues of the sixth-century pope Gregory the Great, and to present himself as a paterfamilias. Thomas Smith inspects the College of Cardinals of Honorius III, elected in 1216, and questions whether this was literally as well as metaphorically a 'household of brothers'. Although the ties that bound its members involved kinship as well as merit and political alliance, Smith concludes that Honorius does not deserve his reputation as a shameless nepotist. Monastic communities, meanwhile, operated as surrogate families for men and women who took vows of chastity that separated them from the rest of humanity. In turn, these supplied a template for the lives of the devout laity. And when monks and nuns were expelled from their religious houses, as Cunich demonstrates, the homes of the pious gentry and nobility provided a natural place of refuge. Such intersections underline the reciprocal influences exerted by the cloister on the world and vice versa. These also emerge from Sarah Foot's study of the cult of St Edmund in Anglo-Saxon East Anglia: the 'new social brotherhood' and 'holy kindred' formed by those who renounced blood ties to enter monasteries paralleled the multifarious ways in which their lay neighbours articulated their emotional attachment to their local saint. Together they formed 'an imagined household', 'a spatially scattered network' that functioned as a kind of *familia*.

By rejecting clerical celibacy, the Reformation created a new kind of family comprising a married minister and his wife and children. The biographies of some of these divines are treated briefly in my own essay, which emphasizes how difficult it is to extract the lived reality of these paragons of patriarchal zeal and religious moderation from the pious myths that have accumulated around them. In her contribution, Sara Slinn examines the role played by Georgian clerical households in preparing non-graduates for ordination. Although they were eventually superseded by theological colleges, these domestic seminaries had a significant impact on the spiritual and intellectual formation of several generations of Anglican clergy. In this respect, they bear comparison with the Dissenting academies that burgeoned in the same era. A century later, as John Tomlinson's analysis of the 1881 census returns for Lincolnshire indicates, some vicarages still doubled as informal educational institutions, taking in students of theology as boarders, as well as younger pupils for private tutoring. Parsonage families in this period were distinguished by their mobility, private wealth, resident servants and the older age of their male heads. The Oxford Movement is usually associated with the rejection of marriage and the embrace of sexual asceticism, but John Boneham's study of the writings of John Keble, Isaac Williams and Edward King reveals that they held a more positive view of family life. Like medieval religious these men believed that single life offered the best means of building a close relationship with God, but they also recognized the household as a location in which faith and sanctity could be cultivated.

CHRISTIANIZATION, DECHRISTIANIZATION AND THE FAMILY AND HOUSEHOLD

The final theme explored in this collection is that of the role of the family and home as a site of spiritual conversion and its alter ego, self-conscious rejection of religion. For early Christians, medieval heretics and early modern Protestants and Catholics alike the household was a critical forum in which people experienced internal religious change and were persuaded to embrace an alien faith as their own. David Maxwell's essay focuses upon the domestic dimensions of an early twentieth-century Pentecostal mission to the Belgian Congo. He shows how the missionary home was an arena for 'intimate evangelism' as well as ethnographic observation and how Western values struggled to sustain themselves in a challenging environment. Death and disaster sometimes deprived the missionaries of their own children, but also created strong attachments with indigenous orphans. Maxwell's research shows how African Christianity developed an internal dynamic of its own and how the Western Pentecostalists' encounters with the inhabitants of central Africa fundamentally transformed them in turn.

Maxwell's emphasis on the crucial part played by gender relations in these processes resonates with Callum Brown's essay on the breakdown of 'the family chain of memory' and its role in dechristianization since the 1960s. Building on his earlier thesis that women were key agents of secularization in the era of demographic revolution brought about by sexual liberation and mass contraception, Brown's analysis of the self-narratives of British, Canadian and American women uncovers a clear link between rejection of family and loss of faith, often catalysed by a feminist awakening. The life stories of the women he interviews contain intriguing echoes of the intergenerational tensions and hierarchical inversions examined by Cooper in the context of the late Roman empire. The decline, no less than the rise, of Western Christianity has been accompanied by conflicts within the household and has given rise to moments in which unbelieving parents are converted by contact with their more religiously committed children. Brown's essay is a preliminary report on a wider project, but it lays a suggestive foundation for future studies of post-Christian society. It is hardly surprising the household has been identified as a key space in which to investigate these developments. Gay marriage, infertility treatments, surrogacy and techniques of genetic manipulation are effecting dramatic changes in the ways families are created, redefining the relationships between their constituent members, and altering the parameters of everyday life. And once again these shifts are provoking political comment, moral controversy and ecclesiastical division. The nexus between religion and the household and between the family and the Church continues to be both compelling and fraught.

Inevitably, this volume cannot explore these connections from every angle and direction. There are numerous aspects of the topic that require deeper evaluation. Nevertheless, it is hoped that this collection will stimulate further work and encourage comparative discussion of many other periods, traditions and contexts. The conversations initiated at Bangor and at Dr Williams's Library in 2012–13 have yielded many important insights and have revealed the rich potential of this field of enquiry.

Alexandra Walsham
Cambridge

JOHN DORAN (1966–2012): AN APPRECIATION

John Doran's sudden and premature death on 31 October 2012 tragically deprived his wife Aleta and their three young daughters of a devoted husband and father. At this moment, too, the Ecclesiastical History Society also lost a part of its future, for John was one of its most loyal and talented younger members, a medievalist whose appointment as one of the two editors of Studies in Church History had been confirmed just three months earlier.

John was a Senior Lecturer and Deputy Head of the History Department at the University of Chester and Co-Chair of the M6 Group of Historians, a gathering of medievalists from the various universities in the North-West. Outstanding on all levels as a teacher, his impressive skill in public speaking had led *The New Statesman* magazine in August 2012 to feature his topical lecture on 'Horses in Warfare' as one of the three most highly recommended talks to attend across the whole country. John's professional career was flourishing. Internationally recognized as a leading authority on the city of Rome and the papacy in the Middle Ages, his monograph, *The Legacy of Schism: Relations between Popes and Romans in the Twelfth Century*, was gradually edging towards publication, another work to add to an impressive collection of articles, chapters, edited volumes and online bibliographies.

In April 1986, John, an undergraduate from Royal Holloway College, came to the then Westfield College to join the 'Pope Innocent III' special subject class and took part in the study visit based at the British School at Rome in September of the same year. This period would lay the foundation of his academic career and reveal his consuming passion for papal history. An excellent linguist, he rejoiced in the opportunity to consult the rich collection of books on history, art and topography in the library of the British School. At the Vatican Library, he met the Prefect, Father Leonard Boyle, and in the Secret Archives, Monsignor Charles Burns, two exceptional scholars with both of whom he enjoyed a deep and lasting friendship.

In June 1987, John was awarded a three-year postgraduate British Academy Studentship to work on 'The City of Rome and the Papacy (1188–1227)', supervised by Professor Jonathan Riley-Smith at Royal Holloway. Subsequently, in 1990 and again in 1991, he obtained grants from the British School at Rome for further research. John's parents were in poor health, and he helped to care for them in Liverpool, taking on part-time lecturing posts at Edgehill and Chester colleges and leading highly successful weekend History courses on the Isle of Man. In 1993, he joined the Ecclesiastical History Society and gave his first paper, today still the only work in English to address the issue of child oblation in the eleventh and twelfth centuries, published in *The Church and Childhood* (SCH 31); a second, on the Latin Mission to Nicaea in 1234, appeared in *Unity and Diversity in the Church* (SCH 32).[1] Both articles revealed the breadth, range and mastery of detail which was to run throughout his work.

Between January and March 1997, John taught an evening class on 'The City of Rome' and there he first met Aleta, whose interests lay in Roman art, architecture and mosaics. They married in July 2000 in Chester. Several members of the society were present and so much enjoyed the wedding reception at Chester College that in July 2001 the Summer Conference was held on its campus. John was called upon to arrange the excursions, the guided tours to Liverpool's outstanding churches and the Saturday trip to Sandbach and Little Moreton Hall. He then assumed the onerous position of Conference Secretary, which involved arranging the Summer Meetings at Leeds (2002), Exeter (2003), attended by Anastasia, then eighteen months old, and an embryonic Cecilia, Liverpool (2004), at which Aleta provided the best picnic lunch that we ever had, Lancaster (2005), Cardiff (2006) and Leicester (2007), as well as the Winter Meetings in January of each year. John's unfailing good humour and excellent organization were rarely in question throughout this period. All the while, Aleta kept his feet firmly on the ground by presenting him with their third daughter, Susanna.

John's academic work and his personal life were inseparably linked. His knowledge of Rome, its history, buildings, rulers,

---

[1] 'Oblation or Obligation? A Canonical Ambiguity', in Diana Wood, ed., *The Church and Childhood*, SCH 31 (Oxford, 1994), 127–41; 'Rites and Wrongs: The Latin Mission to Nicaea, 1234', in R. N. Swanson, ed., *Unity and Diversity in the Church*, SCH 32 (Oxford, 1996), 131–44.

archives and extensive bibliography in so many languages was unparalleled and he was always eager to share his discoveries – and there were very many – with his family and anyone else who was interested. Amongst these were Jonathan Phillips, his supervisor, together with Anne Duggan and Marcus Bull, the examiners of his doctorate, awarded in 2008. He produced two very highly commended *Oxford Bibliographies Online*, on Gregory VII and Innocent III, and, whilst several of his articles were on aspects of Innocent III's pontificate, he by no means confined himself to one pope or even to the city of Rome. Also in 2008, together with Damian Smith, his friend and fellow historian from Royal Holloway, he contributed to and edited a volume on Celestine III, Innocent III's predecessor, whose full sixty years of service in the curia had previously been almost completely ignored. He also worked on Gregory VII, Eugenius III, Alexander III and Honorius III, and three of his articles on these popes remain to be published posthumously. In the collection of essays entitled *Roma Felix*, reviewed by Thomas F. X. Noble of Notre Dame University in the *English Historical Review*, John's discussion of the treatise (*c*.1195) by Lucian, monk of St Werburgh, in praise of Chester and his comparison of the city with Rome was singled out as the most outstanding and original chapter. John was justifiably proud of this commendation.

John's enduring legacy as an historian of international repute has been secured by his friends, Dr Paul Baker of Glasgow and Professor Damian Smith of Saint Louis, who have made possible the eventual completion of his unfinished but extremely important book on Rome and the Romans. John's proposed edited volume on Pope Innocent II is under way and two postgraduate studentships, the John Doran Prize at the Center for Medieval and Renaissance Studies at Saint Louis University for the best graduate paper in the fields of either History or History of Art, and a similar studentship in John's name at the University of Chester, will both be offered for the first time in the autumn of 2013. This volume (50) of Studies in Church History is dedicated to his memory.

None of these practical arrangements should divert us from John's deep Christian faith, which underpinned his whole life. Prayers and masses were said for him by colleagues and friends across the world: from the Frari in Venice to Christ Church Cathedral, Oxford; from Saint Louis University, Missouri, to Pensacola,

Florida; Providence, Rhode Island, St Albans, Cambridge, Chelmsford, London and many other places besides. How appropriate, therefore, that John should have chosen as a subtitle for his article on Alexander III and Rome, published in 2012, 'At last we reached the Port of Salvation'. We who are left behind can do no better than to share in his absolute certainty.

Brenda Bolton

RELATIONSHIPS, RESISTANCE AND RELIGIOUS CHANGE IN THE EARLY CHRISTIAN HOUSEHOLD

by KATE COOPER

Do not suppose that I have come to bring peace to the earth. I did not come to bring peace, but a sword. For I have come to turn a man against his father, a daughter against her mother, a daughter-in-law against her mother-in-law – a man's enemies will be the members of his own household. (Matt. 10: 34–6)[1]

The household was an ideological battleground in antiquity. To 'turn a man against his father' was to challenge deeply held convictions about how society should be constituted. For a free man to raise children in his own image was understood – by Jews, Greeks, and Romans alike – as a right and even a duty. The household was the acknowledged nerve centre for the processes of social control and social reproduction.

It was Edward Gibbon who first saw the importance of the religious history of the household for political history. In Book III of his *Decline and Fall of the Roman Empire*, he famously argued that Christian asceticism had eroded the Roman social order: 'the pusillanimous youth preferred the penance of a monastic, to the dangers of a military, life … the same cause which relieved the distress of individuals impaired the strength and fortitude of the empire'.[2] The wording is intentionally outrageous, of course, and few modern historians would sign on to Gibbon's easily dismissive group psychology. But the connection made by Gibbon between the Christian challenge to the values of the Roman household and the roughly contemporary erosion of the Roman social order remains evocative. Did the

---

[2] Edward Gibbon, *History of the Decline and Fall of the Roman Empire*, Book III, chs 62–4, ed. J. B. Bury (London, 1902).

Christian challenge to the Roman household result in a far-reaching erosion of the social order in the Roman provinces? And if so, did this cause equal and opposite problems after Christianity became central to imperial ideology in the fourth century?

It is beyond the scope of the present essay fully to answer these questions; instead it will propose and develop two central insights. The first is that across the first four centuries Christian writers generated and developed a distinctive discourse of righteous non-participation in the domestic sphere, which justified an individual's refusal to fulfil obligations within the household. Early Christian narratives repeatedly stage a scenario in which missionaries reach past the gatekeepers of the household to engage with its individual members in the interests of religious change. In this context, conflict between wives and husbands, or parents and children, becomes a narrative motif for the moral purity of the individual. These narratives, I suggest, became the focal point for revolutionary developments in the discourse of individual moral agency.

But over the *longue durée* the early Christian discourse of the resisting individual was reshaped and redirected. My second thesis is that over time the values of the Roman empire and those of the Christian community began to come into alignment, and the family of faith was reconciled with the reproductive family in the narrative framework of Christian texts. Already from the second century we see that a new attitude to religious conflict within the household took shape.

In the writings which reflect this alternative view, domestic religious conflict is discouraged. The stories of individuals who break free of the household's bonds of obligation are revised to offer their own resolution. They become stories of successful witness within the household. Instead of repressing the independent voices of their wives and children, husbands and fathers listen carefully and take the witness of subordinate members of the household to heart. By this means Christian ideas were brought into alignment as an element of the tissue binding households into the wider social order. But, I will argue, Christian writers paid dearly for the reconciliation. In developing a new ideal of the resisting individual within the household, they delivered what may have been the fatal blow to older Roman concepts of social cohesion.

Two concepts in particular were eroded under Christian influence. The first was *pietas*, the fearful, affectionate veneration for the gods and for elders and ancestors. Christian writers would adopt the *pietas* ideal in a modified form, but early narratives repeatedly proposed that Christian children could legitimately refuse to follow their parents' judgement in religious matters, and this created a concept of legitimate resistance which would never entirely fade away.[3]

The second endangered ideal was *consensus*, the freely given accord between the two parties of a non-binding contract. Roman thought gave great weight to the idea of non-binding contracts and judgements. In this sense, the Romans were anthropologists before their time, aware that a system of reciprocities based where possible on freely given *consensus* resulted in a more stable and valuable bond than did exacting unwilling cooperation – although the Romans were notoriously good at the latter. Still, the preference for consensus over force was visible in the way Roman society organized itself in areas other than family life. For example, where possible the Roman authorities encouraged arbitration as a means of resolving disputes rather than bringing them under the jurisdiction of the courts.[4]

It must be admitted that the Roman style of power involved copious display of the capacity for force. But we should not underestimate the degree to which the idea of *voluntary* cooperation was preferred in Roman thought. In a famous law of the year 536, the Roman emperor Justinian (d. 565) would pronounce that 'of those things that occur between human beings, whatever is bound is soluble'.[5]

We will see below that it was Christian writers who introduced the idea of binding and ultimately enforceable commitments – such as the marriage vow – as central to the social order. It would not be entirely fatuous to suggest that it was this seemingly intimate development, rather than the barbarian invasions, which propelled the end of the Roman political order in the Latin West.

3 Kate Cooper, 'Gender and the Fall of Rome', in Philip Rousseau, ed., *A Companion to Late Antiquity* (Oxford, 2009), 187–200.

4 For references, see Kate Cooper, 'Christianity, Private Power, and the Law from Decius to Constantine: The Minimalist View', *JECS* 19 (2011), 327–43, at 328–32.

5 Justinian, *Novel* 22 (536), discussed in Philip Lyndon Reynolds, *Marriage in the Western Church: The Christianization of Marriage during the Patristic and Early Medieval Periods* (Leiden, 1994), 63; and John Noonan, 'Marital Affection', *Studia Gratiana* 12 (1967), 479–509.

KATE COOPER

The Power of the *Pater*: Aligning the Household's Pyramid of Authority within the Social Order

In the ancient Mediterranean, the household was expected to fit into the pyramid of relational structures which gave cohesion and order to society. In the best of all possible worlds, the smaller nodes of household and village would support and reflect the relations of authority and social control at the higher levels of city, province and empire. In return, the larger-scale structures were expected to buttress the power of the men in charge at the lower levels. Power within the household was part of the larger fabric of empire.

One of the key questions in recent years has concerned where to locate the household with respect to the public and private spheres. In modern scholarship, the household is sometimes seen as a 'public' space, a visible scene of action in the face-to-face landscape of gossip and mutual surveillance.[6] Certainly, the household was a setting for display, far more socially visible in the communities of the ancient Mediterranean than it has been understood to be in the modern period. Yet at the same time, it remained a symbol of the private interest of the householder, a space of retreat and control. The household was the householder's private enterprise, a platform designed to support his or (in the case of a female head of household) her legitimate aims.

In ancient thought, the household was a symbol both of stability and of danger to the social order. It provided both stage and cast of characters for the rituals of biological and social reproduction, for birthing babies and educating children. But ancient writers were well aware that the intimate business of family-tending could distract a man from his duty to the city and his fellow citizens. Relations within the household were the essential building block of the social order. Yet at the same time, the heightened loyalties within a household could also be turned against the common good. Since Plato, philosophers had warned that men would try to provide for their own dependents better than they saw others doing if they could. Even men who stood above greed could be tempted to hoard resources for the sake of their children.[7]

---

6   Kate Cooper, 'Closely Watched Households: Visibility, Exposure, and Private Power in the Roman *domus*', *P&P*, no. 197 (2007), 3–33.
7   Kathy L. Gaca, *The Making of Fornication: Eros, Ethics, and Political Reform in Greek*

The needs and desires of womenfolk posed yet another snare. The inability of men to resist the charms of their womenfolk was a theme older even than Homer. Of course, the influence of women could be for the good as well as the bad: a good woman could save a man from the brink of destruction and set him on the right path.[8] So the householder tried to pose as a willing upholder of the wider social norms. A figure of authority who was willing to correct subordinates with severity – a parent who refused to indulge beloved children, a husband who refused to be swayed by the charms of his wife – was viewed, on the whole, with admiration. When resistance to social norms was discovered in the household, it was the *paterfamilias* who was held responsible.[9] All parties agreed that a *paterfamilias* could not be worth very much if he could not command the respect of his subordinates. So when members of the household – wives, children, slaves – let it be known that they were following their own inclinations over and above those of the *paterfamilias*, it demeaned his standing in the eyes of the wider world.

The philosophical tradition reaching back to Plato and Aristotle tended to imagine moral agents as idealized citizens in a face-to-face society, but by the end of antiquity the important 'players' were in fact large-scale landowners, men (and sometimes women) who controlled the lives of hundreds or even thousands of slaves and other dependents. As a result, the household's potential to be a force undermining the public order, or contributing to the erosion of Roman values, was no small matter.

RIVAL COGNITIONS AND PARADIGMS OF CONVERSION

Hierarchies require reciprocal recognition, which in turn requires cultural resources. Even the holder of an externally recognized position is only really a leader when the members of the group acknowledge his or her legitimacy. In negotiating reciprocal recognition, interpretative strategies play a central role, as does 'reading' events and relationships to negotiate a mutually agreed-upon

Philosophy and Early Christianity (Berkeley and Los Angeles, CA, 2003).

[8]   Kate Cooper, 'Insinuations of Womanly Influence: An Aspect of the Christianization of the Roman Aristocracy', *JRS* 82 (1992), 150–64.

[9]   Cooper, 'Closely Watched Households', 7.

meaning. The anthropologist Christopher Gregory has coined the term 'rival cognitions' to characterize alternative visions of community which can emerge to challenge the leader.[10] For the ancient household to function, therefore, a tangle of potentially volatile tensions had to be contained.

Most basic was the intergenerational tension between parents and children. In a society with deeply rooted convictions about wifely loyalty and filial piety, turning away from the requirements of duty cannot have been easy. If the role of parents was to guide, nurture and educate their children, the children might nonetheless be tempted to resist the expectations placed upon them. But there were also other tensions in the household, such as those between husband and wife, or slave and master. Anyone who wanted to maintain a rival worldview would need interpretative ammunition against the pressure of conformity.

At least one strand of early Christian literature seems to have been aimed at providing such resources. Writers who wanted to play with the motif of domestic religious dissidence could draw on a key tendency of eschatological discourse, that of hearing authenticity in the voices of those who were less powerful in the here and now. The earliest Christian writers expected the world to end shortly, so they were not deeply interested in upholding the social order. Indeed, the apostle Paul argued that plans for the future are irrelevant because 'the appointed time has grown short' (1 Cor. 7: 29 NRSV).

Written between 53 and 57, Paul's first letter to the Corinthians concedes that established and orderly relationships between married couples are a good thing.[11]

> Now for the matters you wrote about: 'It is good for a man not to have sexual relations with a woman'. But since sexual immorality is occurring, each man should have sexual relations with his own wife, and each woman with her own husband. The husband should fulfil his marital duty to his wife, and

---

[10]   C. A. Gregory, *Savage Money: The Anthropology and Politics of Commodity Exchange* (Amsterdam, 1997), 7–8, 23–6, on reciprocal recognition, with summary and critique of Louis Dumont, *Homo Hierarchicus: The Caste System and its Implications*, transl. Mark Sainsbury (Chicago, IL, 1970), on household polity.

[11]   On sexual ethics and Paul, see the illuminating discussion in Gaca, *The Making of Fornication*.

likewise the wife to her husband. The wife does not have authority over her own body but yields it to her husband. In the same way, the husband does not have authority over his own body but yields it to his wife … (1 Cor. 7: 1–4)

But at the same time, he wants to dissuade the membership from taking on new human commitments:

Because of the present crisis, I think that it is good for a person (*anthrōpōi*) to remain as he is. Are you pledged to a woman? Do not seek to be released. Are you free from such a commitment? Do not look for a wife. But if you do marry, you have not sinned; and if a virgin marries, she has not sinned. But those who marry will face many troubles in this life, and I want to spare you this. What I mean, brothers and sisters, is that the time is short. (1 Cor. 7: 26–9)

For Paul, householding remained a concession rather than an aim, and in this he was to leave a volatile legacy for future generations.

After the destruction of the Temple of Jerusalem in 70, and into the second century, the eschatologically inspired preference against established roles began to be tempered. Communities increasingly saw the need to establish structures that could last into an indefinite future, and this had the effect of encouraging increasingly conservative thinking about relationships in the household. As the idea that power relationships within the household would be suspended by the coming end of the world began to recede, the authority of husbands and fathers began to receive ideological reinforcement from the authority of Christ himself.

At the same time, the responsibility of the husband toward his wife also began to receive new emphasis. The Gospels of Matthew and Mark preserve a cluster of sayings of Jesus about marriage:

Some Pharisees came to [Jesus] to test him. They asked, 'Is it lawful for a man to divorce his wife for any and every reason?' 'Haven't you read,' he replied, 'that at the beginning the Creator "made them male and female", and said, "For this reason a man will leave his father and mother and be united to his wife, and the two will become one flesh"? So they are no longer two, but one flesh. Therefore what God has joined together, let no one separate.' (Matt. 19: 3–6)

It should be remembered that in first-century Judaea, Jewish law allowed a man to acquire as many wives as he could support, and only the man had the right to initiate divorce proceedings, so repudiating a woman was a grave act, and one with potentially disastrous economic consequences for the woman.[12]

> 'Why then,' they asked, 'did Moses command that a man give his wife a certificate of divorce and send her away?' Jesus replied, 'Moses permitted you to divorce your wives because your hearts were hard. But it was not this way from the beginning. I tell you that anyone who divorces his wife, except for sexual immorality, and marries another woman commits adultery.' The disciples said to him, 'If this is the situation between a husband and wife, it is better not to marry.' (Matt. 19: 7–10)

At this early stage, Jesus was by no means in a position to impose norms on his followers; indeed, Christians would continue to divorce with impunity up to the reign of Justinian.[13] But the seed of an idea had been planted.

The 'household tables' of the New Testament, compiled in the later first and earlier second centuries, reflect an emerging thread of emphasis on paternal rule.[14]

> Wives, be subject to your husbands as you are to the Lord. For the husband is the head of the wife just as Christ is the

[12] Michael L. Satlow, 'Marriage and Divorce', in Catherine Hezser, ed., *The Oxford Handbook of Jewish Daily Life in Roman Palestine* (Oxford, 2010), 344–61, at 344.

[13] Roger Bagnall, 'Church, State, and Divorce in Late Roman Egypt', in *Florilegium Columbianum: Essays in Honor of Paul Oskar Kristeller*, ed. R. E. Somerville and K.-L. Selig (New York, 1987), 41–61.

[14] On the 'household tables', see Ulrike Wagner, *Die Ordnung des 'Hauses Gottes'*, WUNT 2 Reihe 65 (Tübingen, 1994). On marriage and fatherhood in the Pauline literature, see Larry O. Yarborough, *Not like the Gentiles: Marriage Rules in the Letters of Paul* (Atlanta, GA, 1985); Gerd Theissen, *The Social Setting of Pauline Christianity* (Philadelphia, PA, 1982). On attitudes to the family, see Carolyn Osiek, 'The Family in Early Christianity: "Family Values" Revisited', *Catholic Biblical Quarterly* 58 (1996), 1–24. Margaret Y. MacDonald's *Early Christian Women and Pagan Opinion: The Power of the Hysterical Woman* (Cambridge, 1996) and *The Pauline Churches: A Socio-Historical Study of Institutionalization in the Pauline and Deutero-Pauline Writings* (Cambridge, 1988) chart how the attitudes to gender and family became more conservative over time, while Dennis R. MacDonald, *The Legend and the Apostle: The Battle for Paul in Story and Canon* (Philadelphia, PA, 1983), offers what is still the liveliest account of the second-century conflict over changing gender roles.

head of the church, the body of which he is the Saviour. Just
as the church is subject to Christ, so also wives ought to be, in
everything, to their husbands. (Eph. 5: 22–4 NRSV)

At the same time, many of the aspects of Paul's teaching which
tended to destabilize paternal authority remained central. Perhaps
most important was the idea that isolated Christians in a faithless
household could make great gains for the kingdom: 'If a woman
has a husband who is not a believer and he is willing to live with
her, she must not divorce him. For the unbelieving husband has
been sanctified through his wife, and the unbelieving wife has
been sanctified through her believing husband' (1 Cor. 7: 13–14).
Yet we will see below that second-century authors were increasingly inclined to protect the authority of the *pater*, although not
at the kingdom's expense.

Two Models of Conversion: The Philosophical Father and the Independent Wife or Child

By the second century, Christian literature had developed
two complementary paradigms of conversion. In the model
preferred by the Christian apologists, an adult male converts
to Christianity as the result of soul-searching and philosophical
debate. So, for example, the philosopher Justin Martyr's account
of his own conversion in the mid-second century saw religious
conversion as the result of sustained philosophical reflection
and debate.[15]

But a second model recognized the subordinate members of the
household as potential engineers of conversion. Ancient commentators agreed that wives and children were a potential weak point
in the household's ideological armour, and repeatedly worried that
they might be susceptible to the influence of a travelling teacher,
prophet or charlatan. A curious story from Justin Martyr illustrates
the Christian interest in this theme. A female Roman citizen who
was married to a dissolute husband took up with the Christians,
and began to shy away from joining him in his wild life. At first,

---

[15] Anthony J. Guerra, 'The Conversion of Marcus Aurelius and Justin Martyr:
The Purpose, Genre, and Content of the First Apology', *The Second Century* 9 (1992),
171–87.

she tried to stay in the marriage, in the hope of having a good influence on him. But when it became clear that it was beyond her power to change him, she filed for divorce. With an eye to revenge, the husband denounced her, along with her Christian teacher, to the authorities.[16]

The wife and child who embraced the faith against the wishes of the *paterfamilias* would become stock characters in narratives of the second and third century such as the *Apocryphal Acts of the Apostles*.[17] The violent conflict between Thecla and her mother Theocleia in the second-century *Acts of Paul and Thecla* offers the most vivid illustration of this theme, tracing the daughter's refusal of her marriage in order to follow Paul and her mother's angry and increasingly violent response.[18] (In narrative terms, either a wife or a child could make the first move. The details might vary, but the essential element of defying the *pater*'s control over members of his household remained the same.)

When Thecla refuses to marry in the *Acts of Paul and Thecla*, it is explicitly because she has been moved by the preaching of the apostle Paul.

> And those who were in the house wept bitterly, Thamyris for the loss of a wife, Theocleia for that of a daughter, the maidservants for that of a mistress. So there was a great confusion of mourning in the house. And while all this was going on (all around her) Thecla did not turn away, but gave her whole attention to Paul's word.[19]

When Thecla refuses her marriage, the mother takes her to the proconsul, demanding that he condemn her to death for her

[16] The story is told in Justin Martyr, *Second Apology* 2.1–20. Useful discussions of the passage can be found in MacDonald, *Early Christian Women and Pagan Opinion*, 205–13; P. Lorraine Buck, 'The Pagan Husband in Justin, *2 Apology* 2: 1–20', *JThS* 53 (2002), 541–6.

[17] Ross S. Kraemer, 'The Conversion of Women to Ascetic Forms of Christianity', *Signs: Journal of Women in Culture and Society* 6 (1980), 298–307.

[18] *Acts of Paul and Thecla*, in Edgar *Hennecke* and Wilhelm Schneemelcher, eds, *New Testament Apocrypha*, 2: *Writings Related to the Apostles; Apocalypses and Related Subjects*, transl. R. McL. Wilson, rev. edn (Cambridge, *1993*). My own understanding of this text has changed over the years; compare *The Virgin and the Bride: Idealized Womanhood in Late Antiquity* (Cambridge, MA, 1996), ch. 3, 'The Bride that is No Bride'; and now *Band of Angels: The Forgotten World of Early Christian Women* (London, 2013), ch. 3, 'The God of Thecla'.

[19] *Acts of Paul and Thecla* 7.

disobedience. What is proposed is essentially an honour killing, although in the event Thecla is saved by a miracle.[20]

I have argued elsewhere that the literary interest in the resisting wife or child as an agent of conversion reflects an ancient perception that the household was a nerve-centre for Christian mission.[21] Here the sources offer a fascinating parallel to the findings of modern social scientists, who suggest that high-growth new religious movements achieve their membership gains largely through pre-existing friendship and family networks.[22]

The most poignant of the pre-Constantinian martyrdom narratives, the prison diary of Perpetua of Carthage, invites its audience to witness her father's plea that she sacrifice before a Roman procurator. For the sake of discussion, I set aside the question of whether Perpetua's narrative is an authentic first-person work by the martyr herself, though if her voice is a work of pious imagination the point I am getting at would still be valid, since what is at issue here is the narrative world of the text, and the kind of theological resource which the text would have offered to an ancient reader.

Perpetua's narrative proposes a clear alignment between her father's authority and that of the Roman magistrate. Each of her audiences with the procurator is preceded by a session with her father, and the attempt of the Roman state to require conformity from her is recast as a personal battle of will between herself and her distressed parent.

> My father also arrived from the city, worn with worry, and he came to see me with the idea of persuading me. 'Daughter,' he said, 'have pity on my grey head – have pity on me your father, if I deserve to be called your father, if I have favoured you above all your brothers, if I have raised you to reach this prime of your life. Do not abandon me to be the reproach of

[20]   Ibid. 27.
[21]   I have discussed this theme further in 'The Household as a Venue for Religious Conversion', in Beryl Rawson, ed., *A Companion to Families in the Greek and Roman Worlds* (Oxford, 2010), 183–97; and 'Ventriloquism and the Miraculous: Conversion, Preaching, and the Martyr Exemplum in Late Antiquity', in Kate Cooper and Jeremy Gregory, eds, *Signs, Wonders, Miracles: Representations of Divine Power in the Life of the Church*, SCH 41 (Woodbridge, 2005), 22–45.
[22]   On the network theory of conversion, see Rodney Stark, *The Rise of Christianity: A Sociologist Reconsiders History* (Princeton, NJ, 1996), 5–11.

men. Think of your brothers, think of your mother and your aunt, think of your child, who will not be able to live once you are gone. Give up your pride! You will destroy all of us! None of us will ever be able to speak freely again if anything happens to you!'[23]

The reader is invited to empathize with her father's attempts to dissuade her, but only up to a point. In the end, they offer a valuable opportunity for the martyr-in-waiting to practise her skill at holding her own in the face of authority. Standing up to her father is only the first step of a process that will escalate, resulting in a confrontation with the imperial representative Hilarianus, and finally in a public contest in the arena.[24]

Clearly Perpetua means to show far more sympathy with the father's plight than we see in the *Acts of Paul and Thecla*. In a sense, her sympathy is the first step of an evolution. From the third century onward, its place within the constellation of Christian identity strategies began to change. In narrative terms at least, Christian writers began to try to resolve the threat to paternal authority posed by the wife or child who chose the family of faith over the biological family.

ACCEPTING THE MISSIONARY FROM WITHIN

The narrative of resistance from within the household would prove a durable medium for cultivating Christian identity, which would endure into the early modern period as a paradigm of sanctity. Yet in these later narratives there is a twist to the old story. Instead of trying to discipline his dependent, the *pater* converts to Christianity and in many cases follows his wife or child to martyrdom. When the heroic child preaches to the father, or the heroic wife preaches to her husband, the man of the house responds. In the apocryphal *Acts of Thomas*, for example, Queen Tertia is initially

[23] *Passion of the Holy Perpetua and Felicitas* 5, in Herbert Musurillo, ed. and transl., *Acts of the Christian Martyrs*, OECT (Oxford, 1972).
[24] This reading of Perpetua is discussed at greater length in Kate Cooper, 'A Father, a Daughter, and a Procurator: Authority and Resistance in the Prison Memoir of Perpetua of Carthage', *GH* 23 (2011), 686–703.

converted by the apostle's preaching, but after the apostle himself is martyred, a miracle at his grave converts the king as well.[25]

The first expression of this new narrative development seems to emerge in the *Pseudo-Clementine Recognitions*.[26] The *Recognitions* are a third-century Christian romance which follows the family of the future pope Clement through a series of novelistic misadventures, during which the mother, father, Clement and his brothers must try to find one another after being separated by shipwreck and other misfortune.[27] Each family member comes to Christianity by a different route: while the *paterfamilias* engages in debate with a thoughtful fisherman who turns out to be St Peter, the mother and brothers come to the faith through bonds of friendship and ties of affection. Christianity, it seems, has something for everyone.

A martyr romance from the fifth or sixth century picks up the themes of the *Recognitions* and develops the intergenerational storyline further. In the *Passio Sebastiani*, two young martyrs-to-be, Marcellus and Marcellianus, deliver a sermon to their parents and wives about the pursuit of Christian perfection. Here, the young men hold the roles of 'husband' and 'son' simultaneously.

> Learn, most dear parents and wives, let your matrimonial affection learn to place the shield of virtue against the Devil's attack and against all the arrows of the carnal desires of the affections. And learn not to yield to the enemy when among the savage army of the tyrant. Learn to struggle more fiercely, to hold your ground … .[28]

---

[25] *Acts of Thomas*, in Hennecke and Schneemelcher, eds, *New Testament Apocrypha*, 2.

[26] I say 'seems' because the dating of many of the texts in question is uncertain, and the versions to come down to us often include earlier and later story elements; the miracle at the grave of Thomas, for example, probably developed in a later version of the story.

[27] On conversion in the *Recognitions*, see Kate Cooper, 'Matthidia's Wish: Division, Reunion, and the Early Christian Family in the pseudo-Clementine *Recognitions*', in George J. Brooke and Jean-Daniel Kaestli, eds, *Narrativity in Biblical Studies* (Leuven, 2000), 243–64; on the date and context of the narrative, Mark Edwards, 'The Clementina: A Christian Response to the Pagan Novel', *Classical Quarterly* 42 (1992), 459–71, offers an insightful discussion, with valuable starting points for further inquiry.

[28] *Passio Sebastiani* 27 (PL 17, cols 1113–50, at 1124), translations here and below are my own unless otherwise acknowledged.

In the *Passio Sebastiani*, such voices are always persuasive: in due course the parents and wives join forces with Marcus and Marcellianus.

I have argued elsewhere that the tension between the household and the resisting individual was schematized and transformed in post-Constantinian society, and the reintegration of the family bond in martyrdom reflects an attempt to resolve tensions between the monasteries, in which the martyr romances were produced, and the families of the monks and nuns, on whom the monasteries often depended for resources.[29] As the ascetic movement was progressively transformed from a movement of resistance to Constantinian Christianity into institutional monasticism, the relations between biological families and ascetic institutions had to be resolved. It was this paradoxical formula – a faith that both challenged the household and offered the theological resources for reconciling the challenge – that would serve as a basis for Christianity's place in medieval society.

THE RISE OF THE MARRIAGE VOW

The attempt to neutralize the tension between *patres* and their pious dependents coincided with changes in the material relations of the household in later antiquity. Most important among these, I would argue, was the transformation of marriage from a fundamentally voluntary contract – Roman thought saw the freely given and reversible mutual consent (*consensus*) of husband and wife as the foundation of the bond[30] – to a binding and irreversible vow. Even though Christian sources had discouraged divorce from the earliest times, it was condoned by Roman law virtually without restriction up to the time of Constantine (d. 337), and still widely available to Christians, although contested divorce was subject to restriction, up to the time of Justinian (d. 565).[31]

---

[29] Cooper, 'Family, Dynasty, and Conversion', 279.

[30] On consensus, see Susan Treggiari, *Roman Marriage: Iusti Coniuges From the Time of Cicero to the Time of Ulpian* (Oxford, 1991), ch. 2, 'Capacity and Intent', esp. 54–7.

[31] On the fluctuations in divorce legislation, see Judith Evans Grubbs, *Women and the Law in the Roman Empire: A Sourcebook on Marriage, Divorce and Widowhood* (London, 2002), 202–10. On the attitude of clerics 'on the ground' to divorce when it was unwelcome but perfectly legal, see Bagnall, 'Church, State, and Divorce'. See

In the Latin West, the principal thinker in developing the idea of the marriage vow as a binding and lasting commitment which broke free of the Roman ideal of freely given *consensus* was Augustine of Hippo. In his *De bono coniugali* Augustine had put forward the idea that the irreversible vow of marriage – for this vow he used the term *sacramentum* – was one of its central defining goods. The other two were *proles*, offspring, and *fides*, fidelity or faithful obedience.[32]

The Literal Meaning of Genesis, written between 400 and 415, knits these ideas into the story of Adam and Eve as told in Genesis.

> The good of marriage is threefold: fidelity, off-spring, and the oath. Fidelity (*fides*) ensures that no sexual intercourse takes place with another outside the bond of marriage. The off-spring (*proles*) is to be lovingly welcomed, affectionately nurtured, religiously reared. The oath (*sacramentum*) lays down that the marriage is not split asunder, and that a husband or wife rejected by the partner should not be joined to another, even for the sake of offspring.[33]

Although the idea of marriage as one of seven sacraments of the Church would not come into play until the Fourth Lateran Council (1215), the idea of the oath or *sacramentum*, which in Augustine's day evoked the binding vow of obedience unto death of a soldier or gladiator, carried with it the ideal of solemn irreversibility.

It was with the end of Roman rule that the idea of the binding vow of marriage began to acquire unstoppable momentum. The letters of Fulgentius of Ruspe (d. *c.*527), written during his exile from the Vandal kingdom of Carthage during the reign of the Arian King Thrasamund, take up the legacy of his fellow North African Augustine. It is Fulgentius who first explicitly refers to marriage as a vow which cannot be broken. In his letter to Optatus, a North African aristocrat whose wife has taken a deathbed vow of continence and then survived to regret it, Fulgentius pronounces that

also Judith Evans Grubbs, *Law and Family in Late Antiquity: The Emperor Constantine's Marriage Legislation* (Oxford, 1999), 253–60.

[32] Augustine, *The Good of Marriage* (*De bono coniugali*) 9.7.12. On *De bono coniugali*, see R. A. Markus, *The End of Ancient Christianity* (Cambridge, 1990), ch. 4, 'A Defence of Christian Mediocrity'.

[33] Augustine, *The Literal Meaning of Genesis* (*De Genesi ad litteram*) 9.7.12 (CSEL 28, 276).

the pre-existing marriage vow takes precedence over any subsequent commitment, which was made without the power to make
it.

The full ability to vow bodily continence is not available to the
married man or woman, whose body is not in his or her own
power but in that of the spouse … . When someone wishes to
make profession of the continence of his body which is under
the power of his spouse, it is like someone trying to give alms
or offer a sacrifice from what belongs to someone else.[34]

Marriage is no longer a matter of consensus; it has become an
obligation.[35]

Scholarship has still not fully accounted for the significance
of this development.[36] It is probably not a coincidence that in
the Latin West, the beginning of a period of cyclical military and
political crisis serious enough to result not only in regime change
but also in the imposition of diverse and conflicting legal traditions
would result in the replacement of the state by the Church as the
guarantor of reproductive allegiances between families.

At the same time, the establishment of an irrevocable bond
between husband and wife would have seemed a fitting instrument for an increasingly volatile social and political landscape. This
coincided, more or less, with the tendency of barbarian law to
structure the marriage relationship as one of strict dependency.[37]
Under Roman law, a wife belonged to the family of her father,
who had the right and responsibility to protect her, but under
Frankish law, for example, a married woman passed into the power
of her husband.

In all likelihood women's position within the household
changed for the worse, since their husbands were no longer strictly
accountable to their birth families for their treatment. An anon-

34 Fulgentius, *Ad Optatum* 14 (SC 487, 92–4); ET Robert B. Eno, *Fulgentius: Selected Works*, Fathers of the Church 95 (Washington, DC, 1997), 286.
35 Fulgentius, *Ad Optatum*, with discussion in Cooper, *Fall of the Roman Household*, 173–83. Fulgentius allows that it is possible for the spouses to choose continence together, but not for one to choose it without the approval of the other, since this would violate the apostle's doctrine of the conjugal debt (1 Cor. 7).
36 On the marriage vow, see Cooper, *Fall of the Roman Household*, 173–83, and literature cited there.
37 Julia M. H. Smith, 'Did Women have a Transformation of the Roman World?', *GH* 12 (2000), 552–71.

ymous fifth- or sixth-century devotional manual addressed to a married woman likens the marriage bond to enslavement: 'You have been bought, matron, and purchased by the contracts of your dowry agreement (*instrumentis dotalibus*), bound by as many ties as [you have] limbs.'[38] Anthropologically, it can be argued that the stronger marriage bond in fact weakened the connection between the two participating families, since it provided for an irreversible transfer of the wife from one family to the other, although in areas where Roman law was in force she remained technically part of her birth family.[39]

The Dangerous Vitality of Private Power: The Household and the Privatization of the Late Roman Landscape

Historians of the early Middle Ages have long argued that at the end of antiquity the Roman household played a central role in the empire's downfall. Gibbon argued two centuries ago that the fall of the Roman empire could be laid at the door of the household: it was the domestic challenge of Christian asceticism that had sapped the virility of Roman manhood, opening the way for the barbarians at the gates. Christian monks, not barbarian warlords, were the architects of the fall of Rome.[40] The process was not quite what Gibbon imagined, but he may have been right to point to the household's importance in this process of religious and social change.[41]

In the 1970s, John Matthews reframed Gibbon's challenge, a point underlined by Patrick Wormald in a justly famous review

---

[38] Anon., *Ad Gregoriam in Palatio* 7 (CChr.SL 25A, 202). There is an interesting discussion of the passage in Lesley Dossey, 'Wife Beating and Manliness in Late Antiquity', *P&P*, no. 199 (2008), 3–40. My own views on the text can be found in Kate Cooper, *The Fall of the Roman Household* (Cambridge, 2007), ch. 4, '"Such Trustful Partnership": The Marriage Bond in Latin Conduct Literature', with a full translation of the text at 239–83.

[39] Cooper, *Fall of the Roman Household*, 153–6.

[40] Notable recent examples are Peter Heather, *The Fall of the Roman Empire: A New History of Rome and the Barbarians* (Harlow, 2005), who makes a lively case for why the landed gentry might have seen barbarian warlords as attractive sponsors for their property rights; and Bryan Ward-Perkins, *The Fall of Rome and the End of Civilization* (Oxford, 2005), who stresses the long-term detriment to trade and prosperity caused by the resulting fragmentation.

[41] Cooper, 'Gender and the Fall of Rome', 198–9.

of Matthews's book.[42] Nineteenth-century writers had seen the self-interested manoeuvring of the last great Roman landowners as the emergence of private power at the expense of public authority, which would result in a system of seigneurial lordship. For Matthews – and, still more, Wormald and the early medievalists for whom he spoke – the fall of Rome was simply the ebbing away of public order. This was less a 'privatization' of power than a reversion to a 'default setting', or, as Wormald puts it, 'a common sense quest for local solutions to the urgent problem of maintaining a traditional way of life, on the part of an aristocracy whose horizons had always been at least partially local'.[43] This approach has informed English-speaking scholarship on late Roman landowners for a generation.[44] We have moved from the 'bad barons' of historiographical yore to a more sympathetic view of post-Roman elites as social and cultural brokers of a new order.

Such historiographical manoeuvrings do not, however, address Gibbon's fundamental point. Fall the Roman empire did, one household at a time. Christianity may not have brought 'superstition' into Roman homes, but as we have seen it did provide a potentially corrosive language of justified social disobedience. The vital and volatile subculture of the Roman household was able to absorb this challenge to its core idea of *pietas*. But this adaptation was accompanied by new strategies for sacralizing the bonds of domestic obligation, and carried unforeseen consequences. Traditionally, the household had played an integral part in the wider social order. But the new vision of the bonds of family was bound closely to the emerging power of the religious specialists who had supplied its language. It would long outlast the political order within which it had been conceived.

University of Manchester

---

[42] Patrick Wormald, 'The Decline of the Western Empire and the Survival of its Aristocracy', *JRS* 66 (1976), 217–26, reviewing John Matthews, *Western Aristocracies and Imperial Court*.

[43] Wormald, 'Decline of the Western Empire', 222.

[44] For complementary approaches, see Peter Sarris, 'The Origins of the Manorial Economy: New Insights from Late Antiquity', *EHR* 119 (2004), 279–311; Roberta Mazza, 'Households as Communities? *Oikoi* and *poleis* in Byzantine Egypt', in Onno M. van Nijf and Richard Alston, eds, *Political Culture in the Greek City after the Classical Age*, Groningen-Royal Holloway Studies on the Greek City after the Classical Age 2 (Leuven, 2011), 263–86.

MATERIAL CHRISTIANITY IN THE EARLY
MEDIEVAL HOUSEHOLD

by JULIA M. H. SMITH

Tu autem cum oraveris, intra in cubiculum tuum, et clauso ostio, ora Patrem tuum in abscondito: et Pater tuus, qui videt in abscondito, reddet tibi. ('But when you pray, go into your room and shut the door. Pray to your Father in private, and your Father, who sees into concealed places, will reward you': Matt. 6: 6)

Manuscript D.V.3 in the Biblioteca Nazionale of Turin is a fat, late eighth-century volume of martyr narratives. Produced at Soissons, probably in the nunnery of Notre-Dame, it may be no coincidence that eighteen of its forty texts concern female martyrs.[1] A further four address familial groups in which wives or mothers play prominent roles. The earliest Latin version of the passion of St Adrian (*BHL* 3744) is among them: one of many late, 'novel-esque' accounts of martyrdom, it is constructed out of clichéd formulae and predictable tropes for post-persecution audiences, like others of its genre.[2] Lacking any historical verisimilitude about the age of persecutions, the passion of Adrian is characteristic of this group of hagiographies in offering valuable insights into domestic Christianity in the age in which it was composed: it brings into sharp focus links between women and material Christianity within the late antique household, the theme this essay pursues into the Carolingian period.

It remained a popular text throughout the Middle Ages. Figure I illustrates a compressed version of its narrative, whose full plotline runs as follows: Adrian, chief official at the court of the tyrant

---

[1] E. A. Lowe, *Codices Latini Antiquiores: A Palaeographical Guide to Latin Manuscripts prior to the Ninth Century*, 11 vols + supplement vols (Oxford, 1934–71), 4: 13 (no. 446); Albert Poncelet, 'Catalogus codicum hagiographicorum latinorum bibliothecae nationalis Taurinensis', *AnBoll* 28 (1909), 417–59, at 419–22; T. A. M. Bishop, 'The Scribes of the Corbie *a–b*', in Peter Godman and Roger Collins, eds, *Charlemagne's Heir: New Perspectives on the Reign of Louis the Pious (814–840)* (Oxford, 1990), 523–36, at 535–6.

[2] The classic discussion of novel-esque hagiography is Hippolyte Delehaye, *Les passions des martyrs et les genres littéraires*, 2nd edn (Brussels, 1966), 227–30.

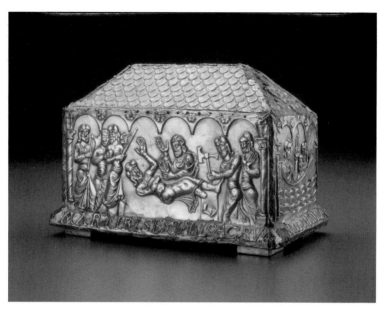

Fig. 1: Twelfth-century Spanish reliquary-casket. Silver repoussé over oak core, 15.9 x 25.4 x 14.5 cm. Left to right: Adrian is led away to his execution; Natalia holds up her husband's severed hand; the executioner lops off Adrian's feet; Natalia steals away with Adrian's hand; Natalia sails away carrying Adrian's hand (end panel). Kate S. Buckingham Endowment, 1943.65, The Art Institute of Chicago. Photography © The Art Institute of Chicago.

Maximian (286–305) at Nicomedia, oversaw a round-up of Christians, but was so impressed by their steadfastness under threat of death that he converted and was thrown into jail alongside them. His wife Natalia came from a very high-ranking Christian family, but had hitherto kept her religion secret. Rushing to the jail, she fell at her husband's feet, kissed his chains, confessed her true Christian identity and exhorted him to persevere in his new-found faith. Much of the first part is taken up with Natalia and the other noble ladies of the city caring for the Christian prisoners, cleansing their festering wounds and exhorting them to keep strong in their faith; when the captives were finally led before the emperor, all except Adrian had suffered so much from the appalling conditions in the prison that they could not stand and were too weak to be tortured. So they were sent back to jail, where the executioners arrived with butcher-blocks and cleavers. Natalia insisted that Adrian must be the first: she steadied first one then the other of his feet on the butcher-block while it was chopped off and his thigh smashed; she then did likewise for his hand. Then the other Christians met the same end. Their job finished, the executioners made a pyre of all the bodies, but a sudden thunderstorm and torrential downpour (with an earthquake for good measure) sent them fleeing in fear and extinguished the fire. The women were retrieving relics (*reliquiae*) from the pyre when one of Nicomedia's leading Christians appeared and announced he was leaving for the safer environment of Byzantium, a short sail across the Sea of Marmara. The first part of the story ends when the women gratefully accepted his offer to take the pile of bodies with him.

This gruesome episode prefaces an exemplary tale of elite household Christianity in which a woman is the principal character and her chamber is the setting, for Natalia is now a young widow, beautiful and wealthy. While the executioners were chopping up the other Christians in the prison, she had smeared herself in her husband's blood and concealed his severed hand in the folds of her cloak. Unbeknownst to anyone, she returned home with it, anointed it with myrrh, wrapped it in purple cloth and placed it at the head of her bed. Soon thereafter, she accepted an offer of marriage from the tribune of the city, but asked for three days in which to prepare for the wedding. She used the interval to return to her bedroom (*cubiculum*) where her husband's hand was, and, falling on her face in prayer, asked God to help her preserve Adrian's marriage bed from defilement. After further adventures, she escaped to Byzantium, where she placed Adrian's hand upon his body, knelt down in prayer alongside it and then fell into an exhausted sleep. As she slumbered, a vision summoned her to join the other martyrs in heaven; the story ends with her burial alongside them.[3] The sleeping-chamber or *cubiculum* is thus the place where Christian moral codes of sexual self-restraint, fidelity and honourable widowhood are enacted: it is also where relics are kept, heartfelt prayers uttered and visions received. Here, the gospel injunction to private prayer merged with the ethical and material practices of the Christianity of the age.

---

[3] 'De S. Adriano martyre et sociis', ed. L. Surius, in *De probatis sanctorum historiis*, 6 vols (Cologne, 1570–5), 5: 123–31.

★ ★ ★

The *passio Adriani* may well have been composed to appeal to a readership of fifth- or sixth-century pious aristocratic wives and widows. It is certainly redolent of life in fifth-century elite households, whose religious practices, as Kim Bowes has observed, had three principal characteristics.[4] Firstly, they were largely independent of the diocesan Church, even though some heads of households had themselves been ordained to the priesthood. Secondly, they commonly involved extemporized forms of familial asceticism practised within and for the household, especially – but by no means exclusively – by women. Thirdly, in addition to prayer, religious beliefs were expressed in and through the material culture of the home, in the form of paintings, textiles, floor tiles, lamps and other everyday objects with explicitly Christian scenes and iconography (see Figs 2–4).[5] Within the domestic milieu, these were coupled with a 'tactile piety' of material substances: eucharistic bread, phials of oil or water from saints' shrines and biblical locales, together with anything portable blessed by a holy man that could be taken home from a pilgrimage and bring its therapeutic powers of spiritual and physical healing into the home (see Figs 5–7).[6] Although we are not told what the 'relics' were which Natalia's female companions rescued from the martyrs' pyre in Nicomedia – perhaps other lopped-off limbs, perhaps items of clothing or personal adornment, perhaps kindling – nor what they did with them, the narrative certainly reflects a world in which martyr relics were as common in the home as the flasks of holy oil, water or dust which pilgrims

---

[4] Kim Bowes, *Private Worship, Public Values, and Religious Change in Late Antiquity* (Cambridge, 2008); and, from a different perspective, Kate Cooper, *The Fall of the Roman Household* (Cambridge, 2007).

[5] Eunice Dauterman Maguire, Henry Maguire and Maggie J. Duncan-Flowers, *Art and Holy Powers in the Early Christian House*, Illinois Byzantine Studies (Urbana, IL, 1989); Blake Leyerle, 'Pilgrim *eulogiae* and Domestic Rituals', *ARG* 10 (2008), 223–37; William Anderson, 'The Archaeology of Late Antique Pilgrim Flasks', *Anatolian Studies* 54 (2004), 79–93, at 86–7, for ampullae found in domestic buildings; Jonathan P. Conant, *Staying Roman: Conquest and Identity in Africa and the Mediterranean, 439–700* (Cambridge, 2012), 343, for scenes of saints on terracotta tiles.

[6] Derek Krueger, 'Christian Piety and Practice in the Sixth Century', in Michael Maas, ed., *The Cambridge Companion to the Age of Justinian* (Cambridge, 2005), 291–315, quotation at 303; Helen C. Evans and Brandie Ratliff, eds, *Byzantium and Islam: Age of Transition, 5th–7th century* (New York, 2012), 89–92; Gary Vikan, *Early Byzantine Pilgrimage Art*, 2nd edn (Washington, DC, 2010).

Figs 2a–2b: Glass bottle with stylite saint. Mould-blown dull green hexagonal bottle, probably of Syrian manufacture, mid-fifth to seventh century, 22.5 x 6.5 cm. Two of the six sides have a lattice pattern, while two depict palm-fronds, one a cross on a column, and one a stylite saint. British Museum 1911,0513.1. Images © Trustees of the British Museum.

Fig. 3 (left): Lamp with Chi-Rho monogram, North Africa/Tunisia, mid- to late fifth century, hard-fired clay, 5.0 x 14.0 x 8.0 cm. Malcove Collection, University of Toronto Art Centre, Gift of Dr Lillian Malcove 1982, M82.354. Courtesy of the University of Toronto Art Centre. Photography by Toni Hafkenscheid.

Fig. 4 (right): Reliquary amulet, Early Christian/Byzantine, date unknown, bronze, 2.5 x 7.5 x 3.2 cm. Presumably designed to be fastened to a belt or a horse's harness, this miniature cart contains a compartment for a relic or other sacred object. The cross on its sliding lid and the XP within the magical inscription make its Christian meaning explicit. Malcove Collection, University of Toronto Art Centre, Gift of Dr Lillian Malcove 1982, M82.387. Courtesy of the University of Toronto Art Centre. Photography by Toni Hafkenscheid.

Fig. 5: Pilgrim token or disc depicting St Menas, Early Byzantine/Coptic, fifth to sixth century, terracotta, diameter 7.0 cm. The iconography of a pair of camels kneeling at the saint's feet is characteristic of this popular Egyptian shrine at the desert oasis of Abu Mena, 45 miles west of Alexandria. Malcove Collection, University of Toronto Art Centre, Gift of Dr Lillian Malcove 1982, M82.260. Courtesy of the University of Toronto Art Centre. Photography by Toni Hafkenscheid.

acquired at shrines, the twigs and pebbles they gathered at biblical sites, or the fruit and bread blessed by holy men.

Relics are particularly useful 'clues' to domestic Christianity because they invite attention to the household as a space within which objects, words, gestures and cosmologies converged into religious behaviours and practices. Moreover, women's contributions are especially significant when viewed from domestic and familial perspectives.[7] Although Merovingian and Carolingian hagiography frequently emphasizes the social context of early medieval Christianity, it commonly gives preference to its practice outside the home, in churches and at saints' shrines. Similarly, although Carolingian thinkers constructed a cogent vision of the early medieval household as a moral entity by fusing the discourses of marriage, patriarchal authority and the control of sexuality, it nevertheless reveals little about the actual practices – as distinct from aspirations – of Christian living.[8] Recent research, however, has trans-

[7] As I argued in Julia M. H. Smith, 'Did Women have a Transformation of the Roman World?', *GH* 12 (2000), 552–71.

[8] See Valerie Garver, *Women and Aristocratic Culture in the Carolingian World* (Ithaca, NY, 2009); Rachel Stone, *Morality and Masculinity in the Carolingian Empire* (Cambridge,

Fig. 6 (left):   Pilgrim flask. Terracotta, sixth century, from the shrine of St John the Evangelist, Ephesus, 5.0 x 5.0 x 1.8 cm. Musée du Louvre, MNB2066. Image: Marie-Lan Nguyen, © Wikimedia Commons.

Fig. 7 (right):   Pilgrim flask of St Sergios. Tin-lead alloy, 5.4 x 3.81 x 1.59 cm. This sixth- or seventh-century flask depicts the saint on horseback, surrounded by the inscription ΕΥΛΟΓΙΑ ΚΥΡΙΟΥ ΤΟΥ ΑΓΙΟΥ ΣΕΡΓΙΟΥ ('Blessing of the Lord of Saint Sergios') and in all probability was made at (or for) his shrine at Sergiopolis (Rusafa, Syria). Walters Art Museum, 55.105. Image: © Wikimedia Commons.

formed knowledge of early medieval homes as places where men and women lived, loved, worked and prayed. Archaeological excavation has revealed elite lifestyles based on conspicuous consumption in complex residences, to which historians are now adding the textual evidence for furnishings, dress, personal adornment and status-specific occupations for aristocratic men and women.[9] We

2012), with full earlier bibliography in both. See also Julia M. H. Smith, 'Gender and Ideology in the Early Middle Ages', in R. N. Swanson, ed., *Gender and Christian Religion*, SCH 34 (Woodbridge, 1998), 51–73.

9   I summarize drastically: see Christopher Loveluck, 'The Dynamics of Elite Lifestyles in the "Rural World", AD 600–1150: Archaeological Perspectives from northwest Europe', in François Bougard, Régine Le Jan and Rosamond McKitterick, eds, *La culture du haut moyen âge: une question d'élites?* (Turnhout, 2009), 139–70; idem, 'Problems of the Definition and Conceptualisation of Early Medieval Elites, AD 450–900: The Dynamics of the Archaeological Evidence', in François Bougard, Hans-Werner Goetz and Régine Le Jan, eds, *Théorie et pratiques des élites au haut moyen âge* (Turnhout, 2011), 21–68; Robin Fleming, 'The New Wealth, the New Rich and the New Political Style in Late Anglo-Saxon England', *Anglo-Norman Studies* 23 (2001), 1–22; Valerie Garver, 'Textiles as a Means of Female Religious Participation in the Carolingian World', in Sari Katajala-Peltomaa and Ville Vuolante, eds, *Ancient and Medieval Religion in Practice* (Helsinki, 2014), 133–44. I am grateful to Val Garver for allowing me access to her work in advance of publication.

can, then, turn to household Christianity with at least an outline awareness of its physical setting and material context.

Despite their relative grandeur, Merovingian, Carolingian and late Anglo-Saxon aristocratic homes lacked the multiple rooms and spatial complexity that characterized late Roman aristocratic villas.[10] Instead, a residence was essentially a large hall with one or two, or at most three, sleeping chambers (*cubiculum, camera*) opening off it, and a cluster of other buildings nearby, sometimes but by no means invariably including a chapel.[11] It would be misplaced to project onto early medieval halls the arrangement of Roman villas into varying levels of openness and seclusion, let alone any modern, bourgeois notion of 'privacy', for although an emphasis on conjugal sexual privacy and Christian distaste for nakedness had emerged in the late antique Mediterranean, household slaves, servants and officials nevertheless scurried in and out of bedrooms.[12] Furthermore, rumour and political gossip about sexual improprieties commonly originated in the chamber, and, at least in Anglo-Saxon England, royal governance might on occasion also be conducted in the king's chamber, his *būr*. King Alfred (871–99) is famously reported to have heard a lawsuit while washing his hands in his *būr*.[13]

We should envisage early medieval chambers as porous rather than private, oscillating between accessible and reserved spaces. This pertained in religious as well as political matters. Demons, sexual temptation, sickness and death might lurk in bedrooms, where the faithful kept relics of saints to combat them. To ward off demons at night, the fifth-century ascetic Theodoret, bishop of Cyrrhus (Syria), for example, slept with a flask of oil from the

[10] Bowes, *Private Worship, Public Values*, 125–52; Leslie Dossey, 'Sleeping Arrangements and Private Space: A Cultural Approach to the Subdivision of Late Antique Homes', in David Brakke, Deborah Deliyannis and Edward Watts, eds, *Shifting Cultural Frontiers in Late Antiquity* (Farnham, 2013), 181–97.

[11] Loveluck, 'Definition and Conceptualisation', 52–7; idem, 'Dynamics of Elite Lifestyles', 154–7. Of the five royal estates inventoried in the so-called *Brevium exempla* from the reign of Charlemagne, only one had its own chapel: MGH Capit. 1, 254–6, no. 128, cl. 25–39, chapel in cl. 32.

[12] Dossey, 'Sleeping Arrangements'.

[13] *Charters of Christ Church Canterbury*, ed. N. P. Brooks and S. E. Kelly, 2 vols, Anglo-Saxon Charters 17–18 (Oxford, 2013), 2: 853, 855 (no. 104), with comments at 860–1. For Old English *būr* as equivalent to *cubiculum* or *camera*, and for examples of royal business conducted there, see the *Old English Dictionary: A to G Online*, at <http://www.doe.utoronto.ca>, last accessed 25 July 2013.

martyrs' shrines above his bed, and the cloak of St James under his pillow.[14] Eligius, goldsmith to King Dagobert and future bishop of Noyon (*c.*590–660) did likewise. His friend and biographer, Dado of Rouen, describes in some detail the bedroom of the house Eligius inhabited at court, and twice remarks on the numerous relics of saints which hung above the bed, so close that, one night while he was experiencing a divine vision, 'the sweetest drops … like balsam' fell from them onto Eligius's head and perfumed his chamber with their heady scent. In his bedroom, Eligius kept a revolving bookstand containing many books of Scripture which he read eagerly, and he also spent much of each night prostrate in prayer on a hair shirt on the floor beside the bedstead.[15]

Early medieval bedrooms, then, could be sites of intense religious experience. As a place for prayer, relics and (for the literate) books of Scripture, the *cubiculum* continued to function as an informal prayer space at the heart of the household.[16] Its religiosity was also porous, for material substances might transfer its sacred charge to the wider world. Gerald of Aurillac (d. 909) was a late ninth-century aristocrat who led a highly unusual celibate and semi-ascetic life on his family estates in the Auvergne, which he in due course turned into a monastery, although he never formally took the habit himself. His almsgiving and peaceable conduct gave him a reputation for holiness which was enhanced by the actions of others: according to his tenth-century biographer Odo of Cluny, the infirm were accustomed to steal the water in which he had washed his hands, and to cure themselves with it.[17] More frequently, however, it seems to have been beds and bedding themselves which conveyed this miracle-working capacity to others,

---

[14] Leyerle, 'Pilgrim *eulogiae*', 225.

[15] *Vita Eligii* 1.8, 12 (MGH SRM 4, 675, 679).

[16] For similar practices in other medieval periods and places, see Judith Herrin, 'The Icon Corner in Medieval Byzantium', in Anneke B. Mulder-Bakker and Jocelyn Wogan-Browne, eds, *Household, Women and Christianities in Late Antiquity and the Middle Ages* (Turnhout, 2005), 71–90; Diana Webb, 'Domestic Space and Devotion in the Middle Ages', in Andrew Spicer and Sarah Hamilton, eds, *Defining the Holy: Sacred Space in Medieval and Early Modern Europe* (Aldershot, 2005), 27–47.

[17] *Vita Geraldi confessoris* 9; *Catalogus codicum hagiographicorum Latinorum antiquorum saeculo xvi qui asservantur in Bibliotheca Nationali Parisiensi*, 3 vols (Brussels, 1889–93), 2: 399. I accept the arguments of Matthew Kuefler that Odo of Cluny wrote the *vita brevior* of Gerald but not its longer version: 'Dating and Authorship of the Writings about Saint Gerald of Aurillac', *Viator* 44/2 (2013), 49–97, and am grateful to him for sharing his work with me in advance of publication.

whether it was the straw slipped secretly under the mattress on which Germanus of Auxerre (375–448) lay when staying with a pious priest and his wife, the hair shirt which Queen Radegund (c.520–87) put on when she left her husband's bed at night to prostrate herself in prayer beside the privy, or the 'little bed' on which Gertrude of Nivelles (628–58) rested between her vigils and prayers.[18]

Gregory of Tours also tells many stories about the curative properties of beds and bedding. Two concerned his own mother, Armentaria, one of his favoured sources of information. She came from a distinguished senatorial family in eastern Gaul. Relics, including beds, had been central to her own household religion ever since an occasion during her childhood when she had been cured of the quartan fever by slipping into the bed of her saintly grandfather, Bishop Gregory of Langres.[19] As a grown woman, she was among the many people who cut fibres from the rope-bed of a different bishop, Silvester of Chalon-sur-Sâone (which had been moved into his cathedral because of its curative powers), and took them home to hang round the neck of a fevered girl.[20]

Additional stories handed down to Gregory by his mother give us an even fuller insight into the domestic ownership, use and meaning of relics in the sixth century. Armentaria had been widowed early and left with two young sons whom she raised with the help of episcopal relatives.[21] Among her inheritance from Gregory's father Florentius was a gold locket containing the ashes of unnamed martyrs. Her husband had acquired it soon after their marriage, and had always carried with him to protect himself from bandits, floods and other attacks.[22] In her widowhood, Armentaria wore these relics round her neck, and on one occasion, their intercession saved the piles of newly threshed grain from a fire at harvest time. When Gregory, in his turn, inherited these relics, he carried

---

[18] Constantius, *Vita S. Germani* 22 (ed. René Borius, *Vie de Saint Germain d'Auxerre*, SC 112, 164–7); Venantius Fortunatus/Baudonivia, *De vita Sanctae Radegundis* 1.5, 2.15 (MGH SRM 2, 366–7, 387); *De virtutibus sanctae Geretrudis* 4 (MGH SRM 2, 466).

[19] *Liber vitae patrum* 7.2 (MGH SRM 1/2, 238).

[20] *Liber in gloria confessorum* 84 (MGH SRM 1/2, 352).

[21] On Gregory, his family and familial saints' cults, see Raymond Van Dam, *Saints and their Miracles in Late Antique Gaul* (Princeton, NJ, 1993), 50–68.

[22] For a photograph of a small sixth-century gold locket-style reliquary of Byzantine manufacture but found in Spain, see Vikan, *Early Byzantine Pilgrimage Art*, 59 (fig. 36).

them in his pocket, and also benefitted from their protection while travelling.[23] For the bishop of Tours, then, these unnamed martyr remains combined the memories of his parents with the presence of the saints. Both heirloom and reliquary, the tiny, gold medallion encapsulated family identity and saintly protection, whether on the road or around the house and its estates. Safeguarding body, personhood and property, it exemplifies the domestic potency of relics in sixth-century Gaul. As befitted her senatorial background, Armentaria may well have inhabited a many-roomed late Roman villa. Her home certainly had a separate prayer room (*oratorium*) in which she had placed relics of St Eusebius of Vercelli, which also played a meaningful role in her life.[24] Gregory's tales of his mother also take us back to beds, bedding and what was perhaps the greatest threat to any early medieval household: fire. One winter night, she passed the evening in pleasant conversation beside a well stoked fire. Then, after all the household had gone to bed, Armentaria got up and moved her bed near the hearth, and while she slept there, sparks from the embers rose up into the roof-beams and set one of them alight. She slept on, the beam blazing above her, until at last she awoke and called her servants to throw water onto it. That the other rafters and the roof itself did not catch fire was, Gregory firmly believed (as presumably did his mother), due to the presence nearby of Eusebius's relics.[25]

Armentaria's relic-centred domestic piety finds many parallels in other tales which Gregory recounted. To be effective, relics did not need to be located in a distinct prayer space or to belong to persons of elite status, but they did need to be cared for appro-

---

[23] *Liber in gloria martyrum* 83 (MGH SRM 1/2, 94–5), but he does not reveal where he placed it at night. Gregory has numerous other stories of relics which protect crops, vines and fruit trees.

[24] For a detailed description of an estate *oratorium* as a separate building with windows, locked door and its own custodian, see *Liber in gloria martyrum* 8 (MGH SRM 1/2, 43). See Margarete Weidemann, *Kulturgeschichte der Merowingerzeit nach den Werken Gregors von Tours*, 2 vols, Römisch-Germanisches Zentralmuseum Monographien (Mainz, 1982), 2: 130, for other *villae* with their own *oratoria*. As early as 517, the Council of Epaone, cl. 25, railed against saints' relics kept in estate prayer rooms in places where there were no diocesan clergy in the vicinity and tried to prevent the ordination of clergy to these private chapels unless they were properly resourced: *Concilia Galliae A. 511–A. 695*, ed. C Munier, CChr.SL 148A, 30.

[25] *Liber in gloria confessorum* 3 (MGH SRM 1/2, 300–1). Gregory's details of sixth-century domestic furnishings are assembled by Weidemann, *Kulturgeschichte*, 2: 358–62.

priately. Two of his exemplary stories are set in modest lodgings, perhaps one-roomed huts. Before Gregory's episcopal ordination, one of his household servants kept a relic in his *hospitiolum* that he had taken from the wooden railing around St Martin's bed, but he did not care for it properly and all his family fell ill until he surrendered it to Gregory, who put it with great veneration in a 'worthy place', whereupon they all recovered their health. The other incident concerns one of Gregory's deacons, a man who had been healed by a flask of rose oil which he had placed at St Martin's shrine. Thereafter, he kept it hanging on the wall of his dirt-floored dwelling. When a demon shattered the vessel and spilled the precious oil, a servant carefully gathered up the fragments of glass and the oil-soaked dust, which Gregory reconstituted into another flask. Its quantity increased and its healing properties cured many other people.[26]

* * *

Late antique habits of domestic Christianity thus persisted into the Merovingian era. Whether we conceive of the household as the narrow family of parents and children, the co-residential group of master or mistress with servants and slaves, or, in a more extensive sense, as the productive, socioeconomic unit of a landed estate, the material stuff of sanctity and miracle-working was widely diffused around it, at least according to Gregory of Tours. Relics were to be found on the walls, in bedrooms and prayer rooms and in the fields. Equally, they were worn around the neck or carried in the pocket, blurring any distinction between sacred and non-sacred space. They offered tangible and unmediated access to biblical history and to the protective help of Christian saints.

Nevertheless, the place of relics in household Christianity did not remain completely static throughout the early Middle Ages. To be sure, members of the Carolingian lay elite continued to own them and to bequeath them to their heirs, and on occasion relics continued to work miracles. But, by the Carolingian era, methods of storing and venerating relics had altered as their spiritual meaning evolved. At the same time, attitudes of Carolingian

---

[26] *Liber de virtutibus sancti Martini episcopi* 1.35, 2.32 (MGH SRM 1/2, 155, 170–1).

churchmen to the domestication of relics and miracles became far less tolerant than they had been in earlier centuries.

Both changes are brought into sharp focus in the writings of Einhard (*c.*770–840), best known as Charlemagne's biographer. A lay scholar who passed his entire life in an ambiguous relationship to both the secular and the ecclesiastical worlds, Einhard spent the second half of his career in the interstices between Louis the Pious's imperial court and his own religious foundations at Michelstadt and Seligenstadt. He had masterminded the audacious theft of the relics of Sts Marcellinus and Peter from Rome's cata-combs in 827–8, to be installed in first one, then the other, of the churches under his direct lordship. He then commemorated their arrival north of the Alps with a fulsome, if tendentious, narrative. This authenticated the relics in their new homeland by detailing Einhard's careful dissemination of fragments around various churches and reporting their many miracles on Carolingian soil. Almost all the saints' exploits occurred when their relics were in churches, either Einhard's own or those to which he distributed portions of their ashes.[27]

Einhard reported his relics' activities in Frankish churches staffed with clergy who performed the liturgy of the offices and mass in front of their shrines, but on two occasions he punctuated his account with stories of miracles in household settings. The first ones took place in the urban setting of the imperial capital of Aachen, after Einhard had recovered a portion of the relics which had been stolen by the staff of Hilduin, the imperial arch-chaplain, but before he had transported them on to Seligenstadt. Having processed them with crosses and candles to his own home, he briefly installed them there in a makeshift *oratorium*, where they worked miracles. The clear implication is that – unlike Hilduin's residence – Einhard's own townhouse lacked a separate, formally constituted prayer room, but that he felt the presence of the relics required one to be created in a hurry, so that the offices could

---

[27] This paragraph summarizes my earlier articles, 'Einhard: The Sinner and the Saints', *TRHS* 6th ser., 13 (2003), 55–77; and '"Emending Evil Ways and Praising God's Omnipotence": Einhard and the Uses of Roman Martyrs', in Kenneth Mills and Anthony Grafton, eds, *Conversion in Late Antiquity and the Early Middle Ages: Seeing and Believing* (Rochester, NY, 2003), 189–223. See also Steffen Patzold, *Ich und Karl der Große. Das Leben des Höflings Einhard* (Stuttgart, 2013).

be recited in front of them.[28] Even though the relics' stay in his Aachen residence was brief, Einhard wanted them to be located amidst crosses, candles and clerical liturgy in a clearly designated part of the house. The miracles performed in this temporary resting place signalled the stolen relics' pleasure at being returned to their rightful owner and his appropriate veneration of them.

On the other occasion when Marcellinus and Peter worked miracles in a domestic setting, Einhard admitted to being puzzled.[29] On his way from Seligenstadt to the court at Aachen in November 828, he had stopped at the royal villa of Sinzig for the night, and, although it emerges that he did have some of the relics with him, their precise location is never vouchsafed. After the evening meal, Einhard withdrew with his servants into the seclusion of his bedroom. He was preparing to sleep when his butler rushed in and announced that two miracles had taken place down in the cellars, where drink was being handed out to the servants. One concerned beer that turned into wine, the other a candle which relit itself. After giving thanks to God and ordering his butler away, Einhard settled into bed and lay awake for a long while. 'Why', he pondered, 'had a miracle of this sort occurred in a royal house rather than in the place where the most blessed bodies of the sacred martyrs were enshrined [i.e. Seligenstadt]?' He was unable to answer his own question.

For Einhard, then, relics belonged in sacred spaces and needed special care. They ought to be under clerical guardianship in places equipped for the liturgy. He certainly did not expect miracles to occur outside such a setting.[30] His opinion conformed to that of other Carolingian authors, for on the few other occasions when miracles are reported inside houses, their context is always clerically controlled or validated. They take one of two forms. In one no relics at all are involved, but something happens which leads to the miraculous appearance of an object which is immediately taken into clerical keeping. Alternatively the relics are taken, or sent, into lay homes by clergy, or on their instruction. Illustrative of the former is a poor peasant couple who wanted to visit the shrine

[28] *Translatio SS. Marcellini et Petri* 2.3 (MGH SS 15/1, 246); ibid. 2.5 (247), for celebrating vespers and nocturns there.

[29] Ibid. 3.11 (251–2).

[30] Ibid. 4.8 (258–9), for a further example of a miracle in an atypical setting.

of St Gall during the 740s. The wife wove a piece of cloth to take as a gift to the church and when she had finished it, she wrapped a small cake of wax in it and put it in her linen chest. Before they could set out on their journey, however, their house burned down, with all its contents. When the couple returned to see if they could retrieve any iron implements, they discovered the cloth and the wax remained unscorched amidst the embers. So they immediately hurried to the monastery, told their tale to the monks and donated the cloth upon the altar, where it remained as a sign for a long time.[31] The stole of Folcuin, bishop of Thérouanne (d. 855), illustrates the second pattern. This was renowned for helping women in childbirth, and seems to have been used as an early medieval precursor of the Marian birthing girdles of the later Middle Ages, for when women's labour dragged on for days it was taken from the altar of his church into their homes to bring them back from the brink of death.[32] These vignettes, and others like them, indicate the way in which relics participated in the productive and reproductive rhythms of the Carolingian household.

These objects and the accounts of miracles associated with them tied women and households to the Church in ways which sustained ecclesiastical priorities. They suggest an antipathy to miracle-working relics 'on the loose' coupled with a reluctance to countenance unsanctioned thaumaturgical activity. A similarly heavy weight of institutional pressure fuelled the hostility evinced by the Carolingian ecclesiastical establishment towards wonder-working ascetics as well as towards those saints' cults that eluded its direct control.[33] These stories from pious households indicate that Carolingian churchmen resorted to the additional tactic of seeking guardianship of miracle-working objects so that they could be corralled into clerical custody.

It is impossible to gauge just how deeply household Christianity

---

[31]   *Vita Galli vetustissima* 9 (MGH SRM 4, 255). For a similar story of the domestic generation of a relic in the diocese of Thérouanne, see *Annales de Saint-Bertin*, ed. Félix Grat, Jeanne Vieillard and Suzanne Clémencet (Paris, 1964), 92 (*s.a.* 862).

[32]   Folcuin of Lobbes, *Vita Folquini episcopi Morinensis* 14 (MGH SS 15/1, 430). For analogous examples, see *Miracula S. Reginae* (ActaSS Sept. 3, 42); Hincmar, *Vita Remigii episcopi Remensis* 26 (MGH SRM 3, 322–3).

[33]   Paul Fouracre, 'The Origins of the Carolingian Attempt to Regulate the Cult of Saints', in James Howard-Johnston and Paul Anthony Hayward, eds, *The Cult of Saints in Late Antiquity and the Early Middle Ages* (Oxford, 1999), 143–65.

was affected by efforts to assert institutional control over charisma and miracles. Relics do sometimes feature in domestic spaces in other Carolingian sources, but are presented as thaumaturgically inert. Did they perform miracles, but stories about them fail to cross from oral to written form? Did ecclesiastical authors deliberately and consistently suppress all mentions that reached their ears? Was Einhard's puzzlement about why his relics had performed miracles in a house a literary tactic to distance himself from conventions that he deliberately breached? Before concluding that the Carolingian household was not normally a space of miraculous activity, a glance forward to the high and late Middle Ages is helpful. In later centuries, the predilection of layfolk for seeking out relics, taking them into their home and being open to their miracle-working capacity is clear. So too are the various authorial strategies which churchmen used to filter, edit and control stories about domestic miracles.[34] In this regard, the material Christianity of the Carolingian household remains far more elusive than that of subsequent centuries, as well as preceding ones.

★ ★ ★

More readily detectable is a significant reconfiguration in the meaning of sacred stuff in household Christianity in the course of the early Middle Ages. It reflected the maturation of a slow but fundamental alteration in the relationship between life on earth and the hereafter, one which had massive consequences for the 'imaginative content of religious giving [and] the flow of wealth from earth to heaven'.[35] As the early medieval search for Christian salvation came to place ever greater emphasis on intercessory monastic prayer and saintly patronage, so saints and their relics were reconceptualized as landowners in their own right. Some elite landowners transformed their personal *oratorium* into a

---

[34] See, for example, Rachel Koopmans, *Wonderful to Relate: Miracle Stories and Miracle Collecting in High Medieval England* (Philadelphia, PA, 2011), 141, on the domestic origins of Thomas Becket's cult in the hours immediately following his murder. I am very grateful to Rachel Koopmans for drawing my attention to the numerous Becket miracles in household settings narrated by Benedict of Peterborough but omitted from other Becket miracle collections.

[35] Peter Brown, *Through the Eye of a Needle: Wealth, the Fall of Rome and the Making of Christianity in the West, 350–550 AD* (Princeton, NJ, 2012), 479–526, quotation at xxv.

family mausoleum, assigned it a separate landed endowment and appointed their own clerical staff to ensure the commemoration of those buried in it, to say prayers of intercession for their souls in the afterlife, and to take care of the relics. Others separated the spaces and resources for familial asceticism away from those of the rest of the household.[36] In brief, as lordship over family monasteries with relic chapels at their centre comes into historical focus, so household asceticism, domestic relics and the bedchamber as a place of prayer all retreat from prominence.

Careful attention to the exact location of relics in personal ownership reveals the extent of this transformation. Einhard had admitted to having relics of Marcellinus and Peter with him when he travelled back and forth between Seligenstadt and Aachen, and it is in travellers' company that domestic relics are perhaps most readily visible. It is little surprise to find missionaries such as Boniface, Liudger and Willehad travelling with them; they and other ecclesiastics sometimes wore them around their necks.[37] At other times, churchmen placed the sacred remains on portable altars in temporary accommodation, as did Fardulf, abbot of Saint-Denis, who took relics of St Denis with him when he accompanied Charlemagne on campaign in Saxony. We should note their placement: the clergy into whose care Fardulf entrusted the remains placed them on a wooden altar in premises described as a 'tiny dwelling'. However, the cleric on duty went out and closed the door, and a candle set the altar alight. Much to everyone's relief, neither the relics nor the white altarcloth were damaged.[38] Relics, then, were integral to even a makeshift, temporary prayer room.

Rulers and members of the lay elite likewise relied on portable liturgical equipment when they rested during their travels. Gerald of Aurillac, for example, 'always had relics in his presence', and burned little cakes of wax in front of them. When on the

[36] Susan Wood, *The Proprietary Church in the Medieval West* (Oxford, 2006).

[37] Boniface always travelled with relics: Willibald, *Vita S. Bonifatii* 8 (ed. W. Levison, MGH SRG i.u.s. 57, 49), as did Liudger: *Urkundenbuch für die Geschichte des Niederrheins*, 4 vols (repr. Aalen, 1960), 1: 7 (no. 11). Willehad was saved from death when the reliquary around his neck deflected an assassin's blow: *Vita S. Willehadi* 4 (*ActaSS* Nov. 3: 843). See also Widric, *Vita S. Gerardi Tullensis* 3 (*ActaSS* Apr. 3: 210), for a cleric in the bishop's retinue who was travelling by boat and lost his locket reliquary into the water.

[38] *Miracula S. Dionysii* 1.20 (*ActaSS* OSB 3/2: 349–50).

road, he placed them in his tent and prayed in front of them: in effect, he created a bedroom-cum-oratory under canvas.[39] Rorigo, count of Le Mans, also evidently travelled with the wherewithal for private prayer, for when he visited an estate he had given out as a benefice, he heard matins, prayed and meditated 'in a little prayer room hastily erected there, as is the custom for the very noble'.[40] A century later, in Wessex, King Alfred's clergy burned candles by night and day in front of the relics which accompanied him everywhere.[41]

The habit of burning candles in front of relics, whether in a tented chapel, a campaign hut, a temporary prayer room or a home, implies that by the ninth century their care often involved something more than hanging them from a bed-frame or peg in the wall. Additionally, it suggests that the nature of the reliquaries themselves now included caskets which could sit upright upon a portable altar or a tabletop. Surviving early medieval reliquaries do indeed suggest that their form was evolving. In late antiquity, the flasks and lockets which contained relics in personal ownership were complemented by oval, circular or rectangular caskets placed under or within church altars.[42] None of these types is known to have persisted in production or use into the early medieval Latin West: they were superseded by caskets either in the shape of a house (or sarcophagus) or of a purse made of precious metal and jewels. Both types were designed to be portable but stable on a flat surface, and to reflect the light (Figs 8–10). Art historians have noted the change, but not pursued its underlying rationale.

The evolution of form hints at alterations in meaning, use and placement, as a rare account of relics in a Carolingian bedchamber makes clear. In 852, Liudolf, duke of Saxony, and his wife Oda appointed one of their many daughters, the twelve-year-old Hathu-

[39] *Vita Geraldi confessoris* 6, 15 (*Catalogus ... in Bibliotheca Nationali Parisiensi*, 2: 397, 401).

[40] Odo of Glanfeuil, *Historia translationis S. Mauri* 2.16 (*ActaSS* Jan. 1: 1055).

[41] *Asser's Life of King Alfred* 104, ed. W. H. Stevenson (Oxford, 1904), 90.

[42] For overviews and bibliography, see Martina Bagnoli et al., eds, *Treasures of Heaven: Saints, Relics and Devotion in Medieval Europe* (New Haven, CT, 2010); Anton Legner, *Reliquien in Kunst und Kult: zwischen Antike und Aufklärung* (Darmstadt, 1995); Cynthia Hahn, *Strange Beauty: Issues in the Making and Meaning of Reliquaries, 400 – circa 1204* (University Park, PA, 2012).

Fig. 8 (top): The Emly Shrine. Irish house-shaped shrine, late seventh to early eighth century. Champlevé enamel on bronze over yew wood with gilt bronze mouldings and inlay of lead-tin alloy, 9.2 x 4.1 x 10.5 cm. Museum of Fine Arts, Boston, Theodora Wilbour Fund in memory of Charlotte Beebe Wilbour, 52.1396. Image: © 2014 Museum of Fine Arts, Boston.

Fig. 9 (left): Purse-shaped reliquary. Carolingian, third quarter of the eighth century (?), from Enger (Germany). Gold- and silver-alloy with gems, pearls and cloisonné enamel, over oak core, 16.0 x 14.0 x 5.3 cm. Twelve gemstones, including four antique cameos, surround a central stone ringed with pearls and are linked by a double cross. Kunstgewerbemuseum, Berlin, 1888,632. Image source: Wikimedia Commons.

Fig. 10 (right): House-shaped reliquary. Italian, tenth century. Bone and copper-gilt on wood, 19.7 x 18.6 x 8.3 cm. The Metropolitan Museum of Art, The Cloisters Collection, 1953 (53.19.2). Image: © The Metropolitan Museum of Art.

moda, as abbess of their newly founded community of female ascetics at Brunshausen (which was transplanted in 881 to nearby Gandersheim). As abbess, the young Hathumoda kept the foundation subject to her family's dynastic lordship and supportive of its priorities, but she died of fever aged 34 and was buried next to her father at Brunshausen in 874. Shortly afterwards, Agius, a monk of Corvey (and possibly Hathumoda's uncle) wrote a short prose *vita* and long verse *epitaphium* for her. He had himself attended her deathbed, and painted a touching scene of her mother, aunt and sisters clustered in anxious prayer around the sickbed, from the frame of which hung a crystal flask filled with saints' relics. In her final hours, he says, Hathumoda worried about whether the saints really could help the living: we are invited to envision the young abbess anchoring her thoughts on the relics which hung beside her as she prepared herself for whatever might be in store, her family at her side.[43] The picture is domestic, familial and pious – but not miracle-working. Nor does Agius represent the relics as protective, warding off danger to body and soul. Rather, their meaning is intercessory: they embody the salvific grace of the saints of heaven.

During the Carolingian era, lay possession of relics becomes most readily apparent at the point of transfer from personal into ecclesiastical ownership. When donations or bequests of landed property were supplemented by moveable goods, portable relic shrines often featured among the gifts.[44] These could be elaborate, costly and jewelled. On the occasions when liturgical vestments and altar vessels for clerical use accompanied land and reliquaries, lay donors were evidently transferring into ecclesiastical ownership their private family chapels, along with their fittings and the endowments assigned to them. When these wills and charters do not include the liturgical furnishings which would indicate a separate chapel with its own designated priest, the reliquaries presumably derived from an informal domestic prayer space in an inner chamber of the house. In both scenarios, donors wanted 'their' relics to belong

43 Agius, *Vita Hathumodae* 15, 22 (MGH SS 4, 171–2, 173–4). Frederick S. Paxton, *Anchoress and Abbess in Ninth-Century Saxony: the Lives of Liutbirga of Wendhausen and Hathumoda of Gandersheim* (Washington, DC, 2009), 40–7, 58–72, supersedes previous discussions.

44 For moveable wealth in the Frankish lands, see Régine Le Jan, *Famille et pouvoir dans le monde franc (VIIᵉ–Xᵉ siècle). Essai d'anthropologie sociale* (Paris, 1995), 60–8; and, for adjacent regions, François Bougard, 'Trésors et mobilia italiens du haut Moyen Age', in Jean-Pierre Caillet and Pierre Bazin, eds, *Les trésors de sanctuaires de l'Antiquité à l'époque romane* (Paris, 1996), 161–97; Wendy Davies, 'Notions of Wealth in the Charters of Ninth- and Tenth-Century Christian Iberia', in Jean-Pierre Devroey, Laurent Feller and Régine Le Jan, eds, *Les élites et la richesse au haut moyen âge*, Collection Haut Moyen Age (Turnhout, 2010), 265–83; Julia Crick, 'Women, Wills and Moveable Wealth in pre-Conquest England', in Moira Donald and Linda Hurcombe, eds, *Gender and Material Culture in Historical Perspective* (Basingstoke, 2000), 17–37. Selected references to relics in lay charters of donation are noted by Wood, *Proprietary Church*, 455–7.

to monasteries: these transfers would have enhanced the relics' intercessory value while simultaneously ensuring that benefactors' names were commemorated in perpetuity.[45]

Whether house-, sarcophagus- or purse-shaped, surviving reliquaries from the Carolingian era were adapted to sit on an altar or table in a house, tent, chapel or church. The cavity inside their wooden core was stuffed with relics.[46] The exterior was wrapped in metal foil, ranging from the sumptuousness of silver-gilt and gem stones or cloisonné to modest claddings of copper alloy panels with repoussé decoration. All were designed to scintillate in the light of the candles placed around them, whether stationary on a table-top or altar, or while being carried in imposing liturgical processions. Additionally, ones shaped like a purse evoked scriptural injunctions to direct wealth to spiritual ends.[47] We cannot tell whether they really were thaumaturgically inert but they certainly were valuable objects in their own right. To possess one was a material marker of elite status, perhaps especially for women: their meaning was as much about family and social standing as piety and the veneration of relics.[48]

---

[45] For emphasis on personal ownership of relics, see *Urkundenbuch des Klosters Fulda*, ed. Edmund E. Stengel, Veröffentlichungen der Historischen Kommission für Hessen und Waldeck 10 (Marburg, 1956–8), 1/2: 227–31, 372–9 (nos 154, 264). In 784, when Emhilt endowed a nunnery on land inherited from her parents she formalized the transaction 'in the presence of the relics of St Mary which are my very own, which I myself acquired and which are in my very own casket' (ibid. 229, no. 154); fifteen years later, she handed the nunnery over to Fulda, complete with all the reliquaries and other liturgical furnishings in its church (ibid. 377, no. 264). Cf. *Anglo-Saxon Wills*, ed. and transl. Dorothy Whitelock (Cambridge, 1930), 20–1, 24–7 (nos 8, 10), for the will of the late tenth-century Anglo-Saxon ealdorman Æthelmær (no. 10) securing himself burial rights in Winchester New Minster with a grant of land, gold and 'my shrine', and the will of his contemporary, the noblewoman Ælfgifu (no. 8), whose request for burial in Winchester Old Minster included 'her shrine with her relics' as well as much else.

[46] 'Our reliquary, inside which we have placed as many relics as possible' was part of the initial endowment from Roger, count of Limoges, and his wife Euphrasia for the monastery of Charroux in *c.*773: *Chartes et documents pour server à l'histoire de l'abbaye de Charroux*, ed. D. P. de Monsabert (Poitiers, 1910), 60. Cf. the grant made in 802 by Waluram (father of Hrabanus Maurus) to Fulda of his own church at Hofheim, with its landed endowment and all its fittings, including its 'relics in caskets and in crosses': *Urkundenbuch des Klosters Fulda*, ed. Stengel, 1/2: 410–12 (no. 283), at 411.

[47] Cynthia Hahn, 'Metaphor and Meaning in Early Medieval Reliquaries', in Giselle De Nie, Karl F. Morrison and Marco Mostert, eds, *Seeing the Invisible in Late Antiquity and the Early Middle Ages*, Utrecht Studies in Medieval Literacy (Turnhout, 2005), 239–63, at 243–9.

[48] Julia Crick ('Women, Wills and Moveable Wealth') has noted that the 'unusually

★ ★ ★

The documentation concerning Gisela, an aristocratic wife and widow, unites the themes of ownership of relics within elite families with the search for saintly intercession on behalf of both the living and the dead. Daughter of Emperor Louis the Pious (814–40) and sister of Charles the Bald (840–77), Gisela had received a dowry of royal land upon her marriage to one of the most wealthy and influential of her father's court circle, Eberhard of Friuli (d. 864x866). In c.854, they had founded a monastery on Gisela's lands – 'our church' – at Cysoing (Flanders), where they installed their third son, Adelard, as its abbot, and obtained relics of the martyred pope Calixtus to enhance it. Then in 863–4 they drew up a joint will, to take effect after they had both died. It records the meticulous division of their vast fortune into unequal shares for their eight surviving children, and the lengthy details of the costly furnishings of their chapel (capella nostra) shed light on the material culture of the family's household Christianity. Among much else, it mentions fourteen reliquaries, specified as caskets, crosses, crowns, lockets and boxes, which are variously described as made from gold, silver, ivory, crystal and garnets. Far more concerned to document the precious materials than the actual relics themselves, the will identifies only two of them, a splinter of wood of the True Cross and a relic of St Remigius of Rheims: there can be no clearer indication of the role of relics and reliquaries as signs of status than this subordination of their sacral identity to their external trappings and ornamentation.[49]

Because status was inextricably associated with lineage, relics

close' association between women, wills and moveable wealth in late Anglo-Saxon England has interesting parallels in episcopal wills: the continental evidence would benefit from a similar analysis.

[49] *Cartulaire de l'abbaye de Cysoing et ses dépendances*, ed. Ignace de Coussemaker, 2 vols (Lille, 1880), 1: 1–5 (no. 1). For its wider significance, see Rosamond McKitterick, *The Carolingians and the Written Word* (Cambridge, 1989), 245–8; Paul Kershaw, 'Eberhard of Friuli, a Carolingian Lay Intellectual', in Patrick Wormald and Janet L. Nelson, eds, *Lay Intellectuals in the Carolingian World* (Cambridge, 2007), 77–105; Cristina La Rocca and Luigi Provero, 'The Dead and their Gifts. The Will of Eberhard, Count of Friuli and his Wife Gisela, Daughter of Louis the Pious (863–864)', in Frans Theuws and Janet L. Nelson, eds, *Rituals of Power from Late Antiquity to the Early Middle Ages* (Leiden, 2000), 225–80.

might pass through the generations. Two can be tracked with some confidence. In all likelihood, the 'golden crown with [a piece of] the True Cross' which Gisela and Eberhard bequeathed to their eldest son Unruoch originated as a gift from Gisela's father, who seems to have bestowed a piece of it on each of his children, a gift of specifically imperial connotations.[50] The other, a 'crystal phylactery adorned with gold', apparently passed to their grandson Elbuncus, bishop of Parma. His will, testimony to an opulent life-style, selects one of his many reliquaries for special mention: a phylactery 'decorated with gold, gems and pearls, with a beryl carved with the crucifixion set in its middle' which he had inherited from his father, King Berengar of Italy (888–924), Gisela's son.[51] Whereas the relics of St Calixtus remained in their shrine at Cysoing under the guardianship of first Adelard and then his younger brother Rudolph, all the portable reliquaries moved around the family, passing from one household to another across the generations.

Eberhard had died and been buried in Italy. In her widowhood, Gisela took charge of the family's property and religious activities. She built a funerary chapel next to the front of the main church at Cysoing and gave additional land for its support, to ensure that she would in due course be interred there and that lights would always burn at its altar.[52] She had the body of 'my lord Eberhard, of sweet memory' brought from Italy for reburial, and endowed commemorative feasts for her imperial parents and brother, and for all her children.[53] At Cysoing, the tomb of a martyred pope became the focus for the family's liturgical commemoration in a monastery endowed with lands from its founders' patrimony and governed by an abbot drawn from within the family. Gisela thus ensured that a new and enduring forum for familial Christianity was established even as the relics from the original household chapel were dispersed among the siblings.

---

[50] Eric Goldberg, '"More devoted to the Equipment of Battle than the Splendor of Banquets": Frontier Kingship, Martial Ritual and Early Knighthood at the Court of Louis the German', *Viator* 30 (1999), 41–78, at 61–2.

[51] As argued by La Rocca and Provero, 'The Dead and their Gifts', 254. For the full text of Elbuncus's will, see *Le carte degli Archivi Parmensi dei sec. X–XI*, ed. Giovanni Drei, 2nd edn (Parma, 1930), 51–6 (no. 9).

[52] *Cartulaire de Cysoing*, 7–9 (nos 3–4).

[53] Ibid. 10–11 (nos 5–6).

★ ★ ★

Gisela was mindful throughout of the precept 'Lay up to your-selves treasure in heaven' (Matt. 6: 20).[54] For her, as for many others in the Carolingian era, the yearning for heaven involved endowing monastic foundations where donors would be commemorated and intercessory prayer for their salvation maintained.[55] But back in the fifth century, as Gregory of Tours reported (paraphrasing Paulinus of Périgueux), a man took candle wax from the tomb of St Martin and placed it under the inner room of his house 'as a heavenly treasure'.[56] The same reason had prompted Natalia to keep her husband's hand in her bedroom: it brought a little piece of heaven into the inner recesses of the household. As Christian uses of wealth shifted from late antiquity to the Middle Ages, so too did the place and meaning of relics within the household. Their transfer from flasks on walls and bedsteads or boxes under the floor to ostentatious altar-top containers accompanied the emergence of that characteristically medieval Christianity which bound material wealth to formalized saintly intercession in the search for the remission of sin and the hope of salvation. That realignment endowed women with new roles while maintaining their pivotal place within the household Christianity of early medieval centuries.

University of Glasgow

---

[54] Ibid. 8–11 (nos 4–5).
[55] Eliana Magnani, '"Un trésor dans le ciel". De la pastorale de l'aumône aux trésors spirituels (IVᵉ–IXᵉ siècle)', in Lucas Burkart et al., eds, *Le trésor au moyen âge. Discours, pratiques et objets* (Florence, 2010), 51–68.
[56] *Liber de virtutibus sancti Martini episcopi* 1.2 (MGH SRM 1/2, 139).

HOUSEHOLDS OF ST EDMUND

by SARAH FOOT

Theodred, bishop of London, who also held episcopal authority in Suffolk and Norfolk, drew up a statement in the 940s of how he intended to leave his property after his death.[1] Despite his German name, he was probably a native of Suffolk, for he bequeathed a number of Suffolk lands to close relatives living in the region.[2] His most generous bequests were to his cathedral church of St Paul in London, but he made a substantial grant of four estates in Suffolk to the church of St Edmund. Theodred's will provides one of the earliest datable references to the existence of a religious household charged with maintaining the cult of St Edmund. King of the East Angles, Edmund had died in 869, having been defeated in battle by a Danish army which went on to conquer his kingdom. Later generations remembered him as a martyr, although contemporary sources said little about the circumstances of his death.[3] A community of St Edmund was well established at Bury by the middle years of the tenth century, inspiring not only the generosity of the local bishop, but also his confidence in the efficacy of the congregation's prayers. Theodred bequeathed land to the church of St Edmund as the property of God's community there, for the good of his own soul. Exactly when a religious congregation first assembled to preserve the memory of the martyred king, and when it erected a wooden church to house his shrine remains, however, debatable.[4]

---

[1] P. H. Sawyer, *Anglo-Saxon Charters: An Annotated List and Bibliography* (London, 1968), revised version by S. Kelly and R. Rushforth, online at: <http://www.esawyer.org.uk/>, no. 1526, AD 942x951 [hereafter: S]. All charters cited in this article are from the archive of Bury St Edmunds unless otherwise stated; full details of the manuscripts in which each survives may be found in Sawyer's *List*.

[2] D. Whitelock, *Some Anglo-Saxon Bishops of London* (London, 1975); repr. in her *History, Law and Literature in 10th–11th Century England* (London, 1981), no. II, 17–21.

[3] King Edmund's death was recorded in the *Anglo-Saxon Chronicle* under the year 870; since in this period the chronicler's year began in September, the king's death on 20 November actually occurred in 869. Asser, basing his narrative of ninth-century events on the *Chronicle*, took its report to mean that the king died in battle: *Life of Alfred*, ch. 33, ed. W. H. Stevenson (Oxford, 1904, repr. 1959), 26.

[4] For the early history of Bury, see A. Gransden, 'The Legends and Traditions Concerning the Origins of the Abbey of Bury St Edmunds', *EHR* 100 (1985), 1–24;

The uncertainty surrounding the origins of the religious household of St Edmund led me to propose this paper on the theme of 'Religion and the household'. The president invited contributors to consider the household not just as a physical space and setting for worship and personal piety, but also as a network of people bound together by ties of kinship, emotion, service or obligation. That offers a potentially profitable way of exploring how the cult of St Edmund emerged in East Anglia, particularly in Suffolk, and the role in that process of the local East Anglian aristocracy, who showed particular affection for their local saint. The unconventional nature of the surviving written record from the pre-Conquest abbey of Bury St Edmunds sheds significant light on this question. That evidence requires some detailed exposition for which I need the reader's patience, but cumulatively it offers a picture of which we need not to lose sight.

Unlike almost every other Anglo-Saxon monastic house from which an archive of pre-Conquest charters has survived, the abbey of Bury St Edmunds in Suffolk preserved no document resembling a foundation charter, nor one that the abbey could use for that purpose. Lacking the conventional sort of royal or episcopal diploma which established the institution as a religious community and provided the core of its landed endowment, the monks of Bury kept instead a slightly eclectic collection of pre-Conquest documents. Mostly written not in Latin but in Old English, the majority were not royal diplomas (or writs issued by the king, of which Bury also had a substantial collection), but private charters and the wills of members of the local aristocracy, both men and women.[5] This unparalleled archive reveals much about the inheritance strategies of different local families but, more significantly for our purposes, it casts light on the relationship between the local nobility and the religious household dedicated to the memory of Edmund, king and martyr.

T. Licence, 'The Origins of the Monastic Communities of St Benedict at Holme and Bury St Edmunds', *Revue bénédictine* 116 (2006), 42–61.

[5] The research for this essay forms part of the preparation for a new edition of the Anglo-Saxon charters of Bury St Edmunds in Suffolk, undertaken collaboratively with Dr Kathryn Lowe, for publication with the British Academy. For discussion of the archival policies of Bury's monks, see my 'Internal and External Audiences: Reflections on the Anglo-Saxon Archive of Bury St Edmunds Abbey in Suffolk', *Haskins Society Journal* 24 (2013), 166–94.

The language of the household in Anglo-Saxon England did not differentiate secular from religious social groups but applied the language of kindred to both. One Latin noun, *familia*, could describe both a family living in the world (generally in our period a nuclear family of husband, wife and children)[6] and also an ecclesiastical community living under vows. In the vernacular the Old English nouns *hiwisc* and *hired* were similarly ambiguous and applied to both sorts of household.[7] This translation of language between the realms of the secular and the sacred is mirrored in the way that relationships within the cloister were modelled on those of the worldly family.[8] Monks and nuns renounced blood ties when they left their kin to cleave to Christ and to his saints, above all to their patron saint; yet inside the cloister they formed a new social brotherhood, a holy kindred encompassing the living, but joined through prayer and liturgical commemoration to a community's dead.[9] Their lay neighbours, although living in social groups outside the spiritual family, had various ways of articulating their shared emotional attachment to the local saint, including the donation of land or moveable wealth to the custodians of his shrine. Some of the local East Anglian families who showed their devotion through generous donation to the church of St Edmund might also, this essay will argue, claim to be considered as households of the local saint.[10]

In a search for the origins of the congregation of St Edmund it may prove significant that one of the two earliest surviving wills to mention the community comes from the local bishop. Theodred became bishop of London early in the reign of King Æthelstan in either 925 or early 926, and rapidly rose to prominence at the

---

6   H. R. Loyn, 'Kinship in Anglo-Saxon England', *Anglo-Saxon England* 3 (1973), 197–209; David Herlihy, *Medieval Households* (Cambridge, MA, and London, 1985), 2–3, 57; Thomas Charles-Edwards, 'Kinship, Status and the Origins of the Hide', *P&P*, no. 56 (1972), 3–33; Elisabeth van Houts, 'Family, Marriage, Kinship', in Julia Crick and Elisabeth van Houts, eds, *A Social History of England 900–1200* (Cambridge, 2011), 133–41, at 133–5.
7   Sarah Foot, 'Anglo-Saxon Ecclesiastical Households', in Benjamin T. Hudson, ed., *Familia and Household in the Medieval Atlantic World* (Tempe, AZ, 2011), 51–71, at 55–7, 69.
8   Henry Mayr-Harting, *The Venerable Bede, the Rule of St Benedict and Social Class*, Jarrow Lecture 1976 (Jarrow, 1977), 16.
9   Foot, 'Anglo-Saxon Ecclesiastical Households', 60–1.
10   Cf. Barbara Rosenwein, *To be the Neighbor of St Peter: The Social Meaning of Cluny's Property, 909–1049* (Ithaca, NY, 1989), and see further below.

king's court.[11] From his will (which must date from after 942, when King Edmund gave him an estate at Southery in Norfolk mentioned in the text, and before his death between 951 and 953) we see that Theodred held authority not just in London but over the East Anglian see (vacant since around the time of the death of King Edmund), which he ran from a *bishopriche* (episcopal seat) at the church of Hoxne in Suffolk.[12] As already noted, the terms of his bequest to St Edmund's indicate the presence in his day of a household devoted to the martyred king at the town which we call Bury St Edmunds, but which he knew as *Beodricesworth*.[13]

Other evidence also associates Theodred with the cult of St Edmund. In his *Passio* of the saint, written to a commission from the monks of Ramsey Abbey in Cambridgeshire during the 980s,[14] Abbo of Fleury reported that Theodred, 'the pious bishop of the province', had verified the incorruption of the saint's body before it was translated from its original burial place to *Beodricesworth*.[15] He further showed his affection and veneration for the saint by impulsively pronouncing a sentence of death by hanging on thieves who attempted to steal from the shine. Theodred immediately regretted that decision (since the act violated canon law which forbade clerics to impose a death sentence), but not in time to prevent the hanging; thus he did penance for his sin. Abbo associated that penance with the washing of the martyred king's incorrupt body and its reclothing and placing in a wooden coffin.[16] We should probably follow Abbo in connecting Bishop Theodred with the translation of Edmund's remains to *Beodricesworth*, and

---

[11] S. E. Kelly, *Charters of St Paul's, London* (Oxford, 2004), 117.

[12] Mary Anne O'Donovan, 'An Interim Revision of Episcopal Dates for the Province of Canterbury, 850–950: Part 1', *Anglo-Saxon England* 1 (1972), 23–44, at 39–40; Whitelock, *Some Anglo-Saxon Bishops*, 20; T. Pestell, *Landscapes of Monastic Foundation: The Establishment of Religious Houses in East Anglia c.650–1200* (Woodbridge, 2004), 83–5.

[13] *Beodricesworth* means the 'worþ', or homestead, of a person called Beaduric: see E. Ekwall, *The Concise Oxford Dictionary of English Place-Names*, 4th edn (Oxford, 1960), *s.n.* 'Bury'.

[14] Marco Mostert, 'Le séjour d'Abbon de Fleury à Ramsey', *Bibliothèque de l'École des Chartes* 144 (1986), 199–208.

[15] Abbo, *Passio sancti Eadmundi* 15, ed. Michael Winterbottom, *Three Lives of English Saints* (Toronto, ON, 1972), 83; F. Hervey, *Corolla Sancti Eadmundi* (London, 1907), 47.

[16] Abbo, *Passio* 15, ed. Winterbottom, 84–5 (Hervey, *Corolla Sancti Eadmundi*, 47–51); for the first mention of the body's incorruption, see. ibid. 14, ed. Winterbottom, 82 (Hervey, *Corolla Sancti Eadmundi*, 45).

thus date that move to the reign of King Æthelstan (924–39).[17] Bishop Theodred's close connection with the religious community of St Edmund reveals nothing, however, of the origins of the first household which had charge of the king's remains in their original resting-place, a question to which we will have to return.

After Theodred's death, the East Anglian see of Elmham was re-established. Bury's archive contains the wills of two local eleventh-century bishops, Ælfric and Æthelmær, who made bequests of land to St Edmund's, both proving strikingly more generous to that monastic house than to their own episcopal church at Elmham.[18] Later generations of monks at Bury went out of their way to claim that their house had always remained free of any interference from the local diocesan bishop.[19] Yet the evidence of their own archive of vernacular documents suggests that at least some bishops of Elmham had significantly closer relationships with Bury than with the clergy at their diocesan seat. A note, recorded in the margins of a set of Easter tables in the so-called Bury Psalter (now in the Vatican) and at the end of the abbey's bilingual copy of the *Rule of St Benedict*, further indicates a direct connection between abbey and bishop. It reports the involvement of Bishop Ælfwine (bishop of East Anglia 1012x1017–1023x1038) in establishing the rule of monks in the monastery of St Edmund early in the reign of Cnut.[20] We would be hasty, however, in associating the religious household of St Edmund, both in its earlier manifestation as a community of secular priests and after its reform into a Benedictine abbey, only with the episcopate. The local laity took an equal pride and interest in the shrine of their sainted king and the congregation that preserved his memory through prayer and

---

[17] I am grateful to my graduate student Richard Purkiss for discussion of the implications of this close reading of Abbo.

[18] S 1489, 1499.

[19] See T. Licence, 'The Norwich Narrative and the East Anglian Bishopric', *Norfolk Archaeology* 45 (2007), 198–204; idem, 'Herbert Losinga's Trip to Rome and the Bishopric of Bury St Edmunds', *Anglo-Norman Studies* 34 (2012), 151–68; S. Foot, 'The Abbey's Armoury of Charters', in Tom Licence, ed., *Bury St Edmunds and the Norman Conquest* (Woodbridge, forthcoming 2014).

[20] The 'Bury Psalter', BAV, MS Reginensis lat 12, fol. 17ᵛ: 'Hic sub Cnutono rege constructam basilicam beate memorie archipresul Aegelnoðus consecrauit eam in honore Christi et sancte Marie sanctique Eadmundi'; the same note occurs also in Oxford, Corpus Christi College, MS 197, fol. 105ʳ: discussed by David N. Dumville, *English Caroline Script and Monastic History: Studies in Benedictinism* (Woodbridge, 1993), 31–5.

liturgy. Together the lay populace of Norfolk and Suffolk created an imagined 'household' of St Edmund, in the sense of a spatially scattered network characterized by its members' devotion to this saint's cult.

Some of the lay documents preserved in Bury's archive show how the interest of local families in the church of St Edmund persisted across more than one generation. Ealdorman Ælfgar drew up his will at much the same time as Bishop Theodred (between 946 and 951). Through his various bequests he promised to make great heiresses of his two daughters: Æthelflæd, the childless widow of King Edmund, and her younger sister, Ælfflæd, wife of Ealdorman Byrhtnoth, also as yet without children.[21] However, Ælfgar tied much of his daughters' inheritance to his possible future grandchildren, and stipulated ultimately that most of the bequests made initially to his relations should revert to the Church. His careful statement of his intentions for his landed wealth bound past, present and future generations of the family in mutual obligation. Bury stands out as the first of the ecclesiastical beneficiaries named by Ælfgar, because of the loyalty shown to St Edmund not only by the ealdorman but by both his daughters, who punctiliously obeyed their father's wishes, both adding a fresh estate to the land destined for Bury, even though they each had close connections with other English monasteries.[22] This prominent local family, despite the more immediate personal links with the church that it had founded at Stoke-by-Nayland (where several of its members were buried), showed especial devotion for St Edmund, demonstrating that affection over more than one generation. Its affinity to the saint bound Ælfgar's family emotionally with other lay kin groups who expressed the same devotion to East Anglia's martyred king. Although physically remote from the site of the saint's cult, their personal loyalty, articulated through

[21] S 1483; P. Stafford, 'Women and the Norman Conquest', *TRHS* 6th ser. 4 (1994), 221–49, at 232.

[22] S 1494, 1486; Pestell, *Landscapes*, 149. Æthelflæd had links with the nunnery at Barking, a community of nuns at Damerham, and Glastonbury Abbey, while Ælfflæd and her husband Byrhtnoth (who died at Maldon in 991) were notable benefactors to Ely: A. Wareham, *Lords and Communities in Early Medieval East Anglia* (Woodbridge, 2005), 46–60. For the significance of female decisions to bequeath to particular religious houses and specifically the choices of this family, see J. Crick, 'Women, Posthumous Benefaction, and Family Strategy in Pre-Conquest England', *JBS* 38 (1999), 399–422, at 401–3.

generous donation, linked them directly with the prayerful household in Bury and, in the imagination, with their neighbours who
shared an equal attachment.

Another pair of texts in Bury's archive sheds light on the
inheritance strategies of a different local family, this time based in
Norfolk.[23] Some rather laboured wording conveys fairly straightforward transactions: two brothers, Edwin and Wulfric, who owned
land in Norfolk, planned that, after their lifetimes and that of their
sister's son, one estate should go to St Benet at Holme and the other
to Bury St Edmunds. Otherwise, Edwin made only small grants to
local Norfolk churches. Their nephew, Ketel, confirmed his intention to pass on the land he received from his uncles to Bury, and
made a fresh arrangement with his wife's daughter to ensure that,
should they die while journeying to Rome on pilgrimage, an
additional piece of land would pass to St Edmund's for the souls
of himself, his wife and his daughter.[24] While we might expect
Norfolk landowners to make donations to the nearby Benedictine
abbey at Holme, their preference for granting land to St Edmund,
rather than to the historic community at Ely or the newer foundation at Ramsey, indicates a fondness for the local saint. The
dispersed network of people who identified themselves with the
family of St Edmund thus extended beyond the Suffolk nobility.

The families of Ælfgar and Edwin are noteworthy both for the
complexity of their testamentary arrangements and for the willingness of children to fulfil the expressed wishes of their parents'
generation. In their expressions of devotion to Edmund, king and
martyr, their wills are, however, unremarkable when read in the
context of the unique sequence of pre-Conquest lay statements of
testamentary intent which the monks of Bury kept (and continued
to recopy) in the later Middle Ages. Only one of those texts takes
the form of a straightforward Latin diploma making a direct grant
to the abbey: the charter in the name of Wulfstan of Dalham dated
963 giving four hides at Palgrave to St Edmund's at *Beodricesworth*.[25] All the rest are in Old English, a few just brief memoranda
recording straightforward donations to the abbey,[26] while others

[23] S 1516.
[24] S 1519.
[25] S 1213; see Wareham, *Lords*, 29–45.
[26] e.g. S 1219, 1225.

record reversionary grants, by which named individuals arranged
to enjoy the use and produce from an estate during their lives
before it passed to the abbey at Bury once all the parties had
died.[27]

In a number of texts we see the church of St Edmund as just
one among several ecclesiastical beneficiaries. Ælfric Modercope,
who drew up a will before going overseas on pilgrimage, and
Thurstan, son of Wine, bequeathed land to all the Benedictine
houses in the region: Ely, Ramsey, and St Benet at Holme, as well
as to Bury, and in Thurstan's case additionally to the metropolitan
see at Christ Church, Canterbury.[28] More commonly, however,
testators who made bequests to Bury also gave to St Benet's at
Holme, or to small churches in their own localities, as for example
did Thurketel, known by the by-name Heyng, who made grants to
St Edmund and St Benedict;[29] Thurketel of Palgrave, who made a
gift to the bishop and his local church;[30] and Æthelric of Bocking
who shared an estate between St Gregory's at Sudbury (Suffolk)
and St Edmund's.[31] In order to fulfil her dead husband's post-
mortem intentions, Leofgifu bequeathed land to a church at Earl's
Colne in Essex and to the bishop of London; another widow,
Sifflæd, may similarly have followed the wishes of others in conferring grants on her local church at Marlingford in Norfolk and St
Mary's, Norwich.[32] However, in many of these cases and in all of
those wills and other future-tensed statements of intent where no
other religious house apart from Bury benefitted from the testa-
tor's generosity, we may note the prominence given to St Edmund
and the household responsible for his cult.[33] Men and women,
married and widowed, living in Essex, Suffolk and Norfolk all
testify not just to generosity to the church of St Edmund, but
arguably to a particular affection for the local saint; together –

[27] S 1224, 1537.
[28] Ælfric: S 1490; Thurstan: S 1531.
[29] S 1528.
[30] S 1527.
[31] S 1501.
[32] S 1525–1525a.
[33] Bury was only ecclesiastical beneficiary of the wills of Ulfketel (S 1219), Stigand
(S 1224) and Thurketel (S 1225), and of the reversionary grants made by Thurkil and
Æthelgyth (S 1529) and Wulfgeat and his wife (S 1470). For general discussion of all
these wills, see Pestell, *Landscapes*, 119–22.

despite their geographical separation – they constituted a network bound by their common devotion to Edmund.

For monastic houses to establish significant links with the nobility of their local area and maintain those connections across several generations was of course entirely usual, not just in England but elsewhere in early medieval Europe. Barbara Rosenwein has shown from a study of the charters of Cluny how that abbey capitalized on the relationships it built with its immediate neighbours, who used land grants to create and affirm a special relationship with St Peter, to whom the abbey was dedicated.[34] The Benedictine abbey at Ely, refounded in the 960s by Bishop Æthelwold of Winchester as part of the revolution in monastic observance of the mid-tenth century, contrived to ensure the continuing loyalty of local nobles by retaining its dedication to its early Anglo-Saxon saintly founder, St Æthelthryth. Although an archive of vernacular documents such as that preserved at Bury no longer survives, Ely's house-history, the *Liber Eliensis*, testifies to a similar loyalty among local benefactors to that shown to Bury, by recording abstracts and summaries of donations made to the monks by their noble neighbours.[35] In Somerset, Glastonbury Abbey kept a catalogue of all the land grants it received from generous benefactors, the so-called *Liber terrarum*.[36] Yet in one important consideration, Bury St Edmunds stands apart from each of these examples and others one might cite. All these other abbeys preserved a narrative of their origins, supported by documents that, with varying degrees of plausibility, testified to their foundation and the lands with which the monastery was first endowed.[37] For Bury, no such document exists. The pre-Conquest archive now contains just seven Latin royal diplomas, the sorts of text that constitute the majority of documents in other monastic and cathedral archives. And only one of those charters is genuine in the form in which it has survived.[38]

---

[34] Rosenwein, *To be the Neighbor of St Peter*.

[35] *Liber Eliensis*, ed. E. O. Blake (London, 1962).

[36] Used by William of Malmesbury to write his history of that abbey: John Scott, *The Early History of Glastonbury: An Edition, Translation and Study of William of Malmesbury's De antiquitate Glastonie ecclesie* (Woodbridge, 1981).

[37] For discussion of monastic foundation legends as the fruits of imaginative memory, cf. Amy G. Remensnyder, *Remembering Kings Past: Monastic Foundation Legends in Medieval Southern France* (Ithaca, NY, and London, 1995).

[38] S 703 survives as a single-sheet apparent original written by the charter scribe 'Edgar A'; the others – S 483, 507, 980, 995, 1045, 1046 – all display suspicious features.

Arguments from silence present numerous well-acknowledged problems. The failure of Bury to preserve a royal (or episcopal) foundation charter does not, of course, mean that such a document never once existed. But Bury's first post-Conquest abbot, Baldwin, showed considerable skill in crafting for himself a portfolio of documents with which to argue successfully, in front of the king at a council held in Winchester in 1081, that the abbey had never been subject to the authority or interference of the diocesan bishop, and so preventing the then bishop of Elmham from relocating his seat to Bury. Confronted with Bury's barrage of written proofs, the bishop had recourse only to his rhetorical skills and the oral testimony of the man who had kept his predecessor's dogs; he lost ignominiously.[39] On that occasion, Bury clearly had no need of a foundation charter. Was this because such a document did exist but inconveniently failed to mention the critical issue of independence from the episcopate and so was quietly left behind in Suffolk, or even destroyed? Or did Baldwin forbear to order the invention of such a document because a collective memory that that community's origins owed nothing to the generosity of a royal founder acted as a brake on his diplomatic creativity? One wonders what sort of remembered past could have proved so powerful that Bury's monks chose to reject the obvious recourse (the one adopted by so many other early English monasteries) of forging their own royal title deed.

We need to return to the only narratives the abbey did retain about its earliest days: the account found in the *Passio* of St Edmund written in the 980s by Abbo of Fleury and Herman the archdeacon's *Miracula*, composed *c*.1100. Neither can claim contemporaneity with the events they describe, but both witness to the same phenomenon: that the cult of St Edmund emerged from the bottom up. After his death (whether in battle or, as Abbo claimed, following his torture by the victorious Danish army), it was the local, country people of the region who found the king's body and buried it in a humble place – called *Haegilsdun* by Abbo, Sutton by Herman.[40] We might see that act as a manifestation of the grief of

39 David Bates, *Regesta Regum Anglo-Normannorum: The Acta of William I (1066–1087)* (Oxford, 1998), no. 39.
40 Abbo, *Passio*, ch. 11, ed. Winterbottom, 79–80; Herman, *De Miraculis sancti Eadmundi*, ch. 1, ed. T. Arnold, 3 vols (London, 1890–6), 1: 27. See D. Whitelock, 'Fact

the ordinary people of East Anglia at the death of their king, a grief that time would dull, without diminishing the population's loyalty and commitment to the promotion of Edmund's cult. Despite the lowliness of that first chapel,[41] the saint attracted attention through his miracles and was memorialized in a coinage dedicated to his memory issued by the local Danish rulers.[42] After an indeterminate period of time, the local people – encouraged it would seem by the bishop of London, himself a Suffolk man – discovered the incorruption of the saint's body and had it transported for reburial at *Beodricesworth*. Whatever the arrangements for the memorialization of Edmund's cult at his first burial-place, we should imagine that a community of secular priests took charge of the shrine and maintained regular worship in the newly built wooden church. In strictly ecclesiastical terms, this became the first household (*familia*) of St Edmund.

Yet in consigning their martyred king to the formal structures of the Church, the local people did not relinquish their particular care for him. He was their king, and they remained his people. The East Anglian population – especially the ranks of the lesser nobility, the thegns, together with their wives, but also the ealdormen and local bishops – identified themselves closely with their royal saint.[43] Bury's own distinctive archive, with its preponderance of vernacular texts recording small donations from local people, together with the evidence of the abbey's landholdings in the Domesday Book, demonstrate the intensity of the regionalism of the cult of St Edmund and the extent to which devotion to the saint pervaded all of East Anglian society.[44] Care of the saint's relics and the maintenance of a regular liturgical cycle of prayer and devotion lay in the hands of the family of priests, later monks, who lived in the church of St Edmund at *Beodricesworth*, later Bury

and Fiction in the Legend of St Edmund', *Proceedings of the Suffolk Institute for Archaeology and History* [hereafter: *PSIAH*] 31 (1969), 217–33; Susan Ridyard, *The Royal Saints of Anglo-Saxon England: A Study of West Saxon and East Anglian Cults* (Cambridge, 1988), 218–21; and, for a radical suggestion, Keith Briggs, 'Was *Hægilsdun* in Essex? A New Site for the Martyrdom of Edmund', *PSIAH* 42 (2011), 277–91.

[41] Cf. John Blair, 'A Saint for every Minster? Local Cults in Anglo-Saxon England', in A. Thacker and R. Sharpe, eds, *Local Saints and Local Churches in the Early Medieval West* (Oxford, 2002), 455–94, at 486.

[42] C. E. Blunt, 'The St Edmund Memorial Coinage', *PSIAH* 31 (1969), 234–55.

[43] Crick, 'Women', 402–3; Wareham, *Lords*, 59–60.

[44] Pestell, *Landscapes*, 118–19.

(*on byrig*). But the households of St Edmund were scattered across East Anglia, forming a network among the descendants of the subjects of the king who first provided fitting burial for his mutilated remains and ensured that his memory endured.

Christ Church, Oxford

'A FAITHFUL AND WISE SERVANT'? INNOCENT III (1198–1216) LOOKS AT HIS HOUSEHOLD

by BRENDA BOLTON

Arriving at the Lateran on 8 January 1198, officials conducted Innocent III (born Lotari dei Conti di Segni) ceremonially to his apartments within the palace, there to rest, pray and dine.[1] Foremost amongst his concerns was the household, last reformed by Gregory I (590–604). Whilst Innocent clearly adopted Gregory as his model, both for the shaping of his personal life as pope and for his understanding of the papal office,[2] the young pope's efforts to make his household as exemplary as that of his great predecessor have not received the attention they undoubtedly deserve. Gregory's finest *Life*, composed *c*.875 by John, a Roman deacon, uses material from the early *vitae*, thus avoiding the 'scrappy and grudging' biography of the *Liber pontificalis*.[3] Instead, John draws extensively on Gregory's letters and the crumbling but then still extant papyrus volumes of the *Registrum* to demonstrate how this pope transformed his household into monastery, hospice and refuge.[4] Three centuries later, the author of the *Gesta Innocentii* or *Deeds of Innocent III* could do no better than to adapt portions of John's *Life* to highlight reforms not evidenced since the sixth century.[5] Like Gregory, Innocent wished to restore

[1] *Le* Liber censuum *de l'église romaine*, ed. P. Fabre, L. Duchesne and G. Mollat, 3 vols (Paris, 1889–1952), 1: 311–13.

[2] John Doran, 'In whose Footsteps? The Role Models of Innocent III', in Andrea Sommerlechner, ed., *Innocenzo III. Urbs et Orbis,* Atti del Congresso Internazionale Roma, 9–15 settembre 1998, 2 vols (Rome, 2003), 1: 56–73; Christoph Egger, '"The Growling of the Lion and the Humming of the Fly": Gregory the Great and Innocent III', in *Pope, Church and City: Essays in Honour of Brenda M. Bolton*, ed. F. Andrews, C. Egger and C. M. Rousseau, The Medieval Mediterranean 56 (Leiden, 2004), 13–46 (the appendix, 39–46, contains a hitherto unpublished sermon by Innocent on Gregory).

[3] *Le* Liber Pontificalis: *Texte, introduction et commentaire*, ed. L. Duchesne, Bibliothèque des Écoles françaises d'Athènes et de Rome, 2nd ser. 3, 2nd edn, 3 vols (Paris 1955–7), 1: 312–14; Jeffrey Richards, *The Popes and the Papacy in the Early Middle Ages 467–752* (London, 1979), 169–70.

[4] Commissioned by John VIII (870–82). John the Deacon, *Sancti Gregorii Magni vita, a Joanne Diacono scripta libris quatuor* (PL 75, cols 87A–125B (Book 2)); R. A. Markus, *Gregory the Great and His World* (Cambridge, 1997), 2, 14–15, 123; Philippe Lauer, *Le Palais de Latran* (Paris, 1911), 74.

[5] J.-P. Migne, *Gesta Innocentii PP. III* (PL 214, cols xvii–ccxxviii); David Gress-

the ideas of the apostolic age to the Church.[6] And where better to begin the spiritual renewal than within a reformed household? His inaugural sermon as pope on St Matthew's faithful and wise servant accords perfectly with John the Deacon's view of Gregory as *paterfamilias Domini*, head of the Lord's household.[7] Innocent, therefore, regarded the household not only as a metaphor for the congregation of the faithful but also, like Gregory before him, as a model to be used by missionaries to plant and nurture the faith throughout Christendom. Whilst the ongoing conversion of Livonia would provide Innocent with a rare opportunity to inculcate the Christian household within a pagan society,[8] in the Patrimony of St Peter he diverged from Gregory's path by purposeful itineration with his *familia*, thus initiating a public role for the household.

Apart from John the Deacon's meticulous research, little information exists for the activities or personnel of any papal household during the six centuries separating Gregory I and Innocent III. The *Liber pontificalis* presents its serial biographies and continuations through the prism of Rome's architectural and liturgical

---

Wright, 'The *Gesta Innocentii III*: Text, Introduction and Commentary' (Ph.D. thesis, Bryn Mawr College, 1981; publ. in microfilm Ann Arbor, MI, 1994). See also James M. Powell, ed. and transl., *The Deeds of Pope Innocent III by an Anonymous Author* (Washington DC, 2004); Frances Andrews, 'Umkämpfter Raum im Rom Innocenz' III.: Die *Gesta Innocentii papae III.*', in Nikolaus Staubach and Vera Johanterwage, eds, *Außen und Innen. Räume und ihre Symbolik im Mittelalter*, Tradition – Reform – Innovation. Studien zur Modernität des Mittelalters 14 (Frankfurt am Main, 2007), 133–50.

[6]   John W. Baldwin, *Masters, Princes, and Merchants: The Social Views of Peter the Chanter & His Circle*, 2 vols (Princeton, NJ, 1970), 1: 343; Christoph Egger, 'A Theologian at Work: Some Remarks on Methods and Sources in Innocent III's writings', in J. C. Moore, ed., *Pope Innocent III and his World* (Aldershot, 1999), 25–33; idem, 'Gregory and Innocent', 32–8.

[7]   Matt. 24: 25; Innocent III, *Sermo II. In consecratione pontificis maximi* (PL 217, cols 653–60); *Pope Innocent III. Between God & Man. Six Sermons on the Priestly Office*, transl. Corinne J. Vause and Frank C. Gardiner, Medieval Texts in Translation (Washington, DC, 2004), 16–27; *Innocenzo III. I Sermoni*, ed. Stanislao Fioramonti (Vatican City, 2006), 610–23; John the Deacon, *Vita Gregorii* 2.26 (PL 75, col. 97B).

[8]   Barbara Bombi, 'Innocent III and the *praedicatio* to the Heathens in Livonia (1198–1204)', in Tuomas M. Lehtonen and Kurt Villads Jensen, eds, *Medieval History Writing and Crusading Ideology*, Studia Fennica, Historica 9 (Tampere, 2005), 232–41; eadem, Novella Plantatio Fidei*: Missione e Crociata nel nord Europa tra la fine del XII e i primi decenni del XIII secolo*, Istituto Storico Italiano per il Medio Evo, Nuovi Studi Storici 74 (Rome, 2007), 131–43; Torben K. Nielsen, 'Mission and Submission: Societal Change in the Baltic in the Thirteenth Century', in Lehtonen and Jensen, eds, *Medieval History Writing*, 216–31.

revolution,[9] Zacharias (741–52) alone receiving praise for his restoration of the Lateran *triclinium* or dining hall.[10] Cardinal Boso's *Lives of the Popes*, composed during the 1160s and 1170s, concentrate on political activities within the city,[11] whilst papal officials remain largely anonymous. Nonetheless, Benjamin of Tudela, passing Rome on his way to Jerusalem, identified Jews in the household of Alexander III (1159–81),[12] amongst them, the papal steward, Rabbi Yehiel from Trastevere.[13] By the 1190s, when Cencius, the chamberlain, composed his *Liber censuum* or *Book of Taxes of the Roman Church*, he listed various groups of craftsmen and ceremonial assistants who were specifically attached to the papal household.[14] Some were obliged to swear oaths of obedience to the pope and the status of each group was reflected in the number of representatives invited to dine in his presence on great feast days throughout the year.[15] The *Gesta Innocentii* is thus the first biography since John the Deacon's *Vita Gregorii* to provide information on the household. Composed by one of Innocent's chaplains,[16] the anonymous author completed his first version in 1204, but after 1208 simply stopped writing.[17] An invaluable source, it does not,

[9]   Rosamond McKitterick, 'Roman Texts and Roman History in the Early Middle Ages', in Claudia Bolgia, Rosamund McKitterick and John Osborne, eds, *Rome across Time and Space: Cultural Transmission and the Exchange of Ideas, c.500–1400* (Cambridge, 2011), 19–34, at 28–31.

[10]   *Le Liber Pontificalis*, ed. Duchesne, 1: 426–39; John Osborne, 'Papal Court Culture during the Pontificate of Zacharias (AD 741–752)', in Catherine Cubitt, ed., *Court Culture in the Early Middle Ages* (Turnhout, 2003), 223–34.

[11]   John Doran, 'Remembering Pope Gregory VII: Cardinal Boso and Alexander III', in Peter D. Clarke and Charlotte Methuen, eds, *The Church on its Past*, SCH 49 (Woodbridge, 2013), 87–98, at 87–91.

[12]   Michael A. Signer, ed., *The Itinerary of Benjamin of Tudela: Travels in the Middle Ages*, (Malibu, CA, 1983), 63.

[13]   Marie Thérèse Champagne and Ra'anan S. Boustan, 'Walking in the Shadows of the Past: The Jewish Experience of Rome in the Twelfth Century', *Medieval Encounters* 17 (2011), 464–94, at 468–71.

[14]   *Le Liber censuum*, ed. Fabre, Duchesne and Mollat, 1: 305–6.

[15]   Susan Twyman, *Papal Ceremonial at Rome in the Twelfth Century* (London, 2002), 190–3.

[16]   James M. Powell, 'Innocent III and Petrus Beneventanus: Reconstructing a Career at the Papal Curia', in Moore, ed., *Innocent III and his World*, 51–62; Giulia Barone, 'I *Gesta Innocentii III*: politica e cultura a Roma all'inizio del Duecento', in *Studi sul Medioevo per Girolamo Arnaldi*, ed. G. Barone, L. Capo and S. Gasparri (Rome, 2001), 1–23.

[17]   Gress-Wright, '*Gesta Innocentii III*', 109*–14*; John C. Moore, *Pope Innocent III (1160/61–1216): To Root up and to Plant*, The Medieval Mediterranean 47 (Leiden, 2003), 124 and n. 68.

however, begin to match the detailed household accounts of Innocent's contemporary, King John (1199–1216),[18] no papal equivalent existing until the end of the thirteenth century.[19] Intriguing
glimpses in the *Gesta* and contemporary chronicles alike, however,
reveal Innocent as the first 'mobile' pope as he journeyed with his
household around the patrimony.[20]

From St Peter to the present, the papal household remains the
consummate private space, a complex and secretive enclave for
men, assiduously protected from the outside world. And yet, in
what manner, with whom and where a pope lives, the physical
setting for his private worship and personal piety, the nature and
extent of his service for the common good and the quality of his
advisors must always be matters of importance to any congregation
in establishing the credentials of their shepherd. Innocent revealed
his understanding of this need within six weeks of his election
when, on 22 February 1198, following his consecration as bishop
of Rome, he preached on a theme from Matthew 24: 25, 'Who
then is the faithful and wise servant whom the Lord hath made
ruler over his household?'[21]

Examining his own identity and the nature of the papal office,
Innocent claims to be both the servant of Matthew's text and the
head of the household.[22] As 'the servant of servants',[23] his duty is
to exercise ministry rather than dominion[24] by offering faithfulness
of heart, wisdom in works and food in season.[25] Had not Christ

[18] Doris Mary Stenton, *English Society in the Early Middle Ages (1066–1307)*
(Harmondsworth, 1951), 24–30.
[19] A. Paravicini Bagliani, 'La mobilità della corte papale nel secolo XIII', in S.
Carocci, ed., *Itineranza Pontificia: La mobilità della curia papale nel Lazio (secoli XII–XIII)*,
Istituto Storico Italiano per il Medio Evo, Nuovi Studi Storici 61 (Rome, 2003), 3–78;
T. di Carpegna Falconieri and F. Bovalino, '"Commovetur sequenti die curia tota".
L'impatto dell'itineranza papale sull'organizzazione ecclesiastica e sulla vita religiosa',
ibid. 101–75.
[20] Michele Maccarrone, *Studi su Innocenzo III*, Italia Sacra, Studi e Documenti di
Storia Ecclesiastica 17 (Padua, 1972), 123–48; Brenda Bolton, '"The Caravan Rests":
Innocent III's Use of Itineration', in Omnia disce – *Medieval Studies in Memory of
Leonard Boyle, O.P.*, ed. Anne J. Duggan, Joan Greatrex and Brenda Bolton (Aldershot,
2005), 41–60.
[21] Leonard E. Boyle, 'Innocent III's View of Himself as Pope', in *Urbs et Orbis*, ed.
Sommerlechner, 5–17, at 7.
[22] *In consecratione* (PL 217, col. 653D).
[23] 'Plane servus, et utique servus servorum': ibid. (col. 655C).
[24] 'Et ideo ministerium mihi vindico, dominium non usurpo': ibid.
[25] Ibid. (col. 656B).

himself, the supreme example of faithfulness, promised Peter that his faith would not fail?[26] Innocent confesses that his own faith is so essential to him that the Church may only call him to judgement for a sin against it – all the other sins are judged by God alone.[27] Faith and wisdom in works are thus inextricably linked.[28] Innocent, the servant whom Christ has placed over the family and entrusted with its care, and whose episcopal consecration happens to fall on the Feast of St Peter's Chair in Antioch, is proud to proclaim his succession to Peter.[29] Christ, having raised Peter to the fullness of power as head of the Church, enjoined him to feed his sheep.[30] Innocent insists that, as the head of the household, he is bound to provide his family with spiritual food, in word, in sacrament and by example, so that the apostles' work may be continued.[31] In return, he begs all faithful Christians to pray that he may be worthy of fulfilling the office of apostolic service, lest it becomes a charge too great for his weak shoulders to bear.[32]

Having thus so publicly expounded his thoughts on the metaphorical household, Innocent imposed Gregory's transformational changes on his own household and ensured that his *familia* understood their importance. Hence a reading from John the Deacon's *Vita Gregorii* formed part of Innocent's revision to the daily office of the papal court[33] while on Gregory's feast day (12 March) his chaplains heard no fewer than nine *lectiones*, three from his predecessor's homilies, three from John the Deacon's *Vita Gregorii*,[34] and three more from *Statuit illi Dominus*, a sermon he composed in the

---

[26] '[U]t non deficiat fides tua': Luke: 22: 32; *In consecratione* (col. 656C); Boyle, 'Innocent III's View', 8.

[27] '[P]ropter solum peccatum quod in fide committitur possem ab Ecclesia judicari': *In consecratione* (col. 656C); Boyle, 'Innocent III's View', 8.

[28] *In consecratione* (cols 656D–657A); Boyle, 'Innocent III's View', 8.

[29] *In consecratione* (cols 657D–658A).

[30] John 20: 15.

[31] *In consecratione* (cols 659D–660A).

[32] '[Q]uatenus hoc apostolicae servitutis, quod est meis debilibus humeris importabile': ibid. (col. 660C).

[33] '[S]icut enim lectio de vita ipsius euidenter ostendit': Egger, 'Gregory and Innocent', 46; Stephen J. P. van Dijk, *The Ordinal of the Papal Court from Innocent III to Boniface VIII and Related Documents*, Spicilegium Friburgense 22 (Fribourg, 1975), xx–xxi, 419, 467.

[34] 'Gregorius de genere Romanus': John the Deacon, *Vita Gregorii* 1.1 (PL 75, col. 63A); van Dijk, *Ordinal*, 379; Egger, 'Gregory and Innocent', 36 n. 90.

late pope's honour.[35] Innocent's resident biographer was thus fully conversant with Gregory's actions, his account in the *Gesta* closely mirroring John's themes and even the language of the *Vita Gregorii*.

Innocent, well acquainted with Gregory's family monastery of S. Andrea al Celio in Rome, was thoroughly imbued with his predecessor's twofold determination to impose the perfection of the monastic cloister on his household and to restore episcopal institutions to the Church.[36] As the first monk-pope, Gregory had excluded all lay servants or *cubicularii* from his *cubiculum* or private chamber at the Lateran, surrounding himself with regulars as he had been whilst *apocrisiarios* or papal representative at Emperor Maurice's court in Constantinople.[37] On 5 July 595, Gregory wrote to the canons of St Peter's, informing them of the need to restore episcopal privacy by forbidding secular *cubicularii* to robe bishops and decreeing that this task should be performed by clerics or monks in order to prevent scandal and avoid breaching clerical modesty.[38]

Innocent likewise acted to remove lay *cubicularii* from his household, surrounding himself instead with *religiosi*, monks and clerics.[39] He challenged the luxurious living of the higher clergy by personal example, limiting his own meals to three courses, those of his chaplains to two. Henceforth, as his biographer states, laymen were no longer to serve at his table but only those in regular orders. Only on feast days or other solemnities as required were the nobles to perform their customary service.[40] Precious vessels of gold and silver were replaced by glass and wood, costly furs by lambskins,[41] the pope's humble woollen attire being independently

---

[35]   *Sermo XIII de Sanctis: In festo D. Gregorii Papae, hujus nomine I* (PL 217, cols 513C–522A); *Innocenzo III. I Sermoni*, ed. Fioramonti, 363–75.

[36]   John the Deacon, *Vita Gregorii* 2.12 (col. 92C).

[37]   Ibid. 2.15 (col. 93B).

[38]   '[U]t quidam ex clericis vel etiam ex monachis electi ministerio pontificalis obsequantur': *Gregorii papae I Registrum epistolarum* 5.57 (MGH Epp. 1–2), 1: 362–7, at 363 (2), lines 20–1; *The Letters of Gregory the Great* 5.57a, transl. John R. C. Martyn, Pontifical Institute of Mediaeval Studies, Mediaeval Sources in Translation 40, 3 vols (Toronto, ON, 2004), 2: 388–92, at 389 (2) n. 236.

[39]   '[R]emotisque laicis, viros religiosos adhibuit ad quotidianum ministerium mensis, ut ei a personis regularibus honestius serviretur': Migne, *Gesta*, CXLVIII (col. ccxxvi); Gress-Wright, '*Gesta Innocentii III*', 353 lines 14–16; Powell, ed. and transl., *Deeds of Pope Innocent III*, 266 (CXLVIII).

[40]   *Le Liber censuum*, ed. Fabre, Duchesne and Mollat, 1: 305–6; Twyman, *Papal Ceremonial*, 190–3; Stenton, *English Society*, 31–2.

[41]   Migne, *Gesta*, CXLVIII (col. ccxxv); Gress-Wright, '*Gesta Innocentii III*', 353 lines

confirmed by the anonymous Cistercian chronicler from S. Maria de Ferraria near Teano in the Regno.[42]

Whilst endemic famine in Rome caused crowds to flock daily to beg at the doors of the papal household,[43] Gregory reorganized the administration of charity and almsgiving to the infirm and needy, channelling it through the Lateran Palace to each district of Rome. John the Deacon reports that, as paterfamilias, the pope distributed money to the poor each month as well as various seasonal foodstuffs, making the Church appear as a great *horreum* or universal storage barn.[44] Each day, in alleyways or at crossroads, cooked food was handed out to the sick on Gregory's orders, whilst a *veredarius* or special courier delivered meals to the disabled.[45] In order to mitigate the embarrassment of those of every condition who sought help, each dish received an apostolic blessing from Gregory's table before being handed to the grateful recipient.

Innocent's biographer records his works of piety at similar periods of famine, particularly when the price of grain rose to thirty *solidi*. Then he returned immediately from Anagni to Rome to arrange the urgent distribution of necessities through his household to those threatened with starvation.[46] He sent his almoner to seek out diligently the poor and weak, empowering him to issue seals or tokens so that he might send money for food to those who returned them, often as much as fifteen pounds each week. Like Gregory, Innocent displayed special care towards the noble poor who were too embarrassed to beg in public and secretly handed out a sum sufficient to support them for a whole week. Others of all conditions, in 1203 said to number eight thousand

---

8–10; Powell, ed. and transl., *Deeds of Pope Innocent III*, 266 (CXLVIII).

[42] *Chronica Romanorum pontificum et imperatorum ac de rebus in Apulia gestis*, in *Chronica ignoti monachi Cisterciensis S. Mariae de Ferraria*, ed. A. Gaudenzi (Naples, 1888), 1–71, at 34, *s.a.* 1207.

[43] John the Deacon, *Vita Gregorii* 2.16 (col. 93C); *Chronica Ferraria*, ed. Gaudenzi, 32–3; Hans Eberhard Mayer, 'Two Unpublished Letters on the Syrian Earthquake of 1202', *Medieval and Middle Eastern Studies in Honor of Aziz Suryal Atiya*, ed. Sami A. Hanna (Leiden, 1972), 295–310, at 303–5, repr. in idem., *Kreuzzüge und lateinischer Osten*, Collected Studies Series 171 (London, 1983), no. X (same pagination).

[44] '[I]ta ut nihil aliud quam communia quaedam horrea, communis putaretur': John the Deacon, *Vita Gregorii* 2.26 (col. 97B).

[45] Ibid. 2.28 (col. 97C).

[46] Migne, *Gesta*, CXLIII (cols cxcvi–cxcviii); Gress-Wright, '*Gesta Innocentii III*', 343–4; Powell, ed. and transl., *Deeds of Pope Innocent III*, 257–8 (CXLIII).

begging publicly, were to receive bread, money and clothing every day from the almonry.[47] The biographer adds that whilst Innocent exhorted the rich and powerful by word and example to give alms, he secretly ordered a tenth of his entire income to be set aside and distributed for this work. Innocent also encouraged poor and needy children to come up to his table at the end of a meal to receive any left-over food. These commitments clearly required a highly supervised and efficient administrative system, as well as a devoted and motivated group of officials to implement it, thereby bringing the rudiments of a more centralized household organization into existence.

A considerable achievement by both popes was the bringing together within their respective households of regulars and seculars, who observed different rules and professions in one *vita communis* or common life.[48] Indeed, so impressed was John the Deacon at the bonds thus forged between monks and clerics that he compared the church in Rome under Gregory's rule to that of the apostle Luke, or to Alexandria under Mark the Evangelist.[49] Innocent likewise imposed the model of the apostolic community on semi-pagan Livonia, taking this opportunity to introduce the ideal of the Christian household there. In 1200, Albert, bishop of Riga (1199–1229), dispatched the Cistercian, Theoderich of Treiden,[50] to Rome for decisions on several matters. Writing on 19 April 1201, Innocent ordered monks, canons regular and preachers to come together in *unum regulare propositum*, to dress similarly and follow identical observances so that neophytes and pagans alike would come to regard them as one unified community.[51] In a novel ruling which reversed that of Gratian on the

---

[47] Ibid.

[48] M.-D. Chenu, 'Monks, Canons, and Laymen in Search of the Apostolic Life', in idem, *Nature, Man and Society in the Twelfth Century: Essays in New Theological Perspectives in the Latin West*, ed. and transl. Jerome Taylor and Lester K. Little (Chicago, IL, 1967), 202–38, at 206–8.

[49] '[E]t in diversis professionibus habebatur vita communis, ita ut talis esset tunc sub Gregorio penes urbem Romam Ecclesia, qualem hanc fuisse sub apostolis Lucas, et sub Marco evangelista penes Alexandriam Philo commemorat': John the Deacon, *Vita Gregorii* 2.12 (col. 92C).

[50] Theodore of Treiden (d. 1219), O.Cist., abbot of Dünamünde and bishop of Estonia.

[51] *Is qui ecclesiam suam*. Text in Maccarrone, *Studi*, 335–7; idem, 'I papi e gli inizi della cristianizzazione della Livonia', in *Gli inizi del cristianesimo in Livonia-Lettonia. Atti del Colloquio Internazionale di Storia Ecclesiastica, in occasione dell'VIII centenario della*

custom of Levirate marriage in Livonia,[52] the pope agreed that men might continue to marry their deceased brothers' widows on the grounds that to refuse would prejudice future baptisms and thus hinder the formation of Christian families.[53] Innocent, using John the Deacon's account of the mission to the Anglo-Saxons,[54] was thus appealing directly to precedents by which Gregory, six centuries earlier, had reconciled converts to Christianity.[55] In following his predecessor's advice to the missionaries on how to win over rulers,[56] Innocent welcomed into his household Caupo, a local Livonian leader who accompanied Theoderich of Treiden to Rome. Greeting both men warmly, Innocent offered them gifts, to Caupo one hundred golden coins and to Theoderich a splendid copy of Gregory's Bible.[57] Caupo's visit to Rome in 1203 gave him the opportunity to reside for some time in the papal household, observing its customs and liturgical life.

Innocent's household was not only the residence of the pope but sometimes even a hospice or refuge for bishops. One such refugee was Henry Kietlicz, archbishop of Gniezno (1199–1219) who, fleeing his diocese for Rome late in 1206, gave an eyewitness account of the dire state of the Polish Church.[58] Kietlicz marvelled at the solemnity of the liturgies and stational masses of Rome which were so lacking in his homeland. His visit resulted in *Cum decorum*, Innocent's decretal letter of January 1207 to the Polish

---

chiesa in Livonia (1186–1986), Roma, 24–25 giugno 1986, Pontificio Comitato di Scienze Storiche, Atti e Documenti 1 (Vatican City, 1989), 31–80, at 78–80; *CICan*, X 3.1.11; X 4.19.9; X 5.38.8.

[52] Deut. 25: 5–10.

[53] James A. Brundage, 'Christian Marriage in Thirteenth-Century Livonia', *Journal of Baltic Studies* 4 (1973), 313–20, repr. in idem, *The Crusades, Holy War and Canon Law*, Collected Studies Series 338 (Aldershot, 1991), no. XVIII (same pagination).

[54] John the Deacon, *Vita Gregorii* 2.38 (col. 102A).

[55] 'Ad haec sanctae memoriae Gregorii papae praedecessoris nostri adjaerentes': Maccarrone, *Studi*, 336 lines 46–7; Gratian, *Decretum*, C.35 q.3 c.20 (*CICan*, X 4.19.9).

[56] R. A. Markus, 'Gregory the Great and a Papal Missionary Strategy', in G. J. Cuming, ed., *The Mission of the Church and the Propagation of the Faith*, SCH 6 (Cambridge, 1970), 29–38, at 33–6; Neilsen, 'Mission and Submission', 217–19, 224–6.

[57] Henricus Lettus, *The Chronicle of Henry of Livonia*, ed. and transl. James A. Brundage, new edn (New York, 2003), 43.

[58] Brenda Bolton, 'Message, Celebration, Offering: The Place of Twelfth- and Early Thirteenth-Century Liturgical Drama as "Missionary Theatre"', in R. N. Swanson, ed., *Continuity and Change in Christian Worship*, SCH 35 (Woodbridge, 1999), 89–103, at 95–7.

bishops on clerical behaviour at religious festivals, which entered into Gregory IX's *Liber Extra*.[59]

All popes need advisors and a crucial element of Gregory's household reform was his erudite and talented inner circle with whom, according to John the Deacon, he debated both day and night.[60] Four clerics – Peter the Deacon (his interlocutor in the *Dialogues*), the notaries Aemilianus and Paterius, the latter responsible for compiling a digest from his writings,[61] and John (the *defensor*) – together with four monks, Maximianus and Marinianus from S. Andrea al Celio (his monastery in Rome), and Probus and Claudius from the Ravennate, served this function. In a similarly worded but much longer list, Innocent's biographer identified twenty-two chaplains who served the pope and were promoted by 1208.[62] Of these, eight, namely Hugolino, cardinal deacon of S. Eustachio (1198–1206),[63] Leo Brancaleone, cardinal deacon of S. Lucia in Septasolio (1200–2),[64] John Odelus, cardinal priest of S. Maria in Cosmedin (1200–13),[65] Peter de Sasso, cardinal priest of S. Pudenziana (1206–19),[66] Nicholas *de Romanis*, cardinal bishop of Tusculum (1204–18/19),[67] John of Ferentino, cardinal deacon

---

[59] *CICan*, X 3.1.12.

[60] John the Deacon, *Vita Gregorii* 2.12 (col. 92A).

[61] '[E]x libris ipsius aliqua utillima defloravit': ibid.

[62] Migne, *Gesta*, CXLVII (cols ccxii–ccxxv); Gress-Wright, '*Gesta Innocentii III*', 352 lines 11–28; Powell, ed. and transl., *Deeds of Pope Innocent III*, 265–6 (CXLVII); Reinhard Elze, 'Die päpstliche Kapelle im 12. und 13. Jahrhundert', *Zeitschrift der Savigny-Stiftung für Rechtsgeschichte* 67/3 (1950), 145–204, at 175–87.

[63] *Papae consobrinus*, legate to Sicily (1202), cardinal bishop of Ostia (1206–27), legate to Germany (1207–9): W. Maleczek, *Papst und Kardinalskolleg von 1191 bis 1216: Die Kardinäle unter Cölestin III. und Innocent III.*, Publikationen des Historischen Instituts beim Österreichen Kulturinstitut in Rom, Abhandlungen 6 (Vienna, 1984), 126–33; idem, 'Zwischen lokaler Verankerung und universalem Horizont. Das Kardinalskollegium unter Innocenz III.', in *Urbs et Orbis*, ed. Sommerlechner, 102–74, at 141–6 (no. 2).

[64] Cardinal priest of S. Croce (1202–24), legate to Lombardy (1202), to Bulgaria (1204), to Germany (1207–9): Maleczek, *Kardinalskolleg*, 137–9; idem, 'Zwischen lokaler Verankerung und universalem Horizont', 148 (no. 7).

[65] Chancellor of the Roman Church (from 1205), *consanguineus* and perhaps *nepos* of Innocent: Maleczek, *Kardinalskolleg*, 136–7; idem, 'Zwischen lokaler Verankerung und universalem Horizont', 147–8.

[66] Papal agent in Terracina (1202–4), legate and *rector* in Campania and the Marittima, legate to Germany (1216): Maleczek, *Kardinalskolleg*, 163–4; idem, 'Zwischen lokaler Verankerung und universalem Horizont', 153 (no. 18).

[67] Legate to England (1213–14): Maleczek, *Kardinalskolleg*, 147–50; idem, 'Zwischen lokaler Verankerung und universalem Horizont', 158 (no. 18).

of S. Maria in Via Lata (1204),[68] Octavian, cardinal deacon of SS Sergio e Bacco (1206–34),[69] and John Colonna, cardinal deacon of SS Cosma e Damiano (1206–17),[70] functioned variously as legates and administrators throughout Christendom.

Innocent raised three of his chaplains to archbishoprics, appointing Raynaldo to Acerenza (1199–1200),[71] another Raynaldo to Capua (1208–22),[72] and Blasio to Torres in Sardinia (1203–c.1218),[73] with a further ten promoted to bishoprics. The *Gesta* name Paul (c.1200 – October 1206), elevated to the diocese of Orte,[74] Benedict to Fondi (1199–1210),[75] Rainier to Viterbo (1199–?1217),[76] John of Casamari to Forcone (1204),[77] Egidius to Gaeta (February 1203 – 30 November 1210),[78] Albertus Longus to Ferentino (1203–?1210),[79] Peter to Mileto (25 August 1207 – 1213),[80] Saxo to Teramo (February 1207 – 1214),[81] Bartholomew to Trani (1203–25),[82] and Odo to Valva (1206–24).[83] In February 1204, Innocent intervened to quash the election of the Cistercian abbot of Corazzo to the Benedictine monastery of Santa Euphemia, appointing in his place

---

[68] Chaplain until 1203 when he entered the Chancery, legate to England (1206), cardinal priest of S. Prassede (1212–15), papal *auditor* (1215): Maleczek, *Kardinalskolleg*, 146–7; idem, 'Zwischen lokaler Verankerung und universalem Horizont', 150.

[69] *Consobrinus noster*, canon of St Peter's, *camerarius* (June 1200 – 20 April 1204): Maleczek, *Kardinalskolleg*, 163.

[70] Ibid. 154–62.

[71] Papal notary: Norbert Kamp, *Kirche und Monarchie im Staufischen Königreich Sizilien: Prosopographische Grundlegung: Bistümer und Bischöfe des Königreiches 1194–1266*, 4 vols (Munich, 1973–5), 2: 774; Conrad Eubel, *Hierarchia Catholica medii aevi*, 6 vols (Regensburg/Munich, 1913–67), 1: 70.

[72] Papal *procurator* (1199): Kamp, *Kirche und Monarchie*, 1: 112–16; Eubel, *Hierarchia*, 1: 164.

[73] Maleczek, *Kardinalskolleg*, 348; Eubel, *Hierarchia*, 1: 503.

[74] Eubel, *Hierarchia*, 1: 278. Orte was on the Tiber and the Via Flaminia between Rome and Ravenna.

[75] Ibid. 1: 256.

[76] Ibid. 1: 532 n. 1.

[77] O.Cist., *acolytus noster*, legate to Bosnia and Bulgaria (20 June 1204 – 1205), bishop of Perugia (1207–30): Kamp, *Kirche und Monarchie*, 1: 18–20; Eubel, *Hierarchia*, 1: 98.

[78] Kamp, *Kirche und Monarchie*, 1: 82–4; Eubel, *Hierarchia*, 1: 258.

[79] Canon of Anagni: Eubel, *Hierarchia*, 1: 246.

[80] Kamp, *Kirche und Monarchie*, 2: 818–19; Eubel, *Hierarchia*, 1: 340.

[81] Kamp, *Kirche und Monarchie*, 1: 52–3; Eubel, *Hierarchia*, 1: 95.

[82] Kamp, *Kirche und Monarchie*, 2: 552–4; Eubel, *Hierarchia*, 1: 491 and n.1.

[83] Kamp, *Kirche und Monarchie*, 1: 65–6; Eubel, *Hierarchia*, 1: 513.

John, monk of La Cava.[84] John, last on the *Gesta*'s promotion list, displayed conspicuous religiosity and proven probity, both at La Cava and subsequently in the papal chaplaincy.[85] Indeed, Innocent's chaplains, particularly those nominated to dioceses in the Regno,[86] worked hard to extend control and supervision after November 1198 when the pope began to act as regent for the young Frederick II.[87]

Whilst Gregory I's inner circle had consisted of seculars and regulars in equal if small numbers, Innocent maintained a similar balance by advancing the Cistercians, Luca of Sambucina to Cosenza (1202/3–27)[88] and Gerald I of Casamari to Reggio Calabria (?1209/11–?1217), the two metropolitan sees of Calabria.[89] On a more prosaic level in the daily routine of the papal household, Innocent chose as his closest and most influential advisors simple, spiritually-minded Cistercians. He selected Brother Nicholas, his personal chaplain, referred to as 'nonnus Nicholaus', to be a 'wise' head on account of his age,[90] whilst his personal confessor, the charismatic Rainier of Ponza (d. 1207/9), monk of Fossanova, diplomat and facilitator, friend and associate of Joachim of Fiore,[91]

---

[84] *Die Register Innocenz' III. 6 Pontifikatsjahr 1203/1204*, ed. O. Hageneder, J. C. Moore and A. Sommerlechner (Vienna, 1995), 393–5 (no. 233).

[85] 'Dilectum itaque filium I, quondam capellanum nostrum, virum religione conspicuum et scientia commendandum, in monasterio Cauensi et in capellania nostra probatum': ibid. 394–5; Elze, 'Die päpstliche Kapelle', 148.

[86] Acerenza, Capua, Gaeta, Fondi, Mileto, Trani and Forcone. Santa Euphemia lay in the diocese of Nicastro.

[87] Norbert Kamp, 'The Bishops of Southern Italy in the Norman and Staufen Periods', in G. A. Loud and A. Metcalfe, eds, *The Society of Norman Italy* (Leiden, 2004), 185–209, at 204–5; G. A. Loud, *The Latin Church in Norman Italy* (Cambridge, 2007), 251–4.

[88] Kamp, *Kirche und Monarchie*, 1: 833–9; Brenda Bolton, 'From Frontier to Mission: Networking by Unlikely Allies in the Church International, 1198–1216', in Jeremy Gregory and Hugh McLeod, eds, *International Religious Networks*, SCH S 14 (Woodbridge, 2012), 67–82, at 73–4.

[89] Kamp, *Kirche und Monarchie*, 1: 922–6; F. Farina and I. Vona, *L'abate Giraldo di Casamari, amico fraterno di Gioacchino da Fiore, legato pontificio in Germania, in Francia, in Inghilterra, promotore del nuovo complesso monastico, arcivescovo di Reggio Calabria*, Bibliotheca Casaemariensis 3 (Casamari, 1998).

[90] '[E]t nonno Nicholao, domini Papae capellano': J.-M. Canivez, *Statuta Capitulorum Generalium Ordinis Cisterciensis ab anno 1116 ad annum 1786*, 1: *Ab anno 1116 ad annum 1220* (Louvain, 1933), 304 (no. 42).

[91] G. L. Potestà, 'Raniero da Ponza, *socius* di Gioacchino da Fiore', *Florensia* 11 (1997), 69–82; M. P. Alberzoni, 'Raniero da Ponza e la curia romana', ibid. 83–114; G. Cariboni, '"Huiusmodi verba gladium portant": Raniero da Ponza e l'Ordine cistercense', ibid. 115–35.

certainly fuelled the pope's eschatological expectations.[92] From 1205, Stephen of Fossanova, deacon of Sant'Elia in Ceccano and friend of St Dominic, served the pope as chamberlain of the household until his elevation in 1213 as cardinal priest of SS Apostoli.[93]

Innocent revealed his concern for the physical setting of his household from the beginning of his pontificate. The fabric of the Lateran Palace was strengthened and repaired. He ordered a new chamber to be prepared over the chaplaincy, where previously no pope had lived, creating an additional little room (*camerula)* above the apse and establishing a small infirmary (*camera egestiva*) there.[94] Throughout the palace, he installed high and wide wall sconces to improve the lighting, repaved the consistory and installed marble steps and a new furnace. Whilst these improvements were modest, Innocent's private chapel of St Laurence in the Lateran, known as the *Sancta sanctorum* for its wealth of relics, appeared in vivid contrast to the austerity of his household. Filled with the richest and most beautiful gold vessels, pontifical vestments, glowing jewels, gloves and liturgical sandals, all to the greater glory of the Lord, the pope said the daily office within this twenty-foot-square space which held no more than fifteen of his chaplains.[95]

Innocent regarded himself as paterfamilias of his household and based his care for, and appreciation of, his chaplains on his position. On the papal summer retreat 'at that arid Segni' in either 1211 or 1212, he ordered them to say a shorter series of suffrages as the nights were so hot.[96] In the chapel at the Lateran, dedicated to St

92 F. Robb, 'Joachimist Exegesis in the Theology of Innocent III and Rainier of Ponza', ibid. 137–52; Christoph Egger, 'Joachim von Fiore, Rainer von Ponza und die römische Kurie', in *Gioacchino da Fiore tra Bernardo di Clairvaux e Innocenzo III. Atti del 5 Congresso internazionale di studi gioachimiti, San Giovanni in Fiore 16–21 settembre 1999*, ed. Roberto Rusconi, Opere di Gioacchino da Fiore: testi e strumenti 13 (Rome, 2001), 129–62.

93 O.Cist., cardinal (1213–27): Maleczek, *Papst und Kardinalskolleg*, 179–83; V. J. Koudelka, 'Notes pour servir à l'histoire de Saint Dominique, I. Le cardinal Étienne de Fossanova, ami de Saint Dominique', *AFP* 35 (1965), 5–15.

94 Migne, *Gesta*, CXLVI (cols ccxi–ccxxii); Gress-Wright, '*Gesta Innocentii III*', 351 line 28, 352 lines 1–8; Powell, ed. and transl., *Deeds of Pope Innocent III*, 265 (CXLVI).

95 Julian Gardner, 'L'architettura del Sancta Sanctorum', in idem, *Sancta Sanctorum* (Milan, 1995), 19–37.

96 Van Dijk, *Ordinal*, 162 lines 4–9; idem and J. Hazelden Walker, *The Origins of the Modern Roman Liturgy: The Liturgy of the Papal Court and the Franciscan Order in the Thirteenth Century* (London, 1960), 97, 267, 462.

Nicholas and given to the chaplains by Calixtus II (1119–1124),[97] they celebrated their patronal feast by singing solemn vigils of three lessons in the evening and then enjoyed a gift of 'good sweetmeat and wine excellent and plentiful' from Stephen, the papal chamberlain.[98] In September 1215, as a fierce contagion reportedly spread through Rome, the papal household still remained in Anagni. Innocent was committed to return to the city to make final preparations for the Fourth Lateran Council but, since the sickness was considered more likely to affect younger people, he ordered his more youthful chaplains to flee to the Campania, there to escape the 'burning and raging summer' and await the arrival of more clement weather.[99]

Innocent conducted his comprehensive programme of itineration around the patrimony not only to control the region but also because most of his subjects there had not seen their bishop for more than a generation.[100] Absent from Rome for thirteen summer journeys, each lasting at least a month and often longer, he established several physical settings for his household at Segni, Corneto,[101] Anagni, Ferentino, Rieti and Viterbo.[102] Sources reveal that the *familia* occupied temporary accommodation, sometimes even staying under canvas and hence enjoying far less privacy than was usual. An exceptional letter from Subiaco in the summer of 1202, probably written by a chaplain, provides both insight and light relief. The doctor to the papal encampment, a certain Master Romanus, was 'in every way experienced and endowed with estimable qualities', and Innocent regarded him with great honour and esteem.[103] On another level, the chaplains nicknamed their head

---

[97] *Le* Liber pontificalis, ed. Duchesne, 2: 323 line 20; Elze, 'Die päpstiche Kapelle', 172–3.

[98] Van Dijk, *Ordinal*, 357 lines 3–7; idem and Hazelden Walker, *Origins*, 98.

[99] E. Heller, 'Der kuriale Geschäftsgang in den Briefen des Thomas von Capua', *Archiv für Urkundenforschung* 13 (1935), 198–313, at 259.

[100] Neither Clement III (1187–91) nor Celestine III (1191–8) left Rome during their pontificates: Maccarrone, *Studi*, 8–9.

[101] Anna Maria Voci, 'I palazzi papali del Lazio', in Carocci, ed., *Itineranza Pontificia*, 211–49, at 228–9.

[102] Brenda Bolton, 'A New Rome in a Small Place? Imitation and Re-creation in the Patrimony of St Peter', in Bolgia, McKitterick and Osborne, eds, *Rome across Time and Space*, 305–22.

[103] '[M]agistrum duxi Ro[manum] subtiliter consulendum, virum utique maturum et laudabili virtute firmatum': Karl Hampe, 'Eine Schilderung des Sommeraufenthaltes der römischen Kurie unter Innozenz III. in Subiaco 1202', *Historische Vierteljahrsschrift* 8 (1905), 509–35, at 535; Brenda Bolton, 'Subiaco – Innocent III's version of Elijah's

cook Nabusardan, after the general of the army in 4 Kings 25: 8 who destroyed the walls of Jerusalem[104] and accused 'this Prince of Cooks' of destroying the walls of the soul! A unique glimpse into the household was recorded in July 1207 when William, Cistercian monk of Andres and petitioner to the curia, met Innocent, then in Viterbo.[105] Innocent, awakening from his midday siesta, received him with the papal kiss and informed him that, while a student in Paris, he had stayed at Andres on the way to Canterbury. William, delighted, was permitted to sit at the pope's feet to explain his case.

Innocent III, elected pope at only thirty-seven, selected wisely in choosing Gregory the Great as model and father figure. As theologian, liturgist and author, his knowledge of his predecessor's work was already encyclopaedic and he sought to implement Gregory's advice in many fields. Innocent's vast knowledge of the Bible brought him to realize the significance of the household, not only as a metaphor for the whole Church but also as the perfect environment by which to inculcate the values of the apostolic age. But it was Innocent's close reading of John the Deacon's *Vita Gregorii* and his anonymous biographer's skill in adapting John's ninth-century compilation to late twelfth-century conditions which encouraged him to create an exemplary household which looked back to the sixth century. Innocent, however, moved beyond Gregory's reforms, transforming the hitherto exceptionally private role of the papal household to one which, through the increased mobility of itineration, became far more public during the course of the thirteenth century. When he looked at his household, Innocent showed that he knew how to choose and uphold his personnel and support their work in the same way as the faithful and wise servant of Matthew's Gospel.

Queen Mary & Westfield College, University of London

Cave', in Peter Clarke and Tony Claydon, eds, *God's Bounty? The Churches and the Natural World*, SCH 46 (Woodbridge, 2010), 111–23.

[104] 'Nabusardan cocorum princeps': Hampe, 'Eine Schilderung des Sommeraufenthaltes', 531.

[105] *Chronica Andrensis* 155–8 (ed. I. Heller, MGH SS 24, 684–773, at 737–78) for the visit of 1207. See also Werner Maleczek, 'Der Mittelpunkt Europas im frühen 13. Jahrhundert. Chronisten, Fürsten und Bischöfe an der Kurie zur Zeit Papst Innocenz' III.', *Römische Historische Mitteilungen* 49 (2007) 89–157; Bolton, 'A New Rome?', 315–16.

THE COLLEGE OF CARDINALS UNDER HONORIUS III: A NEPOTISTIC HOUSEHOLD?*

by THOMAS W. SMITH

The College of Cardinals constituted the innermost circle of the medieval papal household – arguably one of the most important households in Christendom – whose influence was sought by envoys pursuing diplomatic affairs and petitioners looking to secure grace and justice. The relationships between the pope and the cardinals of his household, and of the household with those outside the papal curia, were integral to the operation of papal government. The college consulted with the pope on matters of politics and everyday church administration, and its specific roles included the election of new popes, the concession of privileges, auditing legal cases heard at the papal curia, deployment of its members as legates *a latere*, and the administration of important curial departments.[1] Although the pope could not dismiss existing cardinals, it was the personal prerogative of the reigning pope to select clergy for appointment to this elite household, although his decisions seem to have been subject to ratification by the existing members of the college, whose exact level of involvement in appointments remains unclear.[2]

This essay analyses the nature of the ties within the household of the college which bound cardinals to the pope and each other, ties which derived from a mixture of nepotism and kinship, the influence of contemporary politics, and elements of meritocracy. The pope and his cardinals constituted a household of brothers; in papal documents such as a letter issued by Pope Honorius III (1216–27) on 10 April 1220 popes referred to their discussions

* I wish to express my gratitude to Barbara Bombi, Sarah Foot, Bernard Hamilton, Christopher Tilley and the editors of Studies in Church History for commenting on this essay.

[1] Walter Ullmann, *A Short History of the Papacy in the Middle Ages*, 2nd edn (London, 2003), 232; Pierre Jugie, 'Cardinal (jusqu'au concile de Trente)', in Philippe Levillain, ed., *Dictionnaire historique de la papauté* (Paris, 2003), 277–81, at 277–8; Colin Morris, *The Papal Monarchy: The Western Church from 1050 to 1250*, OHCC (Oxford, 1989), 570.

[2] Ullmann, *Papacy*, 232; Morris, *Papal Monarchy*, 210; I. S. Robinson, *The Papacy 1073–1198: Continuity and Innovation* (Cambridge, 1990), 45–7.

'*cum fratribus nostris*' ('with our brothers').[3] Given the pope's role in appointing cardinals, it has been assumed that the college was a nepotistic household, with popes simply selecting relatives and friends to fill the top jobs. Bernhard Schimmelpfennig argued that nepotism and family power struggles were rife in the thirteenth-century College of Cardinals, and stated that Pope Innocent III (1198–1216) had appointed relatives to important positions in the college and removed rivals in the process, supposedly including Cencius *Camerarius*, the future Honorius III.[4] Colin Morris similarly claimed that Cencius had lost power under Innocent III.[5] Schimmelpfennig maintained that when Cencius was elected as Pope Honorius III in 1216 'the carousel turned again' and Innocent's kinsmen were ejected and replaced by Honorius's.[6] In summary, Schimmelpfennig argued that 'a change of popes promised to bring with it a saturation of the control of the favoured clan'.[7] This was questioned in passing by Sandro Carocci, but Honorius's college has yet to be subjected to modern historical analysis.[8]

Cencius did not belong to the Roman Savelli family as traditionally claimed; rather, he was of humble origins, and stated in the *Liber censuum* (a book of payments owed to the Church which he finished compiling in 1192) that he owed everything in life to the Church.[9] Werner Maleczek suggests plausibly that he might have belonged to a minor Roman family and worked his way up through the Church.[10] Matthias Thumser posits that he belonged

3   Vatican City, Archivio Segreto Vaticano, Registra Vaticana [hereafter: Reg. Vat.] 10, fol. 171^v; *Regesta Honorii Papae III*, ed. P. Pressutti, 2 vols (Rome, 1888–95; repr. Hildesheim, 1978), no. 2392.

4   Bernhard Schimmelpfennig, *The Papacy*, transl. James Sievert (New York, 1992), 175. The most recent German edition maintains this argument: idem, *Das Papsttum: Von der Antike bis zur Renaissance*, 6th edn, rev. Elke Goez (Darmstadt, 2009), 196–7.

5   Morris, *Papal Monarchy*, 570.

6   Schimmelpfennig, *Papacy*, 175.

7   Ibid.

8   Sandro Carocci, *Il nepotismo nel medioevo: Papi, cardinali e famiglie nobili* (Rome, 1999), 116.

9   Sandro Carocci and Marco Vendittelli, 'Onorio III.', in Manlio Simonetti et al., eds, *Enciclopedia dei papi*, 3 vols (Rome, 2000), 2: 350–62, at 350–1; Werner Maleczek, *Papst und Kardinalskolleg von 1191 bis 1216: Die Kardinäle unter Coelestin III. und Innocenz III.* (Vienna, 1984), 111–12; *Le Liber Censum de l'Église Romaine*, ed. P. Fabre, L. Duchesne and G. Mollat, 3 vols (Paris, 1889–1952), 1: 2.

10   Maleczek, *Kardinalskolleg*, 112.

to the Capocci family, but this too has been questioned by Sandro Carocci.[11] Cencius's date of birth is unknown, although he must have been born in the mid-twelfth century, probably in the 1150s or 1160s; the curialist Jacques de Vitry referred to Cencius as '*senex*' in 1216.[12]

Cencius had been appointed to a canonry at S. Maria Maggiore and held the position of chamberlain at the curia since 1188. He was appointed cardinal deacon of S. Lucia in Orthea by Celestine III in 1193, and was made chancellor in 1194, combining it with his position as chamberlain. Between 1191 and 1198 Cencius acted as an auditor at the curia, and in 1196 was chosen to negotiate with Emperor Henry VI (1191–7). Cencius's dual role as chancellor and chamberlain was abolished by Innocent III, but he was promoted to cardinal priest of SS. Giovanni e Paolo in 1200.[13]

This essay questions whether Honorius III's college was the simple nepotistic household Schimmelpfennig claimed. Such a study is much needed: while prosopographical studies of the college under Innocent III and Gregory IX (1227–41) have been conducted by Maleczek and Agostino Paravacini Bagliani, there remains a significant historiographical gap for Honorius III's reign in the intervening period, which this essay addresses.[14]

To assess Honorius's influence over the college, its composition on his accession must be outlined. Honorius inherited twenty-two cardinals from Innocent III.[15] Innocent's influence on the college had been significant, for he made thirty appointments throughout his eighteen-year pontificate, nineteen of whom were still living at the time of Honorius's succession.[16] Of the other three cardinals

[11] Matthias Thumser, *Rom und der römische Adel in der späten Stauferzeit* (Tübingen, 1995), 60–1; Carocci, *Nepotismo*, 117.

[12] Jacques de Vitry, *Lettres de la Cinquième Croisade*, ed. R. B. C. Huygens, transl. G. Duchet-Suchaux (Turnhout, 1998), 24; see also Jane E. Sayers, *Papal Government and England during the Pontificate of Honorius III (1216–1227)* (Cambridge, 1984), 1.

[13] Maleczek, *Kardinalskolleg*, 112.

[14] Maleczek, *Kardinalskolleg*; idem, 'Zwischen lokaler Verankerung und universalem Horizont: Das Kardinalskollegium unter Innocenz III.', in *Innocenzo III: Urbs et Orbis, Atti del Congresso Internazionale Roma, 9–15 settembre 1998*, ed. Andrea Sommerlechner, 2 vols (Rome, 2003), 1: 102–74; Agostino Paravicini Bagliani, *Cardinali di curia e 'familiae' cardinalizie dal 1227 al 1254*, 2 vols (Padua, 1972).

[15] For a full list, see Maleczek, *Kardinalskolleg*, 59–62. Maleczek counted twenty-three cardinals on Innocent III's death: ibid. 288. Robinson counted twenty-seven: Robinson, *Papacy*, 44.

[16] Maleczek, *Kardinalskolleg*, 287–8.

bequeathed to Honorius, one had been appointed by Alexander III (1159–81), and two by Clement III (1187–91). On his election as pope in July 1216, Cencius was the only surviving cardinal (of five) appointed by Celestine III (1191–8).[17] The makeup of the college in 1216 was overwhelmingly Italian, specifically Roman: of the nineteen cardinals whose origins are certain, twelve came from Rome and its environs, and one each from Viterbo, Benevento, Capua and Vercelli. Of three non-Italians, one came from Spain, another from England, and the last from southern France.[18] Innocent drew many of his thirty appointees from other curial offices: nine cardinals were created from papal chapel staff, three from the chancery, and one from the camera.[19] Many were highly educated *magistri*, although relatively few were drawn from religious orders.[20] Neither Celestine III nor Innocent III were immune to accusations of nepotism, having both appointed blood relations as cardinals.[21]

The next step in analysing the household is to identify how it changed under Honorius. The number and identity of cardinals that Honorius is claimed to have created varies greatly, with numbers ranging from five to fourteen. Confusion stems from the unreliable but influential list of thirteen cardinals given by Alphonsus Ciaconius in the seventeenth century.[22] Drawing on Ciaconius, Lorenzo Cardella printed a similar list in the eighteenth century, substituting one cardinal for another, but keeping the total number at thirteen.[23] In the nineteenth century Johannes Clausen reprinted Ciaconius's list and added an extra cardinal not seen before, bringing the total to fourteen.[24] More than half of these alleged creations were incorrectly ascribed to Honorius.

---

[17] For Celestine's five appointments, see ibid. 111–24.

[18] Ibid. 293.

[19] Ibid. 293–4. On Innocent III's household, see, in this volume, Brenda Bolton, '"A faithful and wise servant"? Innocent III (1198–1216) looks at his Household', 59–73.

[20] Maleczek, *Kardinalskolleg*, 294–5.

[21] Ibid. 295.

[22] Alphonsus Ciaconius, *Vitae, et res gestae pontificum romanorum et S.R.E. cardinalium*, ed. Augustus Oldoinus, 4 vols (Rome, 1677), 2: 43–66.

[23] Lorenzo Cardella, *Memorie storiche de' cardinali della santa romana chiesa*, 9 vols (Rome, 1792–7), 1/2: 232–43.

[24] Johannes Clausen, *Papst Honorius III. (1216–1227): Eine Monographie* (Bonn, 1895), 397–8.

At the beginning of the twentieth century Conrad Eubel removed the erroneous attributions and published a new list of five cardinals appointed by Honorius: Egidio Torres (cardinal deacon of SS. Cosma e Damiano, 1216); Conrad of Urach (cardinal bishop of Porto e S. Rufina, 1219); Nicholas da Chiaromonte (cardinal bishop of Tusculum, 1219); Peter Capuanus (cardinal deacon of S. Giorgio in Velabro, 1219); and Oliver of Paderborn (cardinal bishop of Sabina, 1225).[25] This was the most accurate list to date, although Aldebrand Orsini (cardinal deacon of S. Eustachio, 1216; cardinal priest of S. Susanna, 1219; cardinal bishop of Sabina, 1221), whom Eubel listed as one of Innocent III's creations, but whom Maleczek did not identify as one of that pope's appointments, should also be included, because of Honorius's patronage of him.[26] The witness lists of papal privileges confirm these identifications and do not reveal any unknown cardinals, although Honorius may have created cardinals of whom no documentary traces remain. The total number of cardinals known to have been created by Honorius III thus stands at six.[27]

Having spent over a quarter of a century in service at the curia before becoming pope, Honorius must have owed some of his greatest allegiances to his former peers, the cardinals who now made up his own household – men appointed by Celestine III and Innocent III – which may explain why he made so few appointments to the college. Given his age and humble origins, Honorius was probably neither surrounded by ambitious young men, nor had relatives suitable for immediate creation as cardinals; that Honorius only appointed two cardinals in 1216 is perhaps evidence

---

[25] Conrad Eubel, *Hierarchia catholica medii aevi*, 2nd edn, 6 vols (Münster, 1913–58), 1: 5.

[26] Ibid. 5.

[27] Matthias Thumser, 'Aldobrandino Orsini (1217–1221), ein Kardinal Honorius' III.', *Römische Historische Mitteilungen* 32/33 (1990/1), 41–9, at 42 and n. 5; Falko Neininger, *Konrad von Urach († 1227): Zähringer, Zisterzienser, Kardinallegat* (Paderborn, 1994), 159. In 1217 Honorius also promoted four cardinals created by Celestine III and Innocent III: Bertrand from cardinal deacon of S. Giorgio in Velabro to cardinal priest of SS. Giovanni e Paolo; John Colonna from cardinal deacon of SS. Cosma e Damiano to cardinal priest of S. Prassedes; Cinthius from cardinal priest of S. Lorenzo in Lucina to cardinal bishop of Porto and S. Rufina; and Peter Collivaccinus of Benevento from cardinal priest of S. Lorenzo in Damaso to cardinal bishop of Sabina. In 1221 Honorius promoted Guido Pierleoni from cardinal deacon of S. Nicola in Carcere Tulliano to cardinal bishop of Preneste: Maleczek, *Kardinalskolleg*, 170, 158, 106, 174, 141 respectively. They are not recorded as having had special connections to Honorius.

for this. However, although Honorius did not appoint any rela-tives as cardinals, he did appoint kinsmen to lower positions in the Church. A papal letter of 22 January 1218 despatched to the legate in England, Guala, cardinal priest of S. Martino, reveals that after eighteen months in office Honorius could still proudly claim that 'we do not recall having provided any of our own kinsmen to a living, so that they murmur against us', before promptly appointing just such a familiar, John de Tebaldo, to one of the 'better prebends' in England.[28]

In the first consistory, held in December 1216, Honorius made two appointments to the college. Honorius created Aldebrand Orsini cardinal deacon of S. Eustachio, promoted him in 1219 to be cardinal priest of S. Susanna, and elevated him a second time to become cardinal bishop of Sabina in 1221, making him the only cardinal promoted twice by Honorius. Thumser argues compel-lingly that Aldebrand belonged to the Orsini family, rather than the Caietani as traditionally thought.[29] The Orsini were a powerful Roman noble family that had flourished under Celestine III: the family founder, Orso, was Celestine's nephew.[30] Aldebrand's ances-tors had served at the curia under Honorius's predecessors, and his swift appointment at the start of the pope's reign and subsequent promotions suggest that Aldebrand was known to Honorius before 1216.

After his appointment Aldebrand used his position at the curia to advance his own relatives: a papal letter was issued on 22 March 1217 to the archbishop and chapter of York that secured a prebend for his relation Gimundus.[31] Aldebrand exerted his influence again when another papal letter was issued on 13 April 1221 to the bishop and chapter of Paris, ordering that a Paris prebend which he had possessed when cardinal priest of S. Susanna be awarded

---

[28] Reg. Vat. 9, fol. 201^v (*Regesta*, ed. Pressutti, no. 1015); ET Nicholas Vincent: *The Letters and Charters of Cardinal Guala Bicchieri, Papal Legate in England, 1216–1218* (Woodbridge, 1996), lxxiii, 144–5 (no. 177); John Doran kindly brought this reference to my attention.

[29] Thumser, 'Aldobrandino', 44–6.

[30] Sandro Carocci, *Baroni di Roma: Dominazioni signorili e lignaggi aristocratici nel duecento e nel primo trecento* (Rome, 1993), 387–8; John Doran, 'A Lifetime of Service in the Roman Church', in idem and Damian J. Smith, eds, *Pope Celestine III (1191–1198): Diplomat and Pastor* (Farnham, 2008), 31–79, at 78.

[31] Reg. Vat. 9, fol. 127^v (*Regesta*, ed. Pressutti, no. 458); Thumser, 'Aldobrandino', 48.

to his nephew James and thus be retained within his family.[32] As a cardinal, Aldebrand functioned as an auditor at the curia on a number of occasions.[33] He also maintained close links with France. In 1219 the chapter of Paris chose Aldebrand as bishop, a decision which Honorius reversed.[34] He was also recorded as a contact of King Philip Augustus (1180–1223) at the papal curia.[35]

The second appointment in December 1216 was a Spaniard, Egidio Torres, whom Honorius created cardinal deacon of SS. Cosma e Damiano.[36] Egidio was employed as an auditor throughout Honorius's reign.[37] He also secured favours for his relatives and friends. On 2 May 1218 Honorius issued a mandate to the bishop, cantor and a *magister* of Burgos, ordering that Egidio's relative, 'P. *canonicus*' of Zamora, be awarded an archdeaconry.[38] Another papal letter of 3 January 1219, sent to the dean and chapter of Orense, reveals that Egidio secured a prebend there for another relative, Arius Petrus.[39] On 10 May 1219 Honorius issued a document to the bishop of Palencia granting Egidio's request for a cleric named Bartholomew to be awarded a dispensation to hold an ecclesiastical benefice.[40] On 21 April 1220, the bishop and chapter of Zamora were ordered to admit Egidio's chamberlain, also named Egidio, to the first available prebend.[41] Such nepotism, spreading outwards from the papal household after a cardinal's appointment, was commonplace.

Honorius made no more appointments until 1219, when he created three new cardinals in January and September consistories. Conrad of Urach was drafted into the college's top rank when he was created cardinal bishop of Porto e S. Rufina in Janu-

---

[32] Reg. Vat. 11, fol. 107ʳ (*Regesta*, ed. Pressutti, no. 3241).

[33] *Regesta*, ed. Pressutti, nos 1177, 2095, 2096; *Acta Honorii III (1216–1227) et Gregorii IX (1227–1241) e registris vaticanis aliisque fontibus collegit*, ed. A. L. Tautu (Vatican City, 1950), 98–9 (no. 69).

[34] Reg. Vat. 10, fols 145ᵛ–146ʳ, 152ᵛ (*Regesta*, ed. Pressutti, nos 2279, 2286); Klaus Ganzer, *Die Entwicklung des auswärtigen Kardinalats im hohen Mittelalter: Ein Beitrag zur Geschichte des Kardinalkollegiums vom 11. bis 13. Jahrhundert* (Tübingen, 1963), 165.

[35] Thumser, 'Aldobrandino', 47.

[36] Eubel, *Hierarchia*, 5.

[37] *Regesta*, ed. Pressutti, nos 723, 1479, 1533, 1556, 2064, 2851, 3212, 3436, 3794, 4029, 4081, 4809, 4981, 5011, 5261, 5614, 5798, 6138, 6206, 6211.

[38] Reg. Vat. 9, fol. 249 (*Regesta*, ed. Pressutti, no. 1277).

[39] Reg. Vat. 10, fols 43ᵛ, 46 (*Regesta*, ed. Pressutti, nos 1781, 1798).

[40] Reg. Vat. 10, fol. 92ᵛ (*Regesta*, ed. Pressutti, no. 2055).

[41] Reg. Vat. 10, fol. 173ʳ (*Regesta*, ed. Pressutti, no. 2405).

ary.[42] Conrad came from a noble German family, being the son of Count Egino IV of Urach and his wife Agnes, the daughter of Duke Berthold IV of Zähringen, and had enjoyed an education in the household of his great-uncle, Rudolf of Zähringen, bishop of Liège, where he was a cathedral canon. Conrad had pursued a successful church career before his appointment: in 1199 he entered the Cistercian abbey of Villers in Brabant, and rose to become abbot in 1208/9. He became abbot of Clairvaux in 1213/14, and was abbot of Cîteaux by 1216/17.[43]

The appointment of a German Cistercian marked Honorius's choice as doubly distinct from his predecessors' preferences, and probably reflects the nature of papal diplomacy at this time, which was focused on Emperor Frederick II's crusade. Indeed, Conrad was related to Frederick II (1220–50) in four or five degrees through his mother – something that Honorius must have recognized when despatching him as legate to Germany in 1224, and perhaps even when appointing him.[44] Conrad spent the majority of his career as cardinal on legation. He worked as a legate *a latere* to combat heresy in the south of France from 1220 to 1223.[45] In March 1224 he was selected as legate *a latere* to Germany to preach Frederick II's crusade, where he remained until 1226.[46] Soon after his appointment to Germany, however, in May 1224 he returned to France to conduct follow-up negotiations in Paris with King Louis VIII (1223–6).[47]

In the consistory of January 1219 Honorius also appointed another Cistercian, Nicholas da Chiaromonte, to the college's upper echelon, creating him cardinal bishop of Tusculum.[48] Honorius's two creations from the Cistercians represented one-third of his total appointments, and probably signal an affinity with the

---

[42] Eubel, *Hierarchia*, 5; Neininger, *Konrad*, 157.

[43] Neininger, *Konrad*, 64.

[44] Ibid. 75.

[45] Honorius III, *Opera omnia*, ed. C. A. Horoy, 5 vols (Paris, 1879–82), 3: 373; *Regesta*, ed. Pressutti, no. 2301; Neininger, *Konrad*, 64.

[46] Reg. Vat. 12, fols 183, 183ᵛ–184ʳ (*Regesta*, ed. Pressutti, nos 4903, 4904); Neininger, *Konrad*, 64.

[47] Reg. Vat. 12, fol. 178ᵛ (*Regesta*, ed. Pressutti, nos 4921, 4922); Neininger, *Konrad*, 207.

[48] Eubel, *Hierarchia*, 5, not to be confused with his predecessor as cardinal bishop of Tusculum (1204–18/19), also named Nicholas.

order.[49] We have only fragmentary knowledge of Nicholas's background. Falko Neininger wrote that he was an abbot and also a chaplain of Innocent III.[50] Nicholas Vincent has argued that he was the papal penitentiary who served in England under the legate Guala in 1217, although this has been queried by Patrick Zutshi.[51] However, Vincent's case is convincing, and supported by circumstantial evidence: a papal letter of 29 November 1217, sent to the former abbot of Lagny, refers to the penitentiary in England, Nicholas, as a monk of Casamari.[52] The abbey of Casamari was not only a Cistercian foundation, but also enjoyed the favour of Emperor Frederick II, to whom Nicholas was later sent as legate.[53]

If we accept that Nicholas already had experience of international diplomacy in the service of an important legate and came from an abbey which enjoyed close relations with Frederick II, it may explain why he was quickly chosen for high-profile legations. Nicholas was first despatched as legate *a latere* to Frederick II's court in 1220 to prepare for the emperor-elect's coronation, then again in November 1221, and later to southern France in 1223 to fight heresy.[54] The name Chiaromonte appears to indicate that Nicholas originated from the Kingdom of Sicily, which, at a time when papal-imperial diplomacy revolved around the status of the kingdom and its relationship to the Holy Roman Empire, adds another dimension that perhaps sheds light on his creation as cardinal and selection as legate to Frederick II. When not on legation Nicholas also worked as an auditor at the curia.[55] The spread of nepotism from the curia was demonstrated once again on 23 September 1219, when Nicholas influenced the production of a papal document that ordered Bertrand, cardinal priest of

---

[49] Neininger, *Konrad*, 157.

[50] Ibid. 159.

[51] *Letters*, ed. Vincent, lxxxvi, 110–12 (no. 142); Patrick Zutshi, 'Petitioners, Popes, Proctors: The Development of Curial Institutions, *c.* 1150–1250', in Giancarlo Andenna, ed., *Pensiero e sperimentazioni istituzionali nella 'Societas Christiana' (1046–1250)* (Milan, 2007), 265–93, at 277 and n. 51; see also Emil Göller, *Die päpstliche Pönitentiarie: Von ihrem Ursprung bis zu ihrer Umgestaltung unter Pius V.*, 2 vols (Rome, 1907–11), 1: 82–3, 86, 131.

[52] Reg. Vat. 9, fol. 176^r (*Regesta*, ed. Pressutti, no. 493).

[53] Attilio Stendardi, 'Casamari', in André Vauchez, Barrie Dobson and Michael Lapidge, eds, *Encyclopedia of the Middle Ages*, 2 vols (Cambridge, 2000), 1: 247–8, at 247.

[54] Reg. Vat. 11, fols 37^v, 166 (*Regesta*, ed. Pressutti, nos 276, 3581); *Opera*, ed. Horoy, 4: 492–3 (*Regesta*, ed. Pressutti, no. 4646).

[55] *Regesta*, ed. Pressutti, nos 2043, 2204, 4447, 4562, 5449, 5639, 6000.

SS. Giovanni e Paolo, to provide a benefice for Nicholas's cleric, *magister* William.[56] On 19 November 1219 Nicholas, lacking a residence in Rome, was granted one by the pope.[57]

Honorius's third creation was made in the September 1219 consistory when he made Peter Capuanus the Younger cardinal deacon of S. Giorgio in Velabro.[58] Peter was a distant nephew of the elder Peter Capuanus (d. 1214), who had served as a cardinal under Innocent III, most notably as legate on the Fourth Crusade (1202–4).[59] Both Peters belonged to a prominent Amalfitan family, but the elder Peter's major role under Innocent III would surely have lent the younger Peter *gravitas* in Rome.[60] Peter seems to have been inspired to follow his namesake's career path, and as a young papal subdeacon he followed in the elder Peter's footsteps to study at the University of Paris, where he earned the title *magister* and a doctorate, and subsequently held a chair of theology.[61] The patronage of the elder Peter may have secured him a canonry in Sens, a benefice from the chapter of Saint-Martin at Tours, and perhaps also a canonry in Paris.[62] Before his appointment as cardinal Peter had already been chosen as Latin patriarch of Antioch by Honorius, who cited the younger Peter's pedigree in a letter of 25 April 1219 to the dean and chapter of Antioch.[63] Peter did not pursue as illustrious a career as his uncle: there is little documentary evidence for his role, though he spent some time working as an auditor.[64] That Honorius proposed Peter as patriarch of Antioch before reversing his decision to create him cardinal points to favouritism: Honorius was apparently anxious to further Peter's career. It seems plausible that this derived from Peter's blood tie to the elder Peter Capuanus, with whom Honorius had served under Innocent III.

In August or early September 1225 Honorius made his final appointment, creating Oliver of Paderborn as cardinal bishop of Sabina, transferring him straight into the college's upper eche-

---

[56] Reg. Vat. 10, fol. 131ᵛ (*Regesta*, ed. Pressutti, no. 2201).

[57] Reg. Vat. 10, fol. 140ᵛ (*Regesta*, ed. Pressutti, no. 2261).

[58] Eubel, *Hierarchia*, 5; Werner Maleczek, *Petrus Capuanus: Kardinal, Legat am vierten Kreuzzug, Theologe († 1214)* (Vienna, 1988), 282.

[59] Maleczek, *Petrus*, 62.

[60] Ibid. 51; family tree ibid. 313–18.

[61] Ibid. 281–2; Eubel, *Hierarchia*, 93.

[62] Maleczek, *Petrus*, 281.

[63] Reg. Vat. 10, fols 86ʳ, 152ʳ (*Regesta*, ed. Pressutti, nos 2031, 2285); Ganzer, *Entwicklung*, 165.

[64] *Regesta*, ed. Pressutti, nos 2321, 3449, 3793, 6232; Maleczek, *Petrus*, 282.

lon.[65] As cardinal, the papal registers only record that Oliver was employed as an auditor in an affair regarding Cologne.[66] We know more about Oliver's career before his appointment. At the end of the twelfth century, Oliver was a cathedral canon at Paderborn, before moving in 1201 to teach at the cathedral school of Cologne. Between 1205 and 1207/8 he preached the Albigensian Crusade, and made contact with the other curialists Robert of Courson and Jacques de Vitry at the University of Paris. After preaching the Fifth Crusade between 1213 and 1215, Oliver attended the Fourth Lateran Council in November 1215. He participated in the Fifth Crusade (1217–21) and wrote its most influential account, the so-called *Historia Damiatina*. Subsequently, he preached Frederick II's crusade in 1223.[67] On 7 April 1225, a matter of months before his creation as cardinal, Honorius confirmed Oliver as bishop of Paderborn.[68] Oliver therefore had an enviable record of papal service, which points to a more meritocratic creation by Honorius. The second appointment of a German cardinal also probably reflected the intensity of papal-imperial negotiations over Frederick II's crusade, of which Oliver had personal experience. Indeed, soon after his creation as cardinal Oliver was present at the papal-imperial colloquium at San Germano in July 1225 to plan Frederick's crusade.[69]

The identification of six cardinals appointed piecemeal throughout Honorius's reign permits us to conclude that Honorius did not sweep away Innocent III's household and flood the college with his own kinsmen on his accession. In fact, the college as it operated under Honorius was mostly staffed by Innocent's appointees. The college did not change greatly in size under Honorius, although on his death in 1227 the membership had fallen slightly to eighteen.

The ties which bound Honorius's household together included nepotism, but also political necessity and aspects of a meritocracy.

---

[65] Eubel, *Hierarchia*, 5; H. Hoogeweg, ed., *Die Schriften des kölner Domscholasters, späteren Bischofs von Paderborn und Kardinal-Bischofs von S. Sabina* (Tübingen, 1894), l.

[66] *Regesta*, ed. Pressutti, no. 6235.

[67] Giancarlo Andenna and Barbara Bombi, eds, *I cristiani e il favoloso egitto: una relazione dall'Oriente e la storia di damietta di Oliviero da Colonia*, Verso l'Oriente 4 (Milan, 2009), 13–14; Rudolf Hiestand, 'Oliver Scholasticus und die Pariser Schulen zu Beginn des 13. Jahrhunderts: Zu einem neuen Textfund', *Jahrbuch des Kölnischen Geschichtsvereins* 58 (1987), 1–34, at 1–2.

[68] Hoogeweg, ed., *Schriften*, xlix.

[69] Ibid.

The sources do not tell us much about the pope's personal links with the men he appointed. The fact that he was appointing non-Romans, rather than Roman family and friends, suggests that they were known to him prior to their creation.[70] Honorius bucked the trend for appointing Roman cardinals that had predominated under his predecessors: half of his creations were not even Italian, let alone Roman. Honorius's creations of two cardinals from Germany and one from the Kingdom of Sicily appear political given the papal-imperial diplomacy that dominated his reign. The aversion to appointing Roman cardinals perhaps reflected a prioritization of imperial affairs over relations with the Roman nobility, and he may have intended to regain a modicum of independence from their influence, which had been embraced following the papacy's return to Rome under Clement III.[71] By favouring the appointment of Cistercians, Honorius again seems to have adopted a different approach to that pursued by Celestine III and Innocent III, who – proportionately – created relatively few cardinals from religious orders.[72] Some of the cardinals whom Honorius appointed had strong nepotistic tendencies and the pope connived in this. Nevertheless, the idea that Honorius transformed the college on his accession, purging rivals and flooding it with family and close friends, is flawed. Forms of nepotism certainly existed in Honorius's household, but they were more complex than has been recognized. Honorius had a shorter reign than Innocent III and created fewer cardinals: his six appointments actually made little impact on the composition of the college. Indeed, viewed solely in terms of its overall composition, Honorius III's College of Cardinals was still very much Innocent III's household.

Royal Holloway, University of London

---

[70]   See Vincent's point regarding Innocent III's creation of Guala Bicchieri: *Letters*, ed. Vincent, xxxiv.

[71]   Doran, 'Lifetime', 31–2.

[72]   Maleczek, *Kardinalskolleg*, 294. Innocent III, however, made considerable use of Cistercians to combat heresy in southern France: John C. Moore, *Pope Innocent III (1160/61–1216): To Root up and to Plant* (Leiden, 2003), 152–3.

PERFECTION AND PRAGMATISM: CATHAR ATTITUDES TO THE HOUSEHOLD

by BERNARD HAMILTON

When the Cathar Church was first established in southern France in the twelfth century it was generally tolerated by the secular authorities. At that time its hierarchy recognized only one type of Cathar household, which consisted of single-sex communities of initiated members known as 'the perfect'. After the introduction of the Papal Inquisition in Languedoc in 1233, the Cathar Church was systematically persecuted and one consequence of this was that its leaders' conception of what constituted a Cathar household became diversified. The traditional households of the perfect retained their central place in Cathar life, but the hierarchy also recognized a new type of Cathar household. This consisted of families of committed believers and their dependants, whose work was seen to be vital to the survival of their Church. This essay examines how this change in attitude came about and what its practical consequences were for Catharism.

In order to answer these questions, it is first necessary briefly to describe the Cathar faith. 'God is very good. In this world nothing is good. It therefore follows that God did not make anything which is in this world.' This statement made by Pierre Garsias of Toulouse in 1247 is the most succinct expression of Cathar belief.[1] The Cathars, who flourished in some parts of western Europe, notably the Languedoc in southern France, and north and central Italy, between *c*.1150 and *c*.1320, considered themselves to be the true Church.[2] For reasons of space, discussion here is restricted to

---

[1]   The text of Pierre Garsias's testimony from which this statement comes was published by C. Douais, *Documents pour servir à l'histoire de l'Inquisition dans le Languedoc*, 2 vols (Paris, 1900), 2: 90–114, quotation at 92; ET W. L. Wakefield, *Heresy, Crusade and Inquisition in Southern France 1100–1250* (London, 1974), 242–9, quotation at 244.

[2]   The precise date of the first appearance of Cathars in Southern France is difficult to determine. They were certainly well established there by 1165, when their representatives took part in the Synod of Lombers: *Acta Concilii Lumbariensis*, in M. Bouquet, ed., *Recueil des Historiens des Gaules et de la France*, 24 vols (Paris 1738–1904): 14: 431–4. The last trial of southern French Cathars by the inquisition was held in 1321.

southern France. The Cathars based their teachings solely on the New Testament and some parts of the Old, but they understood the Christian faith in a radically different way from their Catholic contemporaries.[3] The Cathars differed among themselves about some matters of doctrine, but they all agreed that the material creation was the work of an evil God or of an evil demiurge, who had trapped angelic souls created by the good God in the physical bodies of human beings and of warm-blooded animals. At death those souls were reborn either as human beings or as animals, and were unable to escape through their own efforts from this perpetual imprisonment in an evil universe. The good God had sent his Son Jesus in the appearance of a man, though not in human flesh, to save the angelic souls from captivity. Jesus had taught human beings about their true condition, had founded the Cathar Church to continue his work after his earthly ministry had ended, and had given to it the one sacrament of salvation. This was the *consolamentum*, baptism in the Holy Spirit by the laying on of hands. The Cathar churches had bishops, who were assisted by deacons, and the bishop was the normal minister of the sacrament, but at need it might be conferred by any initiated Cathar of either sex.[4]

The sacrament was conferred only on adults, and postulants had to undergo a long period of instruction in the Cathar faith and of training in the austere Cathar life.[5] The *consolamentum* was a liturgical service which culminated in the minister holding the Book of the Gospels over each candidate and saying: 'Holy Father, receive thy servant in thy righteousness and send thy grace and thy Holy Spirit upon him / upon her.'[6] The Cathar Church taught that in this sacrament the candidates received the Holy Spirit, who remained with them throughout their lives, and that when they died their souls would return to the paradise of the good God and

---

[3] The fullest account of Cathar doctrine in its various forms is that of J. Duvernoy, *Le Catharisme. La religion des Cathares* (Paris, 1976).

[4] The same was true of the sacrament of baptism in the medieval Catholic Church.

[5] The Cathars appear to have defined adults as those of marriageable age, fixed in canon law as twelve for girls and fifteen for boys.

[6] L. Clédat, ed., *Le Nouveau Testament traduit au xiiie siècle en langue provençale, suivi d'un Rituel Cathare* (Paris, 1887), ix–xxi (transcription of the text with a modern French translation), 471–9 (a lithographic reproduction of the manuscript text).

the powers of evil would no longer have dominion over them. Those who received this sacrament were known in the Cathar churches as the perfect.[7] The efficacy of the sacrament was not automatic but was conditional on conversion of life and perseverance in that new way of life until death.

The way of life of the perfect was extremely austere. They undertook never to swear an oath, which was a declaration of their separation from public life, since oaths of fealty and legal oaths played a central role in Western society in the Middle Ages.[8] They were required to sever all family ties, to renounce all social status and to surrender all claims to personal property: their property might be given to members of their own family, or to the Cathar bishop to administer on behalf of the Church. In that way the Cathar Church acquired houses, quite ordinary houses in towns or villages, which had been given to them by the perfect, and which varied in size according to the social status of the donors before their profession.[9] The bishop decided what way of life the perfect should follow: a few were seconded to the work of active ministry, but the majority were allocated to single-sex households, in one of the houses which belonged to the Church. The perfect of both sexes dressed in black robes and wore sandals. They were required to live in complete chastity. Unlike the Catholic Church, the Cathar churches made no distinction between marriage and sexual licence.[10] In their view all forms of sex were equally wrong, but especially those which led – as marriage was meant to – to the procreation of children, since this was the mechanism devised

[7]   Alan of Lille, *De fide catholica contra haereticos sui temporis* (PL 210, col. 351).

[8]   In the Latin text of the Cathar Ritual the postulant was required to vow 'quod nunquam iurabitis voluntarie aliqua occasione, nec per vitam, nec per mortem' before he/she was consoled: *Rituel Cathare*, ed. C. Thouzellier (Paris, 1977), 250.

[9]   William of Puylaurens, who completed his chronicle in 1275–6 but had grown up in Languedoc before the crusade, says that before 1209 the Cathars 'had their houses in towns and fortified places … and procured large houses in which they openly preached … to their believers': *The Chronicle of William of Puylaurens*, Prologue, transl. W. A. and M. K. Sibley (Woodbridge, 2009), 8.

[10]   Rainerius Sacconi, who had been a Cathar 'minister' (perhaps a deacon) for seventeen years before being converted to Catholicism and joining the Dominican order, wrote: 'Item communis opinio Catharorum est omnium quod matrimonium carnale fuit semper mortale peccatum, et quod non punietur quis gravius in futuro propter adulterium vel incestum, quam propter legitimum coniugium': *Summa Fratris Raynerii … de Catharis et Leonistis et Pauperibus de Lugduno*, ed. F. Sanjek, *AFP* 44 (1974), 31–60, at 43.

by the evil god to keep angelic souls in captivity. The perfect were bound by strict dietary laws: they were forbidden ever to eat meat (and that included poultry), or any animal product such as eggs or cheese, or to use animal fat in cooking. This was a corollary of their belief that animals also had angelic souls. The perfect were also forbidden to take the life of warm-blooded animals even if threatened by them, as in some areas of southern France they might be by bears or wolves. They did eat fish, I suppose, although I cannot document it, because the gospels relate that Jesus had eaten fish. The Cathars also drank wine, again, perhaps, following the Lord's example.[11]

The Cathar household in the twelfth century therefore consisted of a group of the perfect, either of men or of women, which varied considerably in number in accordance with the size of the house. Communities of men were expected to be self-supporting: some undertook market gardening to produce their own food, while others formed workshops for the weaving for sale of woollen cloth.[12] There is less clear information about the work of communities of women: some of them certainly fostered orphaned girls whose parents had been supporters of the Cathar Church.[13] The life of a Cathar community centred on a rigorous timetable of prayer. During each twenty-four hour period the household assembled to recite set prayers fifteen times.[14] This must mean that the night was broken by communal prayers about every two hours, which was consonant with the belief of the Cathars that the body was evil and that it was therefore essential to subdue all physical appetites, including the desire to sleep.

The Cathar household in theory consisted of the perfect alone. They did not employ servants, and because the communities had no property they did not have any tenants to care for. Postulants who wished to receive the *consolamentum* were sent by their bishops to live in Cathar communities to test their vocations, although their acceptance was by no means certain. Theoretically the perfect had no social links with the rest of the community, but this counsel of perfection

---

[11]   John 21: 9–13; Matt. 11: 19.

[12]   Examples of this in Duvernoy, *La religion des Cathares*, 198.

[13]   A. Brenon, *Les femmes cathares* (Paris, 1992), 122–36.

[14]   'Et isto modo orent XV vicibus inter diem et noctem': 'Le *Tractatus de Hereticis* d'Anselme d'Alexandrie, O.P.', ed. A. Dondaine, *AFP* 20 (1950), 234–324, at 316.

was not always observed. When Philippa, Countess of Foix, with her husband's consent, became a Cathar perfect, it was said that Count Raymond-Roger (1188–1223) regularly came to the house of Cathar ladies in which she lived in order to have supper with his wife.[15] What is certainly true is that whereas the ideal of Cathar communities was to remain aloof from secular society, the very fact that the perfect lived in ordinary houses, which were not purpose-built like Catholic monasteries but were situated in the middle of towns and villages, necessarily brought them into contact with their neighbours.

The perfect were highly respected by many of the people among whom they lived because their ascetic lifestyle resembled that of the holy men and women who in the central Middle Ages were considered the most outstanding practitioners of the Christian life.[16] Many people who listened to Cathar preachers and believed what they taught did not wish to embrace the austere life of the perfect, although they wanted to receive the *consolamentum* before they died. Such people were loosely known as believers, but they were not members of the Cathar Church and they were not bound by its laws. They married and had children, they ate meat and hunted animals, and some of the men were trained warriors and continued fighting. Believers might, if they wished, take part in Catholic worship, but when they were dying many of them sent to the nearest house of Cathars and asked to receive the *consolamentum*. A shortened form of service was drawn up for use in these circumstances.[17] The sacrament was considered as effective when administered to the dying as it was to those who devoted their lives to the practice of the Cathar faith. In the view of the Cathar hierarchy, the households of believers were not Cathar households, and indeed those who lived in them did not all necessarily share the same religious views.[18] The term 'Cathar households' was reserved for groups of the perfect.

This was the situation in southern France from c.1150 until the eve of the Albigensian Crusade in 1209.[19] The crusade led for a

[15]   M. Roquebert, *L'épopée cathare*, 5 vols (Paris, 1970–98), 1: 140.

[16]   See the important study of T. Licence, *Hermits and Recluses in English Society, 950–1200* (Oxford, 2011), which in fact relates to the spirituality of the whole Western Church in that period.

[17]   Clédat, ed., *Nouveau Testament*, xxii–xxvi, 480–2.

[18]   J. H. Mundy, *Men and Women at Toulouse in the Age of the Cathars* (Toronto, ON, 1990).

[19]   For a brief account of the crusade and its effects on Catharism, see B. Hamilton,

time to the abandonment of Cathar houses and the dispersal of communities of the perfect in areas occupied by the invaders. It also led the perfect to discard their distinctive dress and wear ordinary clothes so that they could move freely in territory held by the crusaders. The crusade undoubtedly taught the Cathar community survival skills, but it was not a suitable instrument with which to suppress heresy, nor was it intended to be so. The Albigensian Crusade was launched in order to dispossess lords who would not cooperate with the Church authorities in enforcing the heresy laws and to replace them by Catholic lords who would be willing to do so. As soon as the crusade ended, Cathar communities were re-established in Languedoc and the perfect practised their faith openly once again.[20] A substantive change came about only after the Papal Inquisition had been established there by Gregory IX in 1233.[21] The inquisition had few powers, but it soon developed effective methods of identifying and interrogating Cathars and devised excellent methods of record keeping. Moreover, it had the full support of the Capetian crown, which cooperated fully with the Catholic Church in seeking to suppress heresy.

The Cathar response to the persecution instituted by the inquisition with support of the Capetian officials was to withdraw to the protection of fortresses held by southern French lords who were sympathetic to their cause. The most important of these was Raymond of Perelha, Lord of Montségur: three Cathar bishops made their headquarters on the mountain of Montségur and most of the communities of Cathars in their dioceses withdrew there, building wooden cabins on the slopes of the mountain, where they maintained their traditional way of life. The bishops seconded some of those perfect to go into what had become enemy territory in order to minister to believers. They worked in pairs, as they had always done, but adopted lay dress, and as a result of this believers were able to receive the *consolamentum* when they were dying, and indeed were able to listen to Cathar preaching and maintain a knowledge of the faith. Montségur fell to the forces

'The Albigensian Crusade and Heresy', in D. Abulafia, ed., *The New Cambridge Medieval History*, 5: c.*1198* – c.*1300* (Cambridge, 1999), 164–81.

[20] E. Griffe, *Le Languedoc cathare au temps de la croisade (1209–1229)* (Paris, 1973), 149–234.

[21] The best study of the work of this tribunal is James B. Given, *Inquisition and Medieval Society: Power, Discipline and Resistance in Languedoc* (Ithaca, NY, 1997).

of the French crown in March 1244, and the Cathar perfect who were captured there, having refused to be converted to Catholicism, were summarily burnt.[22] Other fortresses of this kind, which sheltered Cathar perfect, though not as many of them as Montségur had done, were gradually captured by the crown forces. The last important one of these was Quéribus, which fell in 1255.[23] As their aristocratic patrons in France were defeated, the Cathar bishops devised a new strategy and withdrew their headquarters to Lombardy.[24] The inquisition existed also in north Italy, but was less effective there than in southern France because of political divisions between the cities of the Lombard League, the Emperor Frederick II and his heirs, and the papacy. The Cathar bishops of Toulouse and Albi established their headquarters in Cremona c.1250. The surviving communities of perfect from their French dioceses joined them there, and the bishops seconded some of their number to undertake the work of ministry in Languedoc. So traditional households of the southern French perfect continued to exist in Lombardy, and they were an essential part of the Cathar Church's organization. They alone could train southern French believers who sought to be initiated as perfect while they were in the prime of life, once there were no longer any communities of this kind in Languedoc. But in Languedoc at that time the term 'Cathar household' came to mean something different.

It was very dangerous in the second half of the thirteenth century not only to be a Cathar perfect operating in Languedoc but also to be a Cathar believer giving support to the perfect. The anti-heretical legislation codified by the Fourth Lateran Council (1215) had specified that all Cathar believers, and all those who, even if they did not believe Cathar teaching, gave protection or hospitality of any kind to the perfect, should be excommunicated and should lose their civil rights (to hold public office, to inherit property and to make a legal will) unless they were reconciled to

---

[22] J. Duvernoy, ed. and transl., *Le dossier de Montségur. Interrogatoires de l'Inquisition 1242–1247*, 2 vols (Toulouse, 1998).

[23] F. Niel, *Quéribus. La dernière forteresse cathare* (Paris, 1988).

[24] The evidence about southern French Cathars in Lombardy during the later thirteenth century is discussed by M. Roquebert, *Les Cathares. De la chute de Montségur aux derniers bûchers, 1244–1329* (Paris, 1998), 346–68; A. Roach, 'The Relationship of the Italian and Southern French Cathars, 1170–1320' (D.Phil. thesis, Oxford, 1989).

the Catholic Church within a year.[25] Those who refused to be reconciled could be tried by the inquisition and imprisoned until they satisfied the tribunal of the sincerity of their submission to the Church's laws: and during that time their property would be confiscated by officers of the French crown. It also became the practice in southern France that if it could be proved that Cathar meetings had been held in the house of a believer, the authorities had the right to demolish the house as a warning to other Cathar sympathizers.

The Cathar perfect who returned to Languedoc to minister to believers therefore spent much of their time living in woods and caves and held meetings of believers in the open air by night. Normally they only entered towns or villages to administer the *consolamentum* to dying believers.[26] This system worked comparatively well because the Cathar Church continued to be well organized. The bishops in exile set up a network of agents in Languedoc. These were men who were familiar with the distribution of believers in a particular district, and with the topography of the area. They met the perfect as they came through the mountain passes from Lombardy, escorted them to the region in which they were going to work, and acted as liaisons between them and families of believers in that area. They arranged the secure hiding places where the perfect might stay, and alerted the believers to their presence. The perfect continued, as far as possible, to maintain their routine of liturgical prayer fifteen times a day, but they relied on believers for the physical necessities of life, particularly food. Women played a prominent role in this, preparing the food of the perfect which was taken to them secretly at night-time. Groups of believers went out at night to attend Cathar meetings, at which the perfect preached and recited prayers.

Cathar believers had, in the time before the Albigensian Crusade, been made up of people with a very variable range of commitment: on the one hand there were men and women who respected the perfect but were not very enthusiastic about imitating their way of life, while on the other there were people who intended

---

[25] The basis of anti-heretical legislation was Canon 3, *De haereticis*, of the Fourth Lateran Council: *Conciliorum Oecumenicorum Decreta*, edidit Istituto per le scienze religiose (Bologna, 1973), 233–5.

[26] J. Duvernoy, *Le Catharisme. L'histoire des Cathares* (Toulouse, 1978), 297–314.

to become perfect themselves when they could responsibly do so, for example when their children had grown up. During the time of persecution this changed. The believers were by definition men and women who were convinced that the Cathar faith was true and were prepared to risk their freedom and their property in order to support it. They formed the new Cathar households. Their members had to be united in faith: a non-believer among them could denounce the rest to the inquisition. They supported the work of the perfect and attended their meetings; and crucially the next generation of perfect was recruited from these families. Yet although the perfect had become dependent on these households of believers, the theology of the Cathar Church about the spiritual status of believers did not change.

Believers had not been consoled and therefore were not members of the Cathar Church. The only modification to this rule which had been introduced during the Albigensian Crusade was to allow believers to make an agreement, or *convenenza*, with the Cathar Church, stating their intention of receiving the *consolamentum* before they died. In that case the sacrament could be administered to them even if when they were dying they had lost consciousness or the power of speech, provided that they were still breathing.[27] The problem in the age of persecution was that it was essential to have a perfect present to administer the sacrament, and if one could not be found in time, then the angelic soul of the believer would be once again subject to reincarnation and be trapped in the physical creation of the evil God. A second and more immediate restriction applied to Cathar believers: before receiving the *consolamentum* they could not directly pray to the good God. Their only link to him was through the prayers of the perfect, because they had been liberated from the power of evil whereas believers had not been. The believer knelt before the perfect in a ceremony known as the *melioramentum* and said, three times: 'Bless us, have mercy upon us'.[28] The Catholic authorities called this ceremony 'adoration', but that was a misnomer: the believers were not venerating the perfect, but asking them for their prayers because the perfect were their only link to the good God.

---

[27] Duvernoy, *La religion des Cathares*, 159–60.
[28] This is described most clearly by Anselm of Alessandria: *Tractatus*, ed. Dondaine, 316–17 (ch. 9).

Nevertheless, the households of believers were a source of strength to the Cathar Church precisely because believers were not members of that Church. Because they were not bound to observe its rules, in time of persecution they were indistinguishable from Catholics. A Cathar household of believers consisted very often of a married couple with children. The wife might cook the food of the perfect to support them when they were in the district, but the members of the household ate ordinary food, including meat and eggs and cheese. The men of the family could take part in warfare if required to do so; if they were landowners they could hunt; if they were farmers or farm labourers they could kill animals for food. The household could even attend services in the local Catholic church, although some Cathar believers felt scruples about making their communion there. Paradoxically, it was this freedom which believers enjoyed of disregarding Cathar observances which made the survival of the Cathar Church in Languedoc possible during the age of persecution.

Yet this was not a permanent solution, since the Cathar Church could not survive without perfect, because they were its only members. The Papal Inquisition became more effective in Lombardy in the later thirteenth century, and the hierarchy of the Cathar churches of Languedoc in exile there had been virtually eliminated by 1300.[29] This meant that there were no longer any communities in existence in Italy to train southern French perfect, which in turn meant that the missions to Languedoc could not be sustained. Catharism died out in southern France by *c.*1321, when the last known perfect were executed. Cathar households of believers may have survived there longer, but they had no capacity to practise their faith, and no perfect to instruct them and to administer the *consolamentum* to them. Pierre Autier, one of the last perfect traditionally trained for the work of public ministry in Languedoc, said to the crowd as he was led to the stake in 1311: 'If it were lawful for me to preach you would all accept my faith'.[30] To the end, there was no lack of courage and conviction

[29] J. Duvernoy, 'La hiérarchie de l'église occitane', in idem, *L'histoire des Cathares*, 347–51.

[30] 'Petrus Auterii hereticus … quando debuit comburi, dixit quod si permitteretur loqui et predicare populo, totum populum ad suam fidem converteret': cited by J. M. Vidal, 'Les derniers ministres d'Albigéisme en Languedoc: leurs doctrines', *Revue des questions historiques* 85 (1906), 57–107, at 75 n. 2.

among the Cathar perfect or their believers. Yet although the existence of households of Cathar believers undoubtedly prolonged the
survival of Catharism in Languedoc, the restriction of membership
to the perfect alone made it impossible for the Cathar Church to
survive organized persecution once all the traditional households
of the perfect had been destroyed.

University of Nottingham

DAILY COMMODITIES AND RELIGIOUS IDENTITY IN THE MEDIEVAL JEWISH COMMUNITIES OF NORTHERN EUROPE[*]

by ELISHEVA BAUMGARTEN

The Hebrew chronicle written by Solomon b. Samson recounts the mass conversion of the Jews of Regensburg in 1096.[1] The Jews were herded and forced into the local river where a 'sign was made over the water, the sign of a cross' and thus they were baptized, all together in the same river. The local German rivers play another role in the accounts of the turbulent events of the Crusade persecutions. They were also the place where Jews evaded conversion, drowning themselves in water, rather than being baptized by what the chronicles' authors call the 'stinking waters' of Christianity. [2] Reading these Hebrew chronicles, one is immediately struck by the tremendous revulsion expressed toward the waters of baptism. Indeed, in his analysis of the symbolic significance of the baptismal waters for medieval Jews, Ivan Marcus has suggested that baptism by force in the local rivers was so traumatic that they instituted a ritual response during the twelfth and thirteenth centuries. One component of the medieval Jewish child initiation ceremony to Torah study was performed on the banks of the river, expressing Jewish aversion to baptism (see Fig. 1).[3]

[*] I am grateful to Alexandra Walsham for inviting me to explore these themes. Judah Galinsky, Debra Kaplan and Julia Smith made important comments on this article and I thank them for their critique and suggestions. My research was supported by grant no. 420/10 of the Israel Science Foundation.

[1] I have used the recent edition of the Hebrew Crusade chronicles: Eva Haverkamp, ed., *Hebräische Berichte über die Judenverfolgungen während des Ersten Kreuzzugs* (Hanover, 2005), 481.
[2] The expressions *mei tsahanatam* and *mei tinufam*, meaning 'stinking waters', recur regularly in the chronicles as terms for baptismal water: ibid. 263, 271, 277, 347, 373, 379, 385, 395, 447, 461.
[3] See Ivan Marcus, *Rituals of Childhood: Jewish Acculturation in Medieval Europe* (New Haven, CT, 1996), 106–8. Another instance of polemic concerning water is the Saturday night ritual related to Miriam's well: see Israel M. Ta-Shma, *Early Franco-German Ritual and Custom* (Jerusalem, 1992), 201–20, esp. 214–6 (Hebrew), and the study by my student Inbar Gabai-Zada that expands the discussion of this ritual: 'Miriam's Well in Ashkenaz in the Middle Ages' (MA thesis, Bar-Ilan University, 2013). See also Ephraim Shoham-Steiner, 'The Virgin Mary, Miriam, and Jewish Reactions

Fig. 1:   Leipzig, UL, MS Voller 1102/I, Leipzig Mahzor (Worms, c.1310), fol. 130ᵛ.

Whilst these polemical episodes undoubtedly reveal central facets of Jewish life in medieval Europe, they also obscure other no less significant ones. The negative reference to the waters of the river underscores the distinctiveness of Jews among Christians in medieval Europe. Yet the story of medieval northern European Jewry is not just that of an alienated minority.[4] These medieval Jews lived and shared an environment with their Christian neighbours, and whilst they were a minority amongst a Christian majority, and despite some of the persecution they experienced during the high Middle Ages, they were also a central part of European commerce and growth. In the case of the water of the local rivers, medi-

---

to Marian Devotion in the High Middle Ages', *Association for Jewish Studies Review* 37 (2013), 75–91.

    4   Kenneth R. Stow used this term as the title of his book, which remains a standard work: *Alienated Minority: The Jews of Medieval Latin Europe* (Cambridge, MA, 1992). A different attempt at outlining the history of these communities can be seen in Jonathan Elukin, *Living Together, Living Apart: Rethinking Jewish-Christian Relations in the Middle Ages* (Princeton, NJ, 2007).

eval Jews, like their Christian neighbours, were regular consumers of this water found within their urban surroundings. They drank, cooked and utilized this water on a daily basis.[5] Expressed differently, the Jews were part of an entangled existence in which they were both part of their surroundings and a distinct minority.[6]

This essay explores how medieval Jews made use of some common substances within the household and how they instilled them with religious meaning that expressed their distinct status and position within medieval Christian culture.[7] In some cases, these were materials also used by Christians for their own ritual purposes; in others, the Jewish community chose to imbue them with religious difference. Specifically, I will consider how four basic commodities were utilized regularly by Jews: two foods, water and bread; and two household necessities, candles and cloth, all of which were used by medieval Christians as well. I will describe how these were infused with religion and in turn how they served as religious signifiers within the medieval urban environment. The last section of the essay will compare briefly the household and the synagogue, contrasting individual and communal space. The

5 Roberta J. Magnusson, *Water Technology in the Middle Ages: Cities, Monasteries, and Waterworks after the Roman Empire* (Baltimore, MD, 2001); Catherine Gouedo-Thomas, 'Les fontaines mediévales: Images et réalité', *Mélanges de l'École française de Rome. Moyen Âge, Temps modernes* 104 (1992), 507–17.

6 The term 'entangled history' is often used by those who propose the importance of the methodology of *histoire croisée* ('connected history'): see Sanjay Subrahmanyan, 'Connected Histories: Notes towards a Reconfiguration of Early Modern Eurasia', *Modern Asian Studies* 31 (1997), 735–62; Bénédicte Zimmerman et al., eds, *Le travail et le nation. Histoire croisée de la France at de l'Allemagne* (Paris, 1999), for a survey of these terms and methodologies. See also the recent somewhat different but complementary use of this term by David B. Ruderman, *Early Modern Jewry: A New Cultural History* (Princeton, NJ, 2009), 12.

7 A note for readers unfamiliar with Jewish legal texts: one of the most basic and at the same time complex aspects of studying medieval Jewry, and especially the medieval Hebrew sources, is the need to constantly move from the Bible, the Mishnah and Talmud written in late antiquity to the medieval communities within which the Jews lived and their contemporaneous surroundings. This motion back and forth, to and from late antiquity, is essential not only because of the links medieval Jews saw between themselves and their ancestors but because the Mishnah and Talmud form the basis of the Jewish *halakhah* or legal literature and the medieval Hebrew texts were often organized around the themes and order of the late antique literature. As a result, in the interest of simplicity, the different examples I trace in this article will all follow the same pattern – moving from medieval practice to late antique Jewish ritual instructions back to the Christian urban centres within which medieval Jews lived.

conclusion will draw attention to some possible directions for future research.

MEDIEVAL JEWISH HOUSEHOLDS

Writing in the late nineteenth century, the British scholar Israel Abrahams suggested that the home was the place where medieval Jews were most distinct and where their Judaism was best manifested and preserved. He affirmed:

> The Jewish home was a haven of rest from the storms that raged round the very gates of the ghetto, nay, a fairy palace in which the bespattered objects of the mob's derision threw off their garb of shame and resumed the royal attire of freemen. The home was the place where the Jew was at his best. In the market place he was perhaps hard and sometimes ignoble; in the world he helped his judges to misunderstand him; in the home he was himself.[8]

By way of this quotation, let us enter the Jewish households in the urban centres of medieval Germany and northern France often called Ashkenaz in modern scholarship. While opinions differ on the extent to which these communities can be examined as a single unit, there was much intellectual and social crossover between them throughout the Middle Ages and, following many other scholars, for the purpose of this essay I will consider them as a shared cultural area.[9] Whereas the Jewish communities in medieval Germany are known and documented from the late ninth century, in northern France the earliest documentation is slightly later.[10] In both communities the more substantial documentation begins in the period after the First Crusade in 1096. Later, the face of

---

[8] Israel Abrahams, *Jewish Life in the Middle Ages* (repr. London, 1932), 129.

[9] For a discussion of these differences, see Israel M. Ta-Shma, *Ritual, Custom and Reality in Franco-Germany 1000–1350* (Jerusalem, 1996), 16–19 (Hebrew); David J. Malkiel, *Reconstructing Ashkenaz: The Human Face of Franco-German Jewry* (Stanford, CA, 2009), 2–10. The Jews of medieval England saw themselves, and were seen, as belonging to the same Ashkenazic cultural milieu. However, due to the nature of the extant sources concerning the Jews of England, who were the first of the northern European Jewish communities to experience expulsion in 1290, many of the matters I will explore concerning their daily life are unrecorded.

[10] See the classic studies by Avraham Grossman, *The Early Sages of Ashkenaz*, 3rd edn (Jerusalem, 2001), 1–26 (Hebrew); idem, *The Early Sages of France* (Jerusalem, 1995), 13–45 (Hebrew).

northern European Jewry changed due to expulsions and migration, especially following the Black Death, and the latest sources I will examine are from this period of the fourteenth century.

The main sources written by Ashkenazic Jews during the high Middle Ages are religious texts stemming from the male elite. They include legal texts, often arranged according to the Talmudic tractates, biblical chapters or specific issues that arose; liturgical manuscripts, including daily prayers but also and especially holiday prayers alongside the *piyyutim*, poems recited on holidays and special communal occasions; and a small number of chronicles, such as those written after the First Crusade.[11] Alongside these texts written by the Jews themselves, archaeological finds, especially from synagogues, Latin texts written by theologians and by city officials, and some fiscal documents survive. The Hebrew sources are at the heart of this study.

Medieval Jews in Germany and northern France lived in the burgeoning urban centres and were active traders and merchants within the medieval economy.[12] As members of their urban surroundings they were part of the comings and goings of the town, players in local affairs and finances. They were part of a more general religious trend that also characterized the lives of their Christian neighbours. The Jewish communities of medieval Ashkenaz saw themselves as a *kehilah kedoshah*, a holy community, and the sources indicate that many members of these communities were searching for ways to raise the level of piety in their lives.[13] During this same period, their Christian neighbours were doing something similar: medieval Christian society in Germany and in northern France was characterized by growing numbers of men and especially women who chose to further their closeness to God

[11] For a recent survey of many of these genres, see Ephraim Kanarfogel, *The Intellectual History and Rabbinic Culture of Medieval Ashkenaz* (Detroit, MI, 2012).

[12] Michael Toch, *The Economic History of European Jews: Late Antiquity and Early Middle Ages* (Leiden, 2012), 65–102.

[13] See Haym Soloveitchik, 'Religious Law and Change: The Medieval Ashkenazic Example', *Association for Jewish Studies Review* 12 (1987), 205–21; Ivan Marcus, *Piety and Society: The Jewish Pietists of Medieval Germany* (Leiden, 1981); Ephraim Kanarfogel, *Peering Through the Lattices: Mystical, Magical and Pietistic Dimensions in the Tosafist Period* (Detroit, MI, 2000); Israel J. Yuval, 'Heilige Städte, heilige Gemeinden – Mainz als das Jerusalem Deutschlands', in Robert Jütte and Abraham P. Kustermann, eds, *Jüdische Gemeinden und Organisationsformen von der Antike bis zur Gegenwart* (Vienna, 1996), 91–101.

in a variety of ways, whether by joining religious orders or by seeking to live their daily lives in a more pious manner.[14]

Recent scholarship in the area of Jewish Studies has sought to find a way to understand the complex situation of medieval Jews. On the one hand, these Jewish communities shared many features both mundane and spiritual with their Christian neighbours. At the same time, the Jews were a minority group within Christian society and pressure – at times extreme – was exerted on them to convert. As a result, the members of the Jewish community, and especially their leaders, constantly sought ways to strengthen Jewish identity and solidarity, especially in the light of the ever-present and not insignificant numbers of converts to Christianity.[15] In this context, an emphasis on Jewish piety served to increase the level of sanctity in everyday Jewish life, as well as to erect barriers between Jews and their surroundings. Christians were seen as 'the other' par excellence, representing the religion of which all Jews were to beware. Concurrently, the medieval Church throughout the period increasingly sought ways to impose barriers between Jews and their neighbours, for reasons both theological and social. However, and despite the pointed rhetoric that often accompanied those Jewish-Christian exchanges that have survived, the shared features of the two faith communities, taken in conjunction with their common living quarters, suggest that in many ways Jews and Christians were not as distinct as their polemic might lead one to presume.[16]

Returning to the statement of Israel Abrahams, one can question the extent to which the household was indeed a haven, a Jewish space. A look at Jewish households within medieval Christian cities certainly gives rise to doubts on this matter. During the high Middle Ages, Jews did not live in ghettos, which were an early modern invention.[17] Although Jews did tend to live together,

[14] Robert N. Swanson, *Religion and Devotion in Europe, 1215–1515* (Cambridge, 1985); André Vauchez, *The Laity in the Middle Ages: Religious Beliefs and Devotional Practices*, transl. Margaret J. Schneider (Notre Dame, IN, 1993).

[15] Marcus, *Rituals*, and Elukin, *Living Together*, have both proposed ways to examine these tensions.

[16] Recent scholarship has suggested the affinity between Jews and Christians within polemics as well: see Israel J. Yuval, *Two Nations in Your Womb: Perceptions of Jews and Christians in Late Antiquity and the Middle Ages* (Berkeley, CA, 2006).

[17] See Robert Bonfil's work on the significance of the ghetto for the life of early

in the close quarters of a number of streets, in most cases they lived amongst Christian neighbours who shared courtyards, ovens and wells with them.[18] Moreover, Jewish homes were constantly populated by non-Jews. Every Jewish home had a number of servants as well as wet-nurses, and these were on the whole non-Jews.[19] Although the Church raged against the employment of Christians by Jews, the practice was common.[20] Both medieval Jewish sources and city maps indicate that people lived in accommodation grouped around courtyards, in which some entrances led to Jewish households whilst others led to Christian ones. Moreover, Jewish business was often conducted within the home, so that Christians constantly entered Jewish homes.

In light of the constant Christian presence in Jewish households, the question of household religion becomes even more multifarious. In order to understand how Jews practised their religion within the household, we must briefly turn to some of the basic characteristics of Jewish tradition, which was a religion of practice, not of doctrine. According to these guidelines, every action one took – from rising in the morning to seeing a blooming tree or a rainbow – was acknowledged by ritual formulae. The elaborate system of blessings and prayers recited when performing everyday activities was set out in the Mishnah and the Talmud, compiled in the first centuries of the Common Era and further elaborated and expounded by subsequent generations of scholars.[21] As a result, Jews constantly ritualized their everyday activities, including those performed within the household. Not only were acts infused with religious meaning; objects were as well.[22] It should be noted

modern Italian Jews and for their relations to Christians, *Jewish Life in Renaissance Italy* (Berkeley, CA, 1994), 19–77.

[18] On the layout of Jewish living quarters within medieval European cities, see, for example, from the early twentieth century, Alexander Pinthus, *Die Judensiedlungen der deutschen Städte. Eine stadtbiologische Studie* (Berlin, 1931); some more recent work is documented in Christoph Cluse, ed., *The Jews of Europe in the Middle Ages (Tenth to Fifteenth Centuries)* (Turnhout, 2004), esp. the articles in section V.

[19] Jacob Katz, *The 'Shabbes Goy': A Study in Halakhic Flexibility*, transl. Joel Lerner (Philadelphia, PA, 1989); Elisheva Baumgarten, *Mothers and Children: Jewish Family Life in Christian Europe* (Princeton, NJ, 2004), 119–53.

[20] Solomon Grayzel, *The Church and the Jews in the Thirteenth Century*, 2nd edn (Philadelphia, PA, 1966), 23–6.

[21] Louis Jacobs, 'Judaism', in Michael Berenbaum and Fred Skolnik, eds, *Encyclopedia Judaica*, 2nd edn, vol. 11 (Detroit, MI, 2007), 511–24.

[22] As noted at the outset, my focus is not on ritual artefacts that were specifically

that although all the texts discussed in the pages that follow were written by the male elite (the rabbis in the different communities), the materials I am examining were handled daily by all – children, women and less educated men. This is a point to which I shall return in the conclusion.

WATER

I have already underlined water's perilous qualities from a Jewish perspective in times of danger and forced baptism. At the same time, water was used daily and had sacred qualities on this quotidian level. For example, Jews regularly purified their bodies in water, immersing themselves in live springs or ritual baths,[23] whereas Christians baptized believers with water, and sought saints at wells and fountains spread across the medieval countryside. Jews and Christians also drank water and used it for cooking.[24] It is to this use that I now turn in order to discuss one of many practices that had to do with water, the practice known as the *tekufah*.

The word *tekufah* (pl. *tekufot*) literally means 'season'.[25] In medieval Ashkenaz it was used to denote very specific times: the equinoxes and solstices. These times of year were occasions when water was prohibited for use. Medieval Jews believed that drinking water or using water drawn during the hours of the solstice and equinox was dangerous. The Jews of medieval Germany and northern France in particular adapted very stringent beliefs and customs related to the use of water at the *tekufah*, among them the idea that

---

identified with Judaism, such as phylacteries (*tefillin*) or Torah scrolls that were distinctive Jewish objects, but rather on the way different everyday materials were ritualized, as is evident in discussion of daily blessings as well as in many other settings.

[23] For a description of customs relating to the use of ritual baths, see the collection edited by Rahel R. Wasserfall, *Women and Water: Menstruation in Jewish Law and Life* (Hanover, 1999).

[24] Haym Soloveitchik, *Wine in the Middle Ages* (Jerusalem, 2008), 30–1, 75 (Hebrew); Elisheva Baumgarten, '"Remember that Glorious Girl": Jephthah's Daughter in the Middle Ages', *Jewish Quarterly Review* 97 (2007), 180–209; Elisheva Carlebach, 'Water into Blood: Custom, Calendar and an Unknown Yiddish Book for Women', in Deborah Dash Moore and Marion Kaplan, eds, *Gender and Jewish History* (Bloomington, IN, 2011), 59–71.

[25] The expression used in this way originates in Ex. 34: 22; see also Sacha Stern, *Calendar and Community: A History of the Jewish Calendar Second Century BCE – Tenth Century CE* (Oxford, 2001), 50–3.

anyone who drank water at these times would become bloated and ill and might even die.[26]

Explanations for this custom and the dangers were varied, but were connected to the belief that all waters were guarded by angels and that during these significant solar moments the angels were changing guard, thus leaving the water unprotected.[27] This explanation was augmented by medieval German and northern French Jewish commentators who explained that these moments were especially precarious because each one commemorated a portentous biblical event. According to this explanation, the autumn equinox represented a remembrance of the biblical sacrifice of Isaac; the spring equinox commemorated the waters of the Nile that turned to blood; the summer solstice was explained by Moses' hitting the rock (rather than speaking to it); and the winter solstice was a memorialization of Jephthah's daughter from the book of Judges. These traumatic events of the past were said to have endangered the water so that it would harm any who drank from it during these specific hours (see Fig. 2).[28]

The many tables detailing the exact calculation of the *tekufah* that appear in medieval Jewish prayer books alongside liturgical calendars (see Fig. 3) suggest that the observance of the *tekufah* was very important to medieval Jews. In fact, these lists of *tekufot* were among the most popular texts added to the liturgy,[29] and there is evidence that in some Jewish communities the *tekufah* was observed until the Holocaust.[30]

Interestingly, although the custom seems to have been strictly observed in northern Europe, there were many who objected to it in southern Europe, specifically in Spain. The 'southerners' claimed that the idea that water drawn and drunk during the *tekufah* would

---

[26] See Avigdor Aptowizer, 'Issur shetiyat mayim be-she'at ha-tekufah', *Ha-tsofe me-erets Hagar* 2 (1912), 122–6; Abraham J. Klein, 'Ha-sakanah lishtot mayim beshe'at ha-tekufah veha-segulah le-hishamer mimenah be-sifrut ha-halakhah', in *Jubilee Volume in Honor of Prof. Bernhard Heller*, ed. Alexander Scheiber (Budapest, 1941), 86–100; Israel M. Ta-Shma, 'The Danger of Drinking Water during the Tequfa – The History of an Idea', *Jerusalem Studies in Jewish Folklore* 17 (1995), 21–32 (Hebrew); Baumgarten, 'Remember'; Carlebach, 'Water into Blood'.

[27] Ta-shma, 'Danger', 21–32.

[28] For a list of medieval texts where this passage was repeated, see ibid.

[29] See Elisheva Carlebach, *Palaces of Time: Jewish Time in Christian Paris* (Cambridge, MA, 2011); and we await Justine Isserles's study of medieval calendar manuscripts.

[30] Klein, 'Ha-sakanah lishtot mayim'.

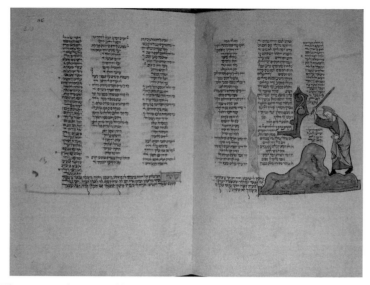

Fig. 2: London, BL, Add. MS 11639, North French Miscellany, fol. 309ʳ, Moses hitting the rock. © The British Library Board.

cause its drinkers to become bloated and then lead to death was an old wives' tale (*sihat hazekenot*).[31] Despite this southern critique, in northern Europe the custom seems to have been more and more strictly observed as time progressed. During the high Middle Ages it was a common observance and references to the four biblical events commemorated by the practice were widespread.

Abstention from water was significant to the running of the household. The rabbis who wrote the texts which have reached us focus on the consequences of using this water at one specific time of year, the spring equinox. This date often fell around the same time as Passover, when the community gathered to make *matzah*, the special unleavened bread consumed during the seven days of the holiday.[32] *Matzah* was made on the day before Passover and if this day was also the day of the *tekufah* then the consequences were believed to be dire. As a result it became accepted and common practice to put water aside for at least twenty-four hours before

[31] Baumgarten, 'Remember', 205.
[32] Ta-Shma, 'Danger', focuses on this season.

Fig. 3: BL, Add. MS 11639, North French Miscellany, fol. 643ᵛ, List of *Tekufot*. © The British Library Board.

making *matzah* with it; in this way the dangers of the *tekufah* could be avoided (see Fig. 4).

The *tekufah* and its perils were relevant four times a year. Some Jewish sources suggest that Christians were also careful not to use water at these times.[33] Whether or not Christians believed that water was dangerous specifically at the times of equinox and solstice, they most certainly celebrated and made note of the solar calendar. St John the Baptist's Day was celebrated on 24 June, at the summer solstice; the ember days fell on the other solstice and the equinoxes. These Christian holy days affected life on the streets, in the markets and within the houses of medieval urban centres.[34] I would suggest that these Christian celebrations on the streets were very attractive to the urban Jews who viewed the festivities around them. At this very time, one of the most basic of household activities – drawing water and its use for drinking and cooking – reminded the Jews of their difference. In other words,

[33] *Mahzor Vitry*, ed. Shimon Horowitz (Nürnberg, 1898), Addendum, 14.
[34] This is a topic I hope to develop more in future study. At the moment one can note the references in Hebrew texts to Christian holidays, e.g. in the Crusade chronicles: *Hebräische Berichte*, 407, 473.

Fig. 4: Jerusalem, Israel Museum, 180/057, *Matzah* Baking: the Bird's Head Haggadah (Southern Germany, *c.*1300), fols 25^v–26^r.

by emphasizing the danger of water on this day, those who might have been enticed by the outside local activities, for example the St John the Baptist's Day fires which celebrated the summer solstice, were reminded of their religious identification. In this way the customs surrounding the *tekufah* were understood by Jews as a unique Jewish observance with its own internal religious message, but one which also served to distance Jews from Christians. Just as water was a basic substance, everywhere present, the *tekufah* and its occurrence permeated the lives of all layers of Jewish society – elite men, women and men in their homes.[35]

To sum up this first example, the use – or rather the non-use – of water during the four moments of the *tekufah* was a house-hold and communal ritual known to, and noted by, all within the Jewish community, and parallel to communal rituals taking place on the streets of medieval European cities. Jews were reminded, if just for a few hours, of their connection to the Bible and through

---

[35] The *tekufah* was a rare occasion in the calendar in that it had household conse-quences more than communal ones. While the *tekufot* were important for calendric computations, no prayers or fasts accompanied the days of the solstices and equinoxes.

it of their connection to God and to other Jews, and thus they internalized their Jewish identity in contrast to Christian activities around them.

BREAD

We have already seen the centrality of water for the baking of the Passover *matzah*. *Matzah* and its preparation served to distinguish Jews from their Christian neighbours during one week of the year, the week of Passover. However, Jews also ate bread on a more regular basis, and this forms our second example. Bread, like water, was a basic necessity; indeed it has been called the most central component of the medieval diet.[36] Before addressing the medieval context, a note concerning Jewish food restrictions is in order. Already in the Bible some aspects of Jewish law were meant to promote the distinctiveness of the Jews as a discrete group, an effort that was often defined in terms of sanctity. Food was a central category in this endeavour and the lists of animals that can or cannot be consumed are examples of this biblical theme.[37] In the first centuries of the Common Era, the rabbis expounded on the topic of Jewish food prohibitions and produced a plethora of instructions concerning food over and above the biblical restrictions. Among these directives were qualifications pertaining to basic foodstuffs such as wine, bread, milk and oil.[38] The late antique list determined that bread baked by non-Jews should not be eaten by Jews, with the central line of explanation being that these shared foods should be avoided so that Jews would not hold weddings together with their non-Jewish neighbours; in other words, this was a measure against intermarriage.[39]

In the Middle Ages this prohibition was not vigilantly observed by Jews in all diasporas. In northern Europe, amongst the Jews of Ashkenaz, widespread disregard of this injunction led to much discussion in the high Middle Ages and an expression of a more general desire to adhere to the law in as pious a way as

---

[36] Melitta Weiss Adamson, *Food in Medieval Times* (Westport, CT, 2004), 1.

[37] Lev. 11. This was further expanded in late antiquity: see David Friedenreich, *Foreigners and their Food: Constructing Otherness in Jewish, Christian and Islamic Law* (Berkeley, CA, 2011).

[38] Babylonian Talmud [hereafter: BT] Shabbat, 17a.

[39] Ibid.; see also BT Avodah Zarah, 36a–b.

possible, which was characteristic of the period.[40] As David Strauss has outlined, the reasons for the non-observance of the directive against bread baked by non-Jews were many, but a central explanation has to do with the material reality of medieval urban culture: bread was not regularly produced at home since its baking required a large oven, a *furnum*. As a result, bread was baked by professional bakers, who were not Jews. Many bakeries were situated within monasteries and religious houses. Often, the customers would bring their own dough to the baker, marked with a stamp.[41] While I am not claiming that bread was never baked at home, to do so was not the general custom in urban centres.

The Jews in medieval Ashkenaz dealt with the question of whether or not Jews could eat bread prepared by a gentile on many different levels. A first trend that can be seen is a gradual dismissal of adherence to this rule. Whilst eleventh-century rabbinic sources note that this restriction was generally observed, sources from the twelfth century negate this picture, suggesting that in northern France all Jews ate bread baked by gentiles, whereas in Germany the Jews would make sure that a Jew was involved in the baking process, for example by helping to light the fire in the *furnum*, but the bread would then be made by the non-Jewish baker. In some cases, the Jews prepared the dough themselves in their homes, marking it with a Jewish seal and then bringing it to be baked.[42]

Although the rabbis in medieval northern France seem to assume that all Jews ate bread baked by Christians without any qualms or hesitation, a linguistic distinction remained. They still called this bread 'non-Jewish bread', *pat goyim*, signifying that it was not baked within the Jewish household or community. German sources suggest that most Jews ate bread baked by gentiles, although there were some who did not out of piety. They also noted that

---

[40]   See n. 13 above.

[41]   I have based my discussion on a Master's thesis by David L. Strauss that remains the most exhaustive treatment of this subject to date, 'Pat 'Akum in Medieval France and Germany' (Bernard Revel Graduate School, Yeshiva University, 1979); see also Jeffrey Woolf, 'The Prohibition of Gentile Bread during the Ten Days of Repentance: On the Genesis and Significance of a Custom', in *Studies on the History of the Jews of Ashkenaz: Presented to Eric Zimmer*, ed. Gershon Bacon et al. (Ramat Gan, 2008), 83–99.

[42]   Strauss, '*Pat 'Akum*', 3–5; Woolf, 'Prohibition of Gentile Bread', 88–91.

the bread that especially pious Jews ate, which was baked by Jews alone, was of inferior quality and taste.[43]

The term *pat goyim* represents the complexity I am trying to explicate. The Jews called this 'non-Jewish bread', using a special term in Hebrew, yet they did so while speaking in the local vernacular, as they communicated inside and outside the house in the local French or Middle High German (which would later become Yiddish). A similar amalgamation of language can be seen in medieval Hebrew texts that include references to baked goods prepared at and bought from local (non-Jewish) bakeries. For example, discussions of the preparations for Jewish circumcision festivals include references to typical French pastries such as *oublies*, *canesteles* and *cantilles*.[44] Thus Jews were aware of the non-Jewish character of these baked goods, but also included them in their ritual celebrations.

A change can be documented during the thirteenth century. At this point the rabbis began to ask whether the baked goods from the local bakery were indeed the best fare to serve at Jewish celebrations. More importantly, the question of bread prepared by non-Jews became noticeably more prevalent. The rabbis insisted more vocally that Jews should participate in the process of baking bread, even if the assistance consisted of throwing a splinter into the fire once a week.[45] This insistence was not without danger: the rabbis were not eager to promote close contact between Jews and Christians, so they sought to determine what the minimum level of Jewish participation necessary was so as to uphold the rabbinic restriction and yet to stay as far away as possible from contact with the bakers. Thus an interesting phenomenon emerged. Jews upheld the restriction on eating bread baked by non-Jews, and they ate the bread as well. By the late thirteenth century, an additional custom is reported in some sources that further underlines the contrast between the ideal and actual practice. Although Jews, on the whole, ate bread baked by non-Jews, they were careful to eat Jewish baked bread during one specific week of the year, the week

43 Strauss, '*Pat 'Akum*', xx.
44 *Mahzor Vitry*, nos 506–7.
45 Strauss, '*Pat 'Akum*', 8–9; Woolf, 'Prohibition of Gentile Bread', 89–90.

between Rosh Hashanah (New Year) and Yom Kippur (the Day of Atonement). During this week, Jews prepared bread at home.[46]

As part of an attempt to explain both how the practice of eating bread baked by non-Jews took hold and why the medieval rabbis did not insist on enforcing the rule that only Jewish-baked bread should be consumed, scholars have noted some of the social customs that accompanied breaking bread. When Jews ate bread they washed their hands and made a ritual blessing before and after eating. The blessing made after eating the bread, at the end of the meal, included a special choral blessing recited when three or more people ate together.[47] This was true on weekdays and on the Sabbath, when bread was a required food (along with wine) three times during the day, at each meal. Medieval European Jews used bread made by Christians for these purposes. Perhaps one can say that bread made by gentiles was socially and ritually sanctified while being consumed.

In the context of the theme of religion in the household, we can see, once again, how the most basic foodstuffs were marked by relations between the two faiths. Bread was a most basic part of the diet and the compromise I have presented from medieval northern Europe allowed the expression of religious difference even when Jews and Christians were eating the same bread. The sensitivity showed by medieval Jews towards Christian food was based on late antique guidelines adjusted to medieval reality; it was mirrored by Christian discussions of Jewish food. Christian authorities were very sensitive to the Jewish abstention from Christian meals. Thus at a council in in 1248 it was stated: 'since in disdain of us, Jews do not use any of our food or drink, we strictly forbid any Christians to use theirs'.[48] The situation I have described is unique to

---

[46] Woolf's article attempts to explain how this custom emerged: ibid. 92–9. In addition, some especially pious women when preparing for the Sabbath would be careful to prepare their own dough to bring to the *furnum*, so as to separate the dough as outlined in the Bible, a commandment that was considered a female responsibility: see Edward Fram, *My Dear Daughter: R. Benjamin Slonik and the Education of Jewish Women in Sixteenth-Century Poland* (Portland, OR, 2007), 132.

[47] The medieval rabbis demonstrated considerable concern regarding the proper way to go about the grace after meals if bread made by non-Jews was outlawed: Strauss, '*Pat 'Akum*', 19, 31.

[48] 'Et quia in contemptum nostrum Judei aliquibus cibis nostris et potibus non utuntur firmiter inhibemus ne aliqui Christiani audeant uti suis': Solomon Grayzel, *The Church and the Jews in the Thirteenth Century* (New York, 1966), 336–7.

northern Europe. In southern Europe, as in North Africa, Jews ate local breads without significant discussion of the practice.

CANDLES

Like bread and water, candles, the third example, were a basic necessity. Candles were not just household items, they were also ritual artefacts, used in both church and synagogue. Medieval churches and their rituals are sufficient evidence of the importance of candles practically and in terms of belief. Candles were prepared, lit, exhibited and donated as part of religious processions, devotions and prayers.[49] Medieval Jews, like their ancestors, were well aware of the sacred significance of candles within the worship of other faiths and in fact prohibited the use by Jews of candles previously used for non-Jewish ritual.[50] At the same time, Jews could not abandon the use of candles. Moreover, Jewish rituals also sanctified the use of candles dating back to the ancient ritual in the Temple where the ritual Menorah was lit by the High Priest. Medieval texts emphasize the use of candles in circumcision rites, which in medieval Ashkenaz included the ritual preparation of twelve candles for the ceremony by the infant's mother and her friends; candles were lit before the beginning of the Yom Kippur (Day of Atonement) fast with deep devotion.[51] These candles were all lit in the synagogue. However, candles were also lit in the home for ritual purposes, with Sabbath candles being the most emblematic of Jewish culture.

Candles and lights had a double function in Jewish culture. They were used regularly as part of Jewish ritual, but the prohibition on lighting a fire or any kind of flame on the Sabbath was

---

[49] I have found no study of candles per se, but their use in daily life and ritual is evident in many texts. One example is provided by their use as part of the liturgy throughout the year, especially in connection to Marian rituals: see Gail McMurray Gibson, 'Blessing from Sun and Moon: Churching as Women's Theater', in B. A. Hanawalt and D. Wallace, eds, *Bodies and Disciplines: Intersections of Literature and History in Fifteenth Century England* (Minneapolis, MN, 1996), 139–57.

[50] In medieval European codices this prohibition was repeated: see, for example, R. Isaac b. Joseph of Corbeil, *Semak* (repr. Jerusalem, 1979), no. 59, who discusses how one can use candles used by Christians; R. Eleazar b. Judah of Worms, *Oratio ad Pascam*, ed. Simcha Emanuel (Jerusalem, 2006), 25 and footnotes.

[51] E.g. Louis Finkelstein, *Jewish Self Government in the Middle Ages* (New York, 1924), 123, where these candles are noted in community ordinances.

at the heart of one of the biblical interdictions which became a hallmark of Jewish tradition.[52] Candles thus symbolized the holiness of the Jewish Sabbath as they were lit to mark the beginning of the Sabbath and then lit once again at its end as part of the *havdalah* (that is 'distinction') ritual.

Already in late antiquity the lighting of the Sabbath candles was being discussed in detail. The second chapter of *Tractate Shabbat* enumerated all the types of kindling not permitted for use on the Sabbath:

> With what may they light and with what may they not light? They may not light with cedar fibre or with uncarded flax or with floss silk … or with tallow. Nahum the Mede says they may kindle with boiled tallow. The Sages say, Whether it has been boiled or has not been boiled, they may not light with it.[53]

One detail of this detailed discussion is of great import for the medieval European context: homes in medieval northern Europe, Jewish and Christian, were often lit by tallow lamps, in contrast to churches, synagogues and other public spaces, which were illuminated by more expensive alternatives such as beeswax candles. Tallow candles or lamps were frowned upon in public spaces since their light was not clean and they smelled.[54] At first glance, one could assume that the implication of this prohibition was obvious. Jews must have used tallow candles during the week but did not do so on the Sabbath. However, reading the medieval sources from northern Europe, where olive oil (the primary choice of Mediterranean Jews) was not readily available and was much more expensive, it immediately becomes evident that medieval Jews were indeed lighting tallow candles for the Sabbath.[55] For example, R. Isaac b. Moses (1180–1250) commented: "'Wherewith may we kindle the Sabbath lights and wherewith may we not … we may not with

[52] Ex. 35: 3.

[53] Mishnah Shabbat, *Mishnayoth: Order Mo'ed*, transl. Philip Blackman (New York, 1963), ch. 2, Mishnah 1.

[54] Jean Verdon, *Night in the Middle Ages*, transl. G. Holoch (Notre Dame, IN, 2002), 76–7.

[55] I have outlined this matter in greater detail in my article: 'A Tale of a Christian Matron and Sabbath Candles: Religious Difference, Material Culture and Gender in Thirteenth-Century Germany', *Jewish Studies Quarterly* 20 (2013), 83–99.

tallow". (Mishna, Sabbath 2: 1) I do not know what source we depend on that we kindle with tallow on Sabbath eve.'[56]

As in the case of bread, creative legal solutions were sought, including using a small amount of oil mixed together with tallow so that the Sabbath lamp would not be dependent only on tallow. However, as we saw with bread, by the early thirteenth century some rabbis were suggesting that those who were pious would not use tallow at all. As R. Judah the Pious, one of the proponents of special stringencies, related in his exempla: 'Once there was a person who lived a long life and they could not find any merit for him excepting that he did not light with tallow on sabbath eve, rather he lit with olive oil.'[57]

Before returning to the material substance of candles, let us turn to the last passage in this chapter in the Mishnah. Providing guidance to the actions and utterances one must perform before the Sabbath begins, the Mishnah instructed: 'Three things a man must say within his house on Sabbath eve towards dusk: Have you tithed? Have you prepared the Erub? And: Kindle the lamp.'[58] Whereas the man of the house was supposed to give these instructions, the women were supposed to execute these actions. They were supposed to make sure the food was properly prepared, to define the household space according to the Sabbath rules,[59] and especially to light the candles, a practice that over the generations had become associated with Jewish women.[60]

Thirteenth-century discussions of this passage elaborate upon it. They indicate that in medieval Europe there was no need to define

---

[56] R. Isaac b. Moshe, *Sefer Or Zaru'a* (Jerusalem, 2010), 2 (Laws of Sabbath Eve, no. 12, cf. nos 28, 34, 35). See also *Mahzor Vitry*, no. 114; *Mahzor Vitry*, ed. Aryeh Goldschmidt (Jerusalem, 2004), Hilkhot Shabbat, no. 68.

[57] I have used the facsimile *Sefer Hasidim Parma H 3280*, intro. I. G. Marcus (Jerusalem, 1985), no. 623, and the earlier published *Das Buch des Frommen*, ed. J. Wistinetzki, intro. J. Freimann (Frankfurt, 1924), no. 623. References are to the Parma version [hereafter: *SHP*]. For variants I have utilized the Sefer Hasidim Database at Princeton University, online at: <https://etc.princeton.edu/sefer_hasidim>.

[58] *Mishnah Shabbat*, ch. 2, Mishnah 7. An *eruv* was a line delineating an area within which certain activities could be practised on the Sabbath.

[59] On the history of the *eruv* as well as some of its gendered implications, see Charlotte E. Fonrobert, 'Une cartographie symbolique: L'eruv en Diaspora', *Les cahiers du Judaïsme* 25 (2009), 5–21; on the medieval *eruv*, see Micha Perry, 'Imaginary Space Meets Actual Space in Thirteenth-Century Cologne: Eliezer ben Joel and the Eruv', *Images* 5 (2011), 26–36.

[60] This connection is already made in *Mishnah Shabbat*, ch. 2, Mishnah 6; see Fram, *My Dear Daughter*, 44, 294.

the space (the *eruv*) before the Sabbath, nor were tithes given to those of priestly descent as in the period when the Temple was standing. However, they underline that it was a man's duty to ensure that his wife was lighting Sabbath candles on time. The rabbis suggested how men might do this. If they were already at the synagogue, the men were supposed to send their sons home to instruct their mothers. Although some rabbinic authorities specified that men should not terrorize their wives or instil so much fear in them that they would live in an unpleasant environment, they were resolute about the importance of having men confirm that their wives were lighting their candles on time.[61]

The instructions about, and the supervision of, women's candle lighting practices were compounded by the tallow restrictions. By the late thirteenth century, men were instructed to guide their wives to use lighting materials other than tallow. For example:

> R. Meir b. Barukh (d. 1293, Wurzburg and Rothenburg o.d. Tauber) would say to his wife each Sabbath Eve: you have separated the dough. Light the candle and put oil in the tallow lamps because he said it is forbidden to have tallow, even melted tallow in the lamp without oil. And once when he did not have oil to put in it (the lamp), he squeezed a walnut into it.[62]

There is a significant difference between the examples of water and bread and that of tallow. Tallow was not only forbidden by ancient sources, but more importantly it had symbolic import in the medieval inter-faith world. Tallow (*helev*) was forbidden for consumption in the Bible. As a result, Jews did not eat tallow or use it for cooking. This meant that medieval Jews used tallow for household tasks and medicinal needs but they did not consume it.[63] Over time, tallow came to signify the ultimate non-kosher food, somewhat like pork, although to a lesser degree (and in some cases tallow was in fact derived from mutton fat). Tallow became a metaphor for all that was not kosher and not Jewish. At the same time, tallow was a widespread substance in northern Europe.

---

[61] See for example, R. Eliezer b. Joel, *Sefer Ra'aviah*, ed. V. Aptowizer (Berlin, 1913), Shabbat, no. 199; *Sefer Hasidim*, ed. Mordechai Margaliyot (Jerusalem, 1960), no. 455.

[62] R. Samson b. Tzadok, *Sefer Tashbetz* (Jerusalem, 1974), no. 2.

[63] Baumgarten, *Mothers*, 137.

In the Jewish-Christian context, tallow became a marker of difference and conversion. Thus when Jews underwent forced conversion during 1096, one of the comments made about those who wished to return to Judaism was that they tried, as far as possible, not to eat tallow when pretending to be Christian. Amongst Jews, converts were referred to as 'tallow eaters'.[64] Returning to candles and Sabbath lamps, one can see how this material substance became a symbol for that which was forbidden within the household, even though it was used with certain restrictions.

CLOTH

Cloth, a fourth everyday substance, will serve as a way to draw together some of the strands in this essay. Following the biblical interdiction, Jews did not mix cloths, or, more precisely, did not wear wool woven with linen, known in Hebrew as *sha'atnez*.[65] We have few discussions of *sha'atnez* in medieval texts before the thirteenth century; however, multiple sources from that century discuss the biblical prohibition and suggest ways to avoid wearing mixed cloths. Jewish merchants from England, for example, report how to examine wool garments and ensure that they are stitched together permissibly, suggesting that Jews regularly checked garments to see how they were made and whether their manufacture was in accordance with halakhic guidelines.[66]

There is some evidence that Jews did in fact wear clothing made of mixed cloths and some concern was expressed regarding this practice. Some sources note that Jews would wear clothes left as pledges by Christians who borrowed money and that these clothes were made of mixed cloths.[67] Jews who travelled were advised to have an extra set of clothes, usually a monastic habit

---

[64] Haverkamp, *Hebraische Berichte*, 483. This idea also comes across in R. Barukh b. Isaac, *Sefer haTerumah* (Warsaw, 1897), no. 63.

[65] Lev. 19: 19; Deut. 22: 11.

[66] R. Jacob b. Judah of London, *Sefer Etz Hayim*, ed. Israel Brodie, 2 vols (Jerusalem, 1962), 2: 119; R. Elijah Menahem b. Moses of London, *Perushei R. Eliyahu meLondrish* (Jerusalem, 1956), 5, no. 1 (Hebrew numbers).

[67] *SHP*, no. 1792; Paris, BN, MS Paris héb. 363, R. Eleazar b. Judah, 'Sefer Rokeah', fol. 8b. Haim Sha'anan, 'Piskei Rabenu R'i MeCorbeil', in idem, *Sefer Ner LiShemaya* (B'nei Berak, 1998), 21, no. 41, where he debates the extent to which one can wear clothes belonging to a non-Jew that are left as a pawn and also discusses the issue of *sha'atnez*. He stipulates that one can surely wear gentile clothes if one's life is in danger.

which they could wear as disguise on the road. In the early thirteenth century R. Judah the Pious instructed those who wished to be pious to make sure that they had a special set of 'Christian clothes' for travelling, ones that were not made of mixed cloths.[68] In this case the implication seems to have been that a Jew would obtain the clothing from Christians but re-stitch it so that it was not made of two cloths but rather stitched with thread out of the cloth it was made of. If this was the case, then, after buying clothing from Christians, Jews were taking this clothing apart and reassembling it.

This example takes us out of the household onto the roads. To some extent, leaving the house is not all that remarkable since the boundary between inside and outside the home was permeated constantly and even more so because, as noted at the beginning of this essay, non-Jews were a constant presence within the household. Yet leaving the household illuminates some of the qualities of the ritual conducted within the household and outside it. Water, bread, candles and cloth were used by Jews and their Christian neighbours. More precisely, the same water, bread, candles and cloth were used by members of both faiths and at times within Jewish households themselves, not only by Jews but also by Christians. Jews 'judaized' their bread, water and candles by ritual blessings said before drinking, eating and lighting. But this was not enough to underline the distinctions between the members of the two religions. At specific moments in the year, these distinctions were further emphasized: with water, around non-Jewish festivals; with bread, for one week a year before high holidays and of course during the week of Passover; with candles, on all festivities and especially when marking holy days such as the onset and end of the Sabbath and holidays as well as when celebrating life cycle events such as weddings and circumcisions. The adjustments made to Jewish law in the light of local settings, circumstances and conditions are remarkable. At the same time, the adherence of Jews as a group to the ancient principles and especially the insistence of the local rabbinic authorities on doing so emerge as well.

Two processes can be detected in the examples considered. The first is that medieval Jews in Germany and northern France changed their attitudes and practices towards some of these basic

---

[68] *SHP*, nos 259, 261.

substances during the course of the Middle Ages. Whereas the late eleventh- and twelfth-century texts suggest that most Jews consumed bread baked by Christians, that they lit candles made of tallow every Sabbath, and that some even drank water during the *tekufah*, by the thirteenth century Christian bread was being eaten with more caution and restrictions, the *tekufah* was being more strictly observed, and tallow lamps were being supplemented by oil. Cloth too was being more carefully supervised and marked in contrast to the marked lack of concern with *sha'atnez* before the late twelfth century. The motivation for drawing distinctive lines between Jewish and Christian substances was both internal and external. Jews in Christian Europe were facing intensifying calls for conversion and they in turn were erecting higher barriers between the religions. At the same time, the particular flavour of thirteenth-century piety called for a return to ancient practices and texts; as a result the rabbis were re-examining the way ancient principles were, or were not, being observed.

A second interesting process emerging from these examples has to do with gender. I noted that the practice of the *tekufah* was scorned by some as *sihat hazekenot* or 'old wives tales'. Nevertheless, this observance became more and more pronounced in the fourteenth and fifteenth centuries.[69] Here we can see women's beliefs feeding into the rabbis' objections. In the case of bread, for example, it was the women who were in charge of baking the bread and they insisted increasingly on preparing the dough alone, going to the baker with dough from which they had removed the traditional tithes, and eating bread made of dough they themselves had made. This insistence went hand in hand with the rabbis' insistence that Jews should remain part of the baking process in the local *furnum*. Finally, although women were those who lit the Sabbath candles, we saw that the thirteenth-century rabbis insisted that their wives should not light tallow candles and began to supervise them much more closely. Here we have two tensions: the first, between figures of authority and women in their communities. The women held beliefs that were not always in line with the written law known mainly to elite and educated men. As the medieval period progressed, the women were more and more carefully overseen. This came about through growing concern

---

[69]   Baumgarten, 'Remember'; Carlebach, 'Water into Blood'.

with Jewish-Christian difference, a matter that both women and community leaders were trying to emphasize. To a large extent, even though Jews were eating Christian bread, lighting the same candles and for the most part drinking the same water, the small distinctions involved in how they did so served to 'judaize' the process and thus to accentuate religious differences. The interplay of religious difference and gender divisions constitutes a theme worthy of further study.

I will conclude by turning to a building that to a large extent could be seen as an antithesis to the house, the synagogue. In larger Jewish communities there were synagogues, some of which were quite magnificent, as attested by the transformation after the Black Death of many synagogues into churches in honour of the Virgin Mary.[70] In smaller communities, the home could become a synagogue, lacking another location. Looking at the ways in which water, bread and candles were used in the synagogue in comparison to their use in the home allows further reflection on religion in the household. The *tekufah* water customs had little impact on synagogue liturgy and prayer, although the tables by which the *tekufah* was calculated were often housed in the synagogue within ritual prayer books. As for bread, it was rarely consumed in the synagogue, as meals were held outside, in courtyards and private homes. The synagogue was lit by candles, but these were expensive and therefore not made of tallow; they were specifically candles not bought from gentiles who intended to use them for the church. So a similar type of restriction applied here to that in the home. Finally, the biblical prohibition on mixed cloths pertained only to clothing worn on the body. Fancy materials and cloths for churches were adapted for use in the synagogues and made by the same craftsmen, much as Hebrew illuminated manuscripts were made by Christian artists.[71] To what extent was the synagogue similar to the house and to what extent was it different? How was the use of everyday substances such as water, bread, candles and cloth negotiated in this public space in comparison to the

---

[70] Mary Minty, 'Judengasse into Christian Quarter: The Phenomenon of the Converted Synagogue in the Late Medieval and Early Modern Holy Roman Empire', in Robert Scribner and Trevor Johnson, eds, *Popular Religion in Germany and Central Europe, 1400–1800* (Basingstoke, 1996), 56–86.

[71] Sarit Shalev-Eyni, *Jews among Christians: Hebrew Book Illumination from Lake Constance* (Turnhout, 2010).

house? While further research is required to define these differences, in light of the examples examined here I would suggest that negotiation within the medieval Jewish community was far more nuanced and delicate than those who study religious polemics might assume. At the same time, medieval authors and their texts suggest that these small variations made all the difference and that within these blurred and porous boundaries, a minority culture emerged whose distinctiveness would have been evident to medieval Jews and Christians, much as the stitching on the 'Christian clothing' worn by Jewish travellers could reveal who was a Jew even when the Jew was purposely disguising him- or herself.

The examination of religion within the household as well as in formal public space such as the synagogue brings into question the relationship between religion and space. To what extent did space reinforce religious difference? In the synagogue the import of the space was definitive, yet within the household it was harder to classify space so clearly, both because of the non-Jews within the house who were constantly present and because of its more individual features. Perhaps within the household time rather than space served to reinforce the religious difference: not the actual bread eaten, but when it was or was not consumed; not the candles lit, but when they were or were not lit. These are possible directions for future research.

Hebrew University, Jerusalem

HOLY FAMILIES: THE SPIRITUALIZATION OF THE EARLY MODERN HOUSEHOLD REVISITED

by ALEXANDRA WALSHAM

The household has been a compelling metaphor for the Christian Church since biblical times. In his epistle to the Ephesians (3: 15), St Paul wrote of 'the whole family' of Christ's followers 'in heaven and earth'; in Galatians 6: 10, he equated the congregation of the elect with 'the household of faith'. But these were merely variations on a more ancient theme. In the Old Testament too the language of kinship is deployed to describe the community of God's chosen people, the Jews, while the idea of the family as the basic building block of human society and the state has its roots in the fourth century BCE, in Aristotle's celebrated treatise on *Politics*.[1] The interrelated tropes of the household as a microcosm and nursery of the Church and commonwealth continued to be invoked throughout the medieval period and they proliferated in the wake of the religious upheavals inaugurated by the Reformation. Expressions of these commonplaces abound in sixteenth- and seventeenth-century England. A long succession of Protestant ministers compared families with 'seed-plots' and 'seminaries' in which the tender plants of godly religion and good citizenship were nurtured, and with '[bee]hives, out of which swarm the materials for greater assemblies'.[2]

This essay explores the relationship between the family and household and the religious cultures engendered by the Protestant

---

[1]   See, for example, Ps. 107: 41. Aristotle, Politics, ed. Steven Everson (Cambridge, 1988), 2–3 (1.2).

[2]   For some examples, see R[ichard] C[awdrey], *A godlie forme of householde government*, ed. John Dod and Robert Cleaver (London, 1612 edn), 13; Thomas Wats, *The entrie to Christianitie, or, an admonition to housholders* (London, 1589), sig. A4ᵛ; William Perkins, *Christian oeconomie: or, a short survey of the right manner of erecting and ordering a family, according to the Scriptures* (London, 1618), dedication, in *Workes*, 3 vols ([Cambridge], 1618), vol. 3; John Downame, *A guide to godlynesse or a treatise of a Christian life* (London, 1629), 330; Daniel Cawdrey, *Family reformation promoted in a sermon on Joshua, chap. 24. ver. 15* (London, 1656), sig. A5ᵛ; John Tillotson, *Six sermons … II. Family Religion* (London, 1694), 83; Samuel Slater, *An earnest call to family religion* (London, 1694), 158. See also Albert Peel and Leland H. Carlson, eds, *Cartwrightiana*, Elizabethan Nonconformist Texts 1 (London, 1951), 159: 'houses are the nurseryes of the church'.

and Catholic movements for institutional reform and evangelical renewal. It endeavours to reassess how far, why and with what consequences these parallel Reformations stimulated a spiritualization of the household and an intensification of domestic piety.[3] It examines the role of the home in the plantation and entrenchment of the new faith and in the survival and resurgence of the old; and it probes the texture and dynamics of personal interactions within the family and between its constituent members. The analysis that follows turns on a series of paradoxes: I shall argue that the household functioned simultaneously as a critical bulwark and ally of the ecclesiastical status quo and as a site and agent of clandestine resistance to it. It buttressed patriarchal and political authority but it was also a forum within which the hierarchies of gender, age and social subordination were tested, strained and sometimes overturned. And it contributed significantly to cementing confessional diversity even as it helped to facilitate the emergence of arrangements that permitted coexistence and toleration.

The ensuing discussion treats the household both as a group of people bound by ties of blood and obligation and as the physical space in which they resided. Commensurate with contemporary usage, it adopts a capacious and elastic definition of family and employs the term to encompass not merely a couple and their children, but also relatives, servants and apprentices who cohabited with them under one roof.[4] Although demographers have demonstrated beyond doubt that the nuclear household was predominant in Britain and northern Europe,[5] I build here on recent research that has emphasized the multiple functions and long tentacles of the family as an institution and recognized the presence of a wider penumbra of living and dead kin, who hovered on the perimeter of

---

3   Since the delivery of this lecture, a collection of essays addressing related issues has appeared: Jessica Martin and Alec Ryrie, eds, *Private and Domestic Devotion in Early Modern Britain* (Aldershot, 2012).

4   See *OED*, *s.vv.* 'family' and 'household'; Naomi Tadmor, 'The Concept of the Household-Family in Eighteenth-Century England', *P&P*, no. 151 (1996), 111–40. See also her *Family and Friends in Eighteenth-Century England: Household, Kinship, and Patronage* (Cambridge, 2001). For a recent collection of essays reassessing the history of family since Lawrence Stone's seminal *The Family, Sex and Marriage in England, 1500–1800* (London, 1977), see Helen Berry and Elizabeth Foyster, eds, *The Family in Early Modern England* (Cambridge, 2007).

5   Peter Laslett and Richard Wall, eds, *Household and Family in Past Time* (Cambridge, 1972), esp. 125–203.

the inner circle and periodically exerted powerful influence within it.[6] Finally, I proceed from the assumption that the household is at once a private realm and part of the public sphere. Defying the binary divide that is the product of more recent times, it exemplifies the highly porous and permeable boundaries that separated these two zones in the medieval and early modern period.[7]

★ ★ ★

The starting point for the first part of this essay is the voluminous body of prescriptive Protestant literature on household government that poured from printing presses in the later sixteenth and seventeenth centuries. As Kathleen Davies and Margo Todd have emphasized, this category of domestic advice book had important late medieval and humanist precursors, notably the Bridgettine monk Richard Whitford's *Werke for Housholders* (1530).[8] Finding classical models in the work of Aristotle and Xenophon, many of its characteristic ingredients were present in St Paul's letters to Timothy and other early Christians. Nevertheless, the Reformation marked an important phase in its development and engendered a fresh wave of texts providing guidance on the inculcation of family piety. Henry Reginald's 1548 translation of the German minister Christopher Hegendorff's *Domestycall or housholde sermons* is an early evangelical specimen, but many more emanated from the pens of a later generation of English puritan writers.[9] William Perkins's *Christian oeconomie* (1609), William Gouge's *Of*

[6] Keith Wrightson, 'Household and Kinship in Sixteenth-Century England', *History Workshop Journal* 12 (1981), 151–8; David Cressy, 'Kinship and Kin Interaction in Early Modern England', *P&P*, no. 113 (1986), 38–69; Rosemary O'Day, *The Family and Family Relationships, 1500–1900: England, France and the United States of America* (London, 1994), 1–28, 125–7; Will Coster, *Family and Kinship in England 1450–1800* (Harlow, 2001), ch. 5.

[7] See Erica Longfellow, 'Public, Private and the Household in Early Seventeenth-Century England', *JBS* 45 (2006), 313–34. On the ambivalence of early modern society about privacy, see Lena Cowen Orlin, *Locating Privacy in Tudor London* (Oxford, 2007).

[8] Margo Todd, 'Humanists, Puritans and the Spiritualized Household', *ChH* 49 (1980), 18–34; Kathleen M. Davies, 'Continuity and Change in Literary Advice on Marriage', in R. B. Outhwaite, ed., *Marriage and Society: Studies in the Social History of Marriage* (London, 1981), 58–80.

[9] Christopher Hegendorff, *Domestycal or housholde sermons, for a godly householder, to his children and family*, transl. Henry Reginald (London, 1548).

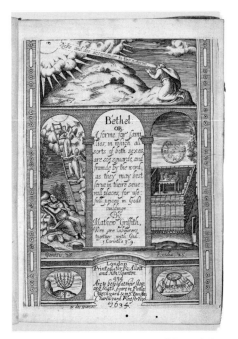

Fig. 1: Guides to domestic piety: Matthew Griffith, *Bethel, or a forme for families* (London, 1634), title page. Reproduced by permission of the Syndics of Cambridge University Library, shelfmark Syn. 7.63.150.

domesticall duties (1622) and Matthew Griffith's *Bethel* (1633) are among the more famous examples of this prolific and popular genre (Fig. 1).[10]

Together with their many cousins and imitators, these books stressed the weighty responsibility of heads of households (and their appointed deputies) to care for the souls of those under their charge and urged them to follow in the footsteps of Abraham, Joshua, David and other Hebrew patriarchs. Aquila, Cornelius, Nymphas and Philemon were widely invoked as worthy precedents from the pages of the New Testament. Presenting the paterfamilias

[10] Perkins, *Christian oeconomie*; William Gouge, *Of domesticall duties* (London, 1622); Matthew Griffith, *Bethel, or a forme for families* (London, 1633). Another is Thomas Carter, *Carters Christian commonwealth; or domesticall dutyes deciphered* (London, 1627). For previous discussions of the household as a religious unit, see Richard L. Greaves, *Society and Religion in Elizabethan England* (Minneapolis, MN, 1981), ch. 7; John Morgan, *Godly Learning: Puritan Attitudes towards Reason, Learning, and Education, 1560–1640* (Cambridge, 1986), ch. 8.

as a kingly and prince-like figure and comparing his office with that of a private pastor, preacher or bishop, their authors outlined an intense and exacting regime of morning and evening prayer, Bible-reading, psalm-singing, catechizing, Sabbath observance and moral discipline that would transform their households into 'holy congregations' and 'little Churches, yea even a kind of paradise upon earth'.[11] Typically they went on to describe the mutual and reciprocal obligations of husbands and wives, parents and children, and masters and servants. While godly and well-ordered families that served the Lord diligently would be the recipients of divine blessing, the curse of God hung over households which were luke-warm if not contemptuous of their religious duties. Instead of arks of piety and sanctuaries of prayer, they became 'dennes of Theeves', 'sinckes of sinne', and 'habitations of divells', and their negligent heads were guilty of nothing less than the spiritual murder of their subordinates.[12] The collective welfare of the household depended on the integrity of its members, as the contrasting fates of the righteous Noah and his family, who were preserved from the Flood, and wicked Achan and his household, who perished, clearly demonstrated.[13]

It was Christopher Hill who first coined the phrase 'the spir-itualization of the household', in an eloquent and persuasive essay published in 1964. For Hill, Protestantism, and more particu-larly puritanism, was the catalyst and midwife of the industrious middle-class family in which capitalist habits and values were born. Refining the earlier pronouncements on this topic by Marx and Engels in a Weberian direction, Hill spoke of the household as the 'dominant productive unit' and described how, by reducing the authority of the priesthood as an intermediary between laypeople and God, the Reformation had elevated that of husbands, fathers and masters, who thereby acquired quasi-sacerdotal status. He

---

[11] Quotations from William Jones, *A briefe exhortation to all men to set their houses in order* (London, 1631), 10; Perkins, *Christian oeconomie*, 670. On the place of reading in family piety, see Andrew Cambers, *Godly Reading: Print, Manuscript and Puritanism in England, 1580–1720* (Cambridge, 2011), ch. 3.

[12] Griffith, *Bethel*, 395; Wats, *Entrie to Christianitie*, sig. B1ʳ; Richard Bernard, *Joshuas godly resolution in conference with Caleb, touching household government for well ordering with a familie* (London, 1612), sig. A3ʳ. For the sins of negligent heads of household, see C[awdrey], *Godlie form of householde government*, sig. A4ᵛ; Thomas Gouge, *A word to housholders*, in his *A word to sinners, and a word to saints* (London, 1670), 226.

[13] Thomas Paget, *A demonstration of family-duties* (London, 1643), 57.

implied that economic individualism was one of the complex side effects, if not the source, of this development.[14]

The same set of prescriptive texts has provided ammunition for a different kind of modernization thesis. Scholars in search of the origins of the emotionally close conjugal family have found in them evidence that the Reformation played a critical part in this process. According to Levin Schücking and Stephen Ozment, Protestantism's repudiation of celibacy and closure of monasteries and convents was accompanied by a celebration of marriage that paved the way for the loving companionate partnership, underlined the duty of procreation, and emphasized the pleasures of sex.[15] Subsequent research by Patrick Collinson, among others, has qualified and nuanced the claim that the Reformation constituted a major watershed in this respect, though it is still acknowledged to have effected a social revolution by creating a married clergy, to have narrowed the parameters of the family by paring away a surfeit of religious allegiances and associations conceived of in quasi-familial terms, and to have diminished the significance of forms of spiritual kinship such as godparenthood.[16] Inspired by the insights of feminist historians such as Lyndal Roper, others have challenged the positive picture of Protestant family life delineated by previous historians. While recognizing the presence of

[14] Christopher Hill, 'The Spiritualization of the Household', in idem, *Society and Puritanism in Pre-Revolutionary England* (London, 1964), 443–81.

[15] This thesis infuses the following works to a greater or lesser extent: C. L. Powell, *English Domestic Relations, 1487–1653* (New York, 1917); Edmund S. Morgan, *The Puritan Family: Religion and Domestic Relations in Seventeenth-Century New England* (New York, 1944); L. L. Schücking, *The Puritan Family: A Social Study from Literary Sources* (1929; London, 1969); Stone, *Family, Sex and Marriage in England,* esp. 141–2; Steven Ozment, *When Fathers Ruled: Family Life in Reformation Europe* (Cambridge, MA, 1983), esp. chs 1–2.

[16] Patrick Collinson, 'The Protestant Family', in idem, *The Birthpangs of Protestant England: Religious and Cultural Change in the Sixteenth and Seventeenth Centuries* (New York, 1988), 60–93; Susan Karant Nunn, 'Reformation Society, Women and the Family', in Andrew Pettegree, ed., *The Reformation World* (London and New York, 2000), 433–59, esp. 433–6. On clerical marriage, see Helen L. Parish, *Clerical Marriage and the English Reformation: Precedent, Policy and Practice* (Aldershot, 2000); on godparenthood, Will Coster, *Baptism and Spiritual Kinship in Early Modern England* (2002). For balanced overviews that focus on England, see Ralph A. Houlbrooke, *The English Family 1450–1700* (Harlow, 1984); Anthony Fletcher, 'The Protestant Idea of Marriage in Early Modern England', in *Religion, Culture and Society in Early Modern Britain: Essays in Honour of Patrick Collinson,* ed. Anthony Fletcher and Peter Roberts (Cambridge, 1994), 161–81.

an ameliorating gap between prescription and practice, they have highlighted the Reformation's role in reinforcing repressive patriarchal structures, inscribing women tightly within the household, and subjecting children to a rigorous programme of indoctrination and socialization.[17]

Here I shall deliberately sidestep these ongoing and convoluted debates.[18] Instead, I wish to focus attention on the broad purchase and widespread diffusion of the ideal of the godly household across the ecclesiastical spectrum in Elizabethan and Stuart England. From the earliest years of the Reformation, the authorities recognized that religious change could not be effected without the cooperation of those who had oversight of the private home. Henrician laws and injunctions required parents and rulers of families to instruct their offspring and servants in the theological matters of the moment and to ensure that they were brought up in an honest calling and the fear of God. In Elizabeth's reign, heads of households were obliged to ensure that children and apprentices attended church on Sundays and feast days and were catechized, and visitation articles regularly enquired about those who defaulted in these tasks. Central government and episcopal directives were supplemented at the local and civic level by even stricter initiatives: according to an order promulgated in the borough of Leicester in 1562, at least one person from each household had to attend Wednesday and Friday sermons on pain of a fine levied on the offending paterfamilias.[19]

Official and semi-official publications like Sternhold and Hopkins's *Whole book of psalmes* (1563) and Richard Day's *Booke of christian prayers* (1569) fed the demand for material to help people structure their domestic devotions, as did a surge of catechisms

---

[17] Lyndal Roper, *The Holy Household: Women and Morals in Reformation Augsburg* (Oxford, 1989). See also Anthony Fletcher, 'Prescription and Practice: Protestantism and the Upbringing of Children, 1560–1700', in Diana Wood, ed., *The Church and Childhood*, SCH 31 (Oxford, 1994), 325–46.

[18] Some of these have been themes of earlier EHS conferences: W. J. Sheils and Diana Wood, eds, *Women in the Church*, SCH 27 (Oxford, 1990); Wood, ed., *Church and Childhood*; R. N. Swanson, ed., *Gender and Christian Religion*, SCH 34 (Woodbridge, 1998).

[19] See, for example, *Elizabethan Episcopal Administration*, ed. W. P. M. Kennedy, 3 vols, Alcuin Club Collections 26 (London, 1924), 2: 93–4, 119, 127–8; 3: 346–7; Greaves, *Society and Religion*, 293–4.

Fig. 2: The godly family: *Tenor of the whole psalms in foure partes* (London, 1563). By permission of the Folger Shakespeare Library, Washington DC, shelfmark 11/9/43.

and works of practical divinity (Fig. 2).[20] Underling the centrality of communal reading in Protestant culture, texts such as Bishop Bayly's bestselling *Practice of pietie* (1613) and John Downame's *A guide to godlynesse* (1622) found a ready market, alongside edifying ballads and instructional tables summarizing the Ten Commandments and key Protestant tenets.[21] Pasted on the walls of humble as well as more expensive dwellings, broadsides like *A short interpretation of the lords praier* (1627) served as mnemonic devices and

---

[20] For a handful of catechisms and family prayer books, see Edward Dering, *Godly private praiers, for housholders to meditate upon, and to saye in their families* (London, [1578]); Richard Jones, *A briefe and necessarie catechisme … for the benefit of all housholders, their children and families* (London, 1583); John Parker, *A true patterne of pietie, meete for all Christian housholders to looke upon, for the better education of their families* (London, 1592); James Leech, *A plaine and profitable catechisme, with certaine prayers adioined, meete for parents and housholders to teach their children and servants* (Cambridge, 1605); *A short catechisme for housholders, with praiers to the same adioyning* (London, 1611); T. P., *A short catechisme for housholders* (London, 1624); Richard Ram, *The countrymans catechisme: or, a helpe for housholders to instruct their families in the grounds of Christian religion* (London, 1655).
[21] See Tessa Watt, *Cheap Print and Popular Piety, 1550-1640* (Cambridge, 1991), ch. 6.

primers both for fathers and masters and those under their charge.[22] Thomas Jenner's engraving *The Christians jewell* advertised itself as fit 'to adorne the hearte and decke the house of every Protestant'. Mimicking the reformed iconography of a reredos in the parish of St Mary Overy, Southwark, it was intended to transform the home into a miniature church.[23] *The good hows-holder* (1607), meanwhile, taught the stern but friendly lesson that wise patriarchs erected the foundations of their families on rock rather than sand and ruled them with 'a warie head and charie hand' (Fig. 3). *The husband's instructions to his family, or household observations*, a late seventeenth-century broadside in the same vein, declared that 'A Family well Govern'd, is like a Kingdom well Rul'd'.[24]

As Tara Hamling's impressive investigations have shown, such texts left a more permanent imprint on the material environment of the middle- and upper-class home. Chimney breasts, firebacks, wall panels and cushion covers were encrusted with admonitory verses and images derived from biblical prints and emblematic title pages. Painted or plastered onto ceilings, they functioned as a reminder that God kept constant watch over the activities of members of the household. Like the CCTV cameras now omnipresent in our cities and towns, nothing escaped the surveillance of the all-seeing eye of the Almighty. Combining fashion with devotion, such pictorial schemes helped to sanctify the interior spaces – halls, parlours and chambers – within which godly families gathered together for private worship.[25] They reinforced Calvinism's diffuse concept of the church as any place where two or three of the faithful gathered together to pray to the Lord.[26]

---

[22] *A short interpretation of the lords praier: necessary for all housholders to learne, and to teach their children and servants* (London, 1627).

[23] *The Christians jewell [fit] to adorne the hearte and decke the house of every Protestant* (London, [1624]).

[24] *The good hows-holder* (London, 1607); *The husband's instructions to his family, or household observations* (London, 1685).

[25] Tara Hamling, *Decorating the 'Godly' Household: Religious Art in Post-Reformation Britain* (New Haven, CT, and London, 2010), especially her discussion of art designed to mimic the gaze and emphasize the presence of God (ch. 6); see also her 'Old Robert's Girdle: Visual and Material Props for Piety in Post-Reformation England', in Martin and Ryrie, eds, *Private and Domestic Devotion*, 135–63; and, in this volume, 'Living with the Bible in Post-Reformation England: The Materiality of Text, Image and Object in Domestic Life', 210–39.

[26] John Calvin, *Institutes of the Christian Religion*, transl. Henry Beveridge, 2 vols (Grand Rapids, MI, 1989 edn), 2: 180 (III.20.30).

Fig. 3: The Protestant patriarch: *The good hows-holder* (London, 1607). © Trustees of the British Museum. Image number AN163671001.

While the ideals embodied in the literature of household government were deeply immersed within mainstream culture, they also formed a distinctive part of the voluntary religion that differentiated puritans from the conformist majority. Indeed, as their efforts to purge the English Church of remaining traces of popery through the medium of Parliament faltered and then failed, it is possible to detect the hotter sort of Elizabethan Protestants placing ever-increasing emphasis on the need for true reformation to begin at home. Puritan divines like Richard Greenham and Matthew Griffith censured those who demanded far-reaching reform but did nothing to sweep their own hearths clean, and lamented the 'supine neglect' and 'wilful contempt of Family-duties' by their contemporaries.[27] It was

[27] Richard Greenham, *A godly exhortation, and fruitfull admonition to virtuous parents and modest matrons* (London, 1584), sigs A7ᵛ–A8ʳ; Griffith, *Bethel*, 2. See also C[awdrey], *Godlie forme of householde government*, sigs A2ᵛ–A3ʳ. Stephen Baskerville, 'The Family in

the want of 'private helpe' that made 'the publicke ministery so unprofitable', declared the Somerset divine Richard Bernard.[28] Writing in 1596, Josias Nicholls had warned that such inattention to the building of the spiritual temple might lead God to remove the candlestick of the gospel and insisted that men who duly ordered their households to engender a 'holy generation' would not only preserve themselves from the coming deluge but might also be the salvation of the Church 'in the time of extreame daunger and darknesse'. 'By the contrarie', he suggested, 'an whole countrie may fall into Idolatry and destruction'.[29] In contexts where godly ministers had been suspended from their livings and where proper catechizing and teaching was lacking, domestic piety was not merely a supplement to publicly ordained services but a substitute and surrogate for them.[30] Sermon repetition and scriptural exposition could function as a stopgap until the magistrate put his hand to the wheel and constructed a true new Jerusalem.

Exemplary attention to household religion is a perennial theme of the funeral sermons and biographical lives of godly divines and laypeople that flourished in the seventeenth century. According to William Hinde, through his earnest performance of household duties the Cheshire gentleman John Bruen had made his home 'a little Bethel' and 'a common nursery for the Churches of God', cultivating the piety of his wife, bringing her by 'wholesome admonitions' and 'mild rebukes' 'to a higher pitch and degree of knowledge and of grace', and applying the 'healing medicine' of the 'rod of correction' to cure the corruptions and misdemeanours of his children and servants.[31] The cameo portrait of John Carter incorporated in Samuel Clarke's well-known anthology praised the diligence in daily prayer and instruction that had transformed his house into a tiny church and oratory, while his account of

Puritan Political Theology', *JFH* 18 (1993), 157–77, argues that the widespread deployment of familial metaphors was indicative of a contemporary sense of crisis within the family.

[28] Bernard, *Joshuas resolution*, 22.

[29] Josias Nicholls, *An order of household instruction* (London, 1596), 'to the Reader', esp. sigs B2^r, B3^v–B4^r.

[30] A scenario discussed in R. R., *The house-holders helpe, for domesticall discipline* (London, 1615), 20–1.

[31] William Hinde, *A faithfull remonstrance of the holy life and happy death, of John Bruen of Bruen-Stapleford in the County of Chester* (London, 1641), 49, 51, 53, 65.

Herbert Palmer highlighted the extraordinary vigilance and painful labours that had made his family akin to 'a garden without weeds'.[32] Ejected from his London living in 1662, Thomas Cawton had been equally assiduous in his domestic duties and a 'true Pater familias' to all those under his jurisdiction.[33] Wives and mothers like Margaret Corbet, who died in 1656, were likewise celebrated as helpmeets to their husbands and commended when they were attentive to the task of instructing their 'hopefull little ones in the holy Scriptures', just as young Timothy was tutored by his mother Lois and grandmother Eunice.[34]

Such narratives must be situated on a continuum with the conduct books and biblical stories which they mirrored in so many particulars. Melding moderation with zeal, they represented an attempt to construct both puritanism and family religion as respectable, conservative and stabilizing forces in English society and to redeem and justify them in the face of the defeat and exclusion of presbyterianism after the Restoration.[35] In a similar way, surviving relatives of the Shropshire minister Philip Henry selectively edited his memoirs to strengthen the impression that he was a perfect 'pattern of Primitive Christianity' in this respect.[36] Part of an ongoing process of polemical myth-making and personal self-fashioning, such texts eclipse strains and dissonances within

---

[32] Samuel Clarke, *The lives of thirty-two English divines, famous in their generation for learning and piety, and most of them sufferers in the cause of Christ* (London, 1677 edn), 135, 190–1. William Gouge was also exemplary in this respect: 'A Narrative of the Life and Death of Doctor Gouge', in William Gouge, *A learned and very useful commentary on the whole epistle to the Hebrewes* (London, 1655), sig. a2ᵛ.

[33] Thomas Cawton, *The life and death of that holy and reverend man of God Mr Thomas Cawton* (London, 1662), 60–1.

[34] Clarke, *Lives*, 414, alluding to 2 Tim. 1: 5. On godly women in conduct books and biographies, see Jacqueline Eales, 'Samuel Clarke and the "Lives" of Godly Women in Seventeenth-Century England', in Sheils and Wood, eds, *Women in the Church*, 365–76; eadem, 'Gender Construction in Early Modern England and the Conduct Books of William Whateley, 1583–1639', in Swanson, ed., *Gender and Christian Religion*, 163–74.

[35] Peter Lake, 'Reading Clarke's *Lives* in Political and Polemical Context', in Kevin Sharpe and Steen N. Zwicker, eds, *Writing Lives: Biography and Textuality, Identity and Representation in Early Modern England* (Oxford, 2008), 293–318.

[36] Matthew Henry, *An account of the life and death of Philip Henry, minister of the gospel* (London, 1698), ch. 4 and preface, sig. A4ʳ. On these editorial strategies, see Patricia Crawford, 'Katharine and Philip Henry and their Children: A Case Study in Family Ideology', in eadem, *Blood, Bodies and Families in Early Modern England* (Harlow, 2004), 175–208.

the Protestant household which can be uncovered if we read them against the grain.

The first of these tensions is the fact that many early households were not harmoniously united but divided by faith. While mixed marriages across the confessional divide were not uncommon, in other instances husbands and wives were, in the words of one writer, 'unequally yoked': similarly, the members of households, young and old, might differ in the style, degree and intensity of their pieties.[37] Such situations provided a recipe for overt or subtle subversions of patriarchal authority. Thus, in the heady atmosphere of Marian persecution in 1556, John Careless counselled a woman enticed to attend mass by her husband, an act that he described as that of a tyrant, to beware that her greatest 'foes' lay within her own household.[38] Later such disagreements focused upon the tricky category of things indifferent. Peter Lake has written of the 'emancipation' of the Chester matron Mrs Jane Ratcliffe and examined how she negotiated the clash between the dictates of her conscience and conventional obligations to her husband.[39] The Baptist prophetess Anne Wentworth similarly defended her wifely disobedience by insisting that she owed ultimate deference to God as divine householder and spouse.[40] Prescriptive handbooks such as Gouge's *Domesticall duties* acknowledged that where the commands of one's earthly superiors crossed with the Lord's commandments, one's duty of subjection to them had distinct limitations. There were situations in which wives, children and servants could legitimately

[37] See the digression on this subject in Hindle, *Faithfull remonstrance*, 52–3. On mixed marriage in the Netherlands, see Benjamin J. Kaplan, '"For They Will Turn Away Thy Sons": The Practice and Perils of Mixed Marriage in the Dutch Golden Age', in *Piety and Family in Early Modern Europe: Essays in Honour of Steven Ozment*, ed. Marc R. Forster and Benjamin J. Kaplan (Aldershot, 2005), 115–33.

[38] John Foxe, *Actes and Monuments* (London, 1583 edn), 1956.

[39] Peter Lake, 'Feminine Piety and Personal Potency: The "Emancipation" of Mrs Jane Ratcliffe', *The Seventeenth Century* 2 (1987), 143–65; cf. Patrick Collinson's scepticism about the capacity of such texts to yield insight into individual lives: '"A Magazine of Religious Patterns": An Erasmian Topic Transposed in English Protestantism', in his *Godly People: Essays on English Protestantism and Puritanism* (London, 1983), 499–525. On spirituality as 'an emotional release from patriarchy', see Diane Willen, 'Godly Women in Early Modern England: Puritanism and Gender', *JEH* 43 (1992), 561–80, at 577.

[40] Warren Johnston, 'Prophecy, Patriarchy, and Violence in the Early Modern Household: The Revelations of Anne Wentworth', *JFH* 34 (2009), 344–68, esp. 353–5; see also Ann Hughes, 'Puritanism and Gender', in John Coffey and Paul C. H. Lim, eds, *The Cambridge Companion to Puritanism* (Cambridge, 2008), 294–308.

defy the directives of the paterfamilias.[41] To this extent there was a kind of Trojan horse inherent in this literature, a domestic form of the resistance theories that emerged in the course of Europe's vicious wars of religion. We might even speak of the household as a kind of monarchical republic itself.[42] Here too allegiances were precarious and contingent.

On the other hand, the total commitment that God required of his disciples could compel husbands and parents to cast aside affection and their duty of care to their dependants in order to obey their divine Father and bear witness to their faith. In Foxe's *Actes and Monuments*, the martyrologist makes clear that abnegation of one's patriarchal responsibilities in favour of dying in the fires of Smithfield was the correct path for an upright Protestant male to take: wives and children, together with friends, were 'lets and impediments' on the 'journey to heaven'. Foxe celebrated the heroic self-sacrifice of John Hullier and Robert Glover, who forsook their beloved families for the cross of Christ. The responsibility of bearing open witness could thus necessitate rejecting conventional models of masculinity.[43] The intimate religious relationships that devout ladies like Mistress Mary Honeywood developed with godly preachers such as Edward Dering who counselled their soteriological neuroses, which Patrick Collinson describes as 'spiritual affairs', must also have injected tension into marital relationships between women and their husbands.[44]

A further symptom of the unsettlement and trouble that swirled beneath the surface of otherwise model Protestant households is the rash of cases of demonic possession that developed in godly families. The mixture of obscenity and piety, blasphemous ravings and edifying speeches, which sprang from the tongues of children and adolescents diagnosed as victims of diabolical invasion,

---

[41] Gouge, *Domesticall duties*, 325–9, 467–9, 636–8.

[42] The allusion is to Patrick Collinson, 'The Monarchical Republic of Elizabeth I', repr. in his *Elizabethan Essays* (London and Rio Grande, OH, 1994), 31–57. On the subordination of the claims of the natural family to the divine authority of God the Father, and the figurative fatherhood of the earthly ruler, see Jonathan Sircy, 'Becoming Spiritual: Authority and Legitimacy in the Early Modern English Family', in Christopher Cobb, ed., *Renaissance Papers 2009* (Woodbridge, 2010), 55–65.

[43] See D. Andrew Penny, 'Family Matters and Foxe's *Acts and Monuments*', *HistJ* 39 (1996), 599–618, esp. 604–7.

[44] Collinson, *Birthpangs*, 75–7; idem, '"Not Sexual in the Ordinary Sense": Women, Men and Religious Transactions', in idem, *Elizabethan Essays*, 119–50.

including the Derbyshire youth Thomas Darling, the Yorkshire lass Helen Fairfax and the London teenager Mary Glover, may be seen as revolts against the strict religious routines and temporary inversions of the strict hierarchies of age and gender that prevailed within the domestic environments within which they were raised. The marathon sessions of fasting, prayer and preaching by which puritan exorcists such as John Darrell released them from Satan's clutches also restored their households to harmony and order. Private chambers became theatres in which ministers wrestled with the Devil for control of the bodies of tormented young people, anxiously watched by assembled relatives, neighbours and friends − a faithful 'company of such as feared god'.[45] Indeed, fervent Protestants regarded such afflictions as a consequence of the sins and delinquencies of the family as a collective entity itself, or as a manifestation of the ill discipline permitted by its head. The 'only effectual means' of protecting one's home from the malice of Satan, declared William Perkins in his *Damned art of witchcraft*, was 'a Sanctification of the places of our habitation' by prayer and Bible-reading.[46] Some contemporaries, by contrast, resorted to techniques that smacked of superstition and magic, concealing objects in blocked niches and hollows and inscribing on beams and near fireplaces ritual marks like the daisywheel, designed to deflect evil spirits and operate as apotropaic devices.[47]

★ ★ ★

From the tensions engendered within the spiritualized household, we must turn to the anxieties for which it provided a focus among outsiders. Even as the Tudor and Stuart regimes regarded the home as a vital forum for the education of the Protestant young,

[45] J. A. Sharpe, 'Disruption in the Well-Ordered Household: Age, Authority, and Possessed Young People', in Paul Griffiths, Adam Fox and Steve Hindle, eds, *The Experience of Authority in Early Modern England* (Basingstoke, 1996), 187–212. The phenomenon of child prophecy reflects similar tensions: see my '"Out of the Mouths of Babes and Sucklings': Prophecy, Puritanism and Childhood in Elizabethan Suffolk', and Susan Hardman Moore, '"Such Perfecting of Praise out of the Mouth of a Babe": Sarah Wight as Child Prophet', in Wood, ed., *Church and Childhood*, 285–99 and 313–24. Quotation from John Swan, *A true and breife report of Mary Glovers vexation, and of her deliverance by fastings and prayer* ([London, 1603]), 8.
[46] Perkins, *A discourse of the damned art of witchcraft*, in *Workes*, 3: 646–7.
[47] Tamling, *Decorating the 'Godly' Household*, 269–73.

they also worried that it might be a breeding ground for dissent and sedition. Although the Act of Uniformity of 1559 exempted worship in the private chapels of the nobility and gentry from its disciplinary provisions, the authorities expressed repeated concern about sacramental activities that took place behind closed doors. Private baptism was only permitted in the cases of the severest necessity and it remained obligatory for wealthy householders to receive communion in their parish churches at least once a year.[48] John Whitgift admitted during the Admonition Controversy that there were occasions when private worship might be acceptable and even commendable, but he firmly repudiated Thomas Cartwright's insistence that 'wheresoever the church meeteth' became temporarily a 'public place', declaring that this did not 'open any window to secret and schismatical "conventicles" (such ... as seek corners)'.[49] Enquiries about secret household meetings in which laypeople and ministers assembled to read, preach or discuss Scripture are ubiquitous in the ecclesiastical records of the period. Thus Richard Vaughan's visitation articles for the diocese of London in 1605 asked if houses, along with barns, fields and woods, were the location of 'any extraordinary expositions of Scripture'. Such conventicles were often described as taking place 'under [the mere] colour or pretext of religion' and thought to be occasions upon which the ecclesiastical and political establishment and the Book of Common Prayer were depraved and brought into disrepute.[50] The Canons of 1604 sought to control another unruly manifesta-

---

[48] See Felicity Heal and Clive Holmes, *The Gentry in England and Wales 1500–1700* (Basingstoke, 1994), 368–9. It is, however, clear that private baptisms continued into the 1630s, although they had become much less common by about 1590: Hannah Cleugh, 'Baptism and Burial in the Reformation Church of England: Theological Tensions and Controversies' (D.Phil. thesis, University of Oxford, 2007), 145–75.

[49] *The Works of John Whitgift, D.D.*, ed. John Ayre, 3 vols, PS (Cambridge, 1851–3), 1: 207–12.

[50] For Vaughan, see *Visitation Articles and Injunctions of the Early Stuart Church*, ed. Kenneth Fincham, 2 vols, CERS 1, 5 (Woodbridge, 1994–8), 1: 38. The phrase 'under color, or pretext of religion' is used, for instance, in Richard Montagu's articles for Chichester (1628): ibid. 2: 24; see also 1: 6–7, 59, 75, 103, 106, 144, 157, 176–7, 181, 194, 205; 2: 14, 52, 58, 89, 129, 138, 197. For similar articles from the Tudor period, see *Documentary Annals of the Reformed Church of England: being a collection of injunctions, declarations, orders, articles of enquiry, &c., from the year 1546 to the year 1716*, ed. Edward Cardwell, 2 vols (Oxford, 1844), 1: 91, 206–7, 245, 293–4, 360, 386, 468; 2: 23–4, 35, 302–4; *Elizabethan Episcopal Administration*, ed. Kennedy, 2: 105, 113, 123, 127–8; 3: 142, 154, 180, 189, 202, 205, 350.

tion of domestic Protestant enthusiasm, private fasts, and firmly prohibited them without a special licence.[51]

One of the underlying concerns behind these various initiatives was fear that the laity were usurping the privileges of the ordained ministry and taking upon themselves the special vocation of prophesying. This was not helped by the fact that many puritan tract writers echoed the marginal note to Genesis 17: 23 in the Geneva Bible, which declared that 'Masters in their houses ought to be as preachers to their families'.[52] The author of *The house-holders helpe* (1615) anticipated the objection that sermon repetition at home verged on 'private Preaching' and noted that 'where that course is continued, men are commonly accounted Puritans, and ... much derided, scorned and mocked for it'.[53] John Bruen's biographer dismissed allegations that in his domestic conferences he had 'trenched too neare' and trespassed upon the office of the clergy and been 'transported with some private spirit of interpretation, above his pitch and place'. His efforts as a diligent householder were not to be confused with the 'fruits of any [such] vain and unwarrantable presumption'.[54] But by the seventeenth century, exuberant household devotion was firmly woven into the satirical caricature of schismatic presbyterianism and puritanism created by the popular press and playhouse, in alliance with official propagandists. In his *Survey of the pretended holy discipline* (1593), Richard Bancroft had castigated the self-styled godly for disdaining to come to their parish churches: 'though they be hard by their dores, they account it dishonourable matter: their parlour-service, and private speaking ... pleaseth them best'.[55]

In the eyes of the Church and state, there was a fine and blurred line between harmless religious exercises confined to a

---

[51] Canon 72 in *The Anglican Canons, 1529–1947*, ed. Gerald Bray, CERS 6 (Woodbridge, 1998), 362–3. Canon 71 renewed the Elizabethan prohibition on preaching or administering communion in private houses.

[52] The comparison had been made by Augustine. It is echoed by Perkins, *Christian oeconomie*, 699; Bayly, *Practice of pietie*, 343.

[53] R. R., *House-holders helpe*, 26.

[54] Hinde, *Faithfull remonstrance*, 76–7. See Heal and Holmes, *Gentry*, 359–74, on gentry household piety.

[55] Richard Bancroft, *A survay of the pretended holy discipline* (London, 1593), 98. See John Earle, 'A She Precise Hypocrite', in his *Microcosmography, or A Piece of the World Discovered in Essays and Characters* (London, n.d.), 72–4; Antibrownistus Puritanomastix, *Three Speeches* (1642), extracts in Lawrence A. Sasek, ed., *Images of English Puritanism: A Collection of Contemporary Sources 1589–1646* (Baton Rouge, LA, and London, 1989), 309–15.

single family and schismatic conventions that jeopardized the unity and integrity of the commonweal. The ambiguity provided some conventicles with legal immunity: presented to the ecclesiastical court for 'using unlawful reading and catechizing in his house by one Faunce of Maldon and John Gardiner of Heybridge' in 1583, William Walker of Cold Norton in Essex claimed that it was 'in his own house and with his own family only' and declared that Faunce was a member of his household.[56] But the barrier between legally defensible annexes to the public liturgy and dissident separatism was all too easily breached. The authorities were probably right to regard the household as a crucible in which gathered churches were forged, though how far this incipient congregationalism was intentional and how far it was a case of 'rudderless drift' out of the expansive embrace of the Church of England remains very debatable.[57] It is striking that some discussions of the godly family emphasized that the visibly profane and unregenerate should be ejected from its presence. Edwin Sandys found support for excising incorrigible members in Psalm 101, declaring 'it is dangerous for any man to nourish serpents in his bosom', and Daniel Cawdrey also recommended barring 'wicked Companions' from the houses of the godly. The late seventeenth-century minister of a London dissenting congregation Samuel Slater urged householders to admit none into their midst 'but those who will keep you company while walking with God': 'let Birds of a Feather get together, what have Birds of Paradise to do with Vultures and Owls'.[58] Others, though, insisted that excommunicating such Corinthians from a private congregation was not permissible and that the intermingling of the wheat and the chaff within the home, as well as within the Church, was God's will.[59]

However, the potential for the pious Protestant household to undercut parochial structures should not be exaggerated. In 1647,

---

[56]   F. G. Emmison, *Elizabethan Life: Morals & the Church Courts; Mainly from Essex Archidiaconal Records* (Chelmsford, 1973), 99.

[57]   The phrase is Patrick Collinson's: 'The English Conventicle', in W. J. Sheils and Diana Wood, eds, *Voluntary Religion*, SCH 23 (Oxford, 1986), 223–59, at 277. Collinson emphasizes that the shift into separation of many conventicles was 'without deliberate intent, indeed directly contrary to intention, and principle'.

[58]   Edwin Sandys, *Sermons*, PS (Cambridge, 1842), 270; Cawdrey, *Family reformation promoted*, 57; Slater, *Earnest call*, 310–11.

[59]   Griffith, *Bethel*, 411; see also 392.

the Scottish General Assembly's Directions concerning 'secret and private worship' censured those who neglected family worship but simultaneously reproved those who withdrew from official services into a domestic world of their own. While in times of 'corruption or trouble' this might be tolerable and even quite commendable, 'when God hath blessed us with Peace and the purity of the Gospel' it was not acceptable.[60] Writing in 1655, Philip Goodwin described 'public and private duties' as 'the two legs of a Christian'; 'if he be crippled on one, he will never go well on the other': both were necessary for the health of the visible Church upon earth.[61] The charitable assumption that every member of society was numbered among the remnant of the elect remained a seductive ideal. It coexisted uneasily with the competing instinct of the self-styled saints to quarantine themselves from the promiscuous multitude in the safe haven of their families and to confine their devotions to the sacred space of their homes.

Unease about household meetings had a long history and drew on ancient stereotypes of heretical deviance that can be traced back to the era of the medieval crusades against Cathars and Waldensians. Especially when such meetings took place under cover of night they were entangled with suspicions about unseemly sexual shenanigans.[62] Echoes of these older images persisted in the early modern period and informed drives against the Lollards, early evangelicals, Anabaptists, Brownists and other sects. It was natural for those driven from open places by persecution to retreat to the relative safety and obscurity of private residences. This was the habitual domain of the 'schools' of Wycliffite heresy kept by figures like Hawisia Moore of Norfolk, who admitted in August 1430 that she had been 'right hoomly and prive' with many heretics

---

[60] *Directions of the General Assembly concerning secret and private worship, and mutual edification* (Edinburgh, 1647), 8; see also Thomas Paget, *A demonstration of family-duties* (London, 1643).

[61] Philip Goodwin, *Religio domestica rediviva: or, family-religion revived* (London, 1655), 115–16.

[62] On the demonization of heretics as sexual deviants, see Jeffrey Richards, *Sex, Dissidence and Damnation: Minority Groups in the Middle Ages* (London, 1994), 57–63. On the link between Cathar activity and the household and family, see Emmanuel Le Roy Ladurie, *Montaillou: Cathars and Catholics in a French Village 1294–1324*, transl. Barbara Bray (Harmondsworth, 1978), 24–30; Malcolm Lambert, *Medieval Heresy: Popular Movements from the Gregorian Reform to the Reformation* (Oxford, 1992 edn), 112–13.

and 'receyved and herberwed [them] in our hous'. Lollardy was a family-centred movement, which frequently spread through the connections of dependency and kin.[63]

The home was likewise the haven into which underground congregations of Freewillers and Protestants retreated during the 1550s.[64] A sense of the affinity with the house churches of apostolic times infuses the language of the letters of the Marian martyrs: Nicholas Ridley farewelled his followers as 'the very household and family of God' just before he went to his death in Oxford in 1555 and John Bradford addressed his congregation as 'his good brethren'.[65] It was also in parlours and chambers that the mysterious disciples of the Dutch mystic H. N. met in East Anglian villages such as Balsham in Cambridgeshire in the mid-Elizabethan period for spiritual sustenance and sociability. A surviving Familist broadside printed in 1575 includes blessings and graces for use at meal times and depicts an affluent family seated around a table (Fig. 4).[66] The very title by which this cryptic sect styled itself – the Family of Love – cemented the negative connection between the household and heresy, as did their convention of greeting each other as brothers and sisters in Christ. With sarcasm thick enough to cut with a knife, fierce critics of these 'monstrous and horrible' heretics like William Wilkinson warned of the 'poyson which dayly floweth from our Lovely Familie'. John Knewstub called it 'the householde of Selfelove'.[67] Similar metaphors shaped the

---

[63] On Hawisia Moore, see Norman Tanner, ed., *Heresy Trials in the Diocese of Norwich, 1428–31*, Camden 4th ser. 20 (London, 1977), 140. For other examples, see Shannon McSheffrey and Norman Tanner, eds, *Lollards of Coventry 1486–1522*, Camden 5th ser. 23 (Cambridge, 2003), 35–6, 102–4, 107, 119, 123, 126, 129, 148–9, 208–9, 212–13. For discussions, see Ann Hudson, *The Premature Reformation: Wycliffite Texts and Lollard History* (Oxford, 1988), 134–7, 175–6, 183, 450; Shannon McSheffrey, *Gender and Heresy: Men and Women in Lollard Communities 1420–1530* (Philadelphia, PA, 1995), ch. 4.

[64] J. W. Martin, 'Tudor Popular Religion: The Rise of the Conventicle', in idem, *Religious Radicals in Tudor England* (London and Ronceverte, 1989), 13–39; Patrick Collinson, 'Night Schools, Conventicles and Churches: Continuities and Discontinuities in Early Protestant Ecclesiology', in Peter Marshall and Alec Ryrie, eds, *The Beginnings of English Protestantism* (Cambridge, 2002), 209–35.

[65] Foxe, *Actes and Monuments*, 1801, 1655.

[66] H. N., *A benedicitie or blessinge to be saide over the table* ([Cologne], 1575); see Christopher Marsh, *The Family of Love in English Society, 1550–1630* (Cambridge, 1994), 89–93.

[67] William Wilkinson, *A confutation of certaine articles, delivered unto the familye of love* (London, 1579), sig. ★3[r] and the Epistle to the Reader; John Knewstub, *A confutation of*

Fig. 4: The Family of Love at home: H. N., *A benedicitie or blessinge to be saide over the table* ([Cologne], 1575). By permission of the Bodleian Library, Oxford, shelfmark Douce. S.Subt. 67 (4).

identity of the early Quakers. In 1677 William Penn addressed a pamphlet to 'the Churches of Jesus Throughout the world', urging them to be 'One Holy Flock, Family and Houshold'.[68] Friends broke their ties with hostile blood relatives only to find new spiritual kin within the Society. In turn their enemies turned the same derogatory vocabulary back against them.[69]

The Restoration renewed concern about the hazy boundary between the family and the illicit conventicle, which was

monstrous and horrible heresies, taught by H. N. and embraced of a number, who call themselves the familie of love (London, 1579), sig. xx5^r. For accounts of household meetings, see the confession of two Familists in 1561, in John Rogers, *The displaying of an horrible secte of grosse and wicked heretiques, naming themselves the familie of love* (London, 1578), sigs I4^v–I5^v.

68 William Penn, *To the churches of Jesus throughout the world. Gathered and settled in his eternal light, power and spirit, to be one holy flock, family and household to the lord, who hath redeemed them from among all the kindreds of the earth* (London, 1677), 2–3.

69 Sheila Wright, '"Truly Dear Hearts": Family and Spirituality in Quaker Women's Writings 1680–1750', in Sylvia Brown, ed., *Women, Gender and Radical Religion in Early Modern Europe* (Leiden, 2007), 97–113.

enshrined in the Clarendon Code. The Acts of 1664 and 1670 defined conventicles as gatherings of more than five people 'over and besides those of the same household' or of a similar number 'where there is no family inhabiting'.[70] But the ironic effect of this legislation was to compel dissent to retreat back into the domestic realm and to foster a spirited resurgence of what conformist and nonconformist writers alike came to define as 'family religion'.[71] Lancashire ministers like Adam Martindale exploited loopholes in the law by dividing their congregations into 'so many parcells' and preaching the same sermon repeatedly (perhaps four or five times a day) in different homes. Thomas Jolly 'fell on the apostolic practice of visiting particular families house by house', and his own at the foot of Pendle Hill was equipped with a purpose-built pulpit that collapsed back into a door and an improvised alarm system to alert those assembled for worship to disperse when pursuivants approached.[72]

Like their puritan forbears, gentlemen such as John Angier organized their own households as if they were 'well disciplin'd armies' and cultivated their daily round of domestic devotion as a badge of distinction and a marker of estrangement from the ecclesiastical establishment.[73] At the same time such practices served to unite moderate dissenters like Richard Baxter with their sympathetic and latitudinarian Anglican neighbours. Baxter's *Catechizing of families* and *Poor man's family book* found a wide readership and functioned both as manuals for humble and wealthy householders and as a makeshift when 'the ministry is defective'.[74] Taking up the text of Joshua 24: 15 ('But as for me and my house, we will serve

[70] 16 Car. II, c. 4; 22 Car. II. c. 1. See also *OED, s.v.* 'conventicle'.

[71] See Gerald R. Cragg, *Puritanism in the Period of the Great Persecution* (Cambridge, 1957), 136–43; Andrew Cambers and Michelle Wolfe, 'Reading, Family Religion, and Evangelical Identity in Late Stuart England', *HistJ* 47 (2004), 875–96.

[72] *The Life of Adam Martindale, Written by Himself, and Now First Printed from the Original Manuscript in the British Museum*, ed. Richard Parkinson, Chetham Society 1st ser. 4 (Manchester, 1855), 173, 176, 194; *The Notebook of the Rev. Thomas Jolly AD 1671–1693. Extracts from the Church Book of Altham and Wymondhouses, AD 1649–1725. And an Account of the Jolly Family of Standish, Gorton, and Altham*, Chetham Society n.s. 33 (Manchester, 1895), xvii, xxi, 63, 133.

[73] *Oliver Heywood's Life of John Angier of Denton, Together with Angier's Diary, and Extracts from his 'An Helpe to Better Hearts': Also Samuel Angier's Diary*, ed. Ernest Axon, Chetham Society n.s. 97 (Manchester, 1937), 84–5, 95.

[74] Richard Baxter, *The poor man's family book* (London, 1674); idem, *The catechizing of families: a teacher of housholders how to teach their households* (London, 1683).

the Lord'), a new wave of handbooks of household government and guides to domestic devotion emerged on both sides of the evolving ecclesiastical divide, including works by William Payne, John Shower, Samuel Slater and the archbishop of Canterbury John Tillotson. Preaching in 1684, Tillotson looked back wistfully to an era before the civil confusions and distractions that had divided the nation in recent decades and prior to the creeping advance of infidelity and atheism, and called for conscientious performance of family religion as a solution to the ills of his 'loose and degenerate Age'.[75] Andrew Cambers and Michelle Wolfe have emphasized the unifying and ecumenical potential of this style of piety in the late seventeenth century, but we should retain a sense of its double-edged quality and its continuing ability to destabilize the status quo.[76]

As the dissenting Lincolnshire minister John Rastrick commented in his memoir on the momentous events of 1688, the Act of Toleration had provided liberty for household gatherings that had hitherto been branded with the brush of schism and treason.[77] It legitimized them, albeit with the proviso that the doors of nonconformist meeting houses were not to be locked. Family religion emerged from the shadows and came out into the open. Simultaneously and somewhat paradoxically, the collapse of the ideal of religious uniformity embodied in the 1689 legislation undermined some of its central pillars and tenets. It did so in the sense that the godly household was a microcosm of the patriarchal Protestant state in which the monarch claimed the right to dictate the religion of his subjects. It was a zone in which husbands, fathers and masters exercised a kind of domestic *cuius regio, eius religio*.[78] Licensed indulgence and coexistence threatened their exclusive control of those over whom they ruled. As early as 1646,

---

[75] See William Payne, *Family religion: or, the duty of taking care of religion in families, and the means of doing it* (London, 1691); Slater, *An earnest call to family-religion*; John Shower, *Family religion in three letters to a friend* (London, 1694); Thomas Bray, *An appendix to the discourse upon the doctrine of our baptismal covenant being a method of family religion* (London, 1699); Tillotson, *Six sermons*, 50, 78–82. T. W., *The godly mans delight or a family guide to pietie* (London, 1679), is a treatise in the vein of Bayly's *Practice of pietie*.

[76] Cambers and Wolfe, 'Reading, Family Religion, and Evangelical Identity'.

[77] Cited ibid. 876, from San Marino, CA, Henry E. Huntington Library, MS HM 6131, fol. 55ᵛ, printed in *The Life of John Rastrick, 1650–1727*, ed. Andrew Cambers, Camden 5th ser. 36 (Cambridge, 2010), 128.

[78] As noted by Morgan, *Godly Learning*, 143.

the presbyterian Thomas Edwards recognized this as a serious threat to male parental authority, saying that if toleration were granted householders would never have 'peace' within their walls. Daniel Cawdrey's *Family reformation promoted* (1656) was likewise clear that this would be a cause of endless rifts and irrevocable divisions within families. It served to discover the iniquity of 'that so much cal'd for cursed Toleration of all Religions'. Institutionalized schism would undermine the foundational unit of society from within.[79] This may be one reason why Dissent appears to have become more endogamous in the eighteenth century. Anxious to preserve themselves intact and strengthen their denominational distinctiveness, the Baptists, for instance, fiercely opposed mixed marriages and asserted tight disciplinary control over the next generation. Similar tendencies among other denominational groups can be detected.[80]

Matthew Henry's *A church in the house* (1704) exemplifies the continuing relevance of these ideals in the changed circumstances of post-Revolutionary England. Henry admitted that family churches were not to be set up in competition with 'publick religious Assemblies' and should be 'erected and maintain'd in Subordination to those more Sacred and Solemn Establishments', but he nevertheless saw them as vital nurseries 'in which the Trees of Righteous are rear'd'. Domestic piety was 'the most effectual Antidote against Satan's Poison', for 'where God hath not a Church, the Devil will have his Chapel'.[81] Henry's book is another index of the extent to which the family was implicated in the prolonged and complicated cultural processes that have been called confessionalization.

---

[79] Thomas Edwards, *Gangraena: or A catalogue and discovery of many of the errours, heresies, blasphemies and pernicious practices of the sectaries of this time, vented and acted in England in these four last years* (London, 1646), 156; Cawdrey, *Family reformation promoted*, 26; see also Keith Thomas, 'Women and the Civil War Sects', *P&P*, no. 13 (1958), 42–62, at 52.

[80] See John Caffyn, *Sussex Believers: Baptist Marriage in the Seventeenth and Eighteenth Centuries* (Worthing, 1988).

[81] Matthew Henry, *A church in the house. A sermon concerning family-religion* (London, 1704), 6, 17, 40, 39. For his own exemplary family religion, see *An account of the life and death of the late Reverend Mr Matthew Henry, Minister of the Gospel at Hackney, who died June 22nd, 1714, in the 52d year of his age*, ed. W. Tong (London, 1716), ch. 3, esp. 124. See also David Jones, *A sermon of the absolute necessity of family-duties, preached to the united parishes of St Mary Woolnoth, & St Mary Woolchurch Haw in Lombard Street* (London, 1692); Oliver Heywood, *A family altar erected … A solemne essay to promote the worship of God in private houses* (London, 1693).

★ ★ ★

The third section of this essay traces the function and fortunes of the family and household in post-Reformation Catholicism. Religion had been a domestic affair in medieval Christianity since the very beginning, but there are grounds for thinking that in the late Middle Ages various currents converged to enhance the importance of the home in spiritual life. The friars were one force behind this reorientation towards the household as the locus of Christian formation and behind the growing cult of the Holy Family: Mary, Joseph and Jesus, as well as his grandmother St Anne and grandfather St Joachim (Fig. 5).[82] Another relevant development was humanism, which placed fresh emphasis on the household as the foundation of an orderly state and inspired a revival of treatises of domestic government, notably Leon Battista Alberti's *Della Famiglia* (1434–41).[83] In northern Europe, the diffusion of Erasmian values helped promote a new vogue for private devotion that bore fruit in the exemplary household regimes of Lady Margaret Beaufort and Sir Thomas More.[84] Late medieval mysticism and monasticism also exerted considerable influence, seeping out of the cloister to shape daily practice among the laity. The example of St Catherine of Siena inspired some to make the home a theatre for contemplative practice and texts such as St Bridget of Sweden's *Liber Celestis* reflected a growing tendency to conceptualize the inner life of the Christian conscience and soul as a household itself. Domestic space became an allegory for religious interiority. New experiments in spirituality like the Brethren of the Common Life were themselves quasi-familial organizations.[85] Whitford's *Werke for*

[82] On the cult of the Holy Family, see Miri Rubin, *Mother of God: A History of the Virgin Mary* (London, 2009), 323–31.

[83] Leon Battista Alberti, *The Family in Renaissance Florence. A translation ... of I Libri della Famiglia,* transl. Renée Neu Watkins (Columbia, SC, 1969).

[84] See Malcolm J. Underwood, 'Politics and Piety in the Household of Lady Margaret Beaufort', *JEH* 38 (1987), 39–52.

[85] See Daniel Bornstein, 'Spiritual Kinship and Domestic Devotions', in Judith C. Brown and Robert C. Davis, eds, *Gender and Society in Renaissance Italy* (London and New York, 1998), 173–92; Gabriella Zarri, 'Christian Good Manners: Spiritual and Monastic Rules in the Quattro and Cinquecento', in Letizia Panizza, ed., *Women in Italian Renaissance Culture and Society* (Oxford, 2000), 76–91; Catherine Batt, Denis Renevey and Christiania Whitehead, 'Domesticity and Medieval Devotional Literature', *Leeds Studies in English* n.s. 36 (2005), 195–250, esp. 209, 213, 228, 237; Anneke B. Mulder-Bakker, 'The Household as a Site of Civic and Religious Instruction: Two

Fig. 5: The extended Holy Family: Mary, Christ, Joseph, Anna and Joachim: woodcut by Albrecht Durer (1511). © Trustees of the British Museum. Reference E.3, 108. Image number AN00551033.

Housholders is representative of a burgeoning devotional literature catering for rising lay demand for guidance on domestic piety, in which the brothers of Syon Abbey specialized.[86] The proliferation of primers, paraliturgical texts and material aids to prayer and meditation such as paternoster and rosary beads ran alongside the sanctification of spaces in which they were handled and read.

Household Books from Late Medieval Brabant', and Sarah Rees Jones and Felicity Riddy, 'The Bolton Hours of York: Female Domestic Piety and the Public Sphere', in Anneke B. Mulder-Bakker and Jocelyn Wogan-Browne, eds, *Household, Women, and Christianities in Late Antiquity and the Middle Ages* (Turnhout, 2005), 191–214 and 215–60; Mary C. Erler, 'Home Visits: Mary, Elizabeth, Margery Kempe and the Feast of the Visitation', in Maryanne Kowaleski and P. J. P. Goldberg, eds, *Medieval Domesticity: Home, Housing and Household in Medieval England* (Cambridge, 2008), 259–76.

[86] On Whitford, see, in this volume, Lucy Wooding, 'Richard Whitford's *Werke for Housholders*: Humanism, Monasticism and Tudor Household Piety', 161–73; see also W. A. Pantin, 'Instructions for a Devout and Literate Layman', in *Medieval Learning and Literature: Essays Presented to Richard William Hunt*, ed. J. J. Alexander and M. T. Gibson (Oxford, 1976), 398–422.

Furnished with images and prie-dieux, bedchambers resembled cells. The interior visual environment of the houses of the affluent echoed and replicated that of public ecclesiastical buildings, and many family chapels were commissioned and built in this period.[87] Whether these trends amount to a privatization of piety and signal the retreat of the gentry from the parish has been hotly disputed by Eamon Duffy in particular,[88] but it is hard to ignore the fact that there was some kind of domestic turn within traditional religion in the century before the Reformation.

The Council of Trent has often been seen as marking a shift in the opposite direction. John Bossy's seminal essay on 'The Counter-Reformation and the People of Catholic Europe' (1970) argued that the Tridentine decrees elevated the enforcement of parochial conformity at the expense of family autonomy and endeavoured to curtail the role of the kin group (both natural and artificial) in religious practice. Reacting against Protestantism's attack on celibacy and eager promotion of the home as the nursery of the Church and commonwealth, Bossy suggested, the Catholic hierarchy 'seems to have taken it for granted that household religion was a seed-bed of subversion'. He saw the hostility of the Counter-Reformation Church towards private masses and its efforts to control confraternities and impose restrictions on the choice of godparents as symptomatic of the translation of a communal Christianity into an atomistic and individualistic one.[89] Other initiatives indicative of Tridentine efforts to supervise house-

[87] For some recent contributions of note, see Diana M. Webb, 'Women and Home: The Domestic Setting of Late Medieval Spirituality', in Sheils and Wood, eds, *Women and the Church*, 159–73; eadem, 'Domestic Space and Devotion in the Middle Ages', in Andrew Spicer and Sarah Hamilton, eds, *Defining the Holy: Sacred Space in Medieval and Early Modern Europe* (Aldershot, 2005), 27–47; Ronda Kasl, 'Holy Households: Art and Devotion in Renaissance Venice', in eadem, ed., *Giovanni Bellini and the Art of Devotion* (Indianapolis, IN, 2004), 59–89; Donal Cooper, 'Devotion', in Marta Ajmar-Wollheim and Flora Dennis, eds, *At Home in Renaissance Italy* (London, 2006), 190–203; Margaret A. Morse, 'Creating Sacred Space: The Religious Visual Culture of the Renaissance Venetian *Casa*', *Renaissance Studies* 21 (2007), 151–84. I am grateful to my colleague Mary Laven for discussions about the relative neglect of this topic in the Catholic context.

[88] Eamon Duffy, *The Stripping of the Altars: Traditional Religion in England c.1400 – c.1580* (New Haven, CT, and London, 1991; 2nd edn 2005), 4, 121–3; idem, *Marking the Hours: English People and their Prayers 1240–1570* (New Haven, CT, and London, 2006), 54–5, 97.

[89] John Bossy, 'The Counter-Reformation and the People of Catholic Europe', *P&P*, no. 47 (1970), 51–70, quotation at 68. For the decree against celebration of the

hold devotion more closely include tighter regulation of hallowed objects and rituals that hovered on the boundary between religion and magic and the crackdown on household altars and private oratories led by Carlo Borromeo of Milan.[90]

But it would be wrong to ignore evidence that the growth of ecclesiastical interest in domestic life remained a feature of Catholicism after Trent and that its protagonists participated in a wider reassertion of the importance of patriarchal and parental responsibilities.[91] To the cluster of treatises on the Christian family that emerged from sixteenth- and seventeenth-century Italy and France may be added Peter Canisius's famous catechism, which included forms of daily prayer designed for domestic settings, and other Jesuit publications.[92] However, Marc Forster has concluded from a study of German Catholicism that the family remained ambivalent and problematic, partly because of its link with privacy and secrecy and its association with the Protestant heresy. It was not a very prominent feature of baroque piety until the eighteenth century. He nevertheless acknowledges that in regions like the Netherlands and Britain, where Catholicism was a proscribed minority religion, the incentives to rely more heavily on the household as an alternative venue for devotion and worship were strong.[93]

In the context of England, there is certainly much to suggest that the home played a critical part in sustaining the faith of beleaguered adherents of the Church of Rome and in providing asylum for the missionary priests who supplied them with the spiritual

eucharist in private houses, see *Canons and Decrees of the Council of Trent*, ed. H. J. Schroeder (Rockford, IL, 1978 edn), 151.

[90] See esp. Philip Mattox, 'Domestic Sacral Space in the Florentine Renaissance Palace', *Renaissance Studies* 20 (2006), 658–73; Morse, 'Creating Sacred Space', 174–5.

[91] On the reassertion of patriarchy in the context of Bavarian Catholic state-building, see Ulrike Strasser, *State of Virginity: Gender, Religion and Politics in an Early Modern Catholic State* (Ann Arbor, MI, 2004).

[92] Peter Canisius, *An introduction to the Catholick faith: containing a brief explication of the Christian doctrine: togeather with an easie method to examine the conscience for a general confession: whereunto is added a dailie exercise of deuout prayers* ([Rouen], 1633). Other examples include the discussion of the 4th [5th] commandment in Benedicti's manual for confessors *La somme des pechez* (1584): see Jean-Luis Flandrin, *Families in Former Times: Kinship, Household and Sexuality* (Cambridge, 1979), 118–45, esp. 121. For Italian works, including Giovanni Leonardi's *Institution of a Christian Family* (1591), see Oliver Logan, 'Counter-Reformation Theories of Upbringing in Italy', in Wood, ed., *Church and Childhood*, 275–84.

[93] Marc R. Forster, 'Domestic Devotions and Family Piety in German Catholicism', in *Piety and Family*, ed. Forster and Kaplan, 97–114.

guidance and sacraments that were essential for their souls' health. As in the case of the Moriscos in sixteenth-century Spain and the crypto-Jewish community that settled in Tudor London, the household functioned as an arena in which English Catholics could exercise agency and perform rites and practices that marked out their opposition to official religion, and which became increasingly politicized (and indeed treasonous) over time. It was a crucial site of covert observance and resistance to the state's attempts to eradicate it; 'the nucleus of a closed society that taught its young to oppose the world outside' and a place in which they engaged in 'domestic subversion'.[94] It is telling that when Lord Vaux of Harrowden was presented, with his entire family and retinue of servants, for refusal to attend Protestant services in May 1581, he claimed 'his house to be a parish by itself', a kind of peculiar or proprietary church.[95] The condition of being a hidden and persecuted religion fostered a powerful sense of identification with primitive Christianity as evoked in the Pauline letters and the writings of Eusebius.

The seigneurial households of the Catholic nobility and gentry upon which recusant historians traditionally focused so much attention have sometimes been seen as an environment in which an old-fashioned style of religiosity as 'a set of ingrained observances' was perpetuated despite the decisive religious and cultural changes that were happening around it. Bossy memorably described the regular weekly and seasonal cycle of feast and fast and traditional celebration of rites of passage that prevailed in this climate.[96] But by the early seventeenth century many upper-class homes were, on the contrary, like glasshouses in which a distinctively Counter-Reformation brand of devotion was nurtured like an exotic flower. Overseen by resident chaplains trained in continental seminaries,

[94]   Mary Elizabeth Perry, 'Space of Resistance, Site of Betrayal: Morisco Homes in Sixteenth-Century Spain', in Nicholas Howe, ed., *Home and Homelessness in the Medieval and Renaissance World* (Notre Dame, IN, 2004), 57–90, at 64, 70; Beverly Nenk, 'Public Worship, Private Devotion: The Crypto-Jews of Reformation England', in David Gaimster and Roberta Gilchrist, eds, *The Archaeology of the Reformation 1480–1580* (Leeds, 2003), 204–20. See also Frances E. Dolan, 'Gender and the "Lost" Spaces of Catholicism', *Journal of Interdisciplinary History* 32 (2002), 641–65, esp. 652–8; Lisa McClain, 'Without Church, Cathedral, or Shrine: The Search for Religious Space among Catholics in England, 1559–1625', *SCJ* 33 (2002), 381–99, esp. 383–6.
[95]   Godfrey Anstruther, *Vaux of Harrowden: A Recusant Family* (Newport, 1953), 113.
[96]   John Bossy, 'The Character of Elizabethan Catholicism', *P&P*, no. 21 (1962), 39–59; idem, *The English Catholic Community, 1570–1850* (London, 1975), ch. 6.

they were incubators of a doctrinally self-conscious piety attuned to the stirrings of conscience and inflected by interior moral rigour.[97] Although our knowledge of these households is refracted through the distorting lens of hagiography, other evidence confirms their characteristic features. The picture that William Palmes painted of Dorothy Lawson's house at St Anthony's near Newcastle upon Tyne and Richard Smith of Lady Magdalene Montague's home at Battle in Sussex (known to locals as 'Little Rome') corresponds with what emerges from more hostile sources.[98] The religious regime of the Babthorpe family at Osgodby in the 1620s, which assembled each evening at 9 p.m. for litanies and every Sunday and holy day for sermons, catechisms and spiritual lessons, and regularly confessed and received the eucharist, offers a curious, near-mirror image of the puritan household.[99] It is also, though, quasi-monastic in character: it mimics the devotion of the religious houses closed, abandoned and displaced as a consequence of the Reformation.[100]

As the inventories of books seized in government raids reveal, reading was a no less central dimension of Catholic than Protestant domestic religion. Clerical exiles and missionary priests fed the apparently voracious appetite of laypeople for spiritual literature by translating Spanish, French and Italian classics, including treatises by Luis de Granada and Francis de Sales, and preparing texts of their own. Robert Persons's *Christian Directory* and Robert Southwell's *Short Rule of Good Life*, written for the Countess of Arundel, Anne Dacre, are the best known. The latter contains guidance on the care of children and servants, but there is in general less

---

[97] See my 'Translating Trent? English Catholicism and the Counter Reformation', *HR* 78 (2005), 288–310, esp. 297–9.

[98] William Palmes, *Life of Mrs Dorothy Lawson, of St Anthony's, near Newcastle-up-on-Tyne, in Northumberland*, ed. G. Bourchier Richardson (Newcastle upon Tyne, 1851); *An Elizabethan Recusant House: Comprising the Life of Lady Magdalen Viscountess Montague (1538–1608)*, ed. A. C. Southern (London, 1954). On Battle, see Michael Questier, *Catholicism and Community in Early Modern England: Politics, Aristocratic Patronage and Religion, c.1550–1640* (Cambridge, 2006), ch. 7.

[99] 'Father Pollard's Recollections of the Yorkshire Mission', in John Morris, ed., *The Troubles of our Catholic Forefathers Related by Themselves: Third Series* (London, 1877), 468.

[100] See Susannah Monta, 'Uncommon Prayer? Robert Southwell's *Short Rule for a Good Life* and Catholic Domestic Devotion in post-Reformation England', in Lowell Gallagher, ed., *Redrawing the Map of Early Modern English Catholicism* (Toronto, ON, and Los Angeles, CA, 2012), 244–71, esp. 247–56.

emphasis on communal and more on individual bibliocentric piety than in the reformed tradition.[101] Although Dorothy Lawson read pious books and saints' lives aloud to her chambermaids and male retainers, silent and meditative rather than communal and oratorical reading may have been the predominant mode.[102] Such households also helped to sustain the flourishing market for sacred objects and articles – crucifixes, *agni dei*, medals, rosaries and portable icons – as well as an underground trade in old and new relics. Among the 'superstitious' items that the authorities confiscated from rooms occupied by the Catholic sisters Elizabeth and Bridget Brome in Boarstall House in 1586 were holy grains and a folding case filled with alabaster pictures, together with pieces of mass cake and a paper upon which the name of the Blessed Virgin was painted.[103] Two years earlier the puritan MP Paul Wentworth had found images in silk, parchment and needlework in the home of Lady Isabel Hampden, one of them of Veronica's veil, as well as various beads and pieces of consecrated bread.[104] At Harrowden, a raid during the reign of James I uncovered a huge haul of reliquaries, altarcloths and vestments, some of which had evidently been rescued from churches and dissolved monasteries during the previous century: these included St Stephen's jawbone set in gold and crystal and a hair shirt of St Thomas Becket from Canterbury, along with various embroidered maniples and tunics, and a gilded picture of Ignatius Loyola.[105] The Staffordshire yeoman Henry Hodgetts kept relics of St Chad in his bedhead as his most precious possession.[106] Living in close proximity with sacred artefacts fostered intense private devotion, even as it promoted relationships that sometimes tested the boundary between authorized and unorthodox religious practice.[107]

---

[101] Robert Persons, *A Christian directory guiding me to eternall salvation* (Rouen, 1607; first publ. as *The first booke of the Christian exercise*, 1582); Robert Southwell, *A short rule of good life. To direct the devout Christian in a regular and orderly course* ([English secret press, 1596–7]), chs 8–9.

[102] Palmes, *Life*, 42; see my '"Domme Preachers"? Post-Reformation English Catholicism and the Culture of Print', *P&P*, no. 168 (2000), 72–123, at 108–13.

[103] London, BL, MS Lansdowne 50, no. 76, fol. 164ʳ.

[104] Kew, TNA, SP 12/16/47.

[105] TNA, SP 14/19/72, cited in Anstruther, *Vaux of Harrowden*, 386.

[106] Henry Foley, ed., *Records of the English Province of the Society of Jesus*, 7 vols in 8 (London, 1877–84), 2: 231.

[107] Cf. Kasl, 'Holy Households', esp. 68, 75.

The presence of these hallowed objects in the chambers and homes of zealous recusants augmented the efforts of their owners and occupants to transform domestic structures and spaces into approximations of churches, convents and oratories. Elizabeth Vaux endeavoured to turn Kirby Hall, near Dene in Northamptonshire, into a place where 'we might as nearly as possible conform ourselves to the manner of life followed in [Jesuit] colleges' and one of Dorothy Lawson's models was St Catherine of Siena, who had pursued her spiritual vocation within her father's house.[108] Such Catholics decorated their private rooms and secret chapels in the most sumptuous baroque fashion: one of the houses in which the Jesuit John Gerard worked at the turn of the seventeenth century was equipped with elaborate silver candlesticks, cruet and lavabo bowls, bells and thuribles of 'exquisite workmanship' and a great gold crucifix carved with a pelican and phoenix. At Battle Viscountess Montague erected an altar enclosed with rails and approached by ascending steps, as well as a pulpit and choir stalls.[109] Following the advice of Robert Southwell, others sacralized their residences and made them 'in a manner a paradise' by dedicating each room to a different saint,[110] or (as in the case of Sir Thomas Tresham's Triangular Lodge and Lyveden New Bield) by constructing them in symbolic shapes and adorning them with Christian imagery such as the Holy Name of Jesus.[111] Above all, though, such houses and households were imbued with holiness by the priests who sheltered inside them and were secreted in concealed closets and cupboards built into the fabric of the building.[112] Some thought that their presence provided supernatural

[108] John Gerard, The *Autobiography of an Elizabethan*, transl. and ed. Philip Caraman (London, 1951), 149; Palmes, *Life*, 8; see also Anstruther, *Vaux of Harrowden*, part II, ch. 6, at 240.

[109] Gerard, *Autobiography*, transl. and ed. Caraman, 195; *Elizabethan Recusant House*, ed. Southern, 43. Dorothy Lawson's chapel was vested 'according to the fashion in Catholick countrys': Palmes, *Life*, 38. See also Richard L. Williams, 'Forbidden Sacred Spaces in Reformation England', in Spicer and Hamilton, eds, *Defining the Holy*, 95–114.

[110] Southwell, *Short rule*, 128–33.

[111] See Richard L. Williams, 'Cultures of Dissent: English Catholicism and the Visual Arts', in Benjamin Kaplan et al., eds, *Catholic Communities in Protestant States: Britain and the Netherlands c.1570–1720* (Manchester and New York, 2009), 230–48, at 240–2.

[112] Michael Hodgetts, '*Loca Secretaria* in 1581', *RH* 19 (1989), 386–95; idem, *Secret Hiding Places* (Dublin, 1989); see also Julian Yates, 'Parasitic Geographies: Manifesting

protection from satanic assault: Anne Vaux believed that whenever a priest was in her house the Devil had no power over it.[113] When these missionaries were captured and executed, the places in which they had hidden acquired the aura of reliquaries themselves, receptacles hallowed by their association with men who had now become glorious martyrs in heaven. They were revered as shrines by later generations of Catholics. The house in Brindle where Edward Arrowsmith had habitually said mass was regarded as a sacred memorial to him by the faithful into the nineteenth century and although the thatched cottage in which Nicholas Postgate lived in Ugthorpe on the Yorkshire moors had been pulled down the site was preserved and his memory cherished.[114]

As on the Protestant side, our inevitable reliance on sources shaped by literary convention and apologetic intention means that the Catholic households they depict can appear to be oases of order and calm. The individuals who comprise them are cardboard cut-out figures who adhere closely to contemporary ideals and expectations of behaviour appropriate to particular stations in life. Once again, though, more careful scrutiny reveals some interesting ripples beneath the surface. It is clear that Catholicism caused ruptures within families as well as between them, and that duty to God could trump the deference owed by wives and children to their husbands and fathers. Bill Sheils's careful study of Yorkshire records has shown that only a minority of recorded Jacobean recusants were members of households containing other Catholic dissenters, while Lucy Underwood's work on the *Responsa Scholarum* and *Liber Primi Examinis* of the English colleges at Rome and Valladolid underlines how often, at least until the mid-seventeenth century, the youths admitted to them were converts, the offspring of parents who remained immersed in the errors of 'schism' or 'heresy'.[115] Embarrassed by their lax practice of Catholicism and/

Catholic Identity in Early Modern England', in Arthur Marotti, ed., *Catholicism and Anti-Catholicism in Early Modern English Texts* (New York, 1999), 63–84.

[113] Clitheroe, Lancashire, Stonyhurst MSS, Anglia A. I. 73; ET in Anstruther, *Vaux of Harrowden*, 189.

[114] Bede Camm, *Forgotten Shrines: An Account of Some Old Catholic Halls and Families in England and of Relics and Memorials of the English Martyrs* (London, 1936), 188, 291.

[115] Bill Sheils, 'Household, Age and Gender among Jacobean Yorkshire Recusants', in Marie B. Rowlands, ed., *Catholics of Parish and Town 1558–1778*, CRS Monograph Series 5 (London, 1999), 131–52, at 137–8; Lucy Underwood, 'Youth, Religious Iden-

or lazy compliance with Protestantism, some did not disdain to reprove their elders, or, like the Welsh Benedictine Augustine Baker, censure them as mere 'neutrals in religion' in memoirs written after their deaths.[116]

The York butcher's wife Margaret Clitherow is the most celebrated example of a woman whose devotion to the Church of Rome led her to break out of the conventional mould prescribed by patriarchy, and to harbour priests in her home, although her pious disobedience was itself in part a construct of her confessor John Mush.[117] More subtle was the strategy of Dorothy Lawson, who 'cloak[ed] the matter' of her monthly confession to a priest 'for her husband's satisfaction' by taking herself away 'as if shee had wanted the conveniencys at home'.[118] The notion that husbands had no authority over the souls of their wives, who should defer in such matters to their 'heavenly spouse', was explicitly articulated in Henry Garnet's 1593 *Treatise of Christian Renunciation*, which encouraged married women to mutiny when they were commanded to commit the sin of 'spiritual fornication' and attend Protestant churches. It also declared to Catholic youngsters that if their earthly fathers sought to sever them from their 'everlasting father', then they were justified in being insubordinate. 'Better it is for you by your owne perseverance to turne away Gods wrath from your family, least he punish it for your parents faultes in you and your children to the fourth generation, than by yeelding to your Parents iniquity, you damne your selves & increase their torments'.[119] The response of one set of clerical casuists who responded to a query about whether was it lawful for wives, children or servants to assist their husbands, fathers and masters in heretical activities (such as preparing meat for them on fast days

---

tity, and Autobiography at the English Colleges in Rome and Valladolid, 1592–1685', *HistJ* 55 (2012), 349–74.

[116] *Memorials of Father Augustine Baker and Other Documents Relating to the English Benedictines*, ed. J. McCann and H. Connolly, CRS 33 (Leeds, 1933), 16.

[117] Peter Lake and Michael Questier, 'Margaret Clitherow, Catholic Nonconformity, Martyrology and the Politics of Religious Change in Elizabethan England', *P&P*, no. 185 (2004), 43–90; eidem, *The Trials of Margaret Clitherow: Persecution, Martyrdom and the Politics of Sanctity in Elizabethan England* (London, 2011), ch. 3.

[118] Palmes, *Life*, 17.

[119] Henry Garnet, *A treatise of Christian renunciation … wherin is shewed how farre it is lawfull or necessary for the love of Christ to forsake Father, Mother, wife and children, and all other worldly creatures* ([London, 1593]), 144–8.

or buying Protestant books) was slippery: they thought that this was allowable 'because of their subjection to their superiors', in whose sins they could not said to cooperate. They admitted that this might cause children to fall from the faith, but they stopped short of recommending outright revolt. William Allen and Robert Persons were stricter: they said that it would 'be much better if they refused to do this sort of service'.[120] The circumstances in which Catholics found themselves could legitimize ignoring the obligations created by the age and gender hierarchies.

This is one of the reasons why post-Reformation Catholicism, at least in its first few generations, has sometimes been described as a matriarchy.[121] This impression has been fostered by the stories of heroic priest-harbourers like Jane Wiseman, Anne Line and Margaret Ward, who were convicted and (in the latter two cases) executed for this crime, and by the notion, embedded in lauda-tory biographies, that many Catholic women were more zealous than their husbands. The high incidence of female recusants with church-papist husbands provoked the concern of Protestants, who discussed various ways of compelling men to bring their unruly wives into line and generally gave short shrift to their excuse that they were unable to coerce them. Whether we should regard this phenomenon as evidence of a surrender of male initiative or alternatively as 'a natural (and mutually agreed) division of labour in the management of dissent' remains a moot point.[122] Both possibilities must be kept in the frame. Reconciling the need to preserve the financial health of the family as well as its spir-itual integrity required a flexible approach to established structures of authority. As Laurence Lux-Sterritt has remarked, 'expediency replaced customary gendered specialization'. The condition of being a Church under the cross effected a shift in the balance of power within Catholic households and gave the 'weaker sex'

---

[120] P. J. Holmes, ed., *Elizabethan Casuistry*, CRS 67 (London, 1981), 119.

[121] Bossy, *English Catholic Community*, 153, and see 150–60.

[122] Alexandra Walsham, *Church Papists: Catholicism, Conformity and Confessional Polemic in Early Modern England* (Woodbridge, 1993), 80–1; see also Marie B. Rowlands, 'Recusant Women 1560–1640', in Mary Prior, ed., *Women in English Society 1500–1800* (London and New York, 1985), 149–80; eadem, 'Harbourers and Housekeepers: Cath-olic Women in England 1570–1720', in Kaplan et al., eds, *Catholic Communities in Protestant States,* 200–15. For one family with a church-papist head, see P. R. P. Knell, 'A Seventeenth Century Schismatic and his Catholic Family', *London Recusant* 1 (1971), 57–70.

more autonomy, ironically partly as a consequence of that fact that married women had no public role or legal status apart from their husbands. It also facilitated the precocious emergence in England of models of female sanctity that emphasized apostolic involvement above contemplative virtues.[123]

Paralleling the close relationships between godly ladies and puritan ministers, the 'ambiguous liaisons' that developed between Catholic gentlewomen and priests also had the capacity to cause discord within the family and interfere with male prerogative. Ultimately derived from St Paul's warnings in 1 Timothy 3: 6 about those who crept into houses and led astray 'silly women laden with sins … with divers lusts', the accusations of sexual impropriety that crystallized around figures like Margaret Clitherow and John Mush are indicative of these simmering anxieties. Although most claims of this kind were probably no more than malicious gossip, such alliances clearly could amount to a kind of 'spiritual cuckoldry'.[124] One case from John Gerard's autobiographical memoir is especially revealing: the story of the conversion of the future Gunpowder Plotter Sir Everard Digby, whose wife embraced Catholicism before her husband and conspired with the Jesuit about the best way to catch him 'in St Peter's net'.[125] The rule of patriarchy was evidently temporarily compromised in this household.

On the other hand, the very fact that the missionaries were so utterly dependent on the wealthy laity for patronage, as well as security and safety, must have sometimes unsettled their status as a superior caste of intermediaries to whom their 'spiritual children' owed deference. What Tom McCoog calls 'the suffocating embrace of the gentry' held the potential to undermine sacerdotal control of religious observance within the family.[126] Priests' sense of obligation to their hosts probably made it more difficult for them to

---

[123] Laurence Lux-Sterritt, '"Virgo becomes Virago": Women in the Accounts of Seventeenth-Century English Catholic Missionaries', *RH* 30 (2011), 537–53, at 538.

[124] Colleen M. Seguin, 'Ambiguous Liaisons: Catholic Women's Relationships with their Confessors in Early Modern England', *ARG* 95 (2004), 156–85. These themes have been further developed by Emma McAlister-Hall in her 2011 Cambridge M.Phil. dissertation, 'Female Harbourers and Helpers in Post-Reformation English Catholicism 1570-1630'.

[125] Gerard, *Autobiography*, 166.

[126] T. M. McCoog, '"Sparrows on a Rooftop": "How we Live where we Live" in Elizabethan England', in *Spirit, Style, Story: Essays honoring John W. Padburg*, ed. T. M. Lucas (Chicago, IL, 2002), 237–64, at 255.

reform habits that did not match with Tridentine priorities: it is possible to detect more than a little tension in Richard Smith's chapter about Viscountess Montagu's humility and 'prompt obedience' to her confessor's will in the matter of her over-rigorous fasting.[127] If in some instances it facilitated tight discipline, in others it must have inhibited missionaries from placing too much pressure on men and women in whose manor and townhouses they were guests and who risked their lives to succour them.

Lower down the social scale, in households that had only intermittent access to priests, people perhaps had scope for greater independence. In the absence of the clergy they had little choice but to take on the roles of catechizing, proselytizing, conducting prayers and reading from devotional books, in a manner more than faintly reminiscent of the Protestant paterfamilias and his pious female helpmeet. They also domesticated liturgical rituals that had been expelled from their parish churches, such as creeping to the cross during Easter week.[128] Furthermore, as Anne Dillon has shown, the family was the critical forum in which sodalities of the rosary emerged. Providing the promise of posthumous help for the dead lingering in purgatory as well as the living, these confraternities effectively turned the home itself into a chantry.[129]

The experience of living in Protestant England, then, promoted a marriage of convenience between Catholicism and the household. It encouraged adherents of the Church of Rome and the priests who served them to enter into alliance with an institution about which the Counter-Reformation felt at best indifference and in some instances real ambivalence. And this development was a source of anxiety to the government, which systematically handed out warrants to officials of the High Commission and Justices of the Peace to enter the homes of its 'popish' subjects in search of prohibited books, papal bulls, scandalous libels and apparatus for performing mass.[130] In a period in which the family was regarded as a realm in which the ecclesiastical and political estab-

---

[127] *Elizabethan Recusant House*, ed. Southern, 37–8.

[128] McLain cites an example from Golborne, Lancashire, where this rite was performed in a private home in 1604: 'Without Church, Cathedral or Shrine', 381.

[129] Anne Dillon, 'Praying by Number: The Confraternity of the Rosary and the English Catholic Community, *c*.1580–1700', *History* 88 (2003), 451–71, esp. 468.

[130] See, for example, Huntington Library, Stowe Temple Religious Papers, folder 5, warrant dated 13 June 1616.

lishment could justifiably intervene in the interests of upholding morality and maintaining social and political order, the idea of fining husbands for failing to discipline their wives and forcibly removing children from their parents for Protestant re-education was entirely defensible.[131] William Chaderton, bishop of Chester, and Henry Stanley, earl of Derby, actively employed the latter technique in the north-west in the 1580s. But new work on the Court of Wards demonstrates that the authorities were generally more reluctant to implement this practice than has been imagined.[132] Revisions to the anti-Catholic bill of 1593, which would have taken the young into official care at the age of seven and imposed punitive penalties on men married to recalcitrant recusants, reveal that the House of Commons was not eager to intrude too far into the domain of the family.[133] The boundaries between public and private were in the process of being relocated.

This may signal a subtle but significant shift in attitudes that found clearest expression in the context of the Netherlands. Here, clandestine Catholic churches like Our Lord in the Attic sheltered behind the architectural façade of Amsterdam townhouses. Their presence was 'an open secret' in which the nominally Calvinist state colluded. The discreet and invisible worship of minorities in such *schuilkerken* allowed contemporaries to turn a blind eye to religious opinions and practices of which they disapproved. It relied on a 'fiction of privacy' by which the family house was regarded as a zone in which freedom of conscience could be exercised. Involving what Ben Kaplan calls a 'fundamental remapping of social space', it is an important moment in the history of toleration.[134] Across the Channel, these arrangements were slower to develop and more informal. But despite the spasmodic raids on

---

[131] See Janay Nugent, '"None Must Meddle Betueene Man and Wife": Assessing Family and Fluidity of Public and Private in Early Modern Scotland', *JFH* 35 (2010), 219–31.

[132] Lucy Underwood, 'Childhood, Youth and Catholicism in England, *c.*1558–1660' (Ph.D. thesis, University of Cambridge, 2012), part II.

[133] John Neale, *Queen Elizabeth and her Parliaments*, 2 vols (London, 1957), 2: 281, 293–4, 297; Bossy, *English Catholic Community*, 155–7; Rowlands, 'Recusant Women', 154–5. The act is 35 Eliz. c. 2.

[134] Benjamin J. Kaplan, 'Fictions of Privacy: House Chapels and the Spatial Accommodation of Religious Dissent in Early Modern Europe', *AHR* 107 (2002), 1031–64, at 1062; see also his 'Diplomacy and Domestic Devotion: Embassy Chapels and the Toleration of Religious Dissent in Early Modern Europe', *JEMH* 6 (2002), 241–61.

known recusant residences that accompanied moments of Jacobite crisis, they were tacitly in place in England too by the eighteenth century. If the household was one of the sources of the problem of religious pluralism unleashed by the English Reformation, paradoxically, eventually it also became part of the solution to it.

★ ★ ★

In conclusion, the relationship between religion and the household during the religious revolutions of the sixteenth and seventeenth centuries was a peculiar mixture of tension and intimacy. Contemporaries on both sides of the theological divide regarded the home as an emblem and bastion of the Church and state, but they also recognized and exploited it as a site of subversion, resistance and dissent. This essay has analysed the sometimes fractious internal family dynamics to which the Reformation gave rise and highlighted some unexpected parallels between Protestant and Catholic domestic practice and experience. Even as it played a key role in inculcating religious uniformity, the household simultaneously fostered fragmentation and facilitated the accommodation of diversity. The spiritualization of the household was a process that operated both at the level of individuals and of the buildings and spaces which they inhabited. It stimulated the creation of a series of confessionally and denominationally distinctive holy families; but it also gave rise to families divided by the different faiths to which their members self-consciously adhered.

University of Cambridge

RICHARD WHITFORD'S *WERKE FOR HOUSHOLDERS*: HUMANISM, MONASTICISM AND TUDOR HOUSEHOLD PIETY

by LUCY WOODING

In 1530 Richard Whitford published *A Werke for Housholders*, for 'them that have gydyng and governaunce of any company | for an order to be kepte bothe in them selfe | and in them that they have in rule and charge'.[1] The work swiftly went through at least seven editions in as many years; Tudor householders clearly found something of value in its advice. Its author was many things: a Bridgettine monk, a humanist, a prolific author of works in the vernacular, and a survivor who went on writing and publishing even after the dissolution of his monastery.[2] He died in 1543. His books provide some important insights into vernacular humanism and late medieval monasticism, and the often unappreciated relationship between the two, which was demonstrated by his reflections on household piety. This essay argues that Whitford's *Werke for Housholders* was rooted in his monastic experience, closely linked to Syon's pastoral role, and that ideas about the early modern 'godly household' should perhaps be adjusted in the light of this connection.

Whitford's humanism and his monastic vocation might initially appear distinct, but they were two sides of the same coin. He joined the monastery at Syon as a humanist scholar with an established reputation, having achieved academic distinction in Cambridge and Paris in the 1490s and secured the patronage of Lord Mountjoy and Bishop Richard Fox and the friendship of Erasmus. When he entered the Bridgettine house in 1511 he brought with him a substantial collection of books for its library. Whitford was no Greek scholar, but his learning was much

---

[1] Richard Whitford, *A Werke for Housholders* (London, 1530), sig. Ai^v.
[2] See *ODNB*; P. Cunich, 'The Brothers of Syon, 1420–1695', in E. A. Jones and Alexandra Walsham, eds, *Syon Abbey and its Books: Reading, Writing and Religion, c.1400–1700* (Woodbridge, 2010), 39–81; A. Hutchison, 'Richard Whitford's *The Pype, or Tonne, of the Lyfe of Perfection*: Pastoral Care, or Political Manifesto?', in *Saint Birgitta, Syon and Vadstena: Papers from a Symposium in Stockholm, 4–6 October 2007*, ed. Claes Gejrot, Sara Risberg and Mia Akestam (Stockholm, 2010), 89–103.

respected. In 1506 Erasmus dedicated his translation of Lucian's *Pro tyrannicida* to Whitford, and when both Erasmus and More had published responses to the work, Erasmus wrote to Whitford and told him 'to compare … with More's, and in this way judge if there be any difference in style', ending with characteristically extravagant fondness, 'as you love both of them equally, so you in turn are equally beloved of them both'.[3]

For Whitford, the monastic life was clearly a logical progression from an academic and clerical career as a humanist, which in itself questions the common assumption that humanism was a 'progressive' option by comparison with monasticism seen as a medieval remnant. The order he joined was a fairly new one: the first professions at Vadstena in Sweden had been in 1384, since when the order had expanded rapidly across Europe. It was also a royal order; its foundation in England was a crucial part of Henry V's self-fashioning and it was positioned across the river from the royal house at Sheen, which Henry VII would transform into Richmond Palace.[4] Established at Syon, Whitford developed a career as a translator and writer, a key contributor to the extraordinary literary output of the abbey in the early years of the sixteenth century, in which *A Werke for Housholders* was perhaps the most significant and certainly the most famous work.[5]

Whitford's book was a response to a growing awareness in late medieval society that religious guidance was needed for the secular household, an awareness which saw the production of vernacular texts across Europe, reaching as far as fifteenth-century Novgorod and the *Domostroy*.[6] Whitford's work was written in simple, direct

---

[3]   Erasmus, Letter 191, in *The Correspondence of Erasmus, Letters 142 to 297 (1501–1514)*, ed. R. A. B. Mynors and D. F. S. Thomson, Collected Works of Erasmus 2 (Toronto, ON, 1975), 113.

[4]   R. Ellis, 'Further Thoughts on the Spirituality of Syon Abbey', in W. F. Pollard and R. Boenig, eds, *Mysticism and Spirituality in Medieval England* (Cambridge, 1997), 219–43, at 219; T. Martyn, 'The History of Syon Abbey', in *Saint Birgitta, Syon and Vadstena*, ed. Gejrot, Risberg and Akestam, 9–26, at 13.

[5]   J. T. Rhodes, 'Syon Abbey and its Religious Publications in the Sixteenth Century', *JEH* 44 (1993), 11–25; C. A. Grisé, '"Moche profitable unto religious persones, gathered by a brother of Syon": Syon Abbey and English Books', in Jones and Walsham, eds, *Syon Abbey and its Books*, 129–54; S. Powell, 'Syon Abbey as a Centre for Text Production', in *Saint Birgitta, Syon and Vadstena*, ed. Gejrot, Risberg and Akestam, 50–70.

[6]   C. J. Pouncy, *The 'Domostroi': Rules for Russian Households in the Time of Ivan the Terrible* (Ithaca, NY, 1994).

prose and was clearly meant to have a broad appeal: it began with the brisk and socially levelling observation that 'all we bene mortall | as well the rych as the poore | the yong as the old | there is no dyfference | none excepte all muste nedes dye'.[7] With this in mind, he recommended a life of hard work and scrupulous morality, as if adapting monastic discipline for the laity. He exhorted his readers to begin each day with prayer, and provided them with the words to dedicate themselves to God. He then expected them to keep busy: 'Let therfore your sayde appoynted occupacion be alwaye good: vertuouse and profytable'.[8] At the end of the day, prayers before bed should involve a strict reckoning of the day's occupations:

> wheder ye wente and what ye dyd … in what company ye were | and what was there youre behavioure and demeanoure | in werke | worde | or thought | and so go forth unto every place | tyme and company as brekefaste | dyner | souper | or drynkyng | and where you fynde or perceyve any thyng that was good | vertuous | and profytable | ascribe and apply that unto oure lorde god | and gyve unto him all the glory | laude and praise therof | for he alone is the gyver of all goodness …[9]

Whitford saw the obligations of the householder as extending to servants and neighbours, and encouraged him to gather these people together on the Sabbath and teach them their Paternoster, Ave and Creed. The work contained a breakdown of each verse of these texts, given in both Latin and English, with an explanation; essentially providing the householder with a basic catechism to use with his dependants. It then went on to do the same with the Ten Commandments, the 'vii princypall synnes' and the five senses.

Whitford's household manual is remarkably readable, and humane. It made no assumptions of knowledge, even giving instructions how to make the sign of the cross 'with your thombe upon your foreheed or front'.[10] It provided a form of words for confession, observing: 'I have knowen many come into confessyon

---

7 Whitford, *Werke for Housholders*, sig. Aii[r].
8 Ibid., sig. Avi[r].
9 Ibid., sig Avi[v].
10 Ibid., sig. Aiii[r].

| that coude nat tell howe to do | or what to saye there'.[11] It dealt shrewdly and kindly with the task of instructing those too old and ashamed to confess their ignorance: 'many that ben aged and can nat say | wyll be abasshed to lerne it openly | and yet if they here it dayly redde after the maner shewed before: they shall by use and custome lerne it very well'.[12] Whitford was also understanding about those too embarrassed to say prayers in front of their bedfellows, appreciating the crowded sleeping conditions of the average sixteenth-century household. He showed particular concern too for children, who were to be taught to pray as soon as they were able to speak, and given moral instruction, probably by the mother, he thought. Discipline was important, but he gave careful instructions:

> let it be done with the charite of our lorde | and with a mylde and softe spirite: that ever it be done for the reformacion of the persone | rather than for the revengyng of the defaute | and therfore shulde you never do any maner of correction whyle you ben vexed | chafed | troubled | wroth | or angry for any cause …[13]

The more high-minded aspects of the book are combined with the popular touch which Whitford displayed in all his published works. He took a particularly firm line on swearing, for example, arguing that the godly householder should no more countenance a blasphemer in his house than he would a leper, and following this up with some fabulous gory stories about what happened to those who swore habitually. One gentleman, who Whitford claimed as 'a friend of a friend', was accustomed to swear 'by God's blood', and suffered a nosebleed in a tavern which rapidly escalated,

> tyll at the last he fell ferther to blede at the eares | at the eyes | at his wrestes | and all the ioyntes of his handes and of all his body… and at other places … shotynge out his tonge in a mervaylous horrible | ugsome and ferefull maner … so that no persone durste come nere him | but stode a farre of | and cast holy water towarde hym.[14]

---

[11] Ibid., sig. Eii[r].
[12] Ibid., sig. Bvi[v].
[13] Ibid., sig. Cvii[v].
[14] Ibid., sig. Ciii[v].

Touches like this made the work both entertaining and unforgettable: these kinds of stories would retain their appeal throughout the sixteenth century, reappearing in later Protestant providentialist works.[15]

At the same time, Whitford's work was also very biblical, with Scripture citations in the margin, and Bible quotations given in both Latin and English; when he wanted to add weight to a point he frequently commented that it was 'the very text and letter of the holy scripture'.[16] He told his householder to know where everyone under his care was on a Sunday, in case there was a chance of a sermon. 'For if there be a sermon any tyme of the daye | let them be there presente all that ben nat occupied in nedefull and lawfull busynes', concluding, remarkably, 'let them ever kepe the preachynges | rather than the masse | if (by case) they may nat here both'.[17]

Sabbath observance was particularly important: after diligent church attendance in the morning, Whitford warned his household to be particularly careful with his charges in the afternoon,

> that in no wyse they use suche vanities as communely ben used | that is to say | berebaytyng and bulbaytyng | foteball | tenesplayng | bowlynge | nor these unlawfull games of cardyng | dycyng … with suche other unthryfty pastymes | or rather losetymes. Wherin (for a suerty) the holy day may rather be broken | than if they wente to the plough or carte upon Ester day | so it were nat done by contempte or dispisyng of the commaundement of the lawe | ne for unreasonable covetyse and love of worldly goodes. For synne doth alway more defoule and breke the holy daye than doth any bodyly werke or occupacion.[18]

These key features of Whitford's work – regular prayer, hard work, the avoidance of dissipation, attendance at sermons, the ordering, education and disciplining of children, servants and neighbours – may all sound strangely familiar. It has been pointed out before that Whitford's godly household was in all essentials

[15] Alexandra Walsham, *Providence in Early Modern England* (Oxford, 1999), 79–80.
[16] Lucy Wooding, *Rethinking Catholicism in Reformation England* (Oxford, 2000), 32.
[17] Whitford, *Werke for Housholders*, sig. Dii[v].
[18] Ibid., sig. Dii[r].

anticipating the puritan households of the post-Reformation period.[19] Rather than see humanism as the precursor of the later movement, however, we could turn the question around and ask how far the puritan 'godly household' was the leftover wreckage after the defeat of late medieval piety. Humanism frequently suffers from being seen as a precursor to Protestantism, but if we examine Whitford's work in its own right what is striking is the intellectual and spiritual rigour which Whitford expected of both his house-holders and of his monastic brothers and sisters, and how this was combined with such a practical and humane approach. His work had qualities which not all its Protestant successors achieved.

Among the many post-Reformation religious texts offering guidance to the householder, there were few as sensible and digest-ible as Whitford's. William Herbert's *Careful Father and Pious Child* of 1648, for example, with its 1,200 questions and answers, and 600 confutations of errors and heresies, all to be learned by heart, might have learnt from Whitford's comparative simplicity of approach.[20] There were of course texts which made a more credible attempt to appeal to the unlearned: William Dickenson's *Milke for babes* of 1628, for example, which suggested that the householder pin the tract to the wall, lest it be swept out with the rubbish.[21] In general, however, the later texts were extremely dense, complicated, forbid-ding works by comparison with Whitford. They were also gloomy. Edward Dering's *Briefe and necessarie catechisme* of 1572 lamented the 'multitude of bookes, full of all synne and abominations' of his time but Whitford wrote in the days when print was perceived to offer more opportunities than dangers.[22] Dering described a church assailed by Satan, who

> hath layd upon it much contempt, many reproches, great povertie, intollerable bondage, so that though the calling be in dede the most precious inheritance under the sun, yet the glory is so darkned unto mortal eyes, that al Nobility is quite

---

[19] Margo Todd, *Christian Humanism and the Puritan Social Order* (Cambridge, 1987), ch. 4; see also H. C. White, *The Tudor Books of Private Devotion* (Madison, WI, 1951), 159, 160.

[20] Ian Green, *The Christian's ABC: Catechisms and Catechizing in England c.1530–1740* (Oxford, 1996), 213.

[21] Ibid. 206–7.

[22] Edward Dering, *A briefe and necessarie catechisme. Verie needefull to bee knowne of all housholders* (London, 1572), sig. Aii[r].

fled from it, the Gentlemen afraid to come unto it, the riche man rather chuseth any other kinde of life …[23]

Whitford wrote with far greater assurance, drawing confidence from the monastic setting in which he worked. Syon was closely involved with the nobility and gentry whom Dering felt the later church had lost; it also had a well-established popular ministry. Rather than look ahead to later puritan developments, we might do better to see the godly household as being derived from the monastic ideals of the pre-Reformation English Church, and in particular, Syon's experience of communicating those ideals to the unlettered nuns and to the laity who flocked to its doors.

Syon was one of the jewels in the crown of late medieval English monasticism, together with the Carthusian house at Sheen on the other bank of the Thames: when, in Shakespeare's *Henry V*, the night before Agincourt, the young king reminds God of the 'two chantries' he has founded in recompense for Richard II's murder, these were the two he meant.[24] Syon was a joint house of sixty nuns and twenty-five monks under the rule of an abbess and it was famed for its learning; the catalogue of its library, begun in 1504 and kept until 1523, included over 1,300 books, including the great humanist editions of the Fathers, Colet's 'Convocation Sermon' (1512), Erasmus's *Paraphrases on the Gospel* (from 1517) and Henry VIII's *Assertio Septem Sacramentorum* (1521).[25] Books were clearly a very important part of the life at Syon: episcopal visitors were instructed to check that the inventory of books was up to date and the books in a good state of repair, that silence was maintained in the library, and that the younger sisters, as part of their respect for their seniors, were 'puttyng to ther handes to helpe them in beryng of hevy bokes'.[26] One of the earliest works to emerge from Syon, *A Ryght Profytable Treatyse* by Thomas Betson, published in

---

[23] Ibid., sigs Aiiii[r], Bij[r–v].

[24] *Henry V*, IV.1: 'I have built | Two chantries, where the sad and solemn priests | Sing still for Richard's soul'.

[25] V. Gillespie, *Syon Abbey* (London, 2001); *Corpus of British Medieval Library Catalogues*, 9 (London, 2001), xlix, liv, lxii. Note, however, that the works were chiefly in Latin, with only one Hebrew and three Greek works.

[26] R. J. Whitwell, 'An Ordinance for Syon Library, 1482', *EHR* 25 (1910), 121–3, at 121.

1500, enjoined its readers always to have a book in their hands, and ended with the parting shot: 'Lerne to kepe your bokes cleane'.[27]

The nuns of Syon were told to bring their books with them when they joined the community; they were allowed unlimited numbers of books for study, and exhorted to read daily.[28] Meanwhile, the monks of Syon had a special responsibility for instructing the nuns in their religion. They were a particularly learned group of men, and were expected to have a certain maturity: significantly, a minimum age of 25 was required to join the order.[29] Their duty towards their sisters next door led to the impressive array of works written in English by the Bridgettine monks which soon found their way into print for a much wider audience. As the translator of *The Myroure of Oure Ladye* wrote with regard to the nuns, 'forasmuche as many of you, though ye can synge and rede, yet ye can not se what the meanynge therof ys: therefore … I have drawen youre legende and all your servyce in to Englyshe', and he went on to say that he had also explained the more difficult part, complaining a bit fretfully meanwhile that 'yt is not lyght for every man to drawe eny longe thyng from latyn into oure Englyshe tongue. For there ys many wordes in Latyn that we have no propre englysshe accordynge therto.'[30] It is clear that Syon's work of translation and religious instruction had a pioneering flavour to it. The move from writing for the nuns to publishing for a far wider readership seems to have been an easy development.

Whitford used his vernacular writings to disseminate the lessons of the monastic life and the *Werke for Housholders* was groundbreaking in being aimed specifically at the laity. It drew on some well-established medieval precedents, such as the twelfth-century treatise by Bernard Sylvester which Whitford translated and appended to some editions of the *Werke*, or the fourteenth-century *Epistle on the Mixed Life* by Walter Hilton, a version of which was also published in 1530, as *The Medled Lyfe*. Whitford's work, however, went much further into the practicalities of bridging

---

[27] Gillespie, *Syon Abbey*, xlvii.
[28] D. H. Green, *Women Readers in the Middle Ages* (Cambridge, 2007), 83, 144.
[29] Cunich, 'Brothers of Syon', 45.
[30] *The Myroure of Oure Ladye*, ed. J. H. Blunt, EETS extra ser. 19 (Oxford, 1873), 3, 7.

the gulf between the religious and secular life. The discussion of morning and evening prayers highlighted one possible difficulty:

> But yet some of you wyll saye. Syr | this werke is good for riligious persones | and for suche persones as bene solitary: and done lye alone by them selfe | but we done lye ii or iii sometyme together | and yet in one chambre dyvers beddes and so many in company | if we shulde use these thynges in presence of oure felowes | some wolde laugh us to scorne and mocke us.[31]

Whitford's response to this was austere: true believers should be prepared to suffer. 'And for the pleasure of god our father | and of our swete savyour Jesus our brother | shulde we be abasshed to take daunger and bere a poore mocke or scorne … ?'[32] The laity might need to adapt monastic ideals for their use, but Whitford saw no reason why layfolk should be less rigorous in their devotions.

Whitford's books bear witness to a close network of monastic brethren and pious lay patrons, in which the monastic community already had close links to the domestic households of the devout laity. He explained in a short preface how he had sent the work to a particular friend, who had then showed it to others, who had, he said, 'instantly requyred me | to put it newely forthe in commune'.[33] This seems to have been standard practice for the Syon community, whose works usually circulated in manuscript, prepared for particular friends and acquaintances, before being produced in print. Simon Winter, confessor to the Duchess of Clarence, wrote his *Life of St Jerome* for her, and told her to copy it, lend it to her friends, and encourage them to copy it too. John Fewterer's *Mirror or Glass of Christ's Passion* was written for Lord John Hussey, and Fewterer signed off the dedication to Hussey as 'your dayly oratour'.[34] When in 1537 Whitford published *A Dayly exercyse and experyence of dethe*, he noted in the preface that he had written the work more than twenty years before for Elizabeth Gibbs, the abbess of Syon, and had copied it many times since.

---

[31] Whitford, *Werke for Housholders*, sig. Aviii^r.
[32] Ibid., sig. Aviii^v.
[33] Ibid., preface.
[34] Alexandra da Costa, 'Ryght Profytable Men: The Literary Community of Syon Abbey Brethren 1500–1539' (D.Phil. thesis, Oxford, 2009), 36–9.

'And bycause that wrytynge unto me is very tedyouse: I thought better to put it in print.' It is clear that Syon was connected to many pious individuals both within and outside the abbey, ministering in particular to nobles or gentry who might spend long periods at the abbey, or even retire there. Various wealthy individuals did this, including Margaret Pole, the Countess of Salisbury, who was maintained there between 1504 and 1509 at the expense of Lady Margaret Beaufort. Others visited regularly: Richard Pace, another humanist and Henry VIII's secretary, spent stretches of time there, as did Thomas More.[35] John Browne, an Inner Temple lawyer, served as steward of Syon 1489–95, and paid for an elaborate altarpiece for the abbey.[36] It was the abbey's friends among the laity who gave refuge to six different groups of religious after the Dissolution, ensuring the survival of the community until the present day.[37] On this occasion, monastic community and domestic household would merge.[38]

Both Syon's manuscript and printed works, therefore, were facilitated by the monastery's links with a small, educated, unusually pious elite; in social as well as religious terms, perhaps, the precursors of the post-Reformation puritans. These monastic humanists, however, had a decided advantage over their later puritan brethren, namely that they had connections with those who did not belong in this elite. Their role within the monastery gave them a connection to popular piety, which some later attempts to spread household piety struggled to establish. On the one hand, Whitford and his associates wrote with the confidence that they were supported by a large, prosperous, learned and respected institution. The abbey gave them credibility, and practical assistance such as the use of Syon's famous library, and its connections with the printing press.[39] This later puritans could perhaps duplicate through their relationship with a university college. But, on the other hand, Syon had what Emmanuel College, Cambridge, for instance, could never

[35] Ibid. 63–4.
[36] Martyn, 'History of Syon Abbey', 17–18.
[37] Ibid. 24–6; Cunich, 'Brothers of Syon', 70–1.
[38] See, in this volume, Peter Cunich, 'The Syon Household at Denham, 1539–50', 174–87.
[39] They could use these connections on behalf of others; the Carthusian work *A Pomander of Prayer* (London, 1530) was printed with their assistance and with a preface by a monk of Syon: Rhodes, 'Syon Abbey', 23.

command, namely a huge popular following at its gates, providing valuable experience of instructing the uneducated.

Pilgrims flocked to Syon, which was renowned for its sermons.[40] Sermon-giving had been important from its inception; when Henry V in his will left his religious books to his twin foundations of Sheen and Syon, all the preaching books went to the latter.[41] The rule for Syon instructed that the brethren were 'bounde to expoune iche Sunday the gospel of the same day in the same messe to all herers in ther modir tonge'. It also permitted any brother who was preparing a sermon to be exempted from choir duties for three days while he prepared it.[42] There were also sermons on feast-days; the mother house at Vadstena preached on fifty additional feast-days every year, and it is highly likely that Syon followed the same pattern. Vincent Gillespie has been sceptical about Syon's humanist credentials, commenting that 'reading was generally more Christian than Ciceronian' and observing that by far the largest genre of books in its library was sermons.[43] This is to take too secular a definition of humanism, however, which could be as much concerned with preaching as with the study of the classics in its pursuit of religious regeneration.[44]

All the evidence suggests that Syon's popular ministry was highly successful. Certainly there were confession houses within the compound to cope with the volume of confessions which pilgrims made there; they were deplored by Thomas Bedyll, one of Cromwell's commissioners in the 1530s.[45] Syon also had ways of reaching out to those who might not have had the wit or learning to understand much from its sermons. In 1500 a papal dispensation allowed brothers to bless rosaries for pilgrims, and Syon was known for both its 'pardon beads' (a string of five beads, linked to a special prayer, with a substantial indulgence attached)

---

[40] Cunich, 'Brothers of Syon', 50–1; S. Powell, *Preaching at Syon Abbey*, Literary and Cultural Studies 29 (Salford, 1997).

[41] V. Gillespie, 'Syon and the New Learning', in J. G. Clark, ed., *The Religious Orders in Pre-Reformation England* (Woodbridge, 2002), 75–95, at 80–1.

[42] Gillespie, *Syon Abbey*, xxxii.

[43] Gillespie, 'Syon and the New Learning', 95, 93.

[44] L. Wooding, 'From Tudor Humanism to Reformation Preaching', in H. Adlington, P. McCullough and E. Rhatigan, eds, *The Oxford Handbook of the Early Modern Sermon* (Oxford, 2011), 329–47; J. K. McConica, *English Humanists and Reformation Politics* (Oxford, 1965).

[45] Da Costa, 'Ryght Profytable Men', 67–9.

and the Bridgettine rosary of sixty-three beads, which was popular before the Reformation but still being used by recusants in the 1620s.[46] The prayers known as the 'Fifteen Oes' of St Bridget were also hugely popular, so much so that they remained in the early Reformation primers, and in a slightly amended form found their way into Richard Day's Protestant prayer book of 1578, which was reprinted as late as 1608.[47]

Syon's brethren had pastoral experience on several levels, therefore: educating the nuns who had no Latin; responding to the pious nobility and gentry who sought their guidance, and ministering and in particular preaching to the great crowds of pilgrims who came to the abbey on Sundays and feast-days. All these features are reflected in Whitford's work, which simultaneously dispensed moral guidance to the wealthy, outlined the fundamentals of the faith to the uneducated and tackled the ethical problems of everyday life. Whitford and his *Werke for Housholders* were the products of the unique and still frequently unsung strengths of late medieval monasticism, which managed to bring together the new insights derived from humanism, and the new opportunities provided by the printing press, with the pious networks which linked the cloister to elite piety, the royal court and the universities, and the well-established traditions of popular outreach, traditional devotion and vernacular preaching.

This nexus between humanism and monasticism can also be found elsewhere, with Benedictines such as Robert Joseph, the scholar-monk of Evesham, or with the Observant Franciscans and other friars who, as Richard Rex has pointed out, often took a leading role as early Protestant reformers.[48] There were also some noted humanists among the monks who contributed to the Marian restoration in the 1550s, such as John Feckenham, abbot of the refounded Westminster Abbey, or William Peryn the Dominican,

---

[46] Ibid. 66; Rhodes, 'Syon Abbey', 12–14.

[47] White, *Tudor Books of Private Devotion*, 216–29.

[48] J. C. H. Aveling and W. A. Pantin, eds, *The Letter-Book of Robert Joseph*, Oxford Historical Society 19 (Oxford, 1967); J. Catto, 'Franciscan Learning in England, 1450–1540', Clark, ed., *Religious Orders*, 97–104; J. G. Clark, 'Reformation and Reaction at St Albans Abbey, 1530–1558', *EHR* 115 (2000), 297–328; idem, 'Humanism and Reform in Pre-Reformation English Monasteries', *TRHS* 6th ser. 19 (2009), 57–93; Richard Rex, 'Friars in the English Reformation', in Peter Marshall and Alec Ryrie, eds, *The Beginnings of English Protestantism* (Cambridge, 2002), 38–59.

who published an English version of Loyola's *Spiritual Exercises*.[49] Theirs was a humanism with a decidedly pragmatic edge, and it helps to explain why Whitford's book was at once biblical, innovative, humane and practical, features which may also explain its popularity in the last decade before Syon was dissolved.

Reformers of every hue were deeply interested in the piety of the domestic household, its problems and its potential. Whitford's work suggests that this concern, far from being a Protestant innovation, was an idea which not only drew inspiration from Christian humanism, but which was also deeply rooted in the communal and pastoral strengths of late medieval monasticism. It suggests strong continuities between the strengths of the pre-Reformation church and the preoccupations of the post-Reformation period. It may be that the puritan godly household should be viewed less as a Protestant creation and more as a survival from the pre-Reformation era which was too valuable to be relinquished. Certainly Whitford's ideas about the household were at once more radical, more populist and more monastic than has often been appreciated.

King's College, London

---

49 William Wizeman, *The Theology and Spirituality of Mary Tudor's Church* (Aldershot, 2006), 140–3.

THE SYON HOUSEHOLD AT DENHAM, 1539–50[*]

by PETER CUNICH

L
ate medieval monastic households shared many features in common with the large secular households of the gentry and aristocracy. Indeed, the language used in describing monastic households had always echoed that of the extended secular family, with 'brothers' and 'sisters' living together under the authority of a superior representing Christ but exercising control of the religious community as a 'father' or 'mother' figure. While the common life of the monastery was very different in many of its details to the lifestyle of a lay family, monastic legislators used the family relationship to describe the *modus operandi* of the monastic community. St Augustine enjoined his monks to 'obey your superior as you would a father', and reminded an errant community of nuns that their superior had been 'the mother not of your body but of your mind'.[1] St Benedict wrote as 'a father who loves you', reminding his followers that God is 'a loving father' and urging them to show each other 'the pure love of brothers' while accepting the abbot as both the 'father of the household' and a 'spiritual father' who would provide for all their worldly and spiritual needs.[2] David Knowles therefore considered the medieval monastic *conventus* to be a 'family' in which a 'simple family life' was led by monks under the care of an ever-present superior who acted as a loving paterfamilias in governing the monastery; the monastery was 'the home of a spiritual family whose life and work begin and end in the family circle'.[3]

Like secular households, monastic households consisted of both an immediate inner 'family' of professed monks or nuns, and

---

[*]   An earlier version of this paper was read at the eighth biennial conference of the Australian and New Zealand Association of Medieval and Early Modern Studies at the University of Otago, Dunedin, in February 2011. This paper makes use of data collected as part of the University of Hong Kong's Monastic Database Project (RGC Project no. HKU7176/97H).

[1]   Boniface Ramsey, ed., *Saint Augustine: The Monastic Rules* (New York, 2004), *Praeceptum (Regula tertia)* 7.1, *Regularis informatio* 7.1, 143, *Obiurgatio* (Letter 211) 4.
[2]   *RB1980: The Rule of St Benedict in English*, ed. Timothy Fry (Collegeville, MN, 1982), Prologue 1, 7.30, 72.8, 2.7, 49.9 respectively.
[3]   David Knowles, *The Monastic Order in England*, 2nd edn (Cambridge, 1963), 302, 404, 300–1, 4.

an outer ring of officials, workers, servants and dependents who together formed the larger monastic *familia*. These households could be quite complex in the great Benedictine monasteries of England, with up to eighty monks and as many or more lay members of the *familia*.[4] Such large unitary households eventually changed in response to the new political realities of the Norman state; from the twelfth century many of the more important monastic households began splitting into two households, one encompassing the convent while a smaller but separate household centred on the abbot.[5] By the beginning of the fifteenth century, when Syon Abbey was founded by Henry V, abbatial households were quite distinct from conventual households in the great monastic houses of England. At Syon, too, it might be argued that two separate households existed from the start – one for the sisters under the abbess, and the other for the brothers under the confessor-general – but it has been suggested elsewhere that these two sides of the Bridgettine double monastery in fact acted together under the ultimate authority of an abbess who always lived in community with her sisters.[6] This feature distinguishes Syon from the other great English religious houses of the period and may help to explain why it was able to survive the Dissolution in 1539 and the numerous vicissitudes of persecution and exile in the following centuries.

In the years immediately before its suppression, Syon Abbey's convent hovered near to the statutory complement of sixty sisters and twenty-five brothers, with its *familia* numbering upwards of eighty-eight persons.[7] The community was famous for its strict observance of St Bridget's *Regula Salvatoris* and its unceasing chanting of the divine office by the sisters and brothers in their specially designed abbey church. The male and female sides of the monastic household went about their daily activities separated by

---

4   Ibid. 440; the word *familia* is used here in its classical sense of the 'household'.

5   David Knowles, *The Religious Orders in England*, 3 vols (Cambridge, 1948–59), 1: 273–4.

6   Peter Cunich, 'The Brothers of Syon, 1420–1695', in E. A. Jones and Alexandra Walsham, eds, *Syon Abbey and its Books: Reading, Writing and Religion, c.1400–1700* (Woodbridge, 2010), 39–81.

7   Known members of the Syon *familia* included 43 lay officials, 7 clerks and servants, 4 priests and 34 annuitants. The domestic servants of the abbey would have added a considerable number to this group.

walls and grilles, but united in the *opus Dei* according to a complex *horarium* and the distinctive Bridgettine liturgy. The Dissolution constituted a crisis for the members of both the professed monastic community and its *familia*, but, unlike the other monastic houses of England, the Syon Bridgettines attempted to continue their monastic calling in smaller pseudo-monastic households from the early 1540s. Although dispersed widely across the Home Counties immediately after the suppression, the several groups of religious, consisting of both male and female members, were able to pursue a form of the regular life in their small household-based secular communities that eventually reunited to form the restored Syon Abbey under Mary Tudor's patronage in 1556.

The most important of these new households was that of the former abbess, Agnes Jordan, which established itself at Southlands, a farm near Denham in Buckinghamshire, very soon after the Dissolution. It was this group of religious that later went into exile on the Continent in 1550 and ultimately formed the nucleus of the Marian refoundation. While the basic elements of this extraordinary survival story have been known since the pioneering work of Canon John Fletcher in the early 1930s, little evidence has survived to illuminate the process by which the community managed to perpetuate its distinctive lifestyle and liturgy during a decade of quiet domestic solitude at Denham.[8] I have suggested elsewhere that the Syon survival strategy was based on a disciplined undertaking by male and female religious to continue living a reduced form of monastic life according to the Bridgettine Rule, a rare example of an English monastic community concealing itself within a lay household.[9] Exactly what did this change of lifestyle mean for the monks and nuns of Syon under the altered circumstances of the 1540s?

The Syon monks and nuns were not, of course, the only Bridgettine community to face a fight for survival during the Reformation; we have evidence from elsewhere in Europe regarding the strategies which other convents employed to preserve their

---

[8] John Rory Fletcher, *The Story of the English Bridgettines of Syon Abbey* (South Brent, 1933), 37–9. Fletcher dealt with the various Syon households in more detail in later manuscript notebooks: see Exeter, UL, Syon Abbey Papers, FLE/12, Canon Fletcher notebooks, 'Syon's Who's Who', 3: 110–14.

[9] Cunich, 'Brothers of Syon', 69–74.

identity. At the Bridgettine mother-house of Vadstena in Sweden, the religious were allowed to stay in the abbey after the reforms of Gustavus Vasa were implemented. It seems, however, that the Bridgettine habit was at least partially banned after 1544, and the nuns were also forced to listen to evangelical preachers after the four remaining Bridgettine brothers were forbidden to administer the sacraments to them. The nuns were nevertheless able to maintain their Bridgettine spirituality for nearly fifty years and when the house was finally closed in 1595 many of the remaining nuns migrated to Maria Brunn Abbey near Danzig to continue the religious life there. It has been suggested that the Vadstena nuns initially made a show of converting to Lutheranism in order to remain in their monastery as a community, but it is also reported that many of them filled their ears with wax and wool to avoid hearing the evangelical sermons that they were forced to attend in the abbey church. This 'passive resistance against attempts to impose Lutheran confessionalization' meant that Vadstena became known as 'a Catholic island in a sea streaming towards Lutheran orthodoxy'.[10] The Vadstena nuns were therefore successful at maintaining their Bridgettine religious identity within the walls of their monastery long after Sweden had officially converted to Lutheranism.

In Denmark the Church Ordinance of the late 1530s was much kinder to religious communities of women, so the royal Bridgettine monastery of Maribo in Jutland continued to function much as it had before the Reformation. The nuns who remained in the abbey were required to wear a cowl, sing in choir and obey the abbess, although they were also instructed to listen to the evangelical sermons of a specially appointed preacher, sing the office in Danish rather than Latin, and adopt a simpler non-Bridgettine habit. We know from an episcopal visitation of 1563 that many of the older nuns adhered to their traditional ways – venerating saints, lighting votive candles, saying their beads and singing the office in Latin – and, like their sisters at Vadstena, they avoided listening to evangelical sermons by surreptitiously reading the old

---

[10] Martin Berntson, 'Reformation and Counter-Culture in Maribo Abbey', in *Saint Birgitta, Syon and Vadstena: Papers from a Symposium in Stockholm, 4–6 October 2007*, ed. Claes Gejrot, Sara Risberg and Mia Akestam (Stockholm, 2010), 216–26, at 219–20, 224; Cunich, 'Brothers of Syon', 80–1.

service books on their laps while the preacher was trying in vain to instruct them in the reformed religion. They even wore their old crowns over their veils in direct disobedience to the injunctions regarding the habit, and some of the old priest-brothers continued to celebrate mass until 1551. While there appears to have been a certain amount of generational conflict at Maribo over what the younger nuns called 'superstitious practices', the community nevertheless clung firmly to the *Regula Salvatoris* and their traditional devotions. Martin Berntson therefore suggests that until its final closure in 1621, the monastery of Maribo managed to maintain its Bridgettine identity by adhering to the banned cult of St Bridget. The aristocratic nuns of Maribo quietly created a Bridgettine counter-culture which united younger and older nuns by preserving the essence of their distinctive religious identity.[11]

Were similar strategies used by English Bridgettine nuns in the years after their monastery was suppressed in 1539? Syon was the most significant of several female religious communities in England that survived the Dissolution as secularized households, but its post-Dissolution existence was in many ways quite different from the continental examples above.[12] Like Vadstena and Maribo, the church and conventual buildings at Syon were initially saved from the general demolition of monastic properties which occurred immediately after the Dissolution, but Syon Abbey was converted into a royal residence after the members of the religious community had been turned out into the world. The members of the Syon community could not, therefore, continue to lead a form of their previous monastic life in the familiar surroundings of the monastery, as was the case at Vadstena and Maribo. The Syon

---

[11] Berntson, 'Reformation and Counter-Culture', 221–3.

[12] Other examples are given in Kathleen Cooke, 'The English Nuns and the Dissolution', in *The Cloister and the World: Essays in Medieval History in Honour of Barbara Harvey*, ed. J. Blair and Brian Golding (Oxford, 1996), 287–301, at 300; Paul Lee, *Learning and Spirituality in Late Medieval English Society: The Dominican Priory of Dartford* (York, 2001), 120; Diane K. Coldicott, *Hampshire Nunneries* (Chichester, 1989), 143–5; John Paul, 'Dame Elizabeth Shelley, Last Abbess of St Mary's Abbey, Winchester', *Papers and Proceedings of the Hampshire Field Club and Archaeological Society* 23 (1965), 60–71; Winifred M. Sturman, 'Barking Abbey: A Study in its External and Internal Administration from the Conquest to the Dissolution' (Ph.D. diss., University of London, 1961), 447. Further examples are mentioned in Mary Erler, 'Religious Women after the Dissolution', in *London and the Kingdom: Essays in Honour of Caroline M. Barron: Proceedings of the 2004 Harlaxton Symposium*, ed. Matthew Davies and Andrew Prescott (Stamford, 2008), 135–45.

community's decision to disperse into small household groups was no doubt a matter of pragmatic necessity, but such was the secrecy of the undertaking that the process has left no formal record. The surviving evidence for the Syon household at Southlands includes records of pension payments and the lengthy will of Abbess Jordan, a document which Mary Erler has used to compare the Denham community with other groups of female religious who managed to preserve some form of community life after the Dissolution.[13] It has nevertheless proven difficult to give this evidence a physical context so that we might understand the type of pseudo-monastic life which the nuns and monks led at Denham between 1539 and 1550. That problem has now been partially solved after a recent survey of the remaining Tudor buildings at Southlands.[14]

Southlands appears to have been built as a large farm house in the early sixteenth century for John Micklowe, who married Peter Peckham's widow, Elizabeth, in 1504. The Peckhams had been settled in Buckinghamshire for several generations and already owned much land in Denham.[15] Peter and Elizabeth Peckham were the parents of Sir Edmund Peckham (*c.*1495–1564; knighted 1542), who started his career in Henry VIII's service as a clerk of the counting house (*c.*1520–2), but rose quickly to become treasurer of the king's chamber (1522–4), cofferer of the royal household (1524–47), and eventually high treasurer of the royal mints (1544–64). He was also a Justice of the Peace for Buckinghamshire (1525–43) and Middlesex (1537–43).[16] The Peckham family had impeccable Catholic credentials and would prove fiercely loyal to the interests of Mary Tudor during the reign of Edward VI and thereafter.[17]

[13] Erler, 'Religious Women', 135–7.

[14] I am grateful to John Martin, the current owner of Southlands Manor, for allowing me to visit his home on 2 December 2010; and to Anthony Emery for his assistance in researching the previous history of Southlands. I am also grateful to Adrian Hirst, rector of Denham, who gave me free access to the church of St Mary the Virgin at Denham and allowed me to use the parish's copy of R. H. Lathbury, *History of Denham* (Uxbridge, 1904).

[15] Lathbury, *Denham*, 240.

[16] S. T. Bindoff, ed., *The House of Commons, 1509–1558*, 3 vols (London, 1982), 3: 78–9.

[17] See Anna Whitelock and Diarmaid MacCulloch, 'Princess Mary's Household and the Succession Crisis, July 1553', *HistJ* 50 (2007), 265–87, at 277, 283–4; Bindoff, *House of Commons*, 3: 80; Erler, 'Religious Women', 136.

Southlands came into the ownership of Edmund Peckham some time after 1522; in 1537 he gave the whole estate to his son Robert at the time of the latter's marriage to Mary Bray. The property at that time consisted of a hundred acres of ploughed land, forty acres of meadow, twenty acres of pasture and six acres of woodland.[18] Robert and Mary Peckham enjoyed possession of Southlands for little more than two years before Abbess Jordan and her companions arrived as their tenants. It is not known whether the Peckham family had any connections with Syon Abbey, but some sources suggest that Agnes Jordan had relatives in the parish.[19] It is also known that one of the Syon nuns at the time of the Dissolution was a Mary Denham, but it is not clear whether she had any connection with the parish; she certainly never joined the abbess's household there and she appears to have lived alone for much of the post-Dissolution period.[20]

The abbess brought with her six sisters, including the senior nuns Bridget Sulyard and Dorothy Slighte, and the more junior Margery Covert, Margaret Lupton, Mary Nevell and Mary Watno. Katherine Palmer probably joined them in 1543. The men who initially arrived with Abbess Jordan were probably only her chaplain Thomas Scudamore (a secular priest) and the lay brother Richard Browne, although it is also possible that a former lay brother, Thomas Godfrey, was travelling with the group at this time. They were later joined by the priest brothers Richard Whitford and Anthony Little (described in Agnes Jordan's will as her 'goostly father'), and the lay brother John Massey. Scudamore seems to have left the household before 1545 and the abbess appointed in his place a new chaplain, probably Leonard Hurst, who was a member of the household in 1546 and attended her in her final illness.[21] Three of the religious died before the abbess's own demise in January 1546 – Margaret Lupton, Richard Whitford and Richard

[18] Lathbury, *Denham*, 211–12. John Micklowe, former treasurer to Henry VII, bought Southlands in 1522.

[19] This suggestion originates from the work of Canon Fletcher, see 'Syon's Who's Who', 3: 117. It is possible that Agnes Jordan's family lived at Jordans, a village five miles to the north-west of Denham.

[20] Mary Denham had a pension of £6 p.a. and was initially with Richard Whitford's household, between October 1540 and May 1541. Her pension was last paid on 10 December 1553 and she appears to have died on 23 August 1554: Kew, TNA, E315/262, fol. 2ᵛ.

[21] Leonard Hurst was rector of Denham c.1550 and died in 1560.

Browne – but there were still at least nine people living at South-lands in 1546.

This large group of ex-religious would have had no difficulty supporting itself on their combined pensions, valued at approximately £260 per annum in 1542 and dropping only slightly to £246 13s 8d per annum immediately before the abbess's death.[22] It is not known how much rent (if any) they paid to Robert Peckham for the lease of Southlands, but even after rent was paid they would have had more than sufficient to lead a comfortable life at Denham until the abbess's death. It is probable that they leased only the house, the agricultural land being farmed by Thomas Legge until his death in 1542.[23] It seems clear from Agnes Jordan's will that she continued to exercise her authority as head of the Syon monastic community, holding all the possessions of the household in her own name, including the furnishings and bedding in each nun's or brother's chamber.[24] The vow of poverty therefore appears to have been observed as far as possible in the changed circumstances which faced the abbess's household. We also know that the pensions of all the ex-religious were collected from the Court of Augmentations at the same time by one agent, so it seems probable that Agnes Jordan continued to exercise control over all the income of the household, not just her own pension.[25]

It is not possible to reconstruct the layout of the house at Southlands in the 1540s because its interior arrangements have changed so much since then, but Agnes Jordan's will indicates that it was large enough to accommodate all the residents of her household, containing at least eighteen rooms in the main residential wings, and nine rooms in the service area, including a kitchen, buttery, larder, ale house, stilling house, store house and laundry.[26] Each

---

[22]   Agnes Jordan's pension was £200 p.a. and Richard Whitford's was £8, while eight of the other religious had pensions valued at between £6 and £6 13s. 8d. The two lay brothers had smaller sums of £2 13s. 8d.

[23]   Lathbury, *Denham*, 212.

[24]   Agnes Jordan's will: TNA, PROB/11/31, dated 28 October 1545, proven 9 February 1546.

[25]   For these payments, see TNA, E315/250, fols 19ᵛ (10 January 1541), 24ᵛ (6 April 1541), 29ʳ (4 July 1541), 32ʳ ([23] October 1541). Thomas Scudamore, the abbess's chaplain, acted as her agent in collecting these pensions.

[26]   The house is described as it was in the early twentieth century by the Royal Commission for Historical Monuments, *An Inventory of the Historical Monuments in Buckinghamshire*, 2 vols (London, 1912–13), 1: 119.

of the occupants had their own chamber, but Agnes Jordan and Anthony Little had two rooms each. Bridget Sulyard had a small altar in her chamber, perhaps indicating difficulty getting to the chapel for services, and we even know that the abbess had green bed hangings. The items of furniture in each room are enumerated in her will, indicating that the occupants of Southlands lived in a degree of comfort that was not perhaps in keeping with the strictures of the Rule. Nevertheless, the scale of the farm buildings was significantly smaller than the massive conventual complex at Syon Abbey and would not have allowed for the fully enclosed and separate lifestyles of male and female religious that was required by the Rule. Indeed, the remaining Tudor buildings at Southlands reveal just how cramped the house must have been for such a large group of people, and this undoubtedly required some major adjustments for men and women who had been accustomed to a highly regulated lifestyle in their spacious abbey.

The main rooms in the house were the hall, which was decorated with wall hangings and furnished with tables and forms, the parlour, which was entered from the main entrance porch, and the richly furnished chapel, but there were several other rooms with specialized functions. The abbess owned a clock with a bell and this stood in its own chamber. There was also a guest's room. A large number of locks and keys to the various doors in the house perhaps indicates that the injunctions in the *Regula Salvatoris* about locking up the monastery continued to be observed on a smaller scale at Southlands. The chapel was the main focus of the abbess's will. It must have been one of the largest rooms in the house and it appears to have been fully set up for the daily round of liturgy and worship. It had its own benches and forms, a bell hanging above the doorway and a holy water stoup. The sanctuary consisted of an altar of wainscot and a 'hallowed superaltar', with a canopy hanging over the reserved sacrament, and a great crucifix above the altar. A full set of velvet and satin vestments and altar-hangings in the various liturgical colours allowed for the dignified celebration of mass and other services. A rich assortment of religious images and devotional items adorned the chapel: a panel of Our Lady with Jesus in her arms, a panel showing Our Lord's Pity, an image of Our Lord standing, an image of Our Lady of Pity with Jesus on her lap, a panel of Our Lord's Maundy with the pageants of his Passion, an ivory carving of Our Lady with two crowns, an image of St George on horseback, a gilt crucifix with Our Lady and St John, an altar-hanging with a pageant of Our Lord's Passion and Resurrection drawn on it, a hanging of blue damask with 'Ihus' embroidered on it, and other images which stood on the altar. This must have been a very impressive array of religious images and devotional paraphernalia and gives some indication of the traditional religious sensitivities of the Syon community after the Dissolution. Given the lavish outlay on the chapel at Southlands, we must presume that the Bridgettine ex-religious continued their daily round of office, heard mass celebrated by one of the priests, listened to sermons, and made their regular confessions as required by the Rule.

It is unclear whether the members of the community continued to wear their habits while living in the secluded privacy of Southlands farm, or instead reverted to secular clothing. I have not been able to find any evidence of the distinctive Bridgettine habit in Agnes Jordan's will. The only items of clothing mentioned are two gowns of 'browne blewe' material and a black kirtle, which seems to indicate that the usual grey habit of the order had been forsaken by 1545. The nuns had not given up their reading habits, however, for Abbess Jordan bequeathed all her remaining books, images and pictures not otherwise specified in her will to the sisters who 'hathe benne most comenly aboute me and hath taken moste paynes with me in my sicknes sythe the dissolvynge of the late monestary of Syon'. Although her will indicates that she was very generous to the remaining members of her household at Southlands, leaving bequests of cash, household goods and devotional items from the chapel, it also seems that it presumed the winding up of the household at the time of her death. Most of the contents of the house and the chapel fittings that had been purchased by Abbess Jordan between 1539 and 1546 were bequeathed to Robert Peckham, presumably as a way of thanking him for the use of the farm. Did Agnes Jordan expect the Peckham family to move back into the house immediately, or was Robert Peckham supposed to act temporarily as trustee for the remaining members of her household until a new superior could be canonically elected? Did the community continue to live at Southlands until Katherine Palmer began to transfer its members to the Bridgettine abbey of Maria Troon in the Low Countries between 1550 and 1552, or did they have to find accommodation somewhere else? These questions unfortunately cannot be answered with any certainty.

Another mystery is the surprising omission from Agnes Jordan's will of the name of Katherine Palmer, the nun who took over the leadership of the scattered members of the Syon community at some time after the abbess's death. Where was she when Agnes Jordan died? The Augmentations pension payments indicate that Palmer was a member of the Southlands household between 1543 and 1546, but by the time Agnes Jordan wrote her will in late 1545 Palmer may well have been sent to the Low Countries to investigate the possibility of moving the household to a continental Bridgettine monastery. The sketchy traditional accounts of Syon's early years of exile suggest that she took a group of nuns to the Low Countries in 1539 and stayed there until the 1550s when she returned to England to re-establish Syon under Mary Tudor, but there is no independent evidence to support this story. Palmer's pension payments were certainly very erratic between the Dissolution and the time when she joined the Southlands household in late 1542. In May 1541 she appears to have been staying temporarily with Richard Whitford's household. The unusual payment record in 1540 and 1541 may indicate an early attempt by Palmer to join a Bridgettine monastery on the Continent.[27] Katherine Palmer's brothers, Henry and Thomas, were both serving the king at Calais in 1540, so it is possible that she received assistance from them in reaching a Bridgettine abbey in the Low Countries, where she may have stayed for a time before returning to England in 1541 or 1542.[28] If she had spent some time on the Continent in 1540–1 it would make sense that she was the one sent by the abbess to arrange a new home for the Southlands household in 1545. This is, of course, pure conjecture, but it would certainly explain her conspicuous absence from Southlands at the end of 1545. We know that she returned in 1546 because Palmer was among the remnants of the abbess's and the prioress's households which combined to form a single household from late 1546, either before or after the death of Bridget Sulyard.[29] Does this mean that Katherine Palmer

---

[27] TNA, E315/250, fol. 27^r; E315/251, fol. 12^{r-v}.
[28] See the biographies of Sir Henry Palmer and Sir Thomas Palmer in *ODNB*, and for Katherine Palmer, online at: <www.oxforddnb.com/view/article/96817>.
[29] Katherine Palmer's new household consisted of Dorothy Slighte, Margery

had been unable to arrange a new home on the Continent, or that the members of the combined household were unwilling to leave England until it became absolutely necessary? Once again, this question cannot be answered.

All the evidence suggests that the three or four remaining households of Syon ex-religious were allowed to continue their secluded pseudo-monastic existence unmolested throughout the last years of Henry VIII's reign, but with the king's death in early 1547 and the imposition of a more overtly Protestant policy by Edward VI's ministers, they probably took fright and began to plan a withdrawal from England. A meeting of representatives from three of the remaining households appears to have taken place on 10 April 1548, after which Katherine Palmer's pension payments again became erratic until 6 May 1549, by which time she had rejoined the combined household.[30] Did this represent another period of travel on the Continent during which she arranged for the transfer of the remaining residents of Southlands to Maria Troon Abbey? Were they even still living at Southlands by this time? These questions cannot be answered, but what is certain is that when the English Bridgettines began arriving at Maria Troon from 24 June 1550, the majority of them were from the original Southlands household, and it was this group that returned to England in late 1556 or early 1557 to re-establish the abbey under Queen Mary.[31] The Southlands household was therefore central to the survival of the Syon monastic community, forming the nucleus for the revived Marian foundation which went into permanent exile after Elizabeth I's accession and stayed on the Continent until the mid-nineteenth century.

Does this leave us any closer to understanding how the members of the Syon household at Denham managed to perpetuate their

Covert, Mary Nevell, Mary Watno, Anthony Little and John Massey from South-lands, Jane Rushe and Anne Dauncy from Prioress Margaret Windsor's household, and Clemence Tresham. The eight women and two men survived on pension payments totalling only £58 13s. 4d. p.a.

30   TNA, E315/257, fols 1ᵛ–7ᵛ; E315/258, fol. 6ʳ.

31   Katherine Palmer was the first to arrive at Termonde/Dendermonde on 24 June 1550, followed on 28 August by Dorothy Slighte and Margery Covert. Anthony Little and John Massey also arrived in 1550, but Mary Nevell and Anne Dauncey came later, in July and October 1552. I am grateful to Mary Erler for providing these dates from Ulla Sander Olsen's edition of the chronicle of Maria Troon Abbey. See also Mary C. Erler, 'The Effects of Exile on English Monastic Spirituality: William Peryn's *Spirituall Exercyses*', *Journal of Medieval and Early Modern Studies* 42 (2012), 519–37, at 528–9.

distinctive Bridgettine identity in the 1540s? While there is not enough evidence to reconstruct their spiritual and community life with any certainty, several features of their survival strategy seem to stand out. First, the initial leadership given by the abbess, Agnes Jordan, and the financial support provided by her substantial pension ensured that this would be the strongest of the several Syon households established after the Dissolution. Second, the abbess and her household were fortunate to have good lay friends such as the Peckhams who were able to support them in various ways, not the least of which was the provision of a house for them to occupy. It is also clear from the abbess's will that she was on good terms with the parish clergy in the parishes of Denham, Uxbridge and Iver, so the pseudo-conventual lifestyle which they adopted at Southlands did not apparently come to the attention of Henry VIII's or Edward VI's ministers. Third, a large and relatively secluded house such as Southlands allowed the household to carry on its communal life in privacy and solitude, something which would not have been possible in a town or village house. Fourth, the private chapel allowed the household to continue reciting the office and performing their other liturgical ceremonies, albeit on a much smaller scale than had been possible at the massive abbey church at Syon. These religious observances were at the heart of their Bridgettine identity. Fifth, the continuing presence of priest brothers in the household provided regular sacramental services and preaching without the need to rely on parochial clergy, and the lay brothers no doubt provided the essential domestic services that any large household required, either with or without the assistance of domestic servants. Finally, after Agnes Jordan's death, the Southlands community was able to rely on a new leader, Katherine Palmer, who may have already established links with continental Bridgettine monasteries, thus ensuring the eventual survival of the community.

It was the timely departure of Katherine Palmer and her household to the Low Countries from the middle of 1550 that rendered Syon's survival possible. The Vadstena nuns left their escape too late, while the Maribo community simply ceased to exist when it was finally suppressed in 1621. By that time, Syon was re-established in Lisbon and attracting a new generation of recruits to a changed, but still recognizably Bridgettine, monastic lifestyle which would preserve the convent's distinctive religious identity into the twentieth century. The preservation of the monastic community had been made possible by the dispersal of the large Syon *conventus* into a number of smaller pseudo-monastic households that appear to have blended so easily into the secular communities in which they were embedded that they have left little evidence of their existence. The Syon example therefore demonstrates that a form of monastic life could be preserved outside the walls of the monastery in post-Dissolution England, but the secular household could only ever be a short-term solution for a contemplative community of religious such as the Bridgettines. Long-term survival required the more specialized household arrangements afforded by the monastic cloister.

University of Hong Kong

REFORMING HOUSEHOLD PIETY: JOHN FOXE AND THE LOLLARD CONVENTICLE TRADITION*

by SUSAN ROYAL

That the *ecclesia* in antiquity met in private homes was well known to first- and second-generation English reformers who sought to reshape the late medieval established Church. In the wake of Catholic accusations of novelty – and thus illegitimacy – evangelicals developed a history of their movement that stretched back through the generations to the early Church itself, and none more successfully than John Foxe (d. 1587), author of *Acts and Monuments* and England's major martyrologist. A crucial link in this historical chain would prove to be the Lollards, medieval English heretics whose 'privy assemblies' saw the reading of vernacular Scripture and its exposition, recitation of the Ten Commandments and the Lord's Prayer, and even hints of liturgical activity, all in the private space of the home.

Scholars have seen Foxe's treatment of the Lollards chiefly in the light of their historical significance for his polemical purposes, and have argued that he shaped his portrayal of their theological emphases so as to temper their more radical ideas. What remains to be studied is how Foxe and other English polemicists handled the ecclesiological legacy of the Lollards, based as it was not in the traditional parish church, but firmly in unconsecrated places, especially the home. I hope to demonstrate that the *Acts and Monuments* offers a more flexible ecclesiology than has previously been thought, and that it provides models for religious practice that go beyond martyrdom, in fact offering a variety of ecclesiological experiences.

Acts and Monuments has long been recognized as among the most influential English books of its age;[1] it aimed to tell the

* I would like to thank Alec Ryrie for his helpful comments on this essay.

[1] For Foxe's incorporation of Lollards as theological models and historical forebears, see Margaret Aston, 'John Wycliffe's Reformation Reputation', *P&P*, no. 30 (1965), 23–51; eadem, 'Lollardy and the Reformation: Survival or Revival?', *History* 49 (1964), 149–70; Patrick Collinson, 'Truth and Legend: The Veracity of John Foxe's *Book*

history of the true Church in England and to provide an answer to Catholics who accused evangelicals of theological novelty. Foxe saw the members of this true Church as an oppressed minority that had existed in Britain since before the Romans (thus Augustine's mission in 597 was portrayed as an invasion that corrupted a flourishing indigenous Christianity) and had stood against the established Church of Rome throughout the Middle Ages. Foxe saw himself and his fellow sixteenth-century co-religionists as the latest in this long line of Christ's true witnesses, and used the Lollards to make a historical connection between the Reformation movement of his own day and the early Church of Christ.

Foxe chose the Lollards because most of their theological beliefs mirrored his own.[2] He consulted medieval court books, combed bishops' registers, and collected oral histories of the persecutions of the 'known men', as Lollards called themselves. What he found buried in fifteenth-century trial records was a rejection of transubstantiation, appeals against images and pilgrimages, and zeal for the vernacular Bible, positions similar to those of the reformers. He also found that after 1414, when a failed rebellion in the name of a Lollard knight fixed an association between Lollardy and sedition, these men and women were forced underground, proselytizing and teaching in private places such as the home.

To show how Foxe uses the household conventicle as an ecclesiological model, it will be helpful to understand the nature of the Lollard gatherings that Foxe presents. As Susan Brigden rightly claims, 'Lollardy was a faith practised in homes, not in churches.'[3] This faith was rooted in the books that gave Lollards the spiritual sustenance missing from their parochial activities, and they gathered to read and listen to them in their homes. Extant evidence suggests that no liturgical or sacramental activities took place; rather, these meetings were centred on the book. Foxe's chronology is replete with examples: Margery Backster of the Norwich group was accused of inviting a neighbour and her maid into

---

of Martyrs', in idem, *Elizabethans* (London, 2003), 151–78; Anne Hudson, *The Premature Reformation* (Oxford, 1988), ch. 10.

   [2] Foxe was by no means the first reformer to make this connection; his mentor and fellow evangelical John Bale found affinity between his own beliefs and those of John Wyclif and his followers, and, even before Bale, William Tyndale had recognized their historical value.

   [3] Susan Brigden, *London and the Reformation* (Oxford, 1989), 93.

her chamber to hear her husband 'reade the lawe of Christ',[4] and Christopher Shoomaker of Great Missenden went to the house of John Say four times to read 'out of a litle boke the wordes whiche Christ spake to his disciples'.[5] Thomas Pope was said to stay up often reading his book until midnight.[6]

While books of Scripture were undoubtedly the Lollards' favourite reading material (Foxe mentions the Acts of the Apostles, the Gospels, and Paul's Epistles), books such as *The King of Beeme* (Bohemia)[7] and *Wyclif's Wicket* are also mentioned, the latter getting John Stilman into trouble when the authorities found it hidden in 'an old oke'.[8] Foxe tells us that when Robert Freeman, a parish priest, was caught reading an unnamed 'suspected booke', he carried it to his chamber.[9] At times Foxe is enigmatic about which books were read, for instance saying that Lollards would meet at the house of Richard Ashford to hear a 'certaine little booke', or that Thomas Carder would meet others to read 'in a certayne Englishe booke'.[10]

Often conventicles contained an element of communing for more than just spiritual food. Nicholas Durdant recited verses out of Paul's letters and the Gospels to his extended family over dinner, clearly intended as a private moment for the family since he asked a boy standing nearby to leave his home before he did it.[11] John Butler, Richard Butler and William King of Uxbridge would sit up all night in the Durdants' home reading Scripture; it seems unlikely that their host would not offer them victuals while there. The notion of eating was closely tied to a common lesson taught in the home: that the eucharist was bread and not the true body of Christ. Foxe tells us that Alice Hardynge taught Richard Bennette what to do if a priest came to his house to administer the sacrament,[12] and that Agnes Grebill had not believed in tran-

---

[4] John Foxe, *The Unabridged Acts and Monuments Online or TAMO* (1570 edn) (HRI Online Publications, Sheffield, 2011), 808, online at: <http://www.johnfoxe.org>.

[5] Ibid. 984.

[6] Ibid. 989.

[7] Ibid. 999. See also Margaret Aston, 'Lollardy and Literacy', in her *Lollards and Reformers: Images and Literacy in Late Medieval England* (London, 1984), 201 n. 37.

[8] Foxe, *TAMO* (1570), 979.

[9] Ibid. 995.

[10] Ibid. 851.

[11] Ibid. 992. This notion of a family activity is echoed in the narrative of John Barret, who was heard reciting the Epistle of James to his wife and maid: ibid. 991.

[12] Ibid. 987. The content of his teaching is not given by Foxe.

substantiation for nearly thirty years and had discussed her beliefs with her husband and sons 'wythin theyr house diuers times'.[13]

Very often Foxe uses the verb 'communed' to describe the actions of these men and women, complete with its connotations of communication, spiritual engagement and eucharistic flavour. Foxe tells us that John Claydon 'communed' in a house with a known heretic, and the Lollard priest William Thorpe reported that he was 'oft right homely & communed with [other known men]'.[14] The notion of conferring and discussing comes across when Foxe tells us that Christopher Tinker suggested to Thomas Clerke that he could show him proof that the bread of the eucharist was not the very body of Christ, but urged him not to tell his wife or her brother, a priest.[15]

This lesson was perhaps laced with secrecy because in these meetings Tinker would foretell the 'day of dome'.[16] Similarly John Ryburne met in 'a close' to prophesy 'that a tyme shall come that no eleuation shall bee made'.[17] John Harrys and his friend Richard Colyns met together with their wives to talk of the Apocalypse, and Foxe tells us that the Lyvord conventicle met to read a book expounding Revelation, and here they 'communed concerning the matter of opening the book with seuean clasps &c'.[18]

Instruction was often less ominous. Learning was at the core of these meetings, which in the records are termed 'scholes of heresy' just as often as 'conventicle'. Notably, Foxe only once uses the term 'schole', which appears to be a term with Catholic associations.[19] Lollard conventicles are described as places of conversation, learning, instruction, teaching and fellowship, while 'schole doctors' are connected to 'canonists and friars'; 'schole matters' are 'subtile sophistry'; and Foxe writes that Agnes Wells, who had

---

[13] Ibid. 1493.
[14] Ibid. 655.
[15] Ibid. 995.
[16] Ibid.
[17] Ibid. 1158.
[18] Foxe, *TAMO* (1583), 856.
[19] In the exception, Foxe writes that one charge against Norwich Lollard Richard Belward was 'that the sayd Richard kepeth scholes of lollardy in the English tounge, in the towne of Dychingham, and a certayne parchment maker bryngeth him all the bookes contayning that doctrine from London'. Belward's trial record is not extant, but we might surmise that Foxe was using this term verbatim from the text: *TAMO* (1570), 803.

refused to confess to her dissenting opinions, eventually caved in 'sone after beyng otherwise schooled, I can not tell how, by the Catholiques'.[20]

Foxe portrays Lollard conventicles as places of teaching and didactic practice. Among other verses, Agnes Asforde of Chesham taught James Morden the words: 'Teende ye not a candle and put it vnder a bushell, but set it on a candlesticke that it may geue a light to all in the house'. We might note the tension between this lesson and the private meeting in which it was taught. The bishops may have had the impression that she had taught many men this way; Foxe tells us they enjoined her not to teach this to any more men, and especially not to her children.[21]

Another man who came to learn from a woman was John Morden, who went to Alice Littlepage to learn the Ten Commandments. In fact, the Littlepages were accused of teaching others the sayings of Solomon, the Ave Maria and the Pater Noster in English; Alice's husband taught fellow Lollards the Apostle's Creed in English as well, which he had learned from his grandmother.[22] On-the-job learning was expected of Agnes Edmundes, who was brought by her father to the house of Richard Colyns 'to seruice, to thee intent that she myght bee instructed there in God's law'.[23] As was often the case in schools, recitation seems to have been part of the curriculum: Robert Pope would join John Morden and his wife to recite the Ten Commandments, and Foxe relays that Alice Colyns (Richard's wife) had an excellent memory, and was often sent for by conventicles of men met at Burford, in order to recite the Ten Commandments and the Epistles of Peter and James.[24]

The idea of learning should not merely be taken to indicate one-way intellectual traffic. Foxe gives numerous examples of neighbours 'resort[ing] and conferr[ing] together' and 'conferring and communing together among themselues'.[25] Thomas Grove used to meet with others in Amersham to 'resort and confer together in matters of Religion', and Foxe did not say that the

[20] Ibid. 987.
[21] Ibid. 988.
[22] Ibid. 991.
[23] Ibid. 999.
[24] Ibid.
[25] For example, ibid. 986, 1001.

conventicle at John Harrys' house read the Apocalypse and the Acts of the Apostles, but that they talked of them.[26]

The move from reading Scripture to discussing its implications is not a great leap. Foxe tells of three Lollards who went to hear Nicholas Field of London in 1530 'to reade a parcell of scripture in English' at the house of John Taylor in Hichenden; afterward, he expounded its meaning, teaching them on matters such as holy days and the eucharist.[27] If this sounds a lot like a sermon, it could be because Field had imbibed the German Reformation's emphasis on preaching while 'beyond the Sea in Almany'. However, the focus on preaching – and preaching anywhere – had been home-grown. As early as 1391, William Swinderby had been accused of preaching and singing in unconsecrated spaces,[28] and John Purvey and other early Lollards were required to abjure the belief that any layman could preach the gospel in every place.[29]

Meeting to hear a 'sermon' and its exposition may have constituted an act of worship; there is evidence of other such acts. Foxe relays John Claydon's belief that people ought to worship in 'meane and simple houses', not in great buildings,[30] and Walter Brute insisted that it was right to pray secretly and in the clothes chamber, juxtaposing this with the public actions of priests.[31] Margery Backster lambasted her neighbour for going to church to worship dead images, declaring: 'And if you desire so much to see the true crosse of Christ, I wyll shew it you at home in your own house.' Foxe writes:

> Which this deponent being desirous to see, the sayd Margery stretching out her armes abrode, sayd to thys deponent, this is the true crosse of Christ, and thys crosse thou oughtest and mayest euery day beholde and worship in thine own house, and therefore it is but vain to run to the church to worship dead crosses & images.[32]

---

[26] Ibid. 991, 996.

[27] Ibid. 1158.

[28] Ibid. 580. Swinderby and other Lollards would meet outdoors or in barns: see Alexandra Walsham, *The Reformation of the Landscape: Religion, Identity, and Memory in Early Modern Britain and Ireland* (Oxford, 2010), 234–6.

[29] Foxe, *TAMO* (1570), 650.

[30] Ibid. 779.

[31] Ibid. 614.

[32] Ibid. 807–8.

Backster's rejection of worship in a place considered consecrated reflects a long-established Lollard suspicion of holy sites. Brute claimed that necromancers and conjurers believe that they could be heard better in one place than in another,[33] and John Clerke claimed that 'all the world was as well halowed as in the Church or churchyard. And that it was as good to be buryed in the field, as in the Church or churchyard.'[34] Coventry Lollard John Blomston claimed that 'a man might as well worship the blessed Virgin by the fire side in the kitchin',[35] and one of Foxe's earliest martyrologies tells of 'a considerable number of citizens and craftsmen … converging in groups in the various ditches of the suburbs, to hear the holy word of the Lord'.[36]

With a better understanding of how Foxe has characterized Lollard conventicles, we can turn to look at how he incorporated the Lollard trials into his book, and then draw out the implications of this material.

In an influential paper, John A. F. Thomson showed that when Lollard beliefs were too radical for the tastes of our magisterial reformer, Foxe was not above suppressing this evidence.[37] When it comes to domestic piety, we see two places where Foxe either adjusts or omits Lollard testimony. One concerns the issue of sacred space generally. According to the trial records of the Norwich Lollards, many of them did not believe that marriages needed to be solemnized in the public church. Foxe is quick to explain that they merely denied that marriage was a sacrament, and that their testimony was twisted by papist 'quarelpickers'.[38] Foxe is clearly reluctant to take the exchange of marriage vows from the oversight of the church – and thus the state.

Foxe also elides information in the case of Joan Baker, a London Lollard, who stated that she could hear a better sermon at home than any priest or doctor could give at St Paul's Cross or anywhere

---

[33] Ibid. 614.

[34] Ibid. 996.

[35] Ibid. 942.

[36] Shannon McSheffrey and Norman Tanner, eds and transl., *Lollards of Coventry*, Camden 5th ser. 23 (London, 2003), 296.

[37] John A. F. Thomson, 'John Foxe and some Sources for Lollard History: Notes for a Critical Appraisal', in G. J. Cuming, ed., *SCH* 2 (London, 1965), 251–7.

[38] Foxe, *TAMO* (1570), 805.

else.[39] Why did Foxe remove it? It would not have been withheld because of its overt anti-clericalism: evangelicals shared this sentiment with their Lollard forebears. Nor does the aspect of place seem to be a crucial factor; after all, Foxe has shown us many examples of Lollards gathering to hear a Scripture reading and exposition thereafter. So where do we go from here? One possibility left is the term 'sermon': perhaps Foxe felt that the words 'hear a sermon at home' would be too overtly subversive. While this is a tempting way to categorize Foxeian omissions, we have to remember the case of John Claydon, the illiterate London Lollard who confessed to having a very expensive book read out to him: this was a book which Foxe clearly states contained a sermon preached at Horsleydown.[40] So we see that the act of hearing a sermon at home does not merit Foxe's exclusion per se, but that these words, unqualified by notions of hearing a sermon read or repeated at home, could have been worthy of censorship.

There may be a more practical (and less ideologically driven) reason for this omission. Recent work by Elizabeth Evenden and Thomas Freeman has shown that the production of the greatly expanded second edition of the *Acts and Monuments* was plagued by a significant paper shortage. In order to accommodate Foxe's rebuttals of several Catholic attacks on the work, and also to include the additional material discovered by Foxe and others, much more paper was needed than his printer, John Day, had planned. Forced to make drastic cuts from the volume in an effort to save precious paper, Foxe omitted documents wholesale, and 'so great was the pressure on Foxe to save even relatively minute amounts of paper that he began to remove excess verbiage from court documents, for no other reason than to save space'.[41] Perhaps in the case of Joan Baker's belief that she could hear a better sermon at home,

---

[39]   Ibid. 966 and the *TAMO* commentary on this page; cf. London Metropolitan Archives, Diocese of London, A/A/005/MS09531/009, fol. 25^{r-v}. We see the same adjustment in the testimony of Agnes Grebill from the Kent group: Foxe, *TAMO* (1570), 805; Norman Tanner, ed., *Kent Heresy Proceedings, 1511–12*, Kent Records 26 (Maidstone, 1997), 18–21, at 20.

[40]   Foxe, *TAMO* (1570), 778. This is likely to be the 'Sermon of the Horsedoun': see Anne Hudson, ed., *Two Wycliffite Texts: The Sermon of William Taylor, 1406; The Testimony of William Thorpe, 1407*, EETS 301 (Oxford, 1993), 133–6.

[41]   Elizabeth Evenden and Thomas S. Freeman, *Religion and the Book in Early Modern England: The Making of John Foxe's 'Book of Martyrs'* (Cambridge, 2011), 165.

Foxe, in an effort to conserve paper, chose to cut out a practice that had been made explicit elsewhere.

With the examples of the Norwich Lollards and Baker, then, I suggest that we re-evaluate Thomson's claims about Foxe's editorial process. Thomson focused on showing that the material Foxe cut from the Lollard records included radical religious claims; but in fact, if we look at what Foxe included in his text, we see evidence of radical ecclesiological practices nearly everywhere in his Lollard narratives. We also see that there were places where Foxe drew the line, such as solemnizing marriages in settings other than a church. Although Thomson is correct to suggest that Foxe might alter the thrust of a statement, he rarely excludes evidence completely, and we should not assume that he omits such evidence because of his religious conservatism.

To see how Foxe could get away with including radical material, we will need to use Patrick Collinson's authoritative essay on 'The English Conventicle'.[42] This, with his other works, illuminates the ambiguous legality of conventicles, and also their inherent separatist potential. He shows that in Foxe's day extraparochial meetings held in homes constituted a grey area in Elizabethan policy, and he characterizes conventicles as not strictly legal or illegal, but 'extra-legal'.[43] This analysis shows exactly how Foxe is able to offer examples of religious practice that have little to do with the parish church.[44] Because of the ambiguous legal status of conventicles, Foxe can use this space to offer a variety of ecclesiological exempla without confronting the legal status quo.

Foxe takes advantage of this flexibility in several ways. First, we see the reformer giving the Lollards high praise for these extraparochial meetings. While it seems characteristic that Foxe would laud those he considered to be his spiritual ancestors, there were aspects of Lollardy that Foxe found hard to square with his own model of reformed faith. Historically, the Lollards presented Foxe with a problem: in a

[42] Patrick Collinson, 'The English Conventicle', in W. J. Sheils and Diana Wood, eds, *Voluntary Religion*, SCH 23 (Oxford, 1986), 223–59.

[43] Ibid. 230.

[44] I say 'little to do with' because, although Collinson argues that Lollards were only semi-separatist, due to their attendance at church, Foxe actually gives at least three examples of Lollards who refused to attend services: see ibid. 237–8. Foxe's examples include Thomas Grove, Thomas Man and Isabel Tracher: *TAMO* (1583), 850, 851, 853.

book about an unbroken chain of martyrs for the true Church, the numerous Lollards who quietly abjured and accepted their penance were a glaring embarrassment. Theologically, they could also be problematic, as we have seen. Foxe uses a number of polemical tools to excuse these anomalies. For instance, he often points out that the times that the Lollards lived in were 'dark and misty times of ignorance'.[45] But there is one area in particular where Foxe has exuberant praise for the Lollards. Of the Chiltern group – whose corporate life Foxe describes as being characterized by their conventicles – he writes: 'To see their trauailes, their earnest seekyng, their burnyng zeales, theyr readinges, their watchynges, their sweete assemblies, their loue and concorde, their godly lyuing, their faithfull marying with the faithfull, may make vs nowe in these our dayes of free profession to blushe for shame'.[46] This passage's significance lies in its uniqueness. It is the only place in the *Acts and Monuments* where Foxe claims that the Lollards are more perfect than their evangelical heirs. And this is not because of correct theological beliefs or their physical sacrifice for the true Church: it is based squarely on their tradition of holding conventicles, their 'sweete assemblies', in the home.

But Foxe shows us that the domicile was a place for more than mutual exhortation. The *Acts and Monuments* reveals more insidious uses for the home. Examples range from the odd wry complaint about the established Church (grumbling about church bells, for instance),[47] through potentially incendiary interchanges (talk of prophecies and the Antichrist),[48] to the outright subversive. Examples of the last of these include John Wikes, who hid heretical fugitives in his home,[49] and Andrew Randal and his wife, who did the same for Thomas Manne while he was on the run.[50] We have mentioned the suggestive relationship between domestic food and the eucharist, and Foxe gives examples of other, more explicit, ties between food and theology. Thus he tells us that John Ryburn ate butter and eggs on the evening before Assumption Day,[51] and

---

[45] Foxe, *TAMO* (1570), 966.
[46] Ibid. 984.
[47] Meeting in a butcher's house, John Eaton and his wife complained about bells: ibid. 1158.
[48] Ibid. 997.
[49] Ibid. 967.
[50] Ibid. 989.
[51] Ibid. 1158.

Marjorie Backster was accused of breaking the Lenten fast when her neighbour entered her kitchen and found bacon and oatmeal baking in a pot.[52] Foxe, then, presents his readers with a picture of the home that goes beyond happy Scripture reading; it can also be a place of private and deliberate defiance. This demonstrates that Foxe was more willing to include challenges to the established Church in the *Acts and Monuments* than Thomson's work suggests.

A few suggestions emerge from this closer look at Foxe's treatment of Lollard conventicles. First, I would like to reiterate that it could be more fruitful for scholars of Foxe to look at what he included in the *Acts and Monuments* rather than concentrate on his omissions. As I have tried to show, a radical or subversive practice omitted in one narrative is, more often than not, present in another – even in the case of conventicling, a contentious issue during the Lollard persecutions as well as in Foxe's day. This in turn forces us to re-evaluate Foxe's own adherence to Elizabethan religious orthodoxy, and the way he coped with religious reform he considered far from complete.

Another suggestion is that Foxe offers a greater variety of ecclesiological models than previously thought. The contemporary legal ambiguity surrounding conventicles allows Foxe to applaud and tacitly commend them, as we saw in the case of the Chiltern Lollards. Conventicles are depicted as a praiseworthy practice for those who do not believe that the established Church is meeting their spiritual needs, and Foxe highlights the household as the centre of fellowship and instruction. As the established Church shifted from Catholic to reformed – albeit not reformed enough for some – Foxe's Lollards could have served as models of religious praxis for discontented separatists and semi-separatists (and even pliant conformists). These Lollard narratives, then, reveal the extent to which Foxe may have considered this a viable alternative for his contemporaries; further, they show that he was willing to suggest to others, through examples of godly ecclesiology, how to supplement, or even replace, their own parochial activities with religious traditions long recognized as edifying and upright by their spiritual ancestors, all taking place in the home.

Durham University

---

[52] Ibid. 808.

THE DECALOGUE, PATRIARCHY AND DOMESTIC RELIGIOUS EDUCATION IN REFORMATION ENGLAND*

by JONATHAN WILLIS

The Decalogue was central to religious education in Reformation England, but this had not always been the case. The early Christian communities sought to distance themselves from the Ten Commandments and what they saw as the legalism of the Jewish faith, while the Middle Ages saw the ascendency of a parallel moral tradition: that of the seven deadly sins.[1] Although the Decalogue never disappeared entirely from Christian life, by the fourteenth century, the parson from Chaucer's *Canterbury Tales* could remark of the Commandments that 'so heigh a doctrine I lete to divines'.[2] The eventual triumph of the Decalogue over the sins during the fifteenth and sixteenth centuries was enormously significant, for the Ten Commandments not only taught religious doctrine; they also conditioned personal and communal devotions and moral and ethical behavioural norms. To an unparalleled extent, the Ten Commandments engendered a sense not only of the individual's bond with God but also of the social and familial bonds they shared with mother and father, brother and sister, master and servant, and the broader community of neighbours wherein they dwelt. This essay will argue that one unintended consequence of the increasing prominence of the Decalogue in the households of sixteenth-century England was that it not only reinforced traditional understandings of household authority: it also modified them significantly. Understandings of gender relations in early modern England have been framed in a number of different

*   This essay comes out of a Leverhulme Trust Early Career Fellowship project on the Ten Commandments and the English Reformation, and I would like to thank the trust for its generous support.
    [1]   Morton W. Bloomfield, *The Seven Deadly Sins* (East Lansing, MI, 1952), 12–60; Ian Green, *The Christian's ABC: Catechisms and Catechizing in England c.1530–1740* (Oxford, 1996), 13–15; John Bossy, 'Moral Arithmetic: Seven Sins into Ten Commandments', in Edmund Leites, ed., *Conscience and Casuistry in Early Modern Europe* (Cambridge, 1988), 214–34, at 219–20.
    [2]   Geoffrey Chaucer, *The Canterbury Tales*, ed. Jill Mann (London, 2005), 770.

ways over the past forty years: in terms of the essential stability of the household,[3] the tightening of patriarchal control,[4] and even in terms of crisis.[5] But what these approaches fail to recognize is that, while the Decalogue undoubtedly reinforced parental (and particularly patriarchal) authority, it did so by stressing in equal measure the responsibility that was also inherent in authority, and the duties of care owed by superiors to inferiors. In both senses of the word, the commandments came to constitute a new, universal 'moral system of the west', given authority by Scripture and ubiquity through catechesis.[6] An important aspect of this system was a much more nuanced understanding of patriarchal responsibility than has often hitherto been recognized.

★ ★ ★

It is important to begin by establishing the formal role of the Ten Commandments in domestic religious education. Starting with the second Henrician Injunctions issued in 1538, the Decalogue began to assume a central role not only in formal, public religious instruction, but in private religious education as well. It was not only the responsibility of clerics to educate children in the rudiments of the faith, but also to admonish 'fathers and mothers, maisters, and governors' to teach their children and servants 'theyr Pater noster, tharticles [sic] of our fayth, and the tenne commandementes in theyr mother tonge ... ofte to

³ Bridget Hill, 'Women's History: A Study in Change, Continuity, or Standing Still?', *Women's History Review* 2 (1993), 5–22, at 13; Bernard Capp, *When Gossips Meet: Women, Family and Neighbourhood in Early Modern England* (Oxford, 2003), 20.

⁴ Lawrence Stone, *The Family, Sex and Marriage in England, 1500–1800* (London, 1977); cf. Alan MacFarlane, 'Review of Lawrence Stone, *The Family, Sex and Marriage in England, 1500–1800*', *History and Theory* 18 (1979), 103–26.

⁵ David Underdown, 'The Taming of the Scold: The Enforcement of Patriarchal Authority in Early Modern England', in A. J. Fletcher and J. Stevenson, eds, *Order and Disorder in Early Modern England* (Cambridge, 1985), 116–36.

⁶ According to Bossy, the change was 'revolutionary'. On this and some of the associated changes, see John Bossy, *Christianity in the West 1500–1700* (Oxford, 1985), 38, 161, 171; idem, 'Some Elementary Forms of Durkheim', *P&P*, no. 95 (1982), 3–18, at 11–12; idem, 'Moral Arithmetic', 216–17; cf. Ethan Shagan, *Popular Politics and the English Reformation* (Cambridge, 2003), 10–20; Simon Ditchfield, 'Introduction', in *Christianity and Community in the West: Essays for John Bossy*, ed. idem (Aldershot, 2001), xxii.

repete and vnderstande'.[7] Later, the Elizabethan Injunctions of 1559 helped to cement the place of the Ten Commandments at the heart of post-Reformation religion by reiterating that 'all parentes and householders' had a duty to teach their children and servants the Creed, Lord's Prayer and Ten Commandments, 'as they are bound by the lawe of God and conscience to do'.[8] In part, then, the memorization and understanding of the Decalogue was imparted through the mechanism of formal catechesis. But from the outset, the household constituted one of the primary arenas in which most children and parents came into contact with the strictures of the law of God, either through a conscious process of teaching and learning or by the more nebulous imparting of a system of belief, ethics and moral obligations.

This was not only the hope of the government, but of a whole host of churchmen, divines and authors. In the introduction to his eight treatises *Of domesticall duties* of 1622, the godly minister and writer William Gouge exclaimed: 'oh if the head and severall members of a family would be perswaded euery of them to be conscionable in performing their owne particular duties … what excellent seminaries would families be to Church and Commonwealth?'[9]

The medical writer Robert Burton heaped nothing but scorn upon parents who, in a desperate attempt to find their daughters husbands, brought them up 'to sing, and dance, and play on the Lute … before she can say her Pater noster, or ten Commandements'.[10] And John Carpenter, in his *Contemplations for the institution of children in the Christian religion*, warned his young audience that 'vntimely' and 'cruell death' was such a real and present danger that, rather than spending out 'the flower of their youth' in 'vaine studies and childish delightes', they should dedicate themselves to 'the vse of things heauenlie and diuine'.[11] This was a familiar argument, and there was nothing in it that applied exclusively to the

---

[7] *Iniunctions gyuen by th auctoritie of the kynges highnes* (London, 1538), fol. [1ᵛ].

[8] *Iniunctions geuen by the Quenes Maiestie* (London, 1559), sig. Aiiiʳ; cf. William Cecil, *Ordinances made … for … the hospitall at Stanford Baron* (London, 1597), 1.

[9] William Gouge, *Of domesticall duties eight treatises* (London, 1622), sig. ¶2ᵛ.

[10] Robert Burton, *The anatomy of melancholy vvhat it is* (London, 1621), 586.

[11] John Carpenter, *Contemplations for the institution of children in the Christian religion* (London, 1601), sigs Aviᵛ–Aviiʳ.

commandments. Thomas Sternhold had used the same language in the dedication of his metrical psalms to Edward VI, 'seeyng furdre that youre tender and Godly zeale doethe more delyghte in the holye songes of veritie than in anye famed rimes of vanitie'.[12] But the ubiquity of the Decalogue, in the catechism, in painted texts in churches, in the liturgy and elsewhere, helped to guarantee its prominence in domestic religious education as well.[13]

The particular value of the commandments in this respect lay in their ability to inform both ethical and doctrinal education, at the rudimentary and advanced levels.[14] They were described by John Hooper in 1548 as containing 'the effect and whole sum of all the scripture': whatever else had been taught by the prophets, apostles, and even by Christ himself, was 'none other thing but the interpretation and exposition of these ten words'.[15] Furthermore, their provenance was impeccable. Numerous authors attested to the fact that the tablets delivered to Moses on Mount Sinai had been inscribed by the finger of God himself.[16] Calvin also pointed out that the numbering of the commandments was no accident, but a divine accommodation to the short wits and limited physiognomy of man: 'for he had giuen us his lawe in so small roome, as euerie man might count it vpon his fingeres ends': the Ten Commandments, in which 'hath God comprehended his whole wil, which is the rule of good life'.[17] The coincidence between the number of fingers of which most men were possessed and the number of the commandments in the Decalogue was also seized upon by the author of an early Elizabethan ballad printed by William Powell, *Some fyne gloues deuised for Newyeres gyftes to teche yonge people to knowe good from euyll*. Laid out visually against a pair of gloves, the commandments hovered above the fingertips, starting with

[12] Thomas Sternhold, *Certayne Psalmes chosen out of the Psalter of Dauid* (London, 1549), sig. Aiii[r].

[13] Cf. Bossy, 'Moral Arithmetic', 232.

[14] Green, *ABC*, 41–3.

[15] John Hooper, 'A declaration of the Ten holy Commandements of Almighty God' (*c.*1548), in *Early Writings of John Hooper*, ed. Samuel Carr, PS (Cambridge, 1843), 271.

[16] E.g. Hooper, 'A declaration', 255; Hugh Broughton, *A reuelation of the holy Apocalyps* (London, 1610), 174; Heinrich Bullinger, *Looke from Adam*, transl. Miles Coverdale (London, 1624), 38; Jean Calvin, *Sermons ... vpon the fifth booke of Moses called Deuteronomie*, transl. Arthur Golding (London, 1583), 391.

[17] Calvin, *Sermons vpon Deuteronomie*, 391.

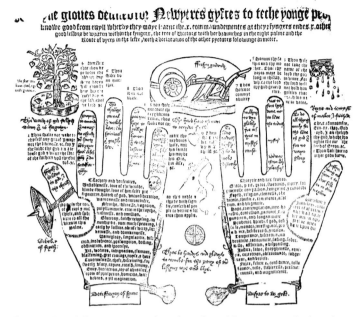

Fig. 1: Detail from T.T., *Some fyne gloves devised for newyeres gyftes* (London, 1559). Reproduced by permission of The Henry E. Huntington Library and Art Gallery, San Marino, California, USA. Image published with permission of ProQuest. Further reproduction is prohibited without permission. Image produced by ProQuest as part of *Early English Books Online*, <http://www.proquest.com>.

the thumb of the right hand and alternating between the fingers of both hands in sequence. On the palms of the right hand were listed the seven virtues, on the left the seven deadly sins, with ten further virtues inscribed on the fingers themselves (Fig. 1).

★ ★ ★

The commandments themselves also contained a clear message about the nature of family relationships, most obviously concerning the divinely instituted importance of hierarchy, authority and obedience. The first commandment, in both number and prominence, was the declaration: 'I am the LORD thy God, which have brought thee out of the land of Egypt, out of the house of bondage. Thou shalt have no other gods before me'.[18] As Heinrich Bullinger explained, the meaning of this precept was 'namely, that wee should take him only for the true and right God, and none else beside or except him: That wee should worship and honour him only, and in no wise to have any other God, comfort, or hope'.[19] It was this principle which formed the head of all the others. Hooper called it 'the ground, original, and foundation, of all virtue, godly laws, or Christian works'; John Brinsley the 'principal duties, which are the very entrances to all true godlinesse'.[20] At stake here was the recognition of the majesty, authority, justice, power and mercy of God himself, a principle of authority from which all other authority stemmed. God had given the Ten Commandments to men as a didactic tool: a remembrancer of the law, a principle of authority that had hitherto been written in men's hearts, but 'when the people had gotten them stony hearts, he wrote the same in tables of stone'.[21]

This image, of a divinely ordained Father, presiding over a simple and wayward people, handing down laws to ensure justice and educating them in the ways of true religion, naturally translated to a range of authority figures in the temporal sphere, from kings and princes to fathers and masters. Jean Bodin, in his *Six bookes of a common-weal*, wrote that 'the right gouernment of the Father and the children, consisteth in the good vse of the power which God (himselfe the Father of nature) hath giuen to the Father ouer his owne children'.[22] The word 'power', Bodin explained, was common to all of those with power of command over others, including princes, magistrates, fathers, masters, captains and lords. But alone of all of these, it was the natural father who was given the right and power to command by nature as well as by divine commandment, 'who is the true Image of the great and Almightie God the Father of all things'. The father was bound by nature to nourish his children 'according to his abilitie and to instruct them in all civilitie and vertue', but children once grown were bound 'with the seale of nature',

---

[18] Ex. 20: 2–3. In the Catholic and Lutheran traditions, the first commandment included the prohibition against the making of graven images, but in the Jewish, Orthodox and Reformed traditions this constituted a second, separate commandment.

[19] Bullinger, *Looke from Adam*, 38.

[20] Hooper, 'A declaration', 255; John Brinsley, *The true watch* (London, 1606), 17.

[21] Bullinger, *Looke from Adam*, 39.

[22] Jean Bodin, *The six bookes of a common-weale*, transl. Richard Knolles (London, 1606), 20.

with a much more straiter bond, to loue, reuerence, serue, and nourish theyr Father and in all things to shew themselves dutifull and obedient vnto them, and by all meanes to hide and couer their infirmities and imperfections, if they see any in them, and neuer to spare their liues and goods to saue the life of them by whome they themselves tooke breathe.[23]

The explicit guarantor of this natural obedience was the fifth commandment of the Reformed Decalogue, 'Honour thy father and thy mother'. Interestingly, in the scheme drawn up by the first-century Hellenistic Jewish biblical philosopher Philo of Alexandria in his treatise *De Decalogo*, this commandment had formed the fifth and final precept of the first table, that is of the list of duties owed not to fellow human beings, but to God.[24] In the Christian tradition, it migrated to become the first commandment of the second table. This gave it a new and special prominence, heading the list of obligations owed by human beings to their fellows. If the first commandment was the ground for all godly laws, then the fifth commandment was the foundation of earthly hierarchy, of civil society and of all natural relationships, 'wherein the Lord takes order for preseruing the honour and dignitie which he hath bestowed vpon euery one'.[25] Such was the importance of this principle, that alone of all the commandments God promised a reward for keeping it: 'Honour thy father and thy mother: that thy days may be long upon the land which the LORD thy God giueth thee.' 'And surely by the worde of the fifte commaundement,' wrote Thomas Becon, 'all mannes life, bothe in the gouernement of a commonaltie, and also of an houshold, is blessed, if so be faithe lacketh not, but that thou doest euery thing obediently, in the name of GOD'.[26] The subjection demanded by the fifth commandment, as well as the benefits of obedience, was applied across the full range of hierarchical relationships, and the nature of these relationships was similarly conditioned by the notion of fatherhood. Nicholas Byfield explained:

---

[23] Bodin, *The six bookes*, 20–1.
[24] *Philo Volume VII*, transl. F. H. Colson, LCL 320 (London, 2006), 3–4, 31, 33.
[25] Brinsley, *The true watch*, 37; cf. Hooper, 'A declaration', 353.
[26] Thomas Becon, *A new postil conteinyng most godly and learned sermons* (London, 1566), fol. 38[r].

God of purpose preserues this title in all superiority thereby to sweeten subiection to inferiors, and to make them think the seuerall dangers, burdens, labors, and subiections in each condition, to be not onely tolerable, but meet to be born, because they endure them vnder parents as it were: and so such superiority, for that reason, should not bee resisted or enuied.[27]

Parental and other forms of obedience were not a simple matter of outward observance, nor to be respected out of fear of punishment: obedience was a state enjoined by nature, by conscience and by divine law.[28]

★ ★ ★

The Decalogue therefore provided a strong foundation for parental, pre-eminently paternal, authority, in the domestic hierarchy as well as in the cosmic, spiritual, political and social spheres.[29] Indeed, their stress on authority and obedience was undoubtedly one of the factors which so recommended the commandments to fathers, masters, monarchs and divines. The Decalogue turned subservience from an ethical question or social expectation into a religious obligation. Servants were obliged to their masters and subjects to their rulers by virtue not of any intrinsic authority possessed by the superior party but because superiors were plenipotentiaries of an authority stemming from God himself. The obedience owed by sons and daughters to their fathers was stronger still, stemming as it did from both nature and the law. And yet the use of the language of fatherhood created a discourse which cut both ways, outlining a duty of responsibility and care alongside alongside the rights, honour and dignity associated with positions of authority. Fathers of all kinds were guaranteed obedience

[27] Nicholas Byfield, *A commentary: or, sermons vpon the second chapter of the first epistle of Saint Peter* (London, 1623), 733.

[28] 'The third part of the sermon of good works', *Sermons, or Homilies, appointed to be read in churches, in the time of Queen Elizabeth* (Dublin, 1821), 49; cf. Henry Parker, *Here endith a compendiouse treetise dyalogue of Diues and pauper* (London, 1493), sig. mii^v; Martin Luther, 'The Fourth Commandment', from 'Ten Sermons on the Catechism', *LW* 51: *Sermons I*, ed. and transl. John W. Doberstein (Philadelphia, PA, 1980), 146; Gouge, *Of domesticall duties*, 441–2.

[29] Bossy, *Christianity in the West*, 116; cf. William Perkins, *A golden chaine* (London, 1600), 67.

by the law, but they were also required to uphold the law and take responsibility for those set beneath them.

The character Theodidactus in the pedagogical discourse *The Christian mans closet* therefore remarked that while it was set down that children should honour their father and mother, 'with what face dare that Father exact of his child the honour commaunded of God in the second Table, when as hee himselfe doth not perfourme his owne duetie'?[30] He lamented that many parents at that time cared more for their horses and swine than their children and family, 'for, twise in one day at the least they giue Meate and Water vnto their hogges and Horses, to eate and drinke to refreshe and comfort them', but they would 'scarscely spare so muche time' to feed their children's minds 'with the wholesome foode of the worde'.[31] If the duty of children was honour, the duties of parents were to nourish, nurture and instruct.[32] A husband's special duties under the fifth commandment, wrote John Brinsley, included wise government, as well as honour for his wife as the weaker vessel, 'especially in couering and bearing with her infirmities'. Wives' duties included offering subjection, loyalty and holy contentment to their husbands. And as parents together, they owed their children education, both in religion and in an honest trade; provision at the present time and in the future; and moderate correction by word and rod.[33] Catechisms such as John Lyster's *A rule how to bring vp children*, a dialogue between a father and his son, rested solely upon this very assumption. 'It is the duty of parents not only to educate and bring vp their Children with meate and apparel, but also to enstruct and teach them in the feare of God, and Christian religion', began the father at the outset of this lengthy catechetical text. He ended in similar vein: 'I Thought it my dutie sonne, to bring thee vp in vertue and knowledge, and in the feare of God, whereof I haue apposed thee, and I thanck GOD thou hast profited well'.[34]

William Perkins explained that the broader obligation of the fifth commandment was, in the affirmative part, to 'preserue the dignitie

---

[30]   Barthélemy Batt, *The Christian mans closet*, ed. William Lowth (London, 1581), fol. 32[r].

[31]   Ibid., fol. 32[r–v].

[32]   Gouge, *Of domesticall duties*, 497.

[33]   Brinsley, *The true watch*, 41–2.

[34]   John Lyster, *A rule how to bring vp children* (London, 1588), fols 1[r], 138[r].

of thy neighbour', and in the negative to 'diminish not the excel-
lencie, or dignitie' of their person. Superiors therefore had a general
duty to yield to their inferiors 'in good matters, as to their brethren',
and a particular duty to rule their subjects in the Lord, justly, fairly
and honestly.[35] Conversely, they were forbidden from harming their
inferiors 'through negligence in gouerning them, and prouiding for
their good estate'. The commandments, or rather their expositors,
were strongly prescriptive about the type of relationship which ought
to exist between husbands, wives, fathers and sons, all of which was
constructed around a firm scriptural infrastructure, including specific
examples from the Old and New Testaments.

Finally, expositions of the commandments made it quite clear
that parents were not only obliged to act with care and conscience
with respect to their children, but that they were obliged more
generally to set a good example through striving to live in godly
accordance with the Decalogue. 'For wordees althoughe they maye
do much', wrote Bullinger, 'yet shall good ensamples of lyuinge
do more to the yougth.'[36] For Gouge, setting a good example
was 'another generall branch proceeding from parents *loue* to their
children'. It was not only for their own sake, but for their children's, that parents were to 'endeauour to *walke vprightly* before
God, and to please him'.[37] There was tangible profit to be had from
such behaviour. Not only would children benefit from observing
a godly parental role model, they would themselves benefit mate-
rially from the divine rewards bestowed upon righteous parents.
These rewards did not extend to grace itself, of course, which
could hardly be passed down the generations along with the family
silver, but it did extend to the fruits of parental righteousness.
Gouge was broadly happy with the notion that parents might
labour after righteousness for their children's sakes, 'for thus doe
they vse the meanes which by Gods word is warranted and sanctified for procuring Gods blessing to their children'.[38]

---

[35] Perkins, *A golden chaine*, 67–72.
[36] Heinrich Bullinger, *The golden boke of christen matrimonye*, transl. Theodore Basille
(London, 1543), fol. lxx[v].
[37] Gouge, *Of domesticall duties*, 502.
[38] Ibid. 503.

★ ★ ★

This essay has been a preliminary investigation into a complex topic, and as such has focused much more on prescription than on practice. Still, the commandments seem to offer an interesting perspective on domestic piety and household religious instruction for several reasons. On the one hand, the commandments, particularly the first and fifth, did an excellent job of outlining and reinforcing a scripturally impeccable vision of patriarchal authority: to disobey a divinely instituted superior was an act of disobedience directed against God himself. On the other hand, what at first glance appeared to be a veritable tyrants' charter came with an important and subtly nuanced subtext. Children were not simply enjoined to obey their parents by reason of duty, fear and obedience. Parents were granted their authority by God and nature, and were to be loved, cherished, cared for, respected and obeyed for conscience' sake. In turn, the office of parenthood granted not only dominion, but also entailed a series of practical, moral and religious responsibilities. Parents were required to care for their children, to provide for their futures, and to be watchful of their spiritual health just as much as their physical well-being. They were also required to live well themselves, both in order to set a good example, and also to share the benefits of the fruits of righteousness with their offspring. It was something of a commonplace in early modern catechisms that the Creed represented the theological virtue of faith, the Lord's Prayer hope, and the Ten Commandments charity.[39] It may be that the Decalogue not only focused peoples' minds on their familial and neighbourly obligations much more effectively than the seven sins had ever managed to, but that they also helped to reshape and refine popular understandings of patriarchy, authority and obedience, both in theory and in practice.

University of Birmingham

---

[39] E.g. John Boys, *An exposition of the dominical epistles and gospels used in our English liturgie throughout the whole yeare* (London, 1610), 120; Robert Bellarmine, *An ample declaration of the Christian doctrine*, transl. Richard Hadock (Roan [English secret press], 1604), 4.

LIVING WITH THE BIBLE IN POST-REFORMATION ENGLAND: THE MATERIALITY OF TEXT, IMAGE AND OBJECT IN DOMESTIC LIFE*

by TARA HAMLING

W hat did it mean to live with the Bible in post-Reformation England? The increased availability from 1560 of printed vernacular Bibles to own and keep in the home marked a profound change in where and how people experienced Scripture. Most authors have concentrated on the impact of this cultural shift on the textual practices of household religion, especially Bible reading or study in the context of daily prayers and associated instruction.[1] More recent research has examined interactions with the Bible as object, especially the common practice of annotating specific passages, recording information or otherwise marking the pages.[2] A turn in humanities disciplines over the past decade towards visual and material culture has emphasized the connotative role of Bibles as signifiers, with important studies of their display function within female piety, as part of the conventional vocabulary of provincial portraits or as staged properties in

* I would like to thank Alexandra Walsham as President of the EHS for the invitation to speak at the 2013 Winter Meeting and for helpful advice and encouragement. I gratefully acknowledge the generous research support provided by a Phillip Leverhulme Prize, which has allowed me to progress the wider project that informs this essay. I am greatly indebted to my research partner for this project, Catherine Richardson, for sharing the fruits of her exhaustive primary research and for informing my thinking.

[1] Since Christopher Hill's wide-ranging account of the 'spiritualization of the household' in *Society and Puritanism in Pre-Revolutionary England* (London, 1964), most work has focused on the educational and disciplinary responsibilities of heads of households, with a separate trajectory focusing on the respective duties of women. An emerging interest in the wider practices, patterns and spaces of household religious observance is reflected in recent publications, including Jessica Martin and Alec Ryrie, eds, *Private and Domestic Devotion in Early Modern Britain* (Farnham, 2012); Andrew Cambers, *Godly Reading: Print, Manuscript and Puritanism in England, 1580–1720* (Cambridge, 2011).

[2] Notably William H. Sherman, *Used Books: Marking Readers in Renaissance England* (Philadelphia, PA, 2008), ch. 4; and Femke Molekamp, '"Of the Incomparable treasure of the Holy Scriptures": The Geneva Bible in the Early Modern Household', in Matthew Dimmock and Andrew Hadfield, eds, *Literature and Popular Culture in Early Modern England* (Farnham, 2009), 121–35, which includes a useful though very brief discussion of 'The Bible as Domestic Object'.

Renaissance drama.[3] Yet despite these contributions there is still an overwhelming focus in the existing literature on the use of religious books in relation to the textual and oral practices of domestic devotion – on readers and reading practices – and a good deal of generalization about the locations for such practices, derived from a particular conceptual model of the country house with clearly defined internal arrangements and designated room functions.

This essay examines physical and documentary evidence to modify this straightforward view of the spatial and material context for encounters with biblical content and associated religious observance by focusing attention on the form, appearance and furnishings of a wider range of house types in early modern England. It contributes a new perspective on the household as a physical space and setting for personal and family piety and extends our understanding of the materiality of Protestant domestic devotion. Acquisition and display of Bibles as domestic objects from the mid-sixteenth century onwards formed part of more general investment in material possessions that reflected the identity, interests and aspirations of householders within the middling ranks of society. Assumptions about the 'iconophobic' nature of English Protestantism have contributed towards a near-comprehensive neglect of its visual and material culture in the established historiography.[4] But the new materialized presence of the Word as a book in the home coincided with a widespread fashion for biblical texts and imagery in the decoration of domestic spaces and crafted wares.[5] This tangible presence of biblical content in a range of media formed a system of texts, images and objects to inform

---

3   Alexandra Walsham, 'Jewels for Gentlewomen: Religious Books as Artefacts in Late Medieval and Early Modern England', in R. N. Swanson, ed., *The Church and the Book*, SCH 38 (Woodbridge, 2004), 123–42; Robert Tittler, *Portraits, Painters and Publics in Provincial England, 1540–1640* (Oxford, 2012), ch. 7; Elizabeth Williamson, *The Materiality of Religion in Early Modern English Drama* (Farnham, 2009), ch. 4.

4   An assumption reinforced by Patrick Collinson's influential article 'From Iconoclasm to Iconophobia: The Cultural Impact of the Second English Reformation', first published as The Stenton Lecture (Reading, 1985), repr. in Peter Marshall, ed., *The Impact of the English Reformation 1500–1640* (London, 1997), 279–308, at 297.

5   Discussed in detail in Tara Hamling, *Decorating the Godly Household: Religious Art in Post-Reformation England* (New Haven, CT, and London, 2010); eadem, 'Old Robert's Girdle: Visual and Material Props for Protestant Piety in Post-Reformation England', in Martin and Ryrie, eds, *Private and Domestic Devotion*, 135–64.

everyday experience in domestic space. Attention to these various means of transmission and reception of Scripture offers a radically different view of post-Reformation Protestant culture to counter the dominant narrative, which invariably casts reformed religious practice as self-conscious separated from material props or concerns.

What follows focuses attention on the nature of experience outside the ranks of the clergy or social elite to examine how ordinary lay people practised their faith in the context of daily life within the home.[6] My sources include extant buildings, their interior decoration and the objects that might be found in them, alongside descriptions of furnished spaces as recorded in probate inventories. This evidence about the visual and material culture of the household is analysed alongside the ideals of devotional practice presented in prescriptive literature and accounts of 'real' behaviours recorded in diaries. I argue that for members of the 'middling sort' the new emphasis on the Bible as the cornerstone of Protestant piety cannot be defined solely in terms of compartmentalized and abstracted experience informed by text, because interactions with biblical content in the form of painted inscriptions and crafted imagery were multi-sensory and rooted in the paraphernalia and bustle of domestic life. The first half of the essay examines the form, function and decoration of domestic rooms to complicate assumptions about where devotional activities might take place and the nature and quality of those experiences. The second half focuses attention on the furnishing of interiors to point towards the wide range of material conditions for domestic life within the middling ranks of society, so that a Bible as a household object could form part of the disarray associated with everyday toil or be set apart within a specialized, exclusive space that was dressed to impress. Awareness of these more particularized contexts for domestic and devotional life, I suggest, affords some sense of the materiality of experience for people within the mainstream of society and belief.

---

6   This interest stems from collaborative research towards a book, authored jointly with Catherine Richardson: *A Day at Home in Early Modern England: The Materiality of Domestic Life* (New Haven, CT, forthcoming 2016).

Locating Devotion

Any attempt to get to grips with the material environment for spiritual experience in the early modern household must first address the powerful but illusory notion of the closet, derived in part from visual depictions showing prayer performed in solitude, located in the confines of a dedicated space and anchored to the text of the Bible.[7] Such imagery reflects a highly constructed model of ideal practice that was achievable only by certain specific members of elite groups, yet the convenient metaphorical simplicity of the closet as locus for personal devotion has contributed towards the power of this deeply entrenched association between practice and space within the historiography.

Modern scholarship has eroded the traditional concept of the closet as private space, even among elite men and women, pointing towards the public implications of withdrawing there and the variety of social activities that might take place within.[8] Then, in her strikingly original account of impediments to privacy in the houses of Tudor England, Lena Cowen Orlin has presented evidence from probate inventories to argue that the dominant purpose of the room that in early modern England was known interchangeably as a closet or study was the safe storage of material goods.[9] Orlin insists that an aggregation of personal possessions was the greatest influence on the rebuilding and use of houses: 'The need to keep goods securely, as also to display them on occasion, was perceptibly more urgent than a desire for privacy.'[10] She concludes that the closet as a dedicated study area was not actual but aspirational in sixteenth-century England and suggests that while the symbolic identity of the prayer closet as a certain kind of private space with devotional functions survived religious reformation as an object of the cultural imaginary, this construct was out of step with social

---

[7]   As, for example, with the printed frontispiece showing Elizabeth I at prayer in Richard Day, *A Booke of Christian Prayers* (London, 1578), and the woodcut of a pious man at prayer in John Hayward, *The sanctuarie of a troubled soule* (London, 1602).

[8]   Alan Stewart, 'The Early Modern Closet Discovered', *Representations*, no.50 (Spring 1995), 76–100.

[9]   Lena Cowen Orlin, *Locating Privacy in Tudor London* (Oxford, 2007), 301. The choice of subheadings for the two sections of this essay acknowledges an intellectual debt to this book.

[10]   Ibid. 311.

circumstance and the closet's variable uses.[11] The implications of this rethinking of the material realities of closets for ordinary people's practice and experience of domestic devotion have yet to be addressed. The possibility of tension between the potentially conflicting desires to secure and display prized possessions is also intriguing and particularly pertinent to consideration of how the Bible as an object with both economic and spiritual value was kept and encountered in the home.

The limited architectural evidence available certainly supports Orlin's view of the closet as a practical storage or working space and equipped as such. There is, however, a major limitation with the extant built evidence as closets in many houses that were remodelled as need arose were probably fairly makeshift partitioned areas within rooms. It is impossible to recover a sense of the form, quality or decoration of these spaces because these non-structural partitions were invariably removed during later renovations to the building.[12] We might expect, however, to find purpose-built closets in newly constructed properties. At Chastleton House in Oxfordshire, built c.1607–12 by the successful clothier Walter Jones to establish himself as a country gentleman, is what seems to be the quintessential prayer closet, as a small inner room beyond a bedchamber. This notion is reinforced by the current presentation of the room by the National Trust as the 'secret closet', because of its slightly irregular position midway between floors. In a 1633 inventory of the property, however, this room was called a chamber, the general designation for upper rooms but one which was becoming increasingly associated with sleeping. It contained 'one bedstead two flock beds one boulster one blanket and a Cov'let one table

[11] Ibid. 325.

[12] Moreover, it seems that these relatively flimsy partitions would afford little sense of seclusion from the hubbub of domestic life; this aural porosity lends a particular perspective to accounts of 'private' prayer being heard outside the closet in some 'godly lives', e.g. the biography of John Carter (d. 1635) who, his son reports, 'prayed constantly in his Closet, whensoever he went into his study … Hee prayed very loud, and mostly very long. For the extension of his voice (I conjecture) he had a double reason; one that by his earnest speech he might quicken up his owne heart and devotion: the other, that he might be a pattern of secret prayer to his Children and Servants': John Carter, *The tomb-stone, and A rare sight* (London, 1653), 12. This account indicates that sense of performance and outreach in the practice of supposedly 'secret' prayer.

& a frame & one old chaire'.[13] The lesser quality of the flock mattresses stuffed with wool refuse compared with the featherbeds in the main chamber suggest that this room provided additional accommodation for servants.

The so-called secret closet at Chastleton is situated in one of the more common locations for smaller adjunct spaces, that is, in the upper section of a projecting porch. This arrangement is represented by more modest late Tudor oak buildings, such as Blakesley Hall near Birmingham and Oak House near Sandwell. These small square chambers with large windows overlooking the frontage of the property are much better suited to keeping an eye on the world than for looking within the self. In other new builds where auxiliary spaces too small to contain a bed adjoin a larger bedchamber, they appear designed as toilets rather than as dedicated spaces for prayer, either with integrated facilities or containing a close-stool (as with another small projecting room on the rear facade at Chastleton), although obviously the two functions are not mutually exclusive. Indeed, none of these spaces preclude the possibility of use for religious practice but the built and documentary evidence does not support the idea that they were created or furnished specifically for that purpose. The material contexts for 'private' devotion were almost certainly more ad hoc and compromised than visual and literary constructions of the closet would allow.

Even if dedicated prayer closets in the form we tend to imagine them existed, only the master or mistress of the house would have had access to them. How might other members of the family have observed their religious duties? Nehemiah Wallington records in his notebooks how as a young man living in his father's house during 1618–19 he would use the 'hie garret', or uppermost attic room, for prayer. On more than one occasion he recounts how the material environment of this space intruded on his thoughts, offering various strategies for suicide; the window was evidently large enough to consider 'leaping out' to his death while another time he was tempted to hang himself there with 'a rope out of the

---

[13] Jonathan Marsden, 'The Chastleton Inventory of 1633', *Furniture History* 36 (2000), 23–42. The secret closet is identified as 'the Chamber adjoyneinge' the 'chamber over the Parlour'.

trash bagge'.[14] While Wallington's response to his environment can hardly be taken as representative of how most people thought, his vivid recall of how material fixtures and domestic clutter framed and disrupted religious practice is perhaps indicative of a wider cultural awareness of the indissoluble relationship between an event and its physical context.

It could be argued that the secondary literature has placed disproportionate emphasis on the rituals of household religion, thus neglecting the routine of spiritual endeavour embedded within the patterns of daily life.[15] The approved practice of daily devotion consisted not only of set prayers in the morning and evening but a continuous and seamless sequence of guided thought to accompany humble actions in between. Commentators repeated the biblical injunction to 'Pray continually' (1 Thess. 5: 17)[16] and devotional texts provided examples of appropriate subject matter to aid this constant diligence in spiritual endeavour. This amounts to an attempt by clerical and household authorities to ritualize the routines of daily life as part of the renewed emphasis on the household as the core social and religious unit in post-Reformation England. In this sense, these approved 'private' and domestic religious practices were intensely public in their implications, intended to impose uniformity in thought and action in daily life across society.

These prescribed quotidian patterns are understudied because of a lack of evidence about if and how they were put into practice, but they are important because they provided a framing context or narrative for the ordered, repetitive actions of the ideal household; an ideal that we may assume aspiring, upright members of the middling sort would wish to be seen to embrace and emulate in whole or in part. While we can speculate that consciousness of the ideal influenced a range of individual or collective behaviours, much of the available evidence about practice tends to offer rather idiosyncratic or extreme examples. Evidence about the devotional behaviours of the conforming majority is much

---

[14] David Booy, ed., *The Notebooks of Nehemiah Wallington 1618–1654: A Selection* (Aldershot, 2007), 33–4.

[15] This is about to change with monographs appearing which focus attention on the lived experience of religion, esp. Alec Ryrie, *Being Protestant in Reformation Britain* (Oxford, 2013).

[16] 'Pray continually' in the Geneva Bible; 'pray without ceasing' in the AV.

harder to find. I would argue, however, that material evidence in the form of domestic decoration represents a concerted effort to express aspects of this prescription and functions in an analogous way, to guide and prompt thought during the diurnal routine of domestic tasks and thereby to transform these practical actions into a series of devotional acts. The quantity of material evidence that has been documented can only represent a fraction of a once ubiquitous trend but can be used to understand the extent to which prescription was absorbed and reinforced by householders about whom we would otherwise know very little. While we cannot be sure how individuals within the household responded to this physical context, there is a synergy in the recurring themes of both prescription and decoration which suggests the power of this dominant discourse in framing and structuring experience. Moreover, decoration applied to the surface of walls provides evidence about how certain kinds of experience were associated with specific physical and spatial contexts.[17]

Bedchamber

According to stricter Protestant advisors, routine activities in the early morning, from first waking until after dressing, were supposed to be accompanied and punctuated by a series of meditations as well as by formal prayer. This places considerable emphasis on the bedchamber as a site for personal devotion. The first authorized book of Christian prayers printed in Protestant England set up a pattern for early morning devotions that was repeated and extended by subsequent theologians and authors of advice. It provided set prayers 'to be sayd at our first waking' and 'at our uprising', which established a formula of appropriate subject matter to contemplate before starting the day.[18] Thomas Bentley's compilation of prayers and advice reflecting a more rigorous form of Protestant piety aimed to elongate the process of morning devotions to include separate prayers and meditations to accompany not only waking and rising, but also to respond to cognizance of dawn and the sun's

---

[17] See, in this volume, Michael Ashby, '"My house shall be called the house of prayer": Religion and the Material Culture of the Episcopal Household, *c.*1500 to *c.*1800', 294–306.

[18] Richard Day, *Christian Prayers and Meditations* (London, 1569); revised version, *A Booke of Christian Prayers* (London, 1578).

rising, as well as other external stimuli. In one treatise included in Bentley's collection, the reader is imagined still in bed after waking and is instructed: 'Hearing the clock strike, pray and meditate', and the accompanying set text figures this as a reminder of the trumpet sounding at Judgement Day, requiring constant watchfulness: 'let the houre of thy sudden coming so runne in my mind, and keep me watching'.[19] Lewis Bayly, in his popular devotional handbook, *The Practice of pietie*, published in numerous editions from 1611 onwards, may have had a rural readership in mind with his external sound to prompt meditation: 'if thou hearest the Cocke crow … call to mind that Cocke-crowing sound of the last Trumpet, which shall waken thee from the dead'.[20] Elizabeth Jocelin's legacy of advice to her unborn child, written in 1622, directs: 'So soone as thou hast made thy prayer to God, prepare to rise, and rising use this Prayer'.[21] The action of rising was possibly even more symbolically significant than first waking and most set prayers to accompany getting out of bed develop the theme of resurrection and judgement. In another suggested meditation the puritan zealot Philip Stubbes frames the act of rising as a form of daily prefigu-ration of eventual resurrection: 'Think also that as thy bodie now riseth out of thy materiall bed, so shal it rise out of the bed of thy grave at the great day of the Lord'.[22] Once out of bed, you might shed your nightclothes: 'Putting off your nearest garment, meditate' and 'Beholding your nakedness, meditate'; then: 'Putting on your nearest garment, meditate'.[23] This continual meditative process is explicitly located within, and responds to, the material environment of the bedchamber to exploit the expected sensory interactions with bed, clock, window and garments to prompt and guide devotional activity. All this should take place as preparation for formal prayer, which according to Bayly must be said 'kneeling down at thy bed-side'.[24] An unusual detail from an inventory from Bristol evokes a more specific material context for this practice. The inventory of goods belonging to Richard Hollyester, a fletcher,

---

[19] Thomas Bentley, *The Monument of Matrons* (London, 1582), 363–5.
[20] Lewis Bayly, *The Practice of pietie* (London, 1613), 154.
[21] Elizabeth Jocelin, *The Mother's Legacy to her Unborn Child* (London, 1624), 29.
[22] Philip Stubbes, *A Perfect pathway to felicitie conteining godly meditations and praiers* (London, 1592), sig. B6.
[23] Bentley, *Monument*, 369–71.
[24] Bayly, *Practice of pietie*, 156, 161.

taken in 1625, records a property of three rooms; the shop, the fore street chamber (which contained the majority of his possessions including twenty-three old books, described as 'sum good & sum badde') and the upper chamber, which contained two old half-headed bedsteads with cords and mats, three old coverlets and two rugs, an old flock bed with a flock bolster and a feather pillow, three old chests and, significantly, 'A ould Couchine that he dyd use for to knelle upon when thus he dyd saye prayeres morninge & Eavneinges'.[25] This sort of additional information about the use of an object is extremely unusual in inventories because it was redundant in relation to the purpose of assessing economic value. The detail about the religious habits of the deceased man was probably communicated by his widow, but its inclusion within the context of a legal document underlines the public nature of individual behaviours within the domestic environment. It is also worth noting the two bedsteads in this upper chamber. It is becoming apparent that co-sleeping – with several people sleeping in the same room or even sharing a bed – was extremely common across the middling ranks of society. This complicates the picture of focused meditative activity presented in prescriptive literature; presumably Richard Hollyester performed his routine 'private' prayers either in front of, or with, his family.[26]

The words of these morning prayers might be triggered by, or echo, inscriptions painted on the walls. A great fashion developed for this sort of painted decoration during the Elizabethan period. At 3 Cornmarket in Oxford, a second-floor room is decorated with wall paintings traditionally dated to *c.*1564–81, when the property was occupied by one John Tattleton; the initials 'IT' were recorded in the painted decoration of another room, since demolished. A frieze of text running along the top of two walls includes this direction: 'In the mornynge earlye | serve god Devoutlye | Fear god above allthynge' (Fig. 1).[27] Calico House in Newnham, Kent, was extensively remodelled in the first decade of the seven-

[25] Edwin and Stella George, *Bristol Probate Inventories, Part 1: 1542–1650*, Bristol Record Society 54 (Bristol, 2002), 58.

[26] See also Alec Ryrie, 'Sleeping, Waking and Dreaming in Protestant Piety', in Martin and Ryrie, eds, *Private and Domestic Devotion*, 73–92, for examples of family members participating in 'private' prayer to accompany waking (esp. 86).

[27] E. T. Leeds, 'A Second Elizabethan Mural Painting at No. 3 Cornmarket Street, Oxford', *Oxoniensia* 1 (1936), 144–50.

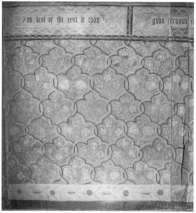

Fig. 1: Wall paintings at 3 Cornmarket St, Oxford, dating from *c*.1564–81. Image courtesy of the Oxford Preservation Trust.

teenth century by a wealthy yeoman, Stephen Hulkes. As part of these renovations a first-floor room was decorated across all four walls with imitation panelling and a frieze above containing texts (Fig. 2). In his will of 1617 Hulkes described this room as 'my painted chamber', suggesting a hint of pride at owning such a fashionably painted room.[28] Though much of the frieze is effaced, it is clear that the texts presented verses from Proverbs 4 and the wording indicates that the inscriptions followed the Bishops' Bible of 1568. The intact fragments (as italicized) suggest that the frieze gave verses 1–4:

> *Heare O ye* chyldren a fatherly instruction, & take good heede, that ye may learne understanding | For I have geven you a good doctrine, forsake not ye my lawe | For when I my selfe was my fathers deare sonne, *and tenderly beloved of my mother* | *He taught me also sayinge, let thyne heart receave my wordes*, kepe my *commaundementes and thou shalt lyve* …

While such painted inscriptions were at the height of their popularity during the later Elizabethan and Jacobean periods, recent discoveries suggest that this trend persisted well into the seven-

---

[28] Rupert Austin and Sheila Sweetinburgh, '"My Painted Chamber" and Other Rooms: Stephen Hulkes and the History of Calico House, Newnham', *Archaeologia cantiana* 130 (2010), 105–44.

Fig. 2: View of the painted wall decoration in the first-floor north-east room at Calico House, Newnham, Kent. Reproduced by permission of English Heritage.

teenth century in some areas. Kathryn Davies has documented an inscription in a stone property in Merioneth dated 1664, which includes the text: 'Ellis Wynne, his chamber' and 'Let me do noe thing, Lord but what may tend to thy glory and my right end'.[29]

The appropriate meditations to accompany getting dressed as provided in devotional texts offer an example of the circular nature of connections between specific activities, the material interactions required by these activities and guided thought. The 'Prayer at the putting on of our Clothes', from *A Booke of Christian Prayers* (1578) has repeated emphasis on the fall of Adam and Eve from grace, which is appropriate in referring to the introduction of clothing as a consequence of sin.

> Most gracious and merciful savyour Jesus Christ, thou knowest how we be borne, clothed, &clogged with the grievous, and

---

[29] Kathryn Davies, *Artisan Art: Vernacular Wall Paintings in the Welsh Marches, 1550–1650* (Almeley, 2008), 200.

Fig. 3: Wall painting of Adam and Eve dating from the second half of the seventeenth century, photographed in an attic room of 'The Springs' farmhouse, Meadle, Buckinghamshire. Reproduced by permission of English Heritage.

> heavy burthen of the first man, who fell away unto fleshly-nesse, through disobedience ... Clothe me with thy self O my redeemer and sanctifier, clothe me with thy self, which art the second man, and hast yealded thy selfe obedient in all things ...[30]

The pattern of the prayer, contrasting the disobedience of Adam with the obedience of Christ, corresponds with the inscription in a wall painting of the subject from a house in Meadle, Buckinghamshire, which once adorned the sloping ceiling of a first-floor room. It reproduces Romans 5: 19: 'As by the disobedience of one man many were made sinners, so by the obedience of one shall many be made righteous' (Fig. 3).[31] There are several extant examples of Adam and Eve iconography depicted in upper chambers, including a carved wooden overmantel dating from c.1612–20 in a second-floor chamber of 90 High Street, Oxford, an extravagant build by an apothecary in the town (Fig. 4). This subject is sometimes found decorating chests, so it might have been encountered

---

[30] Day, *Booke of Christian Prayers*, sigs B.iii^v–B.iiii^v.
[31] Discussed in more detail in Tara Hamling, 'Guides to Godliness: From Print to Plaster', in Michael Hunter, ed., *British Printed Images: Essays in Interpretation* (Aldershot, 2010), 65–85.

Fig. 4:   Carved wood overmantel of *c.*1612–20 in a second-floor chamber at 90 High St, Oxford. Reproduced by permission of English Heritage.

while removing clothes from their place of storage in the room. A carved chest commemorating the marriage of Isaac Walton and Rebecca Floud in 1626, which would have furnished their rented home in London, includes a scene showing the fall and expulsion.[32] In mirroring the message of devotional texts, the presence of the fall of Adam and Eve as large-scale decorative imagery in chambers could serve to put in mind appropriate modes of thought during the routine activity of dressing, providing a spiritual context for the required actions of stripping, being naked and reclothing as a form of ritual cleansing and fortification for the assaults on the soul through the day ahead.

It is possible, therefore, to offer an imaginative reconstruction of how the routine of the early morning might be ritualized through personal devotions if individuals chose to follow prescriptive advice. While we cannot know the extent to which people

32   The chest is now on display at Warwick Castle.

observed these behaviours, or thought in line with prescription, the fact that examples of extant decoration tend to echo the themes identified in devotional texts indicates that for some individuals among the middling sort it was considered desirable to demonstrate a commitment to this ideal of Protestant practice by making permanent additions to the fabric of their houses. While the overall appearance of this sort of wall decoration may reflect a general fashion, the variations in subject matter and the direct address of some inscriptions to the householder, through initials or another kind of 'signature', suggest a greater personal investment in the decoration than simply following a design trend. Adorning the space of the bedchamber in this way establishes an indissoluble connection between the material environment of the bedchamber and the practice of personal piety.

'Some convenient roome'

'When thou hast attired thy [self de]cently & comely, not proudlie, goe forth of thy chamber, and if thou beest a maister of a household, call thy familie together', instructed Stubbes in 1592.[33] This movement from chamber to a more public space punctuates shifts in the nature of continuous devotional activity from a personal and self-regulated spiritual regimen to the communal duties of the gathered household. As Bayly directs:

> if thou desirest to have the blessing of God upon thy selfe and upon thy familie: eyther before or after thine owne private devotion, call every morning all thy familie to some convenient roome; and first, eyther reade thy selfe unto them a Chapter in the word of God, or cause it to be read distinctly by some other. If leasure serve, thou maist admonish them of some remarkeable good notes; and then knelling downe with them in reverent sort ... pray with them.[34]

Bayly does not specify which 'convenient room' might be used for these daily gatherings, possibly because the most appropriate space varied according to house type and plan, especially in relation to urban and rural models but also according to social status.

[33] Stubbes, *A perfect pathway to felicitie*, sig. F3^r–F3^v.
[34] sig. F3^{r-v}.

The decoration of wall surfaces suggests that for some members of the middling sort this group activity defined the quality of the largest, central domestic space, whether a hall, parlour or upper (great) chamber. Embellishing this space with biblical texts served to extend the framing but ephemeral practice of morning devotion so as actively to spiritualize the atmosphere of the household and to encourage further devotional practice throughout the day, so that inscriptions painted on walls, such as the example in a framed panel over a fireplace at Pirton Grange, Hertfordshire, remind members of the household to 'Pray to God continually and learne to know him rightfullie'. A very similar inscription in a frieze within wall decoration in a farmhouse in Kimpton is dated 1605 (Fig. 5).[35] Wall paintings discovered in several houses in Sussex share *memento mori* themes and appear to have been executed by the same craftsman; one inscription in an upper chamber in the White House at Balcombe commands: 'Pray Continually | In all things | Give thanks'.[36] Domestic singing of psalms was supported and reinforced by decoration in an upper room at Great Pednor Manor, where black letter texts in a frieze were taken from the metrical version of the Psalms by Sternhold and Hopkins.[37]

Christ's teachings feature in the painted decoration dated 1603 in a first-floor room at Paramour Grange, near Canterbury. The walls are painted with a bold geometric design which has a recurring pattern featuring Tudor roses, asterisks and ovals, and a frieze running around the top of the room contains verses from the Beatitudes (Matt. 5: 3–12). It is thought that the decoration was carried out by Thomas Paramour, later mayor of Canterbury between 1607 and 1619, although more research is needed to

[35] The wall paintings at Pirton and Kimpton are illustrated in Juliet Fleming, *Graffiti and the Writing Arts of Early Modern England* (London, 2001), 30–1 (figs 6–7). As Fleming points out, the texts are also found in Thomas Tusser, *A hundreth good pointes of husbandry* (London, 1557 and subsequent edns).

[36] Philip Mainwaring Johnston, 'Mural Paintings in Houses: With Special Reference to Recent Discoveries at Stratford-upon-Avon and Oxford', *Journal of the British Archaeological Association* 37 (1931), 75–100, at 82.

[37] E. Clive Rouse, 'Domestic Wall Painting at Chalfont St. Peter, Great Pednor and Elsewhere', *Records of Buckinghamshire* 15/2 (1949), 87–96. On domestic psalm singing, see Linda Phyllis Austern, '"For Musicke is the Handmaid of the Lord": Women, Psalms, and Domestic Music-Making in Early Modern England', in Linda Phyllis Austen, Kari Bohy McBridge and David L. Orvis, eds, *Psalms in the Early Modern World* (Aldershot, 2011), 77–114.

Fig. 5: View of the painted decoration on the cross-wing of a ground-floor room at Ansells End Farm, Kimpton, Hertfordshire. Reproduced by permission of English Heritage.

confirm this connection.[38] Such decoration was also fashionable in more modest urban dwellings. A house in the High Street of Chalfont St Peter, Buckinghamshire, now demolished, had frames containing texts painted on walls and on the sloping portions of the ceiling in one of two rooms on the first floor. The texts were very fragmentary, but one was identified as from Matthew 5: 37, 'But let your communication be Yea, Yea; Nay, Nay: for whatsoever is more than these cometh of evil', and another as from Ephesians 5: 1, 'Be ye therefore followers of God as dear children'.[39] Built as a pair in 1564, 41 and 42 High Street in Exeter represent a new form of urban housing. Each was only one room wide, with a front and back room on each floor and a newel staircase running

---

[38] The paintings were described by Francis Reader, 'A classification of Tudor Domestic Wall Paintings, *Archaeological Journal* 98 (1942), 181–211, at 197–8. They featured in a *Country Life* blog dated 14 September 2009, online at: <http://www.countrylife.co.uk/news/article/397066/Sleep-in-a-Tudor-room-dedicated-to-a-king.html>, accessed 8 February 2013.

[39] Rouse, 'Chalfont St. Peter', 89. As these texts follow the AV they must post-date 1611.

through the centre of each building. The painted colour scheme discovered in a first-floor room in no. 42 includes a band of text that was probably from Scripture, although it is too badly damaged to identify.[40]

The depiction of selected extracts from Scripture as part of the permanent decoration of domestic space may represent an extension of the common practice of marking Bibles, discussed by William H. Sherman and Femke Molekamp. Both authors draw attention to the wide range of marks left by readers, including underlining, circling or annotation of specific passages. Molekamp points out that the Geneva Bible incorporated various formal and paratextual devices to help make the text intelligible to partially literate readers.[41] The summaries, arguments and headings made plain the pertinent theme of the Scripture below and acted as aids to memory. Painted biblical inscriptions could be understood as analogous to these headings, impressing and reinforcing on the memory passages considered especially significant by the householder. These inscriptions can also be understood in the context of page annotations by individual readers which revealed, according to Sherman, 'a set of focused interests that the reader wanted to be able to recall for his own use (or perhaps, that of others)'.[42] As he explains, 'it is clear that many readers found some method of annotation an indispensable practice for digesting and mobilizing the text'.[43] Exhibiting these selected and endorsed excerpts on the walls of houses certainly serves to mobilize the text, sharing the fruits of private engagement with Scripture with a wider community. In this sense these painted inscriptions are a form of commonplacing and might represent a further stage in that process of writing out and sharing selected passages in manuscript form.

We should, however, be wary of making assumptions about the nature of any ongoing reception of these biblical texts once transferred from page to wall. The inscriptions form only part of striking decorative schemes dominated by vivid colour and bold

---

[40]   Photographs held in the Royal Albert Memorial Museum, Exeter.

[41]   Femke Molekamp, 'Using a Collection to Discover Reading Practices: The British Library Geneva Bibles and a History of their Early Modern Readers', *Electronic British Library Journal* (2006), Article 10, 1–13, online at: <http://www.bl.uk/eblj/2006articles/article10.html>.

[42]   Sherman, *Used Books*, 77.

[43]   Ibid. 76.

pattern. They are meant to be looked at and appreciated as well as read. In this regard it is notable that most painted inscriptions employ black letter text. Molekamp has described the use in some Geneva Bibles of the older and more familiar black letter typeface in preference to the more modern roman typeface as a deliberate strategy to engage the common reader. As she points out, 'black letter would have been easier to read for a semi-literate Elizabethan and Jacobean society', because children's reading aids such as the ABC, Lord's Prayer, catechism and psalter were usually printed in this typeface.[44] We might add that black letter as the established typeface associated with these trusted canonical texts also carried greater authority. The semiotic capacity of the form of the inscribed characters could on purely visual terms evoke a sense of reverence or provide comfort through familiarity.[45]

The dining table

In keeping with the Protestant emphasis on constant self-examination and moderation, eating (along with other forms of bodily activity) was loaded with moral and spiritual significance. As John Downame warned:

> For as the devill layeth in every place baites and snares to intrap us, so especially upon our tables, and mingleth the poison of sinful corruption with our meates and drinkes, that if we doe not use them in the feare of God, and keepe a narrow watch over ourselves that we offend not in them, they will proove no lesse dangerous to our soules, then necessary … for the refreshing of our bodies.[46]

In order to prevent such indulgence and abuse of God's bounty, householders were advised to regulate behaviour and thought at mealtimes by reading from the Bible and encouraging individual

---

44 Molekamp, 'Using a Collection', 3.

45 There is no space here to explore the talismanic function of Bibles and associated inscriptions in the home, but interesting connections can be drawn between the use of biblical texts in wall painting and the ritual marking of domestic buildings with crudely incised religious symbols, usually on doors and chimney or window mantels. These marks are generally interpreted as attempts to protect the household from physical or spiritual harm.

46 John Downame, *A guide to godlynesse or a Treatise of a Christian life* (London, 1622), 279.

meditation. Decorating the physical space of the room, as well as items on the dinner table, with religious texts and images could also furnish this spiritual food for thought. By the second half of the sixteenth century, it was becoming increasingly common in larger houses to dine away from the main living space in a parlour or best first-floor chamber. Wall decoration in these higher-status rooms sometimes refers to this function. Recently uncovered paintings in a ground floor room at Cowside Farmstead, Langstrothdale, North Yorkshire, include the texts: 'Whether ye eat, or drink or whatsoever ye do do all to the glory of God [I] Cor[inthians] X: 31' and 'For of him and through him, are all things: to whom be glory for ever. Amen. Rom[ans] XI: 36'.[47] On the east wall is: 'Better is a dinner of herbs where love is than a stalled ox and hatred therewith Pro[verbs] XV: Cha[pter] 17 ver[se].' The same Proverbs reference is included in the painted inscriptions of a frieze in 1 Church Lane, Ledbury, Herefordshire, but here the text follows the Geneva Bible: 'Better is a dinner with greene hearbes where love is, then a fat oxe and hatred therewith' (Fig. 6).

Wall paintings recorded in the 1880s in a first-floor room of a sixteenth-century yeoman's house in Cowden, Kent, include a version of Proverbs 21: 13. 'For hee that will not heare ye crye | Of them that stande in neede | Shall crye him selfe and not be hard | When he doth hope to spede'.[48] This emphasis on Christian charity in the context of dining is also represented by the depiction of biblical stories, such as the Rich Man and the beggar Lazarus (Luke 16: 19–31), in work of 1580 at Pittleworth Manor in Hampshire.[49] The parable of the Prodigal Son also had great potential for scenes of excessive feasting and drinking, as a caution against the extremes of worldly indulgence but also as a comforting reminder of God's potential for forgiveness.[50] I have discussed examples of this imagery in domestic wall painting elsewhere, but here I would add the observation that these subjects were also depicted in items on the dinner table. It is impossible to say how widely imported German stoneware was actually used in England, but there was certainly a dedicated import market and a number of

---

[47]   The property is owned by the Landmark Trust.
[48]   Mainwaring Johnston, 'Mural Paintings in Houses', 84.
[49]   Discussed and illustrated in Hamling, *Decorating the Godly Household*, 132–3.
[50]   Ibid. 156–7.

Fig. 6: Wall paintings at 1 Church Lane, Ledbury, Hertfordshire. Image courtesy of Ledbury Town Council.

vessels with biblical imagery in moulded relief have been recovered in London. These objects also represent a degree of continuity in fashion during the course of reform in the sixteenth century. A small stoneware tankard in the Museum of London is decorated with applied panels in low relief depicting scenes from the parable of the Rich Man and Lazarus, and has been dated to 1525–50.[51] Other examples date from the 1570s to the 1590s, including one dated 1572 with scenes from the parable of the Prodigal Son.[52] A stoneware jug in the collections of the Shakespeare Birthplace Trust depicts the Feast of Herod, with John the Baptist's decapitated head being presented to Herod on a platter. In depicting a scene associated with grand feasting the jug, which probably held ale, sets up a comparison between indulgence in the body and John's rejection of worldly luxuries, while as the precursor

[51] London, Museum of London, accession no. 6333.

[52] Illustrated in Francis Reader, 'Tudor Domestic Wall Paintings, Part II', *Archaeological Journal* 93 (1936), 220–62, facing 251 (plate 24).

of Christ, John's death prefigures his coming sacrifice.[53] In this manner, the object could direct the mind to spiritual concerns during periods of (potentially excessive) bodily indulgence.

A trend for pious inscriptions in pottery is evident especially in items produced by potteries in Harlow, Essex, during the seventeenth century. The characteristic glazed red earthenware with slip-trailed decoration is known as 'metropolitan ware' because of the concentration of finds in the capital. An undated jug in the Museum of London simply states 'FEARE GOD HONOR GOD', but some inscriptions are more sophisticated.[54] Another jug has the inscription 'WHEN THIS YOU SEE REMEMBER ME OBEAY GODS WOURD', which expresses neatly how the sight of this object was intended to prompt remembrance of God's word.[55] The presence of these items, and similar ware, on the dining tables of Protestant houses served as a reminder of the need to show due respect and honour to the ultimate authority during periods of relative relaxation. On the other hand a cup now in the British Museum was presumably meant to offer support during periods of abstinence from food: its text reads 'FAST AND PRAY 1659'.[56]

These examples suggest various ways in which biblical imagery and religious mottoes were materialized around and on the dinner table. In his notebooks, Nehemiah Wallington describes how he took this concept a stage further. On 14 October 1654, he wrote: 'I intend to have the Bible (the food of my soule) to be set on my Table with the food of my body. They will relish well together and one cannot subsist well without the other'.[57] On 19 October, he reflects: 'And tho I layd the word upon my Table at meales (and for want of laying it on my heart) how little did my soule feed upon itt'.[58] By 21 October his habit of bringing the Bible to the table had lapsed: 'And at meale when the word was not in my hart nor on my Tabel'.[59] By 25 October,

[53] The jug is discussed by Victoria Jackson, 'Shakespeare's World in 100 Objects', online at: <http://findingshakespeare.co.uk/shakespeares-world-in-100-objects-number-5-german-panel-jug>, accessed 7 February 2013.

[54] Museum of London, accession no. A4481.

[55] William Burton, *A History and Description of English Earthenware and Stoneware* (London, 1904), between pages 30 and 31 (Fig. 5).

[56] London, British Museum, Registration no. 1887, 0307, D.21.

[57] Booy, ed., *Nehemiah Wallington*, 327.

[58] Ibid. 328.

[59] Ibid. 330.

> in laying my Bible on the Table at mels sometimes I forget
> so apt am I to forget this heavenly word the food of my
> soule: sometims some are offended that I lay it on my Tabel ...
> Sometimes there is no room on the Table for it: so some[times]
> my heart is filed with the world and vainity that there is no
> room in my heart for this heavenly word ...[60]

Wallington's reference to how some people were offended about
this short-lived habit of laying his Bible on the dinner table is
intriguing and needs to be set within the context of his own exaggerated and eccentric puritan behaviours. It does, however, suggest
a degree of sensitivity surrounding propriety in the placing of
Bibles within a domestic context. The second section of this essay
investigates exactly where and how Bibles were kept and encountered within the furnished spaces of the household.

LOCATING BIBLES

Bibles are portable objects – more or less so depending on size
– but even those miniature versions worn or carried would have
come to rest somewhere in the household. Probate records provide
the best evidence for where that was, as long as we accept that
these documents can offer only partial (in both senses of the word)
descriptions of a system of objects interrupted by the very context
of the recording procedure that produced them. One of the many
pitfalls of the inventory as source, as catalogued by Lena Cowen
Orlin, is the absence of items exempted from probate, such as
heirlooms.[61] Inventories would therefore not usually list Bibles that
had already been gifted or bequeathed. At the point of the inventory these books were viewed as commodities to be recirculated
rather than as personal and familial possessions. For the purposes of
this study this objective (if not disinterested) view is quite helpful,
because it is resistant to the tendency evident in modern interpretation to treat Bibles as exceptional items disassociated from

---

[60] Ibid. 332.
[61] Lena Cowen Orlin, 'Fictions of the Early Modern English Probate Inventory',
in Henry S. Turner, ed., *The Culture of Capital: Properties, Cities, and Knowledge in Early
Modern England* (New York and London, 2002), 51–84.

the wider household economies, activities and material settings of which they formed a part.

The placing of Bibles within the home represents the dual nature of the domestic environment as the meeting place of public and personal lives and agendas. Bibles might be stored and secured out of sight in chests along with other precious items, so that William Whittorne (d. 1621), a carpenter of Old Stratford, seems to have kept his 'olde Bible & other small books' in one of four coffers in his lodging chamber along with foodstuffs, 'three strikes of corne & one stricke of malte' and 'bacon and beef', a quantity of yarn, flax and hemp and his working tools.[62] On the other hand these books might be prominently displayed to attract attention and admiration. The vogue, especially in the first half of the seventeenth century, for embellishing Bibles and other religious books with rich, decorative bindings reminds us that these objects formed part of conspicuous consumption and display as well as practical piety. These various strategies responded to the specificities of individual circumstances which produced very different material conditions for living.

It is not possible to generate any meaningful statistical data from the inventories consulted for this essay, largely because of the highly selective nature of the sources that were readily available but also because of omissions and biases in the records themselves.[63] It is possible, however, to glean a general impression of how material settings for Bibles varied according to degrees of status. Some Bibles were presented in a prominent and permanent manner in the most open, public areas of the house. William Hinde's biography of the model godly householder John Bruen explains how:

> in order to exercise the minds and hearts of his own family (and such as might by occasion come to his house) unto godliness and good things [he] brought in, and set up upon a deske, both in his Hall, and in his Parlour, two goodly faire Bibles of the best Edition, and largest Volume … and these hee placed

[62] Jeanne Jones, *Stratford-upon-Avon Inventories 1538-1699*, 2 vols, Dugdale Society 39, 40 (Stratford-upon-Avon, 2002–3), 1: 319.

[63] I have utilized published transcriptions of a complete set of inventories for Stratford-upon-Avon in Warwickshire and selected inventories from the city of Bristol, along with the extensive database of Kentish probate materials for the period 1560–1600 created by Catherine Richardson.

to be continuall residentiaries, the bigger in the Parlour, and the lesser in the Hall.[64]

This reflects a pattern of behaviour amongst those in society with the means to invest in impressive-looking Bibles, whether great in size or quality, to display in main reception rooms as a sign of their commitment to propagating the reformed faith. In the hall of Thomas Post, a draper of Faversham in 1569, was 'an English Bible with a desk'; in the parlour of Richard Lawrence of the same town three years later was 'a great Bible of the last setting out with the desk'.[65] Sometimes there is a glimpse of other decorations in the room; an inventory of 1586 of John Iden of Sandwich, jurat, records in the hall an 'old bible of geneva print', along with 'imagery' described as an 'old story of Joseph', which may have been depicted in painted cloth.[66] In the hall of the Canterbury residence of John Semark, gentleman and alderman, was a Bible along with several other religious books, including a service book and three psalters. This hall was decorated with a 'map of the queens arms set in wainscot'.[67] The depiction of the royal arms in domestic halls and parlours was another trend from *c*.1580, which created a tangible connection with church space where the royal arms were also newly and prominently displayed. The presence in domestic rooms of the royal arms as a stamp of royal and judicial, as well as spiritual, authority appropriated this authority for the householder, possibly as a sign of local office, which seems especially important for the construction of identity within local communities and the social differentiation and competition this entailed. This borrowed authority also bolstered practices of reformed religious observance in the home and helped shape the nature of this experience for the gathered family.

In order to evoke the very different material environments in which Bibles were kept and encountered I want to examine the qualitative details of two inventories. An inventory of 1617

---

[64] William Hinde, *A faithfull remonstrance of the holy life and happy death of John Bruen of Bruen-Stapleford, in the county of Chester, Esquire* (London, 1641), 123.

[65] Canterbury, Cathedral Archives and Library, Probate Records [of the Prerogative Court of] Canterbury [hereafter: PRC], Inventory Registers listed by volume: PRC 10.5.39, Inventory of Thomas Post, draper of Faversham, dated 26 April 1569; PRC 10.7.25, Inventory of Richard Lawrence of Faversham, 2 March 1572.

[66] PRC 10.16.264, Inventory of John Iden of Sandwich, 5 January 1586.

[67] PRC 10.14.152v, Inventory of John Semark, 3 February 1585.

recording the moveable goods of Miles Casse, a tobacco pipe-maker 'in the subburbes of the Citie of Bristol', suggests a very modest household consisting of just two rooms, listed as a 'kitchen' and the 'chamber aforestre' or before (fronting) the street.[68] The 'kitchen' was the main living space and contained all the seating, cooking equipment and tableware, as well as the tools of his profession, including a furnace and 'a long tubb to sift clay in, one board to beat clay upon' and 'a little wicker basket to carry tobaco pipes in'. In the chamber were all the bedding and textiles and four 'old' chests for storage, along with the few items indicative of comfort: two window cushions and a dozen and a half napkins. Apart from these few textiles the overwhelming impression created by the various items described in these two rooms is of a practical working and living environment with almost entirely utilitarian but worn furniture and furnishings; the descriptor 'old' accompanies most of the listings. The chamber had three flock beds, three bolsters and four pillows but only two coverlets and a blanket. That this room had at some stage to sleep a family is suggested by the presence in the kitchen of '4 foormes for children to sit upon' along with two old chairs, six old stools and two 'lesser stooles'. Also recorded there are a 'dozen of woodden dishes' and 'a dozen of pewter spones'; seating and tableware cater for many occupants. Then, amongst the 'old brasse skillet', 'lattin dripping pan', 'old frying pan' and 'old spade' is listed 'one old Bible parte torne out'. We can only speculate as to how this Bible listed with items associated with food preparation, possibly by the hearth, came to have a part torn out. Is this evidence of constant use and wear, the result of a child's innocent or intended vandalism, or purposeful extraction of paper as resource? Perhaps the damage was not inflicted by this household; the Bible might already have been second-hand when it entered into Casse's possession. In any case the appraisers assigned this sorry-sounding Bible a value of one shilling, so it was still deemed resaleable, which suggests that the 'parte torne out' was loose but still present, probably due to a broken binding. Analysing the detail of this inventory and picturing a worn and torn Bible amongst the paraphernalia of humble domestic and occupational work in a living room occupied by a family reveals one kind of material context in which ordinary people experienced the Bible in early modern England.

Another quite different context is suggested by a second inventory, also from Bristol. This is the inventory taken in 1623 of the goods of one John Dunn, a fishmonger.[69] While the saleable assets of the Casse household totalled £7 9s 6d, the relative prosperity of the Dunn household is indicated by the total valuation of £460 9s 4d. This house had at least twelve rooms, including three with beds dressed with quality bedding. Additional, apparently unused, bedsteads were listed in several other rooms. The best 'standing bedsteed', with truckle bed underneath, 'curtaines & frindge with curtaine rods', feather mattresses and bolsters and 'three downe pillows', was listed 'in the Parloure' along with a range of other quality, showy items. Parlours were multi-functional spaces but were usually more comfortably fitted out than the hall or kitchen and therefore served as the best room for receiving and entertaining guests. In larger houses parlours could be reserved for occasional or more specialized uses. Dunn's parlour conforms to this model and was clearly intended for entertaining and associated display; along with the impressive bedstead and furnishings (probably reserved for visitors) it contained a table and frame, twelve joined stools and a form for dining, and a sideboard. It also contained upholstered furniture and an abundance of cushions for comfortable seating: 'two chaires of needle worke & six cushions of the same', 'fower stooles of needle woorke' and 'eighteen cushions to sitt on'. The sizeable company that could be seated comfortably on these cushions might be entertained by someone playing the 'paire of virginalls with the frame'. Two aspects of the listing for this room stand out; the quantity of textile items, which also include 'six side board clothes' and 'two doore clothes', and the additional details about the nature of materials throughout the listing, for example, a *turkie* carpett', 'two *arras* [tapestry] Coverlids' for the bed, and 'a *spruce* chest' (my italics). These notable, quality materials evidently made an impression on the appraisers, as they were intended to do in the context of this display space. It is therefore significant that also listed in this room were 'a Twiggen [wicker] Chaire, two Bibles and pictures about the Roome', assigned a total cost of sixteen shillings. The grouping of the Bibles with the pictures is

---

[69]   Ibid. 41–3.

intriguing, as if they too were meant to be looked at. While it is necessary to exercise caution in interpreting the assemblages listed in inventories as evidence for any physical proximity or association between specific items it certainly appears that these two Bibles were part of a coordinated display of luxury objects to be seen and admired in company. The impression of conspicuous display is reinforced by the fact that the room contained none of the usual collections of household necessities such as linen, utensils or vessels as listed in most of the other rooms. Indeed, 'his Furniture and bookes and other small things' were listed in the kitchen. These particular Bibles were therefore set apart from the other books and the rest of the practical household furniture and living spaces, to form part of a showpiece of quality material possessions.

Comparing these two inventories offers an indication, albeit anecdotal, of the very different ways in which people within the middling ranks of society lived with their Bibles; in the context of a modest two-room dwelling a Bible could be located at the heart of family and working life. But for those with the ability to exercise choice in selecting a specific setting for their Bible, locating this object in the showy parlour of an impressive twelve-room residence set it apart from the everyday routine of domestic life, to be encountered in the context of ostentation and leisure time. Between these extremes is the middling sort of middling-level house, represented by the inventory of Thomas Rogers, maltster, from Stratford-upon-Avon.[70] Taken in 1639, it lists seven rooms in the main house, with a kitchen and other outbuildings. The total value of his goods was appraised at £86 13s. Unlike John Dunn's parlour described above, Rogers's parlour appears to function as a practical living space; it appears modestly equipped with minimal furnishings, especially when compared with the contents of another sitting room, the 'joyne chamber', which apparently functioned as the showier space with a 'joyne bedsteed', court cupboard with cloth, carpet and seven cushions.[71] The contents of

---

[70] Jones, *Stratford-upon-Avon Inventories*, 2: 72.

[71] The contents of 'ye parlour' are listed as: 'one half-headed bedsteed, two tables, one foarme, one chaire, one stoole, one bible, a paire of handirons, one fire shoole, a paire of bellis with linckes & tongs'. In 'ye joyne chamber' was 'one table board & frame, two foarmes, one chaire, two stooles, one joyne bedsteed, one court cupboard, one chest & one coffer, one carpet, one cubberd cloth & cushion, six other cushions'. It is possible that other items were present but unrecorded, if claimed by kin.

the parlour were valued at £1 10s compared with the £5 valuation for goods in the 'joyne chamber'. Yet here it was the more modestly furnished room that contained the Bible. This underlines the variable nature of domestic floorplans, room designations, functions and furnishings which makes it impossible to generalize about the nature of the spaces in which people kept or used their Bibles.

This inventory is particularly significant because the building to which it relates is still extant. The townhouse known as 'Harvard House' in Stratford-upon-Avon was rebuilt in 1596 by Thomas Rogers's father, a butcher and cattle dealer. Unfortunately no trace of the original layout of the ground floor survives; it is now one large open space. But the original plan appears to have been only two rooms deep divided by a chimney stack and staircase, so if we follow the inventory this suggests a hall off the street with the parlour at the rear of the property. The historic wood panelling which might explain the given name of the 'joyne chamber' above the hall on the first floor is still *in situ*, along with a decorated plasterwork overmantel above the fireplace displaying royal emblems. In the chamber on the upper floor are remains of *trompe l'oeil* wall painting mimicking panelling. Although the original form and appearance of the parlour cannot be reconstructed, the design and decoration of these other rooms are evidence of investment in material enhancements to living spaces occupied by average members of the 'middling sort', of which a Bible as a household object formed a part.

CONCLUSION

In the century or so following the Protestant religious settlement in England practices of so-called 'private' domestic devotion took place throughout the whole household – in bedrooms, halls, parlours and upper chambers – multi-functional spaces equipped with all manner of domestic goods and furnishings. Most individuals made use of whatever 'convenient' spaces were available to them, whether a garret or upper chamber, to perform their religious duties, although these shared or cluttered spaces were far removed from the abstracted ideal of the closet. For those with the means to do so, fashioning their material environment – including the decoration of rooms with painted biblical texts and images or the royal arms, and the display of ceramics with religious scenes or mottoes – served to express the piety of the household but also helped to shape it. Recurring texts and iconographies could help focus the mind on prescribed patterns of thought and on the core doctrinal message of the Christian faith, creating an environment of biblical truths which underpinned and informed the routine habits of domestic life. The research outlined above challenges some of the more settled assumptions about the context and nature of household religion in post-Reformation England, highlighting the wider range and complexity of spaces used for devotional activity as well as the considerable extent to which lay observance of the Protestant faith retained a reliance on visual and material apparatus to support the performance of piety in the home. It is time, therefore, to modify our assumptions about the physical context of the household for practices of Protestant piety in post-Reformation England, to look beyond the closet and to investigate the spaces and sensory qualities of the range of domestic environments in which ordinary people lived with the Bible, not only as a book to be read but as a multifarious and diffused presence in their daily lives.

University of Birmingham

ADORAMUS TE CHRISTE: MUSIC AND POST-REFORMATION ENGLISH CATHOLIC DOMESTIC PIETY

by EMILIE K. M. MURPHY

Adoramus te Christe, et benedicimus tibi, quia per crucem tuam, redimisti mundum. Hoc signum erit in caelo, cum dominus ad iudicandum venerunt.[1]

O n the Feast of the Invention of the Holy Cross, 3 May 1606, Henry Garnet was hung, drawn and quartered in St Paul's churchyard, London. In his last dying speech Garnet adapted the liturgy from the office hours of the day and he proclaimed in Latin: 'We adore thee, O Christ and we Bless thee, because by thy Cross, thou hast redeemed the world. This sign shall appear in heaven, when the Lord shall come to judgment'. Finally, beseeching God to let him always remember the cross, he crossed his arms upon his chest and was turned off the scaffold.[2]

Within the historiography of early modern Christianity, scholars such as Thomas Freeman, Brad Gregory and Anne Dillon have recently drawn attention to the fundamental role that martyrs and those executed for maintaining the seal of confession – such as Henry Garnet – played in the formation of devotional identities, and in particular the fraught construction of post-Reformation Catholic identity.[3] Anne Dillon's monograph on post-Reformation English Catholics demonstrated how manuscript and printed martyrdom narratives, such as John Mush's account of the life and martyrdom of Margaret Clitherow in 1586, imparted Tridentine ideals to the beleaguered laity.[4] Catholics were implored to admire the martyrs as figures

---

[1] Oxford, Bodl., MS Eng. Th. B. 2, 135.

[2] Ibid.

[3] Thomas S. Freeman, *Martyrs and Martyrdom in England* (Woodbridge, 2007); Brad Gregory, *Salvation at Stake* (London, 1997); Anne Dillon, *The Construction of Martyrdom in the English Catholic Community* (Aldershot, 2002). For a literary perspective, see Susannah Brietz Monta, *Martyrdom and Literature in Early Modern England* (Cambridge, 2005).

[4] Dillon, 'A trewe report of the li[fe] and marterdome of Mrs. Margaret Clitherowe', in *Construction of Martyrdom*, 277–322. For full printed edition of the original manuscript, see J. Mush, 'A True Report of the Life and Martyrdom of Mrs. Margaret

of consolation and devotion and also to emulate them, embracing the characteristics of humility, constancy and piety in their daily lives. Moreover, texts such as Mush's *Life* presented recusancy itself as a form of martyrdom. As well as emphasizing the eucharistic elements of martyrdom by focusing on the martyr's body and blood and the privileged status of the priesthood, these narratives exemplify the complexity of the discourse occurring within the persecuted community, which enabled its members, as Dillon has shown, 'to express and make sense of the events which they had witnessed'.[5] This essay will suggest that such a focus on martyrs and the related narratives served as a substitute for much that the English Catholic community had lost; it will reveal that English Catholics shared both determination and ingenuity in piecing together new forms of devotional life.

In particular, this essay will highlight the potential of music when it came to reaffirming post-Reformation Catholic identity. Reminding scholars that most texts were written to be read aloud or, in the case of ballads, sung, Alison Shell has provided another facet to our understanding of this discourse in her work on English Catholic oral culture.[6] Shell has highlighted the importance of Catholic martyr-ballads in encouraging people to view martyrs as exemplary figures, and has also explored the complexity of these texts by demonstrating how they could 'blur the distinction not only between audience and congregation, but between earth and heaven, powerfully reminding the listeners that their prayers and praises should be united with those of the saints'.[7] Following Dillon and Shell, this essay adds to our understanding of this martyr-discourse by examining the role that music and 'musical culture', distinct yet inextricably bound to oral and literary culture, played not only in the production but also in the performance of martyrdom narratives in Catholic households.[8]

It is widely held by scholars that devout family households were a mainstay of post-Reformation English Catholicism.[9] The house-

---

Clitherow', in John Morris, ed., *The Troubles of our Catholic Forefathers Related by Themselves*, 3 vols (London, 1872–7), 3: 331–440.

[5] Dillon, *Construction of Martyrdom*, 107.

[6] Alison Shell, *Oral Culture and Catholicism in Early Modern England* (Cambridge, 2007), 2.

[7] Ibid. 122.

[8] Dillon, *Construction of Martyrdom*, 109.

[9] This is not to suggest that Catholicism 'retreated' to the households of the aris-

hold was a multifaceted institution for Catholics, and could be a focus for devotion and piety whilst simultaneously functioning as a 'seedbed of subversion'[10] and site of resistance. Households, particularly wealthy ones, became focal points for local Catholics.[11] To cite the well-known example of the arrangements made for Lady Magdalene Browne (1538–1608) in her family mansion at Battle in East Sussex:

> she built a chapel in her house (which in such a persecution was to be admired) and there placed a very fair altar of stone, whereto she made an ascent with steps and enclosed it with rails, and, to have everything conformable, she built a choir for singers and set up a pulpit for the priests, which perhaps is not to be seen in all England besides. Here almost every week was a sermon made, and on solemn feasts the sacrifice of the Mass was celebrated with singing and musical instruments, and sometimes also with deacon and subdeacon. And such was the concourse and resort of Catholics, that sometimes there were 120 together, and 60 communicants at a time had the benefit of the Blessed Sacrament. And such was the number of Catholics resident in her house and the multitude and note of such as repaired thither, that even the heretics, to the eternal glory of the name of the Lady Magdalen, gave it the title of *Little Rome*.[12]

Whilst the Council of Trent had explicitly banned the celebration of mass in non-ecclesiastical settings, the domestication of the mass after the Reformations in England may, as Alexandra Walsham has suggested, have allowed for the possibility of direct supervision

---

tocracy. See, for example, Michael Questier, *Catholicism and Community in Early Modern England: Politics, Aristocratic Patronage and Religion, c.1550–1640* (Cambridge, 2006).

[10] This now well-known phrase was coined by John Bossy in his discussion of Tridentine Europe and the aftermath of the Council of Trent, 'The Counter-Reformation and the People of Catholic Europe', *P&P*, no. 47 (1970), 51–70, at 68. See also, in this volume, Alexandra Walsham, 'Holy Families: The Spiritualization of the Early Modern Household revisited', 122–60.

[11] For an example of a poorer household becoming the focus for local Catholics, see W. J. Sheils, 'Catholics and their Neighbours in a Rural Community: Egton Chapelry 1590–1780', *NH* 34–5 (1998–9), 109–33.

[12] From the contemporary account written in 1627 by Lady Montague's chaplain, Richard Smith, *An Elizabethan Recusant House: Comprising the Life of the Lady Magdalen Viscountess Montague (1538–1608)*, ed. A. C. Southern (London, 1954), 41–2.

and pastoral care of the laity by the priesthood, as advocated by Tridentine leaders.[13] Furthermore, Walsham contends, it might even have been here 'in the inward-looking households of upper-class recusants ... that the early modern Catholic clergy had the best chance of successfully effecting what [John] Bossy describes as the transformation of communal Christians into individual ones'.[14] However, this essay suggests that this is an unhelpful polarity, and that in fact post-Reformation Catholic households formed the locus for both individual and communal piety.

Lisa McClain's investigation of English Catholics between 1559 and 1642 revealed how the individual 'lived experience' of men and women changed after the Reformation, by tracing how Catholic piety evolved through devotions such as the rosary. She also explored ways, such as the redefinition of religious space, whereby Catholics adapted to a religious climate in which clergy and sacraments were not readily available.[15] In order to move away from the marked tendency amongst scholars that use categories such as 'conformity', 'occasional conformity', 'loyalty', 'recusancy' and 'church-papism' as indicators of religious culture and belief, this essay follows and develops McClain's approach in order to engage with how Catholic experience may have been transformed in practice. Through the discussion of how Catholics used music in their devotion, focusing particularly upon a rare piece of music discovered within the manuscript pages of a Catholic 'encyclopaedia' known as the Brudenell manuscript, from a Northamptonshire gentry household, this essay will cast new light on the adaptation of Catholic domestic piety in the midst of persecution.

In 2005 the literary critic Gerard Kilroy drew to the attention of scholars the neglected Brudenell manuscript, two large (28 x 42 cm) volumes that had been sold to the Bodleian Library by the Brudenell family of Deene Park, Northamptonshire, in 1968.[16] The volumes contain over 1,800 pages of theological and historical information in defence of Roman Catholicism and it is likely that they were transcribed between 1605 and 1608. Whilst several

---

[13] Alexandra Walsham, 'Translating Trent? English Catholicism and the Counter Reformation', *HR* 78 (2005), 288–310, at 297.

[14] Ibid.

[15] Lisa McClain, *Lest we be Damned*: *Practical Innovation and Lived Experience among Catholics in Protestant England, 1559–1641* (London, 2004), esp. chs 2–4.

[16] Bodl., MS Th. Eng. B. 1–2.

hands are present, almost all the texts are in the hand of a single scribe. The collections consist mainly of glosses on verses of the New Testament and extracts from theological works of all periods – from the Church Fathers to accounts of contemporary events concerning recusants – arranged alphabetically under 93 headings called 'books', such as 'Of Absolution', 'Of the Holy Eucharist' and 'Of Persecution'. The contemporary material within the volumes stretches back to the early 1580s and the interrogations surrounding Jesuit priest Edmund Campion, who was put to death on 1 December 1581, and forward to the execution of Henry Garnet in 1606.

The volumes are modelled on an illuminated medieval manuscript and music is found on many of the pages. Old music is used, cut up, drawn on and stuck in; moreover, new music has been composed. At the end of Book 59 of the collection, 'Of Martirs', after the description of the events surrounding the execution of Henry Garnet there is a setting of some of his last words, *Adoramus te Christe*. The piece of music (Fig. 1) bears the name of the composer, Thomas Jollett, in two places – as a signature at the top of the page and written in the neat scribal hand within the composition itself at the end of the bass part. The name appears again within the volume in an inscription on the last leaf:

> *Scriptor qualis erat si quis de nomine quaerat | Cunctis noscatur Thomas Jollet sic nominatur.*

> If anyone wishes to know the name of the writer | Let him be known to all, and called as Thomas Jollet.

In view of the mass of material that focuses on Tresham within the manuscript, the range of theological knowledge possessed by the compiler of the manuscript and the fact that Tresham had access to an immense library, Gerard Kilroy has suggested that 'Thomas Jollett' was a pseudonym for Thomas Tresham.[17] Kilroy also argued that the scribe was Mary, Thomas Tresham's daughter, who had married Thomas Brudenell, later the first Lord Cardigan, in the summer of 1605, and that she had endeavoured to transcribe her father's legacy meticulously. Finally, Kilroy argued that this

---

[17] Gerard Kilroy, *Edmund Campion: Memory and Transcription* (Aldershot, 2005), 13–14.

Fig. 1: *Adoramus te Christe*, attributed to Thomas Jollett, *c.*1606–1608, Oxford, Bodl., MS. Eng.Th.B.2.137. Reproduced by permission of the Bodleian Libraries, University of Oxford.

collection was intended to be buried, 'as had happened to all the other Tresham papers' on 28 November 1605, but that Mary simply changed her mind and decided to 'hand them on to posterity'.[18] However, the presence of *Adoramus te Christe* within these volumes makes nearly all of these hypotheses impossible.

It seems clear that 'Thomas Jollett' composed *Adoramus te Christe* specifically to honour the death of Henry Garnet in May 1606; consequently 'Jollett' cannot be a straightforward alias for Thomas Tresham, who had died in September 1605. The Northampton-shire connection with the manuscript remains, due to its Deene Park provenance, the prevalence of material focusing on Tresham and the documents pasted into the second volume relating to the recusancy of Mary Brudenell. Nevertheless, Kilroy's conclu-sion that '[i]n its entirety the book indicates a degree of biblical

[18] Ibid. 14.

and patristic knowledge that Sir Thomas Tresham, alone among laymen, is known to have possessed' is flawed.[19] Tresham was not 'alone among laymen', as recent scholarship by Nicholas Barker and David Quentin has highlighted.[20] Rather, the library was a collaborative venture, started by Tresham; however, from the 1580s (incidentally, around the time of the first contemporary record within the Brudenell manuscript) the library had 'a new purpose, to serve as a broad source of reference for a Catholic community now cut off from other libraries, private or institutional'.[21]

Kilroy's assertion that the Brudenell manuscript was compiled to be buried is challenged by the didactic nature of the volumes and undermined entirely by the simple fact that the piece of music within this manuscript was meant to be performed. Although there are some instances of Catholic music being copied for antiquarian reasons, the music within the Brudenell manuscript certainly does not fall within this category,[22] for on the page facing *Adoramus te Christe* there is another version of the same piece of music that the scribe has crossed out. This version of the music is cramped, only covers half a page and would have been difficult to perform. It was subsequently completely rewritten on the opposite page, explicitly for performance. *Adoramus te Christe*, first and foremost, demonstrates the ability of the household to engage in the practice of domestic music-making.

Jonathan Willis has argued that for post-Reformation Protestants 'music was at the core of both formal liturgical worship and private devotional life'.[23] Without formal liturgical worship, the domestication of music-making and its role in private devotion within Catholic households is even more significant. In looking to the Northamptonshire links with the Brudenell manuscript, it

[19] Ibid.

[20] Nicolas Barker and David Quentin, *The Library of Thomas Tresham & Thomas Brudenell*, Roxburghe Club (London, 2006).

[21] Ibid. 54.

[22] For further information on these antiquarian impulses, see John Milson, 'Sacred Songs in the Chamber', in John Morehen, ed., *English Choral Practice: 1400–1650* (Cambridge, 1995), 161–79.

[23] Jonathan Willis, '"A pottel of ayle on whyt-Sonday": Everyday Objects and the Musical Culture of the Post-Reformation English Parish Church', in Tara Hamling and Catherine Richardson, eds, *Everyday Objects: Medieval and Early Modern Material Culture and its Meanings* (Farnham, 2010), 211–20, at 212; idem, *Church Music and Protestantism in Post-Reformation England* (Farnham, 2010).

is interesting to note that within the Tresham papers are some of Lady Tresham's accounts from Michelmas 1588 to July 1589, which include: 'Other necessaries, as lute stringes, virginall wyer, mendinge of musicall instrumentes, paper and ynke, and bookes for the children; bookes for my lady'.[24] The Tresham household was evidently musical and, as Flora Dennis concluded from her work on fans and handbells in early modern Italy, '[a]lthough music was immaterial, it nevertheless found many facets of material expression, primarily as musical instruments or in richly illuminated manuscripts'.[25] The materiality of music is epitomized by the Brudenell manuscript, as the volume itself reveals much about the performance context of the music it contains.

For domestic music-making, by far the most usual arrangement for performance was the use of part-books, in convenient oblong format and with a book for each person. These were printed, or individual parts were copied into individual manuscript books, and performers sat or perhaps, as the oblong format allowed, stood around a table to perform. Another much less common arrangement for domestic music performance used the 'table-book'.[26] In this all the individual parts were printed – or copied – on the same page and each part would then have faced each performer as they sat around a table.[27] When this unusual format was used by composers, it was most often in secular music for mixed consort, which might include a combination of instruments and voice parts. The earliest English printed source in this format was the first book of lute songs by John Dowland, dating from 1597 (Fig. 2), and between twenty and thirty volumes in table-book format were published during the next twenty-five years, nearly all lute repertoire. Thomas Jollett's decision to set Henry Garnet's last

---

[24]   Cited in S. C. Lomas, ed., *Historical Manuscripts Commission: Report on Manuscripts in Various Collections*, vol. 3 (London, 1904), 48.

[25]   Flora Dennis, 'Resurrecting Forgotten Sound: Fans and Handbells in Early Modern Italy', in Hamling and Richardson, eds, *Everyday Objects*, 191–211, at 192.

[26]   For a more detailed discussion of this unusual format, see John Morehen, Emilie K. M. Murphy and Richard Rastall, 'Table-book', in *Grove Music Online: Oxford Music Online*, at: <http://www.oxfordmusiconline.com/subscriber/article/grove/music/27341>, accessed 16 August 2013.

[27]   For a video representing the table-book format, see the YouTube clip (particularly at 1: 25), online at: <http://www.youtube.com/watch?v=nntri9OfaRY>, accessed 10 July 2012. Sting is singing from a facsimile of Dowland's 1597 publication.

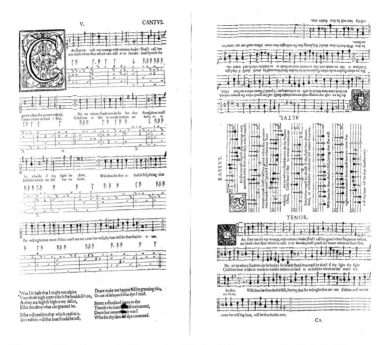

Fig. 2: John Dowland, *First book of Book of Aires*, 1597, fols C1ᵛ–C2ʳ. Reproduced by permission of The Huntington Library, San Marino, California, USA.

words in this way must, then, have been deliberate, particularly as vocal, unaccompanied devotional music in this format was so rare.

Rarer still is the way that *Adoramus te Christe* has been arranged. Whilst working within the table-book tradition, as the two upper and two lower sets of voice parts have been turned around, Jollett's setting is particularly unusual as the two sets face each other. During performance the two sets of voices would have had to read across the other parts to perform, whereas it would have made much more sense if the sets were turned the other way, outwards towards the performers, like other music in the tradition. As the performers were not near to the music, they would not have been able to sit down to sing this, which seems to have been the most usual practice for domestic performance; this is especially odd for table-music. For the performance of *Adoramus te Christe*, the singers would have had to stand in order to be able to see their parts clearly. When this performance context is realized, suddenly the significance of this initially awkward layout is striking. The two sets of singers would have stood facing each other, just as two choirs would have stood facing each other within the chancel of a church.

When the original liturgical context for the performance of *Adoramus te Christe* on the Feast of the Invention of the Holy Cross is considered, Jollett's implicit performance direction assumes further importance because during mass in the new Tridentine rite, introduced from 1570, the choir was standing. When this is combined with the Northamptonshire context of the manuscript, statements by the recusant Lord Vaux gain further significance. In May 1581, Vaux appeared as a recusant in the visitation book of the archdeacon of Northampton, under Harrowden Magna and his excuse for not attending the services of the established Church rested on his claims that his house was 'a parish by itself'.[28] This, in combination with Thomas McCoog's discovery of a curious cipher list – uncovered by the government in 1609 – which highlighted the arrangement of some aspects of the Jesuit mission to England, makes it clear that Catholics considered households literally to be 'churches'.[29] The cipher revealed that in the organization of the Jesuit mission each seminary priest was assigned to particular 'churches'. These were 'not defined geographically but according to families' and thus a household was designated as 'church' in a particular area.[30] In Northamptonshire, the Jesuit John Percy's church was known by the letters A. P. and amongst those under his care was Lord Vaux.

The role that music played in the transformation of household into church was significant. Underlining the fundamental reciprocity between the composer and the performer, the martyr and the confessors, the singers and the audience, Jollett composed music that would emulate a church choir. Through the performance of this music in a domestic household the domestic space became sacred, transformed both aurally, with the devotional music and text to honour Henry Garnet, and physically, with the positioning of the performers. This is in keeping with contemporary literature

---

[28] Cited in Godfrey Anstruther, *Vaux of Harrowden: A Recusant Family* (Newport, 1953), 113.

[29] Thomas McCoog, 'The Society of Jesus in England, 1623–1688: An Institutional Study' (Ph.D. thesis, University of Warwick, 1984), 193–4.

[30] Ibid. 194.

which exhorted Catholics to use their imaginations in order to consecrate space. In the absence of churches, cathedrals and shrines, Robert Southwell's *A Shorte Rule of a good lyfe* – printed by Henry Garnet's printing press in 1596 – directed English Catholic laity to adapt domestic and natural spaces to spiritual use.[31] In expressing devotion to the saints, Southwell directed English Catholic laity to 'take this course':

> I must in every roome of the house where I dwell, imagin in some decent place therof, a throne or chaire of estate, & dedicate the same and the whole roome to some Saint, that whensoever I enter into it, I enter as it were into a chappell or church that is dedicated to such a saint, and therefore in minde doe that reverence that is due to them.[32]

Providing a unique snapshot into the devotional lives of one Northamptonshire Catholic household, *Adoramus te Christe* vividly demonstrates just *how* Catholics may have made domestic space sacred and turned their households into a 'chappell or church', through musical *memoria* to the recently executed priest, Henry Garnet, and through that veneration of the crucified Christ.

Southwell also provided Catholics with suggested rooms where devotion to particular saints might take place, for example 'in the bed chamber, Saints given to short sleepe and watchfulnesse'.[33] He suggested that Catholics 'may in steede of Saints, place some misterie of Christ['s] life or passion: as the last supper in the dining chamber: and such like'.[34] This reference to the dining room, added to the textual and symbolic Christological devotion within *Adoramus te Christe*, vividly enhances our understanding of the innovative ways in which the Catholic laity reimagined the space in their chancel organization, around an ordinary table.

Strikingly, within *Adoramus te Christe*, a text from the Feast of the Invention of the Holy Cross, some of the notes themselves have been arranged in the shape of a cross. In each voice part, where the text for '*hoc signum*' is set, there are four notes in cruci-

---

[31] Lisa McClain, 'Without Church, Cathedral or Shrine: The Search for Religious Space among Catholics in England, 1559–1625', *SCJ* 33 (2002), 381–99.

[32] Robert Southwell, *A Short Rule of a Good Life* (S. Omers [*sic*], 1622), 162.

[33] Ibid. 164.

[34] Ibid. 165.

form. For musical performance, the higher note makes the most melodic sense and the lower note is not meant to be performed, but it serves a purely symbolic function.[35] Directly after the words 'hoc signum' are symbols of a cross, which have replaced the word 'crucis' from the liturgical text; this has not been set in the music and was reportedly not spoken by Henry Garnet on the scaffold. This dual symbolism, of the musical notation and the rebus, is what is known as *Augenmusik* or 'eye music' – apparent to the eye of the performers but not to the ear. This is most commonly seen in the blackness or whiteness of notes; for example, settings associated with images of death and darkness might use very black notation.[36] Setting the four notes themselves into the shape of a cross within musical notation is exceptionally unusual; indeed, this may even be a unique instance.[37] This musical symbolism directed the performers to meditate upon the image of the cross. In each voice part the singers arrive at the text '*hoc signum*' one after the other, so the meditation is both an individual moment of contemplation and, simultaneously, a communal act of performance. The listeners, whilst not being able to see the rebus of the cross or the notational symbolism themselves, directed by the words 'this sign' would have imagined the cross. Perhaps, like Henry Garnet upon the scaffold, they crossed themselves at this moment in the text.

Alexandra Walsham has highlighted how in the context of some English Catholic domestic households missionary priests were able to devote themselves to the creation of doctrinally self-conscious, individualized believers, thoroughly instructed in mental prayer

---

[35] In the performance and recording made for the purpose of my doctoral research in January 2012, several options were tried – singing both the upper and lower notes together, as well as singing just the lower notes. My profound thanks here are due to the members of *Les Canards Chantants*: Soprano, Sarah Holland; Alto, Robin Bier; Tenor, Edward Ingham; and Bass, Graham Bier. From this and the opinions of several musicologists (particular thanks are due to Jo Wainwright, Richard Rastall, John Morehen, Kerry McCarthy, Jeremy L. Smith and Katelijne Schiltz for all their helpful comments on this and on table-music more generally) it is clear that the lower note was not meant to be performed.

[36] See examples in Thurston Dart, 'Eye Music', *Grove Music Online: Oxford Music Online*, at: <http://www.oxfordmusiconline.com/subscriber/article/grove/music/09152>, accessed 29 March 2012.

[37] In his *Grove* entry, Thurston Dart intriguingly asserts that '[t]here is more than one instance of the symbolism of the Crucifixion illustrated by means of a set of notes in the shape of a cross', yet he mentions this after his discussion of canons and unfortunately gives no indication of sources for his statement.

and drawn towards an intimate interiorization of the Christian life. Their lives revolved around regular reception of the sacrament, careful perusal of devotional literature and regular scrutiny of conscience.[38] Yet in the priests' absence, Walsham argued that the culture of print may have acted as 'imperfect proxy and deputy' in order to carry through the policies and messages of the Council of Trent to the beleaguered Catholic laity.[39] In *Adoramus te Christe*, we see how music may also have acted as an 'imperfect proxy', allowing Catholics to identify with the passion of Christ through the last words of Henry Garnet, and provoking performers to meditate upon the symbol of the cross in a devotion that was both communal and individual.

The investigation of devotional music in domestic contexts has significant ramifications for our understanding of how Catholic piety was adapted for the household after the Reformation. Some scholars have argued that despite the efforts of the Counter-Reformation there was a 'shortage of domestic participation', which reinforced missionaries' pessimism about the possibility of widespread and profound family devotion.[40] The Brudenell manuscript demonstrates at least one important exception to this rule, indicating a level of lay piety that is much deeper than many scholars have previously acknowledged. Moreover, this was not an individual piety or literary *memoria* but demonstrative of a vibrant and didactic approach to the practice of Catholicism, as evidenced by the presence of *Adoramus te Christe*.

In the midst of persecution, English Catholics took inspiration and solace from recent martyrs and executed priests such as Henry Garnet. *Adoramus te Christe* is a vivid example of the important role that music played in the culture of martyrdom and, moreover, the subsequent construction of Catholic devotional identities. Responding to Bossy, Walsham has contended that '[w]hereas in Tridentine Europe household religion was regarded as "a seed bed of subversion" in England it came to be the very cornerstone of a Catholic community striving to avoid its own annihilation'.[41]

[38] Walsham, 'Translating Trent'.

[39] Alexandra Walsham, '"Domme Preachers"? Post-Reformation English Catholicism and the Culture of Print', *P&P*, no. 168 (2000), 72–123, at 121.

[40] See J. C. H. Aveling, 'Catholic Households in Yorkshire, 1580–1603', *NH* 16 (1980), 85–101, at 101. Aveling was using John Bossy's phrase.

[41] Walsham, '"Domme Preachers"?', 122.

The role that music played within these households was fundamental, as Catholics found new ways to express their devotion,
which combined individual with communal piety, and fidelity to
the old ways with the invention of new ones. The performance of
Adoramus te Christe around an ordinary dining room table, which
directed those involved to meditate upon the symbol of the cross,
transformed one Northamptonshire household into a 'chappell
or a church'. This essay highlights the creativity and innovation
of post-Reformation English Catholics, who in the absence of
priests were active agents in the transformation of their individual
experience of faith. In the creation and performance of Catholic
music, English Catholics constructed new ways to build relationships with the divine, as well as with one another.

University of York

NEEDLEWORK AND MORAL INSTRUCTION IN ENGLISH SEVENTEENTH-CENTURY HOUSEHOLDS: THE CASE OF REBECCA

by AMANDA PULLAN

In the seventeenth-century household, in which biblically themed decor was fashionable, many needlework projects included images of female biblical characters. Rebecca was among the most frequently embroidered.[1] In both Protestant and Catholic traditions, Rebecca's story, recorded in Genesis 24,[2] was perceived as especially pertinent to the household. Depictions of her story appeared in the sixteenth-century picture Bibles which were dedicated to, and circulated among, Protestant and Catholic audiences in parts of western and central Europe.[3] Rebecca also featured in Erhard Schön's didactic illustrated woodcut, *Zwölf Frawen des Alten Testaments* (*c.*1530).[4] Not all biblical stories

---

[1]   Ruth Geuter has catalogued 770 embroideries from multiple museum collections, which include depictions of 395 biblical stories; she has identified Rebecca as one of the more common subjects, with 31 pieces: V. R. Geuter, 'Women and Embroidery in Seventeenth-Century Britain: The Social, Religious, and Political Meanings of Domestic Needlework' (Ph.D. thesis, University of Wales, 1996), 285. I have found an additional nine pieces with Rebecca, bringing the total to 40.

[2]   Gen. 24: 1–66 tells how Rebecca was chosen to be Isaac's wife. Isaac's father Abraham sent his servant, unnamed here but known as Eliezer (cf. Gen. 15: 2), to find a wife for Isaac among his relatives. Eliezer asked God for a sign to help him make the selection. He then approached Rebecca at the well, and asked for water. She offered to draw water for his camels in addition, fulfilling the sign. Eliezer explained to Rebecca and her family God's providence in the event, and Rebecca returned with Eliezer to Canaan to be Isaac's wife.

[3]   Two of the most eminent sixteenth-century volumes of biblical illustrations were Gerard de Jode, *Thesaurus Sacrarum Historiarum Veteris Testamenti* (Antwerp, 1585); and Jean de Tournes, *Quadrins Historiques de la Bible* (Lyons, 1553). The first edition of de Tourne's *Quadrins* was dedicated to the 'Trereverente Dame, Janne de la Rochefocaud, Abbess de Nostre dame de Xaintes', which suggests an audience which was both female and Catholic. In addition to German and Italian editions, *Quadrins* was also translated into English by Peter Derendel and published in England as *The true and lovely historike portreatures of the Holy Bible* (1553): Alfred Cartier, ed., *Bibliographie des éditions des de Tournes, imprimeurs lyonnais: Mise en ordre avec une introduction et des appendices par Marius Audin et une notice biographique par E. Vial*, 2 vols (Paris, 1937), 1: 348.

[4]   This woodcut may have been produced as an accompanying illustration to Hans Sachs's *Der Ehren spiegel der Zwölf Durchleuchtigen Frawen des Alten Testaments* (1530): Yvonne Bleyerveld, 'Chaste, Obedient, and Devout: Biblical Women as Patterns of

involving female figures were included in these illustrated works, so the inclusion of her story suggests that Rebecca was perceived as a proper model for young women. Moreover, the absence of Rebecca from the large-scale tapestries which throughout the fourteenth to sixteenth centuries commonly depicted biblical scenes provides an important contrast to the popularity of her story in smaller-scale domestic needlework projects.[5]

According to my calculations, after Esther, Rebecca is one of the most common biblical characters to appear in the needlework of this period, and more than 10 per cent of extant biblical needlework pieces feature her.[6] However, these depictions of her have not received due consideration. The popularity of Rebecca's story has been attributed to its focus on marriage and motherhood – states with which seventeenth-century women would identify.[7] Hans Sachs's instructive poem *Der Ehren spiegel der Zwölf Durchleuchtigen Frawen des Alten Testaments* (1530), a 'Mirror' of virtues for women, suggested that it was Rebecca's virtue of obedience to her parents and Isaac that was to be emulated.[8] However, these considerations do not adequately explain why the episode most frequently represented in needlework pieces is Rebecca's offer of water to Abraham's servant. It seems surprising that the emphasis was not on Rebecca meeting Isaac for the first time.[9] What was it about the youthful Rebecca's offering water to Abraham's servant that resonated so strikingly in the seventeenth-century household and

Female Virtue in Netherlandish and German Graphic Art, ca. 1500–1750', *Simiolus: Netherlands Quarterly for the History of Art* 28 (2000–1), 219–50, at 225.

5 Susan Groag Bell, *The Lost Tapestries of the City of Ladies: Christine de Pizan's Renaissance Legacy* (Berkeley, CA, 2004), 52; Guy Delmarcel, *Flemish Tapestry* (Tielt, 1999), 18.

6 Using my updated version of Geuter's inventory, I have identified Rebecca's story on 24 embroidered objects (some objects depict more than one story, each of which I have counted separately according to Geuter's method), from eleven different collections.

7 Mary M. Brooks, *English Embroideries of the Sixteenth and Seventeenth Centuries in the Collection of the Ashmolean Museum* (London, 2004), 40; Tara Hamling, *Decorating the 'Godly' Household: Religious Art in Post-Reformation Britain* (New Haven, CT, and London, 2010), 209; Geuter, 'Women and Embroidery', 292.

8 A. von Keller, ed., *Hans Sachs. Werke*, 26 vols (Tübingen 1870–1908), 1: 203–10, as quoted in Bleyerveld, 'Chaste, Obedient, and Devout', 225 n. 28.

9 Pieces which portray only this scene, Isaac meeting Rebecca, begin to appear in the eighteenth century: see London, Victoria and Albert Museum Collections, T.45–1937; T.122–1930.

made this such a popular image in the repertoire of needlework for young girls?

This essay will examine these extant seventeenth-century needlework projects alongside contemporary texts to address this question. It will argue that while the figure of Rebecca offered a variety of lessons, the virtue of industry and the vice of vanity were the most significant associations with her story. The first section will show how, by depicting Rebecca pouring water for Eliezer at the well, her industry was being praised. The virtue of industry and a woman's readiness for marriage could be demonstrated through her own act of producing needlework. The second section will examine one specific piece in which Rebecca was interpreted typologically as the Virgin Mary. This portrayal of Rebecca as a Marian figure highlights her role in initiating sexual intimacy with Isaac and her identity as a future mother.

The importance of the well scene is crucial to understanding Rebecca's significance. In other visual representations from the period, namely sixteenth-century woodcuts, Rebecca is almost always pictured with a water jug in hand, even if another scene is being represented (Fig. 1).[10] This metonymic device alerts us to the importance of her act of giving water to Eliezer. In needlework, the frequency of occurrence of the scene is striking. Eighteen of the twenty-two pieces representing Rebecca feature her exchange with Eliezer at the well, and in most cases the scene is found on the front or top of cabinets, in areas of high visibility. These eighteen pieces all portray the well scene using similar iconography. The several elements which consistently appear together include a well or fountain, a woman holding a jug, a man (often stylized in the court dress of Charles I) and camels. The standard iconography suggests that women were well versed in the elements of Rebecca's encounter with Eliezer at the well.

On a general level, the multiple representations of the well scene speak to a societal preoccupation with finding a God-ordained match. Having the appearance of virtue was essential for young women hoping to marry. It was even more crucial for their families, who had, as Linda Pollock has so aptly described, 'the problem of transforming girls into the ideal of femininity depicted in the

---

[10] De Jode's *Thesaurus Sacrarum* includes an image of Jacob receiving the blessing from his father with Rebecca in the background holding the water jug.

Fig. 1: Rebecca and Eliezer, from Gerard De Jode, *Thesaurus Sacrarum Histori-arum Veteris Testamenti* (Antwerp, 1585). Reproduced by permission of the Master and Fellows of St John's College, Cambridge.

scriptures'.[11] The seriousness with which this responsibility was taken can be seen in the financial commitment undertaken by many families in funding their daughters' attendance at female academies, apparently with the sole objective of ensuring their eligibility for marriage. One embroidered cabinet with two scenes from the Rebecca narrative, the well scene and the meeting of Isaac and Rebecca, can be traced to a female academy in Hackney; an accompanying note records that the author's grandmother made it there before the outbreak of plague in 1665.[12] This may have been the 'Hackney school' which featured in William Wycherly's comedy, *The Gentleman Dancing-Master*, and which had the reputa-tion of being a route by which women entered the marriage market. In Wycherly's play, Prud recounted how, by finding a 'Monsieur', it was evident that Hipp had 'not been to Hackney school for

---

[11] Linda Pollock, '"Teach Her to Live under Obedience": The Making of Women in the Upper Ranks of Early Modern England', *Continuity and Change* 4 (1989), 231–58, at 237.

[12] For a copy of the letter, see Brooks, *English Embroideries*, 40.

nothing'.[13] If one of the key roles of the educational institution was to prepare a young woman for the vocation of marriage and running a household, we can see why Rebecca would provide an appropriate model for this young pupil at Hackney.

However, Rebecca's significance was not merely as a portrayal of betrothal. The depiction of Rebecca serving water to Eliezer demonstrated industrious behaviour that signified readiness for marriage. It was the specific act of drawing water for Eliezer and his ten camels that cast Rebecca as one who was not idle but willing to work. Texts of the period associate industriousness with Rebecca. The Authorized Version (1611) emphasizes her speed in executing the task. Rebecca's response to Eliezer, 'drink my lord', was followed by the comment 'and she hasted'. Two verses later, she 'hasted and emptied her pitcher into the trough and ranne again unto the well to draw water'. A third time, Eliezer pointed out to Laban, Rebecca's brother, how she had 'made haste and took down her pitcher from her shoulder'.[14] A similar emphasis on Rebecca's industry is found in the Catholic Rheims-Douai translation. A note explains that 'the event sheweth such qualities and vertues in her, as were most agreable to the great charitie and hospitalitie dayly practiced in Abrahams house, most convenient and necessairie for that family and good of manie'.[15] Protestant and Catholic translations both suggest that Rebecca, by drawing water for the servant, showed the necessary industry for the proper running of a household.

Rebecca's industry is highlighted in the contemporary prescriptive literature as well. An important godly tract, *The Golden Boke of Matrimonye* (1542), a translation of the Swiss Protestant reformer Heinrich Bullinger's frequently reprinted *Der christlich Eestand*, explained that Rebecca was 'gentle, serviceable, lowly, given to labour, quick in her busyness, and loving toward strangers'. Beside this text, a note in the margin explained to the reader that these were 'the properties of a maid that should be [in a] chosen wyfe'.[16]

---

[13] William Wycherly, *The Gentleman Dancing-Master. A Comedy, As it is Acted By Their Majesties Servants* (London, 1693), Act I, Scene 1.

[14] Gen. 24: 18–20 (AV).

[15] *The Holy Bible faithfully translated into English out of the authentical Latin, diligently conferred the Hebrew, Greek, & other Editions in divers languages* (Douai, 1635), note on Gen. 24: 14.

[16] H. Bullinger, *The golde[n] boke of christen matrimonye moost necessary [and] profitable*

The author reiterated his approval of Rebecca's 'busyness' in serving Eliezer, commenting: 'When she commeth to the well she maketh no stop: nor bringeth a sorte of young fellowes with her, nether standeth she gasying and wondering upon the strange man, but quickly and straight goeth she her way, and tendeth her own busynesse.'[17]

A century later, John Spencer's *Kaina kai palaia: things new and old* (1658) similarly commended Rebecca for her industry. In his compendium of moral sayings and lessons, Spencer proposed that children should be set to honest employment as the patriarchs had 'their tender daughters brought up in doing Houshold business. Rebecca went with her pitcher on her shoulders to give drink to her Father's camels.' He further postulated that 'such was the harmless simplicity of those days, and such was the obedience of children that even she that was appointed to be the Mother of Patriarchs, Prophets and Kings refused not to set her hand to ordinary employments'.[18] According to Spencer, the young women of the day were not interested in following Rebecca's example of fetching water, but they preferred to use her story to justify the wearing of bracelets and jewellery on the ground that Eliezer had given Rebecca such gifts.[19]

This example of Rebecca as a noble figure who was not afraid to perform tasks beneath her station was also used by John Potter, later archbishop of Canterbury. In his *Antiquities of Ancient Greece* (1699), Potter praised the women of 'the primitive Ages' who were 'accustomed to draw Water, to keep sheep, and feed cows or horses'. He compared Rebecca who 'carry'd a pitcher and drew Water' with the 'rich and noble [from centuries past] who were taken up

---

for all the[m], that entend to liue quietly and godlye in the Christen state of holy wedlock newly set forthe in English by Theodore Basille, transl. M. Coverdale and T. Basile (London, 1542), xliiii. Basile has been identified as Thomas Becon, since the preface in this work is identical to the one among Becon's published works: see *The worckes of Thomas Becon: whiche he hath hytherto made and published, with diuerse other newe bookes added to the same, heretofore neuer set forth in print diuided into thre tomes or parts diligently perused, corrected, and amended: and now finished this present of our Lord* (London, 1564).

[17] Ibid.

[18] John Spencer, *Kaina Kai Palaia: Things New and Old, or A Storehouse of Similies, Sentences, Allegories, Apophthegms, Adagies, Apologues, Divine, Morall, Political, &C. With Their Several Applications* (London, 1658), 482.

[19] Ibid.

with employments of inferior quality'.[20] Potter was reputed to have disinherited his eldest son John for marrying a domestic servant, so perhaps his discourse of work and industry was tempered by an opinion about what kind of labour was acceptable for a person's station in life.[21] Drawing water was not the hard toil that was associated with the 'work' of the labouring classes.[22] Instead it was a dignified task that demonstrated a lack of idleness.

It is not coincidental that the word used most frequently by seventeenth-century women to refer to needlework was 'work'. The equation of needlework with industry is also evident from the frontispiece of a seventeenth-century pattern book which in its twelfth edition depicted the three figures of Wisdom, Industry and Folly. Industry is shown sitting under Wisdom's guidance and she is stitching. The book's subtitle reiterates the implications: *A New Booke wherin are divers Admirable Workes wrought with the Needle. Newly invented and cut in Copper for the pleasure and profit of the Industrious.*[23] Lena Cowen Orlin has traced references to needlework in Shakespeare and concluded that needlework was a way in which women could appear intentionally busy.[24] Those who practised needlework were praised not only for being industrious but also for avoiding idleness. Thus the subtext of a concern with industry appears to be contempt for idleness.

The prominent warnings about vanity and idle behaviour in literature directed to young women were also conveyed through the mermaid and looking glass motif in needlework. This motif has been located on some of the pieces illustrating the Rebecca narrative. It was especially prevalent in the seventeenth century as a warning against the folly of spending too much time in front of the mirror. There is some irony here since it was customary in the latter half of the seventeenth century for the embroidered boxes

[20] John Potter, *Archaeologiae graecae: or, The antiquities of Greece* (London, 1699), 341.

[21] *ODNB, s.n.* 'Potter, John (1673/4–1747)', online at: <http://www.oxforddnb.com/view/article/22612>, accessed September 2012.

[22] Ruth B. Bottigheimer, *The Bible for Children: from the Age of Gutenberg to the Present* (New Haven, CT, 1996), 94–6.

[23] Frontispiece in John Taylor, *The Needles Excellency. A New Booke wherin are divers Admirable Workes wrought with the Needle. Newly invented and cut in Copper for the pleasure and profit of the Industrious* (London, 1631).

[24] Lena Cowen Orlin, 'Three Ways to be Invisible in the Renaissance: Sex, Reputation, and Stitchery', in Patricia Fumerton and Simon Hunt, eds, *Renaissance Culture and the Everyday* (Philadelphia, PA, 1999), 183–203.

to contain mirrors. The external decoration could be seen as a warning against the dangers within the box.[25]

The virtue of industry was an appropriate lesson for young women who belonged to middle- or upper-class households where idleness was a more pressing concern. Lady Anne Halkett made the connection between needlework and idleness explicit. In her autobiography, she praised her mother for the quality of her education and for ensuring that she and her sisters had had the kind of education that prevented idleness, and described how her mother 'kept a gentlewoman to teach us all kinds of needleworke, which shews I was not brought up in an idle life'.[26] Depicting Rebecca's willingness to serve could have accentuated her lack of idleness. As a model for the household, Rebecca may have stood as an antitype of sloth.

Thus far the imagery has been used alongside the literature to suggest that Rebecca was important for her display of industry and her aversion to idleness. The second section of this essay will examine a needlework project recently acquired by the Museum of Lancashire. This embroidered cabinet remained in family hands for over four hundred years until very recently; it was therefore unknown to twentieth-century art collectors and scholars.[27] The needlework of Eunice, the wife of Thomas Bourne of Nether Wyresdale, Lancashire, provides interesting examples of how Rebecca could be understood not only for herself, but as being like Mary. It also suggests that some women perceived modesty and industry differently from the instruction they received from sermons and printed texts.

In the 1660s, Eunice embroidered five scenes for her cabinet. She chose the sacrifice of Isaac (Gen. 22) for the back panel, which formed the backdrop to the other scenes with Rebecca (Fig. 2). On the front panel she depicted Abraham sending out Eliezer (Fig. 3). The top panel was the iconic well scene (Fig. 4). The other two scenes were also common in the iconography of

---

[25] The best example is Port Sunlight, Lady Lever Art Gallery, LL5258, which has the mermaid motif on the lid of the embroidered box containing images of Rebecca: Xanthe Brooke, *The Lady Lever Art Gallery Catalogue of Embroideries* (Stroud, 1992), 183.

[26] *The Autobiography of Anne, Lady Halkett*, ed. John Gough Nichols (London, 1875), 3, quoted in Geuter, 'Women and Embroidery', 173.

[27] The embroidered cabinet (LANMS.2005.4) is currently at the Museum of Lancashire, Preston. Through correspondence with the museum, the Netherhampton Salerooms and Mrs Rachel Kent (née Bourne), provenance details have been established, although lack of historical records has so far made it impossible to identify or date Eunice Bourne with certainty.

Fig. 2: Sacrifice of Isaac, Bourne cabinet. Museum of Lancashire, Preston. Photographs of figs 2–6 by the author, and reproduced by courtesy of Lancashire County Council's Museum Service.

Fig. 3: Abraham sending Eliezer, Bourne cabinet.

Fig. 4: Rebecca and Eliezer at the well, Bourne cabinet.

Rebecca: Rebecca and Eliezer travelling, and the meeting of Isaac and Rebecca. Significantly, however, when it came to the travelling scene, the strong likeness of the depiction of Rebecca to depictions of the Virgin Mary, intensified by her blue gown and the presence of the donkey, are compelling evidence that Eunice here elided the figures of Rebecca and Eliezer with those of Mary and Joseph (Fig. 5). This is particularly interesting because in the surviving embroideries it is highly unusual to represent a scene from the life of Christ as a replacement for a standard trope;[28] indeed, it is uncommon to find any event outside the book of Genesis portrayed in the context of the story of Rebecca, let alone a scene from the New Testament. Moreover, it would be strange for an embroiderer to include all the other scenes from the Rebecca narrative, as Eunice has done, and yet replace one by a New Testament scene, unless she saw a connection between the narratives. Eunice's substitution suggests that she was reading

---

[28] From my analysis of 150 seventeenth-century embroideries, this is the only example in which a scene from the life of Christ has been integrated within the story of Rebecca.

Fig. 5: Travelling scene with Rebecca and Eliezer portrayed as Mary and Joseph, Bourne cabinet.

Rebecca's story typologically, and replacing the Genesis scene with its equivalent in the New Testament. By portraying Rebecca as a Marian figure, it is evident that for Eunice the figure of Rebecca held typological significance. Before Mary, Rebecca had borne children from whom the Messianic line extended.

The reasons for Eunice's substitution are not entirely clear. The substitution of Mary and Joseph is too unusual for it to have been a 'recycling' of the scene from another project, especially since there are no known existing examples of a 'travelling Mary and Joseph' scene. Instead, it is possible that Eunice was Catholic. Unfortunately, neither Eunice nor her husband Thomas can be identified in the extant parish registers for the period. However, parish records do show that four members of the Bourne family refused to take the Protestant Oath of 1641, intended to demonstrate their allegiance to the 'true reformed Protestant religion against Popery and Popish Innovations'. A Thomas was one of those named.[29] It

---

[29] Henry J. Fishwicke, *The History of the Parish of Garstang in the County of Lancaster* (London, 1879), 264–72.

was common for Roman Catholics to abstain from this oath, and their suspect political identity could shed some light on the design and contents of the casket. Eunice's cabinet has a secret drawer, and it also has a smaller container with a false bottom containing an embroidered ovoid reputed to be an acorn from the famed Boscobel Oak. The presence of this royalist relic suggests that the cabinet's maker was loyal to the Stuart crown and quite possibly to the Catholic religion. This seems more probable when considering Eunice's incorporation of Marian typology.

Tantalizingly little is known about Eunice, but her own circumstances may have affected the way she portrayed Rebecca. Her depiction of Rebecca is evidence of the 'domestic subversion' that Alexandra Walsham has recognized as a vital strand of the dynamics at play in the early modern household.[30] Eunice's Rebecca calls into question the behaviour commonly ascribed to her in sermons on marriage. For example, in a sermon printed in 1630, William Gouge pointed to Rebecca as an example of outward reverence.[31] In line with his stated intention to 'stir up Christians to walk worthy of their vocation', Rebecca was offered as a model of female vocation, namely marriage. Gouge emphasized 'outward carriage', which he defined as 'sober behaviour, courteous gesture, and modest attire', and asserted that Rebecca had this kind of 'reverent carriage' because when she approached Isaac for the first time, she covered herself with a veil.[32] On the importance of female modesty, Gouge was not alone in his views. Gervase Markham introduced similar criteria for an ideal wife in his *The English Housewife*, including a section on temperance in behaviour and carriage, and another on garments and modest attire.[33]

With this in mind, Eunice's depiction of the scene in which Rebecca meets Isaac, on the side panel of the casket, is particularly interesting. It shows a curious lack of sober behaviour. No veil is in sight. Instead, Rebecca appears to be seducing Isaac (Fig. 6). Rebecca is lifting her skirt and beckoning with her finger, offering

---

[30]   See, in this volume, Alexandra Walsham, 'Holy Families: The Spiritualization of the Early Modern Household Revisited', 122–60.

[31]   William Gouge, *An Exposition of part of the Fift and Sixt chapters of S. Paules Epistle to the Ephesians* (London, 1630), 21.

[32]   Ibid.

[33]   Gervase Markham, *The English Housewife*, ed. Michael R. Best (Montreal, QC, 1986), 7–8.

Fig. 6: Rebecca meeting Isaac, Bourne cabinet.

an explicit indication as to what comes next. Sexual activity was not an unusual association with the account of Rebecca, but it was not often displayed in needlework. Genesis 26: 8–9 tells how Abimelech, king of the Philistines, observed Isaac sporting with Rebecca, realized that she was his wife and forbade his men to sleep with her. As ministers in the seventeenth century strained to find direct applications of this biblical tale, it was clear they did not find fault with sexual play itself but rather the manner of it.[34] The key difference found in Eunice's needlework is that Rebecca was the one initiating the 'sporting'. This was not sober behaviour according to Gouge, who stipulated:

> Sobriety, as it is a vertue especially belonging to all women, so most especially to wives; and it is opposed to Levity and Wantonnesse … This is not opposed to Matrimoniall familiarity: such as was between Isaac and Rebecca, Gen 26: 8, but such sporting ought … to be in private, when they are alone.

---

[34] Robert Cleaver and John Dod, *A godly forme of houshold government for the ordering of priuate families, according to the direction of God's word* (London, 1621), sig. M2.

It ought to be begun by the husband, as it is there said that (Isaac) sported with Rebecca.[35]

Eunice's Rebecca provides an alternative message of wifely conduct, one that highlights Rebecca's role as a matriarch. The panel which seems problematic, Rebecca seducing Isaac, and which initially caused a museum curator to misattribute it as a scene depicting Solomon and the queen of Sheba, deepens our understanding of how virtue was taught to (and perhaps by) early modern women. Sexual relations for the purpose of carrying on a dynasty were exactly what was considered virtuous. This was particularly true in Rebecca's case, as her sexual relationships would lead to the building of a nation and the birth of Christ. That Eunice also embroidered a pomegranate in the travelling scene is also telling. Representing rebirth and fertility, the pomegranate is a prelude to the action in the final panel, the meeting of the two, and the consequent consummation of the marriage. Eunice's decision to use a motif of strawberries to decorate the top slip sends a similar message (Fig. 6). Strawberries, with their numerous seeds visible on the outside, were emblems of fertility, and could be another reference not only to Rebecca's fecundity but to the Virgin Mary and the birth of Christ.[36] The symbolism of the seed is evident in Thomas Bentley's *Monument of Matrons*, which tells how Rebecca's parents gave her a blessing that she would 'grow into thousands and thy seed possess the gate of thine enemies and be victorious over them … which was afterward fullye accomplished in Jesus Christ'.[37] For Eunice, the ideal of dynastic achievement appears to have become a reality. Burke's *Peerage* records that she bore three children who between them continued the Bourne family line for four centuries.[38]

To return to the main question driving this essay, we can see why Rebecca, as a model of female virtue, would have resonated with the seventeenth-century household. Rebecca's identifiably virtuous conduct in giving water to Abraham's servant was espe-

---

[35] Gouge, *Exposition*, 21.

[36] Susan Frye, *Pens and Needles: Women's Textualities in Early Modern England* (Philadelphia, PA, 2010), 172.

[37] T[homas] B[entley], *The Sixt Lampe of Virginitie: conteining a Mirrour for Maidens and Matrons* (London, 1582), 224.

[38] Bernard Burke, *A Genealogical and Heraldic History of the Landed Gentry of Great Britain and Ireland*, 2 vols (London, 1871), 1: 130.

cially pertinent for young women who were being trained to run a household. This visual narrative provided instruction on the virtue of industry and the vice of sloth. But beyond this traditional message, which is echoed in contemporary literature, we see that the scene between Rebecca and Eliezer had heightened appeal since it represented the aspirations of unmarried women. Rebecca's story was also a way to communicate their understanding of what kind of virtues were important for marriage. Eunice Bourne's representation of Rebecca has indicated that willingness to bear children was more important than the 'modesty' prescribed in conduct books and sermons. Finally, it is important that the Rebecca narrative reached across confessional divides and figured visibly in many seventeenth-century households.

Lancaster University

CATECHESIS, SOCIALIZATION AND PLAY IN A CATHOLIC HOUSEHOLD, *c*.1660: THE 'CHILDREN'S EXERCISES' FROM THE BLUNDELL PAPERS

by LUCY UNDERWOOD

Among the papers of the Blundell family of Little Crosby, Lancashire, are two dramatic sketches entitled 'An Exercise to Embolden the Children in Speaking' and 'Children Emboldened to Speak. By an Exercise'. They were written by William Blundell, recusant, royalist and Lancashire gentleman, in 1663 and 1665 for his daughters and their cousins to perform, probably at Christmas family gatherings. Humorously mingling Catholic catechesis, social education, the exercise of parental authority and childish misbehaviour, these sketches open a rare window onto the life of a Catholic household in the Restoration era.[1] They offer an opportunity to explore the household as the location for the practice and appropriation of religion.

It has often been argued that, during the period of proscription that followed the Protestant Reformation, the 'Catholic household' played a key role in the survival and development of English Catholicism. In particular, the Catholic gentry household has been seen as the main locus of Catholic worship, Catholic culture and Catholic congregations. Such a picture elides a good many complexities, not least because there was no single template of a 'Catholic household', in terms of class or function or religious culture, or even a uniform 'Catholic gentry household'. But it remains the case that family networks and domestic locations were extremely important to the practice of Catholicism.[2] And, like non-Catholic households, Catholic homes were often the places where children first engaged with religious belief and practice.

---

[1] Preston, Lancashire Record Office, DDBL.acc.6121, Box 2, William Blundell, 'Blew Book', fols 27^r–30^r.

[2] John Bossy, *The English Catholic Community, 1570–1850* (London, 1975); Marie B. Rowlands, ed., *Catholics of Parish and Town 1558–1778* (London, 1999); Anne Dillon, 'Public Liturgy made Private: The Rosary Confraternity in the Life of a Recusant Household', in J. Bepler and P. Davidson, eds, *The Triumphs of the Defeated: Early Modern Festivals and Messages of Legitimacy* (Wiesbaden, 2007), 245–70.

A text which offers insight into children's experience of religion within the household is therefore invaluable. The author is an adult, the parent, but his script often implies that he is writing from observation, and he goes out of his way to capture what appears as the perspective of the children, by whom it was intended to be performed.

Despite the burgeoning of scholarship on childhood and adolescence in the early modern period, the experiences of the young within English Catholic communities have been very little studied, although some pioneering work has been done.[3] Historians of childhood have explored various aspects of pedagogy, gendered constructions of childhood, the role of children in religion and religious communities, affective ties in the family, the experience of parenthood and the role of sectarian religious commitment in attitudes to childhood.[4] The Catholic 'domestic drama' we are considering here impinges on all these issues. During the formative decades of the reigns of Elizabeth and James I the engagement

---

[3] See Lucy Underwood, 'Childhood, Youth and Catholicism in England, c.1558–1660' (Ph.D. diss., Cambridge University, 2012). Previous work includes Alison Shell, 'Furor Juvenilis: Post-Reformation English Catholicism and Exemplary Youthful Behaviour', in Ethan Shagan, ed., Catholics and the 'Protestant Nation': Religious Politics and Identity in Early Modern England (Manchester, 2005), 185–206; eadem, 'Autodidacticism in English Jesuit Drama: The Writings and Career of Joseph Simons', Medieval and Renaissance Drama in England 13 (2001), 34–56; Arthur C. F. Beales, Education under Penalty: English Catholic Education from the Reformation to the Fall of James II, 1547–1689 (London, 1963); Caroline Bowden, '"For the Glory of God": A Study of the Education of English Catholic Women in Convents in Flanders and France in the First Half of the Seventeenth Century', in R. Aldrich, J. Coolahan and F. Simon, eds, Faiths and Education: Comparative and Historical Perspectives (Gent, 1999), 77–95.

[4] See, for example, Anthony Fletcher, Growing up in England: The Experience of Childhood 1600–1914 (New Haven, CT, 2008); Linda Pollock, Forgotten Children: Parent-Child Relations from 1500 to 1900 (Cambridge, 1983); P. J. P. Goldberg and F. Riddy, eds, Youth in the Middle Ages (Woodbridge, 2004); Paul Griffiths, Youth and Authority: Formative Experiences in England 1560–1640 (Oxford, 1996); Ilana K. Ben-Amos, Adolescence and Youth in Early Modern England (New Haven, CT, 1994); J. Casey, Family and Community in Early Modern Spain: The Citizens of Granada 1570–1739 (Cambridge, 2007); Carmen Luke, Pedagogy, Printing and Protestantism: The Discourse on Childhood (New York, 1989); C. J. Sommerville, The Discovery of Childhood in Puritan England (Athens, GA, 1992); Anna French, 'Possession, Puritanism and Prophecy: Child Demoniacs and English Reformed Culture', Reformation 13 (2008), 133–61; Alexandra Walsham, '"Out of the mouths of babes and sucklings": Prophecy, Puritanism and Childhood in Elizabethan Suffolk' and Susan Hardman Moore, '"Such perfecting of praise out of the mouth of a babe": Sarah Wight as Child Prophet', in Diana Wood, ed., The Church and Childhood, SCH 31 (Oxford, 1994), 285–300, 313–24 respectively; Sara Mendelson and Patricia Crawford, Women in Early Modern England, 1550–1720 (Oxford, 1998), 75–123, 148–64.

of children with Catholicism was dominated by persecution.[5] This does not mean constantly experiencing oppression, barbarity and hardship, but that a consciousness of being a proscribed minority was a central feature of English Catholic culture and dictated how the young encountered Catholicism. Yet something which the Blundell sketches demonstrate vividly is how, by the 1660s, the emergency had become domesticated.

The Blundell family history was woven into that of English Catholicism. William Blundell (1620–98), author of our sketches, kept copious records of his correspondence and compiled many other papers, including accounts of persecution undergone by his Elizabethan and Jacobean forebears. His own Royalist service in the Civil War, repeated imprisonment, and the costly seques-tration of his estates were also carefully documented.[6] Several of Blundell's daughters – including those featured in these sketches – became nuns, and two of his sons Jesuit priests.[7] Although Blun-dell was a provincial Catholic gentleman, and sometimes chose to emphasize his marginalization, he was deeply engaged in the political and social concerns of his age, as Geoffrey Baker's study has shown.[8] Likewise, the scripts Blundell wrote for his daughters reveal equally the Catholicism which set them apart from their peers, and the social concerns which made them utterly typical. As Shell has discussed in the context of Catholic male education, theatre in various forms was central to early modern pedagogy. Both the exercise of acting, and the content of speeches and plays, helped to form pupils into the kind of adults they were intended to become. Drama was also used by English Catholic communities, within the relatively safe spaces of Catholic households, as a tool to preserve, communicate and defend their faith.[9] In the Blundell girls' plays, William Blundell was inducting his daughters into an

---

[5]   Underwood, 'Childhood, Youth and Catholicism', esp. chs 1–3.

[6]   Cf. his letter to Anne Bradshaigh, 5 February 1657, from Liverpool gaol: DDBL. acc.6121, Box 3, account book 1646–70, fols 61^v–63^r; also (for the sequestration) Blun-dell, *Cavalier*, 40–1, 303.

[7]   DDBL.acc.6121, Box 2, Letter Book 1672–3, fol. 12^r; Box 2, accounts 1663–1680, fols 24–28^v, 87^{r-v}.

[8]   Geoffrey Baker, *Reading and Politics in Early Modern England: The Mental World of a Seventeenth-Century Catholic Gentleman* (Manchester, 2010).

[9]   Shell, 'Autodidacticism'; Paul Whitfield White, *Drama and Religion in English Provincial Society, 1485–1660* (Cambridge, 2008), esp. ch. 5.

educative and religious tradition characteristic of the community to which they were to belong.

The first play opens with a conversation between 'Mall' and her 'father', in which he declares his intention of whipping her for various faults, and she persuades him not to. The father then leaves, and Mall's sisters and cousin appear. Mall begins by lecturing them on good conduct, just as her father had reproved her; but her resolution to 'pray and mend' breaks down, and the girls indulge in some rather disrespectful play with their father's bass viol. The sketch ends with a dance. The second, shorter, piece involves only the children; good behaviour is again the subject of discussion, and again gives way to sparring and teasing.

Catholic catechesis is carefully woven into the playful dialogue of this 'family entertainment'. The youngest child, 'Betty', asks:

> ... will Iustice, Prudence, Fortitude and temperance bring us to heauen? Those are the Cardinal Virtues.
>
> Mall: I ['aye'] hony the Cardinall virtues by all meanes.
>
> Betty: And will Faith, Hope and Charity, bring us to heauen too?
>
> Mall: they will bring us to Heauen Gates. but Faith and hope must go back againe, and only charity must enter into Heauen.

The 'cardinal virtues' were a traditional formulation of the four moral qualities on which virtuous action hinged, and were listed in most early modern Catholic catechisms. Faith, hope and charity, the three 'theological virtues', were not only included in catechisms, but often made the structure for the whole work, with other content being placed under these headings: the Creed under 'Faith', prayers and sacraments under 'Hope', and the Ten Commandments and so on under 'Charity'. Mall's 'only charity must enter into heaven' alludes to 1 Corinthians 13: 13, 'And now there remain faith, hope, and charity, these three: but the greatest of these is charity'.[10] This exchange ends with Bridget asking: 'will not kneading of Cockle bread and turning the Catt in the pan bring a body to Heauen?' and being reproved by Mall, 'O by no means loue. They know the way to Purgatory but not to Heauen'.

---

10   Underwood, 'Childhood, Youth and Catholicism', ch. 3.

Mall's dispute with her father, which takes up the first half of the sketch, also evokes early modern catechisms. Mall offers the argument that 'I haue beene oft at Confession, & I haue confessed the same thing ouer & ouer againe; I had allwise absolution, & I hope God forgaue me my Sins & yet I committed them very often'. Her father probes this proposition:

> Father: … When you got the absolution and pardon which you tell me of, was it only for promising to mend?

> Mall: yes sir, if it please you I did then promise to mend.

> Father: But did you nothing els but promisse.

> Mall: yes sir I was very sorry for what I had don, & I did purposse from my heart to mend. and I did accuse my self and confesse my secret sins which nobody els knew.

> Father: very good. you were sorry for your faults, you purposed to mend and you confessed them all. This was very well: and if this be tru, god that knows your heart hath pardoned all.

> Mall: I trust in God he hath.

Reciting this dialogue on the sacrament of penance would have reminded Mall of the question-and-answer catechisms she would have learnt. Catholic sacraments and the priests who provided them were still forbidden by English law; but for eight-year-old Mary Blundell in 1663[11] they were an integral part of life, bound up with both religious practice and social expectation. There is little sense in the sketch that the religion these girls were being taught was still illegal.

The catechetical echoes make these sketches autodidactic.[12] If Bridget could not previously recite the cardinal virtues, or Mall the components of confession, after learning this 'exercise' they would be able to. Didacticism between the children continues in the 1665 piece, involving Frank, Bridget and 'Peg'. Two years later,

[11]   Mary Blundell was born on 3 February 1654/5, making her just under nine at the date of the first play. Clare Frances was born on 1 August 1656, and Bridget in March 1659/60: DDBL.acc.6121, 'Great Hodge Podge', fol. 184.
[12]   Shell, 'Autodidacticism', discusses autodidacticism (of a different kind) in the school dramas of the Blundell girls' male counterparts.

Frank is now 'the grauest & the most changed woman in the whol World' and offers to teach civility to Bridget.

The fact that the Blundell children in this piece played themselves (while their father presumably played himself) adds to its autodidacticism. William Blundell seems to have written into the script games he had actually seen them playing, and noticeable characteristics. So the children were being asked to observe, and to cooperate in the judgement of, their own behaviour. Mall is permitted (in the script) to argue with her father and as a result to escape punishment; but she is also required to enact the results of such parental indulgence, which (as we shall see) are mayhem and gleeful disrespect for the parent involved. Yet any didactic purpose is woven seamlessly into the humour, the enjoyment, which is the salient feature of these 'Exercises'; there appears to be no conflict between them for the writer. What we can only guess at is how far Blundell has in fact recaptured his daughters' experiences: whether they actually had these sorts of conversations between themselves, discussing the catechism and turning somersaults; whether Mall really did subject her father's disciplinary authority to scrutiny. Much of it rings attractively true – the mixture of pragmatic guile in Mall's desire to evade punishment and the grateful sincerity of her determination to reform when she does; or stage directions like 'Enter Frank driuing her Sister Bridget before her tyed (lyke a horse) with a string in her mouth & c.' And all younger siblings will recognize the older sister's penchant for passing parental injunctions down the pecking order. At the least, we can say that an adult observer found these kinds of interactions both plausible and entertaining.

While the 'Exercises' distinguish the Blundell girls from their Protestant counterparts through Catholic catechesis, they align them with all other English aristocratic girls in the social values conveyed. Both pieces are preoccupied with questions of manners, socially appropriate behaviour, 'civility'. The faults Mall is accused of are 'that rouling untidy gate of yours … that wild carryage of your head … your unreuerent maner of Praying; And of that wild unhandsom laughing of yours'; later Mall chides her sisters' 'too chyldish' behaviour and proposes instead 'fine merry ciuil playes'.

'Civility' was a term increasingly used in the early modern period to denote good manners and social convention. Anna Bryson has argued that its gradual adoption in place of the earlier 'courtesy' reflects a shift in perceptions: 'civility' was an all-encompassing mode of living in a way that medieval rules of courteous behaviour were not, and was linked to an emergent understanding of the word 'civility' analogous to the modern 'civilization'. Personal good manners were inseparable from the good order of society and polity. In England, at least, such values remained wedded to aristocratic assumptions: they were the mark and the duty of those born to rule.[13] Civility became, according to Bryson, a 'practical "science" of sociability, analogous to … the science of political behaviour also required of the "civil" gentleman'.[14] 'Civility' was also related to education and the need to transform the 'natural' lawlessness of children into disciplined, 'civil' behaviour.[15] One conduct book aimed at the young was translated from French (many conduct books were European in origin) by a child of eight (as its publishers advertised). This was *Youth's Behaviour: or Decency in Conversation amongst Men* (1646). The child in question, Francis Hawkins, was a Catholic, and the French version originated at the Jesuit college of Pont-à-Mousson. The concept of civility was one which continental Catholic and English gentry culture shared.[16]

The Blundell texts also make the connection between 'civility' and social station: when Mall tells her sisters she is a reformed character, Frank calls her, ironically, 'the Graue gentlewoman'. Later, when Mall falls in with Frank's antics, the latter comments: 'This is a mad wench Girles is shee not?' But civility is most noticeably linked to maturity and gender. The father reproves Mall: 'you are growne a big Girle & I do not see but your Carryage is still the same that it was 3 or 4 years agoe when you were a chyld lyke your sister Bridget'. Mall tells Frank and Bridget 'this is

---

[13] Anna Bryson, *From Courtesy to Civility: Changing Codes of Conduct in Early Modern England* (Oxford, 1998), esp. 43–74. But John Gillingham qualifies the posited contrast between medieval and early modern concepts: 'From Civilitas to Civility: Codes of Manners in Medieval and Early Modern England', *TRHS* 6th ser. 12 (2002), 267–89.

[14] Bryson, *Courtesy to Civility*, 70.

[15] Ibid. 71–3.

[16] Francis Hawkins, transl., *Youth's Behaviour: or Decency in Conversation amongst Men*, 4th edn (London, 1646); this work was still being reprinted in 1672. Hawkins became a Jesuit in 1649: Bryson, *Courtesy to Civility*, 31; *ODNB, s.n.* 'Hawkins, Francis (1628–1681)'. The 1646 title page describes *Youth's Behaviour* only as 'Composed in French by grave persons for the use and benefit of their youth'; see Bryson for its Jesuit influence.

too chyldish for one of your years. we should now be graue and Womanly'.

The identification of virtue with conduct appropriate to age, sex and social station illustrates the concern of seventeenth-century education with 'socialization', which Anthony Fletcher argues meant training boys for work and the world and girls for 'society' – to be a 'gentlewoman' rather than a 'wench' – and marriage.[17] The work of Richard Allestree (author of the *Whole Duty of Man*), nearly contemporary to the Blundell material, exemplifies a 'gendered' approach to virtue, for instance in his discussion of modesty in *The Ladies Calling* (first published 1673).[18] Modesty is defined as a peculiarly feminine virtue, and Allestree laments that 'such a degenerous age do we now live in, that every thing seems inverted, even Sexes; whilst men fall to the Effeminacy and Niceness of women, and women take up the Confidence, the Boldness of men, and this too under the notion of good breeding'.[19] The virtues essential to a woman before marriage are modesty and obedience: 'there is scarce any thing looks more indecent, then to see a young Maid too forward and confident in her talk'.[20]

The Blundell plays do not entirely fit such models. Their avowed purpose is to embolden the children in speaking, rather than to restrict them. If civility was generally regarded as a masculine concept,[21] Blundell observes no such distinction, even applying 'civil' to feminine as opposed to masculine behaviour: the connection of gender with maturity ('grave and womanly' conduct) equates masculine with childish behaviour. Undisciplined physical activity is 'playes for Boyes'; Mall proposes 'fine merry ciuil playes fit for Girles'. The effect may be to debar older girls from freedoms their brothers continued to enjoy; but 'womanly' conduct is presented as a goal rather than a deprivation. The writer is certainly concerned not to make good behaviour unattractive. Mall, in reproving her

---

[17]   Fletcher, *Growing up in England*, 259–80, although his material focuses mainly on the eighteenth and nineteenth centuries. See also idem, *Gender, Sex and Subordination in Early Modern England 1500–1800* (London, 1985), 364–76. Mendelson and Crawford perceive a similar bias in girls' education: *Women in Early Modern England*, 75–92.

[18]   Richard Allestree, *The Ladies Calling*, in *The Works of the Author of the Whole Duty of Man* (London, 1684), 1–12; cf. Fletcher, *Growing up in England*, 5–6, 25.

[19]   Allestree, *Ladies Calling*, 5.

[20]   Ibid. 58–9, 63.

[21]   Relatively little writing on 'civility' was addressed to women: Bryson, *Courtesy to Civility*, 38–9, 270.

companions, reassures them: 'I have twenty devises in my head of Ciuil fine playes', and asserts: 'I am one (for all this) that can laugh and talke and recreat, as well as you; but still without gapeing and rigging'.

William Blundell's scripts do not bear out Fletcher's thesis that 'it simply did not cross most men's minds that girls could be taught to reason as boys could'.[22] Mall as written is an accomplished rhetorician: she deploys logical argument, appeals to authority and emotional manipulation (playing on her father's evident softness by stressing her 'fear' of him), in order to challenge his right to punish her. After making the analogy with absolution mentioned earlier, Mall continues, 'Sir my duty makes me think you are a good man; yet perhaps you may haue displeased God oftener then one tyme in committing the same fault. God is a louing father to us all & I hope will pardon us'. The child knows that turning the accusation back on the parent is daring: 'my great feares haue put me past feare. Good sir be not angree & pardon this & all together'. But the father is first taken aback, and then acknowledges: 'Chyld I haue offended God oftener in some one thing (I, & ther are many of those som ones too) then you haue offended eyther God or me, in all your faults together'.

The doctrine of original sin, to which Mall's defence refers, is not deployed here to emphasize the essential depravity of children, tainted by sin but not yet redeemed into virtue. Instead, the impression is of relative innocence: children have sinned less often and less seriously than their elders. The father demands: 'Well. And I must not whip nor mortify you (though you vex me every minute) for that good reason you haue shewd me, must I?', to which Mall replies innocently: 'God forbid sir that I should offend so often'.

The conversation does not end here, however. The father continues: 'let us now make use of our reasons a little further, & let you and me dispute'. Mall is then effectively catechized on the sacrament of confession, as we have seen. The father has regained the initiative; he qualifies Mall's defence by pointing out firstly that '[I] … neyther know your sorrow nor yet your purpose', and secondly that 'commonly when God forgiueth our sins he scorgeth us roundly … with worldly afflictions, both to punish what is past and to teach us to mend for the future: And the lesse we haue of those, the more is our Purgatory in an other world.' This is compared to 'the Rod in your fathers hand', which is 'the same to a chyld offending, that purgatory & other temporal paines are in Gods, when he pleaseth to inflict them on sinners'.

Mall interjects with some more advanced theology: 'Most tru deare Father; but I haue heard you say that an act of perfect sorrow (I think you calld it contrition) doth gain a general pardon & freedom euen from purgatory itself': this is probably a reference to the theory of indulgences. But the father remains unconvinced:

> I tell you once againe I am not able to iudge of your sorrow nor of your purpose; your faults are often apparent, and when your pardoned for them (upon promisse of amendment) ther may yet remaine a penance, a little wholsom correction, or memorandum against the next tyme … and this correction I am bound under sin to giue you.

Religion endorses, more than it challenges, parental authority.

Alison Shell argues that this sketch shows a parent 'open to the idea of being exhorted by his child'.[23] Mall certainly 'disputes' with her parent, he admits her accusation, and sentence is revoked. But this is not because Mall wins the dispute: her father is clear that his sinfulness 'doth accuse me but it clears not you'. He concludes that he is still 'bound under sin' to correct her but 'now at this present I hope both you and I may be dispenced with as to that particular – Goe, remember what I tell you, becom a good Gyrle, pray and mend': Mall is not repreived because he should not punish her, but because he does not want to. The dispute, by airing the objection, reasserts the legitimacy of parental authority. Yet it also circumscribes it: the father may be analogous to God, but his justice remains imperfect, because, as he says, he cannot read his child's mind. In confession Mall answers directly to God for the 'secret sins which nobody els knew', while her parent can punish – or pardon – only outward faults.

Mall's repentance is genuine, but mixed with triumph: 'Pray and mend – yes by the Grace of God will I, pray and mend'. She 'neuer came off thus in all my lyfe when my father was so

---

23 Shell, 'Furor Juvenilis', 196–7, quotation at 197.

angree', although her 'I expected no lesse but to haue beene shut up in a darke roome for a weke or a forthenight to gether and to haue dynd and supt upon birchen Rods' can safely be taken as comic hyperbole rather than an accurate description of disciplinary methods at Little Crosby. At this point, Mall's sisters enter, and she announces her conversion: 'I am not that fond idle Girle your sister, who haue hither to beene guilty of far greater extravagances then your self … I am still your sister mall, but not that rude naughty mall that I was an hower agoe'.

After some catechetical revision, the children's discussion moves from the cardinal virtues to Mall's newly-acquired virtue of 'civility'. Frank asks 'how came it to meete with you: for you 2 haue beene very little acquainted?', and Mall explains: 'It came from Heauen in a clap of thunder. And my father was the Thunderer by Gods comand'. Already her penitence is giving way to disrespectful humour; it dissipates completely before Frank's iconoclasm:

> Frank: why this Bass viol is my Father himself. And looke you Cozen Betty, how he thunders Ciuility to my Sister Mary. Mall be Ciuil – Mall be Ciuill – Mall be Ciuill.
>
> Biddy: And what say you sister mall all this whyle?
>
> Mall: I say – Good sir be pleased to pardon me this one tyme and I will allwise be ciuil.

Mall then dresses the viol up in 'a hat and a Gowne and other deuises'. To Frank's warning 'dare you meddle with the Violl? In good truth if my Father com – ', Mall replies airily: 'Feare you no Fathers. My Father and I do now understand one an other'. Her virtuous response to parental lenience has degenerated into licence to misbehave. The girls then order the viol to play for them, and abuse it for failing to do so:

> Mall: You! do you heare? you logger head. you will play anon!
>
> Frank: In truth Sister Mall I do not lyke these ciuil playes of yours. Is ther any Ciuility in this to call one Logger head?
>
> Mall: I call the Bass Viol.
>
> Frank: If it were neuer so base, it is basely don of you, to call it logger head.

> Mall: Why then most louely and worshipfull Bass Viol will you please to let us haue a bit of Musick.

Mall parodies deference to parents: for 'this bass viol is my father himself'. Teasing the viol thus acquires a dangerous relish, savouring of outrageous disrespect: '[Mall:] If we cannot obtain it from you we will strip off your musicall Robes … And naked to the skin, this cold wether, we will kick you down the stayers'. They threaten to hang the viol in the kitchen-chimney 'like a flitch of bacon'. Finally Mall 'puts it out the dore'.

Frank's 'dare you meddle with the viol?' suggests that in reality they were not allowed to touch the instrument, let alone use it to ridicule their father, so that the script authorizes forbidden activity. Since the scriptwriter was (in all probability) the father who originally forbade it, the action ceases to be transgressive, and this can be said of the whole piece. By subjecting his dramatic persona to his children's criticism and turning himself to ridicule (as Allestree might put it),[24] the father both legitimates and controls such behaviour. One is led to wonder how the child actors experienced this legitimation of transgression: did they enjoy it? Did it lessen the attraction of surreptitious disrespect, by demonstrating their father's control of it? Or would such behaviour seem so far beyond the pale as to be simply absurd, such that its condemnation or legitimation was irrelevant? Alternatively, was this part of the script based on observation? It is possible that Mall and her sisters found themselves reproducing, under paternal direction, misbehaviour that they had not realized he was aware of – and that might be the most disconcerting form of rebuke of all.

But primarily this display of indulgent parenting and childish havoc shows a father relishing the humour in his children's games. Blundell was manifestly not threatened by the possibility of his daughters making fun of him behind his back. He did not end the play with retribution: the children's misbehaviour has no consequences, and the finale is a dance. Apparently in fear of further victimization, the now-expelled bass viol 'playes in great hast (with very quick tyme) the old Wiues distes' (presumably operated by Blundell from out of sight). The girls 'dance a Country Dance …

---

[24] Cf. Allestree, *Ladies Calling*, 63.

And haueing made an end, they do speake the Epilogue' (which sadly does not seem to have survived). Disorder ends in harmony. There is nothing like (for example) the depiction of unruly children in Robert Russel's *A Little Book for Children* (1696), in which playing instead of 'reading their Books' leads to name-calling, physical fighting, telling tales and accusations of lying.[25]

The Blundell pieces teach decorum through contained misrule. But their didacticism need not be taken too seriously. The comedy is no more a mere vehicle for moralizing than the educational elements are a mere pretext for entertainment. The didactic points are made in a way that says much for the sensitivity and intelligence of at least one early modern parent; religious catechesis and social education are mingled with humour, play and the gentle ridicule of both father and children.

These texts illustrate how English gentry combined social and religious frames of reference; and how the precepts of catechists and moralists could be simultaneously endorsed, appropriated and played with in an actual seventeenth-century family. The legal framework of the religious persecution of earlier decades remained in place in the 1660s, and would be reasserted violently during such crises as the 'Popish plot' hysteria (1678–81). But in Restoration England children grew up as Catholics in an atmosphere which, although mindful of earlier conflicts, assimilated their religion into a social identity derived from the shared assumptions of English society. William Blundell's dramatic compositions suggest that young girls' experience of both religion and socialization could involve lively intellectual engagement and equally lively humour. Most powerfully, while interweaving all these concerns, the Blundell 'Exercises' are imbued with the delight parents find in their children.

British School at Rome

---

[25] Robert Russel, *A little book for children and youth*, 2 parts (London, , 1693–6), Part 2, 15–16; G. Avery, 'The Puritans and their Heirs', in idem, G. Briggs and J. Briggs, eds, *Children and their Books* (Oxford, 1989), 95–118, esp. 102–3.

'A DOSE OF PHYSICK': MEDICAL PRACTICE AND CONFESSIONAL IDENTITY WITHIN THE HOUSEHOLD

by SOPHIE MANN

In early modern England the place where most people experienced and treated illness was the home.[1] Medical practices were therefore invariably centred on the family, and in many cases, sufferers diagnosed and nursed their ailments without seeking advice from a practitioner, instead favouring the counsel of a family member or friend.[2] Centred on the personal transactions between patients, kin, neighbours, and in some cases a practitioner, how might the religiously plural context of the Reformation era have shaped these close social relationships? The subjects of this study belonged to two Catholic families: Nicholas Blundell (1669–1737) of Little Crosby in Lancashire, and Catharine Burton (1668–1714) of Bury St Edmunds in Suffolk.[3] Focusing on the sickness experiences, lay healing practices and medical treatment described at length in their diaries, this essay asks three central questions. First, in what ways did confessionally opposed families integrate or separate from one another in relation to matters of health? Second, did these subjects forge more exclusive ties with medical practitioners of their own confession, or, conversely, did they find a way to coexist comfortably with, and interact in, the 'medical marketplace'?[4] Third, by examining the practices through which religion and medicine interrelated within the household, I aim to challenge longstanding assumptions concerning the progressive

[1] Andrew Wear, *Knowledge and Practice in English Medicine 1550–1680* (Cambridge, 2000), 24.

[2] Mary Lindemann, *Medicine and Society in Early Modern Europe*, 2nd edn (Cambridge, 2010), 241–2.

[3] This essay, and the case studies it presents, form part of my doctoral work on 'Religion, Medicine and Confessional Identity in Early Modern England', which offers a broader, multi-confessional exploration of the relationship between religion and medicine in daily life and practice.

[4] On the concept of the 'medical marketplace', see Mark Jenner and Patrick Wallis, eds, *Medicine and the Market in England and its Colonies 1450–1850* (Basingstoke, 2007).

'secularization' or 'medicalization' of the sickbed.[5] I hope to shed fresh light on the ways in which medical practices were embedded in social relations and community experiences; and to begin to unravel some of the complex channels through which confessional identity was experienced and expressed in relation to healing.

First, a brief note about our two subjects. Nicholas Blundell and Catharine Burton belonged to a particular stratum of English society, on the edge of the gentry, but their friends and neighbours were drawn from all ranks. The landowner Blundell inherited the manors of Little Crosby and Ditton in 1702 upon the death of his father. He had a prominent public role as squire and his faith did not prevent him from enjoying cordial relations with neighbouring Protestant gentry, clergy and parishioners. However, during the Jacobite rising of 1715 he fell under government suspicion, his diary confirming that the Blundell household regularly provided shelter for members of the Jesuit mission. In 1716 the family travelled into voluntary exile in Flanders and did not return to Little Crosby until 1717.[6] Catharine Burton, the Carmelite visionary and later prioress of the English Carmel at Hopland, was born at Beyton, near Bury St Edmunds, the daughter of the devout recusant yeoman Thomas Burton. She suffered from a debilitating illness between the ages of nineteen and twenty-five, at which time the Burton household in Suffolk operated as a refuge for Jesuits.[7]

There is no reason to suppose that these two contemporaries and their families responded in analogous ways when faced with sickness, as many factors other than religious identity could shape medical choices. Historians of medicine have recently reminded us

5   Recent work tracking these processes includes Michael Macdonald, 'The Medicalization of Suicide in England: Laymen, Physicians and Cultural Change, 1500–1870', *Milbank Quarterly* 67 (1989), 69–91; Andrew Wear, ed., *Medicine in Society: Historical Essays* (Cambridge, 1992); Charles Webster, 'Paracelsus Confronts the Saints: Miracles, Healing and the Secularization of Magic', *Social History of Medicine* 8 (1995), 403–21; Roy Porter, 'The Hour of Philip Aries', *Mortality* 4 (1999), 83–90; Edwin R. van Teijlingen et al., *Midwifery and the Medicalization of Childbirth* (New York, 2000); Ian Mortimer, *The Dying and the Doctors: The Medical Revolution in Seventeenth-Century England* (Woodbridge, 2009).
6   *ODNB, s.n.* 'Blundell, Nicholas', online at: <http://www.oxforddnb.com/view/article/59568?docPos=2>, accessed June 2012.
7   *ODNB, s.n.* 'Burton, Catharine', online at: <http://www.oxforddnb.com/view/article/4122>, accessed June 2012.

that patients had relative freedom to choose the practitioner they liked, selecting therapies and therapists according to their estimation of a practitioner's effectiveness and manners, not to mention availability and cost.[8] Furthermore, we cannot assume that religious groups were perfectly homogeneous in their attitudes to interconfessional relations; some were perhaps more accepting than others. These variables make it difficult to generalize concerning the role religious convictions played in shaping a patient's choice of therapy or healer. That said, by carefully examining healing practices, not only do the relationships between medical choice and confessional identity become more apparent, but we can also qualify longstanding assumptions concerning the progressive 'medicalization' of household responses to illness.

The importance of rooting this investigation in daily practice cannot be overestimated.[9] We currently have a wealth of information concerning the relationship between theological positions and medical theories,[10] but we still know very little about the precise ways in which religious and medical practices interrelated in everyday settings such as the household, the sickbed and the deathbed. The ways in which families of different confessions interacted in these settings are also not at all evident.[11] Whilst there

---

[8] Jenner and Wallis, *Medicine*, 2.

[9] On the relationship between medical discourse and medical practice see, for the eighteenth and nineteenth centuries, Francisca Loetz, 'Why Change Habits? Early Modern Medical Innovation between Medicalization and Medical Culture', *History and Philosophy of the Life Sciences* 32 (2010), 453–74.

[10] John Henry, 'The Matter of Souls: Medical Theory and Theology in Seventeenth-Century England', in Roger French and Andrew Wear, eds, *The Medical Revolution of the Seventeenth Century* (Cambridge, 1989), 87–113; David Harley, 'Spiritual Physic, Providence and English Medicine 1560–1640', in Ole Peter Grell and Andrew Cunningham, eds, *Medicine and the Reformation* (London, 1993), 101–17; idem, 'The Theology of Affliction and the Experience of Sickness in the Godly Family 1650–1714', in Ole Peter Grell and Andrew Cunningham, eds, *Religio Medici: Religion and Medicine in Seventeenth-Century England* (Aldershot, 1996), 273–92; Andrew Wear, 'Puritan Perceptions of Illness in Seventeenth-Century England', in Roy Porter, ed., *Patients and Practitioners: Lay Perceptions of Illness in Pre-Industrial Society* (Cambridge, 1985), 55–101; idem, 'Religious Beliefs and Medicine in Early Modern England', in Hilary Marland and Margaret Pelling, eds, *The Task of Healing: Medicine, Religion and Gender in England and the Netherlands* (Rotterdam, 1996), 145–71; Ronald Numbers and Darrel Amundsen, eds, *Caring and Curing: Health and Medicine in the Western Religious Traditions* (London, 1998).

[11] On the need to explore this issue further, see Alexandra Walsham, 'In Sickness and in Health: Medicine and Inter-Confessional Relations in Post-Reformation England', in C. Scott Dixon, Dagmar Freist and Mark Greengrass, eds, *Living with*

have been attempts to map out general differences in Catholic and Protestant attitudes towards illness,[12] we have yet to understand how these differences manifested themselves in practice. For example, we know that Catholics were encouraged to invoke the aid of saints during periods of sickness and (if able to do so) to make recourse to sacramentals, such as holy water, relics or crosses. If sickness became terminal, they were also advised to call upon a Catholic priest to administer the last rites, which included absolution and extreme unction,[13] practices which Protestants explicitly rejected.[14] Given these differences, when a member of a household fell sick, would the family be happy to call upon the advice, emotional support and treatment of people with whom they were at odds in matters of faith? Would a visiting neighbour or practitioner feel comfortable witnessing religious practices around the sickbed which they deemed to be irreverent? And in what ways was domestic healing employed as a means by which to mark out a household's confessional distinctiveness? It is to these questions that I will now turn.

In household medicine, preventative measures were as important as therapeutic care, and the best means of maintaining health in the humoral system was to practice moderation in the use of the six 'non-naturals' – air, sleep and waking, food and drink, rest and exercise, excretion and retention, and the passions and the emotions.[15] In addition, a variety of home-made remedies were used, most commonly an assortment of time-tested medicines for everyday ills.[16] Learned from books, or from friends with whom they exchanged medical information, women and men often docu-

---

Religious Diversity in Early Modern Europe (Farnham, 2009), 161–83. Francisca Loetz has also encouraged us to think about how individuals gave confessional shape to their daily lives; see her 'Bridging the Gap: Confessionalization in Switzerland', in André Holenstein, Thomas Maissen and Maarten Prak, eds, *The Republican Alternative: The Netherlands and Switzerland Compared* (Amsterdam, 2008), 75–98.

[12]   Wear, 'Religious Beliefs'.

[13]   Ralph Houlbrooke, *Death, Religion and the Family in England 1450–1750* (Oxford, 1998), 148–9.

[14]   Wear, 'Religious Beliefs'.

[15]   The humoral system of medicine remained the dominant conceptual model well into the eighteenth century. Physiologically, it was based on the four humours – black bile, yellow bile, blood and phlegm – and illness arose from their imbalance. Moderation in the use of the six non-naturals was believed to support a healthy humoral equilibrium: Lindemann, *Medicine*, 240–2.

[16]   Wear, *Knowledge*, 49–103; Leong, 'Making Medicines', 145–68.

mented their recipes in manuscript collections.[17] People discussed and distributed home-made medicines within their communities, forming 'exchange relationships' rooted in degrees of trust placed in the supplier or distributor of the recipe. Such practices commonly took place within close-knit social networks, thereby placing the exchange within 'safe' parameters.[18] How might the religious identity of a supplier or distributor have shaped these exchanges?

Nicholas Blundell was an avid collector and dispenser of home-made medicines. The remedies were made in a small 'Apothecary shop'[19] within his household, and he was often visited by neighbours seeking help with everyday ills, such as bruises, falling sickness, dropsy, ague fits and eye disorders.[20] As well as having his own manuscript collection he consulted the recipe books of his wife Frances and his servant Walter Thelwall.[21] His father William Blundell had also been a keen compiler of home-made remedies and it is more than likely that his recipe collection would have been passed down to Nicholas.[22] On a number of occasions we can see exchanges occurring within his own confessional group. He consulted the recipe collections of his wife, and in all probability also those of his father; both were Catholics. As the master of a household attended largely by Catholic servants, he often relied on co-religionists to assist in the making of medicines. For example, he employed his Catholic servant Ned Howerd to help produce a powder for the falling sickness in the summer of 1715, and his Catholic servant Catty Weedow to gather herbs in the family garden 'for Phisick' in the winter of 1718.[23] Members of the Jesuit mission who presided over services at the Blundell family chapel often sought home-made remedies from Nicholas. In the winter

[17]   Wear, *Knowledge*, 21–4, 49–55, 227.

[18]   Elaine Leong and Sarah Pennell, 'Recipe Collections and the Currency of Medical Knowledge in the Early Modern "Medical Marketplace"', in Jenner and Wallis, eds, *Medicine*, 133–52.

[19]   *The Great Diurnal of Nicholas Blundell of Little Crosby*, 2: *1712–1719*, ed. Frank Tyrer and J. J. Bagley (Manchester, 1970), 146.

[20]   *The Great Diurnal of Nicholas Blundell of Little Crosby*, 1: *1702–1711*, ed. Frank Tyrer and J. J. Bagley (Manchester, 1968), 188, 190, 191; ibid. 2: 3, 277, 53 respectively.

[21]   Ibid. 1: 282, 165 respectively.

[22]   See T. E. Gibson, ed., *A Cavalier's Note Book: Notes, Anecdotes and Observations of William Blundell of Crosby, Lancashire* (London, 1880).

[23]   *Great Diurnal*, ed. Tyrer and Bagley, 2: 137, 233.

of 1712 Father Turvil consulted him upon experiencing discomfort in his bowels and was promptly prescribed a 'glister'.[24] In December 1719 Nicholas treated Father Aldred who had 'strained his Anclew'.[25] Father Aldred and Nicholas also exchanged household recipes with one another, as the diarist noted during the winter of 1707: 'I Filter'd some Phisick for Mr Tasburgh by directions of Mr Aldred.'[26]

In other cases, however, an interconfessional approach was adopted. When producing 'Eyebright', which required the gathering of copious amounts of herbs, Nicholas paid the children of his village to gather the required ingredients, regardless, it seems, of their religious affiliations.[27] Similarly, when distributing his medicines to sick members of the community he provided treatments for Catholics and Protestants alike. For instance, in May 1715, he attended to the ailments of the local Anglican parson who 'called ... to beg some Rue to apply to his Rist in order to cuar his Eye'.[28] In addition, his father's recipe collection contained a number of treatments sourced from Protestant suppliers, such as a 'cure for a flux of blood' acquired from his 'old kind friend Mr. Price, the Protestant Bishop of Kildare, who had good experience of it'.[29] The production of home-made remedies was a practice dependent on levels of trust between the donor and compiler of a recipe, or the producer and recipient of a treatment, and the exchanges detailed here demonstrate a marked cooperation between families of divergent faiths. To what extent can similar interactions be detected once family members sought assistance from a medical practitioner?

In her early twenties Catharine Burton was struck down with a violent sickness which lasted for seven years.[30] She experienced a range of symptoms including frequent convulsions, swellings, stomach pains, loss of appetite, pains in her breast and a palsy in her left arm.[31]

---

[24] Ibid. 45. A 'glister' or 'clyster' was an enema or suppository.
[25] Ibid. 277.
[26] Ibid. 1: 152.
[27] Ibid. 2: 34.
[28] Ibid. 135.
[29] Gibson, ed., *Cavalier's Notebook*, 193.
[30] Thomas Hunter, *An English Carmelite: The Life of Catharine Burton, Mother Mary Xaveria of the Angels ... Collected from her own Writings* (London, 1876), 5.
[31] Ibid. 5–61.

Her family sought help from a range of medical practitioners and a number of treatments were employed, including 'strong vomits' administered 'by a French doctress'; remedies from a local physician for 'cooling the fever', and a 'desperate remedy' which the physician hoped would 'abate the violence of the convulsions' and 'hinder [her] death from being so violent'.[32] During this sickness, and following the advice of Father Collins, a member of the Jesuit mission residing in the Burton household, Catharine developed a particular devotion to St Francis Xavier.[33] After beginning a devotion of ten Fridays she 'unexpectedly found the help of the blessed Saint, perceiving some life or agility'.[34] Upon a second devotion she noted: 'So great a joy seized my soul that it diffused itself all over my body, as if new life and blood were infused into me.'[35]

Catharine's health continued to improve until 'in short time' she 'was stronger than ever'.[36] Following this remarkable recovery, a strategy of confession was enacted, whereby the newly healed patient was encouraged to publicize her experience, as she recalled: 'The noise of my sudden recovery being spread abroad, few would believe it but those that saw and conversed with me. Hence I was advised by my confessor to return the many visits which had been made me in my sickness.'[37] Here she records a visit to one of her Protestant neighbours:

> I found myself moved to go visit one of our neighbours, who had always been kind to us and ready to help ... she was so amazed to see me that she could not recover herself ... but said if I was the same person ... it was the greatest miracle the Lord ever wrought ... . I understood ... that this woman was converted.[38]

She continued:

> This was not the only person thus surprised ... . They used to follow me and invite me to their houses. I went to see a

---

[32] Ibid. 43, 63.
[33] Ibid. 64–5.
[34] Ibid. 68.
[35] Ibid. 80.
[36] Ibid. 82.
[37] Ibid. 83.
[38] Ibid.

lady of quality about a mile off. She was so frighted that she was obliged to call for cordials to recover herself ... . She met me afterwards at the parson's house, and ... inquired of him whether he thought miracles were ceased.[39]

Here we see how the domestic healing process could be used to mark out a household's confessional distinctiveness. Moreover, it could operate as an effective proselytizing tool: news of Catharine's recovery apparently encouraged her Protestant neighbours to re-engage with Catholic beliefs.

During a later bout of sickness, a decidedly interconfessional encounter with a local practitioner took place. On returning from a pilgrimage to a well of Our Lady, Catharine fell into a ditch and put her hipbone out of joint. She noted:

My father ... sent for a woman very expert in surgery. As soon as she examined it she said it would be a hard cure, and made me keep my bed for ten days, applying all sorts of remedies but without any effect ... . Despairing, she bid me apply myself to my doctor that had cured me before, meaning St. Xavier. This she seemed to say with great confidence, though she was a rigid Protestant. I followed her advice, and was often much confounded to think that she should be the first that proposed this to me.[40]

In this instance, Catharine's family was happy to employ a practitioner irrespective of religious identity, in the hope that expertise and a cure might be acquired. Moreover, the practitioner's own confession did not preclude their advocating religious practices with which they were, officially, at odds: here we see a Protestant surgeon advising her patient to invoke the aid of a saint.

Turning to Nicholas Blundell, we see that he too invited medical practitioners from across the confessional spectrum into his home. For example, he regularly called upon a local Baptist physician, Dr Fabius. In January 1704 he recalled: 'My Wife sent to Doctor Fabius, he said she was with Child.'[41] The next month: 'My Wife took her first dose of Purging Salts from Dr Fabius.'[42] In the summer of 1704 Nicholas 'went to Low Hill to ... Dr Fabius

39 Ibid. 84–5.
40 Ibid. 86–7.
41 *Great Diurnal*, ed. Tyrer and Bagley, 1: 51.
42 Ibid. 52.

for casting Water'.[43] In August that year a Jesuit missionary staying in the Blundell household was also treated by the Baptist practitioner.[44] That said, the household's favoured local physician was one Dr Lancaster, a Catholic.[45] Illustrative of their close relationship, Dr Lancaster was frequently invited to attend services at the family chapel, and he often provided the household with medical treatment free of charge.[46] Additionally, Nicholas came to rely upon his services at a time of political crisis, the Jacobite Rising of 1715. During this period the family fell under government suspicion and their house was searched three times.[47] They made plans to go into voluntary exile and just before departing Nicholas's daughter fell sick. To assist, 'Dr Lancaster sent an Express with some Physick.'[48] In this case, confessional identity played a complex and multivalent role in shaping clinical interaction. In some instances a practitioner's religious affiliations did not influence their eligibility for employment. But in others the practitioner and patient were co-religionists, enabling employer and employee to support one another in times of crisis, and to participate together in medical and religious practices within the household. The precise manner in which these practices blended in the domestic setting is the final theme I wish to examine.

Despite recent efforts to highlight the close affinities between religious and medical cultures, a number of general assumptions remain intact. These reflect the view that, at the level of domestic healing, distinctions rather than affinities characterized their interrelationship. When discussing the role of seventeenth-century practitioners, Andrew Wear has claimed that 'at the bedside there was usually no mention of a religious ceremony associated with medical treatment'.[49] John Henry has argued that 'at a time when many believed that sickness was visited upon mankind by God, the physician was seen everywhere ignoring such religious consid-

[43] Ibid. 59.
[44] Ibid. 64.
[45] Treatment by Dr Lancaster is noted frequently: ibid. 1: 64, 96–8, 124; 2: 1–15, 60–2, 64, 69, 75, 82, 114, 124, 127, 135, 148–50, 242.
[46] Ibid. 2: 12; 1: 28, 124.
[47] Ibid. 2: 148–9.
[48] Ibid. 150.
[49] Wear, 'Religious Beliefs', 154.

erations and treating sickness in an entirely naturalistic way'.[50] Roy Porter has suggested that death became 'medicalized' in the early modern period through changes in bedside management, with doctor-assisted care gradually replacing that of the spiritual instructor.[51] Similarly, Ian Mortimer's recent work on death in seventeenth-century England has sought to track the process by which the dying spent increasing sums of money on medical practitioners. He infers that the sickbed became 'medicalized', a process he defines as a turn away from divine responses to illness and toward 'professional' medical interventions.[52] Evident in all these assessments is the framing of religion and medicine as distinct, self-evident, categories of practice. In direct contrast, I want to move away from thinking in terms of rigid distinctions – the practitioner's domain the body and the clergyman's domain the soul – because in practice such distinctions could melt away.

An extract from Nicholas Blundell's diary from January 1710, when the author was suffering from an eye disorder, offers a case in point. For two weeks Nicholas was confined to his bed during the daytime, as his eyes were sensitive to light. He called upon the assistance of a Dr Smithson for medical treatment and was prescribed 'Blistering plaisters' and 'Eye Water'. The doctor made a personal visit to the household, let the patient's blood and stayed overnight.[53] Alongside the assistance of Dr Smithson, Father Aldred, the family chaplain, both attended the patient and collaborated with the physician. As Nicholas noted: 'Mr Aldred put oyl'd paper over the Window he kept me company all the after noone … [he] shaved my head and put on three plaisters which he brought from Dr Smithson.'[54] This was not the only occasion when religious attendants engaged in the physical care of a sick body. In the spring of 1712, when Nicholas's daughter fell sick, she was attended to by the Jesuit Father Tasburgh.[55] Similarly, when his wife fell ill in June the following year with 'a sevear Night of Gravell', Nicholas sent for the assistance of the family chaplain.[56]

---

[50] Henry, 'Souls', 89.
[51] Porter, 'The Hour', 83–90.
[52] Mortimer, *The Dying*.
[53] *Great Diurnal*, ed. Tyrer and Bagley, 1: 241.
[54] Ibid. 241–2.
[55] Ibid. 12.
[56] Ibid. 65.

Catharine Burton's recourse to treatment demonstrates similar forms of correspondence between physical and spiritual strategies of care. As previously mentioned, while she was being treated for a dislocated hip, her surgeon advised her to invoke the help of a saint. Following this advice Catharine's condition worsened so much that her father resolved the next morning to send 'for a man surgeon'. When the practitioner arrived at the house, the patient noted:

> I called him to my bedside, acquainted him that I was beginning a devotion to St. Xavier, and begged that no other remedy might be applied, promising that if I were not cured at the end of ten days, I would undergo whatever should be thought fit. Moved with tenderness he condescended to my petition, and with leave of my confessor I began my devotion.[57]

During her previous illness similar cooperation between clerical and medical attendants had taken place. For example, when Catharine's father opted to send for a physician 'who dealt in chemistry', he asked the family chaplain Father Stafford to send a letter to the practitioner detailing the history of his daughter's sickness.[58] Likewise, when, several years into her sickness, it was feared Catharine was approaching death, she recalled: 'The doctor then thought I could not hold out long … hence he ordered me the Last Sacraments out of hand.'[59] These examples suggest that religious responses were not supplanted by medical interventions in practice. Neither, it appears, did any kind of competition or antagonism between medical and religious attendants occur. Rather, these providers of care collaborated within the bedchamber, negotiating treatment strategies and enabling the sufferer to relieve both their physical and spiritual needs.

Two provisional conclusions can be drawn on the basis of this research. First, confessional convictions shaped medical interactions within the household in highly complex and varied ways. Concerning the production and distribution of home-made remedies, we see both intra- and interconfessional exchanges occurring. Regarding recourse to professional assistance, at times practitioner

---

[57] Ibid. 87–8.
[58] Ibid. 37–8.
[59] Ibid. 49.

and patient shared the same religious identity. For religious dissidents this could also provide an important degree of support in periods of political crisis. The medical assistance offered to the Blundell family by their Catholic physician during the Jacobite Rising is a case in point. In other instances, the confessional identity of a practitioner does not appear to have influenced their eligibility for employment. Neither, for that matter, did it necessarily exclude them from recommending religious healing practices which they formally rejected; as in the case of Catharine Burton's Protestant surgeon, who advised her patient to call upon the aid of St Xavier. This suggests that healers may have felt bound by the Christian duty of charity to treat those who espoused rival beliefs. As the clergyman Joseph Glanvill stated in 1669, 'Love obligeth us … to visit the sick', and this duty was 'not to be … confined to the corners of a sect, but ought to reach as far as Christianity itself … [for] the more general it is, the more Christian.'[60] Such encounters were also rooted in the close social relationships that continued to exist between individuals of opposing faiths.

Second, in many of the examples presented we see how religious beliefs and practices constituted an integral part of medical work. Case studies such as these enable us to recover a level of detail that not only deepens our understanding of domestic healing, but also allows us to challenge the assumption that religion and medicine functioned as oppositional domains of conduct and experience. Indeed, it seems that such a polarity would have been inexplicable to contemporary minds as they conceptualized the workings of the body within a fundamentally religious framework. Since God had created man after his own image, attending to the Creator's handiwork constituted a religious as well as a medical act. So the physician Edmund Gayton asserted in 1663 that the human body was 'fitted for Divine contemplation … A physician therefore and divine you see are not inconsistent.'[61] We therefore need to continue rethinking long-established narratives concerning the 'secularization' or 'medicalization' of sickness. Medical practices within the household offer a prime location to do just that.

King's College, London

---

[60] Joseph Glanvill, *Catholick Charity Recommended in a Sermon* (London, 1669), 5–6.
[61] Edmund Gayton, *The Religion of a Physician* (London, 1663), B1–B3.

'MY HOUSE SHALL BE CALLED THE HOUSE OF PRAYER': RELIGION AND THE MATERIAL CULTURE OF THE EPISCOPAL HOUSEHOLD, c.1500 TO c.1800

by MICHAEL ASHBY

Over the past three decades, the study of material culture has become a pervasive feature of historical scholarship. From art to shoes, from porcelain to glass, 'things' are increasingly viewed as a useful medium through which to reconstruct what mattered to historical actors in everyday life.[1] Taking its lead from this vast scholarship, this discussion examines how material culture was integrated into a programme of devotion, edification and religious instruction within England's episcopal palaces, a group of buildings in which the relationship between the material and the spiritual was particularly fraught. Adopting a long chronological span, from 1500 to 1800, it analyses how that relationship evolved into the eighteenth century, a period noted for its proliferation of things and apparently 'secular' character.

Before we proceed, however, it is necessary to examine the two key historiographical stimuli for this discussion in more detail. To begin with, this essay arises from a divergence between the historiography of eighteenth-century religion and broader social and cultural histories of the period.[2] Encouraged by stereotypes of a somnolent Church, many narratives continue to emphasize secularization as one of the eighteenth century's dominant characteristics, whilst others simply ignore religion and the work of ecclesiastical historians entirely.[3] Yet the case for the secularization

---

[1] For a review of the field, see Mary C. Beaudry and Dan Hicks, ed., *The Oxford Handbook of Material Culture Studies* (Oxford, 2010); Ludmilla Jordanova, *The Look of the Past: Visual and Material Evidence in Historical Practice* (Cambridge, 2012).

[2] See Brian Young, 'Religious History and the Eighteenth-Century Historian', *HistJ* 43 (2000), 849–68; Jeremy Gregory, '"For all sorts and conditions of men": The Social Life of the Book of Common Prayer during the Long Eighteenth Century: Or, Bringing the History of Religion and Social History Together', *Social History* 34 (2009), 29–54; idem, 'Introduction: Transforming "the Age of Reason" into "an Age of Faiths": Or, Putting Religions and Beliefs (Back) into the Eighteenth Century', *Journal for Eighteenth-Century Studies* 32 (2009), 287–305.

[3] See Carol Stewart, *The Eighteenth-Century Novel and the Secularization of Ethics*

of eighteenth-century society and culture appears unconvincing, since a body of evidence points to the continued efficacy of both religious institutions and religious structures of understanding in everyday life.[4] Not only were notions of providence, stewardship and charity important long into the eighteenth century,[5] but the English Enlightenment – religion's supposed enemy – was played out within an Anglican context.[6] In short, as Jeremy Gregory has recently argued, the question of secularization is one for historians of the nineteenth, not the eighteenth, century.[7] In fact, Callum Brown has placed the death of 'Christian Britain' far later, in the 1960s.[8]

A second stimulus for this discussion derives from the interrelated historiographies of eighteenth-century consumerism, material culture and the home. Over the past three decades, these historiographies have blossomed and historians now know more about the production, exchange and consumption of goods than ever before.[9] Yet the complex relationship between religious belief and the period's material culture remains unexamined, while scholarship of elite taste, elegance and fashion remains largely secular in tone and content. On the one hand, this state of affairs is unsurprising, given the self-evident hostility between materiality (or the worldly) and religion (the other-worldly). On the other hand, a small body of recent research encourages further study. For

---

(Farnham, 2010). Religion might have received further consideration in Woodruff Smith, *Consumption and the Making of Respectability* (New York and London, 2002).

   4   Jeremy Gregory, 'Christianity and Culture : Religion, the Arts and the Sciences in England, 1660–1800', in Jeremy Black, ed., *Culture and Society in Britain, 1660–1800* (Manchester, 1997), 102–23.

   5   Jonathan Clark, 'Providence, Predestination and Progress: Or, did the Enlightenment Fail?', *Albion* 35 (2003), 559–89; the continued importance of Providence in economic life is explained in Margaret Jacob and Matthew Kadane, 'Now Found in the Eighteenth Century: Weber's Protestant Capitalist', *AHR* 108 (2003), 20–49.

   6   Roy Porter, 'The Enlightenment in England', in idem and Mikuláš Teich, eds, *The Enlightenment in National Context* (Cambridge, 1981), 1–18.

   7   Gregory, 'Christianity and Culture', 123.

   8   See Callum Brown, *The Death of Christian Britain: Understanding Secularization, 1800-2000* (London, 2001).

   9   Neil McKendrick, John Brewer and John Plumb, *The Birth of a Consumer Society: The Commercialization of Eighteenth-Century England* (London, 1982); John Brewer and Roy Porter, eds, *Consumption and the World of Goods* (London, 1993); Maxine Berg, *Luxury and Pleasure in Eighteenth-Century Britain* (Oxford, 2005); Amanda Vickery, *Behind Closed Doors: At Home in Georgian England* (New Haven, CT, and London, 2009).

instance, the success of Lauren Winner's examination of the material culture of domestic religious practice in eighteenth-century
Virginia suggests that study of the material and the spiritual might
also bear fruit in an English context.[10]

In light of the above, this essay focuses on the material
evidence from episcopal households between 1500 and 1800, with
a particular focus on the bishop's palace at Ely. It takes its lead
from Tara Hamling's *Decorating the 'Godly' Household* (2010), which
examines the relationship between decorative arts and reformed
practices of self-discipline and religious worship in elite households. As Hamling explains, the 'permanent presence' of decorative arts showing biblical texts and images 'served to extend the
instruction and guidance provided by the master of the household,
acting as a continual reminder of spiritual matters throughout the
day'.[11] In other words, Hamling shows how a scripturally based
scheme of decoration was a prominent part of Protestant domestic
culture, and to some extent therefore carried forward traditions
established in Catholicism. To be sure, this approach is not perfect,
since it depends primarily on the production, rather than reception, of the household fabric, and in doing so tends to obscure the
many intellectual and emotional responses that fabric might evoke.
Nonetheless, Hamling's methodology remains invaluable and helps
us to chart subtle shifts in religious practice over time, even within
the supposedly 'secular' eighteenth century.

The episcopal palace at Ely, originally built by John Alcock,
bishop of Ely from 1486 to 1500, provides a useful entry point into
the themes of this discussion (Fig. 1). With the exception of the
east tower, very little of Alcock's palace remains intact, since the
fabric was largely destroyed during the Civil War and Interregnum
and was later remodelled by Benjamin Laney (bishop 1667–75) and
Edmund Keene (bishop 1771–81).[12] However, two sources provide

---

[10] Lauren F. Winner, *A Cheerful & Comfortable Faith: Anglican Religious Practice in the Elite Households of Eighteenth-Century Virginia* (New Haven, CT, and London, 2010).

[11] Tara Hamling, *Decorating the 'Godly' Household: Religious Art in Post-Reformation Britain* (New Haven, CT, and London, 2010), 118. See also, in this volume, her 'Living with the Bible in Post-Reformation England: The Materiality of Text, Image and Object in Domestic Life', 210–39.

[12] I am grateful to Mark Hart at the King's School, Ely, for introducing me to the building and to Francis Young for sharing a draft of his book, *A History of the Bishop's Palace at Ely: Prelates and Prisoners* (Ely, 2012). Aside from this, the existing literature on the Ely palace is slim, though basic outlines are provided in the following: Nikolaus

Fig. 1:   G. Hollis, 'The Palace, Ely', engraving in William Stevenson, *Supplement to the Second Edition of Mr Bentham's History* (London, 1817). Reproduced by permission of the Syndics of Cambridge University Library.

useful detail on the building's early history. Firstly, an early nineteenth-century publication by the antiquarian William Stevenson tells us a great deal about the building's late medieval past, as it incorporated observations made by the late historian John Stow (1524/5–1605).[13] Secondly, Ralph Churton's *Life of Alexander Nowell, Dean of St Paul's* (1809) included observations on two inscribed stone tablets that were added by the building's first Protestant occupant, Thomas Goodrich (bishop 1534–54). Although

Pevsner, *Buildings of England: Cambridgeshire* (Harmondsworth, 2002), 378–9; Christopher Hussey, 'Ely Palace, Cambridgeshire', *Country Life* 63 (1928), 850–7; Cambridge, UL, Cam.b.987.42, George Seaman-Turner, 'The Old Bishop's Palace, Ely' (typescript, *c.*1987). The bishop's former London residences, Ely House, Holborn (sold 1772), and Ely House, Dover Street, have received far more attention. In particular, the Holborn residence has been a subject of antiquarian interest since the eighteenth century: see Thomas Boyles Murray, *A Notice of Ely Chapel, Holborn, with some account of Ely Palace* (London, 1840). For the Dover Street house, see Christopher Hussey, *The Story of Ely House, 37 Dover Street, London* (London, 1952).

[13]   William Stevenson, *A Supplement to the Second Edition of Mr. Bentham's History and Antiquities of the Cathedral and Conventual Church of Ely* (Norwich, 1817), 84–5.

these tablets are still extant, the inscriptions are no longer legible, as they were to Churton.[14]

Using Stow's notes, it is worth dwelling on aspects of the palace's interior, as commissioned by the Catholic Bishop Alcock. A visitor to Alcock's palace would notice a series of inscriptions within the windows that served – just as Hamling's Protestant examples would later do – 'to maintain order and discipline' and to provide the household 'with a constant means to salvation'.[15] Thus an unidentified bay window contained no less than twenty-four messages, all of which aided literate inhabitants in exercising self-discipline and temperance. Seven of these were based upon the gifts of the Holy Spirit: fear of the Lord, godliness or piety, knowledge, counsel, fortitude, understanding and wisdom. 'The gyfte of counsell drivite awaye the spirite of covetousnes', thus read one message; 'The gyfte of understandinge removeth the spirite of gluttonye', read a second. Further messages were aimed specifically at the bishop, reciting the seven virtues: chastity, temperance, charity, diligence, patience, kindness and humility. The same window instructed its inhabitants that 'Charite is the vertue of the Church', that 'Patience is the vertue of the Prechars', and that 'Justice is the vertue of Princes and Prelates'. But the warnings and moral instruction did not end there. '[I]n the window of the haull doore' there were a further thirteen messages, stressing the virtues of fortitude, prudence, justice and temperance. 'Temperance', in particular, was emphasized as a means to 'overrule our lustes and pleasures', 'to moderate our passions' and to 'refuse superfluus [sic] things'.[16]

Stow's antiquarian notes serve as a useful source to reconstruct the late medieval religious practice of everyday life. They show, in particular, how bodily and mental self-restraint were intimately linked to the fabric of the household before the Reformation, as it continued to be for Protestant elites after it. However, the notes fail to provide insight into the relationships between specific individuals, particular rooms in the house and inscribed guides to piety. For more information in this regard, we need to turn to a description of Alcock's second palace at Downham, again written by Stow and printed by William Stevenson. The bishop's bedchamber, for

14 Ralph Churton, *The Life of Alexander Nowell, Dean of St. Paul's* (Oxford, 1809), Appendix VI, 'Inscription on the episcopal palace at Ely', 401–2.
15 Hamling, *Decorating the 'Godly' Household*, 118.
16 Stevenson, *Supplement*, 84.

instance, must have been a persistent source of self-reflection, not to mention sleepless nights. Here, the bishop was not only told that a 'good Shepherd gyveth his lyfe for his flocke' (John 10: 11) but was also warned that 'Prelates ought to be more desirous of profting in God's Church, then of authoritie.' Another humbly – and perhaps more challengingly – advised that 'A Bysshope that doth not correct sinnes, is rather to be called an unchaste dogg.'[17] Such messages ought not to be interpreted only as efforts to exercise self-discipline. The bishop's bedchamber was a public as much as it was a private space, and so the messages were very much part of episcopal self-fashioning before a wider audience.

Away from the bishop's chamber, Stow's antiquarian notes also reveal relationships between the individuals of the household. The bishop was the household patriarch and was able to use the building's fabric both for the purposes of self-discipline and for the regulation of others. It was presumably for this reason that a number of messages were located between the bishop's chamber and a 'fayre dininge' chamber, a space used by the servants when serving meals. These (with their biblical references) were:

> Thou good Servaunte, enter thou into thy master's joye
> (Matt. 25: 21)
> Cast out the unprofitable Servant into utter darknes.
> (Matt. 25: 30)
> The butler was receyved agayne into favour.   (Gen. 40: 21)
> And the unfaythfull bakre was hanged.   (Gen. 40: 22)

Throughout the house similar messages were tailored to their specific locations. Texts in another bedchamber were less stern, including the verse, 'Rest in God, and thou shalt be quyet'. The entrance into the 'wyne cellar' explained that 'when a man swallowith up wyne, wyne swallowith up hym'. Finally, the entrance to the chapel depicted the phrase with which this article is entitled: 'My house shall be called the house of prayer' (Matt. 21: 13). Together, these memoranda drew up a complete programme of self-discipline, temperance and godly living.[18]

So far the examples have been taken from the late medieval, and therefore Catholic, interiors of the palace at Ely and the palace

17 Ibid. 85.
18 Ibid. 84–5.

at Downham. It is important to notice, however, that the former continued to be a source of religious contemplation following the Reformation, when bishops not only destroyed the material culture of their predecessors but also created a reformed material culture of their own. Evidence for this continued tradition survives on the exterior of a bow window in the Long Gallery at Ely, built by Thomas Goodrich, the diocese's first Protestant bishop, before his death in 1552. In this case, two stone tablets contain lengthy inscriptions in capital letters with a full point between each word. Today the exact wording is unclear due to weathering, so we are forced to rely on Churton's antiquarian notes.[19] On the east side of the window, the first tablet read:

> OVR DUTIE TOWARDES GOD IS TO BELEVE IN GOD TO FEAR GOD
> AND TO LOVE GOD WITH ALL OVR HERT WITH ALL OVR SOVL
> WITH ALL OVR MYND & WITH ALL OVR POVER TO WORSHIPPE
> GOD TO GYVE HYM THANKES TO PUT OVR WHOL TRUST IN GOD
> TO CALL VPON HYM HONOVR HIS HOLY NAM AND HIS WORDE &
> TO SERVE GOD TRVLY ALL THE DAYES OF OVR LYFE

This tablet reproduced text from the catechism of the 1549 Book of Common Prayer, to which Goodrich had contributed the material dealing with duties towards God and towards neighbour. The second tablet completed the set:

> THE DVTIE TOWARDES OVR NEIGHBOVR IS TO LOVE HYM AS MYSELF
> AND TO DO TO ALL MEN AS I WOLDE THEY SHVHDE DO TO ME
> TO HONOVRE & OBEY THE KYNGE AND HIS MINISTERS TO SVBMIT
> OVR SELFE TO ALL OVR GOVERNORES SPIRITVALL & TEMPORALL TO
> ORDER OVR SELFE LOWELY TO ALL SVPERIORS TO HVRT NO BODY
> BY WORDE NOR DED TO BE JVSTE IN ALL OVR DEALYING TO BEAR
> NO MALYCE IN OVR HERT TO KEP OVR HANDES FROM STELYNG
> & OVR TONG FROM EVYLL SPEAKYNGE TO KEPE OVR BODEYS IN
> TEMPERANCE NOR TO COVET OTHER MENS GOODES BVT LABOVRE
> TRVELY FOR OUR LYVYNGE IN STATE OF LYFE WHICHE PLEAS GOD
> TO CAL VS ON TO

Once again Goodrich's tablets signal that the fabric of the household was used to reinforce patterns of discipline and religious observance. Yet other episodes from the palace's past reveal that the building was also manipulated to reinforce competing

---

[19] Churton, *Life of Nowell*, 401–2.

confessional identities. The clearest sign of this appears on Alcock's surviving tower, where an empty tripartite niche (Fig. 2) testifies to the confessional disputes of the mid-sixteenth century. It is presumed that Bishop Goodrich – a vehement iconoclast – was responsible for removing the statues that once adorned the building.[20] However, during the 1590s Goodrich's gallery was in turn manipulated to reaffirm Roman Catholic identities. Between 1581 and 1600 the diocese was without a bishop, and the palace was used as a prison for recusants arrested by the queen's government. One prisoner, Sir Thomas Tresham, left a detailed account of his third imprisonment, including descriptions of the wall paintings that he and his fellow prisoners completed in the gallery. Tresham's paintings either avoided controversial subject matter or coded it in numerics, geometry or Latin and Greek aphorisms. But other prisoners were clearly less careful. Tresham explained that some had 'the crucifix paynted in ther chambers', which the prison guards had later 'wasshed owte and purposedly defaced'.[21]

Through the scraps assembled by later antiquarians, and through the extant material culture, there is a strong body of evidence to suggest that a close relationship existed between religious practice and the household fabric during the sixteenth century. As we have seen, the building served as the physical backdrop for personal restraint and household discipline for the Catholic Alcock and his Protestant successors. In the case of Tresham, it provided the physical fabric for the expression of politically charged confessional identities. Exactly how the relationship between spirituality and the household fabric continued into the seventeenth century is more difficult to grasp. Antiquarians make little reference to the period other than to explain the damage inflicted on the fabric during the Civil War, while the palace itself provides little insight into that period of its past due to later alterations. Here the chronology is frustratingly vague, but evidence from Ely and elsewhere suggests that it is plausible to follow Hamling's suggestion that the decorative arts continued to express scriptural text and imagery

---

[20] Edward Conybeare, *Highways and Byways in Cambridge and Ely* (London, 1910), 376; *ODNB, s.n.* 'Goodrich, Thomas (1494–1554)', online edn (October 2005), <http://www.oxforddnb.com/view/article/10980>, accessed 16 July 2012.

[21] S. C. Lomas, ed., *Historical Manuscripts Commission: Report on Manuscripts in Various Collections*, vol. 3 (London, 1904), 91–2.

Fig. 2: Tripartite niche on the eastern tower of the Old Bishop's Palace, Ely. Photograph by the author.

until 1660. For instance, the front gable to Bishop Lloyd's early seventeenth-century palace in Chester is decorated with a series of woodwork panels, representing Adam and Eve in the Garden of Eden, the murder of Abel, the sacrifice of Isaac, the Annunciation and Simeon's prophecy to the Blessed Virgin.[22] At Durham Castle seventeenth-century Flemish tapestries depicting biblical episodes survive in what are now the Bishop's Suite and the Senate Rooms. And, finally, the will of John Buckeridge (1562–1631; bishop of Ely from 1628), suggests that similar decoration might have reached the palace at Ely. Buckeridge's private home contained linen damasks depicting 'the story of Judith and Holofernes' and 'the story of daniell'.[23]

The evidence so far presented shows that the sixteenth- and seventeenth-century episcopal palaces were spiritualized households in terms of the decorative arts. The remainder of this

[22] For a brief description, see Rupert H. Morris, 'Bishop Lloyd's Palace', *Journal of the Architectural, Archaeological and Historic Society for the County and City of Chester and North Wales* 6 (1899), 245–8.

[23] Kew, TNA, Prob 11/160/4.

discussion examines the extent to which the same can be said of the eighteenth century, concluding with two overarching points. Firstly, it suggests that the eighteenth century witnessed a change in elite tastes and patterns of interior decoration, which set aside the particular forms and styles of decoration examined above. Secondly, however, it suggests that this shift in styles and forms should not be interpreted as a process of secularization. Instead, it emphasizes continuity across the period, on the basis that religious art fulfilled similar functions to the decorative patterns already discussed. Indeed, even where religiously based art or decoration was absent, Christian tenets such as moderation, stewardship and providence continued to inform the material culture of the household in subtle, unseen, ways.

To begin with, the shift in elite tastes away from the patterns of biblical imagery and inscription discussed above is best revealed by eighteenth-century interaction with older material. Joseph Butler, for instance, took down tapestries at Auckland Castle during his brief spell as bishop of Durham (1750–2), while Thomas Herring did the same at Lambeth Palace as archbishop of Canterbury (1747–57; he was previously archbishop of York from 1743).[24] There may have been practical reasons for these removals, as tapestry is notoriously difficult to maintain. Attitudes, however, had also changed. When Thomas Herring's nephew, another Thomas, observed an old tapestry hanging at Bishopthorpe in 1743, he reacted as if it was something from the distant past: 'the apartment where I now sit is ornamented with the adventures of Samson curiously wrought in old tapestry, the work, perhaps, of some religious dame'.[25]

The palace at Ely also demonstrates a shift in priorities within elite interior decoration. As we have seen, the building had a long and rich history in which material culture was used to provide religious instruction and to express charged confessional identities. By contrast, Bishop Edmund Keene's extensive renovations during the 1770s converted it into a modern and elegant family home. Ornamented with classical urns and wreaths (Fig. 3), and adorned

[24] Thomas Bartlett, *Memoir of the Life, Character and Writings of Joseph Butler* (London, 1839), 194; Tim Tatton-Brown, *Lambeth Palace: A History of the Archbishops of Canterbury and their Houses* (London, 2000), 82.

[25] John Nichols, ed., *Literary Anecdotes of the Eighteenth Century*, 9 vols (London, 1812–16), 2: 535–6.

Fig. 3: Detail from an upstairs fireplace of the palace, Ely, *c.*1771–80. Photograph by the author.

with a grand marble-floored reception and staircase, the palace fabric now fell in line with ordered, classical, architectural tastes. It should be stressed that eighteenth-century Anglicanism did not perceive these classical influences as irreligious. Classical motifs can be conceptualized as expressions of belief in a rational God, while contemporary treatises rarely failed to express the divine origins of classical architecture.[26] Nonetheless, the classical language of Georgian architecture did not provide opportunities for the expression of scriptural themes or passages in the same way that the earlier building had allowed.

Although eighteenth-century tastes cast aside biblical tapestry and scriptural inscriptions in stone, other modes of interior decoration carried forward the close relationship between material culture and religious practice. In oils or on glass, the presence of religious art plays an important role in this story, since art provided a basis for religious devotion, guidance and instruction in similar ways to the decorative patterns described earlier, albeit through a different medium.[27] To be sure, the extent to which episcopal households commissioned or purchased religious art is difficult to measure. Few interiors survive in their eighteenth-century state, while most episcopal wills list 'Pictures' but fail to mention their content. Nonetheless, where available, the surviving evidence indicates that art was a conspicuous feature of eighteenth-century episcopal households. During the 1750s, for instance, Bishop Isaac Maddox commissioned John Rowell (d. 1756) to reproduce

---

[26] Keith Thomas, 'English Protestantism and Classical Art', in Lucy Gent, ed., *Albion's Classicism: The Visual Arts in Britain, 1550-1660* (New Haven, CT, and London, 1995), 221–38; Terry Friedman, *The Eighteenth-Century Church in Britain* (New Haven, CT, and London, 2011), 393.

[27] For a broad perspective on the role of religious art in Europe, see Nigel Aston, *Art and Religion in Enlightenment Europe* (London, 2009).

the Agony in the Garden in stained glass for Hartlebury Castle chapel.[28] Similarly, Martin Benson commissioned William Price the younger (1703–65) to produce stained glass for the palace chapel at Gloucester a decade earlier, with Christ's resurrection and ascension as his chosen scene.[29] In fact, influenced by his time on the Grand Tour as a young man, Benson was one among several bishops to display religious art in his public rooms and even displayed art imported from Catholic Italy.[30] His will listed a 'Holy Family', a 'Madonna with Child' and a scene of the 'Assumption' in the palace dining room, all of which he bequeathed to Catherine Talbot, daughter of Bishop William Talbot and resident of Bishop Thomas Secker's palace at Cuddesdon, Oxfordshire.[31]

Ownership or commission of these scenes cannot be interpreted in any simple or straightforward way, of course. For one thing, the meaning of these works varied according to the room in which they were placed. Religious scenes were more likely to induce devotion when viewed in the chapel, whereas paintings outside the chapel no doubt achieved a social as well as a religious function – to display the bishop's taste or connoisseurship.[32] Moreover, the meaning of these scenes depended greatly on how they were used within the household. As Claire Haynes has shown, eighteenth-century Anglicans had an uneasy relationship with religious art (especially art with Catholic origins). At one level, images provided 'traps for the unwary', which might lead the spectator into sensuous

---

[28] Sidney Gold, *A Short Account of the Life and Work of John Rowell* ([London], 1965), 47–51. Although executed by Rowell, the glass was designed by Dr. John Wall (d. 1776), founder of the Worcestershire porcelain factory. Wall thought his design 'strangely altered in execution': see James Lee-Milne, 'Hartlebury Castle Revisited', *Country Life* 150 (1971), 672–5, 740–3. Bishop James Perowne removed the glass in 1898.

[29] London, BL, Add. MS 5836 fol. 11ʳ; W. S. Lewis, ed., *The Yale Edition of Horace Walpole's Correspondence*, 48 vols (New Haven, CT, and London, 1937–83), 1: 20–1; 35: 153; 43: 42; Bedford, Bedford and Luton Archive Service, Wrest Park MS L30/9/111/86, Mary Yorke to Jemima Yorke, 2nd Marchioness Grey, 29 August 1779.

[30] For religious art at Auckland Castle, see Gabriele Finaldi, 'Zurbarán's Jacob and his Twelve Sons: A Family Reunion at the National Gallery', *Apollo Magazine* 140 (1994), 1–16; Jeremy Musson, 'Auckland Castle, Durham', *Country Life* 197 (2003), 82–7.

[31] Kew, TNA, Prob 11/797/163. Interestingly, Catherine Talbot attempted to paint similar scenes herself: Montagu Pennington, ed., *A Series of Letters between Mrs. Elizabeth Carter and Miss Catherine Talbot From the Year 1741 to 1770*, 4 vols (London, 1809), 1: 41.

[32] Iain Pears, *The Discovery of Painting: The Growth of Interest in the Arts in England 1680-1768* (New Haven, CT, and London, 1988), 31–50, esp. 41–50.

contemplation, superstition and idolatry' if approached uncriti-
cally.[33] Yet amidst these concerns many Anglicans recognized that
well-chosen religious art could edify and instruct when looked at
in the 'correct' (or Protestant) way by men and women of taste and
sound judgement. Indeed, in a comment that connects the role of
religious art to the decorative schemes discussed earlier, art theorist
Jonathan Richardson (1655–1745) made this very point. 'Pictures
are not merely ornamental, they are also instructive', he remarked,
'… our walls … speak to us, and teach us history, morality, divinity;
excite in us joy, love, pity, devotion, &c.'[34] To put it another way,
religious art became an increasingly acceptable component of elite
domesticity during the eighteenth century, as theorists and patrons
argued for its place within a reformed material culture.

Using England's episcopal palaces as a test case, this discussion has attempted to chart the material culture of religious
households across a long chronological span. In one respect, it
confirms Hamling's suggestion that reformed elites integrated
material culture into everyday life, as part of a programme of religious devotion, guidance and instruction. Indeed, both Catholic
and Protestant occupants used the palace at Ely as a canvas for
religiously motivated expression and self-examination. In other
respects, however, this discussion raises further questions. As we
have seen, through religious art, episcopal households carried
forward the close connection between material culture and religious expression into the eighteenth century, a period normally
noted for its apparently secular enjoyment of worldly things. But
did this connection operate outside an episcopal context? And
could mass-produced consumer goods meet the demands of a
Protestant nation? It seems likely the answer to both of these questions will be 'yes'. After all, styles and forms of religious expression
may have changed in the period covered by this essay, but the
overriding need for a material realization of piety did not.

Emmanuel College, Cambridge

[33] Claire Haynes, *Pictures and Popery: Art and Religion in England, 1660–1760* (Aldershot, 2006), 106.

[34] Jonathan Richardson, *Works* (London, 1792), 189, cited in Haynes, *Pictures and
Popery*, 83.

'CONSCIENTIOUS ATTENTION TO PUBLICK AND FAMILY WORSHIP OF GOD': RELIGIOUS PRACTICE IN EIGHTEENTH-CENTURY ENGLISH HOUSEHOLDS

by W. M. JACOB

Households were the basic units of society in England until well into the nineteenth century, providing the focus of much economic activity, as well as education and, as this essay will argue, religious and devotional life. Recent research has revealed the centrality of religious life in the home in early modern England,[1] but the extensive research about eighteenth-century households over the past fifteen years has seldom made reference to the place and practice of religion in the domestic context.[2] This essay, focusing on the corporate religious life of Anglican households rather than on the piety and devotions of individuals, suggests that religion remained at the heart of the home and family lives of Anglican laypeople throughout the period. It was not rediscovered by Evangelicals, nor was it a distinguishing feature of evangelical households, but was a continuing element throughout the period.

Households were quite small, including parents, unmarried children living at home, perhaps a sibling of one or other parent, and, for the middling and better sorts, servants, apprentices and

---

[1] See Ian Green, 'Varieties of Domestic Devotion in Early Modern English Protestantism', in Jessica Martin and Alec Ryrie, eds, *Private and Domestic Devotion in Early Modern Britain* (Farnham, 2012), 9–32; and, for the Restoration period, John Spurr, 'The Lay Church of England', in Grant Tapsell, ed., *The Later Stuart Church 1660–1714* (Manchester, 2012), 101–24.

[2] See, for example, Tim Meldrum, *Domestic Service and Gender 1660–1750: Life and Work in the London Household* (Harlow, 2000); Naomi Tadmor, *Family and Friends in Eighteenth-Century England: Household, Kinship and Patronage* (Cambridge, 2001); Pamela Horn, *Flunkeys and Scullions: Life Below Stairs in Georgian England* (Stroud, 2004); Carolyn Steedman, *Master and Servant: Love and Labour in the English Industrial Age* (Cambridge, 2007); eadem, *Labours Lost: Domestic Service and the Making of Modern England* (Cambridge, 2009); Amanda Vickery, *Behind Closed Doors: At Home in Georgian England* (New Haven, CT, and London, 2009); R. C. Richardson, *Household Servants in Early Modern England* (Manchester, 2010); Brodie Waddell, *God, Duty and Community in English Economic Life 1660–1720* (Woodbridge, 2012), who does argue for the centrality of Christian teaching in the ordering of households and economic and social life generally.

unmarried employees. Households had a degree of fluidity: children might leave or return; nephews or nieces might move in as companions; servants came and went. For those beyond the core members there was an implicit contractual element in membership of a household.[3] Women, as widows or spinsters, might head households. Households might be complex, including as lodgers a number of semi-independent households. The better sort customarily 'took lodgings' when in London for the season, or in Bath or other spas; single people often lived as lodgers in households. In the eighteenth century perhaps half the houses in London contained secondary lodger households.[4]

Households continued to be the basic unit of the Church. Popular clergy handbooks and devotional manuals for laypeople made clear that heads of households should order them on godly lines, following biblical models of household management, reading the Bible and extracts from devotional books aloud to the household; leading them in prayer; catechizing children and servants; and taking them (apart from small children), to church, often sitting together as a household in their allotted pew. Households were seen as communities of prayer. Bishops in visitation charges urged clergy to encourage family prayer. Thomas Wilson (1663–1755), bishop of Sodor and Man, in a much reissued charge urged each of his clergy to introduce family prayers into every family under his care and to 'give neither himself nor his people any rest till he has done all in his power to effect so good a work'.[5] From childhood, people were habituated to daily prayers at home, at charity schools and (for boys) at grammar schools; if they continued to university, there were daily prayers in the college chapel. Authors of devotional manuals assumed that prayers were read in every household.

The Whole Duty of Man Laid down in a Plain and Familiar Way for the Use of All but especially the Meanest Reader with Private Devotions for Several Occasions (1657) was a best-seller for generations.[6]

---

3 For a discussion of the composition of households, see Tadmor, *Family and Friends*, 31–43.

4 Vickery, *Behind Closed Doors*, 240.

5 Thomas Wilson, *Parochialia: or Instructions to the Clergy in their Discharge of their Parochial Duty*, repr. in *The Clergyman's Instructor: or a Collection of Tracts on the Ministerial Duty*, 5th edn (Oxford, 1843), 373–443, at 402.

6 The author was almost certainly Richard Allestree (d. 1681), Regius Professor of Divinity at Oxford and Provost of Eton.

It was aimed at ordinary parishioners: the earl of Leicester in 1722 thought it suitable to give to a stableman.[7] The author urged daily attendance at Morning and Evening Prayer in the parish church, and daily prayers in the family 'carefully attended to by the Master of the Family … to provide for the souls of his children and servants, as to provide food for their families' with 'all that are members of it join[ing] in the common supplications', as well as personal prayers morning and evening. He noted: 'there is none, even the meanest householder but ought to take this care'.[8] Religion should permeate every aspect of a household. Heads of households were advised that: 'by instilling Virtue and Piety into your Children and Servants you take the best Method to secure the Obedience and Tractableness of your Children and the Diligence and Fidelity of your Servants, For when all is done, the Duties of mutual Relations stand most firm upon Principles of Religion'.[9]

In 1792 it was noted: 'A Family is a little Society united together under one Head, … [and the] Governor shall call them together at least twice a day'.[10] In 1724 servants were reminded that 'Masters of families have a Charge of Souls … [and] a Care in chusing Servants to instruct them and refrain from Sin'.[11] In 1747 'Governors of Families' were advised that they should 'lead [servants] into all virtue and godliness of living by your own good Example'.[12]

William Wake, in *The Principles of the Christian Faith Explained*, intended for clergy to distribute to their parishioners, instructed heads of households to 'come every Day to the Publick Prayers of the Church' and if that was not possible, he provided 'A Form of Morning and Evening Prayer for the Use of Families – to be led by the Master of the House, or some Other Person appointed

---

[7]   D. P. Mortlock, *Aristocratic Splendour: Money and the World of Thomas Coke, Earl of Leicester* (Stroud, 2007), 210.

[8]   [Richard Allestree], *The Whole Duty of Man* (London, 1842), 95.

[9]   Anon., *An Earnest Exhortation to House-Keepers To set up the Worship of God in their Families with Daily Prayers for Morning and Evening*, 4th edn (London, 1715), 2. It was in its 22nd edition in 1818.

[10]   Anon., *A Regular Method of Governing a Family, or bringing up Children and Servants in the Service of God*, 2nd edn (London, 1792; first publ. 1729), 29–30.

[11]   Anon., *A Present for Servants from their Ministers, Masters, or other Friends*, 2nd edn (London, 1724), no pagination. It was in its 19th edition in 1821.

[12]   Thomas Broughton, *Serious Advice and Warning to Servants, more especially those of the Nobility and Gentry*, 7th edn (London, 1807; first publ. 1746), iv. Broughton was secretary of the SPCK from 1743.

by him', comprising one of the psalms for the day, a chapter from the New Testament, and prayers and intercessions.[13] He empha-sized the duty of parents and godparents to teach children the catechism, and provided a question and answer method for them to use. Edmund Gibson, as rector of Lambeth, wrote his *Family Devotions* for

> many of the Families under my Care [who] are such as live by the Labour of their Hands and have not much time to spare, and therefore I took Care to comprehend the Matter of both the Prayers in as short a Compass as might be; so short the longest of them may be decently read to a Family in a little less than half a Quarter of an hour.

He commended prayers morning and evening for 'by it chil-dren and servants are trained in habits of devotion, [and] it is a restraint on sin and vice, [and] reforms bad members of families'. He instructed heads of households to train up another member of the family, in their absence, to read prayers.[14] The author of *An Earnest Exhortation* advised: 'If you or any one in the Family can read, let him or her take the Bible and gravely read a Psalm and a Chapter of the New Testament, and then distinctly and reverently on your knees offer up the following Prayers to Almighty God'. He recommended teaching children and servants prayers to be learnt by heart, and 'When they are of a fit Age, go with them to ye Minister and desire him to prepare them for Confirmation'.[15] All manuals for household devotions included graces for before and after meals.

Manuals on household government quoted Scripture to rein-force what people were already familiar with from hearing the Bible read in church and in the household. Servants were reminded of Joseph's trustworthiness as steward of his master's household, even in relation to his wife, and that St Paul in his Epistles to the

---

[13] William Wake, *The Principles of the Christian Religion Explained in a Brief Commen-tary upon the Church Catechism*, 4th edn (London, 1720; first publ. 1699), 120–91. It was still in print in 1841.

[14] Edmund Gibson, *Family Devotion, or an Exhortation to Morning and Evening Prayer in Families with two Forms of Prayer suited to those two Seasons, and also fitted for the Use of one Person in Private* … , 24th edn (London, 1758; first publ. 1699). It was still in print in 1862.

[15] Anon., *Earnest Exhortation*, 5.

Ephesians and Colossians enjoined servants to obey their masters 'not with eye-service, as men-pleasers, but in singleness of heart, fearing God'.[16]

Publishing history suggests a phenomenal public appetite for such works of popular devotion.[17] *The Whole Duty of Man* reached its twenty-eighth edition in 1790; Jeremy Taylor's classic *Holy Living* was into its twenty-sixth edition by 1739, being variously imitated, abridged and adapted for popular use; Robert Nelson's *A Companion for the Festivals of the Church of England* reached its twenty-fourth edition in 1782 and his *Companion for Fasts* its twenty-fifth edition in 1781.

Clergy and devout members of the better and middling sorts energetically provided resources for the religious practice and spiritual welfare of the households of the poorer sort, by distributing manuals and pamphlets published by the Society for the Promotion of Christian Knowledge (SPCK), which were available at half the cost of production to their corresponding members, and to clergy and laypeople on request.[18] Ralph Thoresby (1677–1724) noted receiving an annual parcel, almost certainly of tracts, from the SPCK.[19] George Williamson, curate of Arthuret, near Carlisle, noted in 1742: 'A great deal of Books given to be distributed in ye Parish', including 'Family Devotions, ye Christian Monitor'. He also lent books to parishioners, including 'Nelson's Fasts and Feasts'.[20] Welsh evidence suggests a great demand for SPCK pamphlets.[21]

Susannah Hopton included forty hymns with tunes in her *Devotions in the Ancient Way of Offices*, which suggests that hymns may have been part of family devotions. Mid-eighteenth-century Bristol booksellers advertised collections of settings for psalms and

---

[16] Broughton, *Serious Advice and Warning*, 11.

[17] See John Feather, *The Provincial Book Trade in Eighteenth Century England* (Cambridge, 1985), 38.

[18] W. K. Lowther Clarke, *The History of the SPCK* (London, 1959), 81–4. For much of the eighteenth century the SPCK almost monopolized the publication of popular religious literature.

[19] *The Diary of Ralph Thoresby FRS, 1677–1724*, ed. Joseph Hunter, 2 vols (London, 1830), 2: 196.

[20] *Arthuret and Longtown, 1742–1747: The Diaries of George Williamson, Part 1*, ed. Ted Relph (Crosby Ravensworth, 1997), 24, 62.

[21] See Mary Clement, 'A Calendar of Welsh Letters to the SPCK, 1745–1783', *National Library of Wales Journal* 10 (1957), 1–7.

hymns, perhaps for use in family prayers or for making devotional music at home on Sunday evenings.[22] John Wesley's *Hymns on the Lord's Supper* and *Hymns for the People called Methodists* were written for group and personal use.[23]

Did many laypeople follow all this advice? Prayer and devotional practice, like eating, work and domestic routines, were too commonplace and habitual to be recorded in letters and diaries. Even many diary-keeping clergy seldom recorded household prayers. John Wesley, recording the minutiae of his daily life hour by hour, was exceptional and even he may have omitted some things. In any case only a small number of the middling and better sorts kept diaries and wrote letters. Perhaps novelists, hoping to depict the reality of daily life, at least amongst the gentry, were more accurately depicting household religious practice. With that caveat, we will investigate and evaluate the evidence.

Dr Johnson thought that: 'A well-regulated great family may improve a neighbourhood in civility and elegance, and give an example of good order and piety'.[24] Domestic piety is apparent throughout the hierarchical society of eighteenth-century England. At Court there were daily prayers attended by the royal household.[25] Diaries, letters and buildings provide evidence for religious practice in gentry and aristocratic households. Lord Warrington (1652–94) recommended the procedure laid out in Matthew 18: 15–17 to his sons as the basis for reproving servants: first in private, and without passion; after a second offence, more sharply; and, if again, before the whole family.[26] Ralph Thoresby noted daily family 'prayer and reading' in his Leeds household, and in the

---

[22] First published in 1700 and in its 8th edition in 1765: see Jonathan Barry, 'Charles Wesley's Family and the Musical Life of Bristol', in Nicholas Temperley and Stephen Banfield, eds, *Music and the Wesleys* (Urbana, IL, 2010), 141–53, at 148.

[23] See Robin A. Leaver, '*Psalms and Hymns* and *Hymns and Sacred Poems*: Two Strands in Wesley's Hymn Collections', in Temperley and Banfield, eds, *Music and the Wesleys*, 41–51, esp. 43, 49–51; Nicholas Temperley, *Studies in English Church Music 1550–1900* (Farnham, 2009), 137.

[24] *Boswell's Life of Johnson*, ed. George Hill Birkbeck, rev. L. F. Powel, 6 vols (Oxford, 1934), 4: 296.

[25] See, for example, *The London Diaries of William Nicolson, Bishop of Carlisle 1705–1718*, ed. Clyve Jones and Geoffrey Holmes (Oxford, 1985), 68.

[26] Richard Wroe, *A Sermon at the Funeral of the Earl of Warrington* ([London], 1694), 20–1, quoted in Randolph Trumbach, *The Rise of the Egalitarian Family: Aristocratic Kinship and Domestic Relations in Eighteenth-Century England* (New York and London, 1978), 145.

household of his uncle and aunt in Wakefield. Visiting Wentworth Woodhouse in 1711, he commented: 'I was mightily pleased with the regularity and piety of the Family, which is very numerous, yet all attend the prayer twice every day'.[27] Dr Claver Morris, a physician in Wells who died in 1726, frequently noted on Sunday evenings that he had read *The Whole Duty of Man* to his family.[28] Lady Elizabeth Hastings (1682–1739) at Ledstone in West Yorkshire had devotional reading aloud before family prayers every evening, and devotional works were read aloud to the household, including the servants, in preparation for receiving communion.[29] Sermons, which had very high sales, as well as featuring extensively in issues of the *Gentleman's Magazine*, were often read aloud to households. Thomas Turner, a shopkeeper at East Hoathly in Sussex, noted in the 1750s that every Sunday evening he read sermons aloud to his wife.[30]

Great households often had chapels for daily prayers, rivalling the saloon as the most splendid space in the house, with seating designed to reflect the hierarchy of the household, and conveniently accessible from the different zones of the household. Visitors occasionally commented on daily prayers in chapels, for example at Burley-on-the-Hill, where Richard Pococke noted in 1750 that the earl of Nottingham required a groom to tidy the chapel and ring the bell to call the family and household to prayers twice a day, and to report absentees to him. At Wentworth Woodhouse, he noted: 'There is a handsome chapel, where they have prayers every morning between 10 and 11'.[31] Samuel Richardson, in *The History of Sir Charles Grandison*, described Sir Charles, the ideal gentleman, having married and settled in the country, proposing the chapel

---

[27] *Diary of Ralph Thoresby*, ed. Hunter, 1: 344, 355; 2: 56, 86.

[28] *The Diary of a West Country Physician 1684–1726*, ed. Edmund Hobhouse (Rochester, 1934), 65, 104.

[29] M. G. Jones, 'Lady Elizabeth Hastings 1682–1739', *CQR* 128 (1939), 80–1. The extent to which people prepared for receiving communion is illustrated by *The New Week's Preparation for a Worthy Receiving of the Lord's Supper*, in its 37th edition in 1746, which provided for daily morning and evening meditations during the week before receiving communion, and in the week following. Robert Nelson did not insist on lengthy preparation: perhaps as a layman he realized that such requirements inhibited people from receiving communion.

[30] *The Diary of Thomas Turner 1754–1765*, ed. David Vaisey (Oxford, 1984), 75, 85, 110, 125.

[31] *The Travels through England of Dr Richard Pococke*, ed. James Joel Cartwright, 2 vols, Camden Society n.s. 42 (London, 1888), 1: 66.

to be 'the properest place' for their daily worship, conducted by the chaplain for the family and servants at 8 a.m. and 10.30 p.m.[32]

There was a strong devotional focus at the court of George III and Queen Charlotte, and in aristocratic households.[33] In the 1770s Georgiana, duchess of Devonshire, reported to her mother that the duke had begged the chaplain to read prayers in the chapel at Chatsworth, 'which has not been done for many years'.[34] John Byng mentioned old chapels being refurbished in the 1780s and 1790s at Westwood, Clumber and Bramall, and in 1792 described the chapel at Aston Hall, Birmingham, as 'decent, well-fitted'. However, this was not universal: of Chirk Castle he commented in 1784: 'The chapel is a poor thing, and not in that order that the house of God shou'd be', and in 1789 he thought the chapels neglected at Welbeck, Hardwick and Haddon Hall.[35] In 1814 Jane Austen, describing Fanny Bertram's first visit to Mansfield Park, had Mrs Rushworth comment: 'It is a handsome chapel and was formerly in constant use both morning and evening. Prayers were always read in it by the domestic chaplain within the memory of many; but the late Mr Rushworth left it off'.[36]

Aristocratic and gentry households often had a chaplain.[37] His role was to treat the household as his parish, advising, praying for, exhorting, reproving and teaching,[38] but his position might be ambiguous as to whether he was an upper servant or family. At Longleat, the earl of Bath's chaplain was also librarian, and at Holkham, the earl of Leicester's chaplain and the librarian sat at the same table at dinner as the earl and countess.[39] Chaplains were often tutors to sons, instructing them in the Christian faith and

---

[32] Samuel Richardson, *The History of Sir Charles Grandison*, ed. Jocelyn Harris, 3 parts (London, 1972; first publ. 1753–4), 3: 279–80.

[33] Vickery, *Behind Closed Doors*, 152; Clarissa Campbell Orr, 'The Late Hanoverian Court and the Christian Enlightenment', in Michael Schaich, ed., *Monarchy and Religion* (Oxford, 2007), 317–42.

[34] Chatsworth MSS V50, quoted in Trumbach, *Rise of the Egalitarian Family*, 144.

[35] *The Torrington Diaries, containing the Tours through England and Wales of the Hon. John Byng (later 5th Viscount Torrington, between the years 1781 and 1794*, ed. C. Bruyn Andrews, 5 vols (London, 1970), 1: 46, 180; 2: 11, 16, 31, 202; 3: 222.

[36] Jane Austen, *Mansfield Park*, ch. 6.

[37] For a fuller discussion of domestic chaplains, see William Gibson, *A Social History of the Domestic Chaplain 1530–1840* (London, 1997).

[38] See Jeremy Collier, 'The Office of a Chaplain Enquir'd into', in idem, *Essays upon Several Moral Subjects*, 7th edn (London, 1732), 185–203, esp. 193.

[39] Sarah Markham, *John Loveday of Caversham 1711–1789: The Life and Tours of an*

the classics, and accompanying them on their grand tour. Often, especially if a chaplain was married, he was presented to a local living of which the owner of the estate was patron, to fund him.[40] For Lady Elizabeth Hastings, the vicar acted as chaplain, reading Morning and Evening Prayer daily.[41] In the absence of a chaplain the head of the household read prayers. George Woodward noted when visiting the Pelhams at Stanmer in Sussex in 1756 that Mr Pelham led family prayers when the incumbent was unwell.[42] The earl of Liverpool (1776–1828), when prime minister, himself read Evening Prayer to his whole household once a week, at 5.30 p.m. on Sunday evenings, before dinner.[43]

The Whole Duty of Man recommended: 'Fast Days are to be observed and meat abstained from'.[44] Claver Morris noted that on 8 December 1721, the 'Fast Day to Deprecate the Pestilence now raging in France', they 'did not eat or drink 'till after 6 in the Evening', and on Good Friday 1724 not until 'past 7 in the Evening'.[45] John Wesley, in his rules for Kingswood School in 1748, laid down that on Fridays and in Lent the scholars had vegetables and dumplings for dinner, and no meat.[46]

How far the royal court and aristocratic families, and the better and middling sorts, were examples of good order and piety to the poorer sort, is impossible to estimate. In 1760 James Townley, posing as Oliver Grey, a godly servant, in *An Apology for Servants*, alleged that, in forty-five years' service with fourteen masters, 'I was never showed the way to church but by three of them.'[47]

There is little obvious evidence of how the poorer sort and servants used the vast numbers of manuals and books of prayers given them by their betters and the clergy. Perhaps servants, espe-

Eighteenth-Century Onlooker (Wilton, 1984), 294; Mary-Anne Garry, *Wealthy Masters – 'provident and kind': The Household at Holkham 1697–1842* (Dereham, 2012), 117.

[40] See, for example, R. W. Ketton-Cremer, *Country Neighbourhood* (London, 1951).

[41] Jones, *Lady Elizabeth Hastings*, 80.

[42] Donald Gibson, *A Parson in the Vale of White Horse: George Woodward's Letters from East Hendred 1753–1761* (Gloucester, 1982), 90–1.

[43] Norman Gash, *Lord Liverpool: The Life and Political Career of Robert Banks Jenkinson, Second Earl of Liverpool* (London, 1984), 201.

[44] [Allestree], *Whole Duty of Man*, 40.

[45] *Diary of a West Country Physician*, ed. Hobhouse, 89, 106.

[46] Quoted in J. Wickham Legg, *English Church Life from the Restoration to the Tractarian Movement* (London, 1914), 217.

[47] Richardson, *Household Servants*, 139, quoting Oliver Grey, *An Apology for Servants* (London, 1760), 28.

cially those employed in single- or two-servant households, who could minutely observe, and discuss in the kitchen, the shortcomings of their employers and especially their children, may have resisted household devotions, for masters and mistresses frequently complained of them ignoring the ways in which they instructed them to carry out their duties.[48] How much the poorer sort used such material in their own households is impossible to estimate. Reading some of them raises one's suspicions. The prayers in *The Husbandman's Manual*[49] and most other such manuals are long and gloomy, and it is difficult to envisage them being much used.[50] The exceptions are Edmund Gibson's *Family Devotions*, designed for people 'who have not much time to spare', with short forms of prayer for morning and evening, and *The Whole Duty of Man*. These, one could imagine, might have been used.[51]

It is difficult to know whether household piety declined in the later eighteenth century. Jane Austen's comment that the chapel at Mansfield Park was disused may suggest this. Dr Johnson had claimed that, with the disappearance of minor gentry in serving roles from aristocratic households from the 1720s, chaplains were socially isolated in great households and slowly disappeared.[52] Charles Smyth suggested that when there ceased to be chaplains in households, family prayers were discontinued, because lay men, apart from Evangelicals like the earl of Dartmouth, would not lead prayers themselves.[53] However, chaplains continued to be appointed, and lay people of all sorts of churchmanship continued to lead prayers.

A number of factors may have contributed to a decline. First, apprentices and unmarried employees less commonly lived in their master's households, and, especially among the middling sort, home and work began to be separated; the focus of households became parents and children, and their domestic servants. Second,

---

[48] For a fuller discussion see Steedman, *Labours Lost*, 29, 31.

[49] Anon., *The Husbandman's Manual Directing Him how to improve the several Actions of his Calling and the most usual Occurrences of his life to the Glory of God, and the Benefit of his Soul, by a Minister in the Country for the use of his Parishioners* (London, 1694).

[50] Margaret Spufford, *Small Books and Pleasant Histories: Popular Fiction and its Readership in Seventeenth Century England* (London, 1981), 211–12, noted the gloominess of late seventeenth-century godly chapbooks.

[51] Gibson, *Family Devotions*, 4, 6, 18–19.

[52] *Boswell's Life of Johnson*, 2: 96.

[53] Charles Smyth, *Simeon and Church Order* (London, 1940), 30–1.

the move of manufacturing processes, from workshops adjacent to masters' houses and home working, to factories with much increased workforces, changed the relationship between employers and employees and may have made corporate prayer less acceptable. There is no evidence that late eighteenth-century factory owners employed chaplains as Abraham Cowley had at his iron works.[54] The changed patterns of working may also have reduced people's 'prime time' at home, leaving less opportunity for family devotions. Third, the Methodist movement in its various manifestations from the later 1730s provided, especially for younger and female servants, who seem to have been amongst the most frequent recruits to Methodist societies, an alternative to household prayers. These offered, in self-selected classes and bands, a more varied, exhilarating and participatory devotional experience of prayer, hymn-singing and learning about the Christian faith. They may have provided a means to escape the authority of the head of a household and to assert independence and achieve direct access to God. The absence from, or unenthusiastic attendance at, household prayers of servants of Methodist sympathies may have discouraged others from persisting with the practice.

The limited and circumstantial evidence suggests that there was very strong encouragement for Anglican households throughout the eighteenth century, and not just in evangelical or Methodist families, to be a focus of corporate prayer, as well as catechizing servants and children and edifying one another in reading and listening to sermons. However, such evidence as there is, is from the households of the better and middling sorts. How far the large numbers of publications produced to encourage the poorer sort to household prayers were actually used is an open question.

King's College, London

---

[54] *The Law Book of the Crowley Iron Works*, ed. M. W. Flynn, Surtees Society 167 (Durham, 1952), 162.

SONS OF THE PROPHETS: DOMESTIC CLERICAL SEMINARIES IN LATE GEORGIAN ENGLAND

by SARA SLINN

The late Georgian Church was not exclusively the preserve of the graduate clergyman: Oxford and Cambridge universities produced too few graduates to supply all the titles for orders. My current study of ordination records indicates that between 1780 and 1839 about one in four new entrants to the Church had no degree and that the majority of ordinands in Wales and the Northern Province were non-graduates, generally termed by contemporaries as 'literates'.[1] Why is this relevant to the subject of the household? The answer lies in the way in which these non-graduates prepared for ordination. There were various well-trodden routes: for instance in Wales and north-west England some grammar schools provided tertiary level study. But most non-graduate clerical aspirants followed a schoolboy classical education with private study, often assisted by a clergyman. This essay is concerned with a subsection of this type of preparation, the domestic clerical seminary, in which students prepared for ordination while residing in a clergyman's family. It will consider the markets for such institutions, the nature of the pre-ordination training provided by them, and what a recognition of the operation of these seminaries contributes to an understanding of the channels through which emerging currents of ideology and professional practice flowed in this period.

The market for such domestic tuition came both from those without adequate free or local tuition and from those attracted by the particular reputation of a tutor, either as a teacher or as a fixer of titles for orders.[2] It was also driven by the needs of the clerical

---

[1] Percentage of ordinands who were non-graduates: England and Wales 23.1%; Northern Province 50.1%; Wales 61.9%. For an analysis of the educational backgrounds of those taking orders, see Sara Slinn, 'Non-Graduate Entrants to the Clerical Profession, 1780–1839: Routes to Ordination' (Ph.D. thesis, University of Nottingham, forthcoming).

[2] W. H. Krause believed that Thomas Rogers, a former headmaster of Wakefield Grammar School, Yorkshire, with whom a number of ordinands studied, could obtain

education societies, primarily those based at Elland (Yorkshire) and Bristol, the aim of which was to facilitate the entry into the Church of evangelically minded young men who could not ordinarily have afforded the requisite education, and (to a lesser extent) the Church Missionary Society, which needed tutors to educate their aspirant missionaries in the period before the Church Missionary Institution opened in Islington in 1825.[3] Some domestic tuition thrived under diocesan policies which required non-graduates to study with a clergyman before applying for orders. Such a require-ment operated, for instance, in Salisbury diocese in the 1780s and in York diocese in the late 1820s and 1830s.[4] Domestic seminaries also found students from amongst graduates seeking extra pre-ordination tuition, whether from vocational insecurity, a (prob-ably often justified) sense of academic unpreparedness, or because they had previously been 'plucked' (i.e. failed examination) by a bishop's examining chaplain.[5] Oxford and Cambridge provided almost nothing that specifically prepared ordinands for ordination examinations or for future vocational duties, leaving candidates to muddle their way through lists of recommended reading or find themselves someone to assist.[6] Additionally, men intent on

titles for orders: Charles Stanford, *Memoir of the late Rev. W. H. Krause* (Dublin, 1854), 21.

3   Sara Slinn, 'Archbishop Harcourt's Recruitment of Literate Clergymen. Part 2: Clerical Seminaries for Literates in the Diocese of York, 1800–49', *Yorkshire Archaeo-logical Journal* 81 (2009), 279–309, at 287–95; Eugene Stock, *The History of the Church Missionary Society*, 4 vols (London, 1899–1916), 1: 88–90.

4   For Salisbury, see [C. T. Gauntlett], *Sermons by the late Rev. Henry Gauntlett … with a memoir of the author*, 2 vols (London, 1835), 1: vi–vii. For York, see Sara Slinn, 'Archbishop Harcourt's Recruitment of Literate Clergymen. Part 1: Non-Graduate Clergymen in the Diocese of York, 1800–1849', *Yorkshire Archaeological Journal* 80 (2008), 167–87, at 184–7.

5   Graduate William Watye Andrew prepared with Arthur Roberts of Woodrising, Norfolk: Owen Chadwick, *Victorian Miniature* (Cambridge, 1991), 17. Graduate John Hepworth Gresham read with William Snowden at Bawtry following an unsuccessful appearance at York: York, Borthwick Institute for Archives, Ordination Papers [here-after: BI, Ord.P.], 1836:deacon:Gresham.

6   Some ordinands were clearly given specific advice and assistance by their college tutors, but this lay above and beyond the ordinary B.A. course at Oxford and Cambridge and the few works of divinity studied by all students for the B.A. were basic, popular texts. Graduates from Cambridge, where the B.A. course focused particularly on mathematics rather than classics, were notorious in some circles for their poor performance: see, for instance, Philograntus [James Henry Monk?], *A Letter to the Right Reverend John, Lord Bishop of Bristol, Respecting an Additional Examination of Students in the University of Cambridge, and the different Plans proposed for that Purpose*

entering the Church who needed pre-university coaching, but who wanted it contextualized with reference to their future vocation, often chose (or were sent by family or sponsors) to spend time before matriculation and in vacations at a domestic seminary.[7] For such men their university degree qualified them for orders in the sight of a bishop but they are often described as having prepared for orders with a tutor.[8]

The syllabus of such a seminary focused single-mindedly on the requirements of the ordination examination. The ordinand learnt New Testament Greek and also Latin, and studied basic works of divinity as required by bishops' reading lists.[9] For those young men without a relative or neighbour with an extensive library, access to books is likely to have been a significant incentive to enrol. Many began with a good standard of classical attainment, success at school often being what had led them, their friends and families, to imagine that the literary, clerical life was within reach. But sometimes classical languages needed to be learnt from scratch: William Nunn, preparing for orders in 1810, having begun his '*hic, haec, hoc*' only a few months earlier, had a dream. He was ascending the pulpit in his home parish of Colchester. He looked down to find his text and found to his horror that instead of a Bible, there was a Latin dictionary. The response of his tutor William Hurn, vicar of Debenham in Suffolk was: 'Ay, I can give you the interpretation; you must have a good deal more Latin yet ere you preach.'[10]

The master's motivation might be a commitment to the education of future generations of clergy, but more often seems to have

(London, 1822), 11–12; Eubulus, *Thoughts on the Present System of Academic Education in the University of Cambridge* (London, 1822), 13 (obliquely); Claude Smith Bird, *Sketches from the Life of the Rev. Charles Smith Bird* (London, 1864), 74.

7   Pensioners of the Elland and Bristol clerical education societies were frequently sent to domestic seminaries for assessment; they then prepared either for university or for ordination, or else were dismissed as lacking aptitude.

8   Thomas Clarke's obituary notes that he had 'sent forth many able and excellent ministers into the Church': *Gentleman's Magazine* 63 (1793), 961. Balleine credits Clarke with training Basil Woodd, Edward Burn, Charles Jerram and William Goode for holy orders, although all took B.A. degrees before ordination: G. R. Balleine, *A History of the Evangelical Party in the Church of England* (London, 1909), 121–2.

9   For the ideal of parish-based clerical education, see [William Snowden], *The Church: The Case of 'non-graduate clergymen,' usually called 'literates', dispassionately considered in a letter …* (London, 1830). For Snowden's tutorial work, see Slinn, 'Literate Clergymen. Part 2', 297–301.

10   Robert Pym, *Memoirs of the late Rev. William Nunn* (London, 1842), 56.

been financial: a pupil might bring in between £30 and £50 a year, a considerable amount for the poorer clergy.[11] For John Barber, master of the Clerical Institution at Wilsden, one pupil probably brought him as much as his perpetual curacy.[12] There might be other benefits: William Henry Havergal, at Astley in Worcestershire, unwell for much of his ministry, used pupils for pastoral visiting.[13] Walter Smith, at Almondbury, Yorkshire, used his clerical students to teach the advanced scholars of his grammar school.[14] The number of pupils in the domestic seminary was necessarily limited by the size of both a tutor's accommodation and his family: beds and space at the dining table. Havergal's daughter Jane recalled between two and six pupils living with them.[15] Sometimes there was overspill into lodgings. John Barber advertised for pupils, saying he could 'accommodate two gentlemen in his house, in addition to those already with him, and comfortable lodging may be obtained in the village of Wilsden for others'.[16] The use of lodgings does not necessarily indicate that the domestic character of the tutorial relationship was lost. A man might have slept in lodgings and otherwise have shared worship and meals with his tutor's family.

So did the domestic setting of education add anything characteristic to the nature of pre-ordination training these men received? What impact might it have had on what was learnt, on the assimilation of doctrinal ideas, and on the development of professional character? In terms of academic syllabus, there was little to distinguish literates educated in a domestic seminary from literates who attended a tutor on a non-residential basis, although in the former case there were additional educational opportunities: at Havergal's seminary, breakfast was used to discuss questions

---

[11] In 1813, Thomas Rogers gave William Kettlewell board and instruction for £50 p.a.: Wakefield, West Yorkshire Archive Service [hereafter: WYAS], Records of the Elland Society, C84/1, 8–9 July 1813, 7–8 October 1813. In 1828 William Gill paid him £30 for tuition alone: William Gill, *Memoir of the late Rev. William Gill*, ed. Alfred Gatty (Sheffield, 1880), 4. For Rogers, see Slinn, 'Literate Clergymen. Part 2', 288–92.

[12] The perpetual curacy of Wilsden was worth £46 p.a. For Barber, see Slinn, 'Literate Clergymen. Part 2', 295–7.

[13] Jane Crane, *Records of the Life of Wm. H. Havergal* (London, 1883), 182.

[14] Taylor Dyson, *Almondbury and its Ancient School: Being the History of King James's Grammar School, Almondbury* (Huddersfield, 1926), 114. For Smith, see Slinn, 'Literate Clergymen. Part 2', 294–5.

[15] Crane, *Records,* 27.

[16] *Episcopal Watchman* 2 (1829), 240.

which had been set the previous Sunday, and other mealtimes were used for discussion of politics and new books. Family worship was made the opportunity for practising reading New Testament Greek.[17] The strict focus on a professional syllabus did set the literates apart from the university man and it paid dividends. Adam Sedgwick of Cambridge believed that the bishops, ranking the preparedness of ordination candidates, placed the Oxford graduate first (theoretically a good classicist), followed by the literate, with the Cambridge graduate (whose primary study had been mathematics) as the weakest.[18] But examination success is unlikely to have been indicative of career success. Students in seminaries may have had a more vocationally focused academic education than those from the universities, but the aim of the ordination examination was to ensure the bare competences of scholarship and to regulate admission according to benchmarks of Anglican orthodoxy. The ablest students may have caught the bishops' eyes but simple academic merit rarely led to a successful career in material terms and a popular pulpit ministry or pastoral presence was not predicated on standards of scholarship.

Students living with a practising clergyman might also have opportunities to experience parochial work and other professional duties, and in this they certainly contrasted with men ordained directly from university residence.[19] William Nunn catechized children at Debenham,[20] as did Henry Gauntlett's students at Olney, Buckinghamshire,[21] while Sunday school teaching was undertaken by the students of John Cawood at Bewdley, W. H. Havergal at Astley, Walter Smith at Almondbury and William Snowden at Swillington.[22] Students also visited the poor and sick;

[17] Crane, *Records*, 181–2.
[18] Bird, *Charles Smith Bird*, 74.
[19] At Cambridge, Charles Simeon, fellow of King's College and perpetual curate of Holy Trinity, provided a focus for evangelical ordinands seeking the guidance and skills not offered by their formal course of studies. Simeon held sermon classes from 1792 and conversation parties – fairly formal question and answer sessions – from 1813, both of which were influential in forming evangelical doctrine and practice. Simeon did not provide supported pastoral experience but some undergraduates visited the prison, and assisted in the Jesus Lane Sunday School (founded 1827). For a summary of Simeon's influence on ordinands, see Kenneth Hylson-Smith, *Evangelicals in the Church of England, 1734–1984* (Edinburgh, 1989), 70–6.
[20] Pym, *Nunn*, 52–3.
[21] [Gauntlett], *Sermons*, 1: cxiii.
[22] Anon., *Memoir of the Rev. John George Breay*, 2nd edn (London, 1841), 25, 62–3;

Walter Smith's pupils visited the workhouse.[23] Compared to pupils preparing for the dissenting ministry, opportunities for pulpit practice were limited, since intimation of premature preaching could debar from ordination. But domestic seminaries afforded opportunities for public reading – taking part in family worship and reading lessons in services.[24] John George Breay, when a student of Cawood, conducted a simple Sunday afternoon service in a remote hamlet, reading homilies and ad-libbing printed 'cottage sermons'; lay men were permitted to read the services in domestic settings although ad-libbing sermons, the addition of extempore addresses and prayers, and the assembly of large groups would have tried the tolerance of many bishops. When living with Walter Smith at Almondbury, he composed sermons and had the vicarious pleasure of hearing them delivered by the curate.[25] But, useful as this parochial experience may have been, such pastoral training was apparently not core to the domestic seminaries' role. Two of the tutors approved by Archbishop Harcourt of York, Thomas Rogers and William Snowden, had no direct pastoral responsibilities during their most productive years.[26] This accords with Henry Raikes's *Remarks on Clerical Education*, published in 1831, which devotes a section to preparation for parochial work but does so in terms of providing suggestions for reading.[27]

But above and beyond academic study and parochial experience what might the ordinand have learnt from his residence in a domestic seminary? I mentioned above that mealtimes with Havergal were an opportunity for political and literary discussion. Relationships between pupils and tutors clearly could be close, spiritual and beneficial. The biographer of George Campbell Brodbelt described Thomas Clarke as keeping 'a seminary for pious youths

---

Anon., 'Memoir of the Rev. R. C. Dillon D.D.', *Church Magazine* 1 (1839), 289–95, at 290; Crane, *Records*, 182; BI, Ord.P.1848:deacon:Chapman.

[23] Anon., *Memoir of Breay*, 24, 65, 70–1, 74; Anon., 'Memoir of Dillon', 290; BI, Ord.P.1848:deacon:Chapman; Crane, *Records*, 182; Pym, *Nunn*, 59.

[24] [Gauntlett], *Sermons*, I: cxiii; BI, Ord.P.1848:deacon:Chapman.

[25] Anon., *Memoir of Breay*, 25–7, 67–8.

[26] Their ability to focus on tutorial work, without the distractions of parish duty, probably accounts for their significant output; between them they were responsible for over ninety successful ordinands: Slinn, 'Literate Clergymen. Part 2', 290–1, 297–9.

[27] Henry Raikes, *Remarks on Clerical Education* (London, 1831). Note, however, that some advocated superintended practical experience: see Charles Bridges, *The Christian Ministry*, 3rd edn (London, 1830), 89–90.

intended for the service of the sanctuary; and where primitive manners called to remembrance the description of the sons of the prophets, at Bethel, surrounding the venerable Elisha'.[28] Another student, T. T. Thomason, enthused: 'What a pattern for our imitation have we in him. Oh, that we may be strengthened to walk in his steps! His precepts, his advice, his assistance in our studies, spiritual as well as temporal, make him exceedingly beloved.'[29] Walter Smith was active in his spiritual oversight, giving his pupils advice on the arrangement of their daily spiritual devotions.[30] Is there any evidence that students were moulded by the political, social and doctrinal opinions of their temporary homes, that they adopted particular practices, habits and standards of conduct?

An important aim of many clergy was encouraging the adoption of the practice of family prayer, modelling it in their own households and commending it to their parishioners. It is not possible to attribute a young clergyman's acquisition of the habit directly to emulation of the habits of his tutor; there were many routes of contagion. But where we know anything about the daily discipline of a domestic seminary, family worship morning and evening formed the fixed points of the day, and some tutors were active promulgators of the practice. Samuel Knight, who tutored ordinands at Wintringham (Lincolnshire) and Halifax, published *Forms of Prayer for the Use of Christian Families* in 1791 when such guides were scarce.[31] Thomas Rogers presented it as an essential part of the householder's duty in his lectures on the liturgy.[32] Whilst attachment to the Anglican liturgy was fostered by such devotional practice, these occasions might also model less universal practices. Extempore prayer, associated with evangelical practice, had a place

---

[28] Anon., 'Memoir of the Rev. George Campbell Brodbelt', *Evangelical Magazine* 9 (1801), 378–84, at 379.

[29] J. Sargent, *The Life of the Rev T. T. Thomason* (London, 1833), 31; L. Hicken, 'Thomas Clarke of Chesham Bois', *Churchman* 84 (1970), 130–3. To Hicken's list add 'Philoprepos': see *Christian Lady's Magazine* 14 (1840), 62; and Baptist minister Richard Morris: B. Godwin, *Memoirs of Richard Morris, late Pastor of the Baptist church, Amersham, Bucks*, 2nd edn (London, 1819), 57.

[30] Anon., *Memoir of Bray*, 64.

[31] Samuel Knight, *Sermons and Miscellaneous Works … to which is prefixed a memoir by W. Knight* (Halifax, 1828), xxxvii, xciv. For Knight's work as a tutor for orders, see Slinn, 'Literate Clergymen. Part 2', 292–3.

[32] Thomas Rogers, *Lectures Delivered in the Parish Church of Wakefield in the year 1802*, 3rd edn, 2 vols (London: 1816), 1: 16.

in the daily worship of Thomas Scott at Aston Sandford and with Samuel Knight.[33] The domestic seminary, then, may have been one of the influences which led ordinands to form the habit of domestic worship and which sent out new clergy comfortable and practised in extempore prayer.

Those who had been exposed as students to the operation of an evangelical parish surely absorbed a very full conception of the clergyman's role. The energetic evangelical ministries of John George Breay at Christ Church, Birmingham, and Hugh Stowell at Christ Church, Salford, must have owed something to the example of their evangelical tutors John Cawood and Walter Smith.[34] Even where students had not necessarily embraced the doctrinal principles of their tutors, they may still have emulated their highly active, interventionist parochial presence. In terms of evolving standards of conduct associated with evangelical practice, we know that the pupils of Thomas Scott, who was taking pupils between about 1807 and 1816, saw a Sabbath strictly observed, to the extent that there were no hot meals on that day.[35] Those in Samuel Knight's household, from the 1790s to about 1815, saw amusements eschewed that might encourage a taste for gaiety: his children were not taught to dance.[36] Tutors Rogers and Knight did not countenance field sports. Rogers laid down his gun on ordination.[37] Knight, when asked for advice by Anne Lister of Shibden Hall (to whom he seems to have given the outlines of a gentlemanly education), commented that the most he knew about a gun was what end to point away from himself.[38]

Whilst it is tempting to posit a role for evangelical seminaries in the growth of the evangelical party within the Church, it is difficult to demonstrate, since to a great extent students gravitated to (or were directed to) them. However, there is no evidence that any tutors maintained doctrinal tests, and certainly tutors approved by

---

[33] John Scott, *The Life of the Rev. Thomas Scott*, 2nd edn (London, 1822), 627; Knight, *Sermons*, ciii.

[34] For the ministries of Stowell and Breay, see respectively J. B. Marsden, *Memoirs of the Life and Labours of the Rev. Hugh Stowell* (London, 1868), 46–8; Anon., *Memoir of Breay*, 198–203, 477–88, 492–5, 497–9.

[35] Scott, *Life of Scott*, 612.

[36] Knight, *Sermons*, cii–iii.

[37] Charles Rogers, *Memoir of Thomas Rogers* (London, 1832), 25.

[38] Halifax, WYAS, Shibden Hall Records, SH:7/ML/66.

their diocesans could not very well refuse students sent to them. All the same, domestic seminaries were, from time to time, the setting for individual conversions and theological emulation. William Rose underwent an evangelical conversion when visiting Thomas Clarke's seminary.[39] T. R. Garnsey, once under the influence of the Baringites,[40] returned to mainstream evangelical views under W. H. Havergal, with whom he then prepared for ordination.[41] William Nunn may have taken from his tutor Hurn a wavering orthodoxy. Hurn seceded from the Church in 1822, unable to continue in an 'unfeigned assent and consent' to everything in the Book of Common Prayer, subsequently taking on a dissenting ministry at Woodbridge in Suffolk.[42] His student Nunn remained in the establishment but at the outer edge, embracing high Calvinist doctrines and ministering in a proprietary chapel, barely within episcopal tolerance.[43] Conversely, there are examples of pupils clearly rejecting aspects of their tutors' views. Samuel Walter's pupil Joseph Garside joined the lay Baptist ministry: perhaps Walter's broad pan-evangelical sympathies did little to fasten his pupil to the establishment.[44] However, a domestic seminary is probably best thought of as a node at which new young men of similar views were gathered and then distributed, rather than a place where ideologies were radically transformed. The seminaries are somewhat more intriguing when they can be seen propagating subtler

[39] Hicken, 'Thomas Clarke'.

[40] In 1815 George Baring, vicar of Winterbourne Stoke, seceded from the Church of England and was joined by a small number of other clergy from southwest England. Their doctrines were unstable but they held a high Calvinist view of particular redemption and tended to antinomianism: see Grayson Carter, *Anglican Evangelicals: Protestant Secessions from the* Via Media *c.1800–1850* (Oxford, 2001), 105–51.

[41] Crane, *Records*, 18–19; Carter, *Anglican Evangelicals*, 144, 150–1.

[42] Esther Cooke and Ellen Rouse, *Brief Memorials of William Hurn* (London, 1831), 267–71. During his life Hurn was not explicit about his reason for seceding, his *Reasons for Secession from the Church of England* being published posthumously in 1830. However, his theological perplexities were clear to his pupils. George Laval Chesterton described him as 'an enthusiastic Calvinist', always 'wrestling with obscure doctrinal points' and 'prey to doubt and vacillation': George Laval Chesterton, *Peace, War and Adventure*, 2 vols (London, 1853), 1: 2.

[43] Nunn was with Hurn in 1810 and in vacations until 1813: Pym, *Nunn*, 50–60, 68, 73. For Nunn's subsequent relationship with his bishop, see ibid. 91–106; Ian J. Shaw, *High Calvinists in Action: Calvinism and the City – Manchester and London, c.1810–1860* (Oxford, 2003), 73.

[44] Charles Augustus Hulbert, *Annals of the Church in Slaithwaite* (London, 1864), 140–1.

details of clerical belief and practice. Adoption of the temperance cause and promulgation of congregational hymn singing provide two examples of such transmission.

John Barber at Wilsden was unusual amongst Anglican clergy in embracing the temperance movement from its earliest days.[45] In this minority cause at least four of his pupils followed him.[46] Of these, James Bardsley had, perhaps, the most influence on future generations as canon of Manchester Cathedral, author of the Convocation of York's first report on temperance, and father of a bishop who was also a redoubtable lifelong abstainer.[47] It is possible that Barber's temperance stance attracted at least one pupil: the ordination papers of Thomas Simpson, an Oxford man already in principle qualified for orders, reveal that he spent five months reading with Barber in 1833.[48] Simpson was very possibly bought up as a member of the Cowherdites, a group who practised total abstinence from alcohol.[49] If this is correct then it may even be possible, given that at this stage that Barber was only a signatory to the moderation temperance pledge, that his pupil Simpson played a part in the early adoption by Barber, fellow pupils and temperance supporters at Wilsden of the total abstinence cause.[50]

---

[45]   P. T. Winskill, *The Temperance Movement and its Workers*, 4 vols (London, 1892), 1:156–7, 160–2, 164.

[46]   For Barber's pupils, see Slinn, 'Literate Clergymen. Part 2', 295–7. Winskill, *Temperance Movement*, 1:164, lists four of Barber's students as teetotal clergy 'sent out' from the Wilsden Society: James Bardsley, William Hodgson, William Buxton Marsden and Joshua Laycock.

[47]   Winskill, *Temperance Movement*, 1: 156. James Bardsley, *Report of the Committee on Intemperance: For the Convocation of the Province of York* (Manchester, 1874). His son was John Wareing Bardsley: *ODNB, s.n.* 'Bardsley, John Wareing', online at: <http://www.oxforddnb.com/view/article/30581>, accessed 21 June 2012.

[48]   BI, Ord.P.1833:deacon:Simpson.

[49]   The Cowherdites, or Bible Christians (not to be confused with the Cornish Methodist group of the same name), broke away from a group of Swedenborgians in Salford in 1809 under their leader William Cowherd. Cowherd and his successor James Scholefield preached the necessity of abstaining from meat and alcohol. Never a large group, their few English congregations were in the area around Manchester. See Paul A. Pickering and Alex Tyrrell, '"In the Thickest of the Fight": The Rev James Scholefield (1790–1855) and the Bible Christians of Manchester and Salford', *Albion* 26 (1994), 461–82.

[50]   Edward Royle, *Bishop Bickersteth's Visitation Returns for the Archdeaconry of Craven, Diocese of Ripon, 1858*, Borthwick Texts and Studies 37 (York, 2009), 305 n. 41. Thomas's younger brother James was a lifelong vegetarian, suggesting a Cowherdite upbringing for both brothers: *Proceedings of the Eleventh Annual Meeting of the American Vegetarian Society* (New York, 1860), 9.

While Barber's students imbibed temperance, a remarkable number of students must have heard and experienced the benefits of congregational hymn singing as espoused by their tutors. William Hurn at Debenham, John Cawood at Bewdley and William Henry Havergal at Astley were all authors and circulators of hymns.[51] This period saw the once marginal and distinctively evangelical practice of congregational hymn singing, as opposed to metrical psalm singing, become ever more popular in Anglican worship, particularly after 1820 when Archbishop Harcourt's approval of a local hymn book moved hymn singing onto the right side of the law, at least as far as the Northern Province was concerned.[52] Their students John Nunn, Hugh Stowell and John George Breay went on to publish their own hymn books.[53] Of Havergal's work it seems not improbable that through the network of his pupils – of which there were eighty-one – a love of congregational singing and a receptivity to new works, including the compositions of the Havergal family, were widely disseminated.[54]

These examples of temperance and church music could no doubt be taken much further through networks of association, and through careful piecing together of the networks of influence and association among the clergy. There is also much more to be revealed about the workings of patronage, the trajectories of careers and the spread of religious and political ideologies. This essay has focused on tutors as nodes in the network but an examination of the career-length ties between fellow students would add some depth to what is at present a rather gossamer-like understanding of the social fabric of the clergy.

---

[51] Charles Rogers, Lyra Britannica: *A Collection of British Hymns, printed from the genuine Texts, with Biographical Sketches of the Hymn Writers* (London, 1867), 127 (Cawood), 278 (Havergal); Josiah Miller, *Singers and Songs of the Church*, 2nd edn (London, 1869), 316–17 (Hurn).

[52] Nicholas Temperley, *The Music of the English Parish Church*, 2 vols (Cambridge, 1983), 1: 208–9.

[53] William Nunn, *A selection of psalms and hymns: extracted from various collection, and principally for public and social worship* (Manchester, 1827); Hugh Stowell, *A Selection of Psalms and Hymns suited to the services of the Church of England* (Manchester, 1831); Rogers, *Collection of Hymns*, 529; John George Breay, *A Selection of Psalms and Hymns adapted chiefly to Public Worship* (Birmingham, 1837).

[54] See *ODNB, s.nn.* 'Havergal, William Henry', online at: <http://www.oxforddnb.com/view/article/12632>; 'Havergal, Frances Ridley', online at: <http://www.oxforddnb.com/view/article/12629>; 'Havergal, Henry East', online at: <http://www.oxforddnb.com/view/article/12631>, all accessed 21 June 2012.

This essay began by presenting the domestic seminary as a place where both non-graduate and graduate ordinands might prepare themselves for orders. It has suggested that seminaries were hubs in which likeminded young men were assembled, from which they were disseminated, and at which professional ideas and practices could be adopted. The magnitude of their influence, in terms of the numbers of clergymen passing through them, has not yet been addressed. This is a difficult question: the surviving ordination papers at York, for instance, identify most tutors, at least as far as non-graduates are concerned, but comparable series of records are not available for all dioceses.[55] At York between 1827 and 1836 more ordinands had studied with a clerical tutor than had studied at St Bees Clerical College, the next most important source of non-graduate ordinands.[56] How many graduates resided for study in a clerical household is very much less clear. Biographical sources illuminate individual careers and diocesan material occasionally records that a man had undertaken remedial study, but generally speaking a degree was qualification enough and revealing time spent with a tutor might suggest lack of ability or enthusiastic tendencies which might cast doubts on a subject's orthodoxy. My study of ordinands in the later Georgian period has so far identified in the region of two hundred tutors preparing candidates for orders, although undoubtedly there were a great many more. About many it is not possible to know much. Some acted only occasionally. Many offered tuition but probably not in the domestic setting which has been the focus here. As for the potential output of a tutor who made something of a specialism of it, Havergal had eighty-one students, of whom forty-one became clergy,[57] Thomas Rogers prepared over fifty ordinands,[58] and William Snowden forty.[59]

There is, however, an additional significance to the domestic seminary, which is related neither to the numbers of men who

55 Of dioceses where non-graduates formed a large proportion of ordinands, good series of ordination papers survive for Durham, but not for Carlisle or Chester. Domestic seminaries were not a feature of clerical education in the southern Welsh dioceses.

56 Of 114 literates ordained 1827–36, 39 studied with tutors (although not all on a residential basis); 29 attended St Bees Clerical College, and one each St David's College, Lampeter, and Durham University.

57 Crane, *Records*, 180.

58 M. H. Peacock, *History of the Free Grammar School of Queen Elizabeth at Wakefield* (Wakefield, 1892), 146.

59 BI, Ord.P.1848:deacon:Chapman.

passed through them nor to the resultant networks through which ideas and practices spread. In the domestic seminary it is possible to see that a model of strictly professional education did exist in England during this period: clergy were not entirely products of the unreformed universities or in 'remote' areas (whatever 'remote' might mean) boys fresh from the plough. Instead, in the late Georgian Church some clergy had received a focused, strictly professional education, had been socialized in a clerical household, and had entered their first curacies with some practical experience. Such training was not in the long term to be the way forward. Even if considered effective, domestic seminaries could not have been scaled up to provide an adequate pre-ordination solution for every ordinand. And importantly, the domestic seminary, unlike the university, could not impress on the man of modest background the seal of the gentleman, that uncanonical but nevertheless almost essential attribute of the ever status-anxious Anglican clergy. Instead, as the next decades saw an acknowledgement that ideally the clergy should have a professional education, these small-scale, personal, private, domestic seminaries were largely superseded by larger, formally constituted institutions, both private venture theological colleges and diocesan cathedral establishments. Thus the professional characters of the Victorian clergy were moulded initially in larger, less intimate theological colleges and institutions, rather than the parsonage, that model of the Christian home and family which had played an important, and previously largely unacknowledged, part in moulding many among previous generations.

University of Nottingham

'IDLE READING'? POLICING THE BOUNDARIES OF THE NINETEENTH-CENTURY HOUSEHOLD

by GARETH ATKINS

In April 1805 the *Christian Observer* reviewed George Burder's *Lawful Amusements*, a sermon preached earlier that year in London and recently published. Burder was a leading Independent minister, 'a serious man, employed about serious things', his son later recalled, and the *Christian Observer* might have been expected to approve.[1] Yet it was clear that the reviewer thought he had gone too far. The sermon, he complained, 'might more properly be entitled "Unlawful Amusements"', given that only one out of its thirty-eight pages told readers what they *could* do with their leisure hours.[2] Walking, riding, reading biography, history and natural philosophy, and music 'in moderation' were the only permissible pursuits. 'Visiting the sick and poor in their abodes of penury and pain' was, in Burder's eyes, lawful, but the reviewer doubted whether it was, strictly speaking, an amusement. Nevertheless, to see Burder's comments as symptomatic of a joyless religiosity in which every recreational minute was a minute wasted is to misunderstand them. For, as Evangelicalism gained a foothold in the Church of England during the 1780s and 1790s and came to thrive among well-heeled Nonconformist congregations, there was a growing consensus that leisurely pursuits were permissible and even necessary. However, not everyone agreed as to where the boundaries lay. Those who wrote for the *Christian Observer*, for instance, were clearly more relaxed about pastimes, but took a very dim view of Burder's earthy vehemence. Indeed, one of the reviewer's chief complaints about *Lawful Amusements* was the saltiness of its language, especially its 'very strong, as well as coarse, Philippic against the theatre', from which the reviewer fastidiously declined even to quote.[3]

This essay argues that disagreements as to what constituted 'rational' or 'innocent' amusements were so heated because they

---

[1] H. F. Burder, *Memoir of the Rev. George Burder* (London, 1833), 222.
[2] *Christian Observer* [hereafter: *CO*] 4 (1805), 234.
[3] Ibid. 235.

articulated anxieties about how to safeguard the purity of the household. By the early nineteenth century the 'cult of domesticity' articulated in pious advice literature over the previous two decades was gaining ever more purchase among the respectable middle classes. According to writers like Hannah More, the household was not just a physical location but a spiritual and moral arena within, but separate from, a sinful world.[4] Masters and mistresses were responsible for the religious health of all within it, including servants as well as children; they policed its boundaries. Above all the household was a place for the nurturing of children; a sort of quarantine where they were inoculated against the moral diseases of the outside world. As Leonore Davidoff and Catherine Hall have influentially suggested, for many it was an Eden that had survived the Fall. Visions of domesticity – Cowper's *The Task* above all – were resolutely rural, or at least suburban: and there was a new stress on the garden as a cultivated space away from the fevered world of business, walled off both literally and figuratively for contemplation and innocent familial pleasure.[5] While the aristocratic Whig *ton* regarded a day spent in the country as 'a day given to the grave before one's decease', their bourgeois contemporaries revelled in it.[6] Sir James Stephen's famous reminiscences on 'The Clapham Sect' presented the Surrey villas of his youth as a prelapsarian Eden where children frolicked with clerics and statesmen.[7] Burder's sermons were objectionable, then, because even the mere mention of fashionable peccadilloes intruded sin into paradise.

The rapid spread of such ideas in the late eighteenth and early nineteenth centuries owed much to the proliferation of cheap advice literature. Yet the growing torrent of popular publishing also posed problems for moralists, who became increasingly anxious about what people were reading. Hannah More and the Cheap Repository Tract Society, for example, tried in the revolutionary

4   Anne Stott, *Wilberforce: Family and Friends* (Oxford, 2012) is the most recent work on the subject, while Doreen M. Rosman, *Evangelicals and Culture* (London, 1984) remains the fullest and most comprehensive treatment. See also Leonore Davidoff and Catherine Hall, *Family Fortunes: Men and Women of the English Middle Class, 1780–1850* (London, 1987), 149–92, 317–96; John Tosh, *A Man's Place: Masculinity and the Middle-Class Home in Victorian England* (New Haven, CT, 1999).
5   Davidoff and Hall, *Family Fortunes*, 357–75.
6   Joseph Jekyll, *Correspondence of Mr Joseph Jekyll with his Sister-in-law, Lady Gertrude Sloane Stanley* (London, 1894), 147.
7   [James Stephen], 'The Clapham Sect', *Edinburgh Review* 80 (1844), 251–307.

1790s to drive out the 'poison' of scurrilous chapbook literature by providing 'safe books' for the poor to read.[8] The literary
canon, as William St Clair has shown, took a markedly conservative turn in the same period.[9] And in the 1820s, prosecutions by
those Vic Gatrell labels 'The Enemies of Laughter' put paid to a
hitherto thriving culture of bawdy and lewd prints.[10] But even so,
there was a nagging awareness that other, more insidious enemies
remained. 'Who suspects the destruction which lurks under the
harmless or instructive names of *General History*, *Natural History*,
Travels, *Voyages*, *Lives*, *Encyclopedias*, *Criticism*, and *Romance?*' asked
one concerned commentator.[11] Fevered commentary in the pages
of newly founded pious periodicals bears witness to a growing
realization that new forms of print rendered the boundaries of the
household dangerously permeable. On the one hand, then, as this
essay will show, the opening decades of the nineteenth century
witnessed the development of new conventions surrounding
domestic reading habits. On the other it also saw the evolution
of new forms of literature; for while prevention seemed increasingly unrealistic, it might be possible to divert the attention of the
innocent towards safer fare.

'Children', commented Edward Bickersteth in a much repeated
phrase, 'are creatures of imitation.'[12] Lockean theories about youthful
impressionability meant that pious parents took upon themselves
awesome responsibility. The mind of the newborn infant, Locke
had influentially insisted, was a *tabula rasa*, a blank slate ready to
receive the indelible writing of its upbringing, whether good
or bad, and his *Essay Concerning Human Understanding* and *Some
Thoughts Concerning Education* remained immensely influential well
into the nineteenth century. The Bible seemed to corroborate this.
'Train up a child in the way he should go', exhorted the book of
Proverbs, 'and when he is old, he will not depart from it.'[13] It was
this training that necessitated the sort of hour-by-hour household

[8]   Anne Stott, *Hannah More: The First Victorian* (Oxford, 2003), 169–90.
[9]   William St Clair, *The Reading Nation in the Romantic Period* (Cambridge, 2004),
268–92.
[10]   V. A. C. Gatrell, *City of Laughter: Sex and Satire in Eighteenth-Century London*
(London, 2006), 415–547.
[11]   John Bickersteth, *Brief Memoir of a Wife* (London, 1831), 14.
[12]   Edward Bickersteth, *Works of the Rev. E. Bickersteth* (New York, 1832), 159.
[13]   Prov. 22: 6.

supervision vividly described in Thomas Fry's *Domestic Portraiture* (1833). 'From the cradle to the grave,' warned Fry, 'a succession of hourly events and influences of a thousand kinds will gradually and ultimately establish habits, and give a capacity for happiness or misery on an entrance into the eternal world according to their result.'[14] True, few were quite so rigorous as its subject, the preacher and author Legh Richmond, who kept his family in isolation from other children and forbade fishing, field sports, dancing, the theatre, oratorios and all games of chance. But many would have identified with his parental angst. 'All the benefits of a useful education', declared the MP Thomas Babington, 'may be lost by acquaintance with children of bad habits.'[15] Lest his readers assume, like Rousseau, that children were naturally good, Babington was at pains to correct them: education was the conducting of 'an immortal creature' from the power of Satan to God.[16] 'Let [the father] never forget … the evil existing in his family,' concluded Babington, 'or relax in his endeavours to remove it.'[17]

Fortunately for worried parents, a growing corpus of conduct literature existed to guide them through this minefield.[18] John Tosh calls Evangelicalism 'essentially a *domestic* religion', and this was due in no small part to the religious practices within which growing children were cocooned: family prayers, Sabbath-day recreations, the supervision of morals.[19] Particular care was to be taken in religious education. Watts's *Hymns for Children*, many agreed, was a good starting point, to be followed by Mrs Trimmer's *Bible History*, Watts's catechism (because the vocabulary was simpler and less antiquated), and then – often even for non-Anglicans – the Church of England catechism.[20] Catechists were to be sympathetic and gentle, to expect imperfect answers and to guide

---

[14]   [Thomas Fry], *Domestic Portraiture; or, the Successful Application of Religious Principle in the Education of a Family* (London, 1833), 2.
[15]   Thomas Babington, *A Practical View of Christian Education in its Earliest Stages* (Boston, MA, 1818), 157.
[16]   Ibid. 69–71.
[17]   Ibid. 105.
[18]   Louisa Hoare, *Hints for the improvement of early education and nursery discipline*, 2nd edn (London, 1819); Charles Jerram, *Tribute of Parental Affection* (London, 1823); Isaac Taylor, *Home Education* (London, 1838). A classic text, Philip Doddridge's *Sermons on the Religious Education of Children* (1732), was reprinted in 1811.
[19]   Tosh, *Man's Place*, 5.
[20]   Babington, *Christian Education*, 74–9.

their charges gently towards the truth. Perhaps most interestingly, given the reputation of Evangelicals for bibliolatry, many recommended reserving the Bible for when children had already developed a taste for it. Even then, parents needed to be careful which parts of it their offspring read. David's ardent devotions, thought Babington, were strong meat; and there were plenty of other Old Testament stories which were deemed racy or violent and therefore unsuitable for infants. Outside the sacred books there were also items of national literature that required selectivity if they were to be admitted into the household. Thomas Bowdler's *Family Shakspeare* (1818), for example, censored the rude passages and in doing so added a new verb, 'to bowdlerize', to the dictionary. 'I can hardly imagine a more pleasing occupation for a winter's evening,' Bowdler proudly announced, '… than for a father to read one of Shakespeare's plays to his family circle. My object is to enable him to do so without falling unawares among words and expressions which are of such a nature as to raise a blush on the cheek of modesty.'[21] Although mocked, Bowdler's *Shakespeare* was massively successful and much imitated: by 1900 there were fifty expurgated editions on the market. Others bowdlerized for themselves: the Thornton children at Clapham in 1810 sat 'for half an hour after tea … to hear the *proper* parts of Don Quixote read'.[22] One of the reasons pious families sent their sons to board with clergyman-tutors and their families was that similar control could be exerted over their reading, especially of the classics. Here, and at university, too, the boys were essentially being passed into the care of another 'household', albeit a male-dominated one.

Carefully controlled readings were one thing, but evangelical educators agonized over how to regulate the habits of those who could read for themselves. Henrietta, the wife of John Bickersteth, inscribed scriptural texts inside books presented to members of her family: perhaps a crude attempt to render a book safe, or at least to guide the thoughts of the reader.[23] There was a deep-seated ambivalence here. On the one hand Evangelicals knew that private reading paved the road to self-improvement and, crucially, to being able to read the Bible; but on the other they saw it as a habit 'preg-

---

[21] Thomas Bowdler, *The Family Shakspeare* [*sic*], 10 vols (London, 1818), 10: x.
[22] Cited in Stott, *Wilberforce*, 157.
[23] Bickersteth, *Memoir*, 61.

nant with the greatest evils'.[24] It was not just the ideas that books contained that could pollute the household; it was the patterns of behaviour that reading inculcated. Superficial reading, warned Hannah More, caused 'indolence of spirit' and a lack of taste for anything more challenging.[25] Sir James Stephen put it succinctly. 'Watch against idle reading', he told his son. 'Books will be your best or your worst company.'[26] Some of the direst warnings were reserved for sensational fiction. The idea that novels paved the pathway towards dissipation and vice was well established. On the *Evangelical Magazine's* much-reproduced 'Spiritual Barometer', for example, novel reading was part of a downward progression that moved from 'Indifference' through 'House of God forsaken' and 'Much wine, spirits &c.' via 'Love of Novels' to 'Infidelity' and finally 'Death. PERDITION'.[27] The normally sensible *Christian Observer* even suggested a link between novels and prostitution. 'The annals of the Magdalen and Lock Hospitals,' it mused, 'and of the Guardian Society, if the secret history of the first aberrations of the heart could always be known, would too probably furnish many a record of the baneful habits of novel-reading on ignorant and inexperienced minds.'[28]

It was not that moralists were insensible to the attractions of novels. Many devoured them avidly: like everyone else in Europe, William Wilberforce relished Scott's Waverley novels, while Hannah More found it hard to sit still while waiting for the latest title in the series.[29] Yet there was something unsettling about the scale of Scott's success: while *Ivanhoe* was far removed from circulating library trash like *Fatherless Fanny*, might it act as a stepping stone nevertheless?[30] Novels of whatever sort aroused the passions; they glorified romance; they blurred the lines between heroes and villains; they dulled the palate to worthier but less exciting fare. Such was their fatal attraction that some journals refused even to

[24] Babington, *Christian Education*, 148.
[25] Hannah More, *Strictures on the Modern System of Female Education*, 11th edn, 2 vols (London, 1811), 1: 213.
[26] Christopher Tolley, *Domestic Biography: The Legacy of Evangelicalism in Four Nineteenth-Century Families* (Oxford, 1997), 39.
[27] *Evangelical Magazine* 8 (1800), 526.
[28] *CO* 21 (1822), 241.
[29] St Clair, *Reading Nation*, 201.
[30] *CO* 24 (1825), 164.

quote from them. (It took the *Christian Observer* seven years to review one of the Waverley novels; and even then it spent most of the time wrangling over the rights and wrongs of doing so.)[31] There was, of course, often a gap between the narrow prescriptions of advice literature and the realities of lived experience. But while some pious parents were strikingly open-minded about the sort of books allowed into the home – the young Macaulays, for example, devoured the gothic mysteries of Anne Radcliffe and Madame de Staël's sensational *Corinne* – others were deeply concerned about the dangerous fascinations of literature for young minds.[32] In her *Personal Recollections* (1841), Charlotte Elizabeth (Tonna) recalled how, in reading *The Merchant of Venice* at the tender age of seven, she 'drank a cup of intoxication under which my brain reeled for many a year'. 'Page after page', she went on, 'was stereotyped upon a most retentive memory', so much so that she found it difficult to think about anything else.[33] 'Stereotyped': the image brought Locke's *tabula rasa* terrifyingly up to date with the aid of the latest print technology.

Yet if the reading habit was impossible to break, it could at least be diverted onto safer ground. Although Charlotte Elizabeth, like many of her contemporaries, recommended complete abstinence from secular literature, it was clear that the ban did not extend to novels with a moral or religious character. One of the reasons that Hannah More's *Coelebs in Search of a Wife* (1809) and John William Cunningham's *The Velvet Cushion* (1814) were so popular was that they were set in recognizably realistic domestic settings and exalted everyday virtues. By the time Charlotte Elizabeth was serializing her bestsellers in the 1840s – *Judah's Lion*, *Helen Fleetwood* and *The Wrongs of Woman* – the religious novel was an established genre that could be found in numerous households that once would have eschewed fiction entirely. Evangelicals were increasingly keen to claim that the best poetry, too, came from pious pens, citing Milton, Cowper, the clergyman and gothic poet Edward 'Night Thoughts' Young (*c.*1683–1765), and Henry Kirke White (1785–1806), whose youthful death of consumption at Cambridge put paid to a glit-

---

[31] Ibid. 21 (1822), 163–72, 237; 33 (1834), 731.
[32] Stott, *Wilberforce*, 186–8.
[33] Charlotte Elizabeth, *Personal recollections*, 3rd edn (London, 1841), 25–9, 38–41, 62–5.

tering short career as an essayist and versifier and made him a satisfactorily romantic alternative to Coleridge and Wordsworth.[34] Here too competition was deemed better than prophylaxis. In part all this represents a concession to the increasingly adventurous tastes of pious families. Rosman argues that by the 1830s parents and preachers tended not to proscribe but to channel reading in roughly the right direction.[35] While commentators still discussed where the appropriate division lay between 'secular' and 'religious' writing, what ought to be permitted in the household and what ought to be kept out, the distinction was almost impossible to maintain in practice. Evangelicals themselves realized that when they tried to portray vice as unappealing it looked unconvincing, and that the laboured goodness of domesticated 'heroes' and 'heroines' like Coelebs made them appear priggish and stilted.[36] It was clear, moreover, that prohibition only heightened the appeal of illicit texts: the bookshelves of John Ruskin's strictly evangelical parents, for example, were stocked with Scott, Wordsworth and even Byron.

Another problem was that Evangelicals told their children always to tell the truth. Fiction could be regarded as challenging household conventions by portraying scenes that were 'false'. More than one childish innocent set out after reading Bunyan's *Pilgrim's Progress* determined to seek the way to the Celestial City.[37] 'There would be little occasion for works of fiction,' complained the *Evangelical Magazine*, 'were a due attention paid to the narratives of those who have actually figured on the stage of life.'[38] The growth of religious biography in the first half of the nineteenth century was closely intertwined with this desire to provide alternative reading. While novels used hair's-breadth escapes and whirlwind romances to quicken the pulse, biographies worked within the bounds of real lives. If they were less thrilling, they were also more nourishing. They enabled readers to trace the dealings of Providence with an individual and to see that struggle as well as triumph was part of the Christian's lot. In this sense it was also significant that

---

[34] White was a protégé of Charles Simeon: Rosman, *Evangelicals*, 177–8.
[35] Ibid. 166–202.
[36] Ibid. 169–71.
[37] M. O. Grenby, *The Child Reader, 1700–1840* (Cambridge, 2011), 268–71.
[38] *Evangelical Magazine* n.s. 5 (1827), 342.

the family biographies cited earlier offered their readers examples drawn from 'people like us'. They shared the same failings, the same faith and the same God. 'We have the certainty that none of their more estimable excellences are hopelessly removed beyond our attainment', reminded one writer.[39] Most biographies spent plenty of time on their subjects' upbringings and later family lives. They provided readers with realistic – albeit challenging – models of how to live and how to die. In Fry's *Domestic Portraiture*, for example, deathbed scenes take up a substantial part of the book, while a similarly drawn-out demise occupies about a third of Charles Jerram's *Tribute of Parental Affection* (1824), a fact noted approvingly in the *Christian Observer*. In fiction, it reminded its readers, such scenes were drawn 'as *we* please', but in biography 'it is as *God* pleases'.[40] For the famous preacher Thomas Scott, a life well lived was a 'living sermon', worth a hundred flimsy fictional heroes.[41]

This trend towards truth had noticeable effects on publishing fashions. The success of Legh Richmond's tales of village life, *The Dairyman's Daughter*, *The Young Cottager* and *The Negro Servant*, owed much to his refusal to embroider the stories, which drew on his experience as curate of Brading on the Isle of Wight, and were based on the lives of real parishioners. The cottage of 'Little Jane', home to one of the heroines, even became a tourist attraction. Printed first in the *Christian Guardian* between 1809 and 1814 and then reprinted by the Religious Tract Society as *The Annals of the Poor*, some two million copies were published in the author's lifetime in English alone.[42] It was around this time that publishers began to recognize the demand for safe and improving texts designed specifically for different age groups, and here too a similar trend can be traced. In 1815, for instance, when a juvenile literature section first appeared in the Religious Tract Society catalogue, biographies and works that made much of their being 'drawn from life' made up a large proportion of the titles. The same can be said for the Society for Promoting Christian Knowledge,

---

[39] Robert Wilson Evans, *Scripture Biography*, 3 vols (London, 1834–48), 1: 4.
[40] *CO* 24 (1825), 168.
[41] Cited in Tolley, *Domestic Biography*, 117.
[42] *ODNB, s.n.* 'Richmond, Legh (1772–1827)', online at: <http://www.oxforddnb.com/view/article/23595>, accessed 26 July 2013.

which followed suit in 1817. Edward Bickersteth's *The Christian's Family Library*, a venture aimed at readerships on both sides of the Atlantic, included almost as many biographical works as it did devotional and theological texts.[43] Such ventures aimed to provide an approved corpus for household consumption.

If religious biographies were regarded as safe, it is worth stressing that they were not intended to be dull. In the age of mass readerships and the steam press, there was a growing awareness among religious commentators of all shades that one source of stimulation needed to be displaced by another, even (and perhaps especially) within the bounds of the home. 'If good be not provided, evil will only too easily be found', warned the Tractarian novelist Charlotte Yonge in *What Books to Lend and What to Give* (1887).[44] Ben Fischer has recently argued that missionary narratives provided Evangelicals with 'spiritually constructive light reading' as part of a 'countercultural assault' on prevailing mores.[45] This may offer a reminder that such works were not just defensive: they were also a way of aggressively exploiting the permeability of household boundaries in order to evangelize where tracts or domestic visitors might be denied access. As we have seen, however, this 'assault' also extended into other non-fiction genres like biography and history. Charlotte Elizabeth, for example, saw Shakespeare as dangerous, but had no qualms about immersing herself in the gruesome details of *Foxe's Book of Martyrs*. Although an expurgated edition appeared in 1838, other Protestant publicists were happy to ladle out the gore in the form of lantern slides, children's editions, cheap abridgements and so on.[46] Cultured Evangelicals spent their childhoods in homes filled with books about 'Christian Heroes'. All tastes and purses were catered for: Religious Tract Society biographies ranged from the grandiose *Lives of the British Reformers, from Wickliffe to Fox* (9 s. bound in calf) to the lowly *Memoir of W. O. Esq., of St John's College,*

43 Oxford, Bodl., MS Bickersteth, Ms.Eng.c.6397, fol. 5, Edward Bickersteth to Robert Seeley, [*c.* February 1832].

44 Charlotte M. Yonge, *What Books to Lend and What to Give* (London, 1887), 5.

45 Benjamin L. Fischer, 'A Novel Resistance: Mission Narrative as the Anti-Novel in the Evangelical Assault on British Culture', in Peter Clarke and Charlotte Methuen, eds, *The Church and Literature*, SCH 48 (Woodbridge, 2012), 232–45, at 233, 240.

46 Vivienne Westbrook, 'Mid-Victorian Foxe', in *The Unabridged Acts and Monuments Online* (HRI Online Publications, Sheffield, 2011), Editorial commentary and additional information, online at: <http://www.johnfoxe.org>, accessed 26 July 2012.

Cambridge (8 *d.* in neat cover with gilt edges).[47] While such books were certainly read, they were also valued as consumer objects, as part of a household material culture which religious scholars have been slow to investigate.[48] Such was the range of books available that Edward Bickersteth's *Christian Student* (1829) could recommend appropriate selections of lives for the nursery, the youth, the poor man, the lady, the tradesman and the 'private Christian in middle life', as well as lists tailored for a minister, a curate and a missionary. 'Few subjects', Bickersteth declared, 'are more edifying than the lives of good men.'[49]

Biographies also glamorized domestic ideals in more unexpected ways. Janice Cavell has recently argued that the mania for Arctic exploration was rooted in the self-presentation of explorers like Ross, Parry and Franklin as religious father-figures.[50] If the reality of such journeys was often harsh, reassuring accounts of crews overwintering in their bunks and regaling one another with favourite scriptural passages were central to the publishing success of works like Franklin's *Narrative of a Journey to the Shores of the Polar Sea* (1823). The *Narrative* became a blueprint for later biographies of soldier-saints like Henry Havelock and General Gordon, which were devoured by eager evangelical readers. One of the bestsellers was Catherine Marsh's posthumous *Memorials of Captain Hedley Vicars, Ninety-Seventh Regiment* (1855), which sold over 119,000 copies. While this and other books appealed to the militaristic temper ushered in by the Crimean War and Indian Mutiny, they also presented their subjects as paternal figures who cared for and prayed with their men. John Tosh contends that the period from around 1830 to 1870 marked the apogee of the domestic ideal.[51] Such was its strength – and the depth of the market for accounts of it – that for a time it reshaped even notions of masculine heroism. It was only with the rise of 'high imperialism' in the later nineteenth century that more jingoistic accounts rose to fashion.[52]

[47] John Foster, *A Brief Memoir of Miss Sarah Saunders* (London, *c.*1850), endpaper.

[48] Leah Price, *How to Do Things With Books in Victorian Britain* (Princeton, NJ, 2012).

[49] Edward Bickersteth, *The Christian Student* (London, 1829), 526.

[50] Janice Cavell, *Tracing the Connected Narrative: Arctic Exploration in British Print Culture, 1818–1860* (Toronto, ON, 2008), 92–115.

[51] Tosh, *Man's Place*.

[52] Ibid. 174–5.

When an undergraduate at Magdalene College in the 1790s caught one of the fellows reading *Tristram Shandy*, it is difficult to say who was more surprised.[53] The fellow, William Farish, was a pious man; Sterne's novel was decidedly colourful stuff; and Magdalene was an evangelical citadel – a safe 'household' for the sons of pious parents. Such incidents, however, emphasize one of the chief points of this essay: that the reservations expressed in prescriptive literature did not always reflect reality, and that moralists knew it. Attitudes to 'idle reading' varied from household to household, and even if some tried to distinguish between 'sacred' and 'secular' literature, the burgeoning quantity and variety of material on offer made the division hard to discern and impossible to maintain. As a consequence, Evangelicals devoted growing resources to producing exciting but safe alternatives: religious novels, Bible stories, moral tales. This is important because, although we know a great deal about attitudes to fiction, much more remains to be said about the explosion in biographical works that transformed religious publishing and culture.[54] Excellent work, for example, has been done on early modern conversion narratives, but their more variegated and widespread nineteenth-century counterparts remain comparatively unexplored.[55] In surveying that ground this essay points the way towards a fuller and richer understanding of how evangelical households came to terms with the consumer world of nineteenth-century religion.

Magdalene College, Cambridge

[53] John D. Walsh, 'The Magdalene Evangelicals', *CQR* 159 (1958), 499–511, at 508.

[54] Elisabeth Jay, *The Religion of the Heart: Anglican Evangelicalism and the Nineteenth-Century Novel* (Oxford, 1979).

[55] D. Bruce Hindmarsh, *The Evangelical Conversion Narrative* (Oxford, 2005); Phyllis Mack, *Heart Religion in the British Enlightenment* (Cambridge, 2008).

THE SPIRITUAL HOME OF W. E. GLADSTONE: ANNE GLADSTONE'S BIBLE

by DAVID BEBBINGTON

'Popery is the religion of Cathedrals', wrote J.W. Cunningham, the evangelical vicar of Harrow in his novel *The Velvet Cushion* (1815), ' – Protestantism of houses'.[1] It is a commonplace in the secondary literature that the household was the citadel of the evangelical version of Protestantism in nineteenth-century England. 'Evangelicalism', according to a representative comment by Ian Bradley, 'was above all else the religion of the home.'[2] The head of the household conducting family prayers was the embodiment of the evangelical spirit. It is not the purpose of this essay to question that received image, but it does suggest that a clearer picture of the religious atmosphere of the evangelical home can be obtained from sources other than the manuals published for the paterfamilias to read to the assembled household. The books of family prayers tell us what was prescribed; but alternative sources show us what was practised. Spiritual journals, reflective meditations and candid correspondence can often be more revealing. Nowhere, however, is the kernel of household piety more evident than in the Bibles that some zealous believers annotated for their own benefit. The study of the Bible, as Edward Bickersteth, a leading evangelical divine, put it in his book *A Scripture Help* (1816), was 'a great and important duty'.[3] When members of evangelical families retired to the privacy of their own rooms, they might spend time in devotional reading of the Scriptures and leave a record of their reflections in the margins. Such Bibles, one of which is to be examined here, are treasuries of authentic domestic spirituality. They show something of the heartbeat of evangelical religion.

The family was the fundamental unit of the evangelical strategy for the conversion of the world. At any particular juncture blood

---

[1]   J. W. Cunningham, *The Velvet Cushion* (London, 1815), 17, quoted by Elisabeth Jay, *The Religion of the Heart: Anglican Evangelicalism and the Nineteenth-Century Novel* (Oxford, 1979), 132.

[2]   Ian Bradley, *The Call to Seriousness: The Evangelical Impact on the Victorians* (London, 1976), 179.

[3]   Edward Bickersteth, *A Scripture Help*, 17th edn (London, 1838), 46.

relations could influence each other for good and, above all, it was through fathers and mothers that the faith was to be transmitted over time. 'It is through the institution of families', according to Henry Thornton, a key figure in the Clapham Sect, 'that the knowledge of God and of his laws is handed down from generation to generation.'[4] Parents, according to Scripture, bore the responsibility of bringing up their children in the truth. Although the effect (as novelists such as Samuel Butler trenchantly recorded) could be to quench rather than nourish faith, Doreen Rosman has shown that ideal and reality alike were normally less forbidding than might be imagined. The advice of Louisa Hoare, the pre-eminent evangelical parenting mentor, was to treat children as children and not to represent religion as a gloomy affair. In due time her son Edward entered a light-hearted conspiracy with his father in order to keep his mother in ignorance of his rowing, which she was sure would damage his health.[5] Yet a certain solemnity attached to the institution of family prayer that was the core of household religion. When the Eclectic Society, a largely clerical discussion group of Evangelicals, considered the subject in 1800, the members unanimously felt that, although not explicitly commanded in Scripture, family prayer was essential for spiritual wellbeing. 'My happiest moments', declared Thomas Scott, the biblical commentator, 'are during Family Worship.' It was so obviously a duty, according to the Congregationalist John Clayton, that 'to me it is as plain as if delivered from Sinai'.[6] The gathering for daily devotions functioned as an ideological bond between family members. It announced the allegiance of the whole household.

In the evangelical home of the Gladstones, where the future prime minister William Ewart Gladstone was brought up, his forceful father John, a Scot who had become an immensely successful Liverpool merchant, regularly conducted the corporate worship. In later years he used Henry Thornton's *Family Prayers*, a copy of which survives containing his signature, the date 1841 and various textual amendments,[7] but before the publication of

---

[4]   Henry Thornton, quoted by Standish Meacham, *Henry Thornton of Clapham, 1760–1815* (Cambridge, MA, 1964), 52.

[5]   Doreen Rosman, *Evangelicals and Culture* (London, 1984), 102, 107.

[6]   John H. Pratt, ed., *The Thought of the Evangelical Leaders* (Edinburgh, 1978; first publ. 1856), 199, 198.

[7]   Henry Thornton, *Family Prayers*, 10th edn (London, 1839), copy in author's

this classic of the genre in 1834, he presumably employed one of the many other devotional aids available. On a Sunday evening he sometimes read a sermon, in one instance in 1814 by William Cowper, for his wife and children to hear.[8] In the Gladstone home, however, it was John's wife Anne who played the leading role in determining the religious atmosphere. The currents of her personal devotional life flowed in deep evangelical channels. A dedicated promoter of gospel causes in and about Liverpool, Anne secured a governess for her children on the recommendation of the evangelical author Hannah More.[9] Although in old age William recalled his early religion as 'a sad blank',[10] he learned, probably from his governess, to love John Bunyan's *Pilgrim's Progress*. At the age of six he assured his father that he liked *Pilgrim's Progress* much better than the *Arabian Nights*.[11] Three years later he selected as a gift for his parents from 'their affectionate and dutiful son' a two-volume set of the sermons of the Scottish divine Archibald Bonar.[12] About that time Anne wrote that she believed her son to be 'truly converted to God'.[13] Since conversion was the overriding aim of the evangelical household, in William's case the home proved an effective influence.

It was, if anything, even more powerful an influence over William's older sister Anne. When, in 1816, she was thirteen and William was six, their mother obtained a Bible for her daughter. The gift of the Bible symbolized the mother's hopes that the girl would explore and deepen the body of faith they already shared. The hopes were fully realized. The younger Anne, though a spirited girl who enjoyed Scott and Byron, became a highly conscientious believer, in many ways the lynchpin of the family, especially through correspondence when its members were away

collection.

[8]   Peter J. Jagger, *Gladstone: The Making of a Christian Politician* (Allison Park, PA, 1991), 11.

[9]   Ibid. 7.

[10]   John Brooke and Mary Sorensen, eds, *The Prime Ministers' Papers: W. E. Gladstone*: I. *Autobiographica* (London, 1971), 19.

[11]   Jagger, *Gladstone*, 13.

[12]   Archibald Bonar, *Sermons Chiefly on Devotional Subjects*, 2 vols (Edinburgh, 1815), copy in author's collection.

[13]   Perry Butler, *Gladstone: Church, State and Tractarianism: A Study of his Religious Ideas and Attitudes, 1809–1859* (Oxford, 1982), 12.

from home.[14] As William's godmother, she wrote to him when he was confirmed at Eton in 1826 with a rather gushing form of exhortation: 'oh! my beloved William, the more we see of this world – or the nearer we may seem to approach Another, how unspeakably important do the years of youth appear'.[15] William, perhaps surprisingly, appreciated his sister's close interest and made her his confidante as he began exploring theological issues on the eve of going up to Oxford. In old age he recalled her character as 'most devout and fervent'.[16] Anne helped shape Gladstone's early faith. For that reason her Bible, the main subject of this essay, does more than illustrate the ethos of an evangelical home: it lays bare the content of the piety that formed one of the most significant and powerful personalities of the nineteenth century.

Anne's Bible remained at Fasque, the Gladstone family home in Scotland in the 1830s and 1840s, down to the disposal of the library at auction in 2008, when it was acquired by the author of this essay. The Bible was an extremely cheap stereotyped edition published in 1815 by the British and Foreign Bible Society, the name of which was stamped on its very traditional style of calf cover. It was of the type produced by the society for free distribution and so wasted no space: the first chapters of books of the Bible began on the same pages as the last chapters of the previous books. Anne's mother, who was treasurer of the Liverpool women's auxiliary of the British and Foreign Bible Society, must have given it with an eye to practicality rather than attractiveness. Originally, as a note on the title page declares, it was to function as a pew Bible, but within a short while of receiving the book Anne began to read it in her private devotions, using it as a study Bible. She annotated the volume, often copiously, during her scrutiny of the text, using pencil or ink, apparently indiscriminately. Sometimes, as at John 14, both pencil and ink were employed, apparently at different times. The diligent teenager was undertaking a voyage of personal discovery, as is evident in the frequent appearance of 'A. M. Gladstone', 'A. M. G.', 'Anne Gladstone' and 'A. G.' in the text

[14] S. G. Checkland, *The Gladstones: A Family Biography, 1764–1851* (Cambridge, 1971), 89–91.

[15] Hawarden, Flintshire County Record Office, MS Glynne-Gladstone, Anne M. Gladstone to W. E. Gladstone, 7 February 1827.

[16] *Autobiographica*, ed. Brooke and Sorensen, 140.

at the conclusion of a day's reading. There were occasional doodles when her concentration waned – a sum in the margin at Leviticus 25: 29, a basket of fruit at Lamentations 2 – but in general the task was pursued with single-minded dedication. The young girl was conscious of her setting. On one occasion she recorded that her reading was done in Liverpool; three other times she noted that it was completed at Seaforth, the family home outside Liverpool that she loved. It was as though her thoughts were generated by the domestic context. Certainly the sizeable house provided Anne with the opportunity for quiet reflection on the text.

Taking as her motto 'Search the scriptures' (John 5: 39), a phrase inscribed on one of the front endpapers, Anne proceeded fairly systematically in her studies. Her method, which was recommended in Bickersteth's *Scripture Help*, was to read a whole book of the Bible through before starting on another. She also followed Bickersteth's advice of reading the two Testaments in parallel.[17] She must have consulted at least one commentary, again a practice commended by Bickersteth, for there were occasional references to Hebrew, a language she did not command, but it is unclear which work she used. It does not appear to have been the standard evangelical commentary, Thomas Scott's multi-volume work, since the phrasing of Anne's comments, as at Genesis 6: 5, does not match the language of Scott.[18] Apart from the unspecifiable commentary, there are no indications that she drew from publications. Essentially the task of exploring the text was a solitary adventure. We can follow Anne's method because she often, though not consistently, added the day's date at the end of the passage she read. Normally she studied twenty verses at a time, usually significantly less than a chapter, although at times she could reduce the length to ten, twelve or fifteen verses. By means of taking such blocks each day, Anne read through the bulk of the Scriptures. She began, soon after receiving her Bible, with the book of Job, perhaps because attracted by the poetic style, and carried on through the Old Testament, reaching the end of Jeremiah by 9 March 1817 and the end of Malachi by 19 August that year. In April she added a New Testament passage each day, perhaps read at a different time, starting

---

[17] Bickersteth, *Scripture Help*, 57–8.

[18] Thomas Scott, *The Holy Bible … with Explanatory Notes, Practical Observations, and Copious Marginal References*, new edn, 6 vols (London, 1832), 1: note on passage.

with Luke and proceeding as far as Revelation 15: 4 by 11 February 1818, the last recorded date. In order to make up the omissions at the start of the Testaments, she also read Matthew and Mark from July 1817 and the Pentateuch from just before the date at which she completed Malachi. The result was that she had read virtually all except the historical books over something like fourteen months. It was a remarkable feat of assiduous application.

In the process Anne marked the margins of her Bible with a variety of words, lines and symbols. A large proportion consists of cross-references, adding the type of marginal references that more expensive Bibles often contain on publication. Many of the other words are designed simply to register information. Thus at Genesis 16 the difference between the meanings of the names of Abraham's wife is spelt out: 'Sarai – my princess. Sarah – a princess.' Occasionally these comments are mistaken. Thus at Luke 1: 32 'Emmanuel' is said to mean 'God help us!' rather than 'God with us'. Yet in general the level of accuracy is remarkably high for a girl of fourteen or fifteen. Only infrequently does Anne venture beyond bare explanatory glosses to offer something like expository discussion. A rare instance is at John 13: 34, where the new commandment of Jesus to love one another is said to be 'New in importance & not being observed'. More common are indications of theme: 'Stedfastness' [sic] at Numbers 23 and 'Prayer answered' at Matthew 18. These allusions point to the overriding purpose of gaining edification, not just acquiring knowledge. Dissection of the text in the manner of textual critics was far from the mind of the student, even had she been capable of the task. Bickersteth urged his readers not to take up 'critical niceties',[19] but Anne needed no such warning. Nevertheless she was so attentive to the details of the text that she was aware of points that subsequent critics would raise. Thus at Genesis 20: 5 Anne notes that Abraham's pretence that Sarah was his sister rather than his wife had taken place before, as recorded at 12: 19, one of the repetitions in the book that would lead scholars to elaborate complex theories about the transmission of the text. Even while confining herself

---

[19] Bickersteth, *Scripture Help*, 44.

to low-level comments on the text, Anne showed considerable intellectual acuity.

The lines and symbols enable us to penetrate even nearer the core of Anne's purpose in biblical study. The lines usually mark passages that the teenager considered especially significant. Thus a straight pencil line stands against Genesis 49: 10, in which the elderly Jacob predicts that the sceptre would not pass from Judah. Here Anne, no doubt helped by her commentary, remembered that Jesus was born of the tribe of Judah and so she discerned a messianic prophecy, which was therefore worthy of recording with the line. Again, a wavy line draws attention to Luke 9: 23, according to which Jesus urges each of his disciples to take up the cross daily; and the word 'daily' is underlined. Here the passage is being turned to personal application. The symbols similarly bring out matters relating to primary doctrines or else to spiritual priorities. A key on a rear endpaper shows that three of the symbols, a whorl, a leaf and something like the blades of a pair of scissors, refer respectively to the Trinity, a promise or a petition. The whorl, a circle with curved lines connecting the centre and the circumference, occurs, for instance, at Exodus 23: 20–23, where the Lord declares that he will send his angel to lead the people of Israel against their enemies. Anne evidently understands the angel to be the second person of the Trinity, a doctrine to which she draws attention whenever she can. Even more significant to the annotator are the frequent insertions of a symbol looking rather like a typesetters' paragraph indicator, with two vertical lines intersected by a horizontal u-shaped line. This sign, which occurs most often in the Psalms, emphasizes phrases pregnant with spiritual application. Thus in Psalm 51, a place where it appears as frequently as six times, it accompanies circles round such words as those of verse 2: 'Wash me throughly from mine iniquity, and cleanse me from my sin.' Commonly, as in this psalm, the symbol is associated with the forgiveness of sins, but it can also mark a prayer, an exhortation, a promise, an aspiration or an affirmation. Its appearance brings the reader close to the heart of Anne's faith.

What, then, are the chief features of the piety to which Anne's Bible bears testimony? The characteristic features of the evangelical movement are prominent. Its typical stress on the Bible is evident not only in the whole enterprise of close Bible study but also in some of the annotations. In Psalm 119, a celebration of the law of the Lord, for example, there are several verses where the law, evidently equated with the Scriptures, is marked with the sign like a paragraph marker that has just been discussed. Again, the atonement, another prominent evangelical theme, is highlighted in Anne's markings. Thus at Leviticus 17: 14, where the principle is laid down that the life of a creature is in the blood, there is a comment at the bottom of the page that 'The Blood of Christ cleanseth from all sin.' Conversion, a further evangelical emphasis, is brought out where others might not do so. Thus Jeremiah 31: 18, 'turn thou me, and I shall be turned', has the paragraph symbol in the margin. And the evangelical characteristic of activism puts in an appearance from time to time. Thus Paul's words at Athens, recorded in Acts 17: 29, about the Godhead not being like stone, 'graven by art and man's device', have a footnote inserted: 'Missionaries'. The missionary impulse of the evangelical movement, one of the most striking aspects of its activism, had salience in Anne's thoughts. So the Bible, the cross, conversion and activism had a part in moulding the spirituality of the home. The annotations in the Bible point to the foundations of evangelical faith.

Similarly, the preoccupations of the evangelical movement loom large. The distinction between faith and works is prominent. The enunciation of the Pauline principle in Galatians 2: 16 that justification is not by the works of the law naturally has a marginal line against it. But the idea also appears in less expected places. At Revelation 14: 13 a blessing is pronounced on those who die in the Lord and it is commented that 'their works do follow them'. 'If Works had been justificatory', Anne notes at the bottom of the page, 'they w[oul]d have gone before them.' This artificial dragging in of justification reveals how substantial a place it occupied in the young girl's mind. Again, the residual Calvinism of Anglican Evangelicals is apparent in the Bible annotations. Against 'as many as were ordained to eternal life believed' at Acts 13: 48 is the marginal note 'Pred.', and at the top of the page 'Predestination'. The Calvinism stands behind an element of anti-Catholicism that appears in the notes. The minister serving the church founded by John Gladstone where the family worshipped was remembered by Anne's brother William as a man 'of high No Popery opinions'.[20] Anne no doubt echoes the preacher in commenting at

---

[20] Brooke and Sorensen, eds, *Autobiographica*, 20.

Revelation 13: 'Pope Antichrist'. And a further evangelical preoccupation, sabbatarianism, puts in an appearance. In Nehemiah 13, a book not read through, there is a line against verse 13 relating that the gates of Jerusalem were closed on the Sabbath. Clearly Anne approved. She expressed many of the most salient aspects of evangelical faith in her day.

Yet there are certain features of the annotations that show something of Anne's particular personality. She remained conscious of her role in the household as a daughter. In the Deuteronomic version of the Ten Commandments (Deut. 5: 6–21), for instance, the only one marked apart from the sanctification of the Sabbath is the command to honour one's father and mother. Anne also showed distinctively female concerns. Although there are no markings in the account of the ideal wife in Proverbs 31, Anne did take an interest in the earring mentioned at 25: 12 in the Authorized Version translation of the same book. She singled out the roles of the Syro-Phoenician woman who met Jesus (Mark 7: 25–30), remarking on her 'Strong Faith', and of the woman who anointed Jesus' feet with ointment (Luke 7: 36–50). Most strikingly, Anne related two passages to contemporary life. Paul's discouragement in his first letter to Timothy of elaborate display in female adornment (1 Tim. 2: 9) led her to comment that 'this does not condemn the use of simple things'. Another passage, however, had persuaded a friend to observe strict principles. The instruction not to be yoked unequally with unbelievers (2 Cor. 6: 14), Anne noted, had 'determined Miss E. Johnstone not to go to balls'. The teenager was not convinced by this argument, later attending balls herself. Perhaps the most distinctive feature of the annotations, however, is a series of allusions to royalty. On Psalm 140: 1, which reads 'Deliver me, O LORD, from the evil man: preserve me from the violent man', Anne commented, 'I hear the King (G[eorge] 3ʳᵈ) read this verse with much emphasis at Windsor'. The remark was not inserted in the course of her regular Bible reading, but the news struck her sufficiently for the point to be added subsequently, in March 1817. Later that year, on 19 November, Princess Charlotte, the only legitimate child of the Prince Regent and so the ultimate heir to the throne, died in childbirth. Once more Anne recorded the event in her Bible, even though there was no tangible connection with any passage of Scripture. Three times more, in January and February, she referred back to the loss of Charlotte although there was no warrant in the biblical text. The event clearly made an exceptional impact on the young girl, who we know put on court mourning.[21] It therefore found a place in her Bible.

Perhaps the most conspicuous aspect of the markings in Anne's volume, however, is the wealth of commentary on the Godhead. The 'Power of God' is said to be illustrated by Exodus 14, the 'Divinity of ye holy Spirit' by Ezekiel 8. Most of the remarks, however, refer to Christ. Anne certainly observed the maxim of Edward Bickersteth that one should 'Read the Bible, observing its testimony throughout to Jesus Christ'.[22] Any Old Testament passage that could be interpreted as referring to Christ was marked. The prediction of a star that would come out of Jacob in Numbers 24: 17 had a line against it because it was understood as a messianic prophecy. Other passages such as Jeremiah 31: 31–32 had explicit comments added, in this case 'Pro[phecy] of Christ's Covenant'. Again the abbreviation 'D. C.' was adopted to signalize verses that appeared to constitute evidence for the divinity of Christ. The words put into the mouth of the Lord at Isaiah 43: 11, 'I, even I, am the LORD; and beside me there is no saviour', are interpreted as coming from the second person of the Trinity and therefore receive a 'D. C.' Yet even if the sentiment is understood as Christ's, there is no actual indication there of the divine nature, as opposed to the saviourhood, of Christ. Anne was so eager to build up a powerful case for the divinity of Jesus Christ that she was willing to strain the evidence. It also led her in a Docetic direction. At John 14: 11 the words of Jesus about believing him 'for the very works' sake' have the comment, 'Because he did works no man could'. Jesus is presented here as so much divine that he is no longer human. The numerous uses of the whorl to signify Trinitarianism, with its implication of the divinity of Christ, show a comparable tendency to exaggerate the textual support for the doctrine. Why should there be such a powerful emphasis on the divine standing of Christ? It was partly a result of a standard evangelical desire to bring out the supernatural capacity of the Saviour to save, but there was a reason specific to the Gladstone household. John Gladstone, by birth a Scot, had naturally worshipped initially with the English Presbyterians, but had found them moving in a Socinian direction

---

[21] Checkland, *Gladstones*, 90.
[22] Bickersteth, *Scripture Help*, 73.

and had therefore joined in the creation of an orthodox Scots kirk before moving into the Church of England.[23] The family had itself recently escaped the snare of anti-Trinitarianism. In a letter of February 1818 to Thomas Chalmers, the leading Scottish evangelical Presbyterian, John referred to 'our divine Saviour'.[24] The Gladstone household shaped the religion of its daughter, the author of the biblical annotations.

Anne Gladstone's Bible reveals a good deal about the faith of the home in which her brother William grew up. Her dedicated Bible study, generating copious annotations in the text, shows a firm adhesion to evangelical religion, so that she was insistent on justification by faith, opposition to Roman Catholicism and endorsement of sabbatarianism. Anne was conscious of her role as daughter and a growing woman, taking a special interest in royalty, but her most striking emphasis was on God, with a powerful rejection of anti-Trinitarianism. The faith that Anne expressed was moulded by her family, but went on to help shape William's religion. Anne anchored William's Christian allegiance while he was at Eton, corresponding with him regularly about spiritual matters, and after her early death in 1829 William revered her memory. The intellectual dimension of her religion, well illustrated by her Bible annotations, made her species of Evangelicalism sufficiently firmly based for it to represent the starting point of William Gladstone's spiritual pilgrimage.[25] In subsequent years William would promote a piety with a high church flavour, but his chief method was to conduct a form of family prayer similar to what he had experienced in his original home. He even delivered regular sermons to his own household.[26] The statesman later wrote that in his youth he accepted the religious opinions 'current in the domestic atmosphere' without question.[27] The notes in his sister's Bible reveal much of the evangelical ethos that proved formative for Gladstone.

University of Stirling

---

[23] Checkland, *Gladstones*, 31, 45–6.

[24] MS Glynne-Gladstone, John Gladstone to Thomas Chalmers, 17 February 1818.

[25] D. W. Bebbington, *The Mind of Gladstone: Religion, Homer and Politics* (Oxford, 2004), ch. 3.

[26] D. W. Bebbington, 'Gladstone's Preaching and Gladstone's Reading', *Nineteenth-Century Prose* 39 (2012), 113–36.

[27] Brooke and Sorensen, eds, *Autobiographica*, 140.

THE DEATH OF CHARLOTTE BLOOMFIELD IN 1828: FAMILY ROLES IN AN EVANGELICAL HOUSEHOLD

by ANTHONY FLETCHER

A small collection of family papers provides intimate and illuminating material on the illness and death of a much-loved teenager. Charlotte Bloomfield was the daughter of Lord Benjamin Bloomfield, confidant of the Prince Regent and from 1823 British ambassador at Stockholm.[1] In 1825 Bloomfield had Charlotte painted with pretty golden curls by the fashionable miniaturist Anne Mee (Fig. 1). She holds her pet rabbit. Her story has rich resonances for the study of the evangelical household. This essay explores how a lingering death of this kind could produce a family crisis, which was in effect a test of faith. The case is also interesting in terms of the history of the medical treatment of children at home. Moreover, it shows how memorialization of such a death sustained the evangelical piety of the family in the decades that followed. This account gives particular attention to the particular roles and responsibilities of family and household members.

Linda Pollock's contention, arguing against Lawrence Stone, that most parents between 1500 and 1900 were deeply distressed by the untimely death of children is now generally accepted. Like us, Pat Jalland has written, 'most Victorians believed the death of a child was the most distressing and incapacitating of all'.[2] Yet there was a long tradition of the 'good death', rooted in the Middle Ages, which, as Ralph Houlbrooke has argued, left an example to survivors, 'reconciled them to their loss and strengthened their own Christian belief'. Children as well as adults could die well. The Church had long taught that even young children, facing

---

[1]   ODNB, s.n. 'Benjamin Bloomfield, first Baron Bloomfield (1768–1846)'. The archive and Charlotte's portrait came into my possession following the death of my cousin Ethel Gore-Booth, whose grandmother, Georgiana Bloomfield, was Charlotte's sister.

[2]   L. Stone, *The Family, Sex and Marriage in England, 1500–1800* (London, 1977), 651–2; L. A. Pollock, *Forgotten Children: Parent-Child Relations from 1500 to 1800* (Cambridge, 1983); P. Jalland, *Death in the Victorian Family* (Oxford, 1996), 121.

Fig. 1: Charlotte Bloomfield (1815–28) by Mrs Mee. In the ownership of the author; image reproduced by kind permission of Yale University Press.

early death, might be endowed with powers beyond their years by divine grace.[3] Hannah Newton has argued that children had particularly vivid imaginations of heaven, 'which may explain why they looked forward to going there'. She notes Houlbrooke's suggestion that children may have believed more literally in the afterlife than adults. Newton cites James Janeway's 1671 work *A Token for Children*, in which he declared that if children were not too little 'to go to Hell, they are not too little to serve their great Master, too little to go to Heaven'.[4]

Houlbrooke discussed Janeway's tract at a conference on 'Childhood in Question'. The tract tells the stories of thirteen young lives cut short by early death, some of them between 1632 and 1671. He argued that 'the essential foundation for the sort of good death described by Janeway was personal religious awareness'. A remarkable feature' of several of the stories was 'the early development of spiritual autonomy'. Several of Janeway's dying children read and

---

3   R. Houlbrooke, *Death, Religion and the Family in England, 1480–1750* (Oxford, 1998), 186–7.
4   H. Newton, *The Sick Child in Early Modern England* (Oxford, 2012), 208–20.

prayed by themselves.[5] Newton, studying the period 1580 to 1720 and developing this argument, has suggested that belief in the providential origins of sickness was 'a source of tremendous emotional and spiritual comfort to sick children'. She makes a strong case that, in evangelical circles, whilst hell elicited extraordinary fear, parents could play a large part in helping children achieve confidence about their salvation: 'sometimes feelings of resignation blurred into outright happiness and joy'. The sick child could be 'ill in my body but well in God', that is the child's 'happy emotions could render physical pains more bearable'.[6] In the early 1820s, I would suggest, we are still in this medical and spiritual world.

The illness that led to Charlotte's death seems to have begun in 1825. At an early stage Lord Bloomfield bought her a tiny leather-bound book in which he entered suitable prayers for her to say. The first of these, entitled 'When very ill', began: 'O God who has ordained that I should be a helpless suffering child, make me, I pray thee, perfectly resigned to thy will.'[7] It must have been clear to her father from the start that the doctors were confounded by the problem of how to treat her. He may have begun to resign himself to losing Charlotte as early as 1825. But his work as ambassador in Stockholm preoccupied him, and for most of the period from 1825 to 1828 he was out of England. Charlotte's elder sisters, Harriott and Georgiana, were mostly with their mother in Sweden from 1823. But she, only eight years old in 1823, remained all the time in the charge of her governess at Stud House, Bloomfield's grace and favour residence in Hampton Court Park.

The dying person's social relationships, asserts Houlbrooke, were a key determinant of dying well. In the case of a child's terminal illness, if death was heralded well in advance, there was time for the family to fulfil their special responsibility for spiritual preparation. It was the caring and devoted governess Susan Ridout who, in Charlotte's case, took on this task. Charlotte was a spirited and precocious child, lonely without her sisters.[8] Piety was seam-

5   R. Houlbrooke, 'Death in Childhood: The Practice of the "good death" in James Janeway's *A Token for Children*', in A. J. Fletcher and S. Hussey, eds, *Childhood in Question: Children, Parents and the State* (Manchester, 1999), 37–56.

6   Newton, *Sick Child*, 204, 208–20.

7   Bloomfield archive [hereafter: BA], Charlotte Bloomfield's book of prayers; A. J. Fletcher, *Growing Up in England: The Experience of Childhood* (London 2008), 89.

8   For the role of Miss Ridout in teaching Charlotte the polite accomplishments

lessly integrated into her upbringing. Thus Scripture reading was a regular topic of dialogue between her and the governess. 'I have gone on regularly reading my Testament and have now finished an Epistle of St John', Charlotte reported in a letter to Miss Ridout in December 1825. She quickly received a long reply about her Bible studies. This led to a confession that she had been in trouble understanding two verses in the Epistle of Jude, the ninth and eleventh. Even her nineteen-year-old sister Harriott was unable to remember who Korah was, cited there as falling into false belief.[9]

It may have been Lord Bloomfield himself who prompted a process of questioning Charlotte about her spiritual life during her first bout of illness in 1825. On 2 February 1826, Charlotte wrote in contrition to Miss Ridout about questions she had in front of her: 'I feel that I have not received all the benefit I ought from my late illness. I shall now make use of the questions much oftener and shall hope to find myself improve'. There was a note of childish anxiety: 'I have nearly finished reading Isaiah and will you tell me what I am to read next.'[10]

There was a period in 1826 and 1827 when Charlotte's health somewhat recovered. She began using the teasing nickname Miss Doutty for her governess. But, staying with friends at Bromley in May 1827, she sent news which hinted that she was a child with invalid status: 'we went yesterday to Sundridge Park and they let my carriage go in ... it was so pleasant'. Charlotte's spirit is evident in her goodbye to Miss Ridout: 'I remain ever your affectionate little rogue Chall.'[11] 'I have begun Pilgrims Progress', she related in another letter about this time; 'I have got to where Christian's burthen falls of[f]'.[12]

When a final crisis came at the Stud House, early in 1828, Harriott, Georgiana and their mother were home from Sweden. Miss Ridout may well have been asked to write the account we have of Charlotte's last days, between 17 February and 8 March 1828. Five women – her mother, her governess, an aged retainer (Miss Wall) and two sisters – managed the process of this lingering death with an emotional resourcefulness which sustained the

---

of the age, see Fletcher, *Growing Up*, 236–8.

9   BA, Charlotte Bloomfield to Miss Ridout, 15, 20 December 1825.
10 BA, Charlotte Bloomfield to Miss Ridout, 2 February 1826.
11 BA, Charlotte Bloomfield to Miss Ridout, 3 May 1827.
12 BA, Charlotte Bloomfield to Miss Ridout, n.d. [1827].

child and made it revelatory for them all. Charlotte had written many affectionate letters to Harriott and Georgiana during the previous years.[13] Undoubtedly they were very close to her in her final illness, when they exhibited the qualities of sibling caring and support which were prominent in contemporary prescriptive literature.[14] In the treasured manuscript account of her passing, the process became a positive, even uplifting, experience for the whole household.

Charlotte's illness was never diagnosed but it may have been a brain tumour. Her final days began with severe headaches, for which she was given laxative medicine. On 19 February, she was not well enough for Miss Ridout to read to her. The next day, despite her headache, Lady Bloomfield took her out in the chariot to Bromley. This totally exhausted the little girl, who was carried upstairs on returning in the evening. Her mother promised a journey to the sea at Hastings, probably hoping for a cure there. As a favour, Charlotte begged to tell her governess this news first herself, supposing it 'so agreeable a surprise'.

But this perhaps unwise outing had sapped Charlotte's strength: on Thursday, 20 February, 'she was not moved to her sitting room till 3 o'clock and went back to bed earlier than usual'. Miss Ridout had read her prayers and sat talking with her in the morning. The next day the seriousness of her condition was even more striking: 'I attempted to give her breakfast but she could not eat – did not like the light, nor any sound.' It seems that Harriott and Georgiana were now sharing the nursing care with the governess. When the three of them went out to an uncle's lecture on the 22nd, Charlotte was 'very irritable with her Mama'. In extreme physical pain, it seems that she found it easier, clinging to the person she knew best, to turn to her governess than her mother. The next evening, when Miss Ridout ate her meal with Charlotte, she 'confessed to me how cross she had been the night before to her Mama'. Now, feeling safe, she was 'well enough to feed me with bread and cheese at my dinner'.

This intimacy soon became very close indeed. One day Miss Ridout recorded quite specifically the affection the child showed to her. Charlotte 'thanked me for my good management of her and

---

[13] Fletcher, *Growing Up*, 238.
[14] L. Davidoff, *Thicker than Water: Siblings and their Relations 1780–1920* (Oxford, 2012), 109.

when I said "thank God dear Charlotte" she replied "yes I know that but I thank him for you too"'. 'This is a bad way for you to spend your time, I wish I was better', Charlotte fretted. So Miss Ridout confided how she had recently grieved with her friend, Miss Dickson, about the sickliness of the girl in her charge and was told seriously: 'do you think you love her better than her Saviour does?' Miss Ridout was convinced that Charlotte 'perfectly understood this and I believe acted upon it for she uttered no more wishes.' We can see that it was primarily her governess who was leading Charlotte to God. When it became impossible for the child to participate in their regular prayers, Miss Ridout spoke to her 'of the necessity and comfort of directing our thoughts to God when we could not pray regularly'.

We have to be careful not to overplay the role of this devoted governess because it is, after all, only her account we are left with. Charlotte's sisters must have been constantly in and out of her room. On 25 February, Charlotte 'spoke affectionately of her Papa and described to me the voyage she had made from Dublin to Bristol'. But it was only two days before the end that Lord Bloomfield himself reached the Stud House. Lady Bloomfield's first attempt to summon him from Sweden had been on 22 February.

To Miss Ridout's great joy, when her father eventually arrived home on 5 March, 'she knew him, embraced him fondly … afterwards she attended to a prayer I said to her and kissed my hand'. Next day, she was 'conscious enough to know her Papa and Mama when they approached her'; that afternoon 'she enquired for her sister Harriott and was much pleased to see her … she showed kindness to everyone'. Miss Ridout was now reading her texts at intervals, like 'The Lord is Pitiful', 'God is love' and 'Cast all thy care on him for he Careth for thee'. She could no longer pray herself but 'said distinctly "You pray for me" and she pressed my hand sensibly whilst I was praying'. It is striking in Miss Ridout's account that displays of physical affection between the patient, her parents and her governess were particularly evident in Charlotte's final extremity.

The household care Charlotte received between 17 and 24 February consisted of round-the-clock nursing. Lady Bloomfield, Miss Ridout and Harriott took it in turns to stay with her at night. We have seen how this care was suffused with religiosity; one day Charlotte 'spoke of the Rock of Ages' to the family retainer Miss

Wall. What is striking is the long delay before Dr Bosland, who was alerted early on, turned to surgical remedies. Hannah Newton has noted how, in the eighteenth century, doctors still favoured treatments based on the humours. Certain types of humoral remedies were considered best, especially external remedies which were preferred to surgical ones as gentler and therefore suited to children's tender bodies. Dr Bosland, clinging to this traditional teaching, began by prescribing laxatives and then acid drops which quickly made Charlotte sick. The intention was to expel from the body superfluous or impure humours that had caused the disease. The doctor may have thought these initial measures were essential because Charlotte might die without this immediate treatment.[15]

With her symptoms worsening, Dr Bosland was called on Monday, 24 February. Doctors were sensitive to the issue of children's pain, and he knew Charlotte had screamed at times. But the governess's report that day made him adopt new treatment: 'every bad symptom increased, she ate nothing, was not dressed, could not be induced to move, still greater aversion to light'. Treating a thirteen-year-old, he probably felt that the time had come for surgery and that she might be strong enough to stand this. Bosland now 'cut off her hair – dressed the back with poultice – had her sponged with salt water – gave her calomel, the head kept wet with spirit lotion'. Newton has noticed that physicians from around 1700 became more willing to use blood-letting and blisters than they had been previously, which she attributed to the belief that drastic remedies had to be adopted if a child was to be kept alive.[16]

Before Harriott settled to sleep with her that evening, Miss Ridout left her with a text for the night: 'my flesh and my heart faileth but God is the strength of my heart and my portion for ever'. Over the next two days Charlotte seemed to rally. 'She was less irritable and her pulse rose ... went to her sitting room ... . saw everyone in turn ... looked beautiful'. Her Mama slept in her room one night, and Miss Ridout 'sat up all night' with her the next one. Around 1 March, she began lapsing in and out of consciousness. Miss Ridout mentioned her brother John's name and she recognized it, saying she sent love to him. 'I once

15 Newton, *Sick Child*, 67–9.
16 Ibid. 71–3.

exclaimed aloud to her this day "are you terrified my love? Thanks be to God who giveth us the victory through Jesus Christ our Lord" and she murmured instantly "I know, I know".'

Relatives began to gather to comfort the family. With episodes of screaming and convulsions, several times Miss Ridout thought she was dying. 'Lady Bloomfield was recommended to sit in the room', Miss Ridout's narrative reveals; 'Charlotte certainly knew her Mama and testified her fondness.' On Tuesday, 4 March, her mother spent almost the whole day in her room. She began asking for her Papa who arrived the next day. Dr Bosland was now in more constant attendance. Six new blisters were applied. When she was cold, hot flannels were used to revive her: 'Dr Bosland gave her mulled wine and beef tea.'

Friday, Charlotte's last day, was traumatic for Miss Ridout, as the best doctors available largely took over. There is no record of the emotions of the child's parents, nor of those of her sisters, who were clearly in her room at times: 'she knew everyone and was very grateful in her manner to everyone'. Miss Ridout was with her most of the day: 'she bade me say again a text she liked "Cast all thy care on Him for He careth for thee" and kissed my hand.' A second doctor, Mr Simpson, was called and arrived about six o'clock. He examined her back. 'At seven she was very cold, but was revived by flannels and hot bottles and ether … at half past nine she began to cough, had much difficulty in trying to clear her throat, her mouth bled a little.'

When the two doctors took a break, Miss Ridout resumed her care, remaining with Charlotte all the time from then on. 'I held her up and endeavoured by hot water or tea to assist her … . … but strong convulsions came on … . … at five minutes past twelve the dear child was released'.[17] Her father recorded Charlotte's death on 8 March, in the book in which he had regularly entered prayers for her. This prolonged death had taken almost three years. Lord Bloomfield noted 'this little book was in constant use by my angelic Charlotte from the day I composed the first about April 1825 up to the week preceding her death'.[18]

The manuscript memoir written by Susan Ridout may have been designed, consciously or not, with some long-term didactic

---

[17]   BA, Susan Ridout, account of the last days in the life of Charlotte Bloomfield.
[18]   BA, small notebook with manuscript prayers.

and devotional purpose. It was certainly used in this way, passing to a succession of pious women: Charlotte's sister Georgiana until the 1890s, her daughter Louisa Trench, and then her granddaughter Ethel Gore-Booth, whom I knew as a boy in the 1950s.[19]

Other items in this archive throw light on immediate rituals of mourning in the Bloomfield household. Two days after Charlotte died, one of the family wrote a short verse which reflected, on black-edged paper, about the end to which their 'path of sorrow' had always tended. It expressed gratitude for the largely peaceful manner of Charlotte's death: 'oh from the world thy thoughts set free | and bring thy broken heart to Me'.[20]

'The achievement of a "good" death transformed the process of dying from tragedy into triumph', Ralph Houlbrooke has written. He emphasizes physical and moral support from others as a prerequisite for this.[21] Charlotte, in a house full of servants, sisters and relatives, had it in abundance. The specific evidence that the Bloomfield family resigned themselves quickly to the child's illness is a manuscript written in March 1828, headed 'A Prayer for a Sick Child'. Inscribed on it is a note that this was 'a prayer that was blest to us all the first night of her illness'. The prayer pleaded with God, 'in submission to thy will', to spare the child. But, the writer has underlined, 'if thou art pleased, Lord, to take her away thus early, oh let it be in mercy'. No effort was spared to ensure, 'by the quickest improvement', that Charlotte would be 'perfected in knowledge and grace and made ripe and ready for Heaven and eternal Glory'.[22]

So household care for Charlotte was posited on her redemptive death. She was assumed to be capable of benefiting from her own spiritual awareness. Sickness was part of God's providence. For a child, facing death earlier than most, assistance in making hers a 'good death' was a very special family responsibility.[23] It was probably Georgiana who, when the doctor cut off Charlotte's hair, kept

---

[19] I gave a brief account of this story, soon after the archive passed to me, in my presidential lecture to the EHS: 'Beyond the Church: Women's Spiritual Experience at Home and in the Community, 1600–1900', in R. N. Swanson, ed., *Gender and Christian History*, SCH 34 (Oxford, 1998), 187–203, at 199–200.

[20] BA, verse dated 10 March 1828.

[21] Houlbrooke, *Death, Religion and the Family*, 183–91.

[22] BA, 'A Prayer for a Sick Child'.

[23] Houlbrooke, *Death, Religion and the Family*, 57–70.

a lock of it and attached it by a ribbon to papers onto which she copied the prayers that had been most precious to the little girl, dating this memento 29 February. The hair is as strongly auburn today as it was in 1828. 'We found the leaf turned down at this place, apparently much read for the book opened there', Georgiana noted, above a 'Meditation on Death'. Two other prayers she copied were 'written in the first Testament Charlotte ever had, at the beginning and end of it, the pages almost worn out from constant use'. This was the very best testimony that her sister had lived a deeply religious childhood life.[24]

Lord Bloomfield's daughter-in-law published a memoir of his life in 1884. She had only come to know him late in his life, since she married his son John in 1845. But her testimony about the impact on him of Charlotte's death was certainly accurate. The trials of losing both his mother and youngest daughter in 1826 and 1828, she wrote, had afflicted Bloomfield 'very deeply and by God's grace produced a decided change in his religious opinions'. Returning to Sweden, he came under the influence of a Methodist minister, George Scott, whose counselling induced remorse about his youthful life and the riches he had won through service at the Prince Regent's court at Brighton.[25]

Bloomfield now became strongly sabbatarian. Letters also show the depth of his affection to his surviving daughters.[26] Georgiana's prestigious marriage to Henry Trench of Cangort Park in 1830, bringing into the family an impressive nearby estate to his own at Laughton, thrilled him. In Tipperary a new generation of the young Trenches soon began to appear. Moreover Miss Ridout was there, taking on a new position as governess: 'assure her of my most affectionate regards', Bloomfield wrote to Georgiana. He felt for his native country and wanted to bring spiritual succour there: 'our own poor country is rich in wretchedness', he wrote, 'and I would hold up my petition in behalf of the hungry and naked that abound in Ireland'.[27]

Visiting Laughton in 1833, Lord Bloomfield met a young curate in his parish of Borrisnefarney. James Conolly's memoir of his

---

[24] BA, prayers used by Charlotte Bloomfield and lock of hair, 29 February 1828.

[25] Georgiana, Lady Bloomfield, ed., *Memoir of Benjamin Lord Bloomfield*, 2 vols (London, 1884), 1: 7.

[26] BA, Lord Bloomfield to Georgiana Bloomfield, 1 January, 14, 23 April, 16 July 1830; Lord Bloomfield to the Hon. Mrs Henry Trench, 14 April 1842.

[27] BA, Lord Bloomfield to Georgiana Bloomfield, 'Good Friday'.

friendship with him from 1833 to his death in 1846 is illuminating. 'I was thanked by that good Christian nobleman at lunch', wrote Conolly, for a sermon which had emphasized pardon of sin as primary among 'the fruits which grow on this tree of life, the Cross of Christ'. Bloomfield proposed: 'I would establish a lecture in his house, that wherever he had a house God should have an altar.'

The attendance in the large dining room at Laughton the next week, 'rich and poor from all places around he had himself invited', far outstripped the normal congregation in Conolly's little church. The house became 'a Bethel', where, through Bloomfield's residence, the Lord dispensed 'manna in the wilderness': 'all the neighbourhood were benefited by the example as well as the poor relieved and instructed'. Retiring from official life in 1837, Bloomfield became Commandant at Woolwich, where he continued to promote the gospel in his household. Conolly followed him there and ministered to him during his last illness in 1845 and 1846.[28]

This story emphasizes gender division in the care of the sick child in this period. While Lord Bloomfield, we have seen, prompted Charlotte's systematic prayer and Bible study, it was the women of the household who managed her daily nursing and moral care. Would this have been the case had her father not been abroad? Some historians have suggested that fathers played a more active role in the care of sick children than we might suppose.[29] But Charlotte Bloomfield's 'good death' was enacted by a circle of women whose faith, love and integrity saw her through her last days with merciful tenderness. Thus it illustrates the continuity between the seventeenth century and the nineteenth, in the perception and understanding as well as the treatment of childhood illness.[30]

This treatment was conducted in almost total ignorance, shared with the doctors, of the real cause of her malady. The illness and death of Charlotte Bloomfield indicates how spiritual physic

[28] BA, James Conolly, 'Memoir of Benjamin first Lord Bloomfield', n.d.
[29] J. Bailey, 'A Very Sensible Man: Imagining Fatherhood in England, c.1750–1830', *History* 95 (2010), 267–92; L. Smith, 'The Relative Duties of a Man: Domestic Medicine in England and France c.1685–1740', *JFH* 31 (2006), 237–56; Newton, *Sick Child*, 93.
[30] Newton, *Sick Child*, stresses this continuity. I am very grateful to Hannah Newton for her comments on this essay.

coexisted with medical treatment much longer than some like Ian Mortimer have argued.[31] Lord Bloomfield's subsequent evangelizing in Ireland and at Woolwich, in gratitude for the short life of his 'angelic child', was in part the fruit of this family tragedy. This story illustrates the strength of the evangelical household in Regency England, as a community which bore its own burdens and was able to celebrate the power of faith over mortality when a loved child faced terminal illness.

University of London

---

[31] I. Mortimer, *The Dying and the Doctors: The Medical Revolution in Seventeenth-Century England* (Woodbridge, 2009), 2, 40–1; idem, '"The Triumph of the Doctors": Medical Assistance to the Dying, *c.*1570–1720', *TRHS* 6th ser. 15 (2005), 97–116, at 114.

THE OXFORD MOVEMENT, MARRIAGE AND DOMESTIC LIFE: JOHN KEBLE, ISAAC WILLIAMS AND EDWARD KING

by JOHN BONEHAM

While a number of studies have highlighted the theological and social importance of the household in nineteenth-century Protestant Britain,[1] the significance of domestic life for the leaders of the Oxford, or Tractarian, Movement remains almost completely unexplored. In a sense this is unsurprising, since the movement, which began in the 1830s, emphasized the importance of recalling the Church of England to its pre-Reformation heritage and consequently tended to stress the spiritual value of celibacy and asceticism.[2] Whilst B. W. Young has highlighted the importance of celibacy for John Henry Newman, the movement's main figurehead until his conversion to Roman Catholicism in 1845,[3] and other works have reflected upon the Tractarian emphasis on celibacy and tried to explain its origins,[4] historians of the Oxford Movement have paid very little attention to the Tractarian attitude towards marriage and domestic life.

This essay will argue that the high view of celibacy held by many leaders of the Oxford Movement was tempered by a more positive view of domestic life reflected in the writings of two influential Tractarians who were also married men. John Keble (1792–1866), whose Assize Sermon of 1833 is often seen as marking the begin-

---

[1] E. Jay, *The Religion of the Heart: Anglican Evangelicalism and the Nineteenth-Century Novel* (Oxford, 1979), 131–48; L. Davidoff and C. Hall, *Family Fortunes: Men and Women of the English Middle Class* (London, 1987), 321–9, 357–64; F. Knight, '"Male and Female He Created them": Men, Women and the Question of Gender', in J. Wolffe, ed., *Religion in Victorian Britain*: 5, *Culture and Empire* (Manchester, 1997), 24–57, at 27; A. Stott, *Wilberforce: Family and Friends* (Oxford, 2012), 2–4.

[2] Y. Brilioth, *The Anglican Revival: Studies in the Oxford Movement* (London, 1925), 246–7; for a general introduction to the Oxford Movement, see K. Hylson-Smith, *High Churchmanship in the Church of England* (Edinburgh, 1993), 123–65.

[3] B. W. Young, 'The Anglican Origins of Newman's Celibacy', *ChH* 65 (1996), 15–27.

[4] G. Faber, *Oxford Apostles: A Character Study of the Oxford Movement,* 2nd edn (repr. London, 2008), 215–32; F. M. Turner, *John Henry Newman: The Challenge to Evangelical Religion* (New Haven, CT, 2002), 425–36.

ning of the Oxford Movement, held the University of Oxford's chair of poetry between 1831 and 1841, and served as vicar of Hursley, near Winchester, from 1836. Isaac Williams (1802–65) was heavily influenced by Keble and served as Newman's curate at St Mary's, Oxford, during the 1830s, as well as writing much poetry for the movement.[5] Another significant figure is Edward King (1829–1910), who had come under the influence of Tractarianism as a student at Oriel College in the 1840s and was appointed bishop of Lincoln in 1885. Although a celibate, King emphasized the value of marriage and family life in his writings, which illustrate how a positive view of domestic life was upheld within the movement into the latter half of the nineteenth century.[6]

The close connection between Tractarianism and celibacy was reflected in *The Oxford Movement: Twelve Years, 1833–1845*, R. W. Church's classic account of the movement. According to Church, the Roman Catholic discipline of clerical celibacy was something which attracted many Tractarians as they sought a greater degree of self-denial and asceticism.[7] To fail to live up to this ideal, in their view, was not so much a positive recognition of the value of Christian marriage as a symptom of an 'unmanly preference for English home life, [and] of insensibility to the generous devotion and purity of the saints'.[8] For many of the Tractarians, domestic life and celibacy were to be pitted against each other rather than being seen as complementary vocations. Newman, for example, claimed that marriage was synonymous with worldliness, writing: 'I could not take that interest in this world which marriage requires. I am too disgusted with this world'.[9] Both Newman and his fellow Tractarian Richard Hurrell Froude had a strong dislike for clergymen choosing to marry, and when John Keble married in 1835 Newman saw Keble's silence about his plans as evidence that he recognized marriage as 'a very second-rate business'.[10] Such an emphasis on celibacy represented a clear rejection of the Protestant

5 *ODNB, s.nn.* 'Keble, John (1792–1866)', 'Williams, Isaac (1802–1865)'.
6 *ODNB, s.n.* 'King, Edward (1829–1910)'.
7 R. W. Church, *The Oxford Movement: Twelve Years, 1833–1845* (London, 1891), 294.
8 Ibid. 320–1.
9 *John Henry Newman: Autobiographical Writings*, ed. H. Tristram (London, 1957), 137.
10 *The Letters and Diaries of John Henry Newman*, 5, ed. T. Gornall (Oxford, 1981), 154.

– particularly evangelical – ethos of nineteenth-century Britain, and became one of the main targets for criticism by the movement's opponents.[11]

If many of the Tractarians tended to play down the significance of home life, the little that is known about the domestic experience of John Keble, Isaac Williams and Edward King suggests that the household could play an important role in supporting the Christian ministry. Keble married Charlotte Clarke in 1835, shortly after he was appointed vicar of Hursley, and he lived at the vicarage with his wife and his invalid sister Elizabeth until the latter's death in 1860. His deep devotion to both women was reflected by the fact that he frequently referred to them as being his 'two wives'.[12] Williams married Caroline Champerowne in 1842, after having spent ten years in residence at Trinity College, Oxford, where he had held a fellowship and served as college tutor. Following his marriage Williams left Oxford and served as a perpetual curate to Thomas Keble, John's brother, at Bisley, Gloucestershire, before moving to Stinchcombe in 1848 to serve as curate to his brother-in-law Sir George Prevost. While Keble and his wife remained childless, Isaac and Caroline Williams became the parents of seven children.[13]

Both Charlotte Keble and Caroline Champerowne seem to have shared a concern for domestic affairs which was common among Victorian women.[14] For example, when John Keble was arranging for a new curate to assist him at Hursley, Mrs Keble arranged for a van to move the family's furniture, and she also recommended a number of tradesmen who would be able to assist them in their new home.[15] Following the Williams's marriage it was Caroline Williams who decided which house they ought to live in at Bisley.[16] However, each woman was to make a positive contribution to her husband's ministry which went beyond a

---

[11] Turner, *Newman*, 435; R. Chapman, *Faith and Revolt: Studies in the Literary Influence of the Oxford Movement* (London, 1970), 104–7.

[12] *ODNB*, *s.n.* 'Keble'.

[13] *ODNB*, *s.n.* 'Williams'.

[14] Cf. Knight, '"Male and Female he created them"', 25–31; J. A. James, *Female Piety, or the Young Woman's Friend and Guide through Life to Immortality* (London, 1852), 58.

[15] London, LPL, MS 4923, fols 6–9, J. Keble to C. Anderson, 7 December 1863, Epiphany 1864 (with permission of the Trustees of Lambeth Palace Library).

[16] O. W. Jones, *Isaac Williams and his Circle* (London, 1971), 72–3.

concern for the domestic sphere. Charlotte Keble helped to teach the village lads at Hursley, and she also wrote to her sister-in-law about the progress of the Oxford Movement and the introduction of the daily service at Hursley.[17] Although her frequent ill-health meant that the Kebles often had to be absent from the parish,[18] John Keble's friend Sir John Taylor Coleridge wrote that Charlotte was her husband's 'very helpful and affectionate fellow-worker, comforter and support to the end of his days'.[19]

Caroline Williams assisted her husband by using her artistic talent to provide illustrations for some of his publications.[20] A number of letters from Isaac and Caroline Williams to their eldest son John Edward also shed some light on the nature of the family's domestic life. It is clear from this correspondence that they were in close contact with family and friends who were involved in the Tractarian cause, including the clergyman and family friend James Davies, Isaac's brother-in-law Sir George Prevost, and his brother Matthew Davies Williams.[21] The letters from Isaac Williams to his son recommend a disciplined lifestyle involving early rising and careful study for examinations.[22] Caroline Williams's letters demonstrate that family prayers played an important role in the Williams household,[23] and suggest that she was a woman with a deep grasp of spiritual matters. For example, in her letters to her son she quotes James Davies and discusses with some fervour the importance of baptismal regeneration and of repentance in the Christian life.[24] All this suggests that the Williams home was centred on prayer, discipline and discussion of spiritual matters, and sought to keep in close contact with family and friends. Such a household must have played an important role in supporting Isaac Williams's parish ministry as well as his work of writing and publishing poetry, biblical commentaries and sermons in support of the Tractarian cause.

---

[17] G. Battiscombe, *John Keble: A Study in Limitations* (London, 1963), 178; J. T. Coleridge, *A Memoir of the Rev. John Keble, vol. 1* (Oxford and London, 1869), 242–4.

[18] MS 4923, fol. 4, J. Keble to C. Anderson, 9 November 1863.

[19] Coleridge, *John Keble*, 1: 245.

[20] LPL, MS 4473, fol. 151, W. J. Copeland to I. Williams, 5 June 1845.

[21] LPL, MS 4476, fols 141–2, 153, I. Williams to J. E. Williams, both n.d.

[22] Ibid., fols 137, 149, I. Williams to J. E. Williams, n.d.

[23] Ibid., fol. 140, C. Williams to J. E. Williams, n.d.

[24] Ibid., fols 140, 144, C. Williams to J. E. Williams, n.d.

Edward King's experience of domestic life as a celibate included his involvement with the community life of Cuddesdon theological college, where he served first as chaplain and later as principal while residing at Cuddesdon vicarage,[25] as well as his life in the college environment of Christ Church following his appointment to the chair of Pastoral Theology at Oxford.[26] On becoming bishop of Lincoln in 1885, King decided against living with his widowed sister and her children at the new bishop's palace at Riseholme, some three miles outside Lincoln, in favour of residing alone at the old bishop's palace within the city, which was specially renovated for this purpose.[27] The nature of King's domestic life appears to have enabled him to combine availability to his people with a life of regular prayer and devotion. His home included a private chapel where he celebrated the eucharist daily, inducted clergy to benefices and performed ordinations and confirmations,[28] while his study provided a place where he could write letters to correspondents, meet those who sought his assistance and have recourse to his voluminous collection of theological books.[29] Far from leading a solitary existence, King's daily routine involved reciting the morning office with his chaplain and presiding over prayers for his household, and those who visited their bishop to seek his advice were often invited to dine with him at the episcopal palace.[30] This suggests that for King a celibate existence did not imply a rejection of the value of home life. Ultimately it involved using the domestic sphere as a means of serving the clergy and people of his diocese rather than seeing it as a private domain which provided an escape from the duties of his vocation.

Given the positive experience of domestic life shared by Keble, Williams and King it is not surprising that, whilst they each upheld the spiritual importance of the celibate state,[31] their writings also reflected a high view of Christian marriage. For example, King

---

[25] J. A. Newton, *Search for a Saint: Edward King* (London, 1977), 41–2.

[26] B. W. Randolph and J. W. Townroe, *The Mind and Work of Bishop King* (London, 1918), 64.

[27] Newton, *Search for a Saint*, 83–4.

[28] Randolph and Townroe, *Bishop King*, 132–5.

[29] Ibid. 135–44.

[30] Ibid. 144–9.

[31] *Letters of Spiritual Counsel and Guidance, by the late Rev. J. Keble*, ed. R. F. Wilson (Oxford and London, 1875), 233–4; I. Williams, *The Apocalypse* (London, 1852), 256–7; *Spiritual Letters of Edward King*, ed. B. W. Randolph (London, 1910), 109.

described matrimony as one of the 'greatest mysteries' given by God to humankind on earth. It was 'one of God's greatest gifts, one of the closest symbols of what He is, and of the union between Himself and us'.[32] While many Tractarians saw celibacy as a supreme act of self-denial, King argued that married life could equally be a means of overcoming selfishness through self-sacrifice and thus growing in Christian holiness.[33]

The poem on matrimony from Keble's *The Christian Year*, a volume of poems on each of the Sundays, feasts and rites of passage included in the Book of Common Prayer, presents marriage as a sacred vocation which bestows spiritual as well as temporal gifts. This undermines any attempt to suggest that marriage relates merely to the natural, physical order and has no connection with the spiritual life, as Newman, writing as a Roman Catholic but almost certainly reflecting his thinking as an Anglican, was to claim in his novel *Loss and Gain*.[34] For Keble, addressing a newly-wed couple in his poem,

> All blessings of the breast and womb,
> Of Heaven and earth beneath,
> Of converse high, and sacred home,
> Are yours, in life and death.[35]

This suggests that the joy associated with Christian marriage is not just restricted to natural life but that it also has a clear supernatural focus and enables human beings to experience the blessings of heaven upon earth.

Another poem by Isaac Williams, on the subject of 'Christian Reserve', a principle which was central to Tractarian theology, also emphasizes the spiritual value of human love. Williams defined 'reserve' in two lengthy tracts as a principle which sought to govern the dissemination of religious truth in a refined and measured way and stressed the importance of moral preparation for receiving religious teaching.[36] While Williams's tracts dealt with reserve in relation to theological principles, his poem relates it

---

[32] *Spiritual Letters*, ed. Randolph, 48.
[33] Ibid.
[34] J. H. Newman, *Loss and Gain* (London, 1848), 176–7.
[35] J. Keble, *The Christian Year* (London, 1887 edn), 178.
[36] I. Williams, *Tract 80*, 'On Reserve in Communicating Religious Knowledge', in *Tracts for the Times*, 4 (London, 1838), 3.

directly to the emotions and reflects on its significance for human love. He therefore claims that:

> Things which abide nearest the fountain spring
> Of our affections cannot bear the light
> Of common day, but shrink at ruder sight,
> As so decay. Love is a Heav'n-born thing,
> To live on earth it needs home-cherishing,
> Secret and shade.[37]

While it has been claimed that there was a direct connection in Tractarian theology between the principle of reserve and celibacy,[38] this poem shows that, for Williams at least, the principle was also inextricably linked to human love. In his view, love was not to be seen as something which necessarily detracted from the spiritual life but rather as a heavenly gift full of spiritual significance.

Williams's sermons further develop this theme by speaking about marriage in highly sacramental terms. Marriage is not just a profound symbol of the relationship between Christ and his Church but, through matrimony, the love and fidelity of a man and a woman becomes a means by which they and others experience the love of Christ, not just as a theological concept, but through the concrete reality of everyday living.[39] According to Williams, the human love and fidelity expressed in marriage are in no way inimical to the spiritual life, as those who wished to promote the ideal of celibacy might have wished to imply. Rather, one leads to the other so that human love, which finds its fulfilment in marriage, helps the Christian to grow in love and obedience for God.[40]

Although the writings of Williams and King did not argue that married clergy were better placed deal with pastoral situations than their celibate counterparts, they do reflect a high view of the role of the clergyman's wife. For example, they suggested that a priest's wife had a special vocation to support her husband in his ministry and to attend to domestic duties with an attitude of prayer and

---

[37] I. Williams, *Thoughts in Past Years* (London, 1848 edn), 50.

[38] D. Dau, 'Perfect Chastity: Celibacy and Virgin Marriage in Tractarian Poetry', *Victorian Poetry* 44 (2006), 77–92, at 77–83.

[39] I. Williams, *Female Characters of Holy Scripture* (London, 1870), 18–19.

[40] Ibid. 19.

devotion which sanctified the ordinary duties of daily life.[41] This point was highlighted in a series of addresses delivered by Edward King in October 1883, as Regius Professor of Pastoral Theology at the University of Oxford, to a retreat for the wives of clergy.[42] In these addresses King claimed that, through the pious fulfilment of the ordinary duties of home life, the clergyman's wife had the 'responsibility of showing forth a pattern for households, the lifting up of all … into a higher life' by providing an example of a good Christian marriage.[43] While the view of Williams and King of the vocation of the priest's wife is very much of its time in its emphasis on a woman's duty to support her husband by accepting responsibility for domestic affairs, the fact that they recognized that a woman could make a contribution to her husband's ministry confirms that they valued clerical marriage in a way which was not typical of many of the Oxford Movement's adherents.[44]

The emphasis on the spiritual significance of marriage reflected in the writings of Keble, Williams and King went hand in hand with an understanding of the importance of the home as a place where the faith could be taught and handed on. Each of these men had been brought up in a Christian environment where they learned the faith from their parents.[45] Indeed, Williams felt that his experience at public school did much to undermine the religious principles which he had learned at home.[46] According to King's earliest biographers, his early family life had a profound influence on him and led him in later years to claim that '[o]ur English homes may be said to be the Castles of England, and family religion the keep of the Castle'.[47] This clearly suggests that, although King was to remain unmarried, his childhood experience of domestic life was able to impress upon him the value of the household in helping to pass on the Christian faith within the family, something which

---

[41] Ibid. 205; E. King, *Home Life: Being Addresses given at a Retreat for the Wives of Clergy* (London, 1912), 16–17.

[42] King, *Home Life*, v.

[43] Ibid. 16–17.

[44] J. S. Reed, *Glorious Battle: The Cultural Politics of Victorian Anglo-Catholicism* (Nashville, TN, 1996), 220, quoting J. G. Lockhart, *Charles Lindley, Viscount Halifax*, 2 vols (London, 1935), 1: 255.

[45] Battiscombe, *John Keble*, 7–11; Newton, *Search for a Saint*, 20; Jones, *Isaac Williams*, 8.

[46] LPL, MS 4477, fol. 6, unpublished manuscript of Isaac Williams's autobiography.

[47] Randolph and Townroe, *Bishop King*, 21.

was also reflected in his sermons.[48] Isaac Williams's *Hymns on the Catechism* (1853), which was written specifically for the young, and his *Sacred Verses* (1845), in which illustrations accompanied poems on range of sacred themes,[49] can be seen as providing valuable tools which would have helped parents teach the faith to their children within the household.

Apart from providing a context in which children could learn the faith from their parents, the home was also a place where Christians could grow in sanctity through performing faithfully the duties of daily life. This point was highlighted in Keble's *Christian Year*, where he claimed:

> Around each pure domestic shrine
> Bright flowers of Eden bloom and twine,
> Our hearths are altars all ...[50]

Keble's reference to the 'domestic shrine' highlights the belief that the daily activities of home life ought to be inseparable from the life of prayer and devotion. Far from impeding the spiritual life, the home provides an 'altar' on which the ordinary events of daily living can be offered, a place in which the Christian can grow in holiness.

The spiritual significance of the home was also reflected in King's writings. A letter he wrote to a student as principal at Cuddesdon pointed out that 'in spite of position, honour, money, there is something in the memory of home which speaks of a higher pleasure than those things can give us. It tells us, I think, of the true joy in the eternal home, to which ... we are one by one being taken.'[51] For King, the home and family life did not present obstacles to the pursuit of holiness, but were positive gifts which foreshadowed the true home of heaven.

This point was also emphasized in a sermon which Bishop King preached to mark the seven hundredth anniversary of the death of St Hugh of Lincoln. King highlighted the fact that the saint had always shown a great devotion to his father and had

---

[48] *Sermons and Addresses by Edward King*, ed. B. W. Randolph (London, 1911), 71–3.

[49] I. Williams, *Hymns on the Catechism* (London, 1843), 3; idem, *Sacred Verses, with Pictures* (London, 1857 edn).

[50] Keble, *Christian Year*, 79.

[51] *Spiritual Letters*, ed. Randolph, 17.

'none of that spirit of Corban which would make the formal duties of religion an excuse for neglecting the natural duties of home ties'.[52] Such filial duty was clearly very important to King, who had taken his elderly mother to live with him from 1863 until her death in 1883, and had thus combined his duty as a son with his pastoral and academic responsibilities at Cuddesdon and Christ Church.[53] Although King recognized that, especially during times of religious revival, it was possible for these domestic and religious responsibilities to conflict with each other, he argued that the two should not be seen as being mutually exclusive. Such an attitude created a false dichotomy, he thought, since the duties to God and to one's family found fulfilment in each other. This was reflected in his *Meditations on the Last Seven Words of our Lord Jesus Christ*, where he pointed out that Christ's care for his mother's spiritual and material welfare as he was dying on the cross made it clear that following one's vocation honestly ought always to be combined with love and respect for one's parents, family and domestic responsibilities:

> Upon the ladder of the Cross, it might have seemed to some, that [Christ] was manifesting an ascetic spirit, crushing out the natural affection, and forgetful of home love. Not so; it was then that He turned to His Mother, and said, 'Behold thy son' … He made provision for His Mother, for her comfort while she lived on earth. It was not a spiritual provision so much as an earthly which was contained in the words, 'Behold thy son'.[54]

While the Oxford Movement may generally have lacked the strong emphasis on domestic life which was such an important aspect of the outlook of nineteenth-century Protestant Britain, this theme was not totally neglected. Although many adherents of the movement stressed the importance of the dedicated single life as a means of growing closer to God, the value of marriage and family life as a way of pursuing personal sanctity was also highlighted by Keble, Williams and King. There is evidence to suggest that

---

[52] Newton, *Search for a Saint*, 16, quoting Lincolnshire Archives, Larken Papers IV/I, fols 3–21.

[53] Newton, *Search for a Saint*, 41–2; Randolph and Townroe, *Bishop King*, 64.

[54] *Spiritual Letters*, ed. Randolph, 33–4.

what underlay these varying approaches was a different understanding of the relationship between nature and grace. Barbara
Charlesworth Gelpi, for example, has reflected upon the visit of
Hurrell Froude and John Keble to Tintern Abbey, Monmouthshire,
in July 1825, and points out that, while Froude's response to the
visit reflected his admiration for a monastic existence which would
involve withdrawal from the world, Keble's reaction suggested that
marriage and family life were gifts which could aid one's growth
in holiness and grace.[55]

Gelpi's distinction between Keble's emphasis on recognizing the
presence of God as mediated through human life and creation and
Froude's desire for a transcendent experience of God involving
rejection of the joys and comforts of earthly life is also reflected
in Tractarian poetry. Whilst the use of the imagery of nature in
the poetry of Keble and Williams to reflect on theological themes
upholds a highly sacramental view of the created world as the
means by which divine grace is mediated through the physical
order,[56] the poetry of Froude and Newman contains much less
reference to nature and is much more polemic and didactic in
approach.[57] One of Froude's poems presents the pursuit of sanctity
as a struggle against oneself which requires mortification through
fasting, sackcloth and prayer,[58] and suggests that human nature is
to be seen as something to be overcome in the pursuit of grace
rather than the means of achieving it. If Froude's approach helps to
explain why some Tractarians tended to emphasize the superiority
of celibacy over marriage, it seems likely that the more positive
view of home life expressed in the writings of Keble and Williams
was closely connected with their sacramental view of the created
world as a means of experiencing God's presence and receiving his
grace, which was itself linked to the importance of natural imagery
in their poetry. Since the world was created by God, ordinary

[55] B. C. Gelpi, 'John Keble and Hurrell Froude in Pastoral Dialogue', *Victorian
Poetry* 44 (2006), 7–24, at 11–18.

[56] J. Boneham, 'Reserve and Physical Imagery in the Tractarian Poetry of Isaac
Williams', in Peter Clarke and Charlotte Methuen, eds, *The Church and Literature*, SCH
48 (Woodbridge, 2012), 246–58, at 250–2; A. Härdelin, *The Tractarian Understanding of
the Eucharist* (Uppsala, 1965), 60–5.

[57] G. B. Tennyson, *Victorian Devotional Poetry: The Tractarian Mode* (London, 1981),
114–8, 132–3.

[58] R. H. Froude, poem XXXVI, in J. H. Newman, ed., *Lyra Apostolica* (Derby, 1843
edn), 41.

life had just as much value for the pursuit of personal sanctity as withdrawal from it. This aspect of Tractarian theology offers an interesting alternative to the emphasis on celibacy and asceticism which was upheld by many adherents of the Oxford Movement; it still needs to be explored in greater depth if the movement's approach to marriage and domestic life is to be more completely understood.

Aberystwyth University

ISLAM AT HOME: RELIGION, PIETY AND PRIVATE SPACE IN MUSLIM INDIA AND VICTORIAN BRITAIN, c.1850–1905[*]

by JUSTIN JONES

Allegiance is due, under God, to the head of the family from his dependents, as to a king; and though I confess with shame that I have been a weak and faithless ruler hitherto, the time has come for me to exert my authority in removing the abuses which I have allowed to creep into my jurisdiction ... I have been close to death, and have realised that sooner or later I must give account to God not only for myself but for my family.[1]

In a bleak and diseased Delhi, sometime after the wanton British decimation of the city in the wake of the 1857 rebellion, a Muslim nobleman by the name of Nasuh succumbs to the city's recent cholera epidemic. After Nasuh falls unconscious, his father, who had recently died in the same outbreak, appears to him in a dream. He tells his son that a day of reckoning awaits, and that as a father it is Nasuh's duty to inculcate piety in his home. Surviving his illness, Nasuh sets about correcting the excesses of the various members of his family. These include his eldest daughter, who had such foolish habits as playing all night at cards, reading romances and singing idle songs; and his three sons, who were neglectful of their religious duties, read unsuitable poetry, flew kites and kept company with scandalous friends. Despite these blemishes in their household lives, Nasuh is able to persuade some members of his family of the rightness of his vision, turning his children into (respectively) a God-fearing wife and mother, and upstanding gentlemen with right manners and good government professions. All are thus rewarded both in this world and the hereafter.

The setting of a post-Mutiny and cholera-infested Delhi would have been all too familiar to any of the city's former Muslim

[*] Thanks to David Bebbington, Katherine Schofield and Alexandra Walsham for their advice on aspects of this essay, and to the British Academy for research support.

[1] Nasuh, in a letter to his son Kulleem, in Nazir Ahmad, *The Repentance of Nussooh (Taubat-al-Nasuh)* intro. Frances Pritchett (Delhi, 2004; first publ. 1874), 47.

nobility (*shurafa*), a beleaguered community following the collapse of Mughal rule. But the story itself is fiction, forming the centre-piece of the novel *Taubat-i-Nasuh* ('The Repentance of Nasuh'), written in 1874 by Nazir Ahmad, a Muslim colonial administrator based in Delhi. Frequently cited as significant in the development of the novel genre in Urdu, the work is striking for its develop-ment of a form of moralizing fiction set almost entirely in the domestic sphere, taking place in the male and female quarters (respectively *mardana* and *zenana*) of a noble Muslim household. Departing from the lyrical, rather quixotic tones of the hitherto dominant Perso-Urdu literary traditions of the so-called 'Delhi school' associated with figures such as Ghalib,[2] this tale of the moral renovation of a Muslim household looks much more like a kind of Victorian morality tale: austere, clinical and bathed in the imperative to cultivate proper manners and lifestyle.

Focusing upon the second half of the nineteenth century, a tumul-tuous period that saw both the consolidation of formal British rule and the disenfranchisement of much of the pre-colonial Muslim nobility, this essay explores various efforts to exact reforms upon the conduct of the Muslim household in north India. It examines how the Muslim household became a heavily contested space, subject to scrutiny and manipulation both externally, from the colonial state, and internally, from Muslim intellectuals themselves. It suggests that the colonial state and Muslim reformists concomitantly came to see the domestic sphere as a kind of refuge for Islamic values and morals at a time when Islam had been excluded from the political sphere, and hence made parallel, often complementary and sometimes contradic-tory, efforts to shape its workings and behaviours. As a result of these attentions, the Muslim household found itself thrust into the centre of public discussion.

My focus is the Muslim elite of north India, in particular that clustered in Delhi and the smaller towns of the adjacent region of the North-Western Provinces. Many among the Muslim gentry in these centres had worked in service of the Mughal emperors and other Muslim dynasties, and so felt the consolidation of British imperialism after 1858 acutely. Through the second half of the

---

[2]   For information on the cultural world of pre-1857 Delhi, which included such poetic scions as Mirza Ghalib (1797–1869), see Percival Spear, *Twilight of the Mughals: Studies in Late Mughal Delhi* (Delhi, 1991).

nineteenth century and beyond they found themselves at the heart of a wider discourse seeking an alternative forum for perpetuating Islam: one less reliant upon the advantage of Muslim political power and more dependent upon the household as the arena in which religion could be truly protected and nurtured.

This essay begins by exploring the notion of the 'private' domain as it developed in colonial India. It then turns, first, to new genres of instructive writing which carried a vision of moral perfection centred on the household and, second, to the vision of the role of Muslim women within these discussions of domesticity. Never before, it argues, had the realm of household been seen as so pivotal to the destiny of South Asian Muslim society.

INVERTING ISLAM: RELIGION AND THE CONSTRUCTION OF PRIVATE SPACE IN COLONIAL INDIA

The division of the world into the allegedly separate domains of 'public/political/male' and 'private/domestic/female' had long-established origins in European thought, but it is a distinction that perhaps took on particular significance in Victorian Britain. A raft of literature, largely drawing on the work of Catherine Hall and Leonore Davidoff, has established how an evolving notion of middle-class identity in early and mid-nineteenth-century England was constructed around ideas of public and private space. Of these, the latter – a largely domestic and female realm – was dissociated from public and professional life and associated with the raising of children and cultivation of stringent family values. It was, moreover, a vision profoundly tied to the growth of evangelical Protestantism in Britain, which established the clear separation of public and private, and of corresponding gender roles, as sacrosanct to the notion of a moral society.[3]

However, such a categorization of these so-called 'separate spheres' has been successfully debunked as a starting point for investigating the household in pre-colonial India. Not only did the Indo-Islamic idea of household differ greatly from its mean-

---

[3] For a study of the consolidation of this idea of 'separate spheres', and its close interactions with changing attitudes on questions of gender and religion, see Leonore Davidoff and Catherine Hall, *Family Fortunes: Men and Women of the English Middle Class, 1780–1850* (London, 1987), esp. 149–92.

ings in Europe but, as Ruby Lal points out, such public/private dichotomies bore little meaning in a Mughal context in which such lines were much less clearly demarcated.[4] The fact that such ideas of separate spheres would, over the course of the nineteenth century, come to have self-referential meaning for Indian reformists within their own societies was a product of Indian interactions with the ideas and institutions of nineteenth-century colonialism.

As has been convincingly argued in much literature on nineteenth-century European 'Orientalism', the Muslim household represented a place of mystery, and considerable interest, to European minds. By the 1830s and 1840s a fascination with the appearances and routines of the Indian household was evident among the growing number of British visitors and residents in the subcontinent, as well as observers back home. Travellers sought invitations to visit the private residences of noble families, documenting their experiences in evocative language bordering on the fantastical.[5] Ethnographic studies relayed in great detail the rituals and routines of daily life and special days in Indian Muslim households.[6] As elsewhere, European fascination focused particularly on the *zenana*, the traditionally segregated women's quarters of Muslim (and many Hindu) homes. At once depicted from imagination by Orientalist artists like John Frederick Lewis, and deliberately targeted by evangelical groups like the Baptist Missionary Society as a means of establishing footholds within Indian Muslim communities,[7] the

---

[4] Ruby Lal, *Domesticity and Power in the Early Mughal World* (Cambridge, 2004), 3–5. Lal's work discusses how such allegedly 'domestic' arenas as the *haram* (the female quarters of the Mughal court) took leading roles in defining the social and political affairs of the Mughal state, hence 'question[ing] the very notion of a separate domestic sphere, or of distinct public and private domains': ibid. 5.

[5] Such as the diarist Fanny Eden, recounting a staged *nautch* (private dance) in the home of the Raja of Ramnagar in 1837/8: 'the whole scene looked like the Arabian nights put to life': *Tigers, Durbars and Kings: Fanny Eden's Indian Journals*, ed. Janet Dunbar (London, 1989), 81.

[6] The most famous example is perhaps Mrs Meer Hasan Ali, *Observations on the Mussulmauns of India* (Karachi, 1978; first publ. 1832). This work, written by a British woman who married a Muslim nobleman and resided in Lucknow, was distinctive for the author's access to both male and female quarters of Muslim homes. Beyond India, a comparably ethnographically rich and highly influential work from the same decade, again profoundly focused upon the routines of household life as a means of studying Muslim society, is Edward William Lane, *The Manners and Customs of the Modern Egyptians* (London, 1836).

[7] Brian Stanley, *The History of the Baptist Missionary Society, 1792–1992* (Edinburgh, 1992), 228–32.

zenana became something of an obsession for European observers, a perceived key article of Islamic domestic culture.

What exactly explains the scrutiny projected by European observers towards what scholars have often termed the 'intimate arenas' of Muslim societies? Their interest in Muslim home lives may link to the codes of ritual and spatial purity held by many *sharif* (noble) Muslim households, which in India and elsewhere sometimes curbed the spaces in which social interaction with Europeans could occur, and hence made the home a subject of voyeuristic interest. Alternatively, the obsession with a largely imagined Muslim private sphere may simply speak to circulating European stereotypes of the 'despotic' nature of the Muslim sultans and courtiers of the Orient, for which alleged domestic opulence and excess was vital evidence. In particular, the interest in the *zenana* could be related to the highly sensual, sexualized under-standing of Muslim societies which had (through public famili-arity with works such as *One Thousand and One Nights* from the early 1700s onwards) gained currency as a mysterious, sumptuous and somewhat titillating counterpart to the more stringent moral codes of nineteenth-century Britain.

However, as well as frivolous curiosity, there may have been additional reasons for interest in the Muslim household at admin-istrative and governmental levels. With the 'public arenas' (as they are often called) of print and civic associationism subject to heavy surveillance and censorship by the British Raj,[8] it was these 'private' spaces of household and kinship network that became of most concern to a colonial regime which, after the 1857 Rebel-lion, sustained worries about the loyalty and quietism – or lack of them – of its Muslim subjects. One needs only to look at the ire directed at Muslim 'households' (a term used to refer to the lineages of landlords and soldier-clans often blamed for the Rebel-lion), or the various searches conducted upon the houses of alleged Muslim conspirators in the 1860s,[9] to understand how the colonial state projected its fears of so-called 'Muslim fanaticism' onto the

---

[8]   C. A. Bayly, *Empire and Information: Intelligence Gathering and Social Communication in India, 1780–1870* (Cambridge, 1996), 338–64.

[9]   In the 1860s, the evidence used to convict Muslim 'conspirators' in colonial courts was often obtained from raids on noble Muslim households: see, for example, Muin-ud-Din and Ahmad Khan, eds, *Selections from Bengal Government Records on Wahhabi Trials* (Dacca, 1961; first publ. 1863–5), 85–6.

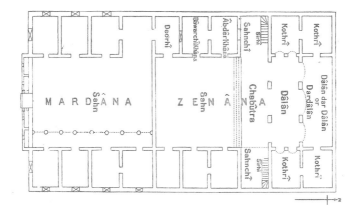

Fig. 1: A sketch illustrating 'the arrangement of native houses of the better sort in the towns of the North-Western Provinces' by M. Kempson (Director of Public Instruction, N.W.P., 1862–78). He emphasizes particularly the *mardana-zenana* (male and female quarters) distinction, adding that the latter is designed 'so that it is impossible for the inmates to be overlooked' from adjacent buildings: M. Kempson, ed., *Taubatu-n-Nasuh*, 2nd edn (London, 1886), 320–1.

domain of the home. The Muslim household became a source of political concern as well as cultural fascination.

The intensity of interest in the household as a means of understanding Islamic society may also denote a general and more fundamental tendency within nineteenth-century British mappings of the separate spheres: namely, the equation of the 'public/political' and 'private/domestic' spheres with, respectively, the realms of secularity and religiosity. These categorizations, drawn from assumptions about the place of religion in society circulating back home,[10] informed the classification and administration of British India. Despite frequent claims to 'non-interference' in matters of religion after 1857,[11] historians have long agreed that British governmental decisions over the course of the nineteenth century

[10] A whole ream of literature has examined what these categories meant in the context of Victorian England: the idealization of a society secularized in its laws, politics and attitudes to worldly progress, but devout and God-fearing in its private lives and cultural spaces: e.g. Jonathan Parry, 'The Disciplining of the Religious Conscience in Nineteenth-Century British Politics', in I. Katznelson and G. Stedman-Jones, eds, *Religion and the Political Imagination* (Cambridge, 2010), 214–34.

[11] Most famously, Queen Victoria's 'Proclamation on Religious Neutrality' (1858).

tended to reflect the pervasive influence of such categories when they encountered matters of 'religious' significance. So, in public and political life, the British often found themselves actively curtailing markers of Islam derived from the Mughal legacy: importing secular languages of politics and development and abolishing Mughal remnants of Islamic law from newly remodelled civil and criminal codes. However, the colonial state's interventions in the personal and family lives of its subjects often carried the assumption that they should be more, not less, committed to the tenets of their religion in private. The classic example was the introduction of what were called 'religious personal laws', with colonial courts adjudicating legal questions pertaining to family affairs like marriage, divorce or inheritance according to amended versions of Hindu, Islamic and other religious laws, drawn from the classical texts of these traditions. Particularly from the 1860s, this process subjected Indians of all religious confessions to generally more rigid, textual and standardized codes of religious family law than anything that had existed in pre-colonial legal adjudication.[12] Hence, while adopting a secular rhetoric of progress deliberately designed to contrast with the perceived dominance of religion in Indian society, the colonial state rather ironically seemed to demand that its subjects adhere in their private lives to the strictures of their faith in ways that had not hitherto been required.

Furthermore, even at the lower levels of observation and administrative practice, British personnel seemed to carry a particular understanding of what religion was, and made value-judgements that legitimized religion as a largely 'private' matter. So, in observations on Indian Muslims, forms of highly visible or 'public' religion were often framed in derogatory or suspicious nomenclatures. Extravagant ceremonials like weddings were frowned upon as indulgences; Sufi rites such as attendance at saints' shrines were dismissed as 'superstitious', 'cultish' or 'pagan';[13] and highly

---

[12] On the British implementation of a form of Islamic law on private/family rather than civil/criminal matters, see Scott Alan Kugle, 'Framed, Blamed and Renamed: The Recasting of Islamic Jurisprudence in Colonial South Asia', *Modern Asian Studies* 35 (2001), 257–313. For the equivalent application of Hindu personal laws, see J. Duncan Derrett, 'The Administration of Hindu Law by the British', *Comparative Studies in Society and History* 4 (1961), 10–52.

[13] These terms are all used to describe such practices in Garcin de Tassy, *Mémoire sur quelques particularités de la religion musulmane en Inde*, 2nd edn (Paris, 1869).

visible or demonstrative public occasions, like Friday prayers or the Muharram festival, were seen as potentially subversive events that often warranted police supervision at sensitive political moments.[14] However, the cultivation of moral perfection in private lives and domestic spaces was often articulated as a more legitimate and worthy form of religion, mirroring as it did the distinctly Victorian, and indeed largely Protestant, values of piety, restraint and moral conscience.

The scholar and missionary William Muir's highly influential biography of the Prophet, published in 1861, offers a clear example of how some Victorian authors perceived true Islamic piety to be manifested in the household sphere. Ruminating in one chapter on the 'rites and ordinances' established by Muhammad in his own 'domestic life', Muir describes how the austere routines of prayer and fasting revealed the 'simplicity', 'abstinence' and 'self-control' of the Prophet and his lifestyle, commendable values that quite contrasted with the 'splendour and luxury' enjoyed by some of his successors.[15] Such descriptions by British philologists seem to reveal an often-ignored complexity to Victorian attitudes to Islam and its figureheads. While Islam's more public and political manifestations were often feared, especially after 1857, such anxieties were tempered with admiration for the private piety of its founders, with their qualities of religious commitment and personal discipline perhaps mirroring the Protestant (Anglican or, in the case of the many Scots in India, Presbyterian) values of many of the Raj's intellectual champions and staff personnel.

This colonial, and distinctively Victorian, imposition upon India of an idea of the 'private' as an abode of religion was, to generalize somewhat, almost an inversion of the treatment of religion by the Muslim rulers of pre-colonial north India. Indeed, one might argue that the Mughal emperors' patronage of public religious processions and festivals, their close personal ties to religious scholars and Sufis of public influence in their cities, and their having prayers in the congregational mosque read in their name, were acts that

---

[14] It seems likely, although rarely evidenced explicitly, that Protestant suspicion of Catholic public ritual and ceremonialism underlay many of these attitudes among British observers and administrators.

[15] William Muir, *Mahomet and Islam: A Sketch of the Prophet's Life from Original Sources*, 2nd edn (London, 1896; first publ. 1861), 80–6.

explicitly established religion as a public affair, as well as one of the mechanisms by which these royal Muslim households could assert their civil and political presence.[16]

Moreover, in the later nineteenth century these novel and colonial-derived constructs of public/political and private/domestic were accommodated and transmitted in the vocabularies of Indian reformers and social activists, many of whom became engaged alongside the colonial state in a form of surreptitious policing of the Indian household. The later nineteenth century is often seen as a period of particular religious revitalization in India: wider availability of printing technology, and increasing literacy among emerging classes of urban literati, led across India's various religious communities to more reflective, self-aware and vaguely puritan forms of religion, ones versed in their own 'great traditions' and eliciting wider lay engagement.[17] A common feature of such movements, despite their diversity, was that they were in large degree located in this newly constructed 'private' space, focusing on personal comportment and domestic behaviour.

Such privatized, behaviourally focused forms of religion were inextricably linked to the experience of colonial subjecthood. With the domination of India's outer public and political arenas by a language of post-Enlightenment European values, Indian reformists increasingly located their own cultural and spiritual identity in a kind of 'inner domain' tied to the behaviours of home and lifestyle, immune to infiltration by the 'outer' cultures and languages associated with the colonial state.[18] However, while the spheres of private space and domesticity may increasingly have become the natural repository for religion in colonial India, this space was very much a product of the encounter with colonialism.

---

[16] The patronage of Delhi's public life and festive occasions by the Mughal emperor and his court in the second quarter of the nineteenth century – by which time the city was under all-but-formal British control – is evoked from interviews with Muslim nobles and intellectuals in C. F. Andrews, *Zakaullah of Delhi* (Delhi, 2003; first publ. 1929), 22–40.

[17] For an introduction, see Kenneth Jones, *Socio-Religious Reform Movements in British India* (Cambridge, 1990).

[18] This idea of the 'inner' and 'outer' domains (with the former being a site of colonial/postcolonial resistance) – categories distinct from, but sometimes coextensive with, private and public – is posited in Partha Chatterjee, *The Nation and its Fragments: Colonial and Postcolonial Histories* (Princeton, NJ, 1993), 6–13.

Private Lives and Public Moralists: Instructing the Muslim Household

It was the importance vested in the domestic space and private lives of Indians that ensured that the household received so much attention from religious reformists in the second half of the nineteenth century. This applied to, for instance, the Hindu middle class of Bengal, whose identity was increasingly articulated around specific codes of domesticity and household behaviours.[19] A comparable process took place in the setting under consideration here, among the north India Muslim *shurafa*.

Internal supervision of the Muslim community came from many angles. First, there was that coming from the *'ulama*, the class of traditionally educated religious scholars. Prior to the formal establishment of the British Raj, the *'ulama* had often served as clients of political elites, but having been disenfranchised of any such state position and patronage after 1857, they were forced to re-craft themselves in the role of guides on personal and family affairs to a notional community of Muslims. This was particularly true of the reformist Deobandi movement, centred upon a *madrasa* (Islamic school) north of Delhi from 1867. Whilst far from the only Islamic reformist movement of late nineteenth-century India, it set a prototype for many others, not least in its focus upon the amendment of Muslim households and lifestyles. In a break from their earlier vocation in state counsel, its *'ulama* issued instructive decisions or edicts (*fatwas*) for the Muslim population, guiding them on all questions related to personal and domestic behaviours. An archetypal example was the *Fatawa-i-Rashidiya*, a compilation of edicts penned by Rashid Ahmad Gangohi, one of Deoband's founding scholars. Originally elicited in response to specific questions, such compilations presented such edicts in the format of a powerful and systematic canon of instructions for proper conduct.[20] By the early twentieth century, a whole genre of such *fatwa* literature was emerging, centred very much on this constructed notion of 'personal' or 'family' (often *a'ili, khandani*) comportment. Such works not only dealt with subjects that

---

[19] See Tanika Sarkar, *Hindu Wife, Hindu Nation: Community, Religion and Cultural Nationalism* (Delhi, 2001), 23–52.

[20] Rashid Ahmad Gangohi, *Fatawa-i-Rashidiyya* (Delhi, 2007; first publ. 1903).

we might narrowly conceive as 'religious', such as how to pray or observe rites or festivals, but also regulated the minutiae of domestic lifestyles, including styles of dress, food preparation and dining, manners of public greeting and social interaction, appropriate leisure activities and pastimes, travel, personal hygiene and bathroom etiquette.[21]

Such texts illustrate two points. First, that religion was seen as intrinsic to the idea of what in Urdu are called *mu'amalat* and *mu'asharat*: respectively, the totality of personal behaviours and the entirety of human social interactions. Such works offered a total body of guidance for all such affairs. Second, and perhaps more instructively, this example seems to show how Islamic scholars, despite their declared opposition to interaction with 'Western' languages, sciences and institutions, found themselves working within the British-derived categorization of religion as associated with the realm of the private. This was, as Barbara Metcalf termed it, an 'inward looking' version of Islam, with matters of state and governance largely ignored in favour of a focus on the private sphere and household.[22] Indeed, the majority of Indian religious reform movements of this period seem to have been working within the effective boundaries put in place by the colonial state.

The *'ulama* were not the only group to participate in this effort to instruct the Muslim domestic sphere. Significantly, many of these interventions came from a new kind of Muslim intellectual in the late nineteenth century, often young, of *sharif* origins and educated in the institutions crafted to harmonize Islamic learning with new Western literatures and sciences.[23] In the post-1857 decades, their graduates had often entered government employment as administrators, lawyers and teachers; but concurrently they were often active in public life as Urdu essayists, journalists and social activists, framing themselves as intermediaries between the colonial admin-

---

[21] E.g. Maqbul Ahmad, *Tehzib-ul-Islam* (Lucknow, 2005; first publ. 1920).

[22] Barbara Metcalf, *Islamic Revival in British India: Deoband, 1860–1900* (Princeton, NJ, 1982), 11–13.

[23] Of these, the operative examples, both staffed largely by British personnel but with teaching in the medium of Urdu, were Delhi's Anglo-Arabic College (taken under British supervision in 1825) and the Muhammadan Anglo-Oriental College at Aligarh (founded 1875). See, respectively, Magrit Pernau, ed., *The Delhi College: Traditional Elites, the Colonial State and Education before 1857* (Delhi, 2006); David Lelyveld, *Aligarh's First Generation: Muslim Solidarity in British India* (Princeton, NJ, 1978).

istration and a supposed Indian Muslim 'community' whom they aspired to represent. Usually, this class of urban Muslim literati has been described as being separate from, or even opposed to, the scholarly *'ulama*; whilst the latter looked to Arabic education and rejected interaction with European knowledge, the former were more willing to draw selectively from European literatures and ideas where appropriate as a means of seeking contemporary Muslim betterment. What they held in common was their focus on the home and domesticity as the centre of their immediate efforts, with the moral perfection of self and household seen as necessary precursors to any form of worldly improvement.

A key example of such a thinker was Nazir Ahmad, the novelist and government administrator referred to earlier. His novels, of which there were several in the 1870s, were inspired less by Indo-Islamic literary traditions and more by the new encounter with European genres of popular writing. This applies particularly to his seminal novel, *The Repentance of Nasuh*, outlined above. Literary critics have shown that the main prototype for this story was Daniel Defoe's *The Family Instructor* (1715), from which Ahmad drew a similar domestic setting and narrative structure, and also the core story, recounting a gentleman's quest for the moral and mannerly improvement of himself and others.[24] Another novel by Ahmad, *Mira't ul-'Arus* ('The Bride's Mirror'), whose very title perhaps recalls the European 'Mirror for Princes' genre of Renaissance-era didactic literature, tells a comparable story of two female characters, Akbari and Asghari (respectively, the 'elder' and 'younger') who take divergent lifestyle paths, the latter meeting spiritual fulfilment and worldly success, and the former failure on both counts.[25] This story, Ahmad himself admitted, was inspired by Thomas Day's popular *History of Sandford and Merton* (1783–9), which charted two boys' moral improvement and was a staple of moral instruction for schoolboys in nineteenth-century Britain.[26]

The influence of eighteenth-century English household morality tales upon nineteenth-century Indo-Islamic fiction tells us much

---

[24] Daniel Defoe, *The Family Instructor, in three parts, relating I. To Parents and Children. II. To Masters and Servants. III. To Husbands and Wives*, 14th edn (Edinburgh, 1750).

[25] Nazir Ahmad, *The Bride's Mirror: A Tale of Life in Delhi One Hundred Years Ago* (Delhi, 2009; first publ. 1869).

[26] Ahmad, *Repentance of Nussooh*, 126–7; Thomas Day, *The History of Sandford and Merton* (repr. Chiswick, 1828).

about the wider context of exchange and translation between British and Indian literatures, in terms of the texts themselves but also of ideas. The exercise we see here of translating one set of values into the words and contexts of meaning of another ensured the assimilation and naturalization of the English prototypes within the wider cultural milieu of the Indian recipients.[27] Authors like Ahmad were not simply reproducing a British-authored code of civility and proper comportment in another tongue; instead, they were engaged in a dialogue which identified commonalities and crossovers between the cultural and moral values of English literatures and those of Indian Islam.

But as well as indicating the depth of cross-cultural inter-action in cities of former Muslim power such as Delhi, Nazir Ahmad's writings also comprise a clear example of how the colonial state sometimes shared with Muslim reformists a common aim of correcting behaviours in the Muslim household. From 1868 onwards, the colonial administration of the North-Western Provinces was drafting a new curriculum for the region's government Urdu schools. Possibly testifying to residual British fears of ongoing Muslim antipathy to their rule, as well as a belief that only intervention into the intimate arenas of Muslim households could ensure their pacification, these reforms included the launching of an annual government literary prize: awards were to be given for the Urdu works that most successfully delivered an appropriate message of educational and moral instruction. In addition to financial rewards, the winning works would be integrated into the educational syllabus, giving them great advantages in circulation.[28] It is perhaps unsurprising that Nazir Ahmad's socially engaged fiction won these prizes on several occasions, at once boosting his personal career and ensuring that these novels would exert huge influence within the north Indian Muslim elite more widely, especially among younger generations. Ahmad's vision of the pious and obedient Muslim household, then, was one both sponsored and

[27] For a comparable perspective on translation as a process of cultural adaptation rather than mere linguistic exercise, see Magrit Pernau, 'Introduction' to eadem, ed., *Delhi College*, 15–19.

[28] C. M. Naim, 'Prize-winning *adab*: A Study of Five Urdu Books written in Response to the Allahabad Government Gazette Notification', in Barbara Metcalf, ed., *Moral Conduct and Authority: The Place of* adab *in South Asian Islam* (Berkeley, CA, 1984), 290–314.

promoted by the British government, which sought to ensure the political quietism of the Muslim community by impressing upon it a particular ethic of civility and restraint via an emerging brand of didactic literature.

We can see Ahmad's novels, and comparable works by other contemporaneous authors, as to a degree exporting the stauncher, more conservative social practices of an emerging Muslim administrative class of intellectuals, professionals and government officials to the wider Muslim population.[29] Indeed, their shared vision of the correction of Muslim domestic lives often seemed to work against a caricature of its opposite: the aristocratic Muslim household, associated with the nobilities clustered around the Mughal court. The emerging Muslim literati of the late nineteenth century came to describe the older Muslim elites, both in their earlier nineteenth-century heyday and their declining present, with some disdain, with their manners of living bearing the brunt of the scorn. An excellent example of such critiques is offered by the Delhi-based author Altaf Husain Hali, a contemporary and acquaintance of Ahmad. Hali's most famous poetic work, *Musaddas-i-jad-va-jazr-i-Islam* ('The Ebb and Flow of Islam'), was an influential rumination on Muslim decline in India which, significantly, rooted much of this decline in the decadence of the Muslim household. One stanza, quite typical of many others, reads: 'The children of the aristocrats are badly raised. Their condition is ruined and their ways are evil. | Some have the vice of flying pigeons, others a mania for quail fighting. | Some are addicted to hemp and cannabis, others to the delights of opiates.'[30]

While commentators on *Musaddas* have often focused upon the author's use of imagery evoking Islam's expansive global reach and presence,[31] it is striking how the poem consistently describes contemporary Muslim decline in language drawn from the home and the neighbourhood. The imagery throughout is of inappropriate dress and bathing rituals, poor eloquence and vulgarity in

---

[29] For an excellent analysis of Ahmad's fiction which emphasizes its reworking of 'respectability' (*sharafat*) within the context of good family values and worldly resourcefulness rather than antiquated courtly pedigree, see Ruby Lal, 'Gender and *sharafat*: Re-reading Nazir Ahmad', *Journal of the Royal Asiatic Society* 18 (2008), 15–30.

[30] Altaf Husain Hali, *Musaddas: The Flow and Ebb of Islam*, intro. Javed Majeed and Christopher Shackle (Delhi, 1997; first publ. 1879), 194–5.

[31] See Majeed and Shackle's introduction, ibid. 1–80.

social gatherings, imperfect diet and table manners, the loss of family reputations, damaging family feuds and the dilapidation of noble dwellings. The overall impression is one of 'the lament in every street, in every house'.[32] This private decline is, equally strikingly, linked throughout to the wider ebb of Islam around the world; the language of decaying manners at home is merged with imagery of the historic collapse of Muslim power in Andalusia, Baghdad, Egypt and, more recently, India. One may insinuate that it would only be through a correction of domestic practice and personal lifestyle, starting at home and working outwards, that Islam might once again assert itself as a global force.

Like Ahmad's novels, Hali's poem was a work of moral instruction that did not seek to flatter its audience. Again employing household imagery, he described its publication as equivalent to inviting a nobleman from Delhi or Lucknow to dine at one's home, and then serving only 'boiled rice and lentils, and spiceless curry'.[33] Hali's work shared with Ahmad's novels both the vision of the disciplined and proper Muslim household and the placing of the household at the centre of efforts to renew Islam in the wider world. Like Ahmad's, Hali's work also received a government prize for suitable Urdu literature and was subsequently included in the school curriculum, again ensuring that over subsequent generations his work – and with it his ideas – would filter into the north Indian Muslim subconscious.

This juxtaposition of old Muslim aristocracy and new Muslim literati also overlapped with the issue of the language of authorship. Before the consolidation of British rule, Persian had been the language of administration of the Mughal and Nawabi courts, as well as being the major vehicle for Indo-Islamic literary traditions. By contrast, these Muslim reformists wrote in Urdu, long the spoken language of north Indian Muslims but less one of literature. Not only was this crucial to widening their readership, but Urdu, used by the British as the language of government administration and education from the 1830s, carried within it suggestive contextual tones of regulation and instruction. By contrast with Persian, with its associations with courtliness and flamboyance, Urdu echoed the values of restraint and professionalism

---

[32] For elaboration, see ibid., esp.142–9, 194–201.
[33] Ibid. 96–7.

that were integral to emerging Muslim middle classes in north India.[34] Alongside these austere connotations, it is also significant that Urdu was the 'domestic' language in north India, spoken in Muslim households.[35] It was thus more suited to communicating prescriptions for the living of proper home lives. These new genres of didactic literature, then, reflect the intersection of linguistic and social transitions during the late nineteenth century.

This focus on a few key works and authors hints at a far wider prevalence of a new brand of instructive, domestically-oriented writing during these decades. Such literature traversed *fatwa* compilations, novels, poems and other genres. And while such literatures were, as implied above, broadly classified between those that looked inwards to Islamic traditions and those that turned outwards to new literary genres and agendas of worldly progress which appeared with the colonial state, there was perhaps more that united than divided them in their surprisingly coalescent visions of flawless piety and domestic comportment.

For the purposes of this essay, one of the most striking features of this renovation of Muslim domesticity in colonial India was its frequent similarity to certain didactic discourses active in Victorian Britain. Three such points of comparison stand out. First is the connection inferred between societal health in public and private spaces. The contributions of such figures as Rashid Ahmad, Nazir Ahmad and Altaf Husain Hali, despite their cultural and ideological differences, all bore within their context more than a passing resemblance to a brand of intellectuals active in Britain evoked by Stefan Collini as 'public moralists': those who inferred links between the twin perfections of 'public virtue' and 'private habit' in their ruminations on the making of a moral society.[36] Such an

---

[34] Significantly, Hali described his *Musaddas*, employing a fairly simplistic metre of rhyme and fairly straightforward language, as 'lacking in whimsy or elegance', and as an antidote to what he called the 'Eastern hyperbole' of Persian literature: ibid. 96–9.

[35] The British Director of Public Instruction, M. Kempson, praised Nazir Ahmad's fiction on these grounds. He described his work as written in 'the words of everyday life in good society, the true Oordoo of the country, and not the high-flown dialect of pedants and poets'. His novels were 'readable every-day book[s], intelligible to common folk, and pure and practical in tone. There is no pandering to the passions or appeal to the marvellous, which appear to be the ordinary passports to popularity among Oriental writers': M. Kempson to R. Simson (Secretary to Government, N.W.P.), 22 July 1869, in Mushirul Hasan, *A Moral Reckoning: Muslim Intellectuals in Nineteenth-Century Delhi* (Delhi, 2003), 260–2.

[36] Stefan Collini, *Public Moralists: Political Thought and Intellectual Life in Britain,*

idea was echoed by these Muslim authors in their tying of the ultimate rejuvenation of Islamic society and culture to the immediate correction of the household.

Secondly, one might fruitfully compare Indian Muslim and British concepts of masculinity which, in this same mid-nineteenth century period, started to focus upon the need of respectable gentlemen to nurture and protect their households. The responsibility of British gentlemen in this era, John Tosh and others have argued, was not simply to provide for their families financially and educationally (through their own professional or 'public' lives) but increasingly to supervise and involve themselves intimately within the workings and daily routines of home life.[37] Such behaviours appear to be mimicked in the ideals of masculine honour and respectability propounded by these social activists in Muslim India.[38] One can therefore see how Victorian Protestant and Indian Muslim households, newly remodelled on comparable values of piety, austerity and restraint, experienced much in common.

Lastly, as in Britain, these new ideas of home-centred virtue had particular affinity with the activities of a developing middle class. Indeed, the fact that authors such as Hali referred to the Muslim home as *ghar*, a largely neutral and plain term for household that carried none of the more palatial connotations of words associated with noble dwellings like *haveli*, *kothi* or *mehel*, may perhaps imply the relatively modest, aspirational social location to which his efforts were directed. Even the private spaces of the humble Muslim middle-class household could become the platform upon which new ethics of piety and religious duty could be actualized, and thereafter perhaps influence the wider world beyond the household itself.

Running the Household: The Agency of Women in Islamic Reform

You must not suppose that women have no share at all in the business of the world beyond eating and sleeping. On the contrary, it is women who do the entire work of housekeeping

---

1850–1930 (Oxford, 1993), esp. 95–110.

[37] E.g. John Tosh, *A Man's Place: Masculinity and the Middle-Class Home in Victorian England* (New Haven, CT, 2007).

[38] Ahmad's Nasuh is a clear example of such a character, whose gentlemanliness is predicated on his perfecting of his household.

… the world is like a cart which cannot move beyond two wheels – man on one side, and woman on the other. Men cannot spare the time from their breadwinning occupations to spend on the little details of household management … God has created women, in comparison with men, of a more delicate physique; but He has given women hands, feet, ears, eyes, intelligence, thought, memory, just the same as men.[39]

God will ask parents: 'Why have you deprived your daughters of knowledge? Why haven't you considered them as precious as your sons? … We haven't created girls to be raised as pets in their parents' homes, and then to go to their husband's homes to pass their lives as slave girls … We created them so they too, like men, could use their minds and benefit humanity, so they could understand good and evil in this world and be prepared for the hereafter.'[40]

While the texts discussed above dealt primarily with paradigms of masculine comportment and private responsibility, a particular burden of attempts to instruct and shape the Muslim household was, unsurprisingly, placed upon women. The custom of female *purdah* (referring to both veiling and seclusion within the home) observed in *sharif* households meant that Muslim women had always been figures of the home, and in the late nineteenth century the observance of this practice was 'more rigid than ever'.[41] And since, as implied above, nineteenth-century discourses of Islamic reformism in India seemed to share with Victorian moralism a comparable classification of the 'separate spheres' of public and private, we see an instinctive conflation of gender and space, linking femininity with domesticity.

If the location of Muslim women's roles did not change greatly, what was new in late nineteenth-century India was a sense of women's significance within Muslim society at large. Through their role in the home, women had profound importance in the shaping of Muslim society and the transmission of religious values within it. Two of the authors discussed above, Nazir Ahmad and

[39] Ahmad, *Bride's Mirror*, 7–8.
[40] Atuji, in dialogue with Bari Begum, in Altaf Husain Hali, *Majalis an-Nisa* (first publ. 1874), in Gail Minault, *Voices of Silence: English Translation of Khwaja Altaf Hussain Hali's* Majalis an-Nisa *and* Chup ki dad (Delhi, 1988), 36.
[41] Ahmad, *Bride's Mirror*, 14.

Altaf Husain Hali, were also leading figures in articulating this
agency newly assigned to Muslim women, using essays, novels and
verse to demand a wider consideration of their social role and
importance. Ahmad's novel *The Bride's Mirror* seemed to offer a
feminine counterpart to the more masculine ideals of behaviour
in *The Repentance of Nasuh*; once again, the work was a recipient
of the government literary prize, presumably implying the colonial state's sanctification of its vision of women as guardians of
domesticity.[42] Equally significant was Hali's novel *Majalis un-nissa*
('Gatherings of women'), published in 1874. Taking the form of a
series of dialogues between women spanning different generations,
this novel unravels the story of a young woman, Zubaida Khatun,
who through her home education at the hands of her parents, is
eventually able to grow into a supportive and resourceful wife
and mother. Embedded within the novel are reams of instructions
on maintaining the household: how and what to cook; how to
manage household staff, including servants, wet-nurses and food-
sellers; how to nurse children and which toys to allow them; how
to store coals; how to maintain household cleanliness and entertain
guests; and so on.[43] Moreover, in addition to portraying a model
of perfect feminine character and behaviour, Hali's composition
of the text in conversational *begamati zaban* ('household' – literally 'wifely' – Urdu) seems to establish not only the text's own
domestic setting, but the intended space within Muslim society
where it would be received.[44]

To modern eyes, such writings may appear inherently patriarchal. The idealized status of these women's confinement to
domestic lives, and their subservience to their husbands, may look
little different from the pre-existing social predicament of Indian
Muslim women. Moreover, the fact that these texts were almost
without exception penned by men seems further to entrench the
sense that this was largely a discussion by men about women, rather
than one actually involving them. However, what was new was the
focus on the importance of the domestic role, and the autonomy
conferred on women in this context. Such were the implications of

[42] Ahmad's 1869 novel reinforces the conflation of femininity and domesticity,
and charges women with needing to be versed in such skills as sewing, cooking and
household management.
[43] Hali, *Majalis an-Nisa*, 46–54, 69–78.
[44] Minault's introduction, ibid. 12.

the domestic sphere for Muslim society that this was now seen as a calling not of mundane routine but of great responsibility. Indeed, one conclusion drawn by both authors is that, because women were the central figures in the Muslim household, they should be properly taught to read and write. Only then could they fulfil the duties expected of them, in particular imparting proper Islamic values to their children, but also providing creditable company for their husbands.[45] So, while the bifurcation of separate spheres and confinement of women to the home remained very much alive, the insinuation was that women broadly shared the same constitution as men, including qualities of rational thinking (*'aql*), which brought responsibility and the demand for self-perfection. As such, despite its inherent social conservatism, this literature granted women the same acumen and social importance as men, and hence would ultimately pave the way for the emergence of more socially innovatory forms of Islamic feminism in the twentieth century.

One vivid example of this new focus on women's behaviour is Hali's poem *Chup ki dad* ('Homage to the Silent'), a simple verse published in a reformist Urdu journal in 1905. Seeking to counter a perceived absence of public discussion concerning the social value of women, it stresses their importance to the protection and sustenance of Islam.[46] It opens with exhortations highlighting women's hard work and their value to society: 'You are the picture of piety, | the counsellor of chastity, | of religion the guarantee. | Protection of the faith | comes from you.' Throughout, Hali's poem reflects upon the perils of a woman's position. It depicts girls grappling with various challenges: the personal stigma of being unwanted children, the difficulties of arranged marriage and the challenges of raising infants. Hali points to the social constraints affecting women, including prohibitions on expressing opinions or socializing freely, their lack of education, and the challenge of being subordinate to their parents and later their parents-in-law. He notes the restrictions on women's personal movement, the worry of widowhood, and (perhaps most empathetically) the harsh reali-

---

[45] Late nineteenth-century discussions on Muslim women's education, an issue considered by reformists of the era almost uniformly in terms of home-schooling rather than institutional instruction, are explored in Gail Minault, *Secluded Scholars: Women's Education and Muslim Social Reform in Colonial India* (Delhi, 1998).

[46] For the full text of the poem, see Minault, *Voices of Silence*, 141–50.

ties of boredom and hard work: 'You're cooking, sewing, mending, all day every day, | You never have a moment to yourself', the reader is told at one point. However, his conclusion appears to be that women simply need to accept the nature of their roles: 'Lay aside your troubles, | grin and bear it, | swallow your anger | as if bile were sherbet'. Nonetheless, taken overall, the poem seems to be a call to recognize the value of women: 'Men know of the importance of your task', the author claims. Hali's poem presents women, despite their silence, as having real agency in ensuring the proper conduct of the household, hence the paramount need for women to be educated so as best to fulfil their role.

To modern eyes, such verse, in a basic metre of Urdu rhyme and with such sentimental language, hardly counts as high literature. However, the simplistic style was an obvious attempt to reach out to women themselves, who would normally have benefitted at best from a basic level of home-schooled literacy, and were thus ill equipped to read more high-flying literatures. Insofar as they were being approached as readers, women were being engaged by Hali as participants in this debate as to their function in Muslim society. Moreover, coming as it did from the pen of a satirist, we should compare this vision of the efficient, steadfast and educated Muslim woman with her predecessor: the ignorant and pampered noblewoman (*begam*) associated with the older Muslim nobilities. Implicit references to such figures show how the assumed decadence of the Muslim past became part of the imagery by which Hali framed his vision of the proper household.

The innovative character of such writings becomes even more obvious when they are compared with references to women in earlier Indo-Islamic literary canons. Until the mid-nineteenth century, much high literature and poetry in India had adopted women as symbols of what is called *fitna*: a state of corruption, sin or disorder. Due to the temptations they offered to men, women were the source of the pollutions and passions that threatened to unravel the pristine order both within the home and the wider world. In nineteenth-century Urdu *ghazzal* poetry, for instance, the enticements of women were frequently evoked in the same language of intoxication as were music, wine and narcotics.[47] This

---

[47] Ghalib's poetry was legendary for its heady combination of wine and women: see Sarfaraz Niazi, *Wine of Passion: The Urdu Ghazals of Ghalib* (Karachi, 2009).

image changed substantively in reformist writing of the 1870s and 1880s. Now, far from women threatening the moral order of Islam, they were placed at the very heart of its preservation and renewal, and held the same responsibility as men to maintain proper conduct. As this perspective on the importance of women within Muslim society changed, so did that of the domestic sphere of which they were custodians. The home moved from the periphery of discussions of moral Muslim society to the centre of efforts to protect its integrity.[48]

As with the literature discussed above, such texts about Muslim women's roles did not simply emerge from the pens of those who might be termed 'modernist' authors. Equivalent works, addressing women themselves, were also produced by the Arabic-educated *'ulama*. The canonical text in this regard was the Deobandi scholar Ashraf 'Ali Thanawi's *Bihishti Zewar* ('Heavenly Ornaments'). This multi-volume opus, written between 1902 and 1905, offered comprehensive guidance for women's behaviour. Discussing Islamic traditions, outlining models set by female exemplars from Islamic history, and offering basic instruction in life skills and religious practices, the work was designed to be read by women themselves. To give one example, Book Seven offers a complete outline for the worthy female life, couched in the same themes of restraint described above, and centred entirely within the home. The reader is told, among many other things, to keep worthy company and avoid association with the rich (again, suggesting the inherently middle-class background of its intended reader-ship); to avoid excessive eating; to maintain personal hygiene; to dress modestly and avoid perfume; to maintain good relations with parents, husband and neighbours; to avoid keeping pet dogs; to avoid sleeping on one's front; and to exercise proper control over emotions at all times.[49]

As a direct engagement with women by the *'ulama* and an admission regarding their intellectual abilities and importance in Muslim society, the work was unprecedented. Moreover, even reading the instructions contained in it necessitated some level of

[48] Faisal Devji, 'Gender and the Politics of Space: The Movement for Women's Reform, 1857–1900', in Zoya Hasan, ed., *Forging Identities: Gender, Communities and the State* (Boulder, CO, 1994), 22–37.

[49] Ashraf Ali Thanawi, *Perfecting Women: Maulana Ashraf 'Ali Thanawi's* Bihishti Zewar, intro. Barbara Metcalf (Berkeley, CA, 1990), 202–21.

education. Indeed, the *Bihishti Zewar* opens with a blueprint for the female reader's own home-schooling: an introduction to the alphabet, practice sentences, numerals, names of days and months, and instructions on how to write letters.[50] Despite the widely divergent agendas for the 'public' lives of Muslims held by the *'ulama* and Muslim modernists, this work shows that their visions for Muslim women were remarkably comparable. Both emphasized the continued confinement of women to the home, but also the agency and autonomy of women within it, and their need for a modicum of education on that basis.

Meaningful comparison can also be drawn with the contemporaneous model of womanhood in Britain. The above section identified a confluence between Victorian and Indian Muslim notions of piety and proper conduct, and this applied also to the role of women. The notion of a 'women's mission' centred upon household management has long been recognized to be a product of Victorian discourses of domesticity, as has the archetype of the 'housewife': one subordinate and confined to domestic roles, but also educated and resourceful within her own sphere of influence.[51] These very same ideas and allocation of duties seem to be emerging in parallel within the separate moral universe of Indian Islam.

Moreover, such roles may, intriguingly, have been particularly pronounced for the wives of British colonial officials at the height of the Victorian Raj. Social histories of British families settled in India and elsewhere have shown how, in expatriate arenas, a particular rigidity and strictness was applied to home life, to shore up the purity of colonial society and prevent its contamination by the wider cultural environment in which it existed.[52] Within this

---

[50] Ibid. 45–62.

[51] A few influential examples include Hall and Davidoff, *Separate Spheres*; Elizabeth Langland, *Nobody's Angels: Middle-Class Women and Domestic Ideology in Victorian Culture* (Ithaca, NY, 1995), 25–60; Ann Oakley, *Woman's Work: The Housewife, Past and Present* (New York, 1974); Patricia Branca, *Silent Sisterhood: Middle-Class Women in the Victorian Home* (London, 1975).

[52] These arguments have been developed by Laura Ann Stoler and a number of other social historians of colonial settler societies. Alison Blunt, focusing upon British housewives within India, has argued that 'feminized discourses of domesticity' outlining 'the appropriate behaviour of women as housekeepers, wives and mothers' established the household as a space inseparably bound up with imperial power, and a site for 'establishing and maintaining imperial power relations'. The household, in other words, was essential in 'reproducing the social, moral and domestic values that

framework, it is an ironic thought that the colonial housewife and the colonized Muslim woman in British India perhaps in some sense shared the same experience, each apparently assigned responsibility for safeguarding their home, and hence their community, against adulteration by the other.

CONCLUSION: CULTS OF DOMESTICITY IN INDIA AND BRITAIN

This essay has argued that, in colonial India, the realm of the private and domestic spaces became central to efforts to manipulate, or hold sway over, the workings and customs of Indian Muslim society. Such attempts were made, on the one hand, by the colonial state, whose perception of religion as a largely private matter, together with its fear of Muslim households as sites of potential rebellion, ensured that it desired tacit influence over the Muslim home. Efforts in this direction, all of which entirely belied claims to non-interference in religious questions, included the subjection of matters of family law to the powers of government courts, and the sponsorship of the publication of suitable, domestically oriented Urdu literatures for a mass audience via school syllabi. On the other hand, such attempts to exert household control were also made by Muslim reformists, authors and social activists, who worked, sometimes in league with the colonial state and sometimes separately, to provide guidance for regulating the household. In a sociopolitical context in which Muslims' access to affairs of state had been curtailed, trajectories of Islamic reform in north India from the 1860s onwards seem to have been heavily directed towards the mundane routines of home and daily life. Religious intellectuals, ranging from the Arabic-trained *'ulama* to English-reading modernists, manifested many differences, but they shared a preoccupation with the same terrain of the household. Family routines, women's roles, daily chores, the raising of children and so on were established as the natural abode of religion, the setting in which a pristine Islam could be recovered.

We could, of course, see this process as signifying the construction of clear public-private boundaries, and perhaps compare it

legitimated imperial rule': 'Imperial Geographies of Home: British Domesticity in India, 1886–1925', *Transactions of the Institute of British Geographers* 24 (1999), 421–40, at 437–8.

to the idea of the 'separate spheres' of public/political/male and private/domestic/female spaces so associated with the Victorian middle class. Perhaps, though, this story is not one of the separation of public and private, but rather one of the private becoming a new kind of public, as the details of behaviour behind closed doors became subject to discussion in printed works and public debate. Quite in contrast to the relative infrequency of deliberations on home life in pre-colonial Islamic literatures, the writers of the late nineteenth century opened the minutiae of household behaviours to unprecedented scrutiny. Indeed, while these moralizing trends have often been spoken about in the language of reform, one might argue that they actually demonstrate a form of co-option or even policing of the Muslim household, as Muslim activists sought to exert control within intimate spaces. Charu Gupta's work has documented the more belligerent consequences of this 'cult of domesticity' within the equivalent trajectories of Hindu religious reform. The Hindu home was, she argues, 'colonised' by the perpetrators of this middle-class domestic model; their interventions comprised the surveillance of the trivia of household conduct, the controlling of women's behaviour and bodies, and the monitoring of perceived 'outside' (usually meaning Muslim or Christian) influences within these intimate spaces.[53] Many of these same features appeared concurrently within Indian Islam, with a parallel internal supervision apparently taking place within the Muslim home.

Most studies of Islamic renewal and reform in colonial India have located such processes in developments internal to Muslim society, such as the expansion of Islamic schools and printing presses. By contrast, this essay has drawn comparisons with certain brands of evangelical and Protestant revitalization emerging concurrently in Britain, which exhibited remarkably similar evocations of the importance of home lives in the moral fabric of society. David Bebbington has noted the 'cult of duty, self-discipline and high seriousness' emerging across Protestant (Anglican, Presbyterian and other) denominations from the 1850s and 1860s, based around, among other things, an emphasis on 'conversionism' (the cultivation of piety both within oneself and one's family circle), social

---

[53] Charu Gupta, *Sexuality, Obscenity, Community: Women, Muslims and the Hindu Public in Colonial India* (Delhi, 2001), 123–95.

responsibility and 'discipline in the home'.[54] All such qualities describe with equal clarity the trajectories of reform in Muslim India during much the same period.

Religious transformation in Muslim India and Victorian Britain often appeared to share comparable classifications of public and private spaces and similar understandings of gender roles, calling for men to exert authority over domestic lifestyles and for women to submit fully to their homely duties. Further comparators include the social location of these religious transformations within emerging middle classes in each society, and their emphasis upon the abolition of household practices of leisure and festivity in favour of more proper, restrained home lives. Similarly striking is their overlapping ethical message of self-improvement and responsibility towards one's household, and the literary strategies employed for communicating these visions of moral conduct. Just as Victorian public moralists framed their directives around stories of individuals who had achieved perfection of 'character and conduct' and who therefore compelled emulation,[55] so too did Indian Muslim authors employ exemplary characters, whether Nazir Ahmad's nobleman Nasuh or Altaf Husain Hali's noblewoman Zubaida Khatun, to embody the qualities of piety, modesty and resourcefulness that they propounded.

These comparable trajectories of social reform, centred on domestic spaces, suggest that considerable cross-cultural pollination was occurring between colonial India and Victorian Britain concerning ideas of religion and household. Some of the examples discussed, such as the translation of English morality tales into Urdu and government patronage of didactic literature, seem to reveal the direct impact of British moral discourses on certain strands of Islamic social activism. But most of the examples offered here suggest that the new notions of piety and domesticity developing during this period were coming as much from within the Islamic tradition as from outside. They were grounded in Persian and Urdu idioms and vocabulary,[56] and very often formulated by

---

[54] David Bebbington, *Evangelicalism in Modern Britain: A History from the 1730s to the 1980s* (London, 1989), 105.

[55] Samuel Smiles produced one of the most famous examples of this type: *Self-Help: With Illustrations of Character and Conduct* (London, 1859).

[56] For instance, some have argued that the long-established Islamic moral concept of *adab*, a notion of respectability, was apparently adapted in this period to refer less to

thinkers who deliberately eschewed any kind of contact with British literatures, language or officials. As such, rather than describing a one-way influence of colonial norms upon the colonized, this essay draws attention to parallel, interactive and often reciprocal relationships between religious change in these two milieus, as the two societies found their fates irrevocably intertwined.[57]

British scholars of Islam in this period often described nineteenth-century religious change in the language of Islamic 'reformation', with Muslim reformists cast as 'puritans': terms that alluded not just to their theological stringency, but to their emphasis on piety, moral responsibility and strict personal comportment as the means to salvation.[58] Such language, implicitly (if inaccurately) comparing late nineteenth-century Islam to sixteenth- or seventeenth-century Christianity, perhaps contained a moral sanctification of British rule, evoking European religion as being more advanced than the faith of the colonial state's Muslim subjects. One might, however, argue that the best comparison for religious change in Islam during this period is not the distant entity of the European Reformation, but the more immediate encounter with the assumptions, strictures and standards of mid-Victorian Christian moralism.

University of Oxford

---

ancestral or noble distinction and more to ideas of personal merit and responsibility. On a comparable reworking of *sharafat*, see n. 29 above.

[57] For an exploration of religious change according to this framework, see Peter van der Veer, *Imperial Encounters: Religion and Modernity in India and Britain* (Princeton, NJ, 2001).

[58] Such assumptions underwrite the works of William Muir cited above. See also the language used in William Wilson Hunter, *The Indian Musalmans* (Delhi, 2002; first publ. 1871), 49–63.

'DOMESTIC CHARMS, BUSINESS ACUMEN, AND DEVOTION TO CHRISTIAN WORK': SARAH TERRETT, THE BIBLE CHRISTIAN CHURCH, THE HOUSEHOLD AND THE PUBLIC SPHERE IN LATE VICTORIAN BRISTOL

by LINDA WILSON

Sarah Terrett died suddenly on 25 November 1889, aged 53, after speaking at a meeting of the White Ribbon Army, the temperance organization she had founded in 1878. Following her death many people sent letters of sympathy to her bereaved husband, William.[1] One of these, from the Rev. W. F. James, a minister of the Bible Christians, makes for especially interesting reading. The Bible Christian denomination, to which Sarah and William belonged, was one of the smaller Methodist connexions, and had its heartland in rural Devon, the area where she had grown up.[2] James recalled the hospitality he enjoyed when visiting the Terretts' home, Church House, in Bedminster, south Bristol:

> Never shall I forget the hearty welcome I invariably received or the Christian kindnesses invariably shown me. No house was better named, and Mrs Terrett made it worthy of the name. She combined in a striking way domestic charms, business acumen, and devotion to Christian work. She was, altogether, one of the most remarkable women I ever knew. While possessing all the tenderness and sympathy of the highest female character she laboured with all the energy and enthusiasm of a stalwart man.[3]

These reflections raise several pertinent issues relating to the Terrett household. The continuing importance of domesticity and hospitality, and the way in which Sarah Terrett crossed bounda-

---

[1] Frederick William Bourne, *Ready in Life and Death: Brief Memorials of Mrs S. M. Terrett* (London, 1893), 148.
[2] Jennifer M. Lloyd, *Women and the Shaping of British Methodism: Persistent Preachers, 1807–1907* (Manchester, 2009), 73. Note that Methodists referred to their networks of churches as connexions, not denominations.
[3] Bourne, *Brief Memorials*, 124.

ries between household, business, church and public life, are all highlighted. The letter also notes 'masculine' aspects of her character. This essay will demonstrate that the household of Sarah and William operated in both private and public spheres, and that Sarah was the dominant partner in at least some aspects of their marriage. It argues that their household reinforces the increasing consensus that the Victorian public/private division was nuanced and complex.

Any discussion of religion and domesticity in this period must engage with the concept of 'separate spheres'. Made familiar through the work of Davidoff and Hall,[4] this theory suggests that the Victorian middle classes regarded the home as primarily the women's sphere of activity and interest, and the public world as belonging to men. The reality, as Davidoff and Hall themselves noted,[5] was of course more nuanced, and recent research, such as that by Sarah Williams, has emphasized this.[6] Many women were involved in philanthropy outside the home, and some, like Sarah Terrett, also founded or participated in businesses,[7] while by the later decades of the century women were becoming more accepted in the public sphere, for instance as lecturers.[8] At the same time, it has been argued that in the middle decades of the century men were also a strong presence in the private sphere.[9] Nonetheless, the concept of separate spheres, when suitably nuanced, continues to offer a useful framework for discussion.

A brief sketch of the background will establish the context for the Terrett household. The family lived in Bristol, 'the unofficial regional capital of the south west',[10] which during the late nine-

---

[4]   Leonore Davidoff and Catherine Hall, *Family Fortunes: Men and Women of the English Middle Class 1780–1850* (London, 1987).

[5]   Ibid. 33.

[6]   Sarah Williams, 'Gender, Religion and Family Culture', in Sue Morgan and Jacqueline de Vries, eds, *Women, Gender and Religious Cultures in Britain, 1800–1940* (London, 2010), 11–31, at 15.

[7]   Noted by Kathryn Gleadle, 'Revisiting Family Fortunes: Reflections on the Twentieth Anniversary of the Publication of L. Davidoff & C. Hall (1987) *Family Fortunes: Men and Women of the English Middle Class, 1780–1850*', *Women's History Review* 16 (2007), 773–82.

[8]   See, for example, Linda Wilson, *Marianne Farningham: A Plain Woman Worker*, SEHT (Milton Keynes, 2007), 151–61.

[9]   John Tosh, *A Man's Place: Masculinity and the Middle-Class Home in Victorian England* (New Haven, CT, and London 2007; first publ. 1999).

[10]   Philip Ollerenshaw and Peter Wardley, 'Economic Growth and the Business

teenth century experienced a continuation of the 'sedate, though always persistent'[11] growth of the previous decades. The city's prominence was due partly to a variety of businesses and industries,[12] including several large firms with strong Nonconformist connections, notably W. D. & H. O. Wills, tobacco manufacturers; E. S. & A. Robinson, paper bag makers; and J. S. Fry & Sons, chocolate producers, as well as many smaller businesses. Several members of these families, together with other Nonconformist men and women, for the most part Liberals, played a significant part in the civic life of the city.[13] Sarah and William Terrett thus lived in a context in which Bristol Nonconformists were developing an increasing public profile.

A variety of sources contribute to our picture of the Terrett household and its relationship to the local chapel and beyond. Of these, the most significant is an account of Sarah's life written by Frederick W. Bourne, a historian of the Bible Christians, who had known her personally. Although his biography focuses heavily on Sarah's involvement in the White Ribbon Army, it also offers significant glimpses of the couple's home life. Bourne's memoir is hagiographical (one commentator has called it 'the most odious book of its kind I have ever read',[14] although this comment is unjustifiably extreme), but a valuable resource, Sarah's own narrative history of the White Ribbon Army makes up a substantial part of the text. Bourne also includes extracts from letters of condolence, such as the one quoted from above. Other material, drawn primarily from local newspapers, supplements his account.

From Bourne we learn that Sarah and William married in 1859, and that most of their married life was spent in Church House, where they brought up their three surviving children. The household, although busy in itself, effectively formed a base for their work, church and other activities. Church House was close to the

---

Community in Bristol since 1840', in Madge Dresser and Philip Ollerenshaw, eds, *The Making of Modern Bristol* (Tiverton, 1996), 124–55, at 124.

[11] Ibid.

[12] John Lynch, *A Tale of Three Cities* (Basingstoke, 1988), 19.

[13] For instance, the establishment of University College in Bristol in 1877 was partly due to the generosity of the Wills family.

[14] Martin J. Crossley Evans, 'Nonconformist Missionary Work Among the Seamen and Dock Workers of Bristol, 1820–1914', in Joseph Bettey, ed., *Historic Churches and Church Life in Bristol: Essays in Memory of Elizabeth Ralph 1911–2000* (Bristol, 2001), 162–95, at 179.

area where they ran a series of small businesses. Like Sarah's father, William was a butcher,[15] and she put her experience in a butcher's shop to good use in helping William with his work.[16] They were both active in their local Bible Christian chapel, and in the wider life of the connexion, the city and beyond. Yet the household remained important to William and Sarah. Bourne observed with approval that 'the best praise of her public work is, that it did not spoil her beautiful home life'.[17] For Bourne, it seems, it was the quality of a woman's domestic accomplishments that validated or invalidated her public involvement.

One aspect of this commendable 'home life' was generous hospitality, a quality highly regarded in the Methodist connexions, whose ministers often had to travel.[18] Sarah and William had frequent visitors or overnight guests, especially ministers. Bourne noted that Sarah 'played the part of hostess to perfection … . A day spent in her home was a study in courtesy and piety',[19] but passing comments indicate that William was also involved in offering hospitality. One minister, the Rev. R. Squire, wrote to William after Sarah's death: 'I shall cherish as a most sacred memory that precious Sabbath I spent with you and yours not long ago.'[20] Other people lived at Church House for longer periods, including two nephews, Robert and Percy Babbage. In 1881 Robert, aged 17, was an assistant in the business, while Percy, 7, attended a local school.[21] Hospitality was thus extended both to actual family members and to the wider family of the Church.

The Terretts also welcomed larger groups of people. For many years 'one of the annual meetings of the Connexional or Finance Committees of the Bible Christian Connexion' was held at Church House, entailing two or three days of entertaining twenty or thirty people, with up to half that number actually staying in the house. Both were involved: Bourne noted that 'notwithstanding the expense

---

[15] Bourne, *Brief Memorials*, 22, notes that she had been her father's 'chief helper'.

[16] Ibid. 30.

[17] Ibid. 151.

[18] Linda Wilson, *Constrained by Zeal: Female Spirituality amongst Nonconformists*, SEHT (Carlisle, 2000), 152–4.

[19] Bourne, *Brief Memorials*, 151.

[20] Ibid. 125.

[21] Kew, TNA, Census Returns of England and Wales, 1881, RG11/2455, fol. 20, p. 33. Babbage was Sarah's maiden name.

and fatigue involved, it always seemed to be regarded as an unmixed pleasure to Mr and Mrs Terrett and their family, as it certainly was to their guests'.[22] Sarah and William also used their grounds for a regular public event: an annual Butcher's Festival, with three hundred sitting down to eat and six hundred attending in the evening; a sermon was preached, and Sarah also gave a talk, which one local newspaper described as 'of considerable length', about her temperance work.[23] Probably much of this hospitality fell to the Terretts because of the size of their house as well as their commitment to the life of the chapel. Containing as it did a library, found only in a minority of houses, usually those belonging to professional men,[24] and a garden large enough to hold a substantial garden party, Church House was an unusually capacious property. The implication is that this hospitality was a pleasure for the couple, and thus that it arose, at least in part, from their own preferences.

The nature of these events demonstrates that the Terrett household was at times a public as well as a private space, thus highlighting the difficulty of clearly distinguishing between them. As noted above, Davidoff and Hall acknowledged this as long ago as 1987, stressing that 'Public was not really public and private not really private despite the potent imagery of "separate spheres".'[25] A nuanced understanding of the concept of separate spheres is needed to allow for the complexities of actual situations.

As well as respectable guests, the Terretts welcomed the disadvantaged into their house on at least one occasion. William reminisced about coming home late one night and 'hearing the sound of a strange, uncouth voice in the library. On entering, I found a rough man sitting by Mrs Terrett's side, listening very attentively to her as she sweetly and plainly described the way of salvation to him.' William joined them, and they knelt and prayed together as the man 'threw down his tattered hat' and asked God for forgiveness.[26] Such hospitality was also a feature of Sarah's temperance

---

[22] Bourne, *Brief Memorials*, 152.

[23] *Bristol Mercury and Daily Post*, 5 July 1881.

[24] Jane Hamlett, 'The Dining Room should be the Man's Paradise, as the Drawing Room is the Woman's: Gender and Middle-Class Domestic Space in England, 1850–1910', *GH* 21 (2009), 576–91, at 583.

[25] Davidoff and Hall, *Family Fortunes*, 33.

[26] Bourne, *Brief Memorials*, 128. On gender and rooms in the house, see Hamlett, 'Gender and Middle-Class Domestic Space'.

organization, the White Ribbon Army, which, rather than being a movement for church members and adherents who wanted to campaign for temperance, was aimed at those who would not normally attend a church gathering. Bourne commented regarding his own ministry in Weston-super-Mare: 'I have visited others when dying who had not entered a place of worship for years until the White Ribbon Army threw open their doors and made the vilest welcome.'[27] A hospitable household led directly to a hospitable mission.

At the heart of the household was the marriage relationship. It is difficult to gain a definite impression of William, but what emerges from the evidence is a marriage founded more in comradeship than in difference, prefiguring a trend Tosh notes as occurring in the 1890s.[28] Sarah appears to have been the stronger character, at times making decisions without consulting her husband. The most important of these was her agreeing to buy the old Bible Christian chapel in Bedminster for £425 for her temperance work, after which she waited several days before telling William.[29] The refurbished building was opened by the mayor of Bristol in early 1881 as a 'Workman's Hall and Mission Institute'.[30] On another occasion Sarah gave one of William's suits to the doorman of the mission without asking his permission, and William only discovered this when he commented to her how well dressed the man had been that evening![31] However, she also took care of William: only a few days before she died, he came back soaking wet from an evening preaching engagement some distance away and she 'herself' (as opposed to a servant or daughter, presumably) 'brought him hot water for a foot-bath', and spoke 'of the delight it gave her to wait on him'.[32] Bourne portrayed her as domesticity personified, as well as a pioneer of faith.

Another significant aspect of the household was its expression and practice of faith. The Terretts regularly held family worship, usually led by William, but sometimes by Sarah,[33] which, while

---

[27] Bourne, *Brief Memorials*, 113.
[28] Tosh, *A Man's Place*, 171.
[29] Bourne, *Brief Memorials*, 54.
[30] *Bristol Mercury and Daily Post*, 29 January 1881.
[31] Bourne, *Brief Memorials*, 59.
[32] Ibid. 137.
[33] Ibid. 151.

unusual for married Nonconformist women, was not unknown.[34] Sarah was also a great believer in personal prayer, and her biography makes frequent references to prayer in different circumstances, such as praying for her husband when he was out speaking.[35] She also believed in faith healing, refusing to consult doctors, although it seems that William and Sarah differed over this question.[36] Faith was foundational for the Terrett household.

Finance was another area in which the household and faith were connected. Sarah and William gave generously to the Bible Christian connexion and to charities. A cameo painted by Bourne suggests that Sarah's opinion generally prevailed over William's in this sphere. At one difficult time, when discussing their finances, 'they both felt their expenses should be lessened'.[37] However, when William questioned their regular giving to the chapel and connexion, Sarah was adamant that stopping this would be a mistake, saying that 'God's work must not be interfered with. We cannot afford to give less'. It was her preference that they followed.[38] In at least some areas of household management, Sarah was the dominant individual.

The rearing of children was another central function of the household. Sarah's own account explains that of the nine children born to her and William, six died in infancy, leaving a son and two daughters who grew to adulthood, although the son predeceased her; however, little else is said about these tragedies.[39] In common with many Nonconformists of the period, Sarah regarded the rearing and educating of children, and the role of mothers, as particularly significant.[40] Girls were to be trained to fulfil this same role themselves in the future. Speaking in Bedminster in 1877, at the stone-laying ceremony for a new chapel, Sarah stressed the importance of backing up Sunday School teaching at home, appealing especially to mothers. Having briefly mentioned boys, noting that '[s]ome of the greatest men the world has ever

---

34 Wilson, *Constrained by Zeal*, 150–3.
35 Bourne, *Brief Memorials*, 137.
36 Bourne devotes a whole chapter to this topic: ibid. 131–5.
37 Ibid. 153.
38 Ibid.
39 Ibid. 125.
40 Wilson, *Constrained by Zeal*, 147–9.

produced have risen from low ranks in society',[41] she turned her attention to girls, arguing that whilst

> we may not be successful in making them Hannah Mores, Elizabeth Frys, Geraldine Hoopers, Florence Nightingales, or Mary Carpenters, yet we may render them capable of making homes happy – domesticated, Christian, loving and devoted wives and mothers. It has been beautifully and rightfully said 'the arm that rocks the cradle rules the world.'[42]

This conveys a contradictory message, an example of the complex relationship between religion and feminism noted by Jacqueline de Vries amongst others.[43] It appears that Sarah's ideal was to raise girls who would be active in the public sphere, particularly in areas related to philanthropy, yet at the same time she suggested that domestic duties and ability should be rated over other achievements. Bourne also spoke of Sarah's strong affection for her own children, noting 'the loving care she lavished on them':[44] a standard comment for the time. We have no reminiscences from her surviving children to support or contradict his statement, and nothing is said about William's relationship with them. Not enough is known to draw firm conclusions about the Terretts' relationship with their children.

Sarah and William belonged to their local Bible Christian chapel. Her role in the household was supplemented by active involvement in this church, teaching in the Sunday School, fundraising and preaching.[45] For instance, in 1877, at the laying of the foundation stones for the new chapel, she delivered a sermon urging people to give money to the chapel funds.[46] The connexion had maintained its early theology which allowed women to preach, and by the end of the century, as Jennifer Lloyd has noted, women were frequently leading missions.[47] As I have argued elsewhere, churches in this

---

[41] Bourne, *Brief Memorials*, 35. Note that her hearers would have been mostly working-class.

[42] Ibid. 36.

[43] Morgan and de Vries point this out: 'Introduction' to eaedem, eds, *Women, Gender and Religious Cultures*, 1–10, at 7.

[44] Bourne, *Brief Memorials*, 152.

[45] Ibid. 159.

[46] Ibid. 32–45.

[47] Lloyd, *Women and the Shaping of British Methodism*, 264.

period can be thought of as a 'third sphere', providing opportunities for women and working men to develop skills and experience an outlet for their abilities beyond their household.[48] These skills, once learnt, could be transferred to the public sphere. Sarah Terrett clearly fits this model. Fluid movement between the private sphere of the household and the wider sphere of the Church was quite acceptable in Bible Christian churches.

Sarah set up her own mission: after purchasing the former Bedminster Bible Christian chapel, she held regular meetings there, including gospel preaching as well as a temperance message.[49] This was in addition to her chapel involvement. Members of the Terrett household were regular participants. One particular Friday, a 'Service of Song' was held: William chaired the evening, Sarah 'gave the readings' and their eldest daughter played the piano.[50] There were many other helpers, but the temperance mission and the Terrett household were closely intertwined.

Both William and Sarah, however, developed interests and responsibilities not only beyond the household but beyond business and the local church and very definitely within the public sphere. Sarah was in her early forties when she founded the White Ribbon Army, which quickly spread throughout and beyond the city of Bristol with a series of local groups. Temperance reform was a nineteenth-century development and had many facets.[51] Frances Knight has argued that by 1890 'the line between … Christianity and temperance had become blurred almost to the point of invisibility'.[52] This was certainly true for Sarah, who called teetotalism 'that angel companion to Christianity'.[53] Branches of her movement were rapidly established in many areas of Bristol, but also in Bath, Drybrook in the Forest of Dean, and as far away as Plymouth, and Dawley in Shropshire. There was also one outpost in

---

[48] Wilson, *Constrained by Zeal*, 210–11.

[49] Bourne, *Brief Memorials*, 58–62.

[50] Ibid. 59.

[51] B. Harrison, *Drink and the Victorians* (London, 1971), is still the standard work on the movement up to 1872.

[52] Frances Knight, 'Recreation or Renunciation? Episcopal Interventions in the Drink Question in the 1890s', in Stewart J. Brown, Frances Knight and John Morgan-Guy eds, *Religion, Identity and Conflict in Britain from the Restoration to the Twentieth Century* (Farnham 2013), 157–73, at 162.

[53] Bourne, *Brief Memorials*, 34.

London.[54] By the time of her death late in 1889, Sarah had become the 'General' of over fifty battalions,[55] and hundreds of individuals and families had been influenced by her organization. She was a popular speaker: announcing her name was a sure way of gaining a full house for an event.[56] William was also active in the White Ribbon Army, although once the leaders were given titles she was the General and he was the Lieutenant-General. When they held large anniversary meetings in Bristol's Colston Hall, Sarah chaired the evenings, while William delivered the report of the previous year's activities and developments.[57] He was clearly the second in command, and in Bourne's account he remains a slightly shadowy figure. Yet William was a man of stature and influence in business and in the Church. He was a preacher, and, although Bourne does not say so, became a local councillor for Bedminster East in 1882.[58] In public and often in private, however, he appeared content to defer to Sarah's stronger character, in seeming contradiction of the expected understanding of gender roles within marriage in this period.

It could not have been easy for Sarah to balance priorities and keep her household running. Her role as leader of her temperance organization frequently involved public speaking. One minister who knew her well recounted how, after dealing all day with 'pressing' family and business matters, she would 'take train for Taunton, Bridgewater or Plymouth, conduct a crowded meeting, sometimes addressing thousands, and, where possible, returning by the night mail to be in her place in the home and business the next morning. She continued these excessive labours for months and years.'[59] The organization depended so heavily on Sarah that after her demise it declined rapidly.[60] In the only hint of criticism in his whole book, Bourne commented that if it had been more organized, the work might have better survived her death.[61]

[54] Ibid. 95 (Bath), 94 (Drybrook), 83–4 (Plymouth), 87 (Dawley), 89 (London).
[55] Bourne (ibid. 111) refers to a 55th battalion.
[56] Ibid. 124.
[57] See, for example, *Bristol Mercury and Daily Post*, 29 November 1882.
[58] Crossley-Evans, 'Christian Missionary Work', 178; *Bristol Mercury and Daily Post*, 2 November 1882.
[59] Bourne, *Brief Memorials*, 124.
[60] Ibid. 109.
[61] Ibid. 99.

Ultimately, her excessively busy lifestyle probably contributed to her early death.

In conclusion, William and Sarah provide an interesting example of an evangelical household in which both wife and husband were active in public, church and private spheres. In their marriage, despite William's being a businessman, preacher and later a city councillor, Sarah appears to have been the dominant partner, not only regarding issues of faith but on occasions in other areas, such as finance. The Rev. M. Brokenshire, minister at the Bedminster Bible Christian chapel, had no hesitation in summing up Sarah's character in his funeral address by the word 'Strength'.[62] Her 'energy and enthusiasm' was less an essentially 'male' character-istic than an expression of her own strong character. Sarah's life and actions challenged gender identity, if inadvertently, whatever conventional phrases she and those around her also used, and her marriage demonstrates the difficulties of making generalizations about relationships in this period.

Although Bourne and others regarded Sarah's leadership of the White Ribbon Army as her main achievement,[63] the house-hold was still at the heart of her life. The Terretts ran a hospitable home in which the boundaries between the household and the wider spheres of Church and business were frequently porous, as they hosted gatherings for regional church business or festivals of butchers. Their household, operating as it did in both private and public spheres, is an example of the complex nature of the Victorian public/private division and demonstrates the need for a nuanced understanding of the concept of separate spheres.

University of Gloucestershire

---

[62] Ibid. 149.
[63] Ibid. 111–30.

WHO IS LIVING AT THE VICARAGE? AN ANALYSIS OF THE 1881 CENSUS RETURNS FOR CLERICAL HOUSEHOLDS IN LINCOLNSHIRE

by JOHN W. B. TOMLINSON

The 1881 census took place on the evening of Sunday 3 April and provides a snapshot of the composition of virtually every household in the UK, including details of age, occupation and birthplace. In Lincolnshire the census returns for 647 ecclesiastical parishes and districts provide a valuable source of information about the households of the clergy. The range of this record, from remote rural villages to urban communities, although limited to one region of the country, can be considered as largely representative of typical clerical households in England in the late nineteenth century.

From the material the census provides important issues arise. With a fifth of parishes lacking a clerical household, how successful were moves to put a parson in every parish or to abolish pluralism? Did lay households gain a greater religious influence in such places? Where it was present, how did the clerical household differ from others in the parish? The census provides hints about the differences mainly in terms of where people were born or where they had lived. Furthermore, it also reveals the number and type of servants present, which is a good indication of the expense of the household. What this study shows is that benefice incomes usually felt short of this expense, and as such there must have been some use of private wealth. This represents an investment in the local church by clerical households that has largely been obscured by a concentration on benefice incomes. It also shows a reliance on the personal income of the clergy which the Church could not depend upon in succeeding generations. In total 673 clergymen of the established Church were recorded in Lincolnshire, a much larger group than either solicitors or doctors, and about the same as schoolmasters, although many of these were declassified clergymen according to the rules of the census.[1] The farmers,

---

[1] *Census of England and Wales, 1881, 3: Ages, Condition as to Marriage, Occupations and Birth-places of the People* (London, 1883), 294–6. The compilers of the census decided to count clergymen who were working as schoolmasters only as schoolmasters.

at 9,470, were a larger group, as were the 24,387 indoor servants. This essay is concerned with the households of incumbents and curates in charge of Anglican parishes, of whom 489 have been identified, ignoring church dignitaries, assistant curates and the not inconsiderable number of clergy designated 'without cure of souls'.

The census was not enumerated according to ecclesiastical boundaries, although these often naturally matched enumeration areas and the census report carefully noted the differences. Clergy were critical of the census process, accusing enumerators of misplacing populations and ignoring local designations, and expressing their indignation in *Crockford's* amongst other places.[2] However, the evidence from much of Lincolnshire, in particular the rural areas, is that clergy were shown a good deal of deference, for instance by placing the vicarage or rectory as the first dwelling in the neighbourhood or as the only house to be accorded a name. The very way the census was carried out and tabulated thus shows the status of the clergy in their local communities.

As the census took place on the evening of the fifth Sunday of Lent, two weeks before Easter, it is not surprising to find most clergy at home. Only five were definitely away for the night: two had left their children behind to be looked after by the servants, another was visiting his curate son in Birmingham, and two wealthy incumbents were probably enjoying better weather abroad.[3]

The number of parishes without a clerical household was not insignificant. Out of the 647 ecclesiastical parishes and districts, 23 were in vacancy, and in at least three the parsonage was being built and the incumbent not fully established in his parish.[4] In addition, a considerable number of places, 114 out of 647, had a church to be serviced but no resident clergyman or minister of any denomination. Many of these were small, with populations of 150 or fewer, but nine were, in Lincolnshire terms, sizeable villages of over 350.[5] In the vast majority of these cases, however, there was an incumbent who lived locally: up to three miles away, or an hour's

---

2   See the introduction to *Crockford's Clerical Directory* (London, 1882).
3   Kew, TNA, Census Returns of England and Wales, 1881, RG11/3238, fol. 92, p. 20; RG11/3222, fol. 32, p. 23; RG11/2957, fol. 65, p. 10; RG11/3213, fol. 43, p. 1; RG11/3374, fol. 72, p. 6.
4   RG11/3221, fol. 60, p. 10; RG11/3293, fol. 39, p. 7; RG11/3298, fol. 28, p. 5.
5   No resident serving clergyman was found in Gunness with Burringham (864 people), Upton-cum-Kexby (562), Elsham (502), Fosdyke (477), Frithville (436),

walk, thus technically within the rules of ecclesiastical pluralism, presumably because he preferred the amenities and society of a larger settlement such as Louth, Sleaford or Folkingham.[6]

The absence of a clerical household in a significant number of places meant that the Anglican ecclesiological ideal of a resident clergyman in every parish could not be achieved. The shortfall was thought to be primarily due to benefice incomes, which were on the decline because of the state of the agricultural economy. However, evidence from the census, as described later, may indicate another reason, the shortage of wealthy clergy. Where Anglican clergy could not be deployed, other denominations, particularly those in which laypeople enjoyed a stronger religious role, had a greater influence.[7] Obelkevich, in his in-depth study of part of Lincolnshire, has shown that Methodism in its various forms was dominant in many of those villages where Anglican clergy were absent.[8] What kept religion alive in these sparsely populated and 'open' villages were the households of Nonconformist laymen.[9] Nonconformist ministers were almost entirely resident in the towns.[10] Indeed, it was in urban areas, even in the cathedral city of Lincoln, with its thirteen Anglican parishes and twenty-four parochial clergy, that the numerical competition between Church of England clergymen and other ordained ministers was at its greatest. In contrast, the clerical household was in its primacy as a model of religious life and influence in the 'closed' villages where society for reasons of economics and tradition revolved around the parish church, as evidenced by higher church attendance in such communities.[11]

Normanby-by-Spital (397), Scredington (397), Eastville with Midville (359) or Forton (357).

[6] Since the 1830s the Church authorities had been successful in reducing this phenomenon: see Frances Knight, *The Nineteenth-Century Church and English Society* (Cambridge, 1995), 142. The three mile restriction was imposed by the Pluralities Act (1850), and this was increased to four miles in the Pluralities Acts Amendment Act (1885). Both Acts also recognize the importance of benefice income.

[7] Anthony Russell, *The Clerical Profession* (London, 1980), 236.

[8] James Obelkevich, *Religion and Rural Society: South Lindsey 1825–1875* (Oxford, 1976), 168.

[9] The terms 'closed' and 'open' respectively describe those villages under the control of one or a few landowners who were usually Anglican and those relatively free from such social influence.

[10] The census records very few non-Anglican ministers in rural areas.

[11] The 1851 Religious Census and later worship registers showed higher attend-

The census shows some significant differences between the clerical households and those of their neighbours. Firstly, clerical households were headed by older men.[12] As might be expected, considering the career progressions available within the Church, only one incumbent was under 30: Walter Peacock, aged 28, was both rector and patron of Ulceby with Fordington, succeeding his father to both positions, and living at the vicarage with his mother, sisters and brother, as he had probably done for most of his life.[13] A third of the incumbents (about 160) were over 60, and thirteen were over 80. Charles Moore, rector of Wyberton, was the oldest at 93, one of only eighty-four men in the county aged over 90.[14] He died soon after the census, allowing the patron, who must have been patient, to appoint her own son to the living later that year.[15] The lack of pension provision kept most clergy in their parishes until they died, although at least one incumbent had made arrangements under the provisions of the Incumbents Resignation Act 1871, for at Long Bennington £150 was deducted from the benefice income as a pension for the former incumbent.[16] Curates provided help where the incumbents had become aged and incapacitated, sometimes becoming part of the clerical household, as at Billingborough and at Hougham.[17] As an occupational group incumbents were significantly older than the population at large, a divergence that increased in subsequent decades as the decline in ordinations took effect from this period. The ages of the wives of the clergy reveal a tendency, replicated in the rest of society, for them to be at least two years younger than their husbands. However, in one or two cases the gap was much larger: thus Henry Browne of Toft next Newton was forty-four years older than his wife.[18]

The mobility of clerical households also often marked them out as different, but there were three contrasting types. Of the incumbents and wives (845 in total), few had been born in the parish (13)

---

ance at the parish church where the majority landowner was Anglican.

[12] Whereas one in three incumbents was over 60, only one in ten men in Lincolnshire had reached or exceeded this age: *Census 1881*, 3: 277.

[13] RG11/3258, fol. 31, p. 13.

[14] *Census 1881*, 3: 277, RG11/3212, fol. 66, p. 13.

[15] Edward Robert Kelly, *Kelly's Directory of Lincolnshire* (London, 1885), 591.

[16] Kelly, *Directory*, 55. The Act allowed retiring clergy to receive a pension from the income of the benefice, up to one third of the benefice value.

[17] RG11/3196, fol. 32, p. 29; RG11/3379, fol. 106, p. 12. In other parishes the census shows that the curate stayed in a different house, usually close to the church.

[18] RG11/3282, fol. 137, p. 3.

or even in Lincolnshire itself (83). Most of these locally born clergy had been appointed through family patronage, as at Spridlington, where the incumbent followed his father-in-law and brother-in-law, and his mother-in-law seems to have been a permanent fixture at the rectory; at Branston, where the Curtois family had held the advowson for over two hundred years and the vicar lived in the rectory built by his grandfather in 1765; and at North and South Elkington where the Smyth family were lords of the manor, chief landowners, local magistrates, patrons and vicars.[19] At the time of the census, this type of clerical household, with its close links to the local gentry, existed in about one in ten of all Lincolnshire parishes, generally those which were better endowed.[20] The second type was the household that became fixed in one location once the head had found a suitable parish, adequately endowed, in which to bring up his family, begin a settled ministry and stay until he died.[21] Like that of the settled farmer or established town professional, these households were unlikely to move again. A third type of clerical household is revealed by the census through the different birth places recorded for children, a litany of previous parishes that spoke of a very unsettled existence.[22] Without the security of a reasonable freehold such clergy would expect to move frequently in search of work, as in the case of William Dixon of Panton, who had lived in five different parishes in thirteen years.[23] The mobility of this clerical household was even greater than that of the poor tenant farmer, clerk or schoolmaster. The census data also shows that some clerical families were subject to the economic depression inflicting agriculture, as at Castle Bytham, where the household of Charles Crackenthorp had no servants but included a son-in-law described as a 'farmer out of work' and about to emigrate.[24] Thus the census reveals clerical households at various points on a spectrum of fortune.

[19] RG11/3246, fol. 17, p. 7, Arthur Hutton, *Some Account of the Family of Hutton* (n.pl., 1897); RG11/3236, fol. 82, p. 20, Kelly, *Directory*, 334; RG11/3263, fol. 123, p. 13, Kelly, *Directory*, 386.

[20] Information is from *Crockford's* and Kelly, *Directory*, and corresponds to national figures provided in Russell, *Clerical Profession*, 245.

[21] RG11/3246, fol. 97, p. 1; RG11/3374, fol. 32, p. 9; RG11/3266, fol. 72, p. 10.

[22] RG11/3221, fol. 25, p. 44; RG11/4696, fol. 106, p. 6.

[23] RG11/3247, fol. 59, p. 2.

[24] RG11/3195, fol. 49, p. 25.

A significant consequence of the mobility of clerical households was that it brought an influence from beyond the county into the local community, particularly important in remote rural parishes which were otherwise populated by locals. The vast majority of incumbents and their wives, over 80 per cent, came from Britain but beyond Lincolnshire, although a not insignificant number, 7 per cent, had been born overseas, perhaps not unsurprisingly in a Church that was increasingly international in its missionary outlook. In contrast, only 15 per cent of the Lincolnshire population were born out of the county and less than 2 per cent were born abroad.[25] This highlights a distinctive characteristic of the clerical household, which was shared with some gentry families, as the census returns show. Furthermore, comments on the census forms reveal a group of clergy who had worked abroad: six examples are Andrew Frost at Croxton, Alexander Johnson at Fulstow and Mathew Lamert at Mavis Enderby, who had all worked in India; Samuel Blackburne at Beesby, formerly a missionary in New Zealand; Samuel Bond at Honington, who had been in South Africa; and James D'ombrain of Sotby, who was 'formerly civil commissioned chaplain at Smyrna'.[26] Such experiences in some clerical households will have helped to broaden the horizons of the local community.

A feature of some clerical households was the 'boarder', who lodged either for educational purposes or to provide an extra income for the clergy, or both.[27] As the census shows, these boarders were usually from other parts of the country. Small groups of pupils were living at the parsonages in Dunston, Dembleby, Messingham, Howell, North Hykeham, Ingham and Horbling,[28] and the incumbent households of West Torrington, Wellingore, Grayingham and Withcall had one pupil each.[29] At Marton the vicar's wife was

---

[25] *Census 1881*, 3: 310–12.
[26] RG11/3285, fol. 107, p. 23; RG11/3266, fol. 107, p. 10; RG11/3255, fol. 95, p. 8; RG11/3260, fol. 93, p. 14; RG11/3234, fol. 44, p. 2; RG11/3247, fol. 87, p. 4; Kelly, *Directory*, 634.
[27] This was noted by Peter Hammond, *The Parson and the Victorian Parish* (London, 1977), 37–8.
[28] RG11/3237, fol. 75, p. 10; RG11/3223, fol. 117, p. 15; RG11/3288, fol. 92, p. 24; RG11/3225, fol. 45, p. 8; RG11/3235, fol. 99, p. 18; RG11/3246, fol. 44, p. 2; RG11/3196, fol. 91, p. 12.
[29] RG11/3247, fol. 23, p. 11; RG11/3224, fol. 72, p. 8; RG11/3293, fol. 104, p. 13; RG11/3263, fol. 69, p. 8.

running a school in the vicarage with eight resident pupils.[30] A 22-year-old student of theology was lodging with his younger brother at Amcotts rectory, perhaps in preparation for ordination.[31] Sometimes the incumbent gave lodging to the schoolmistress, as at Spridlington, or to a 'sowing teacher', as at Cabourn.[32] It is not known why an unmarried brother and sister were boarding at North Cockerington; they had no profession and lived off investments, but came from Portsea, like the vicar.[33] The occupations of some of these boarders give an insight into the restoration work of incumbents: at Brant Broughton, an 'artist glass painter' from London was probably working on the very ornately decorated parish church in that village.[34]

Another valuable element of the census is information on resident servants. The vast majority of clerical households had two or more servants, with only about one in seven recording one servant or none. Two-thirds had two or three servants, on a par with the farmer of two hundred acres or more in the countryside, and the solicitor, the doctor and the larger shopkeeper in the towns. This was an indication of middle-class status. In comparison, Nonconformist ministers, depending on their denomination, usually only had one servant, although Primitive Methodist and Baptist ministers rarely had any. Roman Catholic priests invariably had a housekeeper. About one-fifth of clerical households had four or more servants, with a few heading up households with a large staff: John Cross of Appleby employed eight, including a lady's maid and footman; Thomas Wright of Broughton had nine, including two lady's maids, a footboy, a coachman and a butler; Frederick Ramsden of Uffington also had nine, with a footman and butler; as did Richard Walls, vicar of Firsby, who lived at Boothby Hall.[35]

The presence of servants born beyond the locality again emphasizes the way in which the clerical household was distinctive in reflecting influences beyond the neighbourhood. Only a small minority of servants in parsonages came from the parish, although most came

30 RG11/3298, fol. 17, p. 7.
31 RG11/4699, fol. 90, p. 7.
32 RG11/3246, fol. 17, p. 7; RG11/3279, fol. 82, p. 1.
33 RG11/3265, fol. 11, p. 1.
34 RG11/3374, fol. 38, p. 1.
35 RG11/3286, fol. 90, p. 16; RG11/3285, fol. 25, p. 15; RG11/3194, fol. 74, p. 4; RG11/3257, fol. 153, p. 7.

from within the county and relatively close by. Some had been born in parishes where the clergy or their wives had previously lived. At Alkborough the vicar's wife recruited her maid from her home town of Kirbymoorside, and at Eastoft the vicar's wife and the cook both came from the same village in Suffolk.[36] At Doddington rectory the cook and the parlour maid, apparently twin sisters, were from Huntingdon; while at Kirby-on-Bain the three maids were from the same village in Suffolk; and all the servants at Langton-by-Spilsby rectory were from Essex.[37] Some of the visitors staying over on census night who had no apparent family connection would appear to have been prospective servants far from home. At West Barkwith an 11-year-old girl was visiting from the East Riding; a 12-year-old Irish girl was staying in Barrow-on-Humber; at Louth a 13-year-old girl from Hampshire was present; and at Winteringham an older woman from Leek was looking for work.[38] Occasionally the clerical household included no one at all who had been born in the county, as at Mavis Enderby, Silk Willoughby and Waddingham, while a cook and a maid from Bavaria had found their way onto the staff of the parsonage in Horncastle.[39] At Barrowby, George Welby, brother of the Countess of Lindsey, staffed his rectory with seven servants of both genders from different parts of England and a lady's maid from Belgium.[40] This higher-end clerical household was very similar to those of wealthy laymen, where status was enhanced by male servants, for whom a tax was paid, and servants recruited from outside the county.

Perhaps most importantly, the presence of servants in the clerical households as revealed by the census provides evidence of the private wealth of the clergy. As over 85 per cent of clergy were able to employ at least two, and in many cases several more, servants, it would appear that most clerical households were better off than their rather modest clerical income would suggest.

However, certain factors have to be considered. Servant numbers were greater in households with young children, especially where a newborn child necessitated a 'monthly nurse', who was only a

36 RG11/3286, fol. 116, p. 9; RG11/4700, fol. 97, p. 4.

37 RG11/3236, fol. 4, p. 1; RG11/3252, fol. 32, p. 6; RG11/3256, fol. 88, p. 8.

38 RG11/3247, fol. 20, p. 6; RG11/3290, fol. 4, p. 2; RG11/3262, fol. 55, p. 7; RG11/3286, fol. 56, p. 15.

39 RG11/3255, fol. 95, p. 8; RG11/3223, fol. 97, p. 1; RG11/3281, fol. 143, p. 10; RG11/3248, fol. 50, p. 23.

40 RG11/3234, fol. 11, p. 13.

temporary employee. The census shows that governesses employed to teach the children were a common feature of middle-class homes, particularly in remote rural areas such as Lincolnshire, where good schooling was less readily available. Another factor likely to increase servant numbers was guests who were visiting at the time of the census and had brought their servants with them, or whose advent necessitated the employment of temporary staff. Charles Terrot, vicar of Wispington, was hosting his daughter and granddaughters and as a consequence the number of servants in the house probably increased, while at Burton-upon-Stather one of the lady's maids was recorded as a visitor, and the servants at Lavington vicarage numbered ten, probably at least in part on account of four visitors.[41]

Consideration must also be given to those servants who, although not registered as living under the roof of the incumbent, did live very close by: at Edenham, the young Harry Cotterill in the next house was described as the 'vicars servant', and at Sibsey the vicar's housekeeper and housemaid were listed as neighbours to the vicar, although this may be an enumerator's mistake.[42] Grooms, not strictly indoor servants, lived out at West Keal, Saltfleetby St Peter and Welby.[43] In many places, the census also records several people who were classified as 'domestic servants' but lodging or living at home and whose place of work cannot be accurately known.[44]

Further account must be taken of those who, as part of the household, were not described as servants but who helped with domestic duties. Members of an extended family seem to have lived in several parsonages. How much domestic work they did, if any, and whether they were paid or just received their board and lodging is unknown. At Barholm the governess had the same surname as the vicar; the unmarried vicar of St Michael on the Mount, Lincoln, was being looked after by his sister, as was the unmarried rector of Covenham St Mary; and the widowed rector of Quarrington had two unmarried sisters-in-law to help him look after his six children, which meant that he only had to

---

[41] RG11/3249, fol. 68, p. 12; RG11/3287, fol. 10, p. 13; RG11/3227, fol. 63, p. 10.
[42] RG11/3197, fol. 46, p. 6; RG11/3216, fol. 6, p. 5.
[43] RG11/3255, fol. 69, p. 6; RG11/3265, fol. 74, p. 6; RG11/3234, fol. 130, p. 5.
[44] The unreliability of the census record in this respect is referred to by Lucy Delap, *Knowing their Place: Domestic Service in Twentieth-Century Britain* (Oxford, 2011), 11–12.

employ one maid.[45] There were no servants at the parsonage at Surfleet, but a 38-year-old widowed niece lived with the elderly vicar and his wife, and a similar situation obtained at Addlethorpe; at Tothill the 80-year-old rector shared his home with two females, vaguely described as 'relatives'; and at Dowsby everyone, including the cook and the housemaid, had the same surname as the incumbent.[46]

However, even recognizing these factors, it is still apparent that the number of servants employed by incumbents was generally in excess of what could be afforded from their benefice incomes. In Lincolnshire one-tenth of livings were valued at £150 or less per year, and only a third at £400 or more.[47] Furthermore, these were often speculative amounts that might not be easy to collect, and were subject to taxes, charges and reductions for parish needs. Generally the trend from the 1870s was for these values to decline as the agriculture based on the heavy clay soil of the county became less profitable.[48] Taking into account the provincial nature of Lincolnshire and the benefit of a rent-free house, to have two or three servants, the norm for incumbent households, would require an income of at least £500, well beyond the reach of most incumbents in their capacity as clergymen.[49] It has been argued that parsonages could employ servants more cheaply, on account of possible benefits such as an education, a large well-built house, a respectability and certain status, and (perhaps not insignificantly for young girls away from home) less of a threat of sexual harassment from their employer, though this could not be guaranteed to be absent.[50] Clergy were much concerned about the plight of young female servants at this time.[51] The disadvantages of working at a

---

[45] RG11/3194, fol. 103, p. 6; RG11/3241, fol. 85, p. 38; RG11/3266, fol. 19, p. 14; RG11/3223, fol. 74, p. 2.

[46] RG11/3202, fol. 94, p. 20; RG11/3257, fol. 39, p. 11; RG11/3260, fol. 59, p. 12; RG11/3196, fol. 53, p. 1.

[47] Figures from *Crockford's* 1882; Kelly, *Directory*, 1885.

[48] Hammond, *Parson*, 41.

[49] This is the approximate necessary income suggested by Mrs Beeton in *The Book of Household Management* (London, 1861), section 21, online at: <http://www.mrsbeeton.com>, accessed 24 May 2012; see also Judith Flanders, *The Victorian House* (London, 2004), 93–119.

[50] The balance of power, including sexual, between servant and employer is explored in John Benson, 'One Man and his Servants', *Labour History Review* 72 (2007), 203–14.

[51] See, for example, remarks made at the chapter meetings in north Lincolnshire:

parsonage might include the need to attend household prayers and church more often, and to work in a house where financial economy was important.[52] However, the small advantages of working in a clerical household cannot on their own explain how clergy seemed to employ the number of staff they did.

The presence of servants in clerical households supports the view that the private wealth of the clergy was subsidizing the Church to a large degree, and increasingly so at a time when benefice income was falling.[53] Contemporary sources highlighted this dilemma: 'it is not the Church which maintains the Clergy, but the Clergy who maintain the Church'.[54] If the number of servants is an indication of wealth, then in many cases private income was at least matching that provided by the benefice. One way of measuring wealth is through probate records, though it has to be recognized that these are affected by factors such as longevity and inflation.[55] These records suggest that the number of servants in a clerical household, rather than the benefice income, is a better indication of the wealth of the household. The clergy who in 1881 were incumbents of the most prosperous livings, that is those of £750 a year or more, at their deaths were valued at an average of £15,700 each, a not inconsiderable amount. However, the clergy who hired the most servants in 1881, that is seven or more, at their deaths were worth an average of £30,900. Thus the composition of clerical households as revealed in the census may offer a valuable tool for exploring the extent of private wealth among the clergy. The census data certainly shows that there were rich clergy who chose to serve in relatively poor livings and who from their own means helped to maintain the Church and head up households with a liberal provision of servants.

The 1881 census provides evidence for three important conclusions about the character of clerical households in the Church of England in the last quarter of the nineteenth century. Even when

Lincoln, Lincolnshire Archives Office, RD1/4/2, Ruridecanal Minute Book (Yarborough No. 2), 1871–1897, 18 September 1879, 2 March 1881, 26 June 1884.

[52] See Frank Dawes, *Not in Front of the Servants, Domestic Service in England 1850–1939* (London, 1973), 46–50, 102.

[53] See Alan Haig, *The Victorian Clergy* (London, 1984), 304.

[54] *Crockford's* 1884, ix.

[55] *England & Wales, National Probate Calendar (Index of Wills and Administrations), 1858–1966*, online at: <http://www.ancestry.com>, accessed 24 May 2012.

deployment was at its most abundant because ordination numbers were at a peak, about a fifth of parishes in Lincolnshire had no resident clergyman, and thus the presence of the clerical household was far from universal.[56] It was in the places where they could not be found that lay households, particularly those of other denominations, had a role in maintaining religion, although this has left a fainter historical record. However, where they were present, clerical households brought an important influence from the wider world beyond the county and the nation, in terms of the origin and experience of the members of the clerical family and their servants. Finally, the number of servants in the clerical household provides important evidence that in many cases the household and thus the work of the local church was underpinned by private wealth. The implication is that the fall in benefice incomes, often seen as a key reason for the decline of the clergy, is less significant than some contemporaries and historians have argued. It is important to ask why the wealthy became less willing to take on this clerical role in subsequent generations. These elements of the clerical household made it distinctive and gave a particular character, in terms of outlook and generosity, to the way the Christian faith was expressed at the parish level.

Lincoln College

---

[56] The 870 ordination total for 1885 was never surpassed: see Russell, *Clerical Profession*, 242; Michael Hinton, *The Anglican Parochial Clergy* (London, 1994), 12.

THE MISSIONARY HOME AS A SITE FOR MISSION: PERSPECTIVES FROM BELGIAN CONGO

by DAVID MAXWELL

Nineteenth- and twentieth-century Protestant missionaries considered themselves exemplars of the Christian home. They devoted considerable energy to writing about domesticity and to constructing model homes in the mission field. In spite of their good intentions there was often a large gap between their ideals and the realities of life on mission stations. By means of a case study of a Pentecostal faith mission in Katanga, Belgian Congo, this essay demonstrates how models of the Western Christian home were unsustainable and examines the manner in which missionaries coped with unfulfilled domestic dreams. It shows how Western notions of the Christian home were undermined by the harshness of the tropical environment, the disparity in numbers between male and female missionary vocations, and the persistence of African notions of domesticity. The missionaries endured the material and emotional deprivations of life in the bush through faith in a providential God and by constructing intimate but tense relationships with African Christians. The essay begins with a discussion of some of the most pertinent scholarship on missionaries and domesticity.

In an important article entitled 'The "Christian Home" as a Cornerstone of Anglo-American Missionary Thought and Practice', the prominent historian of mission Dana Robert writes: 'The idea of the Christian home was central to Christian Mission. Endorsed across denominations and national differences, discussed at ecumenical gatherings, and cutting across the dichotomy between civilisation and evangelisation, the 'Christian Home' consistently remained both a means and a goal of Anglo-American missions.'[1] Robert goes on to explain that the Christian home remained

---

[1] Dana Robert, 'The "Christian Home" as a Cornerstone of Anglo-American Missionary Thought and Practice' in eadem, ed., *Converting Colonialism: Visions and Realities in Mission History, 1706–1914*, SHCM (Grand Rapids, MI, 2008), 134–65, at 135.

an enduring component of Anglo-American mission theory because it combined social and evangelistic functions of missions, while simultaneously justifying the movement's existence to western supporters of mission. It provided a rationale for the participation of women in all aspects of mission work, including homemaking, evangelism, fund raising, teaching and even social reform. It also validated a Protestant lifestyle that met the personal needs of expatriate missionary communities.[2]

Other historians have pointed to an even broader significance of missionary ideals of the Christian home. In work that integrates mission history into the history of empire, scholars such as Susan Thorne and Catherine Hall have shown how nineteenth-century English Evangelicals and humanitarians sought to advance the emancipation of female members of the new industrial bourgeoisie by representing them in opposition to colonized women, who were depicted as in desperate need of conversion and liberation. The notion that non-Western cultures lacked adequate norms of hygiene, child rearing, proper sexual practice and gender relations created the intellectual and moral context for evolving new modern metropolitan domesticity which defined middle-class women primarily as wives and mothers.[3] Female missionaries embodied this bourgeois domestic agenda in their encounter with non-Western peoples.[4]

Robert contends, however, that despite its ubiquity in missionary literature the Christian home has tended only to be studied in terms of missionary attempts to impose Western bourgeois notions of domesticity on indigenous peoples, particularly women.[5] This approach highlights missionary assumptions that indigenous women were incapable of intellectual development and needed only to be trained as a servant class. She cites, for instance, a particularly influential article by Deborah Gaitskell which examines the flawed attempts by a range of Anglo-American missions to

---

[2]   Ibid. 136.

[3]   Susan Thorne, *Congregational Missions and the Making of Imperial Culture in Nineteenth-Century England*, (Stanford, CA, 1999); Catherine Hall, *Civilising Subjects: Metropole and Colony in the English Imagination 1830–1867* (Cambridge, 2002).

[4]   Patricia Grimshaw and Peter Sherlock, 'Women and Cultural Exchanges', in N. Etherington, ed., *Missions and Empire* (Oxford, 2005), 173–93, at 178–9.

[5]   Robert, 'The "Christian Home"', 140–1.

prepare South African girls for motherhood and domestic service in a socio-economic context in which white bourgeois ideals of home could not be sustained.[6] As a counter to this emphasis, Robert's own work explores African appropriations of missionary domesticity in Zimbabwe. She shows how contemporary indigenous churchwomen have seized domestic ideals 'as a means of self-reliance, self-respect and control over one's spouse', arguing that 'the Christian home remains a popular idea today because it is a sign and means of Christianisation that women control themselves'.[7] Robert does, however, over-argue her case. Gaitskell's work has shifted from the study of the missionary imposition of domesticity to African appropriations and recognition that Africans and missionaries at times had similar views of the female role.[8] Other scholars have examined African transformation of Western domesticity as a means of increasing female autonomy or creating a new respectable identity.[9] Nevertheless, Robert's observation that the Christian home was a 'pragmatic plastic concept that was shaped according to national, class, and gender interests' remains particularly apt.[10]

Some of the best work on missionary households explores the contests between Africans and Europeans over the meaning and uses of Christian domesticity. In her monograph *A Colonial Lexicon of Birth, Ritual, Medicalisation and Mobility in the Congo*, Nancy Rose Hunt provides a sophisticated examination of missionary domesticity amongst Baptists working at Yakusu in western Belgian Congo during the twentieth century. Her analysis focuses on the quaint tales that were the staple of Protestant mission propaganda. These biographical stories of mission Africans had simple plots

---

[6] Deborah Gaitskell, 'Housewives, Maids or Mothers: Some Contradictions of Domesticity for Christian Women in Johannesburg, 1903–39', *JAH* 24 (1983), 241–56.

[7] Robert, 'The "Christian Home"', 157–8.

[8] See Deborah Gaitskell, 'Power in Prayer and Service: Women's Christian Organisations', in R. Elphick and R. Davenport, eds, *Christianity in South Africa: A Political, Cultural and Social History* (Berkeley, CA, 1997); eadem, 'At Home with Hegemony? Coercion and Consent in the Education of African Girls for Domesticity in South Africa before 1910', in Dagmar Engels and Shula Marks, eds, *Contesting Colonial Hegemony: State and Society in Africa and India* (London, 1994), 110–28.

[9] Teresa Barnes, *'We Women worked so Hard': Gender, Urbanization and Social Reproduction in Colonial Harare, Zimbabwe, 1930–56* (Oxford, 1999); David Maxwell, *African Gifts of the Spirit: Pentecostalism and the Rise of a Zimbabwean Transnational Religious Movement* (Oxford, 2006).

[10] Robert, 'The "Christian Home"', 136.

which recounted lives marked by progress. At their most extreme and compelling the stories told of reformed cannibals eating with knives and forks and female ex-slaves who became house girls, mothers and Bible translators. Visits by Belgian royalty, Christmas dinner and tea parties all figured highly in these tales because they were a means of creating home and domesticating the savage. Good behaviour on the part of Africans was rewarded with greater responsibility in the missionary household and increased access to interior rooms. Domesticated young men moved from kitchens to dining rooms and bedrooms, then on to hospitals, operating theatres and rural health centres as nurses-cum-evangelists. Girls received a parallel formation in housekeeping and maternal training. Marriage between former house girls and house boys, often arranged by missionaries, was the pinnacle of missionary endeavour. [11] Hunt's account of the processes of domesticity amongst African men and women on a mission station is all the more compelling because of her use of fieldwork, including extensive interviews, to show how missionary attempts to remake African subjectivities were 'debated and translated' by those Africans she calls 'middle figures' who strove to forge their own identity as respectable Christian elites. [12]

My own research on the Congo Evangelistic Mission (CEM), based in Katanga in south-eastern Belgian Congo, shares many of Hunt's conclusions about missionary programmes of domesticity. But there are also significant differences. Although Hunt offers a nuanced account of the missionary household as a site of intimate evangelism, she examines the social and intellectual world of African Christians with far more empathy than she does that of missionaries, who are the major concern of this essay. The case of the CEM shows that missionary attempts to build the Christian household were highly contingent. In the opening stage of the encounter the household was flimsy at best; it was often mobile as pioneer missionaries attempted to come to terms with the vast territories under their supervision. Once established, the household remained vulnerable to disease and death, hunger and exhaustion, isolation and loneliness. Missionaries remained reliant upon Africans for material and emotional sustenance. They constructed

---

[11] Nancy Hunt, *A Colonial Lexicon of Birth, Ritual, Medicalisation and Mobility in the Congo* (Durham, NC, 1999), 117–95.
[12] Ibid. 7–8.

deep and lasting relationships with African Christians, although the stresses and strains of the colonial situation meant that they could at times also reject those with whom they formed the closest bonds. The porosity of the missionary household also had implications for the creation of ethnographic knowledge. Scholars are increasingly interested in the contribution of missionaries to colonial science, particularly their role as ethnographers.[13] The contingency of their existence meant that missionaries encountered Africans in circumstances far removed from stereotypical location of the veranda. Their observations were often well grounded, particularly in the self-representations of African converts who were evolving their own response to Christian modernity.

Some of the differences between the Baptist and CEM cases stem from the different methodological approaches of these studies. Hunt offers close readings of the missionary propaganda intended for European supporters. Mission periodicals were filled with optimistic stories of the transformation of African bodies and circumstances and normative statements about the parameters of the African Christian household in order to convince donors and intercessors of the value of the missionary cause. But missionaries also engaged in private correspondence with friends and prayer partners, sharing frustrations and failings as well as successes. The genre of these letters was more that of the embattled and isolated psalmist than the triumphal Evangelical. This personal correspondence was supplemented by a genre of missionary images, usually found in personal photograph albums and sometimes in magic lantern shows, depicting the more intimate side of missionary life. These images, photographs taken by missionaries, can show a far more multifaceted response to Africans than the simple oppositions that the conventions of evangelical prose published for readers back home usually allowed. Private correspondence, magic lantern slides and photograph albums belonging to former CEM missionaries have been deposited in the CEM archives and will be discussed in this essay. Other differences between the CEM and Baptists were theological and material, as will be revealed in the following section.

---

[13] Patrick Harries and David Maxwell, eds, *The Spiritual in the Secular: Missionaries and Knowledge about Africa*, SHCM (Grand Rapids, MI, 2012).

The Congo Evangelistic Mission

The Congo Evangelistic Mission was founded by William Burton and James Salter in Mwanza, near Katanga, Belgian Congo, in 1915. It was intended to be a mission to Luba- and Songye-speaking peoples. As an independent Pentecostal faith mission it was an exemplar of the type of pneumatic Christianity that increased in numerical strength and public presence throughout the twentieth century in Africa, Asia and Latin America to become one of the most dynamic religious movements in the contemporary world.[14] The Congolese Church, which is descended from the CEM, claims over half a million adherents today.[15] In contrast, the Baptist Missionary Society (BMS), founded in 1792, was one of the first Nonconformist missionary organizations. Pioneering in western Congo in 1880, it preceded the Leopoldian state of 1885 and its Belgian successor of 1908. The BMS shared the latter's civilizing mission of health and education, though often differed from it on the vexed issue of labour.[16] Unlike Baptist missionaries, CEM Pentecostals were driven by a millennial imperative to evangelize and shunned the 'incubus' of a large mission infrastructure because it slowed continuous gospel proclamation.[17] Fresh recruits were quickly placed in new stations in order to maximize the chances of reaching the unsaved before the end times. CEM stations resembled neither the 'Little Englands' in the rainforest created by the Baptists nor the vast mission towns – even 'kingdoms' – created by Catholic missions, which benefitted from state patronage.[18] Instead,

---

[14] K. Fiedler, *The Story of Faith Missions* (Oxford, 1994); B. Cooper, *Evangelical Christians in the Muslim Sahel* (Bloomington, IN, 2006).

[15] D. Cartwright, 'Zaire Evangelistic Mission', in S. M. Burgess and E. M. van der Maas, eds, *New International Dictionary of Pentecostal and Charismatic Movements* (Grand Rapids, MI, 2001). The movement split after independence and the sections were later assigned numbers as part of President Mobutu's top-down amalgamation and classification of Protestant denominations. The largest section is now known as *La Trentième* ('The Thirtieth').

[16] B. Stanley, *The History of the Baptist Missionary Society, 1792–1992* (Edinburgh, 1992), 106–39.

[17] P. Kay, *Cecil Polhill, The Pentecostal Missionary Union, and the Fourfold Gospel with Healing and Speaking in Tongues: Signs of a New Movement in Missions*, North Atlantic Missiology Project, Henry Martyn Centre, Position Paper no. 20 (Cambridge, 1996).

[18] Allen Roberts, 'History, Ethnicity and Change in the Christian Kingdom of Southeastern Zaire', in L. Vail, ed., *The Creation of Tribalism in Southern Africa* (London, 1989), 193–214.

one or two missionary families were responsible for vast swathes of territory. Because they were able to offer only limited provision in education and bio-medicine, CEM missionaries were more reliant upon an army of African evangelists to transform African lives.

Burton and Salter had arrived in Katanga as bachelors. Their intent had been to live an itinerant life, planting churches ('assemblies') in African villages by building up a core of faithful believers. Following the ideal of the influential missionary thinker, Henry Venn, their intention was to move on when the assembly was self-supporting, self-governing and self-propagating.[19] However, this plan did not prove possible and so Burton and Salter established the station at Mwanza, where their first house was extremely rudimentary and shared with African brethren. Like many pioneering missionaries, Burton and Salter took their first converts into their home as 'houseboys' in order to enhance their Christian formation. The missionaries' relations with the first of these, fittingly named Abraham, were characterized by a good degree of reciprocity. They taught him the precious skill of literacy and he helped them learn Kiluba, procured them food and gained them an entry into local society. The walls of their first dwelling place were so thin that Burton and Salter were treated to a rare snapshot of how African Christians viewed them. In his hagiographical account of Abraham's life, Salter describes how the missionaries could hear their African companions discuss their faltering attempts at language-learning: '[They] mimicked our voices and accents and exposed our mistakes so faithfully that we had to gag ourselves with bedding or we should have been convulsed with laughter.' Burton and Salter also grasped that their early converts viewed literacy as possessing a talismanic quality. While constructing buildings at different ends of the station Burton and Salter would communicate via messages written on wood chips carried by Abraham. They lived in close enough proximity to him to observe that he had made a collection of these discarded chips among the treasures in his trunk.[20]

In the pioneering phase the CEM household was often mobile as missionaries trekked, preaching to outlying villages accompanied by Christian porters who carried tents, provisions, the camera and other scientific instruments (Fig. 1). The porters relied on the

19 T. Yates, *Christian Missions in the Twentieth Century* (Cambridge, 1994).
20 J. Salter, *Abraham: Our First Convert* (London, c.1933), 8–11.

Fig. 1: William Burton on trek. Reproduced by courtesy of the Central Africa Mission [hereafter: CAM] (Preston 26).

missionary's gun for game and protection, sleeping close to his tent at night. The missionaries depended upon their porters for local knowledge. They were also made aware that once they had retired to their tents at night their African colleagues would translate their 'faltering' attempts at Kiluba into proper gospel preaching, explaining what they had really meant to say.[21] More efficacious still in terms of proselytism was the porters' habit of singing out the gospel in order to ward off dangerous animals and raise their spirits as they traversed alien territory. It was often song rather than preaching that attracted an audience and communicated new Christian ideas.[22] The sojourns in African villages also provided missionaries with a key opportunity to pursue the general activities that make up ethnography: observing, inquiring, conversing, noting and photographing (Fig. 2).

Burton and Salter soon realized that they were not suited to the single lifestyle. Burton was shocked by Luba notions of sexual hospi-

[21] Max Moorhead, *Missionary Pioneering in Congo Forests: A Narrative of William F. P. Burton and his Companions in the Native Villages of Luba-Land* (Preston, 1922), 75, 96.
[22] W. Burton, *Honey Bee: Life Story of a Congo Evangelist* (Johannesburg, 1959), 25, 27.

Fig. 2: Preparing for a trek. Reproduced by courtesy of CAM (Preston 3).

tality. He was also unnerved by the advances of young women and felt unable to proselytize them. In March 1918 he went to South Africa to recruit more missionaries and to marry Hettie Trollip, a young woman from a respectable farming family in the Cape who belonged to the Pentecostal Apostolic Faith Mission. Salter also married quickly, but in 1922 left the field to run operations from England. Henceforth, Burton acted as secretary and *représentant légal* of the CEM. As effective head of the mission he was responsible not only for evangelizing the villages around Mwanza but also for the oversight of the entire field. Between 1918 and 1925, over thirty Pentecostal missionaries joined the CEM, vastly expanding the mission's reach across the entirety of the former Luba territory and subsequently into Songye-speaking areas and later into towns and cities.

Two of the most significant new recruits were Teddy Hodgson and Harold Womersley, who arrived in 1920 and 1924 respectively. Womersley proved particularly skilled at pioneering new stations and in his history of the CEM he describes the first eighteen months of his life in the Congo as that of a 'rough bachelor'. Although engaged to be married, the colonial state took almost two years to process his fiancée's papers. He was first sent alone to Kisanga, where he constructed a simple mud and wattle hut and cooked his own food. Doubtless moved by his loneliness, the villagers presented him with a 'village beauty, smeared head to foot with red ochre and palm oil, hair ridged and bobbed, blue and white beads round her ankles, and a tiny beaded cloth around her waist'. Womersley declined, drawing consolation from the fact that several months of solid isolation would compel him to make rapid progress in speaking Kiluba.[23] From Kisanga he was transferred to Lake Kikondja to pioneer the region with Hodgson. Then in 1927 he and his new wife, Josephine, were sent to a completely new area of Busangu where she was the first white woman the locals had encountered. Seven years later they were moved to another remote location, Kabongo in the far north of the territory. Although Josephine transformed Harold's bachelor hut into a 'comfortable and attractive home', they often worked apart, with Harold embarking on treks lasting several weeks to evangelize outlying villages and conduct mission business.[24] On these occasions Josephine was de facto head of the mission station.

Hodgson was a bachelor until 1932, living a peripatetic existence visiting lakeside fishing villages on his boat. His young wife Linda died of blackwater fever in 1933 and he remained a widow until 1939, when he married Helen, who lived until 1959. As bachelor and widow Hodgson drew much from the companionship of his oarsmen and African evangelists.[25]

A good deal of Burton's correspondence with Salter and with the Myerscough family, who acted as the mission's treasurers, concerned the selection of new recruits. As Pentecostals, applicants had, of course, to have been baptized in the Holy Spirit, to have a passion for soul-winning, and to believe in the eternal damnation of the unrepentant sinner. In addition, new missionaries had to possess the qualities necessary to build Christian households. They had to be 'useful', 'intelligent' and 'hard working'; those who were lazy, dirty and lacked initiative were sent home.[26] Missionary

---

[23] H. Womersley, *Congo Miracle: Fifty Years of God's Working in Congo (Zaire)* (London, 1974), 82, 85.

[24] E.g. ibid. 82.

[25] E. Hodgson, *Fishing for Congo Fisherfolk* (London, 1934); idem, *Out of Darkness: The Story of an Indigenous Church in Belgian Congo* (London, 1946)

[26] Preston, Central African Missions [hereafter: CAM (formerly CEM)], Burton to Myerscough file [hereafter: Myerscough file], William Burton to Thomas Myerscough, 25 March, 18 August 1925.

wives had to be 'all round capable girls'.[27] Given that the ideal was companionate marriage, one might have assumed that applications from single men would have been discouraged, as were those of single women. But the single men were accepted, while single women were viewed as too frail to survive the harsh bush environment and as less useful than African male evangelists, who cost far less to maintain. The bar on single women caused a stir at home, not least because female vocations far exceeded male ones and women were the chief supporters of missionary work. Eventually some single women were accepted by the CEM for missionary service, not least because it was hoped that they might be transformed into wives for the bachelor missionaries.[28]

Letters back home carried advice for new arrivals on the accoutrements of the mission household (Fig. 3). Missionary couples were encouraged to bring with them 'a portable typewriter for men ... small tool chest, bedding and haberdashery and a little special crockery'. A good mahogany dining table, high-quality reed carpets and the essential Singer sewing machine could all be procured locally.[29] The physical dimensions and setting of the mission house formed the first set of object lessons in Christian modernity. Images in magic lantern shows and CEM literature depict the mission house with well-tended gardens and trees, and clear-cut straight paths. There were a good number of shots of brickmaking (Fig. 4). Bricks were far more than building blocks: they were associated with wage labour and new types of kiln; they produced rectangular structures which formed a powerful contrast with the circular structures so prominent in African architecture. Bricks built straight roads and bridges, beat back vegetation, conquered streams and rivers, and kept out animals and some insects.[30] An obituary for the Catholic missionary Emile Callewaert celebrated the fact that he had burnt more than two million bricks

---

[27] Ibid., Hettie Burton to Edith Myerscough, 10 February 1944.

[28] Ibid., Theo Myerscough to William Burton, 23 April 1934.

[29] Ibid., Burton to CEM Home Council, 25 January 1926; William Burton to Edith Myerscough, *c*.1944; W. Burton to the British and Foreign Bible Society, July 1921, cited in Moorhead, *Missionary Pioneering*, 34.

[30] John Mackenzie, 'Missionaries, Science and the Environment in Nineteenth-Century Africa', in A. Porter, ed., *The Imperial Horizons of British Protestant Missions, 1880–1914*, SHCM (Grand Rapids, MI, 2003), 106–30, at 116.

Fig. 3: The Mission house at Mwanza. Reproduced by courtesy of CAM (Preston 53).

during his pioneering work in Katanga.[31] If the CEM missionaries were attempting to reproduce an alien idyllic setting, it was that of the South African Cape.[32] The Burtons imported seeds and livestock from Hettie's family farm.[33]

While it was relatively easy to construct the physical circumstances of a Christian household, social relations were more difficult to engineer and maintain. The axiom that the twentieth-century African Christian movement was 'a woman's movement' did not apply in the Luba context, where women initially proved more resistant to Christianity than young men.[34] Luba culture ascribed women a status complementary to that of men. Through coif-

[31] *Le Messager du Saint-Esprit* [École des Missions (Brabant)] 30/1–3 (January–June 1938), 134.

[32] Myerscough file, William Burton to Phil and Edith Myerscough, 28 January 1938.

[33] William Burton, sermon in South Africa, 1918, cited in Moorhead, *Missionary Pioneering*, 121.

[34] B. Sundkler, 'African Church History in a New Key', in Kirsten Holst-Peterson, ed., *Religion Development and African Identity*, Studia Missionalia Upsalensia 17 (Uppsala, 1987), 73–83, at 83. This was often the pattern in Southern Africa but it did not apply

439

Fig. 4: Brick making. Reproduced by courtesy of CAM (Preston 44).

fures, cicatrization and adornment, their bodies became receptacles of spiritual energy and beholders of political secrets.[35] Missionary strictures about monogamous Christian marriage seemed to limit their chances of biological reproduction, which was the main route to female status in Luba society. As in other East and Central African contexts the first female converts were runaways, women fleeing domestic slavery or abusive relationships. Hettie Burton built a women's refuge which, besides women in flight, attracted other socially marginal women such as widows who lacked the security of living children. The refuge also took in abandoned and orphaned infants.[36] In time, however, other women converted, especially as female missionaries developed their skills in midwifery.

In an autobiographical account of her refuge work, Hettie Burton offered an evangelical critique of institutions which she

to the Yoruba: see J. D. Y. Peel, *Religious Encounter in the Making of the Yoruba* (Bloomington, IN, 2000), 234–40.

[35] M. Nooter Roberts and A. Roberts, eds, *Memory: Luba Art and the Making of History* (New York, 1996), ch. 3. Cicatrizations are 'tattoos' made by cutting incisions in the skin.

[36] M. Wright, *Strategies of Slaves and Women: Life Stories from East Central Africa* (London, 1993).

believed limited women's entrance into Christian monogamy and companionate marriage, such as polygamy and the commoditized bride price. Butanda and Kupata female initiation ceremonies, which were important moments of liminality, education and socialization into Luba culture and history, were a particular target as sources of indiscipline and corrupting sexual mores.[37] The conditions of the typical village, from which girls were to be liberated, were repeatedly contrasted with the Christian home.[38] Ordinary domestic activity was turned into another set of object lessons for African women. Hettie Burton wrote:

> In each group of girls … I select the neatest and most intelligent, bringing them into our home to do some sweeping, scrubbing, dusting etc. … Their quick eyes take in many advantages and conveniences in our manner of life, commencing even with whitewashed ceilings and walls which make our home so light and give a sense of cleanliness. They admire our texts and pictures, making a mental note that they would like such things in their own homes when they get married.[39]

Taking the reader on a tour of the home of Djenipa, one of her prize girls who had married an evangelist, Hettie Burton commented:

> We are at once struck by the general neatness. … The table has a clean white cloth on it, and there are two substantial home-made chairs. A book shelf on their walls was once a brick mould. It holds their precious testaments, hymn books, school books and a few lesser helps.
>
> The food is in the cupboard. The beds are nicely made from planks cut in a near-by forest and are covered by counterpanes of native cloth. There is even a jam-jar of flowers on the table, while the wall is adorned by texts and coloured prints taken from the *Illustrated London News*.
>
> A backroom contains their supply of peanuts, maize, millet and other foodstuffs, stored in big earthen pots with smaller pots on top to keep out dust, rats and insects.

---

37 Nooter-Roberts and Roberts, *Memory*.
38 H. Burton, *My Black Daughters* (London, 1949), 20–30.
39 Ibid. 38.

The little ones are dressed in simple loincloths. ... The elder girls, however [,] have dresses ... All are clean and supremely happy, so different from the dirty, diseased youngsters in the villages around.[40]

In addition, Djenipa and her female Christian colleagues cultivated successful gardens and supported their husbands in evangelistic work.[41] Missionary photographs and slides celebrated these living embodiments of Christian domesticity. A popular image was that of an unnamed African evangelist and his nuclear family, dressed in cotton clothes and posing outside their square brick house. Another favourite was of unnamed 'pastors' wives' in what the Burtons described as 'clean' cotton clothes. Their heads covered with simple turbans rather than complex coiffures, these African women represented a new type of Christian womanhood. The slide was complemented by another photograph of five male pastors, dressed in simple cotton shirts. William Burton argued that clean clothes and homes were the 'beginning of a cleaner moral order'.[42] The images represented to western church audiences the best fruit of missionary labours, providing outward and visible signs of conversion (Figs 5, 6, 7).

As in other African Christian movements it was African women themselves who chose to abandon their elaborate coiffures and cicatrization and to cover their heads and bodies with cotton clothing as markers of respectability.[43] However, because this respectability fused with former notions of rank and honour, Luba and Songye households never quite resembled the missionary ideal of the nuclear family. In villages far away from missionary supervision, the African Christian patriarch might build an extended family of kin and collect a following of clients in order to enhance his esteem, prestige and weight in the community.[44] Moreover, first-generation African evangelists frustrated missionary attempts at matchmaking by preferring to find their own wives, Christian

40 Ibid. 38–42.
41 Ibid.
42 W. Burton, *Congo Sketches* (London, 1950).
43 W. Burton, *Congo Evangelistic Mission Report*, no. 42 (May–June 1933), 693–4.
44 T. C. McCaskie, 'Cultural Encounters: Britain and Africa in the Nineteenth Century' in A. Porter, ed., *The Oxford History of the British Empire*, 3: *The Nineteenth Century* (Oxford, 1999), 668–9.

Fig. 5: An evangelist and his family. Reproduced by courtesy of CAM (Preston 75).

Fig. 6: Pastors' wives: (left to right) Ndokasa, Luisa and Jennifer. Reproduced by courtesy of CAM (Preston 73).

Fig. 7: Pastors: (left to right) Yoela Kapumba, David Katontoka, Samsoni Kashamo, Abraham Nyuki, Tshango Menge. Reproduced by courtesy of CAM (Preston 50).

or not.[45] It was fitting that African Christianization had its own internal dynamic because missionary ideals and schemes so often failed.

DISEASE AND DEATH IN THE MISSIONARY HOUSEHOLD

Missionary photography was an effective tool in recording the transforming effects of Christian modernity, but what it did not reveal was the household's continued vulnerability to disease and stress. Although literary scholars have rightly shown how missionary propaganda emphasized disease and misfortune in order to portray the missionary life as one of heroism, missionaries did in fact fall ill and die, often in great numbers.[46] For most of the colonial era, doctors across Africa were unable to cure a host of diseases, including pneumonia, yaws, tropical ulcers, and other diseases related to colonial underdevelopment and poverty such

---

[45] Interview with Ngoy Kabuya, Ruashi, Democratic Republic of Congo (DRC), 13 May 2007.
[46] Grimshaw and Sherlock, 'Women and Cultural Exchanges', 179.

as tuberculosis and cholera. It was not until the widespread introduction of antibiotics after the Second World War that European
doctors in the continent (and indeed elsewhere) gained a degree
of healing power over these and other afflictions.[47] In West Africa
missionaries died at alarming rates. In 1905 it was noted that the
Catholic Society of African Missions (SMA) had lost 283 members
in the first fifty years of its existence, which amounted to over half
of its then current membership of 480 missionaries. It was esti-
mated that in Dahomey a male missionary lasted three years, and
a missionary nun four.[48] Similar circumstances prevailed in Belgian
Congo. Burton and Salter had originally set out as a group of four,
but one colleague, George Armstrong, died even before he arrived
in Mwanza and the other, George Blakeney, was so demoralized by
a recurrent illness that he very soon returned to the USA.

In his provocative book, *Out of our Minds*, the influential anthropologist Johannes Fabian offers a 'critical study of the objective
conditions that determined knowledge of the Other as reported
in travelogues and early ethnographies'.[49] Seeking to destroy the
myth that field work was conducted in laboratory conditions by
the disembodied anthropologist, Fabian writes:

> More often or not they ... were out of their minds with
> extreme fatigue, fear, delusions of grandeur, and feelings
> ranging from anger to contempt. Much of the time too they
> were in the thralls of 'fever' and other tropical diseases, under
> the influence of alcohol or opiates ... high doses of quinine,
> arsenic and other ingredients from the expedition's medical
> chest.[50]

This model of encounter, framed by the realities of late nineteenth-
and early twentieth-century central Africa, and in particular the
omnipresence of disease and death, sheds light upon the stresses
and strains of the missionary household and the relationships

47 Walima Kalusa, 'Christian Medical Discourse and Praxis on the Imperial Frontier: Explaining the Popularity of Missionary Medicine in Mwinilunga District,
Zambia, 1906–1935', in Harries and Maxwell, eds, *The Spiritual in the Secular*, 245–66,
at 248.
48 E. Isichei, *A History of Christianity in Africa* (London, 1995), 85.
49 J. Fabian, *Out of our Minds: Reason and Madness in the Exploration of Central Africa*
(Berkeley, CA, 2000), 8.
50 Ibid. 3.

which missionaries cultivated with African Christians. However, in the case of the CEM the problem was not so much drugs as the lack of them. As Pentecostals, CEM missionaries believed in divine healing and God's providential care; consequently they preferred to live by faith rather than take prophylactics. Both Burton and Salter experimented with non-drug-taking before deciding to learn from Armstrong's death. However, their colleague Cyril Taylor, missionary pioneer of the adjacent CEM station at Ngoimani, continued to abstain.[51] Of Taylor, Burton wrote in 1923:

> Taylor is himself in a funny condition. He does not seem to have the energy to settle down definitely to do anything, but wanders weakly and listlessly from one thing to another, so that often his natives, despairing of ever making him understand their palavers, come over here, to beg me to explain things to him.[52]

Because of their missionary's condition, Taylor's evangelists acted with a high degree of autonomy. They refused to act as porters for the colonial authorities and were renowned for public displays of tongue-speaking and falling down in the Spirit. Such behaviour unnerved the Belgian colonial state, which was already suspicious of the independence of low church Protestant adepts and fearful of a repeat of the prophetic movement led by Simon Kimbangu in the west of the country.[53] Neither did William Burton's own early abstention from drug-taking facilitate good relations with the colonial state, as a letter to Salter in 1919 illustrates: 'I assure you Jimmy I am so weak I can scarcely walk across Elizabethville. On the day I visited the Vice-Governor General I must have had a temperature of 104 and so I can scarcely remember anything I said to him'.[54]

Salter did begin to take quinine but nevertheless fell victim to the dreaded blackwater fever, doubtless because he was not taking the prophylactic in the right dosage. In May 1917 he set off on an

---

[51] CAM, Burton to Salter Letters and Reports 1919–30 file [hereafter: BS file], Burton to Salter, 29 November 1919.

[52] Ibid., Burton to Salter, 28 April 1923.

[53] Ibid., Burton to Salter, 22 October 1928. On relations with the state, see David Maxwell, 'The Soul of the Luba: W. F. P. Burton, Missionary Ethnography and Belgian Colonial Science', *History and Anthropology* 19 (2008), 325–51, at 331–3.

[54] BS file, Burton to Salter, 29 November 1919.

evangelistic trek for three days to the north of Mwanza to pioneer what would become Taylor's station. When he did not return, a former slave-turned-evangelist, Shalumbo, set out to look for him and located him near death on the edge of a village. Shalumbo nursed Salter back to consciousness, but once the latter could walk he set off again with tent, carriers and a raging fever. Ignoring Shalumbo's protestations he staggered from village to village in a fit of preaching. Eventually he was found in a delirious state by a trader who accompanied him back to Mwanza. One can only imagine what the villagers of Ngoimani region made of their first encounter with Christianity, in the person of a fever-stricken missionary, literally out of his mind in a state of delirium.[55] But perhaps, once again, his African helper Shalumbo explained what he meant to say. This was an extreme example, but, as Harold Womersley has observed, missionaries often trekked with fever that made their heads 'buzz and ache'.[56]

Burton's correspondence with Salter and the Myerscoughs documents many missionary triumphs, but also a catalogue of misfortunes: the death of missionaries and their children, poverty, the persecution of African evangelists, and a host of ailments affecting colleagues such as malaria, blackwater fever, pneumonic influenza, dysentery and nervous stress. Missionaries sent home on furlough returned late due to illness; some never returned. By 1932, eight CEM missionaries had died in the field or in England.[57] It was difficult for missionaries to rest and recuperate on their stations, not least because the household did not equate with privacy. Hospitality had to be offered to officials, traders and other missionaries. There was also a constant stream of African visitors: enquirers, the curious, those in need of advice and the sick and the needy. Missionaries with children suffered the pangs of separation when those of school age were sent away to school, generally in Southern Rhodesia. Those with young children lived in constant fear of their falling ill. Even furloughs could become draining and alienating experiences; there were books and articles to write, and the constant speaking engagements for purposes of

---

55 William Burton, Mwanza, 15 May 1917, cited in Moorhead, *Missionary Pioneering*, 68–9.

56 Womersley, *Congo Miracle*, 93.

57 Burton, *God Working*, 263–4.

fundraising, but also the discovery that they had 'lost much of what made them really English'. As Burton put it:

> [T]he language is a little less perfect, manners and customs change appreciably in those intervening years. Brothers and friends have married. Old chums have now found other interests … . They find that they that they had forgotten how to swing onto a tram-car, and they would far prefer meeting a herd of buffalo to crossing a street with cars rushing up and down. Indeed they have largely become denationalised.[58]

These misfortunes added to the pressures upon the Burtons, who in Mwanza were left holding the fort while their own health declined. In 1928 William Burton recounted to Salter how each mailbag contained forty to eighty letters from donors, to which he was obliged to respond. In addition he was writing half of each bimonthly edition of the *Congo Evangelistic Mission Report*, as well as running the mission and dealing with the colonial state. By this stage his body had been terribly weakened by malaria and he had lost ten inches from around his waist. 'I CANNOT POSSIBLY carry on much longer', he complained.[59] His wife was in a far worse condition, suffering from valvular heart disease. The following year he reported: 'I hate to own it, but the facts are facts. Hettie is losing ground all the time. Her heart is in a really serious condition', and the burden of station responsibility was 'sapping her life'.[60] They struggled on with no relief until 1935 when Hettie's nerves were in such a state that she was sent over the edge into palpitations and breath-loss by crying babies and 'shooting motors' (stuttering engines).[61]

Fabian has observed that Europeans often approached Africa and its population through 'hygiene'. This included keeping clean, but was also a broader notion including ideas of discipline, and was deemed essential in the absence of the social mores and the amenities of civilization. Self-control was a prerequisite for the control of others too, given that the assertion of bodily vigour and the concealment of weakness were crucial

---

58 Ibid. 260.
59 BS file, Burton to Salter, 22 October 1928.
60 Ibid., Burton to Salter, 22 August 1929.
61 Ibid., Burton to Salter, 1 November 1935.

to maintaining white authority. The loss of vigour through illness in front of Africans was deeply unsettling.[62] Worse still, despite Burton's belief in the centrality of patriarchal Christian marriage, wives and single women found themselves in charge of entire mission stations.

To some extent Burton dealt with stress by projecting it onto others. Mwanza became a sacred enclave from which he seemed to do battle with the rest of the world: the Belgian authorities and their Catholic allies, the 'dirty Portuguese', the Protestant Christian Council in Belgian Congo, and even other Pentecostal denominations such as the Assemblies of God. He had little time for colleagues who were incompetent in French or Kiluba. In one of his darkest moments, while recuperating in South Africa, he seems briefly even to have fallen out with his lifelong friend Jimmy Salter, accusing him of raiding his private letters. Salter had not immediately taken his partner's side against a younger missionary who appeared to be as headstrong as Burton himself.[63]

It has been widely noted that missionaries behaved toward and wrote about Africans in a contradictory manner.[64] Burton invested a good deal of creative and intellectual energy in collecting, photographing and painting Luba coiffures and sculptures. His scientific work on the Luba was valued by contemporary social anthropologists and museum curators in South Africa and Belgium, and yet in his missionary writings he derided Luba sculptures as crude idols and complex coiffures were cast as frivolous wastes of time. It is likely that mood swings caused by fatigue and isolation help explain some of this bizarre behaviour. The stresses and strains of the colonial situation also contributed to the schizophrenic behaviour which missionaries exhibited toward progressive African Christians, the very category they had invested most in creating. Those who appeared too westernized were cast as mimics and those who were too autonomous were viewed with suspicion.[65] Like many of his colleagues, Burton appeared unable to come to

---

[62] Fabian, *Minds*, 59–63.

[63] Myerscough file, BS file.

[64] T. Spear, 'Neo-Traditionalism and the Limits of Invention in British Colonial Africa', *JAH* 44 (2003), 3–27, at 4.

[65] D. Maxwell, 'Photography and the Religious Encounter: Ambiguity and Aesthetics in Missionary Representations of the Luba of South East Belgian Congo',

terms with the built-in obsolescence of missionary work, which involved devolving responsibility to an African church and going home. Doubtless this was to do with the sacrifices he himself had made.

Burton's embattled outlook and his wife's recurring health problems probably stemmed in part from the loss of their child.[66] In a tragic letter to Thomas Myerscough in June 1923, Burton recounts that they had been parents for just ten days. Their child, David, named after Livingstone, one of the 'bonniest babies' William had ever seen, died from a small insect bite. He concluded: 'It is a sweet thing to have been a father and mother but we do terribly miss our little boy.'[67] William never wrote about the death of his son again, but in her account of women's work, published years later in 1949, Hettie explained that they had longed for their own child to rear as an example but that God had filled her emptiness with another passion. Henceforth she threw herself into work with girls and women. Her book *My Black Daughters* was prefaced with the words 'God took my one child and gave me many'. Indeed she formed a particularly strong bond of intimacy with a little girl, Mangasa, whom she adopted following the death of the child's mother and cared for until Mangasa married. Hettie devoted a whole chapter of her book to Mangasa, although it is narrated in an dispassionate manner.[68] But her fondness for the child is revealed in her loving gaze captured in a magic lantern slide and in the reminiscences of Mangasa's son, who returned to Mwanza as a school teacher (Figs 8, 9, 10).[69] More generally, African Christian informants spoke of their relations with missionaries with ambivalence similar to that which missionaries displayed towards them. Often deploying the parental idiom, African converts depicted missionaries as kindly people who had taken them into their homes as children, provided material security and given them opportunities to learn new skills.

Comparative Studies in Society and History 53 (2011), 38–74, at 67–72; BS file, Burton to Salter, 11 November 1925.

[66] For another account of the death of a child of missionaries, see Elizabeth Elbourne, 'Mother's Milk: Gender, Power and Anxiety on a South African Mission Station, 1839–1840', in Patricia Grimshaw and Andrew May, eds, *Missionaries, Indigenous Peoples and Cultural Exchanges* (Brighton, 2010), 10–23.

[67] Myerscough file, Burton to Thomas Myerscough, 22 June 1923.

[68] H. Burton, *Daughters*, 2, 59–64.

[69] Interview, Banze Inabanza Jacques, Mwanza, DRC, 22 May 2007.

Fig. 8: Hettie Burton and baby Mangasa. Reproduced by courtesy of CAM (Preston 76).

Fig. 9: Mangasa. Reproduced by courtesy of CAM (Preston 14).

Fig. 10: Banze Inabanza Jacques, Mwanza, Democratic Republic of Congo, 22 May 2007. Photograph by the author.

Less appreciated were the missionary impatience, surveillance and overemphasis on discipline and hard work.[70]

Besides finding succour from sometimes conflicted friendships with African Christians, CEM missionaries were sustained by a theology of action, hope and endurance. They drew encouragement from the Psalms and inspiration from the miracles recounted in the Gospels. They celebrated conversions and movements of the Holy Spirit. They looked for signs of God's providential care in unexpected gifts, the good deeds of others and answers to prayer. Most of all they believed in God's power to heal.[71] The Burtons stayed at Mwanza in spite of recurring collapses of health, including William's cancer of the colon in the 1940s. Hettie remained until her early death in 1952. William was forced to leave Belgian Congo during the violence that followed the secession of Katanga from the newly independent colony in 1960. He stayed on in Southern Africa, living an existence of peripatetic preaching until his death in 1971. In his history of the CEM, aptly entitled *Congo Miracle*,

---

[70] E.g. interviews: Nshimbi Kinekinda Simon, Ruashi, DRC, 8 May 2007; Ngoy Maloba Ngulungu, Ruashi, DRC, 9 May 2007; Mama Andyena, Kyungu Dyese and Mama Numbi Martha, Mwanza, DRC, 21 May 2007. See Hunt, *Colonial Lexicon*, ch. 2, for similar reminiscences from African Christians who experienced extensive missionary tutelage.

[71] W. Burton, *Signs Following* (London, n.d.).

Harold Womersley recounted a similar trajectory of collapses and 'miraculous healings of his body' that punctuated his period in the Congo from 1924 to 1970.[72]

William Burton also took refuge in missionary science and art. At times his letter-writing would digress into lengthy descriptions of African landscapes. He would irritate junior colleagues by extending homeward journeys in order to paint a sunset or an African village scene.[73] He described his art as his 'safety valve'.[74] His most stressful moments seemed to have been particularly productive. In the same 1928 letter to Salter in which he protested that he could not continue any longer, he also described how he had taken about four hundred photographs, some of them 'remarkably fine', and written a thirty thousand-word hagiography of an African evangelist.[75] In this period he also finished an extensive ethnography of the Luba.

Because of the contingency of the missionary household we can be sure that Burton's ethnographic representations were grounded in research, although his reliance on converts as auxiliaries gave his data a particular emphasis. He often wrote of cannibalism but like other missionary writers he never saw evidence of the practice himself; his accounts were always second-hand, generated by his Christian porters on trek.[76] These progressive young men, often the subject of Burton's hagiographical success stories, drew upon idioms of respectability to assert moral boundaries between themselves and their 'pagan', even cannibal, neighbours.[77]

In practice, Euro-American notions of the Christian household were transformed by the realities of life in remote regions of central Africa. Africans entered the most private spaces of missionary homes as servants. Others were brought up as surrogate children,

---

[72] Womersley, *Congo Miracle*, 129–30.

[73] H. Womersley, *Wm F. P. Burton. Congo Pioneer* (London, 1973), 100–3.

[74] BS file, Burton to Salter, 15 June 1933.

[75] Ibid., Burton to Salter, 22 October 1928. The manuscript was probably that of W. Burton, *When God Changes a Man: A True Story of this great Change in the Life of a Slave Raider* (London, 1929).

[76] W. Arens, *The Man-eating Myth: Anthropology and Anthropophagy* (New York, 1979); cf. the nineteen-page account by Hettie Burton, 'A Missionary Exploration of the Ludvidyo Watershed', BS file, Burton to Salter, May 1923.

[77] D. Maxwell, 'Freed Slaves, Missionaries and Respectability: The Expansion of the Christian Frontier from Angola to Belgian Congo', *JAH* 54 (2013), 79–102, at 98.

bottle-fed from birth. Black porters lived in even closer proximity to missionaries on trek and were sometimes compelled to provide them with intimate care. Disease and death took companionate marriage and family life beyond the reach of many. Yet missionaries believed themselves to be exemplars of Euro-American ideals and strove to maintain them. As John Mackenzie observes, they had a self-image as 'a people who controlled their own natural and human environments with the help of their technology, science and western medicine, as well as through their moral aura, their moral force and state of grace'.[78] The Burtons did their best to ensure that the interior of their house resembled a Western home so that white visitors would not feel out of place, and they insisted on maintaining European standards of hygiene and decorum: for instance, visiting missionaries had to wash and change clothing before dinner.[79] The gap between theory and practice added to the stresses of missionary existence.

CONCLUSION

In this essay I have explored what Patricia Grimshaw and Andrew May define as 'the explanatory power of intimate relations and gender' as they were worked out in a mission community.[80] Missionaries lived in closer proximity to African communities than colonial agents. Their agendas for social and moral transformation of African society caused them to engage more deeply with Africans than many colonial officials and settlers whose concerns were often restricted to labour and law. Because missionary designs for the African Christian household were demonstrated by example, they were more likely than first-generation colonial settlers to include women among their workers and thus to face more forcefully the disruption that colonial experience posed to gender relations. Given that childbearing often undermined their wellbeing, the health and energy of wives were more deeply affected than that of their husbands. The responsibility for maintaining a model

---

[78] Mackenzie, 'Missionaries, Science and the Environment', 128.

[79] Myerscough file, William Burton to the Assemblies of God Missionary Council, 3 January 1931.

[80] Patricia Grimshaw and Andrew May, 'Reappraisals of Mission History: An Introduction', in eidem, eds, *Missionaries, Indigenous Peoples and Cultural Exchange* (Eastbourne, 2010), 1–9, at 3.

household and an exemplary family added to their level of insecurity.[81]

By examining the missionary struggle to establish and maintain a Christian household we arrive at a more grounded understanding of missions. In spite of their triumphal accounts of their work for metropolitan audiences, pioneer missionaries often lived fragile existences as sojourners in foreign lands. In order to manage their vulnerabilities, missionaries, both male and female, formed deep bonds of intimacy, affection and trust with African Christians and these meant that missionary lives were as transformed as they were transforming. This embedded and dynamic notion of religious change moves scholarship in an important direction away from an overly dichotomous model of encounter which depicts white missionaries colonizing the minds of black pagans.

University of Cambridge

---

[81] Grimshaw and Sherlock, 'Women and Cultural Exchanges', 181–2.

CHRISTIAN FAMILY, CHRISTIAN NATION: RAYMOND JOHNSTON AND THE NATIONWIDE FESTIVAL OF LIGHT IN DEFENCE OF THE FAMILY

by ANDREW ATHERSTONE

'We reject that morality – death to the family!'[1] So interjected a young female heckler during the inaugural rally of the Nationwide Festival of Light (NFOL) in Westminster Central Hall on 9 September 1971. Although press coverage of the event focused upon more dramatic interventions, such as the attempt by a group of bogus nuns to storm the platform, it was this stark proclamation of 'death to the family' which revealed the primary ideological battleground in the NFOL's morality campaigns of the 1970s. Six months later, Bishop Maurice Wood of Norwich told the follow-up 'Land Aflame' rally in March 1972 that 'in this day of synthetic substitutes there is no substitute for the family'.[2] NFOL was sometimes accused of fighting simultaneously on too many fronts, ranging from pornography and blasphemy to religious education and Sunday trading, but Eddy Stride (rector of Christ Church, Spitalfields, and chairman of the NFOL executive committee) summarized the movement's purpose as being 'to actively promote the values of human dignity expressed in the Biblical view of family life'.[3]

Amy Whipple and Matthew Grimley have recently examined the broad cultural significance of the NFOL as a barometer of conservative Christian values in pre-Thatcherite Britain.[4] The organization collaborated sometimes with the anti-obscenity

---

[1] John Capon, *And There Was Light: The Story of the Nationwide Festival of Light* (London, 1972), 43.

[2] Nationwide Festival of Light Archives [hereafter: NFOLA] (in possession of the author), 'Land Aflame '72', press release, 20 March 1972.

[3] NFOLA, Minutes of the Nationwide Festival of Light Executive, 21 December 1976. Most of the executive minutes are lost, but I am grateful to Penny Howell, the former secretary, for copies of the few which survive.

[4] Amy Whipple, 'Speaking for Whom? The 1971 Festival of Light and the Search for the "Silent Majority"', *Contemporary British History* 24 (2010), 319–39; Matthew Grimley, 'Anglican Evangelicals and Anti-Permissiveness: The Nationwide Festival of Light 1971–1983', in Andrew Atherstone and John Maiden, eds, *Evangelicalism and the*

campaigns of Mary Whitehouse's National Viewers' and Listeners' Association (NVALA), but had a wider aim: to re-establish the nation's Judaeo-Christian moral framework. This essay examines a central aspect of the NFOL's ideology, the teaching on family by Raymond Johnston, the movement's first full-time director from 1974 until his untimely death from pancreatic cancer in 1985 at the age of 58.[5] He was the public face of the NFOL and shaped its priorities. An Anglican evangelical layman, he had worked previously as a schoolteacher and then as a lecturer in education at the University of Newcastle-upon-Tyne, and brought to NFOL what its first historian called 'some much-needed intellectual muscle',[6] injecting philosophical and academic rigour into this 'essentially activist body'.[7] According to the *Church Times* Johnston was 'the antithesis of the popular conception of the Evangelical kill-joy', a man with a lively appreciation of the arts, especially music. Under his leadership the early exuberance of NFOL rallies with their praise-shouts ('Give us a J, give us an E, give us an S – U – S') and Jesus-stickers was replaced by 'temperate and rational argument'.[8] In March 1979 Johnston helped to launch 'CARE for the Family', a NFOL educational division which aimed to provide positive teaching on family life,[9] and the acronym CARE (Christian Action, Research and Education) soon became the new name of the entire organization. After outlining Johnston's model of the ideal biblical family, this essay analyses his cultural diagnosis of family breakdown in modern Britain and his recommended antidotes for family defence and reconstruction. It concludes that he saw a causal connection between the health of the family and the flourishing of the nation.

Church of England in the Twentieth Century: Reform, Resistance and Renewal (Woodbridge, forthcoming 2014).

5   For a brief introduction, see David Holloway, *A Call for Christian Thinking and Action: The Life of Raymond Johnston* (Newcastle-upon-Tyne, 2004); *ODNB*, online supplement (2012), *s.n.* 'Johnston, (Olaf) Raymond (1927–1985)', at: <http://www.oxforddnb.com/view/article/101341>, last accessed 20 September 2013.

6   London, CARE Trust Archives, John Capon, 'Festival Flashback', Nationwide Festival of Light broadsheet, 1979.

7   John Capon, 'Back to Square One', *Crusade*, September 1976, 19–22, at 21.

8   Douglas Brown, 'How the Light Burns 10 Years On', *Church Times*, 11 September 1981, 10.

9   'Is It Well with the Child?', *Nationwide Festival of Light Bulletin*, no. 6 (1979), 3–5.

The Model Family

Johnston's theology of the family was laid out at greatest length in his London Lectures in Contemporary Christianity, delivered at All Souls', Langham Place, in April and May 1978, and published as *Who Needs the Family?* (1979). The *Church Times* welcomed the volume as 'a clarion call … to do spiritual battle for the conversion of England, home and family', and urged it to be taken seriously by those who 'tend to reach for their snuffers at anything to do with the Nationwide Festival of Light'.[10] Although Johnston acknowledged that the Old and New Testaments spoke of the extended 'household', he elided the concepts of household and Western nuclear family ('mum, dad and kids') which he went so far as to call 'the Christian norm'. He believed that the Bible offered a divine 'blueprint' for the proper way in which the family should function, and rejected suggestions that it was culturally conditioned.[11] In Johnston's analysis, this 'Christian family ethic' lay at the very epicentre of the controversy over the permissive society.[12] He himself was part of a nuclear family, married to Peggy Bell, and they raised two daughters who were teenagers in the 1970s.

Johnston maintained that within every family there should be 'a fundamental hierarchy' and took it for granted that the husband was the 'head of the household', a case he argued on the basis of the Genesis creation narrative, the Pauline Epistles and Trinitarian theology.[13] As he explained in a series of lectures at the C. S. Lewis Institute in Washington DC in 1980, '[t]he husband is the leader, the person who is the ultimate fount of discipline, authority and protection.'[14] Although he did not insist rigidly upon the traditional roles of husband as breadwinner and wife as homemaker, he spoke with approval of these 'time-honoured distinctions'.[15] In

[10] Margaret Daniel, 'Stopping the Rot', *Church Times*, 13 July 1979, 6.

[11] Raymond Johnston, *Who Needs the Family? A Survey and a Christian Assessment* (London, 1979), 14, 30, 39.

[12] Raymond Johnston, 'Christian Morality and the Church of England', in Anthony Kilmister, ed., *When Will Ye Be Wise? The State of the Church of England* (London, 1983), 99–122, at 112.

[13] Johnston, *Who Needs the Family?*, 99, 112.

[14] Raymond Johnston, *Caring and Campaigning: Making a Christian Difference* (London, 1990), 106.

[15] Johnston, *Who Needs the Family?*, 52, 55.

his critique of the emerging Charismatic movement, he welcomed especially its conservatism on family matters. For example, Johnston applauded the best-selling paperback, *The Christian Family* (1970), by the American Lutheran Larry Christenson, because it was 'Scriptural and patriarchal in approach … Adam's priority, male headship, the authority of the husband – all these are expounded and applied unashamedly as God-given'. Christenson's book was republished in Britain by the charismatic Fountain Trust and Johnston rejoiced that it 'comes as a shock to *Guardian*-reading Christian intellectuals in England'.[16]

From the book of Proverbs, Johnston deduced that it was primarily the duty of fathers to convey practical wisdom to their children while 'home-making' was 'the unique contribution of the ideal wife', no matter what Germaine Greer might say to the contrary.[17] He saw these innate differences between men and women in the family as part of the wonderful diversity of God's creation, whereas 'the world of the enthusiastic egalitarian, by comparison, is not only inhuman but very drab'.[18] Although contraception was not morally wrong in principle, he believed it was sinful for a married couple deliberately to opt out of parenthood because in so doing they were avoiding family. Johnston explained: 'the family is God's pattern and motherhood is a blessing … . This should be the norm, the duty and the path of obedience as well as of fulfilment for the married woman.'[19] Pregnancy was only to be avoided for very weighty reasons, such as severe health risks or the call of the pioneer mission field. He warned that for wives with small children to be in full-time work 'weakens the family decisively',[20] and urged his Christians hearers to testify to 'the crucial function of motherhood for child, for husband, for family life … and for civilised values'.[21] Without strong marriages it was impossible 'to build happy families and stable, creative communities', and for this reason Johnston objected to the phrase 'one-parent family' as an

---

[16] Raymond Johnston, 'Creation, Culture and Charismatics', *Scottish Bulletin of Evangelical Theology* 2 (1984), 23–31, at 29.
[17] Johnston, *Who Needs the Family?*, 85–6, 111.
[18] Johnston, *Caring and Campaigning*, 70.
[19] Johnston, *Who Needs the Family?*, 84.
[20] Johnston, *Caring and Campaigning*, 115–6.
[21] Johnston, *Who Needs the Family?*, 87.

oxymoron.[22] He called the family 'the micro-church', a place of great potential for healing, encouragement, personal growth and evangelism.[23]

DIAGNOSIS: FAMILY UNDER THREAT

Johnston was in no doubt that Britain in the 1970s was in a desperate moral plight. In an address to the Newcastle Moral Welfare Association in February 1973, entitled 'Must Britain Rot?', he declared that 'The very fabric of our society is being eroded so that eventually we will crumble into political and economic insignificance'.[24] Two years later, at a conference in Leicester for evangelical ministers, he observed: 'Britain today stands on the brink of a precipice … on the point of collapse – culturally, politically, economically and morally.'[25] At the root of this impending national calamity lay the destruction of the family ideal. Johnston marshalled a wide array of statistics in his attempt to show that the key family relationships between husband and wife and between parents and children were unravelling at an alarming rate, pointing to symptoms such as divorce, abortion, child neglect, wife-battery, sexual promiscuity, truancy, vandalism and assault. He argued that the abandonment of 'Christian family values' led inevitably to community damage, positing links between pornography and sexual crimes, between homosexual behaviour and the spread of syphilis, and between broken marriages and disturbed children.[26] Johnston frequently ransacked the latest sociological studies for data which corroborated his theological diagnosis, claiming that the Bible's teaching about happy families meshed with the best secular research 'like a glove to the hand'.[27]

In a paper on 'The Moral Battle' (1976), Johnston suggested that those responsible for undermining family values were an unrepresentative but vocal minority, 'a small group of atheists, humanists,

[22] Ibid. 63, 68–9.

[23] Raymond Johnston, 'Homosexual Relationships', *Reformed Anglican* 5 (January 1980), 16–26, at 24.

[24] London, Latimer Trust Archives, Raymond Johnston Papers [hereafter: RJP], Raymond Johnston, 'Must Britain Rot?' (typescript, 1973), 1.

[25] Raymond Johnston, *Christianity in a Collapsing Culture* (Exeter, 1976), 3–4.

[26] Johnston, *Caring and Campaigning*, 121–2.

[27] Johnston, *Who Needs the Family?*, 61.

anarchists, Marxists of various kinds and non-political perverts', with positions of influence in the arts and the media, allied to financial profiteers.[28] These various sources of 'anti-family propaganda and anti-family activity' featured regularly in his cultural analysis.[29] At the 1972 'Land Aflame' rally in Westminster Central Hall, Johnston warned that revolutionaries were attempting to destroy the Christian family in order to prepare the way for 'the great takeover' of British society, though he was uncertain whether it would be 'Soviet-Marxist, or Chinese-Maoist, or just sheer anarchy'.[30] Elsewhere he observed that the strong nuclear family was a bulwark against totalitarian 'social engineers' because it 'encourages the emergence of citizens with a sense of individual worth'.[31] The Marxist threat was a dominant motif in Johnston's writings. He pointed to the infamous attack in *The Communist Manifesto* upon 'the bourgeois family', and warned that the anti-family policies of Soviet Russia in the 1920s and 1930s, such as easy divorce and abortion on demand, had left that nation 'enfeebled'. When critiquing the writings of the South African psychiatrist David Cooper, author of *The Death of the Family* (1971), he drew attention to Cooper's political rhetoric and the Marxist undertones of his medical theories.[32] Johnston particularly loved to quote from Aleksandr Solzhenitsyn's *Warning to the Western World* (1976), a BBC radio broadcast which drew parallels between the disintegration and moral degeneration of British culture and that of Tsarist Russia on the eve of the Bolshevik Revolution.[33] Closely allied to the Marxists were the 'militant feminists' promoting androgyny, or the cult of the 'aggressive female' and the 'effeminate male', tendencies which Johnston believed to constitute 'a serious threat to civilised life as we know it'.[34]

Alongside the anti-family ideologues were the political activists pushing for immediate change in parliamentary legislation. In *Who Needs the Family?* Johnston explained:

[28] RJP, Raymond Johnston, 'The Moral Battle: The Turn of the Tide?' (typescript, 1976), 1.

[29] Johnston, *Caring and Campaigning*, 104.

[30] RJP, Raymond Johnston, speech at the 'Land Aflame' rally, 16 March 1972 (typescript), 3.

[31] Johnston, *Who Needs the Family?*, 129.

[32] Ibid. 25–8.

[33] Johnston, *Caring and Campaigning*, 23.

[34] Johnston, *Who Needs the Family?*, 70–1.

Their philosophy is a tolerant liberalism, which in the end undermines the family. Many of them are, or have been, our own friends and colleagues. Many have held high political rank in Britain or academic rank in universities. Some of them claim to be Christian. Others are avowed humanists, members of that tiny but influential group of dogmatic atheists, who have been so powerful in the House of Commons (mostly, alas, in the Parliamentary Labour Party) and in the British Broadcasting Corporation over the last twenty years.[35]

Of necessity, NFOL aimed for broad cross-party support. Stride, for example, was a shop-steward in the East End of London before ordination, and at the 1976 'Ten Commandments' rally in Trafalgar Square he made much of the fact that he followed a Tory MP on the platform, although he had 'never voted for that party' in his life.[36] By contrast, Johnston enjoyed the privileged background of public school and Oxford University. He kept his voting pattern secret and did not broadcast his opinion of Margaret Thatcher's rise to power, but he freely criticized the Labour governments of Harold Wilson and James Callaghan (1974–9), especially what he saw as their abdication of responsibility to protect families.[37] Wilson's first period in office (1964–70) had witnessed the decriminalization of homosexuality and abortion, the rise of no-fault divorce, and the weakening of curbs on obscenity in print, stage and screen. Johnston believed there was no popular mandate for these legal reforms which 'so deeply affect family ideals', but that they had been pushed through parliament by vocal lobbyists working to a minority agenda.[38]

There was money to be made from permissive behaviour in the marketing of contraceptives, sex theatres and the abortion industry, and the NFOL's director assailed those who viewed family disintegration as an opportunity for financial exploitation. He warned against 'the ruthlessness of ad men and pornocrats',[39] and welcomed the 1972 Longford Report on pornography as 'a shattering record of commercially inspired corruption' of which 'any civilised nation should be

---

35   Ibid. 131.
36   NFOLA, Nationwide Festival of Light broadsheet, Autumn 1976.
37   Johnston, *Who Needs the Family?*, 118.
38   Ibid. 133.
39   Johnston, 'Land Aflame' speech, 4.

ashamed'.[40] One product of consumerism about which Johnston was especially concerned was the advent of 'family-splitting youth culture' with its 'paraphernalia' of jeans and magazines, rock stars and disc-jockeys.[41] Pop culture had produced millions of teenagers who were encouraged to treat their puzzled parents as 'square' rather than as models for imitation and oracles of wisdom.[42] Particularly alarming were texts such as *The Little Red Schoolbook* (1971), aimed at young secondary school children, which not only bred political anarchism and sexual licence but also fostered 'malevolent mistrust of the adult world'.[43] Such attempts to set children against their parents were, in Johnston's view, a 'perversion of family hierarchy'.[44] He urged parents not to collude in this subversive cultural shift and told the 'Land Aflame' rally to 'reject this hypnotic myth of the "generation gap"' which they had been brainwashed into believing by its frequent and loud repetition.[45]

Perhaps the most powerful source of 'anti-family influence' was the mass media,[46] especially television, which Johnston feared would soon turn Britain into 'a nation of monosyllabic morons'.[47] He observed that possibilities for cultural control only dreamed of by George Orwell had now become a reality as broadcasters reached into almost every home in the country. The BBC, he suggested, was engaged in rewriting history with its 'pseudo-documentary programmes … the ultimate manipulation'.[48] In his critique of two BBC filmstrips from 1969–70 for sex education in primary schools, Johnston thought it highly significant that the word 'family' was used once only in passing, and the words 'husband', 'wife' and 'marriage' never at all. He warned that 'what the BBC offers is God-less, love-less, marriage-less and value-less'.[49] Likewise ITV had succumbed to 'anti-family forces' with

[40] Johnston, 'Must Britain Rot?', 8.
[41] Johnston, *Who Needs the Family?*, 136.
[42] RJP, Raymond Johnston, 'How to Torpedo the Family' (typescript, n.d.).
[43] RJP, Raymond Johnston, 'The Exploitation of Youth' (typescript, 1975), 12.
[44] Johnston, *Caring and Campaigning*, 116.
[45] Johnston, 'Land Aflame' speech, 6.
[46] Johnston, *Who Needs the Family?*, 136; Raymond Johnston, 'The Power of the Media', in Bruce Kaye, ed., *Obeying Christ in a Changing World*, 3: *The Changing World* (Glasgow, 1977), 41–63.
[47] RJP, Raymond Johnston, 'Language Today', *News Extra*, September 1975.
[48] Johnston, 'Exploitation of Youth', 16.
[49] Johnston, 'Land Aflame' speech, 2–3. See further School Broadcasting Council,

its comedy series, *Miss Jones and Son* (1977–8), which portrayed unmarried motherhood as 'acceptable, enjoyable and in no way tragic or damaging'.[50] Johnston complained at the creative licence given to humourists like Dick Emery and Benny Hill to push at the boundaries of sexual decency and coarse language, lamenting: 'A typical night of English television almost suggests that honour, reticence, courage and chastity are dead, courtesy and idealism things of the past.'[51] The cinema was worse, specializing in 'spectacles sickening to the Christian conscience', with extreme violence and sexual perversion on display in early 1970s films like *A Clockwork Orange*, *Straw Dogs*, *Last Tango in Paris*, *The Exorcist* and *Death Wish*. Johnston drew parallels with the popular pastimes of the late Roman Empire at the height of its decadence before its ultimate collapse, and summarized his concern: 'The cinema has long ceased to be family entertainment.'[52]

Another culprit contributing to the collapse of family life in Britain, according to Johnston's diagnosis, was the Christian Church itself, especially the ordained leadership of the Church of England, which he believed was guilty of colluding with, and even actively contributing towards, the disintegration of family ideals. Anti-clericalism was a frequent theme in his discourse. In 1973 he declared that some Anglican bishops and clergy had 'lost the moral vision, or the moral courage, to discern evil and to speak out against it', although there were a few notable exceptions like Bishop Bardsley of Coventry and Bishop Huddleston of Stepney.[53] A decade later, at an evangelical conference in Edinburgh, he despaired that a 'significant proportion' of the Church of England's bishops, theologians and bureaucrats had

> flirted with, if not espoused, Unitarian theology, prelatical autocracy, a Tridentine soteriology and the secular ethical package offered (for example) by *The Guardian*, comprising

'"Where Do Babies Come From?" and "Growing Up": Two Radiovision Sex Education Aids', in Rex S. Rogers, ed., *Sex Education: Rationale and Reaction* (Cambridge, 1974), 239–50.

50 Johnston, *Who Needs the Family?*, 122.

51 Johnston, 'Land Aflame' speech, 5.

52 Raymond Johnston, 'Media Corruption and the Christian Conscience', *Catholic Herald*, 17 January 1975, 3. See also RJP, idem, 'The Effects of Film', paper for a meeting at the House of Commons, 14 May 1975.

53 Johnston, 'Must Britain Rot?', 10.

roughly abortion on demand, euthanasia by request, mildly Marxist politics, Keynsian [*sic*] economics, British imperial guilt, the world over-population scare, nuclear pacifism, divorce by consent and the public defence of sodomy as an acceptable activity.[54]

In *The Reformed Anglican* Johnston wrote of 'moral treachery in our churches' and grieved over the increasingly vocal advocacy by Anglican clergy of homosexual relationships, which he perceived as undermining the biblical pattern of the godly household.[55] It came to him as no surprise that in the *Alternative Service Book 1980* the Ten Commandments had been removed from the Church of England's communion liturgy and consigned to an appendix. In Johnston's opinion, because the clergy had abdicated their responsibility, moral leadership on family matters must come instead from an articulate laity, and he emphasized that NFOL was a 'lay-led and lay-inspired' movement.[56]

Despite the diversity of the sociological and ideological pressures which undermined the ideal of the Christian family in 1970s Britain, Johnston viewed them together as a coherent 'anti-family movement … guided by the ethic of human and family disposability'. He believed that NFOL was engaged in a 'spiritual battle', because these attacks upon the family were ultimately derived from a common satanic source.[57] Ever since the first human family had been expelled from Eden, and one brother murdered the other, the Evil One had striven 'to poison and destroy family relationships'.[58] Johnston argued this most fully in a paper entitled 'How to Torpedo the Family', suggesting that because the family was part of God's providential ordering of society it was a special focus of Satan's malice. For example, he described British tolerance of abortion as 'perhaps the greatest of all Satan's triumphs', destroying hundreds of thousands of 'potential family members' every year,

[54] Johnston, 'Creation, Culture and Charismatics', 23. See also Raymond Johnston, 'The Moral State of the Church of England', in David Samuel, ed., *Concern for the Church of England* (London, 1985), 7–12.

[55] Johnston, 'Homosexual Relationships', 25.

[56] Johnston, 'Christian Morality', 120–2.

[57] Johnston, *Who Needs the Family?*, 137, 144.

[58] RJP, Raymond Johnston, 'The Family Today: What Should the Christian Voice be Saying?' (typescript, *c.*1971), 4 .

and he proclaimed that when families unravelled people were more easily enslaved to the forces of political and spiritual evil.[59]

ANTIDOTE: MENDING AND DEFENDING FAMILIES

Although the diagnosis was stark, Johnston believed an antidote was possible and urged Christians to 're-impregnate the whole of society' with the biblical family ideal.[60] He offered three primary strategies. First, they must model godly family life to prove to their sceptical neighbours that it was ultimately happier and more satisfying than the permissive alternatives. Christians must demonstrate that a family built upon the Ten Commandments or the Sermon on the Mount was 'the best prescription for living'.[61]

Second, Johnston exhorted Christians towards active sociopolitical engagement as shapers of public policy, looking back especially to the seventeenth-century puritan vision of national renewal. He encouraged them to serve as local councillors, magistrates and Members of Parliament: 'The man of God is involved, not insulated. … . There must be no talk of the ghetto and no talk of retreat.'[62] He looked with admiration to the United States of America where the Moral Majority helped to sweep Ronald Reagan into the White House in November 1980, hoping that their example would encourage more British Christians 'to gird up our loins'.[63] Francis Schaeffer's *Christian Manifesto* (1981) sought to mobilize conservative Christians politically and Johnston contributed an enthusiastic foreword to the British edition.[64] Some separatist Evangelicals criticized the NFOL for lack of doctrinal clarity and for muddling the gospel with social reform,[65] but Johnston advocated co-belligerence on family matters on an ecumenical

---

59 Johnston, 'How to Torpedo the Family'.

60 Johnston, *Who Needs the Family?*, 138.

61 RJP, Raymond Johnston, 'Land Aflame' speech (draft), 10.

62 Johnston, *Collapsing Culture*, 22.

63 Raymond Johnston, 'Now is the Time for Pressure', *Church of England Newspaper*, 16 January 1981, 5.

64 Francis Schaeffer, *A Christian Manifesto* (Chicago, IL, 1981; London, 1982). On the significance of this book, see Barry Hankins, *Francis Schaeffer and the Shaping of Evangelical America* (Grand Rapids, MI, 2008), 192–227.

65 'Festival of Light?', *Evangelical Times*, October 1971, 1, 9; 'The Lessons of the Festival of Light', *Evangelical Times*, November 1971, 2; 'NFOL: Falling Between Two Stools?', *Evangelical Times*, September 1976, 13.

platform, especially between Evangelicals and Roman Catholics, within a broad-based Judaeo-Christian framework.[66] At the 1976 'Ten Commandments' rally the director read messages of support from Archbishop Blanch of York, Professor T. F. Torrance (moderator of the Church of Scotland), Cardinal Hume and the chief rabbi.[67] The publicity material carried quotations from Solzhenitsyn, Archbishop Coggan of Canterbury and Pope Paul VI.[68]

When it came to the details of public policy, Johnston believed it was the duty of government to penalize 'family wreckers' and to uphold Christian family values.[69] He proposed a raft of practical legislation which included the need for a legal definition of the 'family'; economic incentives for married couples and for women who stayed at home to look after their own children; a compulsory waiting period of three to six months before marriage to emphasize the seriousness of the commitment; the abolition of no-fault divorce; stronger obscenity laws; and the restriction to married couples of the right to buy contraceptives, adopt children or receive fertility treatments (which must only use the husband's sperm, otherwise it would be 'tantamount to adultery'). Johnston also proposed that parents be given the legal right to inspect all materials used in sex education, and that the promotion of homosexuality should be outlawed in schools, though he did not live long enough to see this wish fulfilled by Section 28 of the 1988 Local Government Act.[70]

The political limitations of the Christian Church were obvious, so Johnston's third strategy for restoring the family ideal was to preach and pray for revival. He hoped for a return to the days of Josiah and Nehemiah, when rediscovery of the law of God led to national renewal.[71] He argued that gospel preaching was 'of tremendous importance in cleansing a culture and in keeping it clean',[72] and celebrated the way in which the revival sermons of John Wesley and George Whitefield had transformed English society in the eighteenth century, including family life: 'We blas-

---

[66] RJP, Raymond Johnston, 'The Way of Salvation' (typescript, 1976).

[67] Nationwide Festival of Light broadsheet, Autumn 1976.

[68] NFOLA, 'For the Love of God and Neighbour', publicity flier, September 1976.

[69] Johnston, *Who Needs the Family?*, 140.

[70] Johnston, *Caring and Campaigning*, 116, 125–31.

[71] RJP, Raymond Johnston, interview with Peter Meadows, 16 September 1976 (transcript).

[72] Johnston, 'Exploitation of Youth', 16.

pheme if we say God could not do that again. Britain need not rot.'[73] In his evocative conclusion to *Who Needs the Family?*, Johnston proclaimed: 'Now one thing only can save the family for our nation. ... There is only one force that can cleanse, heal and restore family order ... and that is an old-fashioned Gospel revival.'[74]

CONCLUSION

In his 'Call to the Nation' in October 1975, Archbishop Coggan insisted: 'Give us strong, happy, disciplined families, and we shall be well on the way to a strong nation. The best way to cut at the roots of a healthy society is to undermine the family.'[75] In his New Year message a few weeks later, the archbishop reiterated: 'The surest bulwark of a stable society is a loving Christian home'.[76] Raymond Johnston concurred with these assessments. He believed there was a close connection between the health of the family and the flourishing of the nation. At the heart of his apologia lay his conviction that 'the family is needed by both the individual and the wider society. Both are threatened if the family disintegrates.'[77] He argued from the Mosaic law that anti-family sins 'pollute a whole community',[78] and claimed that 'Promises broken in the bedroom will lead to promises broken in the boardroom.'[79] Thus NFOL's campaigns to defend the Christian household were part of their desire to revitalize the nation. The cultural and ideological maelstrom of the 1970s had national implications but was most sharply focused in individual homes and family relationships. Some mocked Johnston that with the advent of the permissive society it was now impossible 'to put the clock back', but he doubted the wisdom of this secular non-biblical proverb, and exhorted his fellow Christians to summon Britain back to the national blessings of the 'the old-fashioned family'.[80]

Wycliffe Hall, Oxford

[73] Johnston, 'Must Britain Rot?', 12.
[74] Johnston, *Who Needs the Family?*, 145.
[75] John Poulton, *Dear Archbishop* (London, 1976), 19.
[76] *The Times*, 31 December 1975, 12.
[77] Johnston, *Who Needs the Family?*, 116.
[78] Johnston, *Collapsing Culture*, 18.
[79] Johnston, 'Christian Morality', 122.
[80] Johnston, *Caring and Campaigning*, 118, 128.

UNFETTERING RELIGION: WOMEN AND THE FAMILY CHAIN IN THE LATE TWENTIETH CENTURY

by CALLUM G. BROWN

There is a significant case to be made that women are central to the secularization of the West since the mid-twentieth century. This case has started to be argued in a variety of ways. A number of scholars have linked secularization to women via change to the family. In 1992, French sociologist Danièle Hervieu-Léger theorized secularization not as the collapse of religions but as modernity's transformation of conventional forms of religion (especially Judaism and Christianity) into 'the religious' – a state of sacredness devoid of shared liturgy, even of belief in God, but characterized by belonging to new types of secular institution (notably she cited football clubs), and instigated by the collapse of the nuclear family (what she called 'the traditional family').[1] In this process, she suggested, what modernity had done was to sustain a 'chain of memory' of religious ritual, but not of religious beliefs. At the heart of Hervieu-Léger's narrative of causation of the 'religious crisis' that was ending belief, she identified the collapse of the traditional family through the coming of ultra-low fertility in the 1960s and 1970s.[2] She wrote that the 'collapse of the traditional family' was 'the central factor in the disintegration of the imagined continuity that lies at the heart of the modern crisis of religion', pinpointing the period 'around 1965 with the downturn in the statistics of births and marriages which had risen markedly in the period 1945–50'.[3] With falling fertility and marriage, and rising divorce, cohabitation and births outwith marriage, '[i]ndividual well-being and fulfilment take precedence.' Although the British religious sociologist Grace Davie used Hervieu-Léger's concept in support of her thesis of Christianity's survival through believing without belonging,[4] the

---

[1] Danièle Hervieu-Léger, *Religion as a Chain of Memory* (Cambridge, 2000).
[2] Ibid. 133–4.
[3] Ibid, 133.
[4] Davie wrote an introduction to the English edition of Hervieu-Léger's book

French sociologist was explicitly not sanguine about the fate of the Churches: 'The rise of the religious does not necessarily give rise to religion.'[5] Hervieu-Léger regards the change in the family resulting from the 1960s as putting organized religion in a parlous state in western Europe, whilst Davie sees the secular family as relying vicariously by 2000 on religion for the enactment of a Christian or Jewish liturgy on behalf of the secular.

In sociology, a most interesting study by Kirsten Aune of evangelical women in England has argued that 'evangelicalism does not seem to have succeeded in resisting secularization'. On the contrary, 'while evangelical religiosity continues among women occupying more traditional social positions (as wives and mothers), adherence is declining among those whose lives do not fit the older pattern of marriage and full-time motherhood'.[6] In Aune's work, there is again an acknowledgement of the key role of family in female religiosity. More directly, the form of argument to be pursued here has recently been explored by Lynn Abrams who, writing from the position of a gender historian, rather than as a historian of religion, researching the emerging self-hood of women in the 1960s, has demonstrated the limited manner in which religion featured in the narratives of British women she interviewed: 'religion ceased to provide a framework for the way one chose to live a life'.[7]

The link between women and secularization has been an element of my arguments in a number of works over several years. The issue has been approached through study of discourse change concerning women's piety and domesticity, quantitative analysis of the women's key role in the demographic revolution, and studies using mostly autobiographical sources.[8] In this essay, I explore

in 2000, and then reinterpreted the idea of the chain of memory for her own book of the same year. However, Davie appears to have reversed Hervieu-Léger's meaning: Grace Davie, *Religion in Modern Europe: A Memory Mutates* (Oxford, 2000), 33.

[5] Hervieu-Léger, *Religion*, 166.

[6] Kirsten Aune, 'Evangelical Christianity and Women's Changing Lives', *European Journal of Women's Studies* 15 (2008), 277–94, at 288.

[7] Lynn Abrams, 'Mothers and Daughters: Negotiating the Discourse on the "Good Woman" in 1950s and 1960s Britain', in Nancy Christie and Michael Gauvreau, eds, *The Sixties and Beyond: Dechristianization as History in Britain, Canada, the United States and Western Europe, 1945–2000* (Toronto, ON, 2013), 60–82, at 80.

[8] Including Callum G. Brown, *The Death of Christian Britain: Understanding Secularisation 1800–2000*, 2nd edn (London, 2009; first publ. 2001). I have elaborated the arguments outlined in this essay in 'Gendering Secularisation: Locating Women in the Transformation of British Christianity in the 1960s', in I. Katznelson and G. Stedman

this link further using oral testimony. When rapid secularization came in the 1960s, religious decline in the Europeanized West was transformed from marginal and slow change to rapid collapse of Christian culture. It became something qualitatively different to what it had been before. Women played a significant – arguably the key – part, and one that they had not played before. In this, Hervieu-Léger is right. The conventional family structure as well as its religious dedication were shattered – by rising divorce, the decline of marriage, declining fertility, rising illegitimacy and the ending of the shame (and terminology) of birth outside marriage. Women's changing life destinies, involving trends towards gender equalization in education, work, career, sport and sexual satisfaction, and the rise of cohabitation rather than marriage, tended to be statistically associated with declining religiosity.[9] The fabric of the modern life of secularizing nations in western Europe, Canada and Australia was adapted principally through women's liberation, and gained ideological backing from the ideals of feminism. This is why women only become part of the story of secularization from the mid-twentieth century. Read books about secularization's history prior to 1960, and in most it is entirely about men and male 'things': about church organization, the religiosity of the establishment elites, plebeian male impiety, and social problems of drunkenness, gambling and sex that led to men's lapsing religious observance. It was the sixties that transformed church lapsing into secularization that involved women intimately – into the thoroughgoing eradication of Christian dominance of family life, popular culture, civil law on behaviour, and sexual moralities. It was in this decade that women started to lose religion in significant numbers, and to move towards parity in numbers with

Jones, eds, *Religion and the Political Imagination* (Cambridge, 2010), 275–94; 'Women and Religion in Britain: The Autobiographical View of the Fifties and Sixties', in *Secularisation in the Christian World c.1750 – c.2000: Essays in Honour of Hugh McLeod*, ed. Callum G. Brown and M. F. Snape (Farnham, 2010), 159–73; 'Sex, Religion and the Single Woman *c.*1950–1975: The Importance of a 'short' Sexual Revolution to the English Religious Crisis of the Sixties', *Twentieth Century British History* 22 (2011), 189–215; *Religion and the Demographic Revolution: Women and Secularisation in Canada, Ireland, UK and USA since the 1960s* (Woodbridge, 2012); 'Gender, Christianity and the Rise of No Religion: The Heritage of the Sixties in Britain', in Christie and Gauvreau, eds, *The Sixties and Beyond*, 39–59.

9 The quantitative case for this hypothesis is made in Brown, *Religion and the Demographic Revolution*.

men amongst those who claimed to be of no religion.[10] In this regard, then, the manner of women leaving religion becomes an important topic for research.

LEAVING RELIGION

Between 2009 and 2012, I interviewed twenty-three women and thirty-two men in Britain, Canada and the USA about how they came to be without religion; one further interview of a woman used here was conducted by a colleague, and I obtained written testimony from a further woman and four men.[11] All bar three of the interviewees were born before 1958. These interviews were in a 'whole life' format in which I took volunteers chronologically through their lives, asking them to narrate the nature of their religious attitudes at each point, and, for those who lost faith, to identify the manner, pace and triggers for that loss. The vast bulk of those interviewed were people who ended up as atheists, agnostics, humanists, freethinkers and/or sceptics (and usually a mixture of some, and occasionally all, of these positions), and I recruited most of them through organizations which they had joined to reflect those views. Most developed some level of commitment in non-religious organizations – usually humanist, but sometimes atheist. They represent the actions of a tiny fraction of the people of the countries I am studying. But they do mark out the ways in which defection from religion occurred. They show how alienation from religion of those born in the 1930s, 1940s and 1950s was often in childhood, between the ages of 7 and 12, and how for most people a transition to atheism occurred usually decades later, often after 50; most did not join a non-religious organization until past middle age. More recently, in the 1990s and 2000s, it is clear that the age of adopting atheism has become very much lower, and the

---

[10] Callum G. Brown, 'The People of No Religion: The Demographics of Secularisation in the English-Speaking World since c.1900', *Archiv für Sozialgeschichte* 51 (2011), 37–61, at 58–9.

[11] As is standard in oral history scholarship, all the interviewees are identified by their real names except where they have requested anonymity, in which case a pseudonym is used. All interviews were conducted under the ethics approval regimes of the University of Dundee or the University of Glasgow, and each interviewee signed Informed Consent forms prior to interview and a Copyright Release form afterwards. When the project is complete, the testimony will be deposited in an archive.

process for those born in the 1980s and 1990s is concentrated into a short period of transition.[12]

What emerges from this study is that the manner of the loss of religion, and the self-narration of it, is heavily gendered. In a separate examination of British men losing religion between the 1940s and the present, I have concluded that they locate their loss almost entirely in the context of their application of reason, rationality, science, philosophy and social science (which includes their perception of the social dysfunctionality of religion in places of religious conflict such as Northern Ireland and the Middle East) to the issue of belief in a god or gods. For three men, it was located in the context of combat. For one from Northern Ireland, there was reflection on the role of his mother and grandmother in directing him towards a non-religious path at the age of 16 through their attempt to prevent him from dating Catholic girls. But beyond that, what is significant is the general dearth of reference by men to the family as the context of personal loss or abandonment of religion.[13]

I will introduce selected testimony from amongst my female interviewees, organized into five major groups which signify distinct narrative patterns. One thing is common to all the female interviewees: their location of their religious loss in the context of family – usually their parental family, but occasionally their marital family. This 'family narrative' in recounting religious matters, and loss of religion specifically, is distinctive to women. But within this 'master narrative' there are, if you like, 'sub-narratives', each of which is also distinctive to women. Through looking at these, we see the way in which women relate their loss of religion to family contexts – many of them using an ensemble of the sub-narratives to construct their testimony.

Loss Narrative I: Trauma

In Devon during the 1950s, Annette Horton's childhood was what she calls 'a very conflicted mess'. Her family was Roman Cath-

---

[12] Accounting, for example, for the very young age profile of the group known as Skeptics in the Pub compared to the British Humanist Association.

[13] Callum G Brown, 'Men losing Faith: The Making of modern No-Religionism in the UK 1939–2010', in Lucy Delap and Sue Morgan, eds, *Men, Masculinities and Religious Change in Twentieth-Century Britain* (London, 2013), 301–25.

olic, and one theme of her testimony is how the women of her family were subjected to the constant sexual demands of men. She reported:

> But my mother, as I was saying, she came from a very, very large family of Roman Catholic[s]. There were seventeen live births in the family that I know of anyway, and my grandmother was pregnant almost non-stop from the age of sixteen to forty-nine. And I never met her husband, but they tended to be on the borderland of [a] criminal element, often because they were really poor. I know my grandfather was in and out of gaol, and he was an alcoholic, and my grandmother was an alcoholic, and my mother was. And so all I heard from my mother was about the Catholic Church. I mean, she'd go on and on [about how] she had been physically abused by one of the priests and so had a couple of her sisters, and that it was absolutely terrible being born right in the middle of this huge family. And she's often said she's never forgiven her mother for what she saw as the incongruities between having multiple fathers to her children yet never using birth control. So that was a *really* strong influence in my growing up years. She'd often tell me of her sisters having to do their – do abortions you know. And so that was a *huge* strong influence. It was *very* negative against the Catholic Church.

Annette's father came from a strict Presbyterian background in Scotland, but he became a Buddhist, though his wife prevented him having the Buddhist funeral he wanted. In the midst of this, Annette developed an extreme hostility towards the Roman Catholic Church, and in her teens during the late sixties joined the British Humanist Association; she told me: 'So I don't know when I stopped believing in God, but I can't say I ever did believe in God frankly'. She recalled that two topics were banned at the family meal table: God and Northern Ireland, because she had a different view from her parents on both topics. Annette in her late sixties tried to understand her alienation from religion: 'how come around fourteen I had decided God was rubbish?' And she recalled being sent at fourteen to Majorca to learn Spanish with a family her parents had met on holiday, resulting in her being 'dragged off to mass every single morning with them and it was all in Latin'. But the family was anything but a model of morality:

it was violent, and although their child was religious she was also a shoplifter. They had, she recalls, 'such values that really were not mine, but yet they went to mass every single morning and that really clinched it for me. I just thought, "you know, this is so hypocritical".' And to complete the mess, at the age of 12 she was sexually abused by her parents' best friend, but her mother would not believe her, and she went on to suffer abuse as a young adult.[14]

A significant number of female respondents spoke of trauma in relation to their loss of religion or religious belief. Joan Gibson, born in 1943 in Cheltenham, became a born-again Anglican Evangelical at around 20, after which she married a Church of Scotland minister in 1965. In the early 1980s she developed a strong feminism at the same time as her marriage broke up. She says: 'I mean, I had all these sort of marital personal problems and my father had died of cancer of the oesophagus, which had been horrible, and I think I was just realising that religion didn't have any answers.'[15] From this Joan moved over a number of years to a humanist standpoint. Another Englishwoman, Mary Wallace, was born near Northwich in 1960. She experienced Anglican religious education at school, and for a short period when 13 and 14 became a Pentecostal: 'I was completely hooked for six months and it was an absolutely fascinating little group of people, a very small gathering of people, a very small church but really passionate, passionate people.' Eventually, she reported: 'I just worked out that the whole thing was absolute gobbledegook', and left. But it was some two decades later, when her second child died just after birth, that she became alert to the need to express her absence of faith, asking herself in the week between the death and the funeral: '"What do you do to have a funeral if you don't believe in God? How do atheists do this stuff?" You know, if they don't go to a minister and say "would you conduct a ceremony for me?"' Although a minister conducted a kindly service, this was her 'big turning point' as she received literature from the British Humanist Association on how to conduct funerals and felt: '"Ah that's it, that's it, that's really what we should be doing, that means something to me."' All of the words

---

[14] Annette Horton, b. Plymouth 1949, 1–4.
[15] Joan Gibson, b. Cheltenham 1943, 5.

in that book meant something to me in terms of a connection that I'd never felt before.'[16]

Two more types of trauma are worth noting here. The first was religious trauma, experienced by those facing and deciding to reject intense religious cultures. Two of my interviewees were raised in what they regarded as religious cults, and the leaving was traumatic in the face of intense pressure from specialist agents intending to prevent this eventuality; their experience included the practice of 'shunning' by other family members. But a more widespread phenomenon was merely being raised in a region with intense religious culture. Leslie O'Hagan's father was a scientist, based originally at Stanford in California where she was born, and she moved when she was very young for her father's work to Dallas, Texas, by which time her parents had lost their faith. During her childhood in the 1960s and 1970s, she attended Methodist Sunday school and summer camp, so as to be part of the general activities of her friends. But she was raised religiously as 'nothing'. She reported: 'I guess I felt like an outsider there. Everyone had their church there, and I didn't feel I fitted anywhere.' She reports that she tried very hard to 'accept Jesus into her heart' as she was urged by school teachers, church and friends.

> And I felt nothing; what's wrong with me? I remember a horrifying experience around grade 3 at school. In the Bible belt, everyone has a church and a religion, and everyone assumes you are a Christian. And we had to do a report, an oral report, on our religion, and our church. Well, I didn't have one. And I remember that terror. I had to get up and tell this story – about my Dad was this, my Mom was this. And he didn't believe. And this was humiliating, putting a child through this. … That scarred me. Everyone said: 'She's not one of us.' I grew up in the Bible belt just never feeling that I belonged there.

She finally escaped her trauma when in young adulthood she met a visiting nonbeliever, and they married and moved to Seattle, becoming Unitarian Universalists and humanists.[17]

Finally, there was one accident trauma. Ruth Majors had become an evangelical Christian at the age of 11, and went through

---

[16] Mary Wallace, b. Northwich 1960, 3, 5.
[17] Leslie O'Hagan, b. Palo Alto, CA, 1961.

university undertaking various missionary and charitable endeavours at home and abroad. But in her mid-twenties she developed doubt about her evangelical Christian faith, in part focused on disquiet after experiencing evangelical missionaries' treatment of non-Christian cultures in the Far East. Finally she experienced clarity during a motoring accident in Kent when travelling in a car that overturned. Though nobody was hurt, she recalled this as her 'turning point', reporting: 'as we were flying through the air (laughter) I can remember thinking I don't believe in life after death and imagining this policeman announcing to my mother that we were all dead (still laughing) and I think, I do think that from that moment on I felt I was living a hypocritical life by still going to church'.[18]

Traumas, including grief, sexual abuse, marital breakdown and depression were to be found amongst a significant minority of female respondents; some more will be considered later.

Loss Narrative II: Radicalization

Tanya Long was born in 1944 in an isolated mining town in Ontario. Her parents and extended family were nominally religious, mostly in the United Church of Canada. Here is her story:

> When I was a teenager I went through a period of a sort of a kind of religious fervour. And I even had an experience or two that, like going for a walk and it's being very foggy, and kind of thinking that I heard the voice of God. I think that only happened once, but yes I did have a certain religious fervour throughout my adolescence and then into my young adulthood. And I actually married when I was 21. I met him at university. I married a man who was studying to be a minister. And the reason he came to university was because he had just been converted. And he was full of religious fervour. He really knew, you know, he had been converted, and he was all gung-ho. And I fell in love with him and we got married. And we had this vision of the two of us kind of sailing our ship and he was gonna be the captain and I was gonna be the helmsman, and we were gonna go out there and do all

---

[18]   Ruth Majors (pseudonym), b. London 1941.

these wonderful good deeds [laughs]. Well, that lasted about six months [laughs]. And in a way as the marriage deteriorated, which it eventually did because we should never have gotten married – we were too young and we were both unhappy, needy young people and we should never have married. And as the marriage deteriorated, both of our religious fervours kind of went by the wayside [laughs] along with the marriage. And my husband never did end up becoming a minister. He got disillusioned. In fact, one time he told me that part of why he got disillusioned was because he was so turned off by my fervour that it looked ridiculous to him [laughs].[19]

The thing they shared in their marriage was a strong impulse to work for human rights and social issues. The Anglican church they joined in downtown Toronto in the late 1960s, Holy Trinity, was very liberal and active on these issues, and they were inspired by this radicalism, especially on emerging gay rights, food banks and homelessness. Tanya reported: 'I think we were involved with the church to the extent that we were even – once the religious fervour kind of started to die down, because of that community involvement and because of the liberal ideas that that church represented.' After their marriage broke up, Tanya remained religiously active, moving to a United Church congregation because this was the first Canadian denomination to approve gay ordained clergy in 1972. But she gradually came to realize that she could not handle the sermons, because she lacked a belief in God. She turned first to Buddhism and then in the 1990s to the Humanist Association of Toronto, in which she remained until at least 2010.

Tanya's testimony comes alive with remembrance of the radical liberal Christianity that so energized her and her husband in the late 1960s and early 1970s; she spoke of tears coming to her eyes on hearing of the acceptance of a gay minister. The way in which her liberal radicalism led her to enthuse about religion was shared by some other respondents who then broke away. In the case of Ruth Majors in the 1960s, she became interested in radical causes, going to Cambridge University where she joined the Christian Union, twice went on the CND Aldermaston marches, became active in the evangelical Cambridge University Settlement in Bermondsey,

19 Tanya Long, b. Sudbury, ON, 1944, 2.

and was involved in prison reform and working with prostitutes. After a period in Thailand with missionaries, she finally acknowledged her loss of faith when she returned to England; she went on to become a feminist literary theorist at a Canadian university.

Annette Horton associated her move from her mother's claustrophobic Catholicism with feminist impulses. Her first individualist streak, as she called it, was joining the British Humanist Association while still in her teens, and reading avidly in humanist literature and magazines. Her striving for a career as a doctor was set in the context of reaction to the back-street abortions and excessive pregnancies of her mother and especially her grandmother, and the sexual abuse she experienced, both at the age of 12 and at medical school, when she was raped twice. She became pregnant in 1967, the year before the legalization of the pill for the unmarried in the UK, and had an abortion because otherwise she would have been thrown out of medical school. She felt a calling to assist the poor and non-white ethnic groups, and notably women amongst these groups. After qualifying, she worked first in Cook County Hospital in Chicago, one of America's most dedicated hospitals for poor blacks and Latinos; from there she became a flying doctor, serving mainly the First Nations Peoples in western Canada. Later still, she trained as a psychiatrist specializing in home visits to women suffering from the circumstances of failing relationships, abortions and related issues. But although Annette became a doctor, she does not cite science as the cause of her loss of religion.[20]

Radical causes were by no means limited to female losers of religion. Many of the men I interviewed also felt a calling to support human rights, the cause of assisted suicide and medical charities. No-religionist organizations and individuals have told me of their charitable works of various kinds, ranging from operating a humanist soup kitchen in Glasgow to the humanist Vancouverites' backing of girls' schools in Kenya. But the human rights issues stand out as both distinctive and women-centred. In Montreal during the late 1960s, the president of the Humanist Association of Canada, Dr Henry Morgentaler (1923–2013), opened the city's first abortion clinic at a time when abortion was illegal, instigating nationwide support for decriminalization of medical

---

[20] Horton, 4–6.

abortions, and affirming the long developed alignment of organized no-religionism with birth control and a woman's right to choose over terminations.[21] More broadly, the drive for women's autonomy arising from the radicalism of the 1960s was manifest in various guises in female losers of religion. Underlying many of the testimonies is the sense of acquiring a new freedom from a destiny that would have led them down roads similar to those of their mothers, and thereby to live lives limited by a conventional domesticity unliberated by the surge of second-wave feminism and the women's liberation movement.

Loss Narrative III: Converting the Family

A third sub-narrative is of a different stamp altogether. This is the model of those who were brought up in the 1930s, 1940s and 1950s by religiously indifferent parents, but who became intensely religious, usually evangelical, sometimes fundamentalist, influenced by the strong evangelical movement of the time – including the influence of Billy Graham. Of the twenty-three female interviewees, eight were strongly influenced by religion in this way, amongst whom four converted the rest of their families.

Ruth Majors was born in 1941 in London but, because her father was a serviceman, she spent part of her childhood in Tripoli before he resigned from the army and the family became very poor, with her staying for three years with grandparents in Ramsgate. This was a working-class family, half Catholic, half Protestant, but 'not really churchgoers' as she described them. In Tripoli in 1949 or 1950, she went to an American Baptist church, but her parents hated it and took her away from it. But in Ramsgate in 1952 when she was 11, she became interested in an evangelical church across the road from her grandparents' home, and she became a born-again Evangelical. This led to the conversion of the whole family. Here is her testimony:

> So, anyway, we were living in Ramsgate and I took the 11 plus exam and I got in to the grammar school. It was a girls' school, it was a fairly good school and I was always quite good in school. We were living opposite a church – my parents were not church-

[21] <http://en.wikipedia.org/wiki/Henry_Morgentaler>, accessed 9 July 2013. I am grateful to two anonymous respondents for discussing the significance of this case with me.

goers at all, at least I don't remember ever going to a church with them except to a wedding. And this church was an evangelical church with a very charismatic vicar and vicar's wife who was an even better preacher than he was actually. And they ran the summer camp for kids and all that. So I got roped in to the church when I was 11 and I got quote 'converted' and I marched my parents off to Billy Graham rallies and they got converted. And so we became an evangelical family (much laughter) largely at my instigation, though my brother was also very good at music and he became the organist in the church, so that was his connection. We were living right opposite this church, so it became very much the centre of our life in a way. And I can remember disapproving of my mother because she wore lipstick to church, and being horribly mean to her about it, saying she was an embarrassment; and she did her vacuuming on Sundays which was also very prohibited. So I must have been absolutely obnoxious. (laughing)

So, as she said, 'we became an evangelical family'. There is an interesting phenomenon in mid-century of the nominally Christian family being overtaken by the intensifying religiosity of the child. The family becomes the site for the self-expression of girls and young women, but the process was located in the so-called 'fifties revival', which in many cases pitted the more religious child against the less religious parents.

It is surprising how many children were enveloped in religious culture when their parents were to varying degrees indifferent, negligent or even hostile. Raised in mid-century households that had little religious connection, by various routes the children became religiously active and this impacted on the parents. Joan Gibson grew up in Malaya in the 1950s, where she was placed with other British girls in two Catholic schools successively:

> the whole ambience of the [first] school was very, very peaceful, but there was no sort of proselytising by the Catholics at all. But when I went to the other school, which was multiracial, the non-Catholics had instead of what was supposed to be religious instruction it was I think moral education but in actual fact it was Catholic. That was I think more indoctrination.[22]

---

[22]   Gibson, 2.

Despite this experience, and despite describing herself as 'a Christian probably', she spoke of her family as really quite religiously indifferent: 'my family had no interest in religion and never went to church'. Her father was from the Presbyterian Highlands, but she learned very much later in life that her mother was divorced and that no church would marry the couple; thus Joan was an illegitimate child, and her parents only finally got married when she was three or four years old. She reports her mother as being resentful of the Churches, and traces her mother's ecclesiastical hostility to this cause.[23]

In British Columbia, Grace Daniels's mother was brought up a Seventh-Day Adventist but, according to her daughter, gave this up as soon as she could, and raised her children largely without religion: 'So I was brought up in essentially a non-religious household and I don't think my father had any particular belief, although I'm not really sure if he was brought up in a church or not, I kind of doubt it.' Her mother told her she thought religion was a crutch. But Grace opted as a child aged four or five to go with her friends to church and Sunday school, reporting: 'it sounded kind of cool (laughs), you know sounded like they were doing interesting things'. She went to various churches in her childhood, including summer Bible camp, eventually leaving the churches for ever at the age of nine after the pastor changed church, undermining her sense of certainty in the clergy's steadfastness, and because of being offered candy at the end of each service as a bribe to return the following week. An underlying driver of reason and reasonableness came out, leading her to leave church of her own volition. But the going to church, and the sustaining of a religious belief after that for some time, was done in part to defy her mother:

> I still had a belief in something and, and you know a little bit in this too was a sort of an aspect of, it was rebelling against my mother (laughs) so she was an atheist, and I wanted to rebel against that, right, a little bit of that kind of woven through it. So yeah, it was just like the churches there, you know, was something wrong. So I guess that's just sort of in the back of my mind. There's, there's a God, but [I'm] probably not going to find it in the church.

23   Gibson, 5.

What is interesting here is the ability of children to sustain a religious culture for a very long time in the 1960s and early 1970s despite parental indifference. Grace was drawn in her later teens towards the 'New Age', especially the element influenced by Sufism, reacting in part against the treatment of women in the Seventh-Day Adventist tradition, for instance, over the wearing of jewellery; she became a devotee successively of the Maharishi Mahesh Yogi, founder of Transcendental Meditation, and of Pir Vilayat Khan, founder of the Sufi Order International, attending meditation camps in California, before moving in the following decades towards humanism.[24]

In Trenton, Ontario, Ena Sparks was brought up in a household of fairly lukewarm but conforming Christian parents; her mother took the children to church, the father did not go. But Ena became a practising Christian in her mid-teens, accepting a Gideon Bible and signing a certificate saying she accepted Christ in her life. She joined the Young Life group, an active Christian organization, and went on at 20 to get married in the United Church of Canada. When her husband was killed in a road accident when she was 22, she took to travelling in Europe and the rest of the world, and developing a maturing attitude to religions:

> I realised actually travelling in different countries that I formed some maybe stronger opinions about certain types of religions and certain types of practices and things like that. [I] started, I think, to develop more of a kind of a rejection of the influences that maybe the Catholic churches had for example. It didn't actually interest me to go to any Muslim countries, and I think partly it was just because of how they treat women. And I was starting to tie that thinking into the problems of religion, but it was still kind of thinking of religion as a power as opposed to a faith, and actually a Marxist view, the opium of the masses – I by then was kind of thinking along those lines.[25]

More generally, many respondents spoke of attending Sunday school and even church when their parents did not attend; their drift from religion came when a sense of rationality in favour of

---

[24] Grace Daniels, b. Vancouver 1958, 1–4.
[25] Ena Sparks (pseudonym), b. Trenton, ON, 1954, 1–4.

unbelief won through. Karen Bulmer, brought up in Livingston in Scotland, had a family heritage in the Orange Order, but her parents did not attend church despite sometimes sending her. To this was added religious education at school. But Karen was a doubter from early on, from primary school:

> I remember being deeply sceptical as a child and I've always been should I say anti-religious, organised religion. I've always been sceptical, even would say cynical about it as a child. I remember thinking 'what's this about, this isn't right, how can this — how can this be, how can people, how can men assume that they have understood the message?' To me it was obvious it was entirely manmade as a child.[26]

In Vancouver, Loraine Hardie grew up in the 1940s and 1950s with parents who went to church much less than she went to Sunday school. Her grandparents too were strongly Anglican. But the break came in 1965 when she decided not to have a church wedding. And then she worked in a Jewish nursery in Vancouver where she learned how both Christians and Jews had claims on being chosen people:

> And I was beginning to see the problems, so for me to really let it go was not easy because … my upbringing was quite enjoyable, I wasn't having any problem with church or Sunday School and I really liked the music of the church, and so it was a struggle for me to let go of all of that. So [it] definitely wasn't that I was revolting, it was more just I was just, my own rationality was, you know, telling me that this does not make any sense you know.[27]

LOSS NARRATIVE IV: FEMINISM AND INDIVIDUALISM

Jutta Cahn was born in Berlin in 1925 of an assimilated Jewish father and Lutheran mother, and brought up in a household with very little religion, although she described learning it at Protestant school. But on moving to England at 11, she took herself to the Church of England where she was confirmed.

---

[26] Karen Bulmer, b. Livingston 1975, 2.
[27] Lorraine Hardie, b. Vancouver 1939, 1–2.

The war was on and I was inquisitive at the time and took confirmation classes and got myself confirmed. My parents had no say in the matter, I decided on that. But within a year I left [laughs]. And had had quite enough of the religious teachings that I had taken as a result of becoming confirmed in the Church of England.

The trigger for her was having family in both Germany and Britain during the war:

On the German side the Christians I suppose were asking for their God, so to speak, to smite the enemy, namely the Brits. Where did that leave me? In a state of confusion. And it was enough for me to quit, and I quit for the rest of my life in terms of being a religious person.[28]

The sense of deciding for oneself as a child is strong in quite a number of respondents, both for religion, and in walking away from it.

Some women refer to an assertive individualism as lying at the heart of their rejection of religion. In a sense, in even the most traumatic of accounts, there is a claim to independence, to an autonomous self that demanded separation from the expectations that family and community had for a girl or young woman in the middle decades of the twentieth century. By the 1960s and 1970s, the most striking element of that individualism that led women from the religion of their parents was second-wave feminism. This was important to Joan Gibson: after becoming an Anglican Evangelical at around 20, she married a Church of Scotland minister in 1965. In the early 1980s she developed a strong feminism at the same time as her marriage broke up: her feminism and anti-religionism developed contemporaneously, combining in hostility to the Church's treatment of women.[29]

Women and business also brought forth an individualism that combined capitalism and feminism. By her mid-twenties, Ena Sparks was placing her role in business in the context of feminist thinking about discrimination in pay and careers for women. This view she developed in large part because of her mother's ideas,

---

[28] Jutta Cahn (Poser), b. Berlin 1925.
[29] Gibson, 5.

and her reaction against the more limited career opportunities for women of her mother's generation:

> I thought myself as supporting myself, kind of, sort of a long way too, and I think a lot of it has, some of it has to do with my mom. You know, that women should be independent, they shouldn't necessarily be seen themselves as supporting the man, and being that kind of second place in a relationship. And even more so, I think it is important for women to be able to support themselves and be independent so that they can choose.[30]

Her mother, she reported, 'made me somewhat independent'. Her parents 'had a pretty good equal relationship, although you know it still had its traditional elements as well'. She read feminist literature in her late teens and early twenties, leading her to 'I think feeling much more strongly that religions are very instrumental in keeping women in a place, and things like that'.[31]

Perhaps the most searing account of the conjunction of losing religion with feminism in everyday life comes from Pat Duffy Hutcheon, born in 1926 and brought up in rural Alberta. Her upbringing was very poor, and life became hard in the drought of the thirties and early forties when the mere struggles to stay warm and to eat enough were uppermost. Her overriding concern was that of work: to find an economic role for a woman as daughter and as wife, to keep two families from starvation. Resonant of Carolyn Steedman's study of the economic self-conception of women of the past,[32] Pat's testimony comes back to that relentlessly, even when asked other questions:

> CB: Did you have a settled view of religious matters in your teens?
>
> PH: Oh yes. Yes much before my teens I had a very settled view. I had to go after working – Our family had to split up and I had to try to find a job from grade 9 on, try to find a job. Worked my way through high school by keeping – working as a house helper, home helper and then getting to school and

30 Sparks, 5.
31 Ibid. 6.
32 Carolyn Steedman, *Landscape for a Good Woman* (London, 1986), 125–49.

getting my board and room that way. So that's how I tried to get my high school, and I didn't have much time to worry about other issues [laughs] other than getting fed.

She trained as a teacher, scratching a poor and troubled living in an isolated prairie school, and then things became worse when she married unwisely.

And so I boarded then with a very nice couple. But she had a brother who'd just returned from the war and he had horrible problems and nowadays of course he woulda been treated. In those days it wasn't recognised at all. And I got just kinda trapped. I was feeling so sorry for him and I got told – Before I knew what was happening, I was engaged to him because everyone said 'well you can't turn away from him now cause he's counting on you' and all of this and 'he's got so many problems'. And I knew it was a terrible thing for me to do for my part, but I got trapped, and when you're that age you do some stupid things.

Her liberation from religion becomes a story of economic struggle, on top of which came a decade of living with a physically abusive husband. Her escape came when she left her husband, taking their 10-year-old son with her, and, against seemingly insurmountable odds, established an academic career for herself in the field of education studies in the 1960s. Pat's struggle for survival, autonomy and freedom from religion is an intense story, one she has told not just in oral testimony but in a published autobiography.[33] She died four months after I interviewed her.

Conclusion

Through these overlapping narrative types, we see the way in which women, far more than men, place their journeys from religion in the context of family. This bears out, I believe, the argument I have made elsewhere in terms of quantitative demographic research on Canada, Ireland, the UK and the USA, that women's

---

[33] Pat Duffy Hutcheon, *Lonely Trail: The Life Journey of a Freethinker* (Ottawa, ON, 2009).

experience of the family is central to the rapid secularization that took off in the Western world in the 1960s.[34]

The process that vented rudely upon the West from the sixties has been overwhelmingly a female one. I have previously argued from the British case that one of the ways in which secularization must be observed is as a collapse of a hegemonic discourse that, over the period from 1800 to 1960, combined piety with respectable femininity. I have further argued that the historian can detect popular reflexivity to that loss in the 1960s through oral testimony.[35] The present study, I believe, enhances that detection. Through the scale and character of personal loss of faith, and through the personal narratives of women who have lost religion, we can observe the collapse of discursive Christianity in the wider cultural reconstructions of the age. Where a woman lost religion in the third quarter of the twentieth century, the family seemed no longer to be a conduit for a chain of religious memory. This seems to be because women's walk away from religion at that time was part and parcel of them walking away from the traditional family model and towards a female self. Lynn Abrams, in her oral history study of mid-century British women, concludes that, for women growing up in the post-war decades,

> the religious narrative as a way to make sense of a life was no longer relevant … rather, they acknowledged that there was such a narrative – one that would have been framed by issues of respectability, outward presentation, social convention, and the face one presents to the public – but that it belonged to their mothers' generation. When the daughters were asked questions about religion their answers referred to their parents' and sometimes their grandparents' generation and their own girlhoods.[36]

In these interviews with women, there are two things happening. First, women's stories of losing religion in the middle decades of the twentieth century are situated within the memory frame of the family. This is because, firstly, that is where, for women at least, religion and its effects, especially its moral effects, have traditionally been situated and manifested. Women have traditionally experienced Western

---

34 Brown, *Religion and the Demographic Revolution*, 172–216.
35 Brown, *Death of Christian Britain*.
36 Abrams, 'Mothers and Daughters', 79.

Christianity as a moral impression on their lives, which propelled a woman to take the family as the defining frame of her life and moral respectability; her very essence in nineteenth- and early twentieth-century culture was centred on religious encouragement to be a familial icon — a beacon of righteousness, as homemaker, wife and mother.[37] Secondly, the memory frame of the family is uppermost in a woman's recollection of losing religion because women have a closer and more profound relationship with the family than do men, in terms of discourses of caring and nurture. The family has been widely regarded as providing 'a natural place' for women to locate their sense of self, and it is no surprise that this cultural conditioning led to their narratives being located in that place too. So, what is then happening is a dangerous act: one of rejecting the religion that defines the family self, but locating that act of 'leaving' within that framework still. In other words, there remains a moral imperative to which a woman leaving religion between the 1940s and 1970s felt compelled to accede: to acknowledge that tampering with her religiosity implied tampering with her familial respectability. The women were generally challenging the first (the religion) whilst wanting, initially at least, to leave the family morality either untouched or, perhaps, to have it challenged in a separate act that was separately justified. This does not mean that it was impossible to challenge both simultaneously; some women's autobiographies of the period do record this.[38] But I suspect this was rare. This is not to imply an essentialist position on women's 'natural' connectivity between religion and family; rather, it is to acknowledge the power of the essentialist discourse to which women had to face up in the century's third quarter if they wished to disown organized religion. It would thus be hypothesized that this level of double rejection — of religion and family — lessened or disappeared for a later generation of women. This is certainly something that I have found amongst women born after 1960, but too few have been interviewed to make a significant finding.

Women use the family motif or frame to narrate the story of loss of religion because women locate meanings about life within the family (or at least within relationships). Their communication strategies are different from those of men. They are more likely

[37] Brown, *Death of Christian Britain*, ch. 4.
[38] A good example is Michelle Roberts, *Paper Houses: A Memoir of the '70s and Beyond* (London, 2007).

to situate their stories within networks of other women, whereas men are happier at taking the floor and telling a self-narrative that does not rely as much on relations with others. Oral history theorists speak of this. Kristina Minister and Alessandro Portelli talk about gendered themes for male and female memories – such as war and reason for men, family for women – which orientate life narratives in a gendered fashion.[39] Moreover, there is a theory that women undertake 'narrative labour' within the family; they are often responsible for the passing on of family stories and memories, and thus their stories are located within relationships. By contrast, men's stories are often about self-aggrandisement.[40]

So, in women's way of talking retrospectively about their journeys from religion, the family appears as the central narrative feature. Ultimately, though, the key thing seems to be that the story of 'losing religion' for women concerns finding the *self*-narrative that is unchained from family. That finding of the self involves rejecting, or at least questioning, the values with which they had been brought up. But paradoxically, to do that, to discover an independent female self, women feel compelled to commence their narration within the family frame they may be about to recall leaving. It often first appears in their narratives as something they have had to engage with in their lives, often as a battle. They may have battled with the 'reality' of the family, or against the idea of it, as something to overcome in their life journey. For women, the family is such a crucial element in their lives that, by default, they use it as the framework for narrating their life stories. The dominant discourse that these women have travelled through in their lives, from tradition to modernity, is that the family *should* be at the heart of their lives and identity. In a sense, this is what second-wave feminism has been about but, for individual women, renegotiating their relationship to family remains a work in progress, not an outcome. The walk from religion thus becomes for women a story of walking also from a family of traditional discourse and of a reality to be left behind. As Abrams writes, 'the women at the

[39] Kristina Minister, 'A Feminist Frame for the Oral History Interview', in Sherna Berger Gluck and Daphne Patai, eds, *Women's Words: The Feminist Practice of Oral History* (New York, 1991), 27–41; Portelli as discussed in Lynn Abrams, *Oral History Theory* (London, 2010), 28.

[40] Kristin M. Langellier and Eric E. Peterson, *Storytelling in Daily Life: Performing Narrative* (Philadelphia, PA, 2004), 108–9.

centre of the debate about secularization in Britain negotiated their way through a period characterized by cultural conflict and a clash of values'.[41] The story is, in part, about a journey from the woman in the family to the woman in her self.

The story of religion in the midst of post-1960 rapid secularization becomes one of the chain of memory being severed – neither believing nor belonging. The way this happened over the last seventy years has been heavily gendered, something not dealt with in the accounts of Hervieu-Léger or Davie. The way men lose religion is little changed since the nineteenth century, and probably since the eighteenth century; Bertrand Russell's account of battling as a Victorian teenager with the logic of god is a story replicated in its essence by virtually every one of the thirty-two men I have interviewed.[42] By contrast, none of the women I interviewed claimed reading as triggering loss of religion in the way many of the men did. Equally, none cited science or philosophy as triggers either. Unreason and the unreasonableness of organized religion did come into a minority of accounts, but, again, not to the extent that they did for male interviewees. Stories of women losing religion, which are very, very rare before the 1960s, are constituted recurrently in a story of the loss of the chain of memory of family and family religion – often told in complex, though essentially family-centred, ways. From the 1960s, Western secularization became one with a demographic revolution at whose heart lay women and family. Hervieu-Léger was right to establish the link between secularization in France and collapsing female fertility in the 1960s and 1970s. But clarity is needed to avoid observing this, as Davie has done, in terms of the survival of secular people's vicarious chain of memory, routed through a few Christian philanthropists and likeminded volunteers, with a Christian past.[43] Rather than sociology of religion becoming 'the sociology of the religious', as Hervieu-Léger suggested, the testimonies of women who lose religion show with uncanny unanimity that the changing family lies at the heart of what is swiftly enveloping large swathes of the West – the sociology of the secular.

University of Glasgow

[41] Abrams, 'Mothers and Daughters', 61.
[42] Bertrand Russell, *The Autobiography of Bertrand Russell* (London, 1975), 35.
[43] Davie, *Religion in Modern Europe*.

HOUSEHOLD SOVEREIGNTY AND RELIGIOUS SUBJECTIFICATION: CHINA AND THE CHRISTIAN WEST COMPARED*

by ADAM YUET CHAU

This essay is an attempt to explore the cultural logics behind two very different orientations towards spirits (divinities), one Chinese and the other Christian, and the kinds of religious subjects that are produced by practices informed by these two differing orientations. Specifically, I examine the role the household plays in Chinese religious life as a site and structural unit to host different categories of spirits (gods, ghosts and ancestors), and contrast this with the Christian idiom of being hosted by God. In Christianity, God is the supreme host; humans (Christians) can only be guests at God's banquet but they cannot host God in return. It is explicitly an unequal relationship. And even though they are unworthy of such generous treatment Christians must accept this divine grace and join the communion. The eucharist, the most important Christian ritual for almost all Christians, is

* This essay is part of a larger monograph project on the idiom of hosting in Chinese political and religious culture, which was first conceived when I was an An Wang postdoctoral fellow at the Fairbank Center for East Asian Research, Harvard University, in 2004–5, for the occasion of the conference '"Religion" in China: Rethinking Indigenous and Imported Categories of Thought' (21–22 May 2005). I have subsequently presented papers on the topic at the University of Bristol (2006, East Asian Studies); University College London (2006, Anthropology); the Ecclesiastical History Society Summer Conference on 'Religion and the Household' (2012); Purdue University, at the summer workshop on social scientific studies of religion in China (2012); the University of Oxford, as part of the Wilde Lectures in Natural and Comparative Religion (2013); and the Macau Ricci Institute (2013). Many friends and colleagues have helped nurture my thinking on this topic in the past few years, amongst whom Stephan Feuchtwang, Henrietta Harrison, Craig Clunas, Mary Laven and Nicolas Standaert deserve special mention. I thank Mary Laven for having told me about the 2012 EHS Summer Conference, and Alex Walsham for having encouraged me to contribute a paper. Presenting an earlier version of this essay in front of a group of distinguished church historians was humbling. The audience members took my wild speculations and deliberately provocative comparisons in good spirit, for which I am grateful. The revision has benefitted from comments and suggestions from Mary Laven and the editors of Studies in Church History. Émile Perreau-Saussine took interest in my 'hosting' project and suggested that we read together works on the Catholic mass but this plan could not be realized due to his tragic death in February 2010. I dedicate this essay to his memory.

a constant reminder to Christians that they are guests, and that when they go to heaven, they will be God's guests eternally. In the Chinese case, on the other hand, the household hosts the spirits by providing offerings. Gods, ghosts and ancestors are invited to the bountiful banquet at fixed times of the year and then sent off when the banquets are over. The spirits can only be guests; they do not, and indeed cannot, host human guests. In Chinese religious culture there are no accounts of spirits, be they deities, ancestors or ghosts, hosting humans. In the Chinese hosting of spirits, the guest is accorded honour and respect, but it is the host who is the most active, potent and pre-eminent agent. In other words, agency rests with humans. And the social idiom of hosting enframes the entire cluster of ritual actions.

This essay will explore, firstly, household hosting as an expression of what I call 'household sovereignty'; secondly, the household as a basic unit of religious engagement and hosting as an idiom of religious practice; and, thirdly, the kinds of religious subjectification and religious habitus the two differing orientations towards divinities might produce: Chinese householder 'hosts' on the one hand and 'guestly' Christians on the other.[1] I argue that there has been a historical process of the Christian Church usurping Christians' household sovereignty, by instituting the church as proper site of worship and by the ritual of the eucharist, which is God hosting worshippers through his surrogate the priest. If this sharp contrast has been slightly exaggerated, my goal has been to accentuate the differences between these two orientations and to stimulate debate about the broader questions of the historical evolution of religious subjectification in different societies. I will draw upon insights generated by materials from Shaanbei (northern Shaanxi Province) in north-central China, where I conducted ethnographic fieldwork research on religious life in the late 1990s, as well as my

---

[1] By 'religious subjectification' I mean the process through which a certain kind of person (i.e. religious subject) is produced through engaging in an ensemble of religious practices over a long period of time. The resulting 'religious habitus' in a person issues forth his or her embodied practices. This conceptualization owes its inspiration to theorists such as Louis Althusser, Michel Foucault and Pierre Bourdieu. For a more detailed explication of these concepts, see Adam Yuet Chau, 'Religious Subjectification: The Practice of Cherishing Written Characters and Being a *Ciji* (*Tzu Chi*) Person', in Chang Hsun, ed., *Chinese Popular Religion: Linking Fieldwork and Theory*, Papers from the Fourth International Conference on Sinology (Taipei, 2013), 75–113.

more recent short-term fieldwork in Taiwan.[2] A caveat is in order at this point. As an absolute outsider to ecclesiastical history, many of the things I say about the history of Christianity are inevitably speculative. But this essay is written in the spirit of raising questions relating to the comparative study of religion and the household, so I beg the specialists in the history of Christianity for their indulgence. Just as my exposure to reading on church history has stimulated me to ask new questions about Chinese religious culture, I hope that the questions raised in this essay will achieve similar effects for non-China scholars of religious history in the West and elsewhere.

The Household as a Basic Unit of Religious Engagement in Chinese Religious Culture

The household as a discrete socio-political unit is most likely a product of, and constitutes the most foundational component of, agrarian societies. The traditional agrarian empire in China depended on the patrilineal household and the household patriarch for proper governance, and considered all kinds of social actors outside the household framework suspect, such as celibate monastics, prostitutes, bachelors not belonging to any households, Jesuit missionaries or members of celibate sisterhoods. This pattern of household-centric governmentality has in important ways persisted until today.

In addition to facilitating the management of taxation and security, the household also operates as a sovereign political-economic and ritual unit. Budgeting and most production-consumption decisions (including division of labour, assignment of tasks, migration, household division and marriage) are made at the household level. All members of the household are the responsibility of the head of the household until the sons divide the household and form new households of their own. But the most salient expressions of household sovereignty are the interactions between the household as a discrete ritual unit, on the one hand, and all kinds of spiritual forces (gods, ghosts and ancestors) and ritual special-

---

[2] See Adam Yuet Chau, *Miraculous Response: Doing Popular Religion in Contemporary China* (Palo Alto, CA, 2006); idem, 'Actants Amassing (AA)', in Nicholas J. Long and Henrietta L. Moore, eds, *Sociality: New Directions* (Oxford, 2012), 133–55.

ists, on the other. I contend that the idiom of 'hosting' human and supernatural guests on important hosting occasions lies at the foundation of processes of religious subjectification in Chinese religious culture. Such a process produces 'hosts' who embody gestural and other related protocols of hosting, who need not memorize any catechism or understand any theological arguments, who engage with social and supernatural intimates not as individuals but as members of households who act as a collectivity. Note that I am speaking of hosting in terms of receiving guests who are known and familiar to the host. This concept of hosting contrasts sharply with the more commonly employed concept of 'hospitality', which primarily refers to receiving and being kind to strangers.[3] In fact, in the Judeo-Christian religious tradition the figure of the stranger has theological significance: one had better offer hospitality to the stranger who shows up at one's door since he might very well be an angel or God himself! On the other hand, in the Chinese religious tradition there are hardly any such figures of stranger-spirits.[4]

On key hosting occasions such as funerals, weddings and communal festivals where the households form the basis, the 'sovereignty' of the host household is the most manifest and celebrated. The household courtyard, during the course of the hosting occasion, is transformed into a kingdom with the head of the household as its sovereign. I use the concept of sovereignty to evoke the conceptually analogous connections between the household and the state. The *Chambers 20th Century Dictionary* defines sovereignty as 'pre-eminence; supreme and independent power; the territory of a sovereign or of a sovereign state'. Peasant household event productions such as funerals and weddings are essentially 'host/guest rituals'.[5] They fashion the host household (*zhujia*) as a

---

[3] See Felicity Heal, *Hospitality in Early Modern England* (Oxford, 1990); Jacques Derrida and Anne Dufourmantelle, *Of Hospitality: Anne Dufourmantelle invites Jacques Derrida to Respond*, transl. Rachel Bowlby (Palo Alto, CA, 2000); *Journal of the Royal Anthropological Institute* 18 (2012), supplementary issue on hospitality, ed. Matei Candea and Giovanni da Col.

[4] One may be tempted to speculate that Christianity has retained this stranger-spirit figure which it has inherited from a religion of a nomadic and tribal people, whereas the Chinese, having become sedentary (i.e. living in fixed settlements) for so long, have elaborated on familiar spirits instead.

[5] For an exposition of the concept of event production, see Chau, *Miraculous Response*, ch. 7.

sovereign social unit and the head of the household as the sovereign or master (*zhu*) of this unit. The host household exudes 'preeminence' over and above other households (although of course the structural meaning and position of each host household are derived from its being situated within the constellation of households in the community and beyond, each of which is entitled to host at some point in the course of its 'lifespan'). During these hosting occasions, even though the guests (including both humans and spirits) have to be well treated and respected, it is the *zhujia* that accrues recognition, social prestige, 'face' and symbolic capital by being the host. For the brief period of the event production (two or three days), it is as if the whole world revolves around the courtyard of the *zhujia*. The 'red-hot sociality' (*honghuo* in Shaanbei dialect, *re'nao* in Mandarin, *lau-jiat* in Minnan dialect) produced by the convergence of so many people, noisy firecrackers and music, steamy dishes, colourful decorations and loud banqueting makes the *zhujia*'s house unquestionably pre-eminent.[6]

Hosting is a moral event production because a recognition and acknowledgment of social worth is communicated between, and co-produced by, host and guest, and the hosting event always entails morally inflected judgements of all the details of the whole event (behaviour, utterances, gestures, levels of courtesy, politeness and generosity, and so on). By being host, a social actor or a group of social actors is putting status and reputation on the line. A well hosted event production maintains or augments the host's status and reputation, while a badly hosted event production can drastically drain the host's store of social-relational goodwill and affect his or her social standing. Successfully hosting major household event productions most importantly constitutes the personhood and identity of all members of the household and by extension establishes and confirms the standing and 'sovereignty' of the household in the community.

The household is the most fundamental unit of religious engagement in Chinese religious life because the household is the most basic political, economic and moral-religious building block of Chinese society. To the extent that an individual engages in religious activities, most of the time he or she is engaging in

---

[6] Ibid., chs 7–8.

such activities on behalf of members of the household as an intimate collectivity whose welfare is interdependent. There has been a long-held misconception about Chinese religious life, that since women seem to participate more in religious activities they must be more religious (or superstitious, depending on one's attitude towards such activities). But the truth is that most women participate in religious activities on behalf of all members of their households; they are simply representatives of the household as a unit of religious engagement. The same is true when only the names of heads of households are written on the memorials to be sent (through burning) to the celestial court in communal rituals; on these occasions the heads of households do not act as individuals but rather as representatives of their respective households.

The household is also the site of the worship of various deities and spirits (e.g. ancestral and deity worship at domestic altars, or the stove god). On the more obvious, basic and prosaic level, the household is host to the stove god, heaven and earth (*tiandi*), the immediate ancestors, and perhaps some other common deities found in domestic settings (e.g. the god of wealth, the goddess of mercy Guanyin). Usually represented in the form of spirit tablets (*shenweipai*) on domestic altars, these are like permanent lodgers in the home, to be cared for on a daily basis, usually in the forms of incense (freshly offered in the morning), red electric lamps in the shape of candles, and offerings that need not be replaced too frequently (e.g. fruits made of wax, biscuits and candies in wrappers). Familiarity has made it unnecessary for the host household members to be too ceremonious in interacting with these deities and ancestors. Typically the matron of the household (the wife of the head of the household or the daughter-in-law) assumes responsibility for such 'everyday forms of hosting'. These minor yet recurrent hosting occasions mirror minor social hosting occasions (e.g. friends and neighbours dropping by for a visit). At certain nodal points along the lunar calendrical trajectory the family makes more elaborate and special offerings with more ostentatious gestures of being the host to these spirits and deities, collectively or individually, e.g. on the first day of the lunar New Year, on the anniversary of an immediate ancestor's death, on the birthday of one of the deities such as Guanyin (somehow extremely generalized deities such as heaven and earth, the stove god, and the god of wealth do not have birthdays), or during the 'ghost month' (for banqueting the 'hungry ghosts'). To be sure, not all of these rituals physically take place within the household – for example, the lineage ancestral rites take place at the lineage hall[7] – but there is no mistaking that the household is always the most basic unit of hosting these various kinds of spirits.

When the village or neighbourhood community stages a communal religious festival, such as a temple festival in honour of the spirits enshrined in the community temple, or a New Year's festival, it is the households that serve as the basic participatory building blocks by contributing funds, labour, or both. In fact, in many communal rituals the households stage their own house-hold-based mini-rituals that are embedded in the larger framework of the communal ritual but are nevertheless expressions of the household idiom of religious engagement. For example, during a large-scale Daoist communal cleansing ritual (*jiao*), there are usually two distinct sites of ritual actions. In the temple the main group of Daoist priests and musicians conduct the long and drawn-out rituals for the community at large – but also, significantly, read aloud the names of the heads of households before submitting the communal requests to heaven (i.e. the Jade Emperor) – while indi-vidual (or small groups of) ritualists, usually lower ranking, conduct much briefer and simpler small rites from house to house at the invitation of individual households, receiving separate 'red packets' with cash in them as payment for their services.

There is another important aspect of the household that makes it the most basic unit of religious engagement. In Chinese religious life, the most common and most important activities are in the form of households hiring ritual specialists to conduct rituals on behalf of the household, especially at funerals. The overwhelming majority of these specialists-for-hire are not regular members of any larger religious institution and do not live in special dwellings separate from the common people; rather, they are mostly house-holders themselves, who live amongst the people who constitute their client base. In contrast with clerics who live collectively in cloisters (e.g. monasteries, nunneries, Daoist belvederes and temples), these religious specialists are atomized, living within

---

[7] Traditionally wealthy lineages tend to have lineage halls in which the ancestral tablets of all deceased ancestors of the lineage are held and where the lineage stages regular offering rituals.

the community of prospective clients but sometimes far removed from other similar specialists. I have in mind the proverbial *yinyang* master, the *huoju* (or *sanju*) Daoist priest, the spirit medium, and other similar types of 'householder religious specialists' (or 'householder religious service providers').[8] In fact, the impulse to engage in religious practices at the household level is so strong in many parts of China that there are even 'temple festivals' that take place within the houses of the spirit mediums, whose tutelary spirits constitute the divine guests to be hosted on these occasions.[9] One is also tempted to interpret the so-called 'house churches' in China as having resulted not simply from the state's unwillingness to let the worshippers build proper churches but rather the worshippers' desire to keep worshipping in their own homes, to 'host God' (at least in form if not in theology), and to express and assert their household sovereignty.[10]

We can thus see that, firstly, the overwhelming majority of religious activities in Chinese life use the household as the basic unit; secondly, that most ritual service providers in China are household-based; and, thirdly, that a large number, if not the majority, of religious activities in China involve households engaging with ritual specialists who are themselves householders. These observations will establish what can be called the 'household idiom of religious engagement', in contrast with the corporatist idiom (e.g. lineage collective worship, temple festivals) or the individualist idiom (e.g. individuals engaging in personal-cultivational activities). This also

---

[8]   See Adam Yuet Chau, 'Superstition Specialist Households?: The Household Idiom in Chinese Religious Practices', *Minsu quyi* (*Journal of Chinese Ritual, Theatre, and Folklore*) 153 (2006), 157–202; idem, 'Chinese Socialism and the Household Idiom of Religious Engagement', in Tam Ngo and Justine Quijada, eds, *Religion and Communism: Comparative Perspectives* (Berkeley, CA, forthcoming).

[9]   See Yue Yongyi, 'Jiazhong guohui' ('Making Temple Festivals at Home'), in Yue Yongyi, *Lingyan, Ketou, Chuanshuo* (Efficacy, Kowtow, Legends) (Shanghai, 2010), 169–240.

[10]   There is some tantalizing evidence suggesting such household-centric Christian practices in China. For example, in some places worshippers belonging to officially sanctioned churches attend the Sunday services but gather even more frequently in small groups in one another's homes for small-scale worship and fellowship; some elderly converts are still in the habit of inviting 'the Lord' to come and consume offerings in their homes (i.e. hosting God). See Wang Ying, *Shenfen jiangou yu wenhua ronghe: zhongyuan diqu jidujiaohui ge'an yanjiu* (*The Construction of Identity and Cultural Incorporation: The Case Study of a Protestant Church in the North China Plain*) (Shanghai, 2011).

contrasts sharply with the usual mode of religious engagement in Christianity, where individual worshippers constitute a congregation that supports collectively a priest or equivalent, and where the believers engage with God, at least in theory, as individuals.[11]

THE HOSTING IDIOM AND ITS IMPLICATIONS FOR THE FORMATION OF RELIGIOUS HABITUS

A significant amount of the attraction of Chinese religious activities for the Chinese derives from their employing the idiom of hosting in framing ritual actions. The hosting idiom is attractive because it is a common idiom found in many domains of Chinese social life. In other words, the familiar idioms and models prevalent in Chinese social life have informed and enframed Chinese religious life. More than a cognitive resonance between the religious and the social, the actual 'doing' of religion employs certain key organizational and conceptual idioms that underlie much of Chinese social life. Hosting is one of these key idioms that have been imported to, or captured by, the religious domain. Hosting is a major structuring idiom through which the staging of many ritual actions and event productions in Chinese religious life is made possible.

Yet capturing a key social idiom such as hosting has its cost for the development of Chinese religious traditions: the over-socialization of religious practices and the inability of Chinese religious traditions to disengage from the social to achieve the sort of 'theologicalization' characteristic of Judeo-Christian religious traditions. Asking 'Why did Chinese religions never develop theologies?', just like economic historians in the past asking 'Why did China not develop capitalism?', is of course problematic, although the question can be extremely productive. I suggest that while the religious domain captured hosting as a key conceptual and organizational idiom, hosting as a social practice in turn captured the religious domain to reproduce itself as a sort of 'formal impulse',[12] i.e. an

---

[11] Both historical studies of Christianity and the gradually maturing field of the anthropology of Christianity have revealed very many different forms of practising Christianity. I have no doubt collapsed a wide diversity of possible forms of Christian practices into a generic image, but as I mentioned in the caveat above I have constructed these images in such sharp relief for heuristic purposes.

[12] See Eugene Y. Wang, *Shaping the Lotus Sutra: Buddhist Visual Culture in Medieval*

easily transposable idiom amenable to being mobilized in radically different domains and contexts. We might also call this idiom a 'cultural schema'.[13] This is why in Chinese religious actions the emphasis is put on being a good host and on orthopraxy rather than being a good theologian and on orthodoxy. Hosting is an irreducibly social practice that has prevented the emergence of theologians. The host has to be thoughtful, but he need not think. The hosting has to be done properly, yet the host can be (or must be?) an unthinking host because all the ritual actions have been prescribed and codified. The Chinese themselves seem to have so taken this idiom for granted that they have not theorized about it in any elaborate way (not even the otherwise theory-minded neo-Confucians of the late imperial era!). Through embodying the roles of host and guest in countless social occasions (religious and non-religious), most Chinese act out the hosting idiom without conscious reflection; the idiom becomes part of their 'habitus' (social as well as religious, if indeed these two domains can ever be separated).

As a result of the prominent role hosting plays in Chinese religious culture, Chinese religious practices cultivate a kind of social subjectivity (i.e. hosts and guests) rather than religious subjectivity (i.e. the Judeo-Christian 'believer'). Instead of saying China does not really have any religion (which is too extreme a thing to say), it is more accurate to say that China does not really have a religious subjectivity. In other words, we may say that we find in China neither religion nor superstition but a collection of hosts and guests (some human and some supernatural) united in multitudinous hosting occasions.

What I am trying to argue is not that Chinese religious life is merely hosting. Chinese religious life is of course a lot more than that. No one can deny the richness of Chinese religious imagina-

---

China (Seattle, WA, 2005). This formal impulse has also informed how the Chinese do politics. For example, I have used the hosting idiom to interpret 'Mao's travelling mango cult' during the Cultural Revolution; see Adam Yuet Chau, 'Mao's Travelling Mangoes: Food as Relic in Revolutionary China', in Alexandra Walsham, ed., *Relics and Remains: P&P*, Supplement 5 (2010), 256–75. Upon receiving the mangoes as a gift from the supreme leader, the revolutionary masses turned them into a sort of revolutionary relic that had to be welcomed, hosted, protected, venerated and then passed on.

[13] Sherry B. Ortner, *High Religion: A Cultural and Political History of Sherpa Buddhism* (Princeton, NJ, 1989).

tion, and a Judeo-Christian style of theologizing is far from being the only way to elaborate religious conceptions. Lay religious life is also far richer and varied than the hosting model can summarize. Chinese religious life cannot and should not be reduced to the hosting idiom. Yet one can hardly picture Chinese religious life without the hosting idiom. Take away hosting from Chinese popular religious life and the entire popular religious life at the level of practice will simply collapse or become entirely unrecognizable.

CHRISTIANITY'S USURPATION OF HOUSEHOLD SOVEREIGNTY

The English poet George Herbert (1593–1633) wrote a poem that subsequently became one of his most popular and best loved. The poem is about divine grace in the Christian tradition:

Love (III)[14]

Love bade me welcome, yet my soul drew back,
Guilty of dust and sin.
But quick-ey'd Love, observing me grow slack
From my first entrance in,
Drew nearer to me, sweetly questioning
If I lack'd any thing.

A guest, I answer'd, worthy to be here;
Love said, you shall be he.
I, the unkind, ungrateful? Ah my dear,
I cannot look on thee.
Love took my hand, and smiling did reply,
Who made the eyes but I?

Truth, Lord, but I have marr'd them; let my shame
Go where it doth deserve.
And know you not, says Love, who bore the blame?
My dear, then I will serve.
You must sit down, says Love, and taste my meat:
So I did sit and eat.

---

[14] George Herbert, *The Complete English Works* (New York, 1995), 184. I am grateful to Henrietta Harrison for bringing this poem to my attention.

This beautiful poem, I argue, encapsulates the defining relationship between God and individual Christians in the Christian tradition: God as host and the Christian individual as guest; God as the all-powerful, all-forgiving host and the Christian individual as a completely unworthy guest who is nonetheless made worthy by divine grace, and made to recognize and accept this grace. There are a few details here that are worth noting as important for my argument. Firstly, the setting of this meal (or banquet?) is most likely in heaven, i.e. in God's 'house', even if it is not specified. Secondly, the Christian individual is a solitary guest; the banquet is for him or her alone; the Christian individual is face to face alone with God. Of course one may say that this individual Christian is made to stand symbolically for all Christians, yet the intimate setting evoked by the poem is theologically justified. After all, all sinners must face God and accept his grace individually. In other words, the concept of grace is a powerful religious-subjectificatory force.

The Christian theological formulation of God as the ultimate host in heaven ('the Kingdom'), as poignantly illustrated in Herbert's poem, is translated into this-worldly practice in the idiom of the Church (physically as the church building but also as the collectivity of all believers), which represents the body of Christ. When worshippers go to church for mass or communion, the Church and church personnel are always the host and the worshippers are always the guests. Instead of 'feeding' the deities, as in Chinese popular religion, Christian worshippers are fed the body and blood of Christ at communion in the form of bread and wine (interestingly the bread is known as the 'host' as well, although the etymology is entirely different).[15] Christians stage important life-event productions such as baptisms, weddings and funerals at the church, again relegating sovereignty to it. This church-centred event production structure vitiates the importance of the households as loci of hosting.

But how did this loss of household sovereignty come about? How did the figure of the individual sinner and recipient of grace emerge as the focus of theological attention and the paradigm of

---

[15] I am aware there are divergent views amongst theologians and Christian denominations regarding what happens to the bread and wine but these should not detract from the central imagery of God hosting human beings.

religious engagement? During pre-Christian Roman times, people in the Roman empire practised household-based hosting of deities in ways that were very similar to those found in China. And the early Christian Church very much replicated this household idiom, for instance in the form of household-based assemblies.[16] However, over the course of the development of the Church, it slowly but decisively usurped the agency of the household (what I have called 'household sovereignty'), until the household could no longer host God.[17] The eucharist as a paradigmatic ritual was instituted to *mise-en-scène* this reversed host–guest relationship between humans and spirits. Although some kind of household-based hosting did survive or even flourish in popular practices in medieval Catholicism and so-called 'popular Catholicism' (e.g. in the Mediterranean or the Philippines),[18] the overwhelming tendency has been to eradicate household sovereignty. In its stead individualized religious subjectivities were produced (through images such as God's 'banquet for one' and practices such as confession), as individuals could no longer work alongside other members of the household to host as a collectivity (i.e. the household). Now all members of the parish must gather in God's 'house' (i.e. the church building) to worship, and the priest acts as God's human-faced host to serve Christ's body so that the congregants can, indeed must, 'sit and eat'.

University of Cambridge

[16] See Wayne A. Meeks, *The First Urban Christians: The Social World of the Apostle Paul* (New Haven, CT, 1983).

[17] Mary Laven (private communication) reminds me, however, that the Church and the household long continued to struggle over the proper locus of worship. For example, the Council of Trent brought a renewed emphasis on the importance of the Church for Christian ritual life, as exemplified in its measures concerning domestic masses: see Philip Mattox, 'Domestic Sacral Space in the Florentine Renaissance Palace', *Renaissance Studies* 20 (2006), 658–73.

[18] See William A. Christian Jr, *Person and God in a Spanish Valley*, rev. edn (Princeton, NJ, 1989); Fenella Cannell, *Power and Intimacy in the Christian Philippines* (Cambridge, 1999).